Intellectual Traditions of Pre-Colonial Africa

EDITED BY

Constance B. Hilliard, Ph.D.
University of North Texas

Boston   Burr Ridge, IL   Dubuque, IA   Madison, WI
New York   San Francisco   St. Louis
Bangkok   Bogotá   Caracas   Lisbon   London   Madrid   Mexico City
Milan   New Delhi   Seoul   Singapore   Sydney   Taipei   Toronto

McGraw-Hill

A Division of The McGraw·Hill Companies

INTELLECTUAL TRADITIONS OF PRE-COLONIAL AFRICA

Copyright © 1998 by The McGraw-Hill Companies, Inc. All rights reserved. Printed in the United States of America. Except as permitted under the United States Copyright Act of 1976, no part of this publication may be reproduced or distributed in any form or by any means, or stored in a data base or retrieval system, without the prior written permission of the publisher.

This book is printed on acid-free paper.

1 2 3 4 5 6 7 8 9 0 DOC/DOC 9 0 9 8 7

ISBN 0-07-028898-4

Editorial director: *Jane Vaicunas*
Sponsoring editor: *Leslye Jackson*
Marketing manager: *Annie Mitchell*
Editorial coordinator: *Amy Mack*
Project manager: *Kimberly Hooker*
Production supervisor: *Melonie Salvati*
Designer: *Kiera Cunningham*
Photo research coordinator: *Sharon Miller*
Compositor: *Shepherd Incorporated*
Typeface: *10/12 Times Roman*
Printer: *R. R. Donnelley & Sons Company*

Library of Congress Cataloging-in-Publication Data

The intellectual traditions of pre-colonial Africa
   / edited by Constance B. Hilliard.
      p. cm.
   ISBN 0-07-028898-4 (alk. paper)
      1. Africa—Civilization. 2. Africa—Intellectual life.
   I. Hilliard, Constance B.
   DT14.I575 1998
   960—dc21   97-22527
                                                       CIP

http://www.mhhe.com

To Terrill

About the Author

Constance Hilliard received a B.A., M.A., and Ph.D. from Harvard University in the areas of African History and Semitic Historiography. She has served as a visiting professor at Wellesley College and a visiting scholar at Harvard's Center for Middle Eastern Studies. Ms. Hilliard rejoined academia after serving for several years as a foreign policy staff analyst for the United States Senate and as a columnist for the *Dallas Morning News*. The author is currently an assistant professor at the University of North Texas.

Preface

This book was conceived several years ago in a vibrant lunch conversation with the late Professor Marilyn Waldman, whose lifelong devotion to historiography has been an inspiration to me. We talked at length about the lack of readily available English translations for Africa's rich and diverse intellectual traditions. The repercussions of this lacuna were especially unsettling, for their lack of availability left the often unarticulated but powerful impression within the scholarly community and among the public at large that the continent of Africa existed outside the main currents of human intellectual achievement.

And just as this book project evolved as a celebration and homecoming for the lost, effaced, and misplaced traditions of the African continent, its preparation has served as an intellectual homecoming for me as well. In returning to my scholarly roots in African historiography, I have delighted in reconnecting with Professors John Ralph Willis of Princeton and Martin Kilson at Harvard, both of whom have served in crucial mentoring roles for me over the years. Without their patient encouragement and support I could not have seen this project through.

It also has been my enormous good fortune to receive strong institutional support for this intellectual traditions of Africa project. I am grateful to the Center for Middle Eastern Studies (CMES) at Harvard University, its former Chair, William A. Graham, and CMES administrative assistant Mrs. Barbara Henson for making it possible for me to undertake the research for this project in my capacity as visiting scholar at the Center. I also must thank my colleagues in the History Department at the University of North Texas, in particular Professor Gustav Seligmann, for their patience, support, and enthusiasm for this project. My research assistants, Michelle Bragg and Jamie Carawan, saved me from drowning countless times in the maelstrom of details this project generated. To them I am deeply appreciative. I also must express a special note of thanks to my faculty colleagues at Wellesley College who generously offered the excellent facilities and breathtakingly beautiful setting of that campus for me to complete work on this manuscript.

The composing of a book demands vital inputs from many people. Certainly the most critical in this undertaking has been the creative vision and enthusiasm of my editor at McGraw-Hill, Leslye Jackson. When this evolving project consisted of little more than a few sketchy ideas on paper, Leslye displayed a remarkable talent for conceptualizing it and initiating the arduous process of transforming it into an actual publication. I am deeply grateful to her for making the commitment to shape my ideas into a concrete, scholarly reality, and doing so with enormous patience and good humor. How fortunate indeed I also was to have Kimberly Hooker as project manager for this book. In working together over the course of the past several months, I have developed respect and admiration for her style of ever so gentle prodding, consummate professionalism, and an unflagging commitment to seeing this project through successfully. I also should like to express my appreciation to Fred Lentz, McGraw-Hill's book representative in Dallas. This project would never have been launched without his initial notice of my ideas and truly infectious enthusiasm for the project itself.

I also owe a debt of gratitude to the reviewers who helped shape this manuscript in many ways. My thanks go to the following people for their assistance: Roger B. Beck, Eastern Illinois University; Chouki El Hamel, Duke University; Adrienne M. Israel, Guilford College; Kenneth Mason, Santa Monica College; Cheryl Johnson-Odim, Loyola University (Chicago); David Schoenbrun, University of Georgia; Robert Shell, Princeton University; and Leonard M. Thompson, Professor Emeritus, Yale University.

My family is my most precious intellectual gift. My sister Ida Pipkin whose practical knowledge, my brother John Hilliard whose stress-busting wit, and their families provided the crucial balance demanded of my sanity during the composing of this book. And finally, I owe a debt I cannot possibly ever repay to my husband, Terrill Tripp, for being there as a one-man cheering squad for me, every day and in every possible way.

Contents

The Intellectual Traditions of Pre-Colonial Africa

Introduction 1

Part I
PHARAONIC EGYPT

1. The Old Kingdom: The Resurrection of Osiris from *The Pyramid Texts*   21
2. First Intermediate Period: The Dispute of a Man with His Soul   26
3. The Middle Kingdom: Sinuhe's Triumphant Return Home   31
4. The Second Intermediate Period: Problems 59 and 59B from the *Ahmes Mathematic Papyrus*   36
5. New Kingdom: Thoth—The God of Wisdom and Learning from *The Book of the Dead*   38
6. Queen Hatshepsut: Expedition against Punt (Somalia)   41
7. Scribes: Instructions to Prime Minister Rekh-mi-Ra   45
8. Anonymous: Love Poems   48
9. Amenhotep III: The Great Hymn to Amen   52
10. Amenemope: The Wisdom Teachings   55
11. Pharaoh Akhenaten and Queen Nefertiti: The Great Hymn to the One God Aten   61

Part II
ANCIENT NUBIA

12. General Piankhi: The Kushite Conquest of Egypt from the *Piankhi Stela*   72
13. Shabaka: The Memphite Theology   80
14. Pharaoh Taharqa: Commemorations to the Queen Mother   83

15 Mentemhet: The Building and Restoration of the Monuments in Thebes 85

16 Priests of Meroë: Prayer to the Lion-God Apedemak 90

Part III
HELLENIZED EGYPT AND NUBIA

17 Heron of Alexandria: Approximating the Square Root of a Nonsquare Integer from *Metrica* 98

18 Valentinus: The Gospel of Truth from *The Nag Hammadi Library* 100

19 The Gnostics: The Gospel of the Egyptians 109

20 Hermeticists: Libellus XVI—Epistle of Asclepius to King Ammon from *The Corpus Hermeticum* 118

21 Origen: A Great Theater Is Filled with Spectators from *Exhortation to Martyrdom* 122

22 Plotinus: Are All Souls One? from *Ennead IV* 128

23 Pachomius: Instruction Concerning a Spiteful Monk 133

24 Athanasius: Temporal Afflictions and Eternal Glory from *The Resurrection Letters* 134

25 Synesius of Cyrene (Libya): Letters to Hypatia and Euoptius 137

26 Paphnutius: Abba Aaron and the Miracle of the Nubian's Son from *The Coptic Histories of the Monks of Upper Egypt* 140

27 Coptic Apocrypha: The Death of Joseph from *The Coptic Apocryphal Gospels* 142

Part IV
BYZANTINE AND ROMANIZED CARTHAGE—NUMIDIA

28 Tertullian: Against the Valentinians 153

29 Perpetua: The Martyrdom of Saints Perpetua and Felicitas 162

30 Cyprian: Heretical Baptism—The Issue between Rome and Africa 172

31 Augustine: The Miseries of the Romans in the African Wars from *The City of God* 175

32 Corippus: The Royal Banquet from *In Praise of Justin* 181

Part V
BYZANTINE, COPTIC, AND ISLAMIC NORTH AFRICA

33 Dhu al-Nun of Nubia: Islamic Gnosticism 189

34 Sawirus Ibn al-Mukaffa: The Father Gabriel from *History of the Patriarchs of the Egyptian Church* 192

35 Ahmad Ibn Yusuf al-Misri: Choicest Accounts of Ibn Tulun 196

36 Ibn Tumart: The Muslim Creed 198

37 Mamelukes of Egypt: The Young Man with the Severed Hand and the Girl from *A Thousand and One Nights* 207

38 Ibn Battuta: The Royal Court of the Sultan of Mali from *The Travels of Ibn Battuta* 218

39 Ibn Khaldun: "Sufism" and "Defining the Intellectual Sciences" from *The Muqaddimah* 222

40 The Arabized Berbers: The City Girl and the Country Girl 227

41 Leo Africanus: The Book Trade at Timbuctu from *A Geographical Historie of Africa* 233

42 Ahmad al-Tijani: A Ritual Prayer 235

43 The Mahdi: A Proclamation 236

Part VI
ETHIOPIA AND SOMALIA

44 King Ezana: The Decline and Fall of Meroë 244

45 Isaac: Solomon and Sheba from the *Kebra Nagast* 247

46 Shihab al-Din: The Conquest of Ethiopia from *The Ethiopian Royal Chronicles* 259

47 Royal Chronicler: The Conquest of Ethiopia from *The Ethiopian Royal Chronicles* 264

48 Royal Chronicler: The Empress Berhan Mogasa from *The Ethiopian Royal Chronicles* 266

49 Bahrey: History of the Galla 268

50 Afawark Gabra Iyasus: Fictitious Story 273

51 Qamaan Bulxan: In Praise of a Beautiful Somali Woman 276

52 Mahammed ᵓAbdille Hasan: The Sayyid's Reply 278

53 The Ethiopian Public Health Bureau: Medical Legislation 281

Part VII
WEST AFRICA

54 Ancient Mali: The Foretelling of the Great Sundiata's Birth from *The Epic of Sundiata* 298

55 Mahmud al-Kati of Songhay: The Coming to Power of the Tyrannical Sonni Ali from the *Tarikh al-Fattash* 306

56 Abd al-Rahman al-Sadi of Songhay: The Destruction of Knowledge from the *Tarikh al-Sudan* 309

57 Hausaland: Queen Amina the Great 311

58 Hausaland: Matters of State from *The Kano Chronicle* 313

59 Uthman dan Fodio: The Proper Treatment of Women from *Nur al-Albab* 316

60 Abdullah dan Fodio: The Intellectual Background of the Jihad 318

61 Al-Kanemi/Bello: The Case For and Against Holy War from *Infaq al-Maysur* 321

62 Samuel Anla Ogun Johnson: Yoruba System of Numbers 327

63 The Yoruba of Nigeria: Hymns to the God Shango 333

64 The Ibo of Southeastern Nigeria: Night One from *The Ozidi Saga* 335

65 The Ashanti of Ghana: A Drum Prayer 343

66 James C. Minor of Liberia: Letters 347

Part VIII
CENTRAL AFRICA

67 Afonso of Kongo: The Evils of the Slave Trade 356
68 The Ovimbundu of Angola: Katiukaila and His Wife Ngeve 359
69 The Luba of Zaire: Nkongolo's Origins from *The Luba Genesis Myth* 361
70 The Yaka of Southwest Zaire: Treatment for Female Infertility 367
71 The Nyanga and the Pygmies of Gabon: The New Laws from *The Mwindo Epic* 371
72 The Fang of Gabon and Cameroon: Hymn to the Sun 373

Part IX
EAST AFRICA

73 The Dinka of Southern Sudan: Divorce—A Woman's Song 381
74 John Nyakatura: The Attack on Rwanda from *The History of Bunyoro-Kitara* 385
75 The Buganda of Uganda: Daoura 387
76 The Bahima of Ankole (Uganda): I Who Encircle the Foe 389
77 Chronicler: The Arrival of Vasco da Gama from *The Kilwa Chronicle* 391
78 Chronicler: Intrigues from *The Pate Chronicle* 393
79 Abdallah Ibn Nasir: Lament for Greatness from the *Utendi wa Inkishafi* 398
80 Mwana Kupona: A Dying Woman's Advice to Her Daughter from the *Utenda wa Mwana Kupona* 403
81 The Masai of Kenya: Proverbs 409
82 The Kikuyu of Kenya: The Lost Sister—Two Versions 412
83 King Macemba of the Yao (Tanzania): Facing Invasion 417
84 The Shambaa of Tanzania: The Kilindi Are Born Liars from *The Mbegha Myth* 418
85 The Kamba of Kenya and Tanzania: Medical Treatments 420

Part X
SOUTHERN AFRICA

86 The Shona of Zimbabwe: The Clan Praises of the Daughters of the Moyo Wakapiwa Clan 429
87 The Zulu of South Africa: Shaka and the Princess Mkhabayi from *The Zulu Epic of Shaka the Great* 432
88 The Xhosa of South Africa: Custom Requires the Traditional Response 447
89 William W. Gqoba: The Cause of the Cattle-Killing at the Nongqawuse Period 452
90 Lesotho: Moshoeshoe I 456
91 Botswana: Medicinal Plants 458
92 The !Kung of Namibia: Tactics in Springbok Hunting 461

End of Book Credits   463

Contents Arranged by Subject

Part I
PHARAONIC EGYPT

SOCIAL

  2 First Intermediate Period: The Dispute of a Man with His Soul 26

POLITICAL

  7 Scribes: Instructions to the Prime Minister Rekh-mi-Ra 45

HISTORICAL

  6 Queen Hatshepsut: Expedition against Punt (Somalia) 41

RELIGIOUS

  1 The Old Kingdom: The Resurrection of Osiris from *The Pyramid Texts* 21

10 Amenemope: The Wisdom Teachings 55

11 Pharoah Akhenaten and Queen Nefertiti: The Great Hymn to the One God Aten 61

BELLES LETTRES

  3 The Middle Kingdom: Sinuhe's Triumphant Return Home 31

  8 Anonymous: Love Poems 48

  9 Amenhotep III: The Great Hymn to Amen 52

PHILOSOPHICAL

  5 New Kingdom: Thoth—The God of Wisdom and Learning from *The Book of the Dead* 38

SCIENTIFIC

  4 The Second Intermediate Period: Problems 59 and 59B from the *Ahmes Mathematic Papyrus* 36

Part II
ANCIENT NUBIA

SOCIAL

14 Pharaoh Taharqa: Commemorations to the Queen Mother 83

15 Mentemhet: The Building and Restoration of the Monuments in Thebes 85

HISTORICAL

12 General Piankhi: The Kushite Conquest of Egypt from the *Piankhi Stela* 72

RELIGIOUS

13 Shabaka: The Memphite Theology 80

16 Priests of Meroë: Prayer to the Lion-God Apedemak 90

Part III
HELLENIZED EGYPT AND NUBIA

SOCIAL

25 Synesius of Cyrene (Libya): Letters to Hypatia and Euoptius   137

RELIGIOUS

18 Valentinus: The Gospel of Truth from *The Nag Hammadi Library*   100

19 The Gnostics: The Gospel of the Egyptians   109

21 Origen: A Great Theater Is Filled with Spectators from *Exhortation to Martyrdom*   122

23 Pachomius: Instruction Concerning a Spiteful Monk   133

24 Athanasius: Temporal Afflictions and Eternal Glory from *The Resurrection Letters*   134

26 Paphnutius: Abba Aaron and the Miracle of the Nubian's Son from *The Coptic Histories of the Monks of Upper Egypt*   140

27 Coptic Apocrypha: The Death of Joseph from *The Coptic Apocryphal Gospels*   142

PHILOSOPHICAL

20 Hermeticists: Libellus XVI—Epistle of Asclepius to King Ammon from *The Corpus Hermeticum*   118

22 Plotinus: Are All Souls One? from *Ennead IV*   128

SCIENTIFIC

17 Heron of Alexandria: Approximating the Square Root of a Nonsquare Integer from *Metrica*   98

Part IV
BYZANTINE AND ROMANIZED CARTHAGE—NUMIDIA

HISTORICAL

31 Augustine: The Miseries of the Romans in the African Wars from *The City of God*   175

RELIGIOUS

28 Tertullian: Against the Valentinians   153

29 Perpetua: The Martyrdom of Saints Perpetua and Felicitas   162

30 Cyprian: Heretical Baptism—The Issue between Rome and Africa   172

BELLES LETTRES

32 Corippus: The Royal Banquet from *In Praise of Justin*   181

CONTENTS ARRANGED BY SUBJECT

Part V
BYZANTINE, COPTIC, AND ISLAMIC NORTH AFRICA

POLITICAL

43 The Mahdi: A Proclamation   236

HISTORICAL

38 Ibn Battuta: The Royal Court of the Sultan of Mali from *The Travels of Ibn Battuta*   218

41 Leo Africanus: The Book Trade at Timbuctu from *A Geographical Historie of Africa*   233

RELIGIOUS

33 Dhu al-Nun of Nubia: Islamic Gnosticism   189

34 Sawirus Ibn al-Mukaffa: The Father Gabriel from *History of the Patriarchs of the Egyptian Church*   192

35 Ahmad Ibn Yusuf al-Misri: Choicest Accounts of Ibn Tulun   196

36 Ibn Tumart: The Muslim Creed   198

39 Ibn Khaldun: "Sufism" and "Defining the Intellectual Sciences" from *The Muqaddimah*   222

42 Ahmad al-Tijani: A Ritual Prayer   235

BELLES LETTRES

37 Mamelukes of Egypt: The Young Man with the Severed Hand and the Girl from *A Thousand and One Nights*   207

40 The Arabized Berbers: The City Girl and the Country Girl   227

SCIENTIFIC

39 Ibn Khaldun: "Sufism" and "Defining the Intellectual Sciences" from *The Muqaddimah*   222

Part VI
ETHIOPIA AND SOMALIA

POLITICAL

52 Mahammed ʾAbdille Hasan: The Sayyid's Reply   278

HISTORICAL

44 King Ezana: The Decline and Fall of Meroë   244

46 Shihab al-Din: The Conquest of Ethiopia from *The Ethiopian Royal Chronicles*   259

47 Royal Chronicler: The Conquest of Ethiopia from *The Ethiopian Royal Chronicles*   264

48 Royal Chronicler: The Empress Berhan Mogasa from *The Ethiopian Royal Chronicles*   266

49 Bahrey: History of the Galla   268

RELIGIOUS

45 Isaac: Solomon and Sheba from the *Kebra Nagast*   247

50 Afawark Gabra Iyasus: Fictitious Story   273

51 Qamaan Bulxan: In Praise of a Beautiful Somali Woman   276

SCIENTIFIC

53 The Ethiopian Public Health Bureau: Medical Legislation   281

Part VII
WEST AFRICA

RELIGIOUS

60 Abdullah dan Fodio: The Intellectual Background of the Jihad 318

63 The Yoruba of Nigeria: Hymn to the God Shango 333

65 The Ashanti of Ghana: A Drum Prayer 343

BELLES LETTRES

54 Ancient Mali: The Foretelling of the Great Sundiata's Birth from *The Epic of Sundiata* 298

57 Hausaland: Queen Amina the Great 311

64 The Ibo of Southeastern Nigeria: Night One from *The Ozidi Saga* 335

SCIENTIFIC

62 Samuel Anla Ogun Johnson: Yoruba System of Numbers 327

POLITICAL

58 Hausaland: Matters of State from *The Kano Chronicle* 313

61 Al-Kanemi/Bello: The Case For and Against Holy War from *Infaq al-Maysur* 321

59 Uthman dan Fodio: The Proper Treatment of Women from *Nur al-Albab* 316

HISTORICAL

55 Mahmud al-Kati of Songhay: The Coming to Power of the Tyrannical Sonni Ali from the *Tarikh al-Fattash* 306

56 Abd al-Rahman al-Sadi of Songhay: The Destruction of Knowledge from the *Tarikh al-Sudan* 309

66 James C. Minor of Liberia: Letters 347

Part VIII
CENTRAL AFRICA

POLITICAL

71 The Nyanga and the Pygmies of Gabon: The New Laws from *The Mwindo Epic* 371

HISTORICAL

67 Afonso of Kongo: The Evils of the Slave Trade 356

RELIGIOUS

72 The Fang of Gabon and Cameroon: Hymn to the Sun 373

BELLES LETTRES

68 The Ovimbundu of Angola: Katiukaila and His Wife Ngeve 359

69 The Luba of Zaire: Nkongolo's Origins from *The Luba Genesis Myth* 361

SCIENTIFIC

70 The Yaka of Southwest Zaire: Treatment for Female Infertility 367

Part IX
EAST AFRICA

SOCIAL

73　The Dinka of Southern Sudan: Divorce—A Woman's Song　381

80　Mwana Kupona: A Dying Woman's Advice to Her Daughter from the *Utenda wa Mwana Kupona*　403

81　The Masai of Kenya: Proverbs　409

POLITICAL

83　King Macemba of the Yao (Tanzania): Facing Invasion　417

HISTORICAL

74　John Nyakatura: The Attack on Rwanda from *The History of Bunyoro-Kitara*　385

75　The Buganda of Uganda: Daoura　387

77　Chronicler: The Arrival of Vasco da Gama from *The Kilwa Chronicle*　391

78　Chronicler: Intrigues from *The Pate Chronicle*　393

BELLES LETTRES

76　The Bahima of Ankole (Uganda): I Who Encircle the Foe　389

79　Abdallah Ibn Nasir: Lament for Greatness from the *Utendi wa Inkishafi*　398

82　The Kikuyu of Kenya: The Lost Sister—Two Versions　412

84　The Shambaa of Tanzania: The Kilindi Are Born Liars from *The Mbegha Myth*　418

SCIENTIFIC

85　The Kamba of Kenya and Tanzania: Medical Treatments　420

Part X
SOUTHERN AFRICA

SOCIAL

86　The Shona of Zimbabwe: The Clan Praises of the Daughters of the Moyo Wakapiwa Clan　429

88　The Xhosa of South Africa: Custom Requires the Traditional Response　447

POLITICAL

87　The Zulu of South Africa: Shaka and the Princess Mkhabayi from *The Zulu Epic of Shaka the Great*　432

HISTORICAL

89　William W. Gqoba: The Cause of the Cattle-Killing at the Nongqawuse Period　452

90　Lesotho: Moshoeshoe I　456

SCIENTIFIC

91　Botswana: Medicinal Plants　458

92　The !Kung of Namibia: Tactics in Springbok Hunting　461

Introduction

There is a special beauty in perceiving the African continent as richly diverse and yet organically whole. Perhaps even more to the point, intellectual honesty impels us to do so. One of the most tragic legacies of Africa's slave past and European colonialism was the propensity of earlier Western scholars to rationalize their "civilizing mission" by devaluing Africa's intellectual inheritance and placing the continent outside the main currents of human intellectual development.

The works of such scholars employed two distinct devices—one applied to rural Africa, the other to its influential states—in order to construct African inferiority. The first device dictated a dismissal of Africa's rural intellectual heritage as "unimportant" and primitive by the mere fact of its being oral rather than written. In equating the presence of writing within a society to civilization, such scholars merely ignored Europe's own oral past. The unwritten fount for such classics as the *Iliad, Odyssey,* and others was conveniently forgotten.

The intellectual contributions of urban Africans posed an even greater challenge to maintaining the schema of African inferiority. In this instance Western scholars of a previous era performed unseemly amputations on the body of Africa itself, lopping off vital limbs and reattaching these severed appendages to more politically serviceable parts of the world. Thus, pharaonic Egypt became cartographically redefined as "Mediterranean" or merely "Near Eastern." To be sure, modern scholars now believe that Egypt may have played a far larger role in influencing the culture of ancient Greece and the Near East than previously acknowledged. However, any new appreciation of the powerful influences Egypt exerted on its ancient neighbors should serve to enrich our awareness of this African contribution to Western development rather than efface it.

Just as the sophisticated techniques of modern archaeology have situated the cultural roots of earliest Egypt in Africa among the cultures that evolved along the Nile River Valley, contemporary scholars have also found it necessary to revise once popular paradigms that depreciated the Africanness of other urban societies on that continent as well. In the same way, Western philosophers who in earlier times described early African Christians like Tertullian, Athanasius, and Augustine as merely citizens of Rome now have begun to recognize these seminal figures of early Christianity as products of an African as well as a Latinized cultural context. In other instances, historians once dismissed the rich cultural traditions of Timbuktu in the ancient empire of Songhay and the Swahili coast of East Africa as "Arab" and therefore derivative. But in fact these cases represented the literary output of indigenous ethnic groups who expressed themselves in the script available to their particular culture. As for the Islamic cultural influences, over time certain indigenous African languages, like Hausa, Fulani, and Swahili, began being written using Arabic script in the same way that medieval Europeans once wrote solely in Latin but later began to employ that script to compose texts in their vernacular languages.

HOW ARE "INTELLECTUAL TRADITIONS" DEFINED?

Those works that have proven to be of enduring value to the societies that spawned them are adjudged as "traditions" within this volume. The term "intellectual" may demand a more expansive explanation, however. I have used it in this book synonymously with verbal art. In this way oral literature is acknowledged in equal measure to written. I have found it necessary for practical reasons to limit the book's scope to verbal art, although I do indeed recognize the myriad other forms of human creativity, which includes the plastic arts, music, architecture, textile design, and dance.

Early Europeans often devalued the intellectual wisdoms of the Africans by designating their traditions "folklore" in contrast to the comparable European traditions, to which they gave the descriptor "intellectual." As early as 1927, Arthur B. Spingarn pointed out in his introduction to Blaise Cendrars's work *The African Saga:*

> The traditional literature of Africa, collected assiduously by missionaries, explorers, ethnologists, administrators and philologists, has been considered from many angles, as religion, as folklore, as philology and as an aid to the study of primitive psychology. Rarely, if ever, has it been considered as the expression of the genius of a people, and only incidentally, if at all, has it been read purely as literature.[1]

It is worthwhile to an understanding of the African continent and perhaps all of human cultural achievement to remember that literacy is not the sole measure of intellectual worth. Likewise, the absence of literacy in a society does not preclude wisdom and a reverence for knowledge. To be sure, *griots* or praise-singers, who recite one of the most beautiful oral traditions of all time, *The Epic of Sundiata* (depicting the life of the thirteenth century founder of the West African empire of Mali), reflect this devotion:

> The art of eloquence has no secrets for us; without us the names of kings would vanish into oblivion, we are the memory of mankind; by the spoken word we bring to life the deeds and exploits of kings for younger generations . . . I teach kings the history of their ancestors so that the lives of the ancients might serve them as an example, for the world is old, but the future springs from the past.

Not only must we appreciate the ethnic diversity of African societies, but also the socioeconomic diversity within societies that would influence the lens through which similar traditions or histories were viewed differently. Wherever possible I have therefore tried to present the contrasting presentations emanating from the different classes within a society. In this sense "intellectual" is not merely the cognitive product of

---

[1]Blaise Cendrars, *The African Saga* (New York: Payson & Clarke Ltd., 1927), p. 5.

cities, states, or scribes but also of decentralized societies and oral traditions. After all, even in Western literature, an enjoyment of Shakespeare at the expense of the originally oral Beowulf would be a grievous loss to us moderns, indeed.

Steven Feierman in his work *Peasant Intellectuals* examines the wider usage of the term "intellectual" to transcend the verbal culture of the elites within a society. He explains:

> Intellectuals are defined . . . by their place in the unfolding social process: they engage in socially recognized organizational, directive, educative, or expressive activities. Teachers, artists, political leaders, healers, and bureaucrats are all intellectuals within this definition of the term. The definition is derived, of course, from Gramsci, who explained that it is not possible to define intellectuals simply by the fact that they engage in intellectual activities, because these activities proceed within every social group.[2]

The tendency to ascribe superiority to one's own class, ethnicity, or cultural traditions is certainly not limited to Europeans but rather appears to be a universal trait of human societies. For example, even within the African traditions contained in this volume, we see similar efforts at elitist reframing based on class biases. Sundiata, the founding hero of the empire of ancient Mali, was presented as little more than a mischievous rascal in the written literature composed of Islamized scholars of Mali. This is because they disdained their own rural classes, who were resistant to Islamic influence. Likewise, the peasantry of Mali praised Sundiata as the greatest leader who ever lived, while disparaging later Muslim rulers of that state. The rural masses, in earning their living from the land, were not as strongly influenced by Islam as the urban merchant class, whose livelihood was dependent on the trans-Saharan trade controlled by the Islamic world.

One of the most controversial elements of African intellectual tradition relates to the natural sciences. It is only in recent times that scholars have begun to question the assumptions upon which our understanding of European science have been based. Because Westerners had believed that Africans were incapable of abstract reasoning, virtually all history of science research on the early sciences attributed most of the scientific contributions emanating from Hellenized Alexandria in Egypt to ethnic Greeks. As a consequence, it is only now that Western scholars are beginning to appreciate the powerful amalgam created in Alexandria between the ancient sciences of Egypt and those of Greece. Apart from the civilization of Egypt, the sciences practiced by other societies throughout the African continent were often subsumed and lost in scholarly classification schemes that dismissed all such knowledge as folklore, witchcraft, and magic.

EXTERNAL INFLUENCES ON AFRICA?

This volume represents a modest attempt to celebrate the rich intellectual traditions spawned on the African continent and in so doing contribute to salving the wounds of

---

[2]Steven Feierman, *Peasant Intellectuals: Anthropology and History in Tanzania* (Madison: University of Wisconsin Press, 1990), p. 18.

Africa's amputated history. However, this effort to celebrate the rich traditions that evolved in Africa should not be misperceived. It does not represent an attempt to isolate that continent from the other worlds it touched, influenced, and was influenced by. Nor does it intend to subject Africa, comprising some 11.7 million square miles and the largest number of distinct ethnic and language groups in the world, to a superficial unity of culture and outlook or a simplistic notion of a single nub of diffusion.

The matter of foreign influences in Africa's intellectual traditions is an especially delicate one. This is because in attempting to redress an imbalance it becomes all too easy to go too far the other way. The point is not to perceive of the African continent as having been cut off from the influences of neighboring regions. It is rather to acknowledge the nature of historical distortions as they relate to Africa and thus to redress them by appreciating the fact that all societies have a core; none are a clean slate to be written upon by others. Thus, the extraordinarily rich cultural contributions of Hellenized Egypt to the world from the fourth century B.C. to the Roman conquest in 30 B.C. must be appreciated for the dynamic ways in which they melded the African cultural traditions with the Greek. In like manner, the Latinized early Christian theologians like Augustine, Cyprian, and Tertullian, who were products of Rome's colonization of North Africa, should be understood within their Roman-influenced and African context.

There are areas in which African ideas bear uncanny likeness to the ideas of other regions of the world because they both share the fundamentals of a common humanity. In other arenas African ideas and concepts will indeed have seeded or influenced comparable notions in neighboring regions of the world. As for which constitute elements of separate development of common humanity and which have been diffused, I will not in this volume attempt to surmise, but will rather allow the voices of the ancients to merely speak their piece.

WHO IS AN AFRICAN?

It would be impossible to compose a work on the intellectual traditions of the African continent without first posing the stubborn question, Who is an African? What indexes—culture, geography, or genetics—should be employed to make that determination?

Africa has always been a continent of contrasts and complexities. Empire-building societies that evolved written traditions coexisted alongside culturally prolific but nonliterate populations inhabiting vast decentralized regions of the African continent. However, not very long ago, Western scholars argued that the centralized states in Africa were populated by "Caucasoids," while the rural, decentralized societies were inhabited by "Negroids" (regardless of the actual skin color of the respective inhabitants). Scholars today recognize that the underlying differences between the states and their decentralized neighbors were considerably less cultural than they were ecological, and had nothing whatsoever to do with "race." A sizable proportion of Africa's soils is low in organic matter, erodes easily, and is especially susceptible to overuse. Such factors as fertility and erosion patterns, accessibility to navigable waterways, incidence of tropical diseases, and availability of commercially desirable natural resources determined in large measure which regions would evolve the population density and economic activity needed to develop state systems rather than remain decentralized.

The "Eurocentric" tendency to de-Africanize the most sophisticated urban societies on that continent has over time served to denude Africa of its intellectual heritage. Left in its wake was the flatly sketched imagery persisting to this day of a static continent, devoid of any cognitive traditions at all and locked in an anthropological present of timeless, ahistorical tribal societies. Such a distortion of Africa's past, not surprisingly, fueled the "Afrocentric" backlash. Unwilling merely to question European falsifications of African history, the Afrocentrists often substituted their own romanticized versions of historical events. In recognizing the historiographical quagmire into which African history has sometimes sunk under the weight of competing claims, this anthology strives to steer a course guided by analytical skepticism and a reverence for authenticity.

How then have the works included in this anthology been chosen? Understandably, African authorship represents the first criterion for inclusion in this work. While that single standard may seem straightforward, it in fact constitutes the most controversial aspect of this book. For what defines "African" in the matter of intellectual traditions when the conjoining of these two concepts, i.e., "African" and "intellectual," have been ignored even in learned circles until modern times? This book defines as "African" those works composed by authors who not only resided on the African continent but who were also members of ethnic groups indigenous to Africa. While it is easier to appreciate the indigenous quality of oral traditions, written tradition may require further explanation.

Thus, the Dutch-descended Afrikaners of South Africa have not been included in this work. Nor does this book include the traditions of ethnic Greeks or Romans living in ancient Africa, the Phoenicians, or those of African Jews whose lineage goes back to the ancient Hebrew peoples of the Near East.

It also becomes useful to distinguish between Arabian migrants, for example, and the Arabization of North Africa. There were certainly instances of Arabs settling in North Africa. However, the overwhelming majority of the Arabic-speaking populations of North Africa are descended from the indigenous populations who adopted the Arabic language and culture of the conquerors.

Historians of today look back with chagrin at the so-called Hamitic hypothesis that nineteenth- and early twentieth-century scholars employed to sidestep the indigenous populations in accounting for the existence of sophisticated states in Africa. According to this myth, a purported migration of Caucasian "Hamites" was responsible for whatever "civilizing" influences the African continent evolved. Not only were the ancient Egyptians described in this manner, but the list continued to expand as archaeological research uncovered important ancient state systems in other African regions as well. Before it was finally debunked, the Hamitic hypothesis had come to encompass the Buganda, Berbers, Ethiopians, Nubians, Fulani, and virtually every other African ethnic group, of whatever skin color, for whom historical research revealed sophisticated state systems and literate traditions, of which indigenous Africans were presumed racially incapable. Surely, the most irrational aspect of this once fashionable Hamitic myth was the complete reversal in meaning of the term "Hamite" itself. That is, prior to the nineteenth century, Westerners had employed the term "Hamite" in a depreciating manner to refer to Africans. These so-called biblical descendants of Ham, according to the Babylonian Talmud, were accursed with dark skin and kinky hair to punish Ham's son Canaan for looking upon his father's nakedness. It was only after the Napoleonic expedition to Egypt in 1798, when Europe began to uncover the magnificent remnants of ancient Egyptian civilization, that the race of people referred to as Hamites was suddenly metamorphosed from light-skinned Negroids to swarthy-complexioned Caucasoids. Through taxonomic sleight-of-hand, the West could therefore enjoy the glories of ancient Egypt, tracing its own racial heritage to that civilization.

From the nineteenth century onward, Western scholars adopted the convention of slicing the African continent into two geographical and racial segments, the white North and black sub-Saharan Africa. However, a genetic examination of the gradual changes in skin color of these populations as one moves down the continent does not support these popularly used racial classifications, which are based on social and political rather than biological factors.

WERE THE ANCIENT EGYPTIANS "BLACK"?

In recent years a heated debate has erupted over the racial designation of the ancient Egyptians. While Eurocentric scholars have traditionally asserted that the ancient Egyptians were "white," their Afrocentric counterparts now insist that this remarkable civilization was "black." While this debate remains ongoing, we should remember that the racial categories of "white" and "black" are not biological. Rather, they represent social constructs peculiar to America and certain other societies.

It is true, for example, that at the present time genetic tests may be able to determine who among the sampling of Americans possesses the sickle-cell genes, which would tag them as African-descended or "black." However, such a marker is environmental rather than racial. That is, while the Zulus of South Africa do not possess the sickle-cell marker because their homeland is not afflicted with malaria, many Greeks and other Europeans of Mediterranean origin do, for the same environmental reasons. Scientific researchers now assert that today's more sophisticated understanding of genetics makes it possible to establish a myriad of classification schemes for dividing up human populations. Genetic scientists also insist that scientific codings at the genetic level such as blood types, disease vectors, and so forth do not correspond with the racial classifications that we have inherited from the eighteenth and nineteenth centuries.

As for the ancient Egyptians, they appear to have possessed the same diverse hues of skin colors as do their modern-day counterparts. As for whether they were "Africans," our contemporary understanding is quite solid that indeed they were. There is no indication whatsoever that the ancient Egyptians, nor for that matter the North African Berbers from whom many of the most famous of the early Christian theologians were descended, were Asian or European migrants to Africa.

* * *

The task of selecting works for inclusion in *The Intellectual Traditions of Pre-Colonial Africa* has been a painful one. Great works of elegance and insight must be passed over or excerpted to accommodate necessary space constraints. I could not exhaust the range of traditions on a continent that has spawned thousands of societies and languages in one volume. And perhaps I should expose my fundamental bias at the start. Every society, on every continent, regardless of ethnicity or socioeconomic conditions has contributed its own intellectual products to the collective output of humankind, because the bringing forth of cognitive and creative impulses are as compelling as the bringing forth of offspring. As a consequence, what has been included in this volume, the societies and ethnicities whose intellectual products have been represented, is not to my mind higher on some abstract scale of "intellectualism," or more aesthetically pleasing or even more representative of human wisdom, than what has been left out. I was simply faced with a dilemma. An effort on my part to be all-inclusive would merely have left me with a manuscript so voluminous that it would have been of clearly unpublishable dimensions.

Thus, the texts in this anthology are divided into 10 geographical/historical "Parts." These sections encompass several different types of intellectual products. For example, many selections represent those traditions wholly indigenous to Africa as in the case of all the oral literature presented here in addition to the writings in hieroglyphics of ancient Egypt and Nubia. A truly unfortunate but unavoidable omission from this work is the literature in the Meroitic script of the ancient Nubians of Meroë. While to be technical about it, scholars have in fact succeeded in deciphering this unique script used for texts in Meroë from the second century B.C. until the fourth century A.D., this knowledge remains of little practical use because no one has yet been able to translate the Meroitic language of Ancient Nubia itself. It is also a more haunting reality that whatever was not salvaged in the 1960s and before is lost under the man-made Aswan Dam and will never be retrieved.

Another category of traditions treated in this anthology are literatures unique to Africa such as ancient Ethiopic, also known as Ge'ez, and Swahili but whose genesis can be traced to the intermixing of African languages and non-African written traditions. This case perhaps most closely approximates the process by which Phoenician alphabetic literacy was first transmitted to the Ionian Greeks of the Aegean islands and the western shores of Asia Minor, producing the literary fundaments of the Western intellectual tradition. In like manner, Ethiopic literacy was deeply influenced by the ancient Sabean language of Southern Arabia, while Swahili constitutes a linguistic admix of Arabic and Bantu vocabularies, which were written in the Arabic script prior to the European colonial era when the Latin alphabet came into widespread use for this purpose.

An additional type of intellectual tradition relates to those representing a cultural amalgamation of African and non-African religious or imperialist expansion. Two very different Berber traditions of North Africa exemplify this case. The first is reflected in the writing of Saint Augustine of Hippo, considered to be one of the most influential patriarchs of Western Christianity. Western philosophers have credited this fourth century African, who wrote *The City of God* and *The Confessions,* with having done more to define the later intellectual contours of Western civilization than any other single historical figure. However, they have tended to ignore his geographical identity as a Bishop of African Christianity. However, to do so is to miss the unique essence of St. Augustine's genius and contribution to the intellectual history of the West. While St.

Augustine, who grew up in Roman-dominated North Africa, was indeed a product of his Latin education and milieu, his temperament and thinking could not help but be influenced by the unique character of the African Church founded by Tertullian more than a century before. The singularity of St. Augustine's Christian vision may have emanated precisely from the fact that he was not a product of the Hellenized cities of the East with their humanized gods. He was rather a cultural heir to the peculiar melange of religions in Carthage and Numidia, which lingered on amid the Berber peasantry, coupled with the dualistic theology of Manichaeism, popular in Africa at the time.

Another intellectual giant of Berber ethnicity was the fourteenth century Islamic scholar Ibn Khaldun. His magnum opus, *Al-Muqaddima,* "Introduction to History," offers some of the most penetrating insights ever written on the nature of human society and political organization. And yet his writings are clearly presented from the vantage of a jurist and administrator whose astute observations derived from the environment of his homeland.

In like manner, Muslim West Africa's rich corpus of written traditions in Arabic, as well as indigenous languages employing the Arabic script, resulted from a centuries-long conversion process of the indigenous population to the Islamic religion through trading relations rather than conquest. The resulting literature reflects the Islamic literary tradition, as well as the local African cultural context of its respective authors.

Another important criterion for inclusion in this volume are traditions that predate the modern era. This is not because contemporary African literature in indigenous or European languages have been given all the recognition they deserve. It is rather, since they do enjoy wider availability, a growing public awareness already exists regarding the breadth and richness of this later literature.

The final two criteria for selections included in *The Intellectual Traditions of Pre-Colonial Africa* are that each selection represent an exemplar of the literary heritage of the society that spawned it and that it offer the modern reader some modicum of insight into that particular society's intellectual culture. For ancient Egypt an effort has been made to include literature from some if not all of its major literary genre. While "The Dispute of a Man with His Soul" intimates the social turmoil of the disintegrating Old Kingdom period, "Sinuhe's Triumphant Return Home" represents one of the finest examples of the Classical period of ancient Egyptian belles lettres. The "Hymn to the One God Aten" provides a glimpse into the brief but influential period of ancient Egyptian monotheism. The "Instructions of Amenemope" is an important work of Egyptian wisdom literature, which bears certain striking parallels to biblical Psalm 104, exemplifying the strong cultural influence that Egypt wielded over the ancient Near East. An excerpt from the important Rhind Papyrus presents one of the few surviving texts displaying the mathematical problem solving that Egypt bequeathed to the west. As for Nubia, in the absence of decipherment of the literature of Meroë, what remains most notably are the Kushite or Nubian stellae detailing their conquest of Egypt in the eighth century B.C. and establishment of Egypt's Twenty-Fifth Dynasty.

The two most noted works of Ethiopian literature are the *Kebra Negast* ("Glory of Kings") and *The Ethiopian Royal Chronicles.* The former book of traditions and religious folklore has been venerated in Ethiopia for centuries, because of the unique role it played in articulating their presumed descent from the Hebrew King Solomon. *The Ethiopian Royal Chronicles* represent courtly literature, depicting the life and times of that country's rulers from the thirteenth century onward. The sacred literature of Ethiopia, although not presented in this particular anthology, is fairly extensive. It includes the books of the Old and New Testament in addition to such apocalyptic Hebrew books as the Book of Enoch and the Book of Jubilees, preserved only in their ancient Ethiopic or Ge'ez versions.

The oldest extant literary works from West Africa are sixteenth-century writings from Timbuktu in the empire of Songhay. These chronicles, excerpts from which are translated in this anthology, suggest the existence of other works that have since perished. It was from these intellectual traditions nurtured in Timbuktu that subsequent scholars from Northern Nigeria and Senegal produced their own writings.

For the East African coast, the popular nineteenth century Swahili poem, "Utendi wa Mwana Kupona" ("Poem of Madam Kupona"), written by the wife of a Lamu notable, offers insights into the lifestyle, as well as social and religious mores, of a well-to-do East African household of the century before the European colonization of that continent. The anonymous Swahili Chronicle of Kilwa represents a genre of historical writing that offers important exposure to the cultural lore and history of the society.

This book has been divided into 10 parts to correspond with Africa's broad historical and geographical divisions. While this sectioning should represent a convenience to readers becoming exposed to various traditions of which they may possess little previous awareness, an important caveat must be borne in mind. Namely, availability of traditions are determined by what has not been lost to the ravages of time, as well as the interests and inclinations of translators to present texts in modern English. For ancient Egypt, most of all, scholars have no way of knowing the full extent of the intellectual heritage of this remarkable civilization. All that can be studied is that which has survived. What then constitutes the existing body of Egyptian literature offers a far broader sampling than is commonly known by a public generally unfamiliar with any aspects of Egyptian culture apart from its monumental architecture and religion. While the corpus of Egyptian literature owes its existence to the caprice of fate, this literature offers both aesthetic rewards and hints about the wealth of intellectual traditions that no longer exist.

One final point must be made in explaining the goals of this work. Recent anthropological findings have bolstered contemporary thinking that the African continent served as the cradle of mankind. However, that privilege did not come without costs. Having borne the rewards and burden of human habitation from earliest times, an ecologically fragile Africa is today confronted with the fierce consequences of prolonged contact between humankind and the environment. The Nile River valley, whose extraordinary fertility sustained ancient Egypt's population density and underpinned its wealth, has tragically evolved into one of the most overpopulated and therefore economically troubled areas of the world. The gold reserves that once nourished the wealth of ancient Nubia and the merchant empires of Ghana, Mali, and Songhay are long depleted. The climatic processes of desertification emanating from the once fertile Sahara are intensifying on account of human activity. Overcultivation of poor soils, overgrazing, and excessive cutting of fuelwood have essentially destroyed the agricultural base of the regions bordering the Sahara. In the area once encompassed by the ancient West

African empire of Songhay, the desert has spread more than 350 kilometers in the past 20 years alone. The descendants of the ancient Nubians in what is today the Sudan battle desertification which threatens to envelope what remains of agricultural land at an accelerating pace of 10 kilometers a year. Ethiopia, much of what lies in an ecologically fragile zone also prone to desertification, is today far better known for its devastating periodic famines than the richness of its historical traditions. These relentless processes of ecological decline also represent an integral part of Africa's history, interwoven in the fabric of the rise and fall of states.

Additionally, this volume ends with the advent of European colonialism, which for much of Africa occurred around the turn of the twentieth century. The economic and cultural disruptions engendered by the European colonization of Africa have been overwhelming and profound. For these reasons the selections in this book can also be read with a certain poignancy, because they predate the colonial era.

Some of the most brilliant intellectual work occurred during periods of political instability and imperial decline. The disintegration of ancient Egypt's Old Kingdom, which scholars now believe coincided with a natural disruption of Nile flooding patterns, produced some of its finest, though deeply pessimistic, literature including "The Dispute of a Man with His Soul," presented in this anthology. Certainly the 13 years that Saint Augustine worked on *The City of God* were tumultuous ones for the Roman Empire as he witnessed the disintegration of the old order. Alaric the Visigoth's sack of Rome in A.D. 410 precipitated the work, and barely three years after its completion, the Vandals overran North Africa. The two noted chronicles of the empire of Songhay in West Africa, the *Tarikh al-Sudan* ("History of the Land of the Blacks") and the *Tarikh al-Fattash* ("History of the Searcher for Knowledge"), both describe with intensity of feeling the destruction of this state, which never recovered from the Moroccan invasion of 1591. In this regard, the author of the *Tarikh al-Sudan* introduces his work thus:

> I was present at the ruin of knowledge and at its effacement and saw it disappear at the same time as the gold coins and even the small change [which have also vanished]. And then, because knowledge is rich in its treasures and fertile in information, since it reveals knowledge to man of his homeland, his ancestors, their annals, the names of their heroes and their biography, I asked divine assistance and undertook to write myself all that I was able to gather on the subject of the princes of the Sudan and of the Songhay race in order to recount their adventures, their history, their exploits and their battles. Then, I added to this the history of Timbuktu, from the foundation of this city, the princes who reigned in it, the scholars and saints who inhabited it and other things as well.

From Africa's east coast, one of the most noted Swahili poems of the nineteenth century, the "Utendi wa Inkishafi" ("Poem of Lament"), represents a homily to the collapsed East African sultanate of Pate. Its author, Saiyid Abdallah, laments:

> Where are the brave men of Pate sultanate
>   men of noble and shining mien?
> They have been forced into the mansions of the eternal sands . . .

To read and reflect on the literatures of ancient Africa is to experience the enduring beauty and genius of the human intellect. But it is also to confront the transitoriness of societies and empires. Although the traditions presented in this book may have been eclipsed by time, they are not dead. These works of human genius possess the radiant power to cast long shadows and humble those who in their contemporary arrogance believe that monuments of stone and steel alone are immortal.

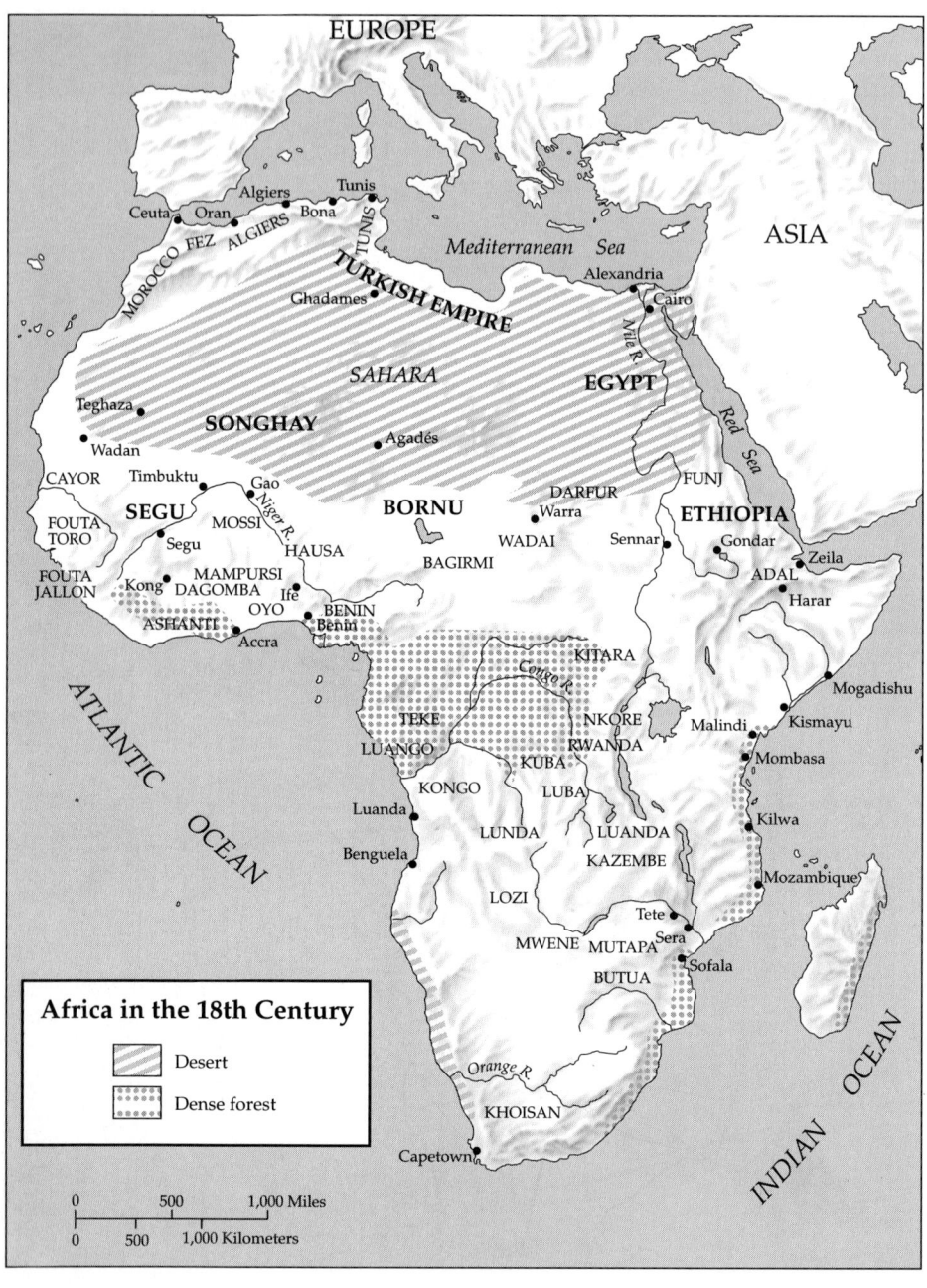

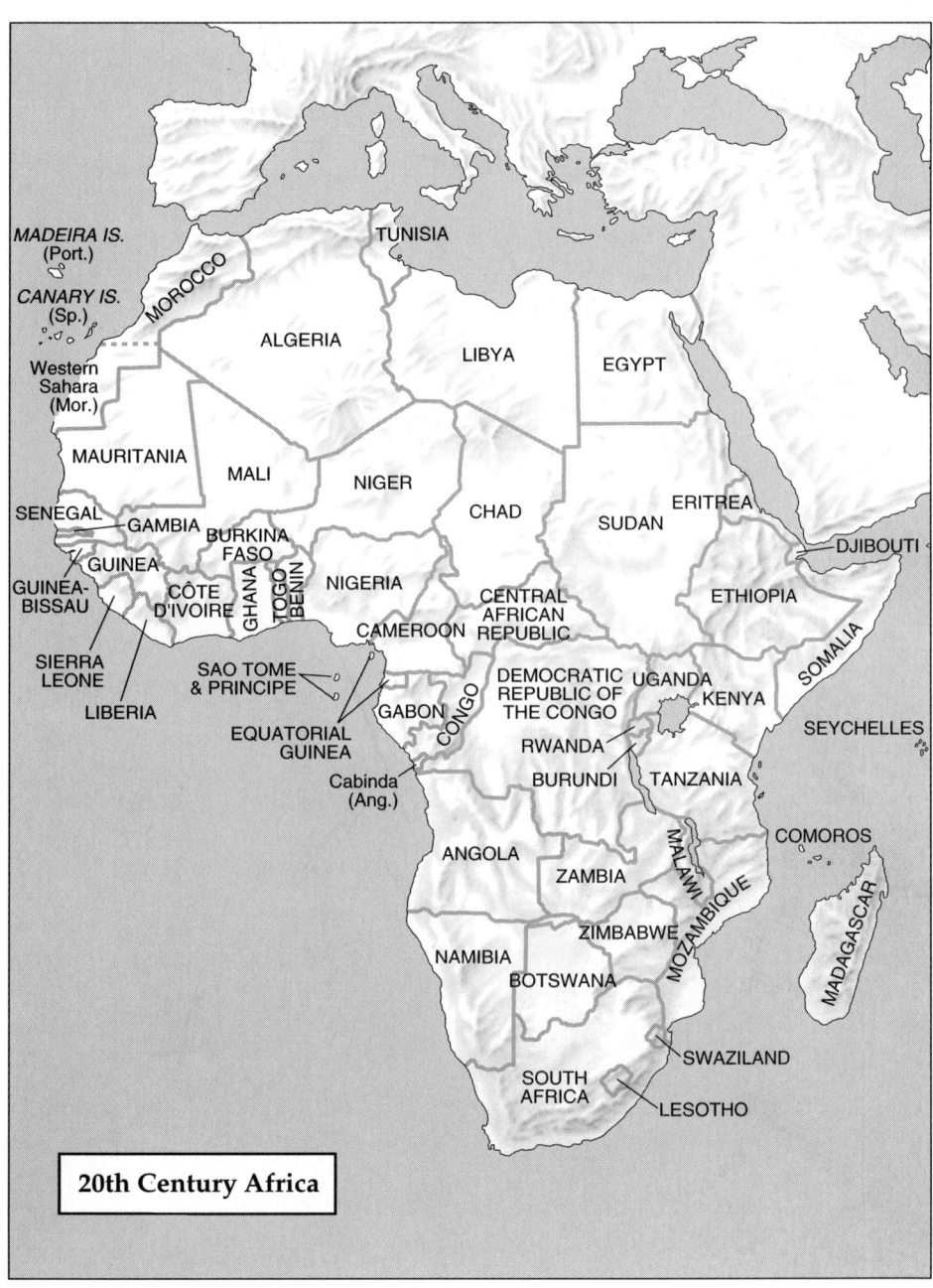

PART ONE

Pharaonic Egypt

The breathtaking imagery of pyramids set against a desert backdrop, gold-encased pharaonic tombs, and monumental statuary devoted to a pantheon of gods represents the ancient Egypt embossed on the contemporary imagination. The decipherment of hieroglyphics is no longer a barrier to our understanding of this remarkable civilization and its people.

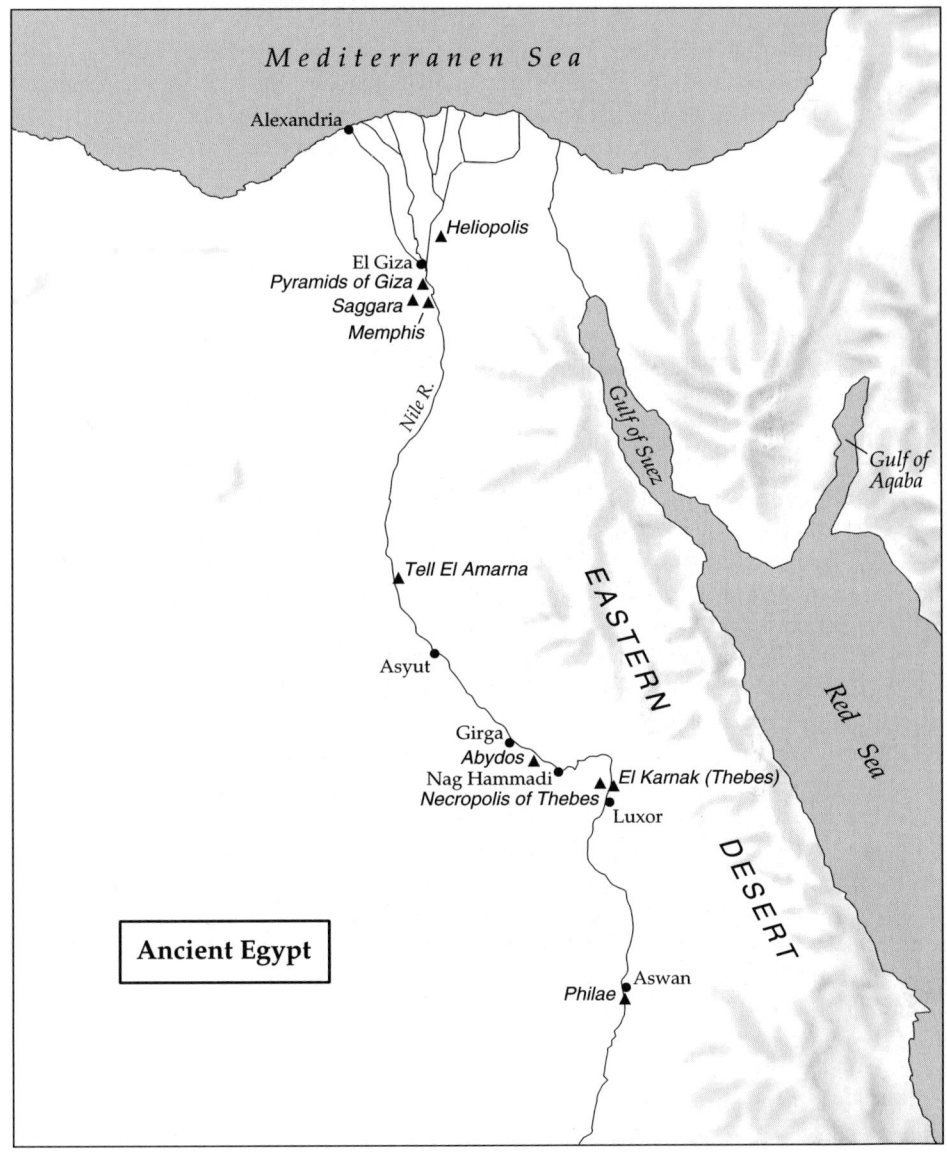

As a consequence scholars are now beginning to recognize that the ideas and humanity reflected in the intellectual culture of ancient Egypt, rather than its pharaonic architecture, may turn out to be that society's most enduring legacy of all.

Lasting for more than 3,000 years, the Nile Valley civilization of Egypt represents the most long-lasting society humankind has yet achieved. Archaeological evidence suggests the existence of settled populations engaged in farming along this stretch of the immensely fertile Nile River valley as early as 10,000 B.C., growing strains of wild barley, sorghum, and millet first cultivated in Nubia to the south. Egypt's dynastic history begins around 3100 B.C. when the first known pharaoh Menes or Narmer emerged from southern, that is, "upper" Egypt and unified that region with the northern part of the country or "lower" Egypt. The godlike nature of the Egyptian king or "pharaoh" is a concept that the Egyptians retained from the cultural influences of the south.

THE DYNASTIES

Contemporary scholars have categorized the dynastic history of Egypt into three kingdoms and two intermediate periods. The Old Kingdom (2700–2200 B.C.) represented the era of ancient Egypt's consolidation and the production of some of its most lasting achievements, including construction of the Great Pyramid at Giza that is the tomb of Pharaoh Cheops. The building of it used 2.3 million stone blocks weighing in at 2.5 tons each. Scholars have also estimated that the pyramid's construction required a workforce of 20,000 men laboring for 23 years in order to complete this massive structure. This period also coincides with the development of a remarkable number of innovations, from the development of this monumental architectural style employing stone to the use of hieroglyphics.

The Old Kingdom's 500-year span of political consolidation and architectural and scientific achievement was followed by the First Intermediate period (2200–2050 B.C.), a time of chaos when the central authority of the pharaoh was lost to the competing interests of provincial leaders. However, by 2060 B.C. a powerful new ruling family had emerged in upper (southern) Egypt at Thebes, bringing about the beginnings of a new period of centralized authority and prosperity for the country. This Middle Kingdom (2050–1780 B.C.) period witnessed an especially strong growth of the arts and literature. For this reason this era is often referred to as Egypt's Classical period. During the 300-year span of the Middle Kingdom, Egypt also extended its boundaries southward into parts of Nubia in order to gain control of a lucrative trade in gold and ivory operating within the Nubian kingdom of Kush.

Ecological evidence suggests that the Second Intermediate period (1800–1500 B.C.) that followed the Middle Kingdom and perhaps even the earlier First Intermediate period of centralized collapse may have been precipitated by changes in the Nile flooding patterns. The changes disrupted agricultural productivity and eroded the surpluses upon which centralized authority was based. In any case invaders from Syria and Canaan, known as Hyksos, assumed the weakened throne of Egypt and ruled until they were finally ousted by a new Egyptian dynasty in 1570 B.C. In this way the New Kingdom came into being and endured for half a millennium. It was during this time in Egyptian history that the powerful Queen Hatshepsut (1486–1468 B.C.) came to the throne and ruled as a king. The New Kingdom was also a period of imperial expansion where Egypt extended its rule into the Near East.

A century after Hatshepsut's reign the "Amarna Revolution" occurred with the coming to power of Akhenaten (1375–1362) who shifted the capital from Thebes to the new city of Amarna. The new pharaoh broke away from the entrenched priesthood in order to establish Egyptian monotheism, through devotion to Aten, the god of the Sun-Disk.

Akhenaten's successor Tutankhamen (1362–1352) is perhaps the most popularly known of all the Egyptian monarchs only because his tomb survived intact so that the modern world could marvel at the extraordinariness of pharaonic culture. Tutankhamen died young but not before returning the Amen priesthood to primacy and the pantheon of gods they acknowledged, while downgrading the monotheistic divinity of Aten.

A period of gradual, irreversible decline set in after 1100 B.C. Nubia gained in strength as Egypt became weaker, and in 730 B.C. the Nubian state of Kush invaded its northern neighbor and established the twenty-fifth dynasty of Egypt. The Kushites were eventually overthrown by the Assyrians, whose brief rule was overturned by the Persians, who ruled until Alexander the Great of Macedon conquered Egypt in 332 B.C. Alexander left his general, Ptolemy, to rule on his behalf, establishing the Greek Ptolemaic dynasty of Egypt.

The Roman period of Egyptian history began with the defeat of Cleopatra and Antony by the Roman General Octavian in 30 B.C. and lasted until A.D. 324. However, by then the 3,000-year-old culture of the Egyptians had become so interwoven into the fabric of the ancient world that it had achieved its own special form of immortality.

HIEROGLYPHICS

In the 1820s a young French scholar named Jean-François Champollion published *Egyptian Grammar* and *Egyptian Dictionary*. These linguistic reference books utilized his decipherments of hieroglyphic inscriptions on a stone tablet discovered by French engineers three decades earlier at Rosetta near the mouth of the Nile. The work of Champollion and other early Egyptologists opened the world of the ancient Egyptians to the West. However, it is only in modern times that a more sophisticated understanding of their language has allowed for translations that do any justice at all to the sophistication and subtleties of Egyptian thought. The contemporary Egyptologist, Joseph Kaster, has noted:

> our intimate knowledge of the language and the accessibility of most of the discovered writings and inscriptions in good scholarly editions, have enabled us to make an intelligent comparative valuation of the civilization of ancient Egypt, and to determine its place in the political and cultural development of mankind. We find, as a result, that the debt of Western civilization to ancient Egypt is far greater than one might be inclined to imagine.[1]

---

[1] Joseph Kaster, *The Wisdom of Ancient Egypt: Writings from the Time of the Pharaohs* (New York: Barnes and Noble Books, 1993), p. 6.

Specifically, Kaster notes such Egyptian cultural contributions to the West as the beginnings of technology, engineering, mathematics, and astronomy, as well as the solar calendar of 12 months. The Egyptian idea of *maat,* that is, "the inner sense of right and justice which is the common heritage of humanity," is a concept articulated by Socrates for the Greeks after the Egyptians had been governing themselves in this manner for more than 2,000 years.[2]

One of the most controversial areas of possible Egyptian diffusion to the West surrounds the alphabet itself. As scholars study the scripts employed by the ancient Egyptians, that is, hieratic and demonic, as well as hieroglyphics, an intense debate has erupted in academic circles as to whether the Semitic scripts of the Near East that developed into the alphabet in Europe might also have evolved from the Egyptian scripts rather than having evolved independently.[3] Joseph Kaster observes that the discovery in 1906 of 10 stone tablets in the Sinai peninsula region of Egypt where the pharaohs had operated turquoise mines led Sir Alan Gardiner to suggest that these signs were a connecting link between hieroglyphics and the Semitic alphabetic script.[4]

EGYPTIAN THEOLOGY

Because it has taken more than a century for Egyptologists to gain sufficient proficiency in the decipherment of hieroglyphics to acknowledge the breadth and subtlety of Egyptian thought, it is only now that the larger public can begin to appreciate the spiritual force that Egyptian religion had on the ancient world. This theology shared by the Egyptians with other African populations of the Nile Valley dramatically differed in attitudes toward death and the afterlife from the Mediterranean peoples, whether of Greece and Rome or the ancient Near East. To the Africans a life after death existed where the human spirit merged with the great god Osiris and those who had lived a righteous life would attain perpetual joy.

The general outline of Egyptian theology emanates from the story of Osiris who possessed two natures, being partly god and partly man, and his sister-wife, the goddess Isis. Osiris was put to death by the wicked Typhon, the hippopotamus, and his limbs scattered to the four winds. Isis collected his body parts and put them together again, returning Osiris to life but not upon earth. He became judge of the dead and his son Horus, depicted in temple art with the head of a hawk, became the last of the gods to reign on earth. The pharaohs or kings of Egypt were believed to be the direct descendants of Horus. Nineteenth century Egyptologist Samuel Sharpe observes the significance of another important element of their theology, that is, the concept of the trinity:

> The gods were very much grouped in sets of three, and each city had its own trinity. In Thebes it was Amun-Ra, Athor and Chonso, or father, mother and son . . . In Abousimbel and Derr in Nubia, the trinity is Pthah, Amun-Ra, and Horus-Ra, and

---

[2]Ibid., pp. 11–12.
[3]Albertine Gaur, *A History of Writing* (London: The British Library), pp. 88–89.
[4]Kaster, *The Wisdom of Ancient Egypt: Writings from the Time of the Pharoahs,* p. 9.

there are the three gods to whom Rameses II is sacrificing the Philistines in the scriptures at Beyrout . . . At Philae the trinity is Osiris, Isis and Horus, a group indeed common to most parts of Egypt . . . Every king of Egypt, even while living, was added to the number of the gods, and declared to be the Son of Ra, which was the title set over the second oval of his name. He was then sometimes made into the third person of a Trinity . . . This opinion of the miraculous birth of the kings is well explained in a series of sculptures on the wall of the temple of Luxor . . . Lastly, the several gods or priests attend in adoration upon their knees to present their gift to this wonderful child, who is seated in the midst of them and is receiving their homage.[5]

Scholars are only now coming to appreciate the power and influence that the Egyptian theological culture had on the ancient world of that time. Siegfried Morenz, author of *Egyptian Religion,* notes the influence of the Egyptian court chronicle upon Hebrew literary forms:

Here we may mention the traces left by the Egyptian royal ritual upon the courts of Israelite rulers, which affected even Isaiah's famous list of appellations for the Prince of Peace. For this, although mutilated, is probably derived from the fivefold titulary of the Egyptian king.[6]

EGYPTIAN LITERATURE

The literature of the Egyptians as with their monumental architecture was intimately bound up with their religious worldview. The Egyptians believed that the god Thoth invented writing. From the period of the Old Kingdom (2700–2200 B.C.), the largest corpus of literature is the pyramid texts and "wisdom" or "instruction" literature presenting proverbs and "precepts for correct living." The political environment of the First Intermediate period, chaotic, famine-ridden, is mirrored in a literature of cynicism that developed during that time. The pyramid texts of the pharaohs are followed during this era by the coffin texts of the nobility, representing a gradual process of religious democratization, whereby not just the pharaoh but the aristocracy receive the promise of life after death. The Middle Kingdom (2050–1780 B.C.) is regarded as the classical period of the Egyptian language, during which some of the most sublime examples of belles lettres were written, including *The Tale of Sinuhe.* It is during this period of Egyptian prosperity and imperial expansion that *The Book of the Dead* emerges as a further adaptation of the coffin texts, broadening the base of their reach into the middle classes.[7] Once again we note a progressive democratizing process of the doctrine of immortality, in that it is now offered to the middle classes of merchants and artisans as well as to nobles and pharaohs. It is into this environment that Christianity arrives in the early years A.D. The Egyptian city of Alexandria becomes a center for the formulation of this new Christian theology, and the descendants of the ancient Egyptian scribes

---

[5]Samuel Sharpe, *Egyptian Mythology and Egyptian Christianity with Their Influences on the Opinions of Modern Christendom* (London: Carter Publishers, 1896), p. 19.
[6]Siegfried Morenz, *Egyptian Religion* (translated by Ann E. Keep) (London: Methuen & Co. Ltd., 1973), p. 252.
[7]Kaster, *The Wisdom of Ancient Egypt: Writings from the Time of the Pharoahs,* pp. 41–42.

become its early theologians, offering Egypt's masses the promise of eternal life through the embrace of a new Savior, Jesus Christ.

EGYPTIAN SCIENCE AND MATHEMATICS

In the past the study of the sciences in ancient Egypt were unfortunately impeded by two problems: a dearth of surviving papyri and the narrow methodological frameworks of traditional Western scholars themselves. The latter issue underpinned a common belief in the West until quite recently that the Egyptians, unlike the Greeks, were incapable of abstract thought, although they were unquestionably accomplished engineers. While scholars would today find such assumptions embarrassing and laughable, such notions tended to define the parameters of our understanding of the Egyptian sciences. And yet what we do know of the Egyptians is that they created a civilization of such consummate sophistication that scientific concepts formed an integral part of its society. While any texts that might elucidate much of their scientific understandings have been lost, their accomplishments in astronomy, engineering, and administration could not have occurred without a highly technical mastery of these subjects. Even our word *chemistry* derives from *al-kemi,* the name the ancient Egyptians gave themselves. We can appreciate the advanced understanding they had of astronomy in their development of the solar calendar and 24-hour timekeeping, since this system is still with us today. In the field of medicine, mummification is only the most visible survival of Egyptian accomplishments. Pharaonic medicine evolved into a highly specialized science embracing effective surgical procedures and herbal pharmacology, which included natural ointments similar to the modern drug Neosporin. In the field of mathematics, several important papyri attest to Egyptian intellectual absorption in algebra, geometry, and trigonometry.

TEXT 1

The Old Kingdom: The Resurrection of Osiris

from The Pyramid Texts[1]

By 5,000 B.C. the earliest populations to inhabit the Nile River valley had shifted from hunting and gathering to cultivation of the extraordinarily rich soils along the river. As the political organization of the societies of the Nile began to congeal, so did their religious traditions. When King Menes of upper Egypt, that is, the southern region bordering Nubia, conquered the north around 3200 B.C., the unification of this new state produced a concomitant synthesis of localized theologies. The birthplace of worship for the Egyptian Divine Ancestor, Osiris, appears to have been in Menes's homeland of upper Egypt or Nubia, where in earliest times Osiris was worshipped as a deity of fertility. The king was then worshipped as the incarnation of Osiris's son, Horus. Devotion to Osiris came to be conjoined over time with that of Ra, the sun-god of lower (northern) Egypt to form the basis of the ancient Egyptian religion. Osiris offered his adherents the hope of resurrection and immortality. As E. A. Wallis Budge has pointed out in the early part of this century:

> [Osiris's] human nature . . . enabled him to understand the needs, troubles, and grief of men, and to listen sympathetically to their prayers, and his divine nature gave him powers to help them in this world and in the next.[2]

It was in fact the legend of Osiris that furnished Egypt with its unifying myth and defined the divinity of the Egyptian pharaoh as the incarnation of his son, Horus. The Egyptian theology of creation predates even the oldest of the pyramid texts, which are the largest bodies of texts written during the Old Kingdom (2700–2200 B.C.). They derived their name from the fact that they were inscribed on the inside walls of pyramids built for kings of the Fifth and Sixth Dynasties.

---

[1]Joseph Kaster, *The Wisdom of Ancient Egypt: Writings from the Time of the Pharoahs* (New York: Barnes and Noble Books, 1993), pp. 83–90.
[2]E. A. Wallis Budge, *Osiris and the Egyptian Resurrection* (New York: G. P. Putnam's Sons, 1911), p. xix.

It is from this "Hymn to Osiris," a portion of which is excerpted below, that derives the most quoted lines in Egyptian theology: "And he rose splendid, and ascended the seat of his father in glory."

[The resurrection of Osiris]

It is your great sister who has collected your flesh, who has gathered your hands, who sought you, who found you on your side on the shore of Nedyt.
Your two sisters, Isis and Nephthys, come to you. They heal you, complete and great, in your name of Great Black, fresh and great, in your name of Great Green!
Osiris, your mother Nut has spread herself over you, that she may hide you from all evil things. Nut has guarded you from all evil; you are the greatest among her children.
O Osiris, he who comes and comes, you shall not be in need! Your mother comes; you shall not be in need!
Nut, you shall not be in need; protectress of the great, you shall not be in need; protectress of the fearful, you shall not be in need!
She protects you, she prevents your need, she gives back your head to you; she collects your bones for you; she brings your heart into your body for you.
Nut has made you to be as a god to your enemy, for you are made young in your name of Fresh Water.
Osiris, who was placed upon his side by his brother Set, he who was in Nedyt stirs; his head is raised up by Ra. His abomination is to sleep; he hates to be wearied!
Osiris awakes in peace; he who was in Nedyt awakes in peace. His head is lifted up by Ra.
He rots not; he stinks not!
"Come, my child!" says Atum. "Come to us!" say they, say the gods to you, Osiris!
"Our brother is come to us—the eldest, the first-begotten of his father, the first-born of his mother."
You support the sky on your right side, having life. You live, because the gods ordained that you live. Osiris supports the sky on his right side, having life. He lives his life, because the gods have ordained that you live!
You lean on the earth on your left side, having joy. You live your life, because the gods have ordained that you live!
Osiris is the blood which came forth from Isis! Osiris is the red blood which came forth from Nephythys!

[Osiris impregnates Isis]

Your sister comes to you, rejoicing for love of you!
Isis comes to you, rejoicing for love of you!
"I have assembled my brother; I have united his limbs. I have come, I lay hold of you; I have put your heart in your body for you. I have come, rejoicing for love of you! O Osiris, this source is within you! I am the water-hole; I am overflowing!"

Source: From *The Wings of the Falcon* by Joseph Kaster, © 1968 by Joseph Kaster. Reprinted by permission of Henry Holt & Co., Inc.

TEXT 1: *The Old Kingdom: The Resurrection of Osiris*

You have placed her upon your phallus, that your seed may go into her, pointed like Sothis. Horus the pointed has come forth from you as Horus who was in Sothis!

[The battle of Horus and Set]

It is Horus! He has come to avenge his father Osiris! He has proclaimed a royal decree of death in the places of Anubis. Everyone hears it and he [Set] shall not live.
Thoth, spare none among those who have wronged the king!

[The first company of the "justified" was born] before there was anger, before there was tumult, before there was strife, before there was conflict, before the Eye of Horus was plucked out, before the testicles of Set were torn away.
Horus falls because of his Eye. The Bull Set collapses because of his testicles.
Horus has moaned because of his Eye. Set has moaned because of his testicles.
Horus has seized Set; he has placed him under you, that he may carry you, and that he may quake under you like the quaking of the earth, for you are more exalted than he, in your name of "He of the Exalted Land."
Horus has caused that you seize him with your hand, without his escaping you. O Osiris, Horus has avenged you! He has done it for his *Ka* in you, that you may be satisfied in your name of "Satisfied *Ka*."

[The return of the organs of Horus and Set after the battle]

Osiris is the messenger of the gods in search of the Eye of Horus. Osiris searched for it in Buto; he found it at Heliopolis. Osiris snatched it from the head of Set, at the place where they fought.
The messenger of Horus, whom he loves, was Osiris, who has brought back to him his Eye. The messenger of Set, whom he loves, was Osiris, who has brought back to him his testicles.
You, Osiris, shall spit in the face of Horus in order to drive the injury away from him. You shall catch the testicles of Set, in order to drive away his mutilation. That one was born to you; this one was begotten by you.
You have been born, O Horus, as one whose name is "him at whom the earth quakes." You are begotten, O Set, as one whose name is "him at whom the sky trembles." That one [Horus] has not a mutilation; this one [Set] has not an injury. This one has not an injury; that one has not a mutilation.

[Horus gives his Eye to Osiris]

Your son Horus has smitten him; he has snatched back his Eye from him; he has given it to you, that you may become glorious thereby, that you may become mighty before the Glorious Ones.
O Osiris, arise! Horus comes, he reclaims you from the gods. Horus has loved you; he has equipped you with his Eye.
Horus has given you his Eye, the hard one. He has placed it for you, that you may be strong, and that all your enemies may fear you. Horus has completely filled you with his Eye, in this his name of "fullness of the god."
Horus has opened your eye for you, that you may see with it, in its name of "Opener of the Way."
[In a variant spell, Osiris eats the Eye:] that which you have eaten is an eye. Your body is full of it; your son Horus parts with it for you, that you may live by it.

[Horus as the Avenger of Osiris]

Horus says: Arise for me, father! Stand up for me, O Osiris! It is I; I am your son; I am Horus your avenger. I have smitten for you him who smote you. I have avenged you, O father Osiris, on him who did you evil!

O Osiris, Horus has found you! He rejoices over you. Go forth against your enemy; you are greater than he!

Horus has caused him to carry you; he has delivered you from your enemy. He has avenged you.

Horus has extended your enemy beneath you. You are older than he [Set] for you were born before him.

Horus has caused Thoth to bring your enemy to you. He has placed you upon his back, and he dares not resist you. Sit you down upon him!

Mount; sit upon him, so that he dare not resist you!

And the Ennead shall not allow Set to be free from carrying you forever!

[Set's lying testimony, and his judgment]

Remember, Set, put in your heart this word which Geb spoke, the threat which the gods made against you in the house of the Prince, in Heliopolis, because you did strike Osiris to the ground!

As you, Set, did say: "I have not done this against him!" that you might prevail thereby; that you might be acquitted, and prevail in spite of Horus.

As you, Set, did say: "It is he who defied me!" As you, Set, did say: "It is he who came too near to me!"

Osiris desires to be justified by that which he has done; since Tefen and Tefnut have justified Osiris, since the Two Truths have heard him, since Shu has been his advocate, since the Two Truths have given verdict, he has encompassed the thrones of Geb; he has raised himself to that which he wished.

So that his limbs are united, which were once hidden. He united himself with those who are in Nun. He concludes his defense in Heliopolis.

[The triumph of Osiris and Horus]

O Osiris, stand up, see what which your son has done for you! Awake, hear that which Horus has done for you!

He has caused Thoth to turn back for you the Followers of Set, and that he bring them to you all together.

Thoth has seized your enemy for you, so that he is beheaded together with his followers; there is not one whom he has spared!

He has beaten for you him who beats you. He has killed for you him who kills you, like a wild bull. He had bound for you him who binds you. He has put him under your great daughter who is in Kedem.

So that mourning ceased in the Two Palaces of the gods!

[The risen Osiris as the ongoing principle of life]

Osiris has come forth this day at the head of the full flood. Osiris is the crocodile with the flourishing green plume, with head erect, his breast lifted, the foaming one who has come forth from the thigh of the Great Tail which is in the gleaming heavens.

Osiris has come to his pools, which are in the land of the flood, in the great inundation, to the seats of contentment—green of fields, which are in the horizon.

Osiris makes green and fertile the fields in both lands of the horizon. Osiris has brought the gleam to the Great Eye in the midst of the field. Osiris receives his throne which is in the horizon.

Osiris rises as Sebek, son of Neith. Osiris eats with his mouth; Osiris urinates; Osiris copulates with his phallus. Osiris is lord of semen which women seize from their husbands, wherever Osiris wishes, according as his heart conceives.

O you whose life-giving tree becomes green, who is over his field; O opener of flowers, he who is on his sycamore; O you whose riverbanks glisten with verdure, who is over his tree of charm!

O lord of green fields, rejoice this day! Osiris will henceforth be among you; Osiris will go forth in his environs. Osiris will live on that upon which you live.

O Bulls of Atum! Make Osiris green! Refresh Osiris more than the Red Crown which is upon his head, more than the floodwaters which are upon his thighs, more than the dates which are in his fist!

TEXT 2

First Intermediate Period: The Dispute of a Man with His Soul[1]

The seventh through the eleventh dynasties of Egypt, covering the period of 2200–2050, have come to be known as the First Intermediate period. The central authority of the king disintegrated, possibly due to the severe economic disruption caused by the period of the irregular flooding of the Nile. The provincial lords were, as a consequence, able to wrest control from the disintegrating central authority. However, the period ushered in became one of political chaos and widespread famine. Not surprisingly, the surviving texts from that era reflect the anxiety and cynicism of those times.

"The Dispute of a Man with His Soul" represents one of the most celebrated works of that epoch. This text in hieroglyphics is contained in the Berlin Papyrus 3024. According to William Kelly Simpson in The Literature of Ancient Egypt, this work:

> consists of a dialogue between a disillusioned and despairing man and his soul on the topic of the use of going on living; the speaker sees death as the only escape from the miseries of the world as he sees it, and yet hesitates to take the plunge; the soul likewise vacillates between living and dying, but finally decides in favor of life.[2]

---

[1] William Kelly Simpson, *The Literature of Ancient Egypt: An Anthology of Stories, Instructions, and Poetry* (New Haven, CT: Yale University Press, 1973), pp. 201–9.
[2] Ibid., p. 201.

[. . .] you in order to say [. . .] their [tongues] cannot ⌜question⌝, for it will be ⌜crookedness⌝ [. . .] payments, their tongues cannot ⌜question⌝.[4]

I opened my mouth to my soul, that I might answer what it had said: / This is too much for me today, that my soul does not argue with me; it is too great for [exaggeration], it is as if one ignored me. Let my soul not depart, that it may attend to it for me [. . .] in my body like a net of cord, / but it will not succeed in escaping the day of trouble. See, my soul misleads me, but I do not listen to it; draws me toward death ere <I> have come to it and casts <me> on the fire to burn me [. . .] / it approaches me on the day of trouble and it stands on yonder side as does a . . . Such is he who goes forth that he may bring himself for him. O my soul, too stupid to ⌜ease⌝ misery in life and yet holding me back from death ere I come to it, sweeten / the West for me. Is it (too much) trouble? Yet life is a transitory state, and even trees fall. Trample on wrong, for my misery endures. May Thoth who pacifies the gods judge me; may Khons defend me, / even he who writes truly; may Re hear my plaint, even he who ⌜commands⌝ the solar bark; may Isdes defend me in the Holy Chamber, [because] ⌜the needy one is weighed down with⌝ [the burden] which he has lifted up from me; it is pleasant that / the gods should ward off the secret (thoughts) of my body.

What my soul said to me: Are you not a man? Indeed you are alive, but what do you profit? Yet you yearn for life like a man of wealth.

I said: I have not gone, (even though) that is on the ground. Indeed, you ⌜leap away⌝, but you will / not be cared for. Every prisoner says: "I will take you," but you are dead, though your name lives. Yonder is a resting place ⌜attractive⌝ to the heart; the West is a dwelling place, rowing [. . .] face. If my guiltless soul listens to me / and its heart is in accord with me, it will be fortunate, for I will cause it to attain the West, like one who is in his pyramid, to whose burial a survivor attended. I will [. . . over] your corpse, so that you make another soul ⌜envious / in weariness⌝. I will . . . , then you will not be cold, so that you ⌜make envious⌝ another soul which is hot. I will drink water at the eddy, I will raise up ⌜shade⌝, so that you ⌜make envious⌝ another soul which is hungry. If / you hold me back from death in this manner, you will find nowhere you can rest in the West. Be so kind, my soul, my brother, as to become my heir who shall make offering and stand at the tomb on the day of burial, that he may ⌜prepare⌝ a bier / for the necropolis.

My soul opened its mouth to me that it might answer what I had said: If you think of burial, it is a sad matter; it is a bringer of weeping through making a man miserable; it is taking a man from his house, he being cast on the high ground; never again will you go up that you may see / the sun. Those who built in granite and constructed ⌜halls⌝ in goodly pyramids with fine work, when the builders became gods their stelae were destroyed, like the weary ones who died on the riverbank through lack of a survivor, / the flood having taken its toll and the sun likewise, to whom talk the fishes of the banks of the water. Listen to me; behold it is good for men to hear. Follow the happy day and forget care.

A peasant ploughed his plot and loaded his harvest / aboard a ship, towing it when his time of festival drew near. He saw the coming of the darkness of the norther, for he

---

Source: From William Kelly Simpson, *The Literature of Ancient Egypt: An Anthology of Stories, Instructions, and Poetry,* © 1973. Reprinted by permission of Yale University Press.

was vigilant in the boat when the sun set. He ⌈escaped⌉ with his wife and children, but came to grief on a lake infested by / night with crocodiles. At last he sat down and broke silence, saying: I weep not for yonder mother, who has no more going forth from the West for another (term) upon earth; I sorrow rather for her children broken in the egg, who have looked in the face of the crocodile-god / ere they have lived.

A peasant asked for a meal, and his wife said to him: There is <. . .> for supper. He went out to . . . for a moment and returned to his house (raging) as if he were ⌈an ape⌉. His wife ⌈reasoned⌉ with him, but he would not listen to her; he . . . and the bystanders were ⌈helpless⌉.

I opened my mouth to my soul that I might answer what it had said:

Behold, my name is detested,
Behold, more than the smell of vultures
On a summer's day when the sky is hot.

Behold, my name is detested,
Behold, <more than the smell of> a catch of fish
/ On a day of catching when the sky is hot.

Behold, my name is detested,
Behold, more than the smell of ducks,
More than a covert of reeds full of waterfowl.

Behold, my name is detested,
Behold, more than the smell of fishermen,
More than the creeks / of the marshes where they have fished.

Behold, my name is detested,
Behold, more than the smell of crocodiles,
More than sitting by ⌈sandbanks⌉ full of crocodiles.

Behold, my name is detested,
Behold, more than a woman
About whom lies are told to a man.

Behold, / my name is detested,
Behold, more than a sturdy child
Of whom it is said: "He belongs to his rival."

Behold, my name is detested,
Behold, <more than> a town belonging to the monarch
Which mutters sedition when his back is turned.

To whom can I speak today?
Brothers are evil
And the friends of today unlovable.

To whom can I speak / today?
Hearts are rapacious
And everyone takes his neighbor's goods.

<To whom can I speak today?>
Gentleness has perished
And the violent man has come down on everyone.

To whom can I speak today?
Men are contented with evil
And goodness is neglected everywhere.

To whom can I speak / today?
He who should enrage a man by his ill deeds,
He makes everyone laugh <by> his wicked wrongdoing.

To whom can I speak today?
Men plunder
And every man robs his neighbor.

To whom can I speak today?
The wrongdoer is an intimate friend
And the brother with whom one used to act is become / an enemy.

To whom can I speak today?
None remember the past,
And no one helps him who used to do (good).

To whom can I speak today?
Brothers are evil,
And men have recourse to strangers for ⌜affection⌝.

To whom can I speak today?
Faces are averted,
And every man looks askance at / his brethren.

To whom can I speak today?
Hearts are rapacious
And there is no man's heart in which one can trust.

To whom can I speak today?
There are no just persons
And the land is left over to the doers of wrong.

To whom can I speak today?
There is lack of an intimate friend
And men have recourse to someone unknown / in order to complain to him.

To whom can I speak today?
There is no contented man,
And that person who once walked with him no longer exists.

To whom can I speak today?
I am heavy-laden with trouble
Through lack of an intimate friend.

To whom can I speak today?
The wrong which roams the earth,
/ There is no end to it.

Death is in my sight today
<As when> a sick man becomes well,
Like going out-of-doors after detention.

Death is at my sight today
Like the smell of myrrh,
Like sitting under an awning on a windy day.

Death is in my sight today
/ Like the perfume of lotuses,
Like sitting on the shore of the Land of Drunkenness.

Death is in my sight today
Like a trodden way,
As when a man returns home from an expedition.

Death is in my sight today
Like the clearing of the sky,
Like a man who . . . / . . . ⌜for⌝ something which he does not know.

Death is in my sight today
As when a man desires to see home
When he has spent many years in captivity.

Verily, he who is yonder will be a living god,
Averting the ill of him who does it.

Verily, he who is yonder will be one who stands in the Bark of the Sun,
Causing choice things to be given / therefrom for the temples.

Verily, he who is yonder will be a sage
Who will not be prevented from appealing to Re when he speaks.

What my soul said to me: Cast complaint upon ⌜the peg⌝, my comrade and brother; make offering on the brazier / and cleave to life, according as ⌜I⌝ have said. Desire me here, thrust the West aside, but desire that you may attain the West when your body goes to earth, that I may alight after you are weary; then will we make an abode together.

It is finished / from its beginning to its end, just as it was found in writing.

TEXT 3

The Middle Kingdom: Sinuhe's Triumphant Return Home[1]

The story of Sinuhe is considered by many Egyptologists to represent the finest work of Egyptian belles lettres. Composed in hieroglyphics during the Twelfth Dynasty in the twentieth century B.C., it relates with great drama the tale of an Egyptian courtier named Sinuhe. Perhaps fearing that he would be implicated in a possible conspiracy upon hearing news of the death of the reigning king, Amenemhat I, in 1961 B.C., Sinuhe flees the country. Intending to journey southward, his rudderless boat is thrown off course and he comes to live in exile in Syria–Palestine. The excerpt presented below narrates his triumphant return to the Egyptian homeland that he loves and has yearned for throughout his life lived in exile.

Sinuhe Wishes to Return to Egypt

O God, whoever you are, who decreed this flight, may you be merciful and may you set me in the capital. Perhaps you will let me see the place where my desire lives. What can be more important than joining my dead body to the land where / I was born? Come, help me! What has come to pass so far has been good. God has given me satisfaction. May He act similarly to better the end of one whom He had made miserable and be concerned about one whom He had shunted off to live in a foreign land. Today He is merciful, and He hearkens to the prayer of a man far off. May He change my region whence I roamed the earth for Him to the place from which He brought me.

The King of Egypt is merciful to me, and I live on his bounty. May I greet the mistress of the land who is in his palace, and may I attend to the errands of her children.

---

[1]William Kelly Simpson, *The Literature of Ancient Egypt: An Anthology of Stories, Instructions, and Poetry* (New Haven, CT: Yale University Press, 1973), pp. 66–74.
Source: From William K. Simpson, *The Literature of Ancient Egypt: An Anthology of Stories, Instructions, and Poetry,* © 1973. Reprinted by permission of Yale University Press.

My body will be youthful again. Old age has come down on me and feebleness has hurried upon me. My eyes are heavy, and my arms are immobile. / My feet stumble, and my senses are exhausted. I am ready for passing on, when they shall send me to the cities of eternity. But may I still serve the Mistress-of-All that she may say something good for me to her children. May she pass eternity above me.

Now this report was made to His Majesty, the King of Upper and Lower Egypt, Kheperkare, who will be judged right, concerning this state in which I was. His Majesty sent to me with provisions of the royal bounty. He rejoiced the heart of this servant as might be done for a ruler of a foreign land. And the king's children who were in his palace had me hear their messages.

The Royal Edict

Copy of the decree brought to this servant regarding his being brought back to Egypt: The Horus Life of Births, the Two Ladies Life of Births, the King of Upper and Lower Egypt, Kheperkare, Son of Re / Sesostris, living forever. The king orders Sinuhe: This decree of the king is brought to you to tell you that you have traversed the foreign countries and have come forth from Kedem to Retenu. By your heart's counsel to you, land has given you to land. What have you done that one should act against you? You have not blasphemed that one should reprove your words. You have not spoken in the council of the elders that one should restrain your speech. This idea, it took over your senses, although there was nothing in my mind against you. This heaven of yours, which is in the palace, she is well and she flourishes today as in her former state in the kingship of the land, with her children in the audience hall. You shall pile up the treasures which they give you, and you shall live off their bounty. When you have come to Egypt, you shall see the capital in which you were born. You shall kiss the ground at the Great Double Gate, and you shall associate with the Companions. Today / old age has begun for you, and potency has left you. You have thought about the day of burial, the passing over to an honored state. The night will be appointed for you with oils and poultices from the arms of Tayet (goddess of weaving). A procession will be made for you on the day of interment, the anthropoid sarcophagus (overlaid) with gold leaf, the head with lapis lazuli, and the sky above you as you are placed in the outer coffin and dragged by teams of oxen preceded by singers. The dance of the Muu will be performed at your tomb, and the necessary offerings will be invoked for you. They will slaughter at the entrance of your tomb chapel, its pillars to be set up in limestone as is done for the royal children. You shall not die in a foreign land, and Asiatics will not escort you. You shall not be placed in a ram's skin as they make your grave. All of this is too much for one who has roamed the earth. Take thought for your dead body and return.

Sinuhe's Reaction and His Reply

When this decree reached me, I was standing / among my tribe. As it was read out to me, I placed myself upon my belly and I touched the earth. I spread it out over my chest. Then I went about my encampment rejoicing and saying: How could such a thing be done for a servant whose senses led him astray to the land of the barbarians?

TEXT 3: *The Middle Kingdom: Sinuhe's Triumphant Return Home*

Indeed, (your) benevolence is excellent. O you who have saved me from Death. Your Ka will allow me to spend the end of my life with my body in the capital.

Copy of the reply to this decree. The servant of the palace Sinuhe says: In peace, in peace. This flight which this servant did in his ignorance is well known by your Ka, O good God, Lord of the Two Lands, whom Re loves and whom Montu, Lord of Thebes, favors, as well as Amun, Lord of the Thrones of the Two Lands, Sobk-Re, Lord of Sumenu, Horus, Hathor, Atum and his Ennead, Sopdu, Neferbau, Semseru, Horus the Easterner, the Mistress of Yemet, may she enfold your head, the council upon the flood waters, Min-Horus in the midst of the desert lands, Wereret, the Mistress of / Punt, Nut, Haoreis-Re, and the gods who are the Lords of the Beloved Land and the Islands of the Sea. They give life and prosperity to your nostrils; they grant you their bounty. They give you eternity without end and everlastingness without limit. Fear of you is repeated in the lowlands and in the highlands, for you have conquered all that the sun disk encircles. Such is the prayer of this servant to his lord who has rescued him from the West.

Lord of perception, who perceives the people, may he perceive in the Majesty of the palace that this servant was afraid to speak. It is a heavy matter to repeat. The great God, equal of Re, knows the mind of one who has worked for him ⌜of his own accord⌝. For this servant is in the hands of someone who takes thought for him; I am set in his guidance. Your Majesty is the conquering Horus; you arms prevail over all lands. May now Your Majesty command that there be brought Meki from Kedem, / Khentiuwash from out of Keshu, and Menus, those who set your authority over the lands of the Fenkhu. They are rulers whose names are worthy and who have been brought up in your love. Not to mention Retenu, for it belongs to you even as your dogs. This flight which your servant made, it was not premeditated. It was not in my mind. I did not prepare it. I cannot say what separated me from my place. It was like a dream: as when a Delta man sees himself in Aswan or a man of the marshlands in Nubia. Yet I was not afraid. No one chased me. I did not hear a word of censure. No one heard my name in the mouth of the town crier. Except that my body cringed, my feet hastened, and my senses overwhelmed me, with the God who decreed this flight / drawing me on. I am not stubborn ⌜in advance⌝. A man is modest when his homeland is known, for Re has placed the fear of you throughout the land and the dread of you in every foreign land. Whether I am in the capital or in this place, yours is everything which is covered by this horizon. The sun disk rises at your bidding, and the water of the river is drunk if you wish. The air of the heavens is breathed if you speak. Now that this servant has been sent for, this servant will hand over (his property) to his children, whom he has brought up in this place. May Your Majesty act as he wishes, for one lives by the air which you give. Re, Horus, and Hathor love your noble nostrils; Montu, Lord of Thebes, wishes that they live forever.

Sinuhe's Return

I was allowed to spend a day in Yaa to transfer my goods to my children. My eldest son was in charge of my tribe. / My tribe and all my possessions were in his hands, as well as all my serfs, my cattle, my fruit, and all my productive trees. This servant proceeded south. I tarried at the Ways of Horus. The commander in charge of the patrol there sent a message to the capital to give them notice. His Majesty had them send a capable overseer of field laborers of the royal estate and with him ships laden with presents of the royal bounty for the Asiatics who had come with me to lead me to the Ways of Horus. I called each one of them by name. I started out and raised sail. Each servant was at his task. (Dough) was kneaded and strained (for beer) beside me until I reached the wharf of Itjtowy.

Sinuhe at the Palace

When dawn came and it was morning, I was summoned. Ten men came and ten men went to usher me to the palace. I touched my forehead to the ground between the sphinxes. / The royal children waited in the gateway to meet me. The Companions who showed me into the pillared court set me on the way to the reception hall. I found His Majesty upon the Great Throne set in a recess (paneled) with fine gold. As I was stretched out on my belly, I lost consciousness in his presence. This God addressed me in a friendly way, and I was like a man caught by nightfall. My soul fled and my body shook. My heart was not in my body: I could not tell life from death.

His Majesty said to one of these Companions: Lift him up and let him speak to me. And His Majesty said: See, you have returned, now that you have roamed the foreign lands. Exile has ravaged you; you have grown old. Old age has caught up with you. The burial of your body is no small matter, for now you will not be escorted by the bowmen. Do not creep any more. You did not speak / when your name was called out. I feared punishment, and I answered with a timorous answer: What has my lord said to me? If I try to answer, there is no shortcoming on my part toward God. Fear is in my body, like that which brought to pass the fated flight. I am in your presence. Life belongs to you. May Your Majesty do as he wishes.

The royal children were then brought in, and His Majesty said to the queen: Here is Sinuhe, who has returned as an Asiatic whom the bedouin have raised. She let out a cry, and the royal children shouted all together. They said before His Majesty: It is not really he, O Sovereign, my lord. His Majesty said: It is he indeed. Then they brought their *menyat*-necklaces, their rattles, and their *sistra* with them, and they offered them to His Majesty. May your arms reach out / to something nice, O enduring king, to the ornaments of the Lady of Heaven. May the Golden One give life to your nostrils, and may the Lady of the Stars be joined to you. The crown of Upper Egypt will go northward, and the crown of Lower Egypt will go southward that they may unite and come together at the word of Your Majesty, and the cobra goddess Wadjet will be placed on your forehead. As you have kept your subjects from evil, so may Re, Lord of the Lands, be compassionate toward you. Hail to you. And also to the Lady of All. Turn aside your horn, set down your arrow. Give breath to the breathless. Give us this happy reward, this bedouin chief Simehyet, the bowman born in Egypt. It was through fear of you that he took flight and through dread of you that he left the land. Yet there is no one whose face turns white at the sight of your face. The eye which looks at you will not be afraid. His Majesty said: He shall not fear, / he shall not be afraid. He shall be a Companion among the nobles and he shall be placed in the midst of the courtiers. Proceed to the audience hall to wait upon him.

Sinuhe Reinstated

When I came from the audience hall, the royal children gave me their hands, and we went to the Great Double Gate. I was assigned to the house of a king's son. Fine things were in it, a cooling room in it, and representations of the horizon. Valuables of the treasury were in it, vestments of royal linen were in every apartment, and first-grade myrrh of the king and the courtiers whom he loves. / Every domestic servant was about his prescribed task. Years were caused to pass from my body. I was dipilated, and my hair was combed out. A load was given to the desert, and clothes to the sand-dwellers. I was outfitted with fine linen and rubbed with the finest oil. I passed the night on a bed. I gave the sand to those who live on it and wood oil to those who rub themselves with it. A house of a ⌜plantation owner⌝, which had belonged to a Companion, was given to me. Many craftsmen had built it, and all its trees were planted anew. Meals were brought from the palace three and four times a day, in addition to what the royal children gave. There was not a moment of interruption. / A pyramid of stone was built for me in the midst of the pyramids. The overseer of stonecutters of the pyramids marked out its ground plan. The master draftsman sketched in it, and the master sculptors carved in it. The overseers of works who were in the necropolis gave it their attention. Care was taken to supply all the equipment which is placed in a tomb chamber. Ka-servants were assigned to me, and an endowed estate was settled on me with fields attached, at my mooring place, as is done for a Companion of the first order. My statue was overlaid with gold leaf, its apron in electrum. His Majesty ordered it to be done. There was no commoner for whom the like had ever been done. So I remained in / the favor of the king until the day of mooring came.

Its beginning has come to its end, and it has been found in writing.

(The traditional colophon marks the end of this story.)

TEXT 4

The Second Intermediate Period: Problems 59 and 59B

from the Ahmes Mathematic Papyrus[1]

*T*he Ahmes Mathematic Papyrus, named after the scribe who copied this text in hieroglyphics around 1650 b.c., may have emanated, according to the copyist, from an earlier lost work dating to 2000 b.c. This text represents one of the oldest mathematical documents in existence. It is also often referred to as the "Rhind" papyrus, after the Scottish Egyptologist Alexander Henry Rhind, who purchased it in 1858 in a Nile resort town. According to An Introduction to the History of Mathematics by Howard Eves, other surviving papyri of mathematical import include:

- 3100 B.C. *In a museum at Oxford is a royal Egyptian mace dating from this time. On the mace are several numbers in the millions and hundred thousands, written in Egyptian hieroglyphs, recording results of a successful military campaign.*
- 1850 B.C. *This is the approximate date of the Moscow papyrus, a mathematical text containing 25 problems that were already old when the manuscript was compiled.*
- 1350 B.C. *This is the date of the Harris papyrus, a document prepared by Rameses IV when he ascended the throne. It sets forth the great works of his father, Rameses III. The listing of the temple wealth of the time furnishes the best example of practical accounts that has come to us from ancient Egypt.*

Although the Ahmes Papyrus merely represents exercises for young students, it does offer some insights into the state of mathematics in ancient Egypt. Problems 59 and

---

[1]Arnold Buffum Chace, *The Rhind Mathematical Papyrus*, Mathematical Association of America, Oberlin (Ohio), plates 59 and 59B.

TEXT 4: *The Second Intermediate Period: Problems 59 and 59B*

59B in the Ahmes Papyrus exemplify geometrical problems relating to pyramids and the relation of the lengths of two sides of a triangle.

Problem 59

    mr   pr–m–wś n · f imy m 12   wḥ^3–ṯb·t n · f imy   m 8
A pyramid, the per-em-us *to it therein is* : 12, *the* ukha-thebet *to it therein is* : 8.

    ir·ḥr · k   w^{3}ḥ–tp m 8   r   gm·t   6 $\dot{2}$ pw   n   pr–m–wś
Make thou the operation on 8 *for the finding of* 6; ½, *this is, of the* per-em-us.

    1   8
   \\$\dot{2}$ 4
   \\4   2.

ir·ḥr · k $\dot{2}$ $\dot{4}$ n 7   mkı   mḥ pw
Make thou ½ ¼ *of* 7; *behold a cubit this is.*

    1   7
   \\$\dot{2}$ 3 $\dot{2}$
   \\4   1 $\dot{2}$ $\dot{4}$.

ḫpr·ḥr · f m šsp   5   2   mk   śḳd · f pw
becomes it : *plam* 5 *finger* 2; *behold the* seked *of it this is.*
my n m

Problem 59B

    ir·ḥr · k   mr   n 12   śḳd · f   m šsp   5   1
Make thou a pyramid of 12; *the* seked *of it is* : *palm* 5 *finger* 1;

    dy · k   rḫ [·y]   pr–m–wś n · f   imy
cause thou that know I the per-em-us *to it therein.*

    ir·ḥr · k   w^{3}ḥ–tp m   5   1 sp 2 r
Make thou the operation on [palm] 5 *finger* 1 *times* 2 *for the*

    gm · t   mḥ   mk šsp 7 pw   ḫpr·ḥr · f m 10 $\dot{2}$
finding of a cubit; behold palm 7 *this is. Becomes it* : 10 ½;

    $\ddot{3}$ · f   m 7   ir   w^{3}ḥ–tp m 12 $\ddot{3}$ · f   m 4
⅔ *of it is* : 7. *Make the operation on* 12; ⅔ *of it is* : 4;

    mk   pr–m–wś pw
behold the per-em-us *this is.*

Source: From Arnold Buffum Chace, *The Rhind Mathematical Papyrus*, © 1929, Mathematical Association of America.

TEXT 5

New Kingdom: Thoth—The God of Wisdom and Learning

from The Book of the Dead

The text popularly known as The Book of the Dead, although titled by the ancient Egyptians The Chapters of Coming Forth by Day, is a collection of magical incantations. Like the coffin texts used during the Middle Kingdom, they were inscribed on papyrus rolls and employed during the New Kingdom (1570–1090 B.C.) to ensure the resurrection of the dead and their safe journey to the Other World.[1]

It is, however, in The Book of the Dead, written in hieroglyphics, that we are able to gain a modicum of insight into the divine person of Thoth, the god of Wisdom and Learning. According to Egyptian theology, it was Thoth who invented writing and became the keeper of all knowledge, human creativity, the repositor of truth, and the astronomical reckoner of distances, time, and seasons. Thoth was originally depicted as the moon god and appeared on inscriptions with the head of an ibis, and the disc and crescent of the moon. As the Greeks became increasingly more familiar with the cosmogony of the Egyptians after 500 B.C., they transmuted Thoth into their Greek god Hermes and referred to the Egyptian deity as "Hermes Trismegistus" or Hermes thrice-great. Derived from the Greek appellation was Hermeticism. The wife of Thoth was sometimes identified as the Egyptian goddess of Truth, "Ma'at," and to later Gnostic Christians as Sophia.

---

[1]Joseph Kaster, *The Wisdom of Ancient Egypt: Writings from the Time of the Pharoahs* (New York: Barnes and Noble Books, 1993), p. 129.

TEXT 5: *New Kingdom: Thoth—The God of Wisdom and Learning*

I am Thoth, the excellent scribe, whose hands are pure, the lord of the two horns, who makes iniquity to be destroyed, the scribe of right and truth, who abominates wrongdoing. Behold, he is the writing reed of the Lord of All, the lord of laws, who gives forth the speech of wisdom and understanding, whose words have dominion over the Two Lands.

I am Thoth, the lord of right and truth, who judges right and truth for the gods, the judge of words in their essence, whose words triumph over violence.

I have scattered the darkness, I have driven away the whirlwind and the storm, and I have given the pleasant breeze of the north wind unto Osiris, the Beautiful Being, as he came forth from the body of her who gave him birth.

I have made Ra to set as Osiris, and Osiris sets as Ra sets. I have made him to enter the secret habitation to vivify the heart of the Weary of Heart, the Holy Soul who is over the West, and to exult in joy to the Weary of Heart, the Beautiful Being, the son of Nut.

I am Thoth, praised of Ra, the lord of might, who brings to a prosperous end that which he does, the mighty one of enchantments who is in the boat of millions of years, the lord of laws, whose words of power gave strength to her who gave him birth, whose voice subdues opposition and fighting, and who makes the praise of Ra in his shrine.

I am Thoth, who made true the voice of Osiris over his enemies.

I am Thoth, who issues the decree at dawn, and whose sight follows on after his overthrow at his season, the guide of heaven and earth and the Other World, and the creator of the life of all peoples. I gave breath unto him who was in the hidden place by means of the might of the magical words of my utterance, that Osiris might be true of voice over his enemies.

I came unto you, O lord of the Sacred Land, O Osiris, Bull of the West, and you were made flourishing forever. I set eternity as magical protection for your members. I came having magical protection in my hand, and I guarded you with strength during the course of each and every day. Magical protection and life were behind this god, and his Divine Essence was glorified with power.

The kind of the Other World, the Ruler of the West, the possessor of the heavens through truth of voice, firmly established upon him is the *Atef*-crown, he is diademed with the White Crown, and he grasps the Crook and the Flail. Unto him, the great one of souls, the great one of the *Wereret*-crown, every god is gathered together, and love of him who is the Beautiful being, and whose existence is forever unto eternity, goes through their bodies.

Hail to you, O you who are over those in the West, who makes mortals to be born again, renewing your youth and always in your season, and who is more beautiful even than anything in your heart! Your son Horus has avenged you, and the dignities of Atum have been conferred upon you, O Beautiful Being! You are raised up, O Bull of the West, you are made firm, made firm in the body of Nut, who unites herself with you and who comes forth with you. Your heart is raised upon that which supports it, and your breast as it was at its beginning; your nose is made firm with life and prospering; you are living, you are renewed and you are young like Ra each and every day. Great, great is Osiris as one True of Voice and he is firmly established with life!

Source: From *The Wings of the Falcon* by Joseph Kaster, © 1968 by Joseph Kaster. Reprinted by permission of Henry Holt & Co., Inc.

I am Thoth, and I have made content Horus and have quieted the two Divine Combatants in their season of storm. I have come, and I have washed the Red One, I have quieted the Stormy One, and I have made him swallow all manner of evil things.

I am Thoth, and I have done the "Things of the Night" in Letopolis. I am Thoth, and I have come daily into the cities of Pe and Depu. I have led along the offerings and oblations. I have given cakes with lavish hand to the Glorious Ones. I have protected the shoulder of Osiris, I have embalmed him, I have made sweet his odor, even as the odor of the beautiful god.

I am Thoth, and I have come each day to the city of Kher-Aha. I have tied the cordage and I have set in good order the *Mekhenet*-boat, and I have brought it from the east to the west. I am more exalted upon my standard than any god, in this my name of "He whose face is exalted." I have opened beautiful things in this my name of *Wepwawet,* Opener of the Ways. I have ascribed praise and accomplished kissing-of-the-earth to Osiris, the Beautiful Being, whose existence is forever and unto eternity.

TEXT 6

Queen Hatshepsut: Expedition against Punt (Somalia)[1]

One of the most remarkable women in ancient Egyptian history and certainly the most powerful was Queen Hatshepsut who ruled Egypt from 1490 to 1468 B.C. Daughter of Thutmose I, she ascended to the throne after the death of her three brothers, inheriting a country whose impirial position by the time of the Middle Kingdom, cultural achievements, and wealth towered over the rest of the ancient world.[2]

As in many other African societies, the Egyptian royal descent was passed down matrilineally. Although women were not, at least until the reign of Hatshepsut, the actual rulers, a man could only be crowned pharaoh by marrying a princess of royal lineage.

When Hatshepsut came to power, she sought to authenticate her rule by producing a priestly statement that presumably emanated from the almighty god Amen affirming that he was her true father. Thus the divine conception of Hatshepsut was inscribed in hieroglyphics on the walls of her magnificently constructed tomb-temple at Dar al-Bahri. She also had artists depict her with the square beard symbolic of a king.

One of the most noted events of her reign was the expedition Queen Hatshepsut led to the land of "Divine Punt" (in present-day Somalia), also inscribed on the walls of her funeral palace at Dar al-Bahri. This ancient country of Punt was the source of myrrh and precious perfumes which the Egyptians prized greatly, in addition to ivory, ebony and cinnamon wood, and wild panther skins. The reliefs depicting this expedition also provide some details of the Puntites, whose king, *Perehu*, graciously received the Egyptians in the company of his rather plump queen, *Eti*, and their children, two sons and a daughter.

---

[1]James Henry Breasted, *Ancient Records of Egypt: Historical Documents from the Earlier Times to the Persian Conquest* (Chicago: The University of Chicago Press, 1906–1907), vol. II, pp. 106–13.
[2]David Sweetman, *Women Leaders in African History* (London: Heinemann, 1984), p. 3.

Inscriptions

253. Sailing in the sea, beginning the goodly way toward God's-Land, journeying in peace to the land of Punt, by the army of the Lord of the Two Lands, according to the command of the Lord of Gods, Amon, lord of Thebes, presider over Karnak, in order to bring for him the marvels of every country, because he so much loves the King of Upper and Lower Egypt, [Makere (Hatshepsut)], for <u>his father</u> Amon-Re, lord of heaven, lord of earth, more than the other kings who have been in this land forever.

Over the Egyptians

255. [The arrival] of the king's-messenger in God's-Land, together with the army which is behind <u>him,</u> before the chiefs of Punt; dispatched with every good thing from the court, L. P. H., for Hathor, mistress of Punt; for the sake of the life, prosperity, and health of her majesty.

Before the Puntites

256. The coming of the chiefs of Punt, doing obeisance, with bowed head, to receive this army of the king; they give praise to the lord of gods, Amon-Re ─────.

Over the Puntites

257. They say, as they pray for peace: 'Why have ye come thither unto this land, which the people know not? Did ye come down upon the ways of heaven, or did ye sail upon the waters, upon the sea of God's-Land? Have ye trodden (⌜the way of⌝) Re? Lo, as for the King of Egypt, is there no way to his majesty, that we may live by the breath which he gives?

Before the Leader of the Puntites

258. The chief of Punt, Perehu.

Before His Wife

His wife, Eti.

Over the Ass

The ass which bears his wife.

Source: Reprinted from James Henry Breasted, *Ancient Records of Egypt,* © 1906, The University of Chicago Press.

TEXT 6: *Queen Hatshepsut: Expedition against Punt (Somalia)*

In the Tent

260. Pitching the tent of the king's-messenger and his army, in the myrrh-terraces of Punt on the side of the sea, in order to receive the chiefs of this country. There are offered to them bread, beer, wine, meat, fruit, everything found in Egypt, according to that which was commanded in the court, L. P. H.

Before the Egyptian

261. Reception of the tribute of the chief of Punt, by the king's-messenger.

Before the Puntites

262. The coming of the chief of Punt bearing tribute at the side of the sea before the king's-[messenger] ─────.

IV. LOADING THE VESSELS

Scene

263. Two vessels heavily laden with myrrh trees, sacks of myrrh, ivory, woods, apes; on shore and ascending the gang-planks, men carrying sacks and trees.

Over Men with Trees on Shore

264. (⌜Loo, to⌝) your feet, yet people! Behold! the load is very heavy!

Prosperity ⌜be⌝ with ⌜us⌝, for the sake of the myrrh tree in the midst of God's-Land, for the house of Amon; there is the place ⌜where⌝ it shall be made to grow for Makere, in his temple, according to command.

Over the Vessels

265. The loading of the ships very heavily with marvels of the country of Punt; all goodly fragrant woods of God's-Land, heaps of myrrh-resin, with fresh myrrh trees, with ebony and pure ivory, with green gold of Emu, (*mw*), with cinnamon wood, khesyt wood, with ihmut-incense, sonter-incense, eye-cosmetic, with apes, monkeys, dogs, and with skins of the southern panther, with natives and their children. Never was brought the like of this for any king who has been since the beginning.

VIII. WEIGHING AND MEASURING THE OFFERINGS

274. The king himself, the King of Upper and Lower Egypt, Makere (Hatshepsut). Taking the measure of the electrum, laying the hand on the ⌜─⌝ of the heaps, first instance of doing the good things. Measuring of the fresh myrrh unto Amon, lord of Thebes, lord of heaven, the first of the harvest ── ── of the marvels of the countries of Punt. The lord of Khmunu (Thoth) records them in writing; Sefkhet counts the numbers. Her majesty herself, is acting with her two hands, the best of myrrh is upon all her limbs, her fragrance is divine dew, her odor is mingled with Punt, her skin is gilded with electrum, shining as do the stars in the midst of the festival-hall, before the whole land. There is rejoicing by all the people; they give praise to the lord of gods, they laud Makere (Hatshepsut) in her divine qualities, because of the greatness of the marvels which have happened for her. Never did the like happen under any gods who were before, since the beginning. May she be given life, like Re, forever.

Over the Myrrh Heaps

276. Heaps of myrrh in great quantities.

Over the Men Measuring

277. Measuring the fresh myrrh, in great quantities, for Amon, lord of Thebes; marvels of the countries of Punt, treasures of God's-Land, for the sake of the life, prosperity and health ———.

TEXT 7

Scribes: Instructions to the Prime Minister Rekh-mi-Ra[1]

Rekh-mi-Ra was an Egyptian nobleman who served in upper Egypt as vizier or prime minister for Pharaoh Thutmose III (1468–1436 B.C.) during the latter half of this conquering monarch's reign. It was during this period that Egypt established its imperial hegemony over Syria in the East. As James Breasted points out in Ancient Records of Egypt:

> We find in [Rekh-mi-Ra's tomb] the fullest known source for the study of the constitution of the state and the administration of the Pharaoh's government under the empire, beside the best-known representations in color of the peoples and products of Punt, Keftyew, Retenu and Nubia.[2]

These inscriptions are taken from the tomb of Rekh-mi-Ra in the upper Egyptian city of Thebes, which borders Nubia.

Regulation laid upon the vizier Rekh-mi-Ra. The council was conducted into the audience hall of Pharaoh, Life! Prosperity! Health! One caused that there be brought in the vizier Rekh-mi-Ra, newly appointed.

Said His Majesty to him: "Look to the office of the vizier; be watchful over all that is done therein. Behold, it is the established support of the whole land.

"Behold, as for the vizierate, it is not sweet; behold, it is bitter, as he is named. Behold, he is copper enclosing the gold of his lord's house. Behold, the vizirate is not to show respect of persons to princes and councilors; it is not to make for himself slaves of any people.

---

[1]Joseph Kaster, *The Wisdom of Ancient Egypt: Writings from the Time of the Pharoahs* (New York: Barnes and Noble Books, 1993), p. 129.

[2]James Henry Breasted, *Ancient Records of Egypt: Historical Documents from the Earlier Times to the Persian Conquest* (Chicago: The University of Chicago Press 1906–1907), vol. II, p. 267.

Source: From *The Wings of the Falcon* by Joseph Kaster, © 1968 by Joseph Kaster. Reprinted by permission of Henry Holt & Co., Inc.

"Behold, as for a man in the house of his lord, his conduct is good for his lord. But lo, he does not the same for another.

"Behold, when a petitioner comes from upper or lower Egypt, even the whole land, see to it that everything is done in accordance with law, that everything is done according to the custom thereof, giving to every man his right. Behold, a prince is in a conspicuous place, water and wind report concerning all that he does. For behold, that which is done by him never remains unknown.

"When he takes up a matter for a petitioner according to his case, he shall not proceed by the statement of a department officer. But the matter shall be known by the statement of one designated by him, the vizier, saying it himself in the presence of a department officer with the words: 'It is not that I raise my voice; but I send the petitioner according to his case to another court or prince.' Then that which has been done by him has not been misunderstood.

"Behold, the refuge of a prince is to act according to the regulation, by doing what is said to him. A petitioner who had been adjudged shall not say: 'My right has not been given to me!'

"Behold, it is a saying which was in the vizieral installation of Memphis in the utterance of the king in urging the vizier to moderation: 'Beware of that which is said of the vizier Kheti. It is said that he discriminated against some of the people of his own kin in favor of strangers, for fear lest it should be said of him that he favored his kin dishonestly. When one of them appealed against the judgment which he thought to make him, he persisted in his discrimination. Now that is more than justice.

"Forget not to judge justice. It is an abomination of the god to show partiality. This is the teaching. Therefore, do you accordingly. Look upon him who is known to you like him who is unknown to you; and him who is near the king like him who is far from his house. Behold, a prince who does this, he shall endure here in this place.

"Pass not over a petitioner without regarding his speech. If there is a petitioner who shall appeal to you, being one whose speech is not what is said, dismiss him after having let him hear that on account of which you dismiss him. Behold, it is said: 'A petitioner desires that his saying be regarded rather than the hearing of that on account of which he has come.'

"Be not wroth against a man wrongfully; but be you wroth at that at which one should be wroth.

"Cause yourself to be feared. Let men be afraid of you. A prince is a prince of whom one is afraid. Behold, the dread of a prince is that he does justice. But indeed, if a man cause himself to be feared a multitude of times, there is something wrong in him in the opinion of the people. They do not say of him: 'He is a man indeed.' Behold, the fear of a prince deters the liar, when the price proceeds according to the dread one has of him. Behold, this shall you attain by administering this office, doing justice.

"Behold, men expect the doing of justice in the procedure of the vizier. Behold, that is its customary law since the god. Behold, it is said concerning the scribe of the vizier: 'A just scribe' is said of him. Now, as for the hall in which you hear, there is an audience hall for the announcement of judgments. Now, as for 'him who shall do justice before all the people,' it is the vizier.

"Behold, when a man is in his office, he acts according to what is commanded him. Behold, the success of a man is that he act according to what is said to him. Make no delay at all in justice, the law of which you know. Behold, it becomes the arrogant that the king should love the timid more than the arrogant!

"Now may you do according to this command that is given you—behold, it is the manner of success—besides giving your attention to the crown lands, and making the establishment thereof. If you happen to inspect, then shall you send to inspect the overseer of the land-measuring and the patrol of the overseer of land-measuring. If there shall be one who shall inspect before you, then shall you question him.

"Behold the regulation that is laid upon you."

TEXT 8

Anonymous: Love Poems[1]

Only fragments of the original Egyptian texts of these poems have survived. Their sources are Egyptian Papyri held at the British Museum and Cairo Museum, dating from 1567 to 1085 B.C.[2] As Barbara Hughes Fowler has pointed out in Love Lyrics of Ancient Egypt:

> The poems of this collection should, in their innocent sensuousness, give the lie to the popular conception of the Egyptians as a gloomy people, obsessed with death. From the very beginnings of their identity as a people, their hieroglyphs—which abound in signs of animals, plants, and birds . . . attest to their delight in the fecundity of the Nile Valley. These signs were, to be sure, originally emblems for the creatures themselves, but their retention as phonemes and determinatives, exquisitely carved and painted, reveals the Egyptians' joy in the flora and fauna of this present world.[3]

WITH CANDOUR I CONFESS MY LOVE

With candour I confess my love;
I love you, yes, and wish to love you closer;
As mistress of your house,
Your arm placed over mine.

---

[1]Ezra Pound and Noel Stock, *Love Poems of Ancient Egypt* (Norfolk, CT: New Directions Books, 1960), pp. 8–10, 17–18.
[2]Ibid., preface.
[3]Barbara Hughes Fowler, *Love Lyrics of Ancient Egypt* (Chapel Hill, NC: University of North Carolina Press, 1994), pp. xiv–xv.
Source: From Ezra Pound and Noel Stock, *Love Poems of Ancient Egypt*, © 1960. Reprinted by permission of New Directions Publishing Corporation.

Alas your eyes are loose.
I tell my heart: "My lord
Has moved away. During
The night moved away
And left me. I am like a tomb."
And I wonder: Is there no sensation
Left, when you come to me?
Nothing at all?

Alas those eyes which lead you astray,
Forever on the loose.
And yet I confess with candour
That no matter where else they roam
If they roam towards me
I enter into life.

The swallow sings "Dawn,
Whither fadeth the dawn?"

So fades my happy night
My love in bed beside me.

Imagine my joy at his whisper:
"I'll never leave you," he said.
"Your hand in mine we'll stroll
In every beautiful path."
Moreover he lets the world know
That I am first among his women
And my heart grieves no longer.

DIVING AND SWIMMING

I

Diving and swimming with you here
Gives me the chance I've been waiting for:
To show my looks
Before an appreciative eye.

My bathing suit of the best material,
The finest sheer,
Now that it's wet
Notice the transparency,
How it clings.

Let us admit, I find you attractive.
I swim away, but soon I'm back,
Splashing, chattering,
Any excuse at all to join your party.

Look! a redfish flashed through my fingers!
You'll see it better
If you come over here,
Near me.

II

Nothing, nothing can keep me from my love
Standing on the other shore.

Not even old crocodile
There on the sandbank between us
Can keep us apart.

I go in spite of him,
I walk upon the waves,
Her love flows back across the water,
Turning waves to solid earth
For me to walk on.

The river is our Enchanted Sea.

III

To have seen her
To have seen her approaching
Such beauty is
Joy in my heart forever.
Nor time eternal take back
What she has brought to me.

IV

When she welcomes me
Arms open wide
I feel as some traveller returning
From the far land of Punt.

All things change; the mind, the senses,
Into perfume rich and strange.

And when she parts her lips to kiss
My head is light, I am drunk without beer.

V

If I were one of her females
Always in attendance
(Never a step away)

I would be able to admire
The resplendence
Of her body
Entire.

If I were her laundryman, for a month,
I would be able to wash from her veils
The perfumes that linger.

I would be willing to settle for less
And be her ring, the seal on her finger.

TEXT 9

Amenhotep III: The Great Hymn to Amen[1]

*P*haraoh Amenhotep III ruled Egypt from 1390 to 1353 B.C. During his reign, he initiated a major construction project, including a funeral palace in Thebes of which the Colossi of Memnon survives and "a major temple in Nubia," a temple in Luxor, and various buildings in Memphis. His wife, Queen Tiy, was a commoner and native of Ikhmin (the city in upper Egypt noted 2,000 years later as the birthplace of one of the early articulators of Islamic Gnosticism or Sufism, Dhu al-Nun).

Amen was originally a local deity of Thebes, in upper (southern) Egypt. Amen's position rose in the pantheon of gods during the rise of the Middle Kingdom centered at Thebes (2050–1780 B.C.). When that city became the capital of Egypt during the Eighteenth Dynasty, Amen likewise rose to a divine supremacy that made him co-equal with the sun god Ra. He henceforth became known as Amen-Ra.[2] The attributes bestowed upon this most important of all the gods was goodness, loving kindness, and the power of universal creation.

Adoration of Amen-Ra, the Bull of Ionu, the chief of all the gods,
   the good god, the beloved, who gives life to all that is warm,
   and to every good herd:

I

   Hail to you, Amen-Ra, Lord of the Thrones of the Two Lands who
      presides in Thebes!
   Bull of his Mother, the first on his field!

---

[1] Kaster, *The Wings of the Falcon* (New York: Henry Holt & Co., Inc., 1968), pp. 92–100.
[2] Ibid., p. 91.
Source: From *The Wings of the Falcon* by Joseph Kaster, © 1968 by Joseph Kaster. Reprinted by permission of Henry Holt & Co., Inc.

Wide of stride, first in upper Egypt,
>   Lord of the Medjoi, and prince of Punt.
Greatest of heaven, eldest of earth,
>   lord of what exists, who endures in all things.
Unique in his nature, like the essence of the gods,
>   Bull of the Ennead and chief of the gods,
Lord of Truth, father of the gods,
>   who made mankind and created the beasts.
Lord of what exists, who created the fruit tree,
>   who made the green herb and sustains life in cattle.
Beauteous form which Ptah fashioned,
>   the beauteous, beloved youth, he whom the gods praise.
Who made them that are below and them that are above,
>   he who illumines the Two Lands.
Who traverses the firmament in peace,
>   King of Upper and Lower Egypt, Ra, True of Voice.
The chief of the Two Lands, great of strength,
>   lord of reverence, who made all the earth.
More eminent of nature than any god,
>   over whose beauty the gods rejoice.
To whom praise is given in the Great House,
>   who is crowned in the House of Fire.
Whose sweet savor the gods love when he comes from Punt;
>   richly perfumed when he comes down from the land of the Medjoi;
>   fair of face, when he comes from the Land of the God.
The gods fawn at his feet, knowing His Majesty to be their lord—
>   the fearful, the terrible, great of will, and mighty in appearance,
>   who abounds in victuals and creates sustenance.
Jubilation to you who created the gods,
>   raised up the sky and spread out the ground!

IV

The sole king, unique among the gods,
>   with multitudinous names, whose number is not known,
Who arises on the eastern horizon,
>   and sets on the western horizon,
Who is born early every day,
>   and every day overthrows his enemies!
Thoth lifts up his eyes, and delights in his excellence,
>   the gods rejoice in his beauty, and the *hetet*-apes exalt him.
Lord of the ship of evening and the ship of morning;
>   they traverse Nun for you in peace.
Your crew rejoices in seeing the enemy overthrown,
>   and how his limbs are consumed by the knife.
The fire has devoured him,
>   and his soul is consumed yet more than his body.
The dragon, an end is made of his going;
>   the gods shout for joy
>   and the crew of Ra is in contentment.

Ionu is in joy: the foe of Atum is overthrown;
   Thebes is content, and Ionu exults.
The gods of Babylon are in jubilation,
   and they of Letopolis kiss the earth when they see him.
The Mistress of Life is glad:
   the foe of her lord is overthrown.
Strong is his might,
   the most mighty of the gods,
Righteous One, Lord of Thebes,
   in this your name of Creator of Right!
Lord of victuals, Bull of provisions,
   in this your name of Bull of his Mother!
Who made all men that are and created all that is,
   in this your name of Atum-Khepri!
Great Falcon, who makes festive the body,
   fair of face who makes festive the breast!
With pleasing form and the tall plumes,
   the Two Serpents rearing on his brow.
He to whom men's hearts come nestling,
   who suffers mankind to come out to him,
      who gladdens the Two Lands with his going forth!
Praise unto you, Amen-Ra,
   Lord of the Thrones of the Two Lands,
      whose arising his city loves!

TEXT 10

Amenemope: The Wisdom Teachings

*T*his composition is believed to have been written during the Eighteenth Dynasty (1570–1320 B.C.), perhaps in the reign of Amenhotep III, father of Akhenaten who initiated the brief period of Egyptian monotheism known as the Amarna Revolution. The preceding period of Amenhotep III's reign was one of great Egyptian prosperity and royal opulence.

Scholars have long debated the historical implications of the remarkable resemblance these instructions have to the biblical wisdom literature, particularly the Book of Proverbs, verses 22:17 through 24:22. While scholars early in this century surmised that this work of Amenemope was derived from biblical wisdom literature, contemporary scholars, with more sources at their disposal for dating, now agree that the similarities are in fact a reflection of the many commonalties of culture shared by ancient Africa and the Near East.

Proverbs in the Bible, Proverbs Chapters 22 (22) through 24 (NIV) read:

Chapter 22

22 Do not exploit the poor because they are poor and do not crush the needy in court,
23 for the LORD will take up their case and will plunder those who plunder them.
24 Do not make friends with a hot-tempered man, do not associate with one easily angered,
25 or you may learn his ways and get yourself ensnared.
26 Do not be a man who strikes hands in pledge or puts up security for debts;
27 if you lack the means to pay, your very bed will be snatched from under you.
28 Do not move an ancient boundary stone set up by your forefathers.
29 Do you see a man skilled in his work? He will serve before kings; he will not serve before obscure men.

Chapter 23

1 When you sit to dine with a ruler, note well what is before you,

2   and put a knife to your throat if you are given to gluttony.
3   Do not crave his delicacies, for that food is deceptive.
4   Do not wear yourself out to get rich; have the wisdom to show restraint.
5   Cast but a glance at riches, and they are gone, for they will surely sprout wings and fly off to the sky like an eagle.
6   Do not eat the food of a stingy man, do crave his delicacies;
7   for he is the kind of man who is always thinking about the cost. "Eat and drink," he says to you, but his heart is not with you.
8   You will vomit up the little you have eaten and will have wasted your compliments.
9   Do not speak to a fool, for he will scorn the wisdom of your words.
10 Do not move an ancient boundary stone or encroach on the fields of the fatherless,
11 for their Defender is strong; he will take up their case against you.
12 Apply your heart to instruction and your ears to words of knowledge.
13 Do not withhold discipline from a child; if you punish him with the rod, he will not die.
14 Punish him with the rod and save his soul from death.
15 My son, if your heart is wise, then my heart will be glad;
16 my inmost being will rejoice when your lips speak what is right.
17 Do not let your heart envy sinners, but always be zealous for the fear of the LORD.
18 There is surely a future hope for you, and your hope will not be cut off.
19 Listen, my son, and be wise, and keep your heart on the right path.
20 Do not join those who drink too much wine or gorge themselves on meat,
21 for drunkards and gluttons become poor, and drowsiness clothes them in rags.
22 Listen to your father, who gave you life, and do not despise your mother when she is old.
23 Buy the truth and do not sell it; get wisdom, discipline and understanding.
24 The father of a righteous man has great joy; he who has a wise son delights in him.
25 May your father and mother be glad; may she who gave you birth rejoice!
26 My son, give me your heart and let your eyes keep to my ways,
27 for a prostitute is a deep pit and a wayward wife is a narrow well.
28 Like a bandit she lies in wait, and multiplies the unfaithful among men.
29 Who has woe? Who has sorrow? Who has strife? Who has complaints? Who has needless bruises? Who has bloodshot eyes?
30 Those who linger over wine, who go to sample bowls of mixed wine.
31 Do not gaze at wine when it is red, when it sparkles in the cup, when it goes down smoothly!
32 In the end it bites like a snake and poisons like a viper.
33 Your eyes will see strange sights and your mind imagine confusing things.
34 You will be like one sleeping on the high seas, lying on top of the rigging.
35 "They hit me," you will say, "but I'm not hurt! They beat me, but I don't feel it! When will I wake up so I can find another drink?"

Chapter 24

1   Do not envy wicked men, do not desire their company;
2   for their hearts plot violence, and their lips talk about making trouble.
3   By wisdom a house is built, and through understanding it is established;
4   through knowledge its rooms are filled with rare and beautiful treasures.
5   A wise man has great power, and a man of knowledge increases strength;
6   for waging war you need guidance, and for victory many advisers.
7   Wisdom is too high for a fool; in the assembly at the gate he has nothing to say.
8   He who plots evil will be known as a schemer.
9   The schemes of folly are sin, and men detest a mocker.

10 If you falter in times of trouble, how small is your strength!
11 Rescue those being led away to death; hold back those staggering toward slaughter.
12 If you say, "But we know nothing about this," does not he who weighs the heart perceive it? Does not he who guards your life know it? Will he not repay each person according to what he has done?
13 Eat honey, my son, for it is good; honey from the comb is sweet to your taste.
14 Know also that wisdom is sweet to your soul; if you find it, there is a future hope for you, and your hope will not be cut off.
15 Do not lie in wait like an outlaw against a righteous man's house, do not raid his dwelling place;
16 for though a righteous man falls seven times, he rises again, but the wicked are brought down by calamity.
17 Do not gloat when your enemy falls; when he stumbles, do not let your heart rejoice,
18 or the LORD will see and disapprove and turn his wrath away from him.
19 Do not fret because of evil men or be envious of the wicked,
20 for the evil man has no future hope, and the lamp of the wicked will be snuffed out.
21 Fear the LORD and the king, my son, and do not join with the rebellious,
22 for those two will send sudden destruction upon them, and who knows what calamities they can bring?
23 These also are sayings of the wise: To show partiality in judging is not good:
24 Whoever says to the guilty, "You are innocent"—peoples will curse him and nations denounce him.
25 But it will go well with those who convict the guilty, and rich blessing will come upon them.
26 An honest answer is like a kiss on the lips.
27 Finish your outdoor work and get your fields ready; after that, build your house.
28 Do not testify against your neighbor without cause, or use your lips to deceive.
29 Do not say, "I'll do to him as he has done to me; I'll pay that man back for what he did."
30 I went past the field of the sluggard, past the vineyard of the man who lacks judgment;
31 thorns had come up everywhere, the ground was covered with weeds, and the stone wall was in ruins.
32 I applied my heart to what I observed and learned a lesson from what I saw:
33 A little sleep, a little slumber, a little folding of the hands to rest—
34 and poverty will come on you like a bandit and scarcity like an armed man.

Chapter 2

Beware of stealing from a miserable man
    And of raging against the cripple.
Proceed cautiously before an opponent,
    And give way to an adversary;
Sleep on it before speaking,
    For a storm come forth like fire in hay is
The hot-headed man in his appointed time.

Source: From William K. Simpson, *The Literature of Ancient Egypt: An Anthology of Stories, Instructions, and Poetry,* © 1973. Reprinted by permission of Yale University Press.

> May you be restrained before him;
> Leave him to himself,
> > And God will know how to answer him.
> If you spend your life with these things in your heart,
> > Your children shall behold them.

Chapter 4

> The hot-headed man in the temple
> > Is like a tree grown in a garden;
> Suddenly it bears fruit.
> > It reaches its end in the carpentry shop;
> It is floated away far from its place,
> > Or fire is its funeral pyre.
> The truly temperate man sets himself apart,
> > He is like a tree grown in a sunlit field,
> But it flourishes, it doubles its yield,
> > It stands before its owner;
> Its fruit is something sweet, its shade is pleasant,
> > And it reaches its end in a garden.

Chapter 5

> Do not take by violence the shares of the temple,
> > Do not be grasping, and you will find overabundance;
> Do not take away a temple servant
> > In order to acquire the property of another man.
> Do not say today is the same as tomorrow,
> > Or how will matters come to pass?
> When tomorrow comes, today is past;
> > The deep waters sink from the canal bank,
> Crocodiles are uncovered, the hippopotamuses are on dry land,
> > And the fishes gasping for air;
> The wolves are fat, the wild fowl in festival,
> > And the nets are ⌐drained¬.
> Every temperate man in the temple says,
> > "Great is the benevolence of Re."
> Fill yourself with silence, you will find life,
> > And your body shall flourish upon earth.

Chapter 6

> Do not displace the surveyor's marker on the boundaries of the arable land,
> > Nor alter the position of the measuring line;
> Do not be greedy for a plot of land,
> > Nor overturn the boundaries of a widow.
> As for the road in the field worn down by time,
> > He who takes it violently for fields,
> If he traps by deceptive attestations,
> > Will be lassoed by the might of the Moon.

To one who has done this on earth, pay attention,
> For he is a weak enemy;

He is an enemy overturned inside himself;
> Life is taken form his eye;

His household is hostile to the community,
> His storerooms are toppled over,

His property taken from his children,
> And to someone else his possessions given.

Take care not to topple over the boundary marks of the arable land,
> Not fearing that you will be brought to court;

Man propitiates God by the might of the Lord
> When he sets straight the boundaries of the arable land.

Desire, then, to make yourself prosper,
> And take care for the Lord of All;

Do not trample on the furrow of someone else,
> Their good order will be profitable for you.

So plough the fields, and you will find whatever you need,
> And receive the bread form your own threshing floor:

Better is the bushel which God gives you
> Than five thousand deceitfully gotten;

They do not spend a day in the storehouse or warehouse,
> They are ⌜no use for dough for beer⌝;

Their stay in the granary is short-lived,
> When morning comes they will be swept away.

Better, then, is poverty in the hand of God
> Than riches in the storehouse;

Better is bread when the mind is at ease
> Than riches with anxiety.

Chapter 7

Do not set your heart upon seeking riches,
> For there is no one who can ignore Destiny and Fortune;

Do not set your thoughts on external matters:
> For every man there is his appointed time.

Do not exert yourself to seek out excess
> And your wealth will prosper for you;

If riches come to you by theft
> They will not spend the night with you;

As soon as day breaks they will not be in your household;
> Although their places can be seen, they are not there.

When the earth opens up its mouth, it levels him and swallows him up,
> And it drowns him in the deep;

They have made for themselves a great hole which suits them.
> And they have sunk themselves in the tomb;

Or they have made themselves wings like geese,
> And they fly up to the sky.

Do not be pleased with yourself (because of) riches acquired through robbery,
> Neither complain about poverty.

If an officer commands one who goes in front of him,
> His company leaves him;

The boat of the covetous is abandoned <in> the mud,
> While the skiff of the truly temperate man ⌜sails on⌝.

When he rises you shall offer to the Aten,
> Saying, "Grant me prosperity and health."

And he will give you your necessities for life,
> And you will be safe from fear.

TEXT 11

Pharaoh Akhenaten and Queen Nefertiti: The Great Hymn to the One God Aten[1]

*T*he son of Pharaoh Amenhotep III and Queen Tiy, Akhenaten ascended the throne in 1367 B.C. and reigned for 17 years. Religious and social revolutionaries, Akhenaten and his Queen Nefertiti ushered in a brief but remarkably influential age of Egyptian monotheism, which historians usually refer to as the Amarna Revolution. Abandoning the capital of Thebes that was controlled by the priesthood of Amen, Akhenaten and his wife constructed a new city devoted exclusively to the worship of the one god of the sun disk, Aten.

The "Great Hymn to the One God Aten," which bears certain striking parallels to biblical Psalm 104, exemplifies the strong cultural influence that Egypt wielded over the ancient world of that time. Psalm 104 reads:

1 Praise the LORD, O my soul. O LORD my God, you are very great; you are clothed with splendor and majesty.
2 He wraps himself in light as with a garment; he stretches out the heavens like a tent
3 and lays the beams of his upper chambers on their waters. He makes the clouds his chariot and rides on the wings of the wind.
4 He makes winds his messengers, flames of fire his servants.
5 He set the earth on its foundations; it can never be moved.
6 You covered it with the deep as with a garment; the waters stood above the mountains.
7 But at your rebuke the waters fled, at the sound of your thunder they took to flight;

---

[1]Kaster, *The Wings of the Falcon*, (New York: Henry Holt & Co., Inc., 1968), pp. 111–16.
Source: From *The Wings of the Falcon* by Joseph Kaster, © 1968 by Joseph Kaster. Reprinted by permission of Henry Holt & Co., Inc.

8   they flowed over the mountains, they went down into the valleys, to the place you assigned for them.
9   You set a boundary they cannot cross; never again will they cover the earth.
10   He makes springs pour water into the ravines; it flows between the mountains.
11   They give water to all the beasts of the field; the wild donkeys quench their thirst.
12   The birds of the air nest by the waters; they sing among the branches.
13   He waters the mountains from his upper chambers; the earth is satisfied by the fruit of his work.
14   He makes grass grow for the cattle, and plants for man to cultivate—bringing forth food from the earth:
15   wine that gladdens the heart of man, oil to make his face shine, and bread that sustains his heart.
16   The trees of the LORD are well watered, the cedars of Lebanon that he planted.
17   There the birds make their nests; the stork has its home in the pine trees.
18   The high mountains belong to the wild goats; the crags are a refuge for the coneys.
19   The moon marks off the seasons, and the sun knows when to go down.
20   You bring darkness, it becomes night, and all the beasts of the forest prowl.
21   The lions roar for their prey and seek their food from God.
22   The sun rises, and they steal away; they return and lie down in their dens.
23   Then man goes out to his work, to his labor until evening.
24   How many are your works, O LORD! In wisdom you made them all; the earth is full of your creatures.
25   There is the sea, vast and spacious, teeming with creatures beyond number—living things both large and small.
26   There the ships go to and fro, and the leviathan, which you formed to frolic there.
27   These all look to you to give them their food at the proper time.
28   When you give it to them, they gather it up; when you open your hand, they are satisfied with good things.
29   When you hide your face, they are terrified; when you take away their breath, they die and return to the dust.
30   When you send your Spirit, they are created, and you renew the face of the earth.
31   May the glory of the LORD endure forever; may the LORD rejoice in his works—
32   he who looks at the earth, and it trembles, who touches the mountains, and they smoke.
33   I will sing to the LORD all my life; I will sing praise to my God as long as I live.
34   May my meditation be pleasing to him, as I rejoice in the LORD.
35   But may sinners vanish from the earth and the wicked be no more. Praise the LORD, O my soul. Praise the LORD.

Praise of *the living Ra, Horus of the Double Horizon, Rejoicing on the Horizon, in His Name of Shu Who is in the Aten,* living forever unto eternity; Aten living and great, he who is in the Jubilee Festival, Lord of all that the Aten encircles, Lord of the Heavens and Lord of the Earth, Lord of the House of Aten in Akhet-Aten. The King of Upper and Lower Egypt, Living in Truth, the Lord of the Two Lands, Nefer-Kheperu-Ra Wa-en-Ra, Son of Ra, Living in Truth, Lord of Diadems, Akh-en-Aten, Great in his Duration, and the Great Wife of the King, his Beloved, the Lady of the Two Lands, Nefer-Neferu-Aten Nefert-Iti, living, healthy, and youthful forever unto eternity. He says:

> Beautiful is your shining forth on the horizon,
>   O living Aten, beginning of life!
> When you arise on the eastern horizon,
>   you fill every land with your beauty.

You are bright and great and gleaming,
   and are high above every land.
Your rays envelop the lands,
   as far as all you have created.
You are Ra, and you reach unto their end,
   and subdue them all for your beloved son.
You are afar, yet are your rays upon earth;
   you are before their face, yet one knows not their going!
When you go down in the western horizon,
   the earth is in darkness, as if it were dead.
They sleep in their chamber, their heads enwrapped,
   and no eye sees the other.
Though all their things were taken while under their heads,
   yet would they not perceive it.
Every lion comes forth from his den,
   and all serpents that bite.
Darkness is without and the earth is silent.
   for he who created it rests in his horizon.

When the earth brightens and you rise on the horizon,
   and shine as the Aten in the day,
When you scatter the darkness and offer your beams,
   the Two Lands are in festival,
They are awake and they stand on their feet,
   for you have raised them up.
They wash their bodies, and they take their garments,
   and their hands praise your arising.
      The whole land, it performs its work!

All beasts are content upon their pasture,
   and the trees and herbs are verdant.
The birds fly out of their nests,
   and their wings praise your Divine Essence.
All wild beasts prance upon their feet,
   and all that fly and alight.
      They live when you shine forth for them!

The ships voyage downstream and upstream likewise,
   and every way is open, since you have arisen.
The fish in the river leap up before your face,
   and your rays are in the midst of the Great Green.

You who bring children into being in women,
   and make fluid into mankind.
Who nourishes the son in the womb of his mother,
   who soothes him so that he weeps not,
      O nurse in the womb!
Who gives breath in order to keep alive
   all that he has made;
When he comes forth from the womb on the day of his birth,
   you open his mouth in speech, and give all that he needs.

The chick in the egg chirps in the shell,
   for you give it breath therein to sustain its life.
You make its completion for it in the egg in order to break it;
It comes forth from the egg at its completion,
   and walks on its feet when it comes forth therefrom.

How manifold are the things which you have made,
   and they are hidden from before man!
      O unique god, who has no second to him!
You have created the earth according to your desire,
   while you were alone,
With men, cattle, and wild beasts,
   all that is upon earth and goes upon feet,
      and all that soars above and flies with its wings.

The lands of Syria and Kush,
   and the land of Egypt,
You put every man in his place,
   and supply their needs.
Each one has provision
   and his lifetime is reckoned.
Their tongues are diverse in speech,
   and their form likewise;
Their skins are distinguished,
   for you distinguish the peoples of foreign lands.

You make the Nile in the Other World,
   and bring it whither you wish,
In order to sustain the people,
   even as you have made them.
For you are lord of them all,
   who weary yourself on their behalf,
The lord of every land, who arises for them,
   O Aten of the day, great of majesty!

All strange foreign lands,
   you make that whereon they live.
You have put a Nile in the sky,
   that it may come down for them,
And make waves on the hills like the sea,
   to water their fields in their townships.
How excellently made are your designs, O Lord of Eternity!
   the Nile in heaven, you appoint it for foreign peoples,
      and all beasts of the wilderness which walk upon feet;
The Nile upon earth,
   it proceeds from the Other World for the Beloved Land.

Your rays suckle every field,
   and when you shine forth
      they live and flourish for you.
You make the seasons
   to cause to continue all you have created:

The winter to cool them,
   and the warmth that they may taste of you.
You have made the sky afar off to shine therein,
   in order to behold all you have made.
You are alone, shining in your forms as living Aten,
   appearing, shining, withdrawing, returning,
      you make millions of forms of yourself alone!
Cities, townships, fields, road, and river,
   all eyes behold you against them,
      O Aten of the day above the earth!

You are in my heart,
   and there is no one who knows you save your son,
Nefer-Khepru-Ra Wa-en-Ra,
   whom you made understanding of your designs and your might.
The earth came into being by your hand,
   even as you have created them.
When you arise they live,
   and when you set they die.
But you have eternity in your members,
   and all creatures live in you.
The eyes look on your beauty until you set;
   all work is laid aside when you set in the west.
When you rise you make all to flourish for the King,
   you who made the foundations of the earth.
You raise them up for your son,
   he who came forth from your body,

the King of Upper and Lower Egypt, Living in Truth, the Lord of the Two Lands, Nefer-Kheperu-Ra Wa-en-Ra, Son of Ra, Living in Truth, Lord of Diadems, Akh-en-Aten, Great in His Duration, and for the Great Wife of the King, his Beloved, the Lady of the Two Lands, Nefer-Neferu-Aten Nefert-Iti, living and youthful forever unto eternity.

PART TWO
Ancient Nubia

Long dismissed as a mere outpost of ancient Egypt, the region of Nubia is now being reperceived in dramatically different terms because of new archeological evidence. The construction of the Aswan High Dam at the First Cataract of the Nile River in 1960 spurred one of the most remarkable salvage operations ever undertaken. In anticipation of the drowning

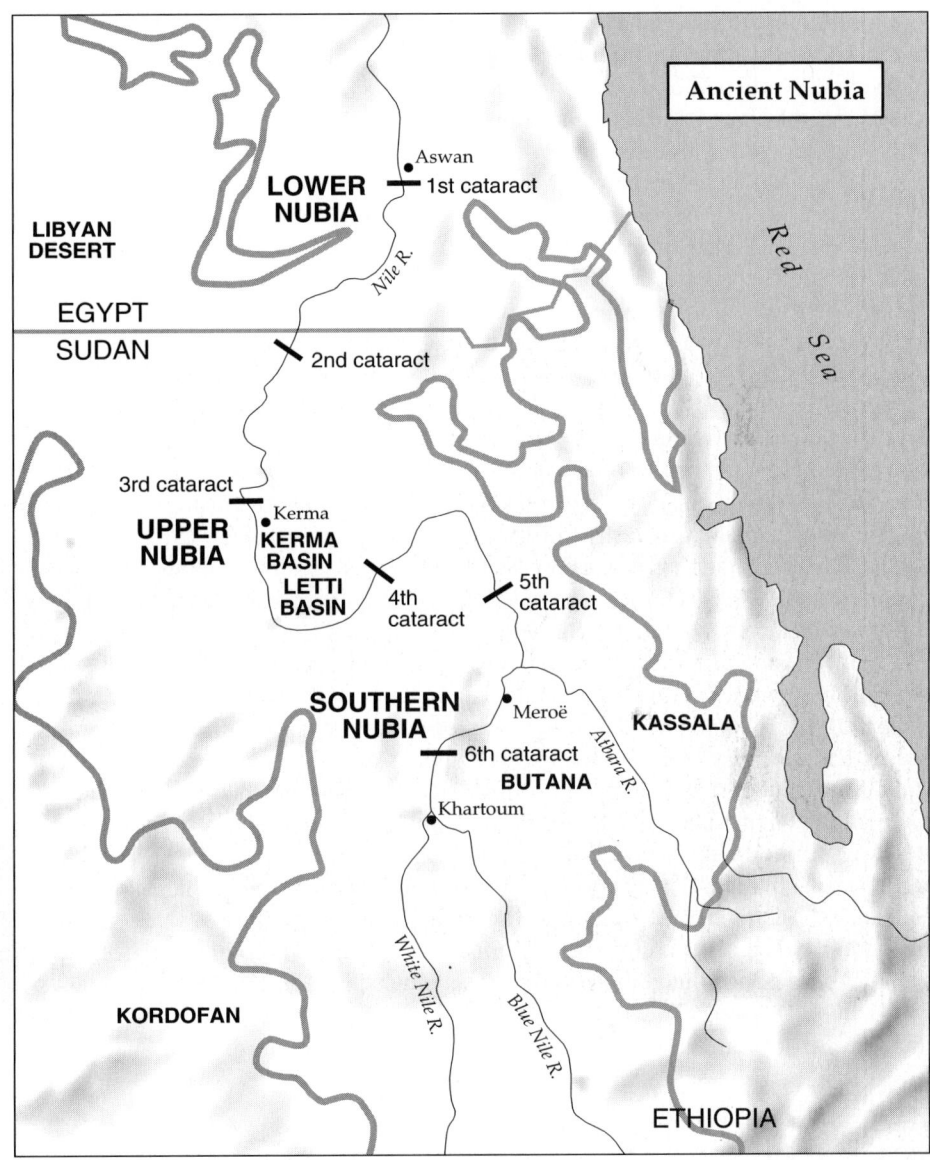

of more than 400 miles of Nubian territory south of Aswan, UNESCO launched an urgent, international appeal to rescue the unique monuments and other artifacts of this millennia-old region. Yeoman efforts were made to save as much as possible. But we simply have no way to gauge what may, as a result of the construction of this much needed water project for the remainder of Egypt, have been lost forever.

Researchers, primarily trained as Egyptologists, were initially unprepared for the picture of Nubia that began to emerge on account of the intensive excavations undertaken. Prior to this effort, the most important work on ancient Nubia had been conducted in the early part of the twentieth century by the Boston Museum in collaboration with Harvard University. This archaeological work had been led by the museum's early curator of Egyptian art and Harvard University archaeologist George A. Reisner (1867–1942) and by his successor Dows Dunham (b. 1890).[1] While the work of Reisner and Dunham unearthed evidence suggesting that Nubia should be examined in its own right, it was only under the emergency conditions of the later Aswan Dam construction that this region began to receive a modicum of the scholarly attention it merited.

What proved most unexpected in these later archaeological discoveries was the uncovering of tombs and other artifacts suggesting that a line of kings lived in the northern Nubian region of Qustul as early as, or perhaps even earlier than, the first pharaohs of Egypt.[2] The archaeologist who uncovered the royal cemetery at Qustul, Bruce Williams, now argues that the earliest recognizable graves in ancient Egypt at Abydos represent the cultural heirs and perhaps even the direct descendants of the Nubian pharaohs of Qustul.[3] While scholars continue to dispute the matter, it is nevertheless clear that a serious process of historical revision is now under way. It will serve to correct our understanding of earliest Nubia, the social evolution along the course of the Nile River valley, and the ways in which these southern societies incubated important cultural elements of ancient Egypt.

Evidence of a different sort also points to an earlier dating of sedentarized populations in the region. It is now known that indigenous wild barley rather than a strain emanating from Mesopotamia (which was originally thought to be the birthplace of this agriculture) was being cultivated by Nubians and Egyptians perhaps as early as 16,000 B.C. and sorghum and millet of African origin were being harvested in the southern region of Nubia by 6,000 B.C.[4]

Apart from the question of dating the earliest of its centralized states, the history of ancient Nubia remains steeped in another controversy as well, that of defining its boundaries. The intensity of this last dispute is fueled by politically charged issues of attribution, as scholars argue which artifacts of the ancient civilizations of the Nile Valley should be attributed to the Egyptians and which to the Nubians.

Usually referred to as the region one-third of whose land area lies within the southern part of modern-day Egypt and the remaining two-thirds in the nation of the

---

[1]Bruce Williams, *Nubia—Its Glory and Its People* (Chicago: University of Chicago Press, 1987).
[2]Torgny Save-Soderbergh (general editor), *Temples and Tombs of Ancient Nubia: The International Rescue Campaign at Abu Simbel* (Philae and other sites, UNESCO, Paris: Thames & Hudson Publ., 1987), p. 207.
[3]Bruce Williams, *The University of Chicago Oriental Institute Nubian Expedition. Vol. III, Part 1: The A-Group Royal Cemetery at Qustul: Cemetery L* (Chicago: University of Chicago Press, 1986), chapter 5.
[4]Kevin Shillington, *History of Africa* (New York: St. Martin's Press, 1989), p. 16.

Sudan, Nubia is also delineated by modern geographers by the cataracts or waterfalls of the Nile River. It is cartographically defined as lying between 18 and 24 degrees north latitude, its northern boundary lying to the south of the Egyptian city of Aswan at the First Cataract of the Nile. Torgny Save-Soderbergh has noted that if, on the other hand, the region of Nubia is defined by the territory inhabited by a Nubian-speaking population, then its northern boundary would encompass the richly monumented city of Aswan itself.[5]

Because the banks of the Nile River in Ancient Nubia were much more narrow, with less arable land than in Egypt, Nubia was in time eclipsed by its more agriculturally fertile Egyptian neighbor. Even so, the agricultural output of the Nubian economy was bolstered by a lucrative trade with Egypt in the natural wealth of its gold mines, ivory, ebony, and incense. In fact, *Nub* (nbw) in the language of the Pharaohs means "gold," a vital commodity of trade between the two regions, which the Nubians mined. The ancient Egyptians also referred to the region of Nubia as *Ta-seti* (Land of the Bow) in deference to the skill of Nubian archers or the "Southern Lands."[6]

KUSH

The term "Kush" first appeared in Egyptian literature as a name for a powerful Nubian state around the second millennium B.C. In later references the kingdom of Kush is the name given specifically to the Nubian empire that was at first centered around the city of Napata in the vicinity of the Fourth Cataract of the Nile River. It came into existence sometime in the ninth century B.C. During the Intermediate periods in Egypt's history, when its own centralized authority became weak, Nubia rose to great prominence particularly because of its ability to retain control of this important trade. However, during periods when Egypt, on the other hand, found itself in political ascendancy, its pharaohs would provoke warfare with their Nubian neighbor in an effort to dominate the trade routes for Egypt's economic benefit. Thus, Egypt was able to seize control of northern Nubia at some time during the Middle Kingdom but lost it to Nubia's political and military resurgence during Egypt's politically chaotic Second Intermediate period. Egypt's colonization of lower (northern) Nubia during the New Kingdom led to the construction of some of Egypt's most massive and impressive monuments in and around the city of Aswan, a vitally important historical area at times defined as upper Egypt and at others as lower Nubia.

Around 730 B.C., the Kushite General Piankhi, son of the Emperor Kashta, reacting to the threat from a Delta prince named Tefnakht, conquered all of Egypt in what has been termed "one of the most memorable episodes in Egyptian history."[7] Piankhi thus established the Twenty-Fifth or "Kushite" Dynasty of Egypt from 730 to 670 B.C. with Kushite pharaohs on the throne in Thebes. Piankhi was succeeded by his brother Shabaka. Later Kushite pharaohs Shebitqo and Taharqa restored many of Egypt's

---

[5]Williams Y. Adams, *Nubia* (Princeton, NJ: Princeton University Press, 1977), p. 337.
[6]Rex Keating, *Nubian Twilight* (New York: Harcourt, Brace & World, 1963), p. 70.
[7]Timothy Kendall, *Kush: Lost Kingdom of the Nile* (Brockton, MA: Brockton Art Museum, 1982), p. 9.

great monuments, had ancient papyri mended, and launched a new period of Egyptian artistic achievement, most noted for its startling realism. Taharqa's (690–664 B.C.) renown was such that he was mentioned in the Bible (2 Kings 19:9) on account of his war against the Assyrian empire. Suffering defeat, the Kushites withdrew back into their Nubian homeland, reestablishing their royal capital at the city of Napata.

MEROË

Gradually, however, the city of Meroë, located further south between the Fifth and Sixth Cataract of the Nile, came to replace Napata. By the second century B.C., the new capital at Meroë was a thriving commercial city located at the juncture of several important river and caravan trade routes. Its culture became increasingly less Egyptianized over time, leading the way for the establishment of a completely different script in their own language of Meroitic. However, the subsequent history of Meroë, a long and vibrant one judging from the archaeological remains, represents one of the most compelling deficits in our historical knowledge of the Nile Valley. Our modern inability to know Meroitic society emanates from the fact that linguists have yet to decipher their writings. Nubian scholar Peter Shinnie noted that "until this language has been successfully read and the inscriptions translated, much of the story of Meroë will remain unknown."[8]

RELIGION AND CULTURE

What is known of the religion of Meroë emanates either from earlier writings in hieroglyphics or from what can be gleaned from temple sculptures and other archaeological artifacts rather than the undeciphered literature of Meroë itself. Its people apparently shared many of the same divinities as the Egyptians. However, the Nubians also worshipped their own local pantheon of deities, the most important of which was the Lion God Apedemak. He exhibited such divine attributes as being the god of war, of sun worship, and of abundance.

Reflecting their local environment rather than the artistic conventions of the Egyptians, the art of Meroë depicted scenes of tropical animals like lions, ostriches, giraffes, and elephants. In their art the Nubians depicted themselves as darker-skinned peoples than the Egyptians, and their women were drawn with an aesthetically pleasing plumpness at variance with the Egyptians' standards of slender feminine beauty.

While both Egyptian and Nubian societies were matrilineal, women played a significant role in Nubian politics, which was not the case in ancient Egypt with the sole exception of New Kingdom Queen Hatshepsut. The title of the Nubian queen mother or *Kandake* was rendered into "Candace" in English and often confused by biblical

---

[8]Peter Shinnie, *Meroë: A Civilization of the Sudan* (New York: Praeger, 1967), p. 132.

and other writers with the name of the monarch herself. As Rex Keating points out in *Nubian Twilight:*

> In theory—if not always in practice—the heir to the throne was chosen from among the sons of the primary sister-wife. Consequently, the king's chief wife as well as his own mother had enormous status. . . [and their] draped garments seem to have been semi-transparent in order to accentuate the shapely outlines of the bodies of the wearers, which tended toward plumpness, according to the Kushite ideal of feminine beauty.[9]

In 24 B.C. Candace Amanirenas led her Nubian troops in battle against the Roman army, defeating three Roman cohorts. While the historical accounts mention her loss of an eye in the ensuing battle, it also narrates the fact that she defaced a statue of Roman Emperor Augustus Caesar, returning to Kush with the statue's head in triumph.

In A.D. 350 Meroë fell to the conquest of Axumite king Ezana. By this time the Nubian kingdom's agricultural base had eroded through overuse within an ecologically fragile environment. This process may have been accelerated by the needs of Meroë's major iron-smelting industry that required ever-increasing amounts of wood for charcoal to feed its smelting furnaces.

CHRISTIAN NUBIA

However, several hundred years later, a new phase in Nubian history opened in a region to the south of Meroë. Three new states, Nobatia, Makuria, and Alwa emerged in the region, all of whom had converted to Christianity by the sixth century A.D. Around A.D. 700 another smaller state to the south, Alodia, joined in a union between Nobatia and Makuria forming a powerful new nation, whose Crown Prince Georgios was received with great diplomatic formality in Cairo and Baghdad.

Scholars have been able to identify a unique style of Christian art emanating from this region, even though its literary traditions have not survived. These art forms include cathedral frescoes, decorated column capitals, crosses, and tombstones. The eighth century frescoes from the Great Cathedral at Fars (today housed at museums in Warsaw and Khartoum) employ paint colors and iconography styles from a period for which no representations have survived in Egypt and Byzantium.

---

[9]Keating, *Nubian Twilight*, p. 70.

TEXT 12

General Piankhi: The Kushite Conquest of Egypt

from the Piankhi Stela[1]

*I*n 730 B.C., responding to a threatened invasion of Thebes by one of the princes of lower Egypt, Kushite King Piye or Piankhi (ca. 747–716 B.C.) surged northward across the Nubian border of Kush, defeating the prince of lower Egypt, Tefnakhte. In a series of battles launched during the eighth century B.C., Piankhi, who had gained control of upper Egypt, continued in his military campaign until he had conquered all of Egypt in what has been described as "one of the most memorable episodes in Egyptian history."[2]

Piankhi recorded his feats of military genius with a directness and forceful, metaphorical style, unknown among Egyptian monarchs at that time, that reflected the unique qualities of his own personality. "Raging like a panther," the Nubian conqueror affirms, taking towns "like a cloudburst" and "turning up his nose at the conquered womenfolk but evaluating horseflesh with the eye of an expert."[3]

The text, written in Egyptian hieroglyphics, was inscribed on the Piankhi Stela, a pink granite column contained in the Museum of Cairo. This particular stela was discovered in 1862 in the temple at Gebel Barkal, a shrine devoted to the worship of the god Amen, in the city of Napata. An early capital of Kush, Napata had been established sometime around 1450 B.C. because of its central location at the intersection of an important caravan route and a Nile River crossing.

---

[1]James Henry Breasted, *Ancient Records of Egypt* (Chicago: The University of Chicago Press, 1906–1907), vol. IV, pp. 419–44.
[2]Timothy Kendall, *Kush: Lost Kingdom of the Nile* (Brockton, MA: Brockton Art Museum, 1982), p. 9.
[3]Ibid., pp. 9–10.

Introduction

817. Command which my majesty speaks: "Hear of what I did, more than the ancestors. I am a king, divine emanation, living image of Atum, who came forth from the womb, adorned as a ruler, of whom those greater than he were afraid; whose father knew, and whose mother recognized that he would rule in the egg, the Good God, beloved of the gods, achieving with his hands, Meriamon-Piankhi."

Announcement of Tefnakhte's Advance

818. One came to say to his majesty: "A chief of the west, the great prince in Neter, Tefnakhte (*T ʾf-nḫt·t*) is in the nome of —, in the nome of Xois, in Hapi (*Ḥʿp*), in — in Ayan, in Pernub, and in Memphis. He has seized the whole west from the backlands to Ithtowe, coming southward with a numerous army, while the Two Lands are united behind him, and the princes and rulers of walled towns are as dogs at his heels. No stronghold has closed [⌈its doors⌉ in] the nomes of the South: Mer-Atum (Medûm), Per-Sekhemkheperre, the temple of Sebek, Permezed, Theknesh (*Ṯ-kʾ-n-š*); and every city of the west; they have opened the doors for fear of him. He turned to the east, they opened to him likewise: Hatbenu, Tozi (*T ʾywḏʾ·t*), Hatseteni (*Ḥ·t-stny*), Pernebtepih (*Pr-nb-tb-yḥ*). Behold, [he] besieges Heracleopolis, he has completely invested it, not letting the comers-out come out, and not letting the goers-in go in, fighting every day. He measured it off in its whole circuit, every prince knows his wall; he stations every man of the princes and rulers of walled towns over his (respective) portion."

Piankhi's Indifference

819. Then [his majesty] heard [the message] with courageous heart, laughing, and joyous of heart.

Second Appeal of the North

These princes and commanders of the army who were in their cities sent to his majesty daily, saying: "Wilt thou be silent, even to forgetting the Southland, the nomes of the ⌈court⌉? While Tefnakhte advances his conquest and finds none to repel his arm."

Submission of Hermopolis to Tefnakhte

820. "Namlot——, prince of Hatweret (*Ḥ·t-wr·[t]*), he has overthrown the wall of Nefrus (*Nfrws*), he has demolished his own city, for fear of him who might take it from him, in order to besiege another city. Behold, he goes to follow at his

---

Source: Reprinted from James Henry Breasted, *Ancient Records of Egypt,* © 1906–1907, The University of Chicago Press.

(Tefnakhte's) heels, having cast off allegiance to his majesty (Piankhi). He tarries with him (Tefnakhte) like one of [his vassals in] the nome of Oxyrhyncus, and gives to him (Tefnakhte) gifts, as much as he desires, of everything that he has found."

Piankhi Commands the Capture of the Hare Nome

821. Then his majesty sent to the princes and commanders (*mr*) of the army who were in Egypt: Purem (*P-wꜣ-r-mꜥ*); and the commander (*ṯś*), Lemersekeny (*Rw-ꜥ-mr-s-k-n-y*); and every commander (*ṯś*) of his majesty who was in Egypt (saying): "Hasten into battle line, engage in battle, surround —, capture its people, its cattle, its ships upon the river. Let not the peasants go forth to the field, let not the plowmen plow, beset the frontier of the Hare nome, fight against it daily." Then they did so.

Piankhi Sends His Army; His Instructions

822. Then his majesty sent an army to Egypt, charging them earnestly: "[⌜Delay⌝] not [day nor] night, as at a game of draughts; (but) fight ye on sight. Force battle upon him from afar. If he says to the infantry and chariotry of another city, 'Hasten;' (then) ye shall abide until his army comes, that ye may fight as he says. But if his allies be in another city, (then) let one hasten to them; these princes, whom he has brought for his support: Libyans (*Thnw*) and favorite soldiers, force battle upon them ⌜first⌝. Say, 'We know not what he cries in mustering troops. Yoke the war horses, the best of thy stable; draw up the line of battle! Thou knowest that Amon is the god who has sent us.'"

Instructions as to Thebes

823. "When ye arrive at Thebes, before Karnak, ye shall enter into the water, ye shall bathe in the river, ye shall dress in ⌜fine linen⌝; unstring the bow, loosen the arrow. Let not the chief boast as a mighty man; there is no strength to the mighty without him (Amon). He maketh the weak-armed into the strong-armed, so that multitudes flee from the feeble, and one alone taketh a thousand men. Sprinkle yourselves with the water of his altars, sniff the ground before him. Say ye to him, 'Give to us the way, that we may fight in the shadow of thy sword. (As for) the generation whom thou hast sent out, when its attack occurs, multitudes flee before it.'"

Reply of the Army

824. Then they threw themselves upon their bellies before his majesty (saying): "It is thy name which endues us with might, and thy counsel is the mooring-post of thy army; thy bread is in our bellies on every march, thy beer quenches our thirst. It is thy valor that giveth us might, and there is strength at the remembrance of thy name; (for) no army prevails whose commander is a coward. Who is thy equal therein? Thou art a victorious king, achieving with his hands, chief of the work of war."

TEXT 12: *General Piankhi: The Kushite Conquest of Egypt*   75

Advance to Thebes

825. They sailed downstream, they arrived at Thebes, they did according to all that his majesty had said.

Battle on the River

They sailed down-stream upon the river, they found many ships coming up-stream bearing soldiers, sailors, and commanders; every valiant man of the Northland, equipped with weapons of war, to fight against the army of his majesty. Then there was made a great slaughter among them, (whose) number was unknown. Their troops and their ships were captured, and brought as living captives (sic!) to the place where his majesty was.

Arrival at Heracleopolis

They went to the ⌜frontier⌝ of Heracleopolis, demanding battle.

List of the Northern Enemy

830. List of the princes and kings of the Northland, namely:

1. King Namlot and
2. King Yewpet (*Yw-wꜣ-p-t*).
3. Chief of Me, Sheshonk, of Per-Osiris (Busiris), lord of Ded.
4. Great chief of Me, Zeamonefonekh, of Per-Benebded (Mendes), together with
5. His eldest son, who was commander of the army of Per-Thutuprehui (*Pr-Ḏḥwty-Wp-rḥwy*).
6. The army of the hereditary prince, Beknenef (*Bk-n-nfy*), together with
7. His eldest son, chief of Me, Nesnekedi (*Ns-nꜣ-ꜥꜣy*, sic!) in the nome of Heseb-ka (*Hsb-kꜣ*).
8. Every chief wearing a feather who was in the Northland; together with
9. King Osorkon, who was in Per-Bast (Bubastis) and the district of Ranofer (*Rꜥ-nfr*).
10. Every prince, the rulers of the walled towns in the West, in the East, (and) the islands in the midst, were united of one mind as followers of the great chief of the West, ruler of the walled towns of the Northland, prophet of Neit, mistress of Sais, sem priest of Ptah, Tefnakhte.

Battle Opposite Heracleopolis

831. They went forth against them; then they made a great slaughter among them, greater than anything. Their ships were captured upon the river. The remnant crossed over and landed on the west side before Per-Peg.

Battle at Per-Peg

832. When the land brightened early in the morning, the army of his majesty crossed over against them. Army mingled with army; they slew a multitude of people among them; horses of unknown number; a rout ensued among the remnant. They fled to the Northland, from the blow, great and evil beyond everything.

List of the slaughter made among them:
People: — men.

Hermopolis Besieged

833. King Namlot fled up-stream southward, when it was told him: "Hermopolis (*Ḥmnw*) is in the midst of the foe from the army of his majesty, who capture its people and its cattle." Then he entered into Hermopolis (*Wnw*), while the army of his majesty was upon the river, in the harbor of the Hare nome. Then they heard of it, and they surrounded the Hare nome on its four sides, not letting the comers-out come out, and not letting the goers-in go in.

Report to Piankhi

834. They sent to report to the majesty of the King of Upper and Lower Egypt, Meriamon-Piankhi, given life, on every conflict which they had fought, and on every victory of his majesty.

Piankhi Determines to go to Egypt Himself

835. Then his majesty was enraged thereat like a panther (saying): "Have they allowed a remnant of the army of the Northland to remain? allowing him that went forth of them to go forth, to tell of his campaign? not causing their death, in order to destroy the last of them? I swear: as Re loves me! As my father Amon favors me! I will myself go northward, that I may destroy that which he has done, that I may make him turn back from fighting, forever."

Piankhi Would Visit Thebes

836. "Now, afterward when the ceremonies of the New Year are celebrated, I will offer to my father, Amon, at his beautiful feast, when he makes his beautiful appearance of the New Year, that he may send me forth in peace, to behold Amon at the beautiful Feast of Opet; that I may bring his image forth in procession to Luxor at his beautiful feast (called): "Night at the Feast of Opet," and at the feast (called): "Abiding in Thebes," which Re made for him in the beginning; and that I may bring him in procession to his house, resting upon his throne, on the "Day of Bringing in the God," in the third month of the first season, second day; that I may make the Northland taste the taste of my fingers."

Capture of Oxyrhyncus

837. Then the army, which was there in Egypt, heard of the wrath which his majesty felt toward them. Then they fought against Per-Mezed of the Oxyrhynchite nome, they took it like a flood of water, and they sent to his majesty; (but) his heart was not satisfied therewith.

Capture of Tetehen

838. Then they fought against Tetehen, great in might. They found it filled with soldiers, with every valiant man of the Northland. Then the battering-ram was employed against it, its wall was overthrown, and a great slaughter was made among them, of unknown number; also the son of the chief of Me, Tefnakhte. Then they sent to his majesty concerning it, (but) his heart was not satisfied therewith.

Capture of Hatbenu

839. Then they fought against Hatbenu (*Ḥ·t-Bnw*), its interior was breached, the army of his majesty entered into it. Then they sent to his majesty, (but) his heart was not satisfied therewith.

Piankhi Goes to Hermopolis

840. First month of the first season, ninth day; his majesty went northward to Thebes, and completed the Feast of Amon at the Feast of Opet. His majesty sailed northward to the city of the Hare nome (Hermopolis); his majesty came forth from the cabin of the ship, the horses were yoked up, the chariot was mounted, the terror of his majesty reached to the end of the Asiatics, every heart was heavy with the fear of him.

Piankhi Rebukes His Army

841. Then his majesty went forth ⌜— —⌝ to hate his soldiers, enraged at them like a panther (saying): "Is the steadfastness of your fighting this slackness in my affairs? Has the year reached its end, when the fear of me has been inspired in the Northland? A great and evil blow shall be smitten them."

Siege of Hermopolis

842. He set up for himself the camp on the southwest of Hermopolis (*Ḥmnw*), and besieged it daily. An embankment was made, to inclose the wall; a tower was raised to elevate the archers while shooting, and slingers while slinging stones, and slaying people among them daily.

The City Pleads for Mercy

843. Days passed, and Hermopolis (*Wnw*) was foul to the nose, without her (usual) fragrance. Then Hermopolis (*Wnw*) threw herself upon her belly, and plead before the king. Messengers came forth and descended bearing everything beautiful to behold: gold, every splendid costly stone, clothing in a chest, and the diadem which was upon his head, the uraeus which inspired the fear of him; without ceasing during many days, pleading with his diadem.

Namlot's Queen Intercedes

844. Then they sent his wife, the king's-wife, and king's-daughter, Nestent (*Nstnt*), to plead with the king's-wives, king's-concubines, king's-daughters, and king's-sisters, to throw herself upon her belly in the harem, before the king's-wives (saying): "We come to you, O king's-wives, king's-daughters, and king's-sisters, that ye may appease Horus, lord of the palace, whose fame is great and his triumph mighty. Grant that he ⎯ ⎯ ⎯ ⎯ me; lo, he ⎯ ⎯ ⎯ him. Lo, ⌜⎯ ⎯⌝ ⎯⎯⎯ [⌜Speak⌝] to him, that he may incline to the one that praises him ⎯⎯⎯ ⎯ ⌜⎯⌝ ⎯⎯⎯."

Piankhi Addresses Namlot

845. "Lo, who has led thee? who had led thee? Who, then, has led thee? Who has led thee? ⎯ ⎯ thou didst [⌜forsake⌝] the way of life. Did heaven rain with arrows? I am [⌜content⌝] when the Southerners do obeisance and the Northerners (say): 'Put us in thy shadow.' Lo, it is evil ⌜⎯⌝ ⎯ ⎯ bearing his food. The heart is a steering-oar; it capsizes its owner through that which is from the god. It seeth flame as coolness ⌜in⌝ the heart ⎯ ⎯. There is no old man, ⌜⎯⎯⎯⎯⌝. Thy nomes are full of youths."

Namlot's Reply to Piankhi

846. He threw himself upon his belly before his majesty (saying): "[Be appeased], Horus, lord of the palace, it is thy might which has done it. I am one of the king's slaves, paying impost into the treasury ⌜⎯ ⎯⌝ their impost. I have brought for thee more than they."

Namlot's Gifts

847. Then he presented much silver, gold, lapis lazuli, malachite, bronze, and all costly stones. Then he filled the treasury with this tribute; he brought a horse in the right hand and a sistrum in the left hand, of gold and lapis lazuli.

Piankhi's Triumphant Entry into Hermopolis

848. Then his [majesty] appeared in splendor in his palace, proceeded to the house of Thoth, lord of Hermopolis (*Ḥmnw*), and he slew bulls, calves, and fowl for his father, lord of Hermopolis (*Ḥmnw*), and the eight gods in the house of the eight gods. The army of the Hare nome acclaimed and rejoiced, saying: "How beautiful is Horus, rest-

ing in his city, the Son of Re, Piankhi! Celebrate for us a jubilee (ḥb-śd), even as thou hast protected the Hare nome."

Piankhi Visits Namlot's Palace

849. His majesty proceeded to the house of King Namlot, he entered every chamber of the king's-house, his treasury and his magazines. He caused that there be brought to him; the king's-wives and king's-daughters; they saluted his majesty in the fashion of women, (but) his majesty turned not his face to them.

Piankhi Visits Namlot's Stables

850. His majesty proceeded to the stable of the horses and the quarters of the foals. When he saw that they had suffered hunger, he said: "I swear, as Re loves me, and as my nostrils are rejuvenated with life, it is more grievous in my heart that my horses have suffered hunger, than any evil deed that thou hast done, in the prosecution of thy desire. It has borne witness of thee to me, the fear of thy associates for thee. Didst thou not know that the god's shadow is over me? and that my fortune never perishes because of him? Would that another had done it to me! I could not but ⌜condemn⌝ him on account of it. When I was being fashioned in the womb, and created in the divine egg the seed of the god was in me. By his ka, I do nothing without him; he it is who commands me to do it."

Disposal of Namlot's Property

851. Then his possessions were assigned to the treasury, and his granary to the divine offerings of Amon of Karnak.

Loyalty of Heracleopolis

852. The ruler of Heracleopolis Pefnefdibast (Pf-nf-dyy-Bꜣs·t) came, bearing tribute to the palace: gold, silver, every costly stone, and horses of the choicest of the stable. He threw himself upon his belly before his majesty; he said: "Hail to thee, Horus, mighty king, Bull subduer of Bulls! The Nether World had seized me, and I was submerged in darkness, upon which the light has (now) shone. I found not a friend in the evil day, who was steadfast in the day of battle; but thou, O mighty king, thou has expelled the darkness from me. I will labor together with (thy) subjects, and Heracleopolis shall pay taxes into thy treasury, thou likeness of Harakhte, chief of the imperishable stars. As he was, so art thou king; as he perishes not so thou shall not perish, O King of Upper and Lower Egypt, Piankhi, living forever.

TEXT 13

Shabaka: The Memphite Theology[1]

The Nubian Pharaoh Shabaka ruled ancient Egypt from 716–702 B.C. during the Twenty-Fifth or Kushite Dynasty of Egypt. He was the brother of the military genius Piankhi, who had first consolidated Kushite control over all of Egypt. Shabaka was most noted for promoting a revival of Egyptian architecture. He constructed new monuments and restored the luster of Egypt's ancient temples that had fallen into ruins, particularly in the region of Thebes.

The text known as The Memphite Theology was inscribed by Shabaka and has survived on a black stela contained in the British Museum. The document deals with certain theological issues shared by the Egyptians and Nubians. For example, the gods Hu, Sia, and Neheh personified authoritative command, intelligence, and the eternal universe. In the Memphite Theology, these divine attributes were represented in the tongue and heart of the god Ptah as well as in all pharaohs. John Kaster in The Wisdom of Ancient Egypt *describes The Memphite Theology as a sort of sacred drama or "mystery play."*[2]

(1) The living Horus: he who makes prosper the Two Lands; [the one of] the Two Ladies: he who makes prosper the Two Lands; the Golden Horus: he who makes prosper the Two Lands; the King of Upper and Lower Egypt: Neferkare; son of Re: Sha[baka], beloved of Ptah South of his Wall, who lives like Re forever. (2) His majesty copied this book anew in the House of his father Ptah South of his Wall. His

---

[1]Marshall Clagett, *Ancient Egyptian Science: A Source Book*, vol. 1 (Philadelphia: American Philosophical Society, 1989), pp. 599–602.
[2]Kaster, *The Wisdom of Ancient Egypt: Writings from the Time of the Pharaohs* (New York: Barnes and Noble Books, 1993), p. 57.
Source: From Marshall Clagett, *Ancient Egyptian Science: A Source Book*, vol. 1, © 1989. Reprinted by permission of the American Philosophical Society.

majesty had found it as a work of his ancestors, which was worm-eaten, so that it could not be known from the beginning to the end. Then his majesty copied it anew so that it was in a better state than it had been in before. [He did this] in order that his name might endure and in order that his monument be made to last in the House of his father Ptah South of his Wall through the length of everlastingness (*dt*), as a work done by the Son of Re [Shabaka] for his father Ptah-Tatenen so that he might be given life forever. . .

(48) The gods who came into being in Ptah:
(49a) Ptah-upon-the-Great-Throne. . . ;
(50a) Ptah-Nun, the father who made (?) Atum;
(51a) Ptah-Naunet, the mother who gave birth to Atum;
(52a) Ptah-the-Great, who is the heart and the tongue of the Ennead;
(49b) [Ptah] . . . who bore the gods;
(50b) [Ptah] . . . .
(51b) [Ptah] . . . .
(52b) [Ptah] . . . , Nefertem at the nose of Re every day.

(53) There came into being in the heart [of Ptah] and there came into being on the tongue [of Ptah] something in the shape (i.e. form) of Atum, for Ptah is the very great one who transmitted [life] to all the gods and to their kas by means of the heart in which Horus has taken shape and by means of the tongue in which Thoth has taken shape, . . . [each] (54) as [an agent or form of] Ptah.

[Thus] it happened that heart and tongue gained mastery over [every] member [of the body] according to the teaching that he (Ptah) is in every body [as heart] and in every mouth [as tongue]: [i.e. in the bodies and mouths] of all gods, all men, all cattle, all creeping things, and of everything which lives. Accordingly [as heart] he thinks out (i.e. conceives) and [as tongue] he commands what he wishes [to exist].

(55) His (Ptah's) Ennead is before him as teeth and lips, [they are] as the semen and hands of Atum, for [it is said that] the Ennead of Atum came into being by means of his semen and his fingers. But the Ennead [of Ptah] is the teeth and lips in this mouth which pronounced the name of everything, from which Shu and Tefnut came forth, (56) and which gave birth to the Ennead.

The sight of the eyes, the hearing of the ears, the breathing of the nose, they report to the heart, and it (the heart) causes every understanding (i.e. completed concept) to come forth, and it is the tongue which repeats what the heart has thought out (i.e. devised). Thus all gods were born and his (Ptah's) Ennead was completed. For every word of the god came into being by means of what the heart thought out and the tongue commanded.

(57) So were made all the kas, and the hemsut were determined, [i.e.] those [spirits or faculties and qualities] which make all foods and provisions, by means of this word [which the heart thought out and which came forth on the tongue]. [Thus justice is done] to him who does what is like [and punishment to] him who does what is disliked. Thus life is given to him who has peace (i.e. is peaceful and law-abiding) and death to him who has sin (i.e. who is a criminal). Thus were made all works and all crafts, the action of the hands and the movement of the legs, (58) and the activity of every member, in accordance with the command which is thought out by the heart and comes forth on the tongue and creates the performance of everything.

And so is said of Ptah [this epithet]: "He who made all and brought the gods into being." He is Tatenen, who gave birth to the gods and from whom every thing came forth: food, provisions, offerings for the gods, and all good things. So it was discovered and understood that he is the mightiest of the gods. And so Ptah was satisfied after he had made everything and all the divine words.

> He gave birth to the gods,
> He made the towns,
> He founded the nomes,
> He put the gods into their (60) shrines.
> He settled their offerings,
> He founded their shrines,
> He made their bodies (i.e. their statues) as they desired [them].
> So the gods entered into their bodies,
> Of every wood, every stone, every clay,
> And of every thing which grows upon him [as Tatenen]
> (61) In which their forms resided.
> Thus all gods were gathered in him, and also their kas,
> Content and united with the Lord of the Two Lands.

TEXT 14

Pharaoh Taharqa: Commemorations to the Queen Mother[1]

Taharqa (690–664 B.C.) is often referred to as the most notable personality of the Twenty-Fifth or Kushite Dynasty of Egypt. Son of Nubian General Piankhi, Taharqa was also mentioned in the Bible (2 Kings 19:9), making reference to the warfare the Kushite ruler waged against the Assyrians.

> Now Sennacherib received a report that Tirhakah, the Cushite king [of Egypt], was marching out to fight against him. So he again sent messengers to Hezekiah. . . .

One fragmentary stele composed in the Egyptian hieroglyphics used by Nubian rulers during that period records such events of Taharqa's reign as a thirty mile cross-country marathon run through the desert in which the king rewarded losers as well as winners.[2] Other fragments found among the ruins of Tanis narrate the coming of his mother from the Kushite capital of Napata to the North (Egypt) to be reunited with her son and a *dedication of a temple in his mother's honor*, cited in the excerpt below. It is known that women played an important role in the leadership structure of Nubia, even though the evidence of female rulers on the Kushite throne dates from a later period. The Roman historian Strabo, for example, records a series of battles between the Kushites and Romans in 23 B.C. in which the Nubian army was led by a queen named Candace, who is also mentioned in the Bible (Acts 8:27). However, the term "Candace" in the Meroitic language actually refers to the title rather than the actual name of the Kushite ruler.

---

[1]James Henry Breasted, *Ancient Records of Egypt,* vol. IV (Chicago: The University of Chicago Press, 1906–1907), pp. 457–58.
[2]A. M. Moussa, "A Stele of Taharqa from the Desert Road at Dashur," *Mitteilungen des Deutschen Archaologischen Instituts Abteilung Kairo* 37, and Kendall, p. 10.
Source: Reprinted from James Henry Breasted, *Ancient Records of Egypt,* © 1906–1907 The University of Chicago Press.

895. [⌜The queen-mother⌝] was in Napata as King's-Sister, amiable in love, King's-Mother _____. Now, I had been separated from her as a youth (ḥwn) of twenty years, [⌜accompanying his majesty⌝] when he came to the Northland (Delta). Then she went north to [⌜the Northland where I was⌝] after a long period (ḥnty) of years, and she found me crowned [⌜as king upon the throne of Horus⌝]. I had taken the diadems of Re, and I had assumed the double serpent-crest, as _____ as the protection of my limbs. She rejoiced greatly [when she saw] the beauty of his majesty, as Isis saw her son, Horus, crowned upon the throne _____ while he was a youth in the marsh of _____ all countries. They bowed to the ground to this King's-Mother, while she _____ ⌜greatly⌝. Their old as well as their young ones [⌜gave praise to⌝] this King's-Mother, saying: "Isis hath received _____ , she hath—her son, King of Upper and Lower Egypt, Taharqa, living forever _____ .

896. Here follow four lines of conventional praise addressed to Taharqa, closing with a comparison of his kindness toward his mother with that of Horus to his mother, Isis:

_____ for his mother, Isis, when thou wast crowned upon the throne.

Taharqa, living forever; he made (it) as his monument for his mother, Mut of Napata; he built for her a temple anew, of fine white sandstone, his majesty having found this temple built of stone, by the ancestors of bad workmanship. His majesty caused that this temple should be built of excellent workmanship, forever.

898. The same hall as the above conclusion has:

He made (it) as his monument for his mother, Mut, mistress of heaven, queen of Nubia (Tꜣpd · t); he built her house, he enlarged her temple anew, of fine white sandstone.

899. A cella beside the main adytum has:

He made (it) as his monument for ⌜his⌝ mother, Mut, Eye of Re, Mistress of Heaven, queen of gods, residing in Napata; building her house of fine white sandstone.

TEXT 15

Mentemhet: The Building and Restoration of the Monuments in Thebes[1]

Son of Kushite Pharaoh Taharqa, Mentemhet continued Nubia's dominion over ancient Egypt. As a member of the Twenty-Fifth Dynasty, Mentemhet embarked on an extensive renovation of the temples and monuments of Thebes that possibly began in 667 B.C., according to James Henry Breasted.[2]

The wealth at Mentemhet's disposal, which made it possible for him to undertake such massive public works projects, must have been considerable. However, in 661 B.C. the Assyrian ruler Ashurbanipal sacked Thebes in a particularly destructive siege of the city, undoing much of what Mentemhet had accomplished by way of restoration.

Titles of Mentemhet

904. _____ all gods, fourth prophet of Amon, prince of Thebes, governor of [the Southland], Mentemhet, son of the prophet of Amon, prince of Thebes, Nesu[ptah]; he saith:

Sacred Barge

I fashioned [the sacred barge of ⌜Amon⌝] of 80 cubits in its length, of new cedar of the best of the terraces. The "Great House" was of electrum, inlaid with every genuine costly stone _____ ⌜of the last day⌝ — equipped _____ .

---

[1]James Henry Breasted, *Ancient Records of Egypt* (Chicago: The University of Chicago Press, 1906–1907), vol. IV, pp. 460–65.
[2]Ibid., p. 459.
Source: Reprinted from James Henry Breasted, *Ancient Records of Egypt*, © 1906–1907, The University of Chicago Press.

Purification of Temples

905. I purified all the temples in the nomes of all Patoris, according as one should purify [⌜violated⌝] temples, — after there had been [⌜an invasion of unclean foreigners in⌝] the Southland. ⌜—————⌝ — all these things which I have brought before you, there is no [lying] speech therein, no contradiction ————— deceit. There is no lie in the place of my mouth.

Prosperity and Plentiful Offerings

906. My mistress is satisfied with all that I have done ⌜for⌝ Thebes, [the Horizon of] him of the hidden name, Eye of Re, Mistress [of temples] ————— I satisfied her lord with the things of his desire, bulls of the largest, and calves of the best. I gave ——— my lord, of good things ————— satisfied with food, and divine offerings, like that which he receives at the beginning of all the seasons, at th[eir] times, ——— I multiplied the amount —————. His granaries swelled with the first fruits [⌜which came to⌝] him down-stream in their season, and up-stream in their time. They made festive ————— in his totals, to celebrate the feasts; that he might provision the prophets, priests, — and lay priests of the temples ————— in the nomes, great and small — — making for me an overflow for my city, the land having moisture, the cities and nomes fatness.

Foreign Invasion

907. ————— it being divine chastisement. [⌜In⌝] the protected Southland in its divine way, while the whole land was overturned, because of the greatness of ————— ⌜—————⌝ coming from the South. I satisfied my — coming from ————— in — [in] going in and in going out by night and by day ————— an excellent refuge for my city. [⌜ I ⌝] repelled the wretches from the southern nomes — — —⌜time⌝.

Family Prosperity and Conclusion

908. ————— following his god without ceasing, — the temple, seeing that which was in it. Every shrine was sealed with [⌜my⌝] seal ————— belonging thereto. I was in the temple —, following the footsteps of my lord. My son was with me ————— priest of his ka, chief prophet of — in Thebes, chief of the phyle, Nesuptah. My children were healthy ————— the prophets knew his counsel —. I spent the day in searching and the night in seeking, searching ————— ⌜summoning⌝ them that passed, calling them that —, and revising the rules that had begun to be ⌜obsolete⌝.

Works for Min-Amon

I brought forth Min-Amon to his stairway in the southern house (Luxor) at his beautiful feast ————— plenty. I presented the oblations of the eight gods in the second month of the third season, twenty-eighth day, in order that ——— of electrum and every splendid costly stone. I fashioned the august image of Khonsupekhrod overlaid with gold (called): "His-Every-Emanation-is ——— Crowns." I made a throne for this god, the legs of pure silver, inlay-figures ——— of his stipulations — — them after a long space (ḥnty) of years, beginning to decay. ——————— [———————] according as a thorough inspection should be made.

Temple of Mut?

910. I built her temple of stone ——————— [the doors were of] new cedar, and kedet (kd·t) wood, mounted with Asiatic copper; the inlay-figures thereon were of electrum, the bolts and fastenings ——————— gold inlaid with every costly stone. I erected for her a hall with thirty-four columns of fine white sandstone ⌜—⌝ ———————. I constructed her pure and beautiful lake of fine white sandstone; I erected for her, her storehouse for the storage of her divine offerings therein; I multiplied the offering-tables ———————.

Works for Khonsu

911. I restored the august image of "Khonsu-in-Thebes-Beautiful-Rest" (called): "Wearer-of-the-Divine-Diadem," with gold and every genuine costly stone. I multiplied their offering-tables of silver, gold, and copper. ——————— ⌜I clothed⌝ Khonsu (called): "The-Plan-Maker-is-an-Emanation," with electrum, as formerly.

Works for Montu

912. I constructed the pure lake of Montu, lord of Thebes, of fine white sandstone like ——————— illuminating his great and august house therewith. I multiplied his offering-tables of silver, gold, and bronze.

Theban Divinities

I fashioned individual vessels. I equipped Wes and Weset, Victorious Thebes, Mistress of Might, as an emanation ———————.

Image of Bast

I fashioned the august image of Bast, residing in Thebes; with staves of electrum and every genuine costly stone.

Works for Ptah

913. I fashioned the august image of Ptah (called): "⌜Thebes⌝-is-Bright-at-His-Appearance," of gold ——————— their offering-tables more beautiful than before.

Images of Hathor

I fashioned [the image] of Hathor, Mistress of the Valley (called): "— - — - — - Bright;" as their glorious emanation, according as a thorough inspection should be made ——————— every one thereof had two staves.

Images of Amon

I fashioned the august image of Amon, lord of Thebes (*Ns·wt-tʾwy*), residing in Thebes (*Wʾs·t*); the august image of Khonsu (called): "Numberer-of-Life;" the august image of Amon, lord of Thebes ——————— every one thereof had two staves.

Statue of Amenhotep I

I fashioned the statue of Zeserkere (Amenhotep I), triumphant; of electrum and every costly stone; with two staves, as it had been before ———————.

Khonsu of Themet

914. [⌈I fashioned the image of⌉] Khonsu, residing in Themet (*Tʾ-mw·t*) ⌈— —⌉ of electrum, with two staves.

Image of "The Great One"

I fashioned "The-Great-One (feminine)-of-the-Garden" as her glorious emanation; I restored her temples, that it might be as formerly.

Wall of Karnak

——————— it of fine white sandstone, to keep off the flood of the river from ⌈it when it came⌉. I hewed a ⌈—⌉ ——————— at his beautiful feast of the fourth month of the first season, twenty-fifth day. I restored the wall of the temple of Amon in Karnak ⌈—⌉ ——————— ⌈— — —⌉. I built a ⌈—⌉ of brick, according as I found it good to make the ancestors ———————.

Works for the Sacred Bull

915. I [⌈fashioned⌉] the bull of Mad (*Mʾd*), as his glorious emanation; I built his house; it was more beautiful than what was therein [⌈ before⌉] ———————.

Temple of Montu

I built the temple of Montu, lord — — — — — its gates shone beautifully ———————.

Works for Uncertain Gods

[I fashioned the image of] — upon his stairway (called: "— - — -of-the-Field-in-Thebes;" of gold, more beautiful than it was before ———— who is lord of the hill-country, residing in Khemkhem (*Ḥmḫm*).

Image of Horus

I fashioned the august image of Horus (called): "The-God-Abides ————."

Image of Min?

916. I [fashioned] (the image of) ⌈Min⌉ (called): "⌈Chief⌉-of-Heaven," as his glorious emanation, overlaid — — ————.

Image of Thoth

I fashioned the august image of Thoth, presiding over Hatibti (*Ḥ·t-ybty*), residing in ————.

Works for Isis

———— I — the emanation of Isis. I fashioned — upon them — — my whole city ⌈— —⌉ — ⌈—⌉ ———— more beautiful than formerly. I constructed a sacred lake for the temple of Isis ⌈— —⌉ — ————.

Works for Osiris

I fashioned the barge of Osiris in this district, of — cubits — — — — of new cedar, according to the accustomed stipulations, ⌈after I had found it of acacia⌉ ———— ———— of brick, after I had found it beginning to fall to ruin ————.

918. Year 24, fourth month of the second season (eighth month), day 23, under the majesty of the king of the Upper and Lower Egypt, Taharqa, living forever.

The god was conducted in peace to the beautiful West, by the hereditary prince, sem priest, master of all wardrobes, prophet of Ptah, divine father, Senbef, son of the divine father, of Sekhetre (*Sḫt-Rˁ*), Enekh-wennofer; born of Neatesnakhte (*Nˀ-ˁˀ-tˀys-nht·t*). His brother, divine father of Sekhetre, Ptahhotep.

TEXT 16

Priests of Meroë: Prayer to the Lion-God Apedemak[1]

Because no clear geographical demarcation exists between upper Egypt and Nubia, it is not surprising that the gods, which Egypt's first pharaoh, Menes of upper Egypt, imposed on the entire country around 3100 B.C., namely Osiris, Isis, and Amen, were deities also worshipped by the Nubians. However, after the fall of the Twenty-Fifth or Kushite Dynasty of Egypt in 650 B.C., a divergent theological culture begins to evolve around the Nubian city of Meroë, to the south of their former capital of Napata.

By the fourth century B.C. Meroë had become a vibrant commercial city, supporting a large iron smelting industry and magnificent temples. A new Meroitic script also began to replace Egyptian hieroglyphics as the writing mode of this Nubian civilization. However, as scholars have yet to decipher Meroitic, we only have access at the present time to those inscriptions that were still being written in hieroglyphics.

One of the most powerful gods of Nubia and Meroë, who was not worshiped in Egypt, was the Lion-God Apedemak; that is, temple ruins devoted to worship of this deity have only been found in the region of Nubia itself. The square-chambered architectural style of such temples with a pylon entrance also differed from characteristically Egyptian temples built in the shape of a rectangle.[2] Other Nubian gods such as Arensnuphis also never became Egyptianized.

While Apedemak's principal attribute appeared to be that of a warrior god, he was also in certain temple depictions placed alongside Isis and Horus to present a trinity. In addition, Apedemak was also presented in a processional that included Thoth, the god of wisdom and learning (whom the Greeks later equated to their god Hermes). Nubian temple inscriptions gave considerable emphasis to this god's south-

---

[1] P. L. Shinnie, *Meroë: A Civilization of the Sudan* (New York: Praeger, 1967), p. 143.
[2] David O'Connor, *Ancient Nubia: Egypt's Rival in Africa* (Philadelphia: The University Museum of Archaeology and Anthropology, University of Pennsylvania, 1993), p. 79.

ern origins, referring to him as "the Lion of the south, the foremost of Nubia" and "Kenset" (a descriptive designation of the lands of the south).³

The prayer to Apedemak has suffered as a temple inscription. It is only because it is written in Egyptian hieroglyphics rather than Meroitic script that scholars have been able to decipher it.

Thou are greeted, Apedemek, lord of Naqa; great god, lord of Musawwarat es- Sofra; splendid god, at the head of Nubia. Lion of the south, strong of arm. Great god, the one who comes to those who call him. The one carries (?) the secret, concealed in his being, who was not seen by any eye. Who is a companion for men and women, who will not be hindered in heaven and earth. Who procures nourishment for all men in this his name 'Perfect Awakener.' The one who hurls his hot breath against his enemy, in this his name 'Great of Power.' Who kills the enemy with —. The one who punishes all who commit crimes against him. Who prepares the place for those who give themselves to him. Who gives to those who call to him. Lord of life, great in his sight.

---

³L. V. Zabkar, *Apedemak: Lion God of Meroë* (Warminster, England: Aris & Phillips Ltd., 1975), pp. 24–35.
Source: From P. L. Shinnie, *Meroe: A Civilization of the Sudan,* © 1967, Frederick A. Praeger.

PART THREE

Hellenized Egypt and Nubia

Three thousand years of Egyptian civilization did not end with the Greek conquest of Egypt in 322 B.C. The new era ushered in by the conquest of Macedonia's Alexander the Great has come to be known as the Ptolemaic period after General Ptolemy I Soter, who ruled Egypt from 323 to 285 B.C. It initiated one of the most vibrant periods

of cultural intermixing that human society has ever known, centered around the city of Alexandria, named after the Greek conqueror.

Over time the commercial and cultural activity that had previously been based around the Egyptian city of Heliopolis shifted to this thriving new commercial center on the Mediterranean Sea at the Delta of the Nile. Alexandria, thus, developed into a cosmopolitan city of Egyptians, Greeks, and Jews. Over the course of centuries, the Alexandrians who continued to call themselves Greeks were more likely to be, in actuality, the descendants of Egyptian Copts who had migrated to the city and over time absorbed its Hellenistic culture.[1] From its earliest beginnings, Alexander the Great had urged his officers to "marry and mix with the local population."

Ptolemy II founded the great Library and Museum at Alexandria around 283 B.C. At its height the library contained 500,000 papyrus rolls, many of which contained more than one book. Alexandria also became the center of the book trade, where works from throughout the ancient world were copied and disseminated among the Greek-reading population inhabiting the Nile Valley. The Library of Alexandria's burning in 48 B.C. during Julius Ceasar's siege of the city has over the course of centuries taken on such mythical proportions that scholars now question whether this collection of a million books were all lost in one conflagration or through a less dramatic succession of political events.

In any case the cultural life of Hellenized Egypt was not restricted to the confines of Alexandria. The Greek alphabet came to replace hieroglyphics and in time became synthesized into the writing of the Egyptian Coptic language, a final evolution of ancient Egyptian, even though seven letters of the demotic script were borrowed from the ancient language. In many ways the Hellenized culture that evolved on Egyptian soil was unique. It could not have been replicated in the cultural milieu of Athens.

ROMAN EGYPT

One of the most captivating narratives of history tells the story of the Egyptian Queen Cleopatra, the last sovereign of the Macedonian dynasty that ruled Egypt. A one-time lover of Julius Ceasar, she later became the wife of Mark Antony. After the Roman armies of Octavian (the future emperor Augustus) defeated their combined forces, Antony and Cleopatra committed suicide, and Egypt fell under Roman domination in 30 B.C. Even though political dominion shifted from the Greeks to the Romans, scholars often encompass this later Roman period under the "Hellenic" label because the cultural fusion of Greek and Egyptian continued unabated. Even though the Roman conquest of Egypt changed the political administration of the country, the language and the culture of the Greeks continued to predominate over Latin in the cultural and intellectual lives of Egyptians during that period.

---

[1] Alvyn Pettersen, *Athanasius* (London: Geoffrey Chapman Publishers, 1995), p. 5.

PART THREE: *Hellenized Egypt and Nubia*

CHRISTIANITY

Western scholars have always recognized the Judaic roots of early Christianity. What they are only now coming to appreciate is the extent to which the church's spread into Africa prior to its diffusion throughout Europe contributed some of Christian theology's most characteristic elements. The religion of the Hebrews, like that of the Greeks, did not promise salvation after death. The concepts of the Trinity, the Eucharist or liturgy of Holy Communion, the Resurrection, and reverence for the Virgin Mary were some of the theological elements that so dramatically distinguished the new religion from Judaism. Contemporary scholars now suggest that these fundamentals of Christian theology and practice may have emanated from the intellectual production of the Egyptian scholars who first defined the theology of the new religion brought to their shores, through the thriving port city of Alexandria, in the early years A.D. by the Apostle Mark.

Egyptians not merely from the Delta region of lower Egypt but also from upper or southern Egypt and Nubia came to embrace the new Christian religion that proffered spiritual shelter from the oppressive dominion of the Roman Empire. In certain ways Christianity proved conducive to traditional Egyptian culture. In others Egyptian theologians in the process of formulating the new theology perhaps made it more so. The ancient Egyptian religion had conditioned its adherents to such beliefs as the resurrection of the dead and an afterlife in which rewards and punishments were meted out in judgment of how one had lived his or her life on earth. The Egyptians were thus able to reject their old gods without altogether having to jettison certain religious tenets they had held onto for more than 3,000 years. For, as the nineteenth century scholar Samuel Sharpe has pointed out:

> [The Egyptians] were used to hearing of a God being put to death, as they had always held that Osiris, though a god, had been put to death . . . of children being born of an earthly mother and having no earthly father, as they held that many of their kings were so born.[2]

It was into this Alexandrian environment that many of the early apostolic fathers of the Christian Church who attained sainthood were born, men like Clement, Origen, and Athanasius.

The oldest Greek translation of the Bible was made in Alexandria during the reign of Ptolemy II Philadelphus (285–244 B.C.). It came to be known as the Septuagint, on account of the seventy translators who participated in this monumental project. Alexandra was likewise the home of Philo Judaeus, one of the most renowned Jewish thinkers of antiquity. Philo represented the thinking of a small but influential number of African Jews whom he believed capable of looking "beyond the letter of the Torah, and, through the lenses of allegory, to discern as the true objective of Jewish revelation a great new immaterial world of mystic accomplishment."[3]

Many thousands of early Christians faced martyrdom at the hands of successive Roman emperors until the conversion of Emperor Constantine in A.D. 312. Even with

---

[2]Samuel Sharpe, *Egyptian Mythology and Egyptian Christianity with Their Influences on the Opinions of Modern Christendom,* (London: Carter Publishers, 1896), p. 105.
[3]Erwin R. Goodenough, *An Introduction to Philo Judaeus* (London: Oxford University Press 1962), p. 46, and Nahum N. Glatzer, *The Essential Philo* (New York: Shocken Books, 1971), p. ix.

the end to Roman persecution of Christians, the church community did not enjoy tranquility as different theological tendencies vied for supremacy. It was in the battle against Arianism, a belief asserting that Jesus Christ did not share his Father's divinity, but neither was he wholly human, that one of the most prominent of the early church fathers, Athanasius, came to the fore. He represented the Bishop of Alexandra at the Council of Nicaea that convened in A.D. 325. The Nicaean Creed established during this tribunal is still used in many Christian denominations.

During the formative years of Christianity in the early centuries A.D., western Europeans were quite willing to follow the theological lead of African Church leaders in certain religious matters. Nineteenth-century Egyptologist Samuel Sharpe described Alexandria's reputation within the larger world of Christendom thus:

> At the end of the third century, Hesychius of Alexandra had published a new edition of the Greek Bible with a corrected text, and such was the credit of Alexandria, as the chief seat of Christian learning, that all distant churches sent there for copies of the scriptures. When Constans wanted copies of the Greek scriptures for Rome, he sent for them to Alexandria and received the approved text for Athanasius. . . . Italy and the West acknowledged Egypt as their best instructress in all ecclesiastical matters.[4]

Egyptian Christians, contrary to the Roman Church, adopted the doctrine of Monophysitism. The Monophysites, in emphasizing the divinity of Christ, denied that Jesus Christ could also have been a normal human being. In 451 the Roman Church declared their doctrine a "heresy," and unrepentant Monophysites were expelled from the official Christian Church, provoking unrepentant Egyptian Christians to form the Coptic Church.[5]

GNOSTICISM AND NEOPLATONISM

Alexandria became the center of the ancient world for intellectual endeavors of all types, with the philosophical studies growing alongside those of the doctrinal elucidation of Christianity. In this religious and philosophical climate, the mainstream church launched an intense battle against the religious philosophy known as "Gnosticism" (even though theologians like Clement and Origen did attempt to integrate some elements of Gnosticism into their religious thinking). A theology of diverse roots, which the Greeks called *gnosis* (knowledge), Gnosticism refers to the special way of knowing that comes through insight rather than reason. In modern parlance it becomes the domain of the subconscious, which is often believed to reveal a deeper truth than empirical fact-finding and the memorization of a proscribed religious dogma. This philosophical school laid special emphasis on the power of human self-awareness, laying a historical basis for the works of the twentieth-century psychologist C. G. Jung who formulated a concept of evil as emanating from the shadow hidden within the self.

The growing influence of Gnosticism in Africa during the formative stages of Christianity was revealed in a corpus of Gnostic texts that have come to be called the Nag Hammadi Library, named after the site in upper (southern) Egypt where these

---

[4]Sharpe, p. 110.
[5]Kevin Shillington, *History of Africa* (New York: St. Martins Press, 1995).

fourth-century papyrus manuscripts were unearthed in 1945. Until the discovery of this document, most of what was known about Gnosticism emanated from the works of the anti-Gnostic church leaders of early Christianity, particularly Tertullian. The Gnostic movement was eventually labeled a heresy by orthodox Christian theologians and forced underground.

Simultaneous to the evolution of Gnosticism, there evolved a non-Christianized philosophic religion reflected in the *Corpus Hermeticum,* the name given to a collection of 17 documents that first surfaced in Europe in the fourteenth century. These texts were written by Hellenized Egyptians of the third century A.D., ascribed fictitiously to Hermes Trismegistus or "Thrice Great Hermes," the name given by the Greeks to the Egyptian god of knowledge, Thoth. Hermes Trimegistus was considered to be the first and foremost teacher of Gnosticism. However, unlike the Nag Hammadi Library of Gnostic texts, the Hermetical writings reveal the thinking of non-Christianized Gnosticism. In this regard Scott has observed that:

> the Hermetic writers recognize no inspired and infallible Scripture; and there is, for them, no written text with the words of which all that they say must be made to conform. . . . Hence there is in the Hermetica a directness and simplicity of statement such as is not to be found in the theological writings of the time, whether Pagan, Jewish or Christian.[6]

The philosophic religion of these Hermetics, or "seekers after God," syncretized the ancient traditions of Egypt with Neoplatonism, the thought of Plato, who had himself studied under the Egyptian priests at one time.[7] This manner of philosophic thought relying on insight over reason eventually reemerged in Europe in the symbolism employed in Masonic rites, and is recalled even today in the depiction of the eye of the pyramid engraved on United States one dollar bills.

THE SCIENCES

In Hellenized Alexandria during the early centuries A.D., great strides were made in pure mathematics, mechanics, physics, geography, and medicine. What is often referred to as "Greek science" was actually the intellectual production of this remarkable period in Alexandria's history, which celebrated the fecund Greek contribution to the accumulated knowledge of Egypt's 3,000-year-old civilization, and that of neighboring Babylonia. Western scholars once assumed without question that, because of their great "innovative genius" and the fact that they wrote in Greek, the scientific thinkers of Alexandria were ethnic Greeks. Now that such outmoded frameworks have been cast aside scholars are now realizing what a rich field of inquiry awaits their attention as they work to uncover more substantive information about the cross-cultural influences of Hellenized Egyptian men and women of science.

---

[6]Walter Scott (ed.), *Hermetica: The Ancient Greek and Latin Writings Which Contain Religious or Philosophic Teachings Ascribed to Hermes Trismegistus* (Boston: Shambahala, 1993), p. 7.
[7]Ibid., p. 4.

TEXT 17

Heron of Alexandria: Approximating the Square Root of a Nonsquare Integer

from Metrica[1]

One of the most powerful intellectual syntheses the world has ever known was that of the Greeks and the ancient Egyptians, which emanated from the Egyptian coastal city of Alexandria. Founded in 332 B.C. by Alexander the Great as a new capital for his conquered prize of Egypt, the city soon grew into the intellectual center of the known world. In time, as the conquering Greeks intermarried with their Egyptian subjects, the traditions of Egypt, which emerged during this period, survived first in the Greek language and later in Coptic. The latter represented a final stage of the ancient Egyptian language, employing the Greek alphabet rather than hieroglyphics. The melding of the Egyptian and Greek cultures, which radiated outward from Alexandria, was known as Hellenic.

Alexandria during this period developed into a remarkably fertile environment for the sciences, laying the basis for scientific knowledge that dominates Western thinking today. Earlier scholars had assumed that these scientific accomplishments were "Greek and Greek alone," and that the nearly 3,000-year-old intellectual traditions of the Egyptians played no role in the seemingly miraculous explosion of scientific knowledge during this period. However, historians of science and mathematics are only now coming to appreciate the full extent of the European and African synthesis of knowledge that made these scientific developments possible.

---

[1]Howard Eves, *An Introduction to the History of Mathematics* (New York: Holt, Rinehart & Winston, 1964), p. 157.

TEXT 17: Heron of Alexandria: Approximating the Square Root of a Nonsquare Integer

One of the many noted mathematicians to emanate from Alexandria was Heron, a Hellenized Egyptian who lived sometime between 150 B.C. and A.D. 250.[2] While many of his works have been lost, at least 14 of his treatises on geometry and mechanics, including descriptions of ingenious mechanical devices, have survived. Heron's most important geometrical work is his Metrica, a copy of which was discovered in Constantinople in 1896. Howard Eves, in An Introduction to the History of Mathematics, notes:

> Book I deals with the area mensuration of squares, rectangles, triangles, trapezoids, various other specialized quadrilaterals, the regular polygons from the equilateral triangle to the regular dodecagon, circles and their segments, ellipses, parabolic segments, and the surfaces of cylinders, cones, spheres and spherical zones. It is in this book that we find Heron's clever derivation of the famous formula for the area of a triangle in terms of its three sides. Of particular interest, also, in this book, is Heron's method of approximating the square root of a nonsquare integer. It is a process frequently used by computers today.[3]

Heron's method of approximating the square root of a nonsquare integer is employed by computers today.

If $n = ab$, then $\sqrt{n}$ is approximated by $(a + b)/2$, the approximation improving with the closeness of a to b. The method permits of successive approximations. Thus, if a_1 is a first approximation to $\sqrt{n}$, then

$$a_2 = (a_1 + n/a_1)/2$$

is a better approximation, and

$$a_3 = (a_2 + n/a_2)/2$$

is still better, and so on.

---

[2]Eves, *An Introduction to the History of Mathematics*, p. 156.
[3]Ibid., pp. 156–57.
Source: From Howard Eves, *An Introduction to the History of Mathematics*, © 1964. Reprinted by permission of Holt, Rinehart & Winston.

TEXT 18

Valentinus: The Gospel of Truth

from The Nag Hammadi Library[1]

By the second century A.D., a clear tension had begun to develop between the mainstream Christian church and the Gnostics, who believed in the divinity within each individual and the attainment of salvation through self-knowledge. Within the vibrant theological community of Alexandria, two theologians of Greek parentage, Irenaeus (c. 120–200) and Titus Flavius Clemens (A.D. c. 150) emerged to lead the theological charge against the Gnostics, and in particular, against the forceful influences of the Egyptian religious philosopher, Valentinus. His doctrine emphasized salvation through gnosis *or self-knowledge.*

Virtually all of the work of the Gnostics were obliterated by the mainstream church during the early centuries of the common era. Its hostility to Gnostic writings is not surprising, since Gnosticism is most noted for its freedom from dogmatism and church establishmentarianism. Until the discovery of the Nag Hammadi Library in 1945, the only surviving knowledge of Christian Gnosticism had come down to us from the refutations of Gnostic doctrines developed by important theologians of Alexandria in the early church.

This version of "The Gospel of Truth" has come down to us in the Coptic language of Egypt.

---

[1]James M. Robinson, *The Nag Hammadi Library in English* (San Francisco: Harper & Row, 1988).

THE GOSPEL OF TRUTH

The gospel of truth is joy for those who have received from the Father of truth the grace of knowing him, through the power of the Word that came forth from the pleroma, the one who is in the thought and the mind of the Father, that is, the one who is addressed as the Savior, (that) being the name of the work he is to perform for the redemption of those who were ignorant of the Father, while in the name [of] the gospel is the proclamation of hope, being discovery for those who search for him.

When the totality went about searching for the one from whom they had come forth—and the totality was inside of him, the incomprehensible, inconceivable one who is superior to every thought—ignorance of the Father brought about anguish and terror; and the anguish grew solid like a fog, so that no one was able to see. For this reason error became powerful; it worked on its own matter foolishly, not having known the truth. It set about with a creation, preparing with power and beauty the substitute for the truth.

This was not, then, a humiliation for him, the incomprehensible, inconceivable one, for they were nothing, the anguish and the oblivion and the creature of deceit, while the established truth is immutable, imperturbable, perfect in beauty. For this reason, despise error.

Thus it had no root; it fell into a fog regarding the Father, while it was involved in preparing works and oblivions and terrors, in order that by means of these it might entice those of the middle and capture them.

The oblivion of error was not revealed. It is not a [. . .] from the Father. Oblivion did not come into existence from the Father, although it did indeed come into existence because of him. But what comes into existence in him is knowledge, which appeared in order that oblivion might vanish and the Father might be known. Since oblivion came into existence because the Father was not known, then if the Father comes to be known, oblivion will not exist from that moment on.

Through this, the gospel of the one who is searched for, which (was) revealed to those who are perfect through the mercies of the Father, the hidden mystery, Jesus, the Christ, enlightened those who were in darkness through oblivion. He enlightened them; he showed (them) a way; and the way is the truth which he taught them.

For this reason error grew angry at him, persecuted him, was distressed at him (and) was brought to naught. He was nailed to a tree (and) he became a fruit of the knowledge of the Father. It did not, however, cause destruction because it was eaten, but to those who ate it it gave (cause) to become glad in the discovery, and he discovered them in himself, and they discovered him in themselves.

As for the incomprehensible, inconceivable one, the Father, the perfect one, the one who made the totality, within him is the totality and of him the totality has need. Although he retained their perfection within himself which he did not give to the totality, the Father was not jealous. What jealousy indeed (could there be) between himself

Source: Pages 209–19 (4,872 words) from *The Nag Hammadi Library in English,* 3rd., completely revised ed. By James M. Robinson, general editor. Copyright © 1988 by E. J. Brill, Leiden, The Netherlands. Reprinted by permission of HarperCollins Publishers, Inc.

and his members? For, if this aeon had thus [received] their [perfection], they could not have come [. . .] the Father. He retains within himself their perfection, granting it to them as a return to him and a perfectly unitary knowledge. It is he who fashioned the totality, and within him is the totality and the totality was in need of him.

As in the case of a person of whom some are ignorant, he wishes to have them know him and love him, so—for what did the totality have need of if not knowledge regarding the Father?—he became a guide, restful and leisurely. In schools he appeared (and) he spoke the word as a teacher. There came the men wise in their own estimation, putting him to the test. But he confounded them because they were foolish. They hated him because they were not really wise.

After all these, there came the little children also, those to whom the knowledge of the Father belongs. Having been strengthened, they learned about the impressions of the Father. They knew, they were known; they were glorified, they glorified. There was manifested in their heart the living book of the living—the one written in the thought and the mind [of the] Father, which from before the foundation of the totality was within his incomprehensibility—that (book) which no one was able to take, since it remains for the one who will take it to be slain. No one could have become manifest from among those who have believed in salvation unless that book had appeared. For this reason the merciful one, the faithful one, Jesus, was patient in accepting sufferings until he took that book, since he knows that his death is life for many.

Just as there lies hidden in a will, before it is opened, the fortune of the deceased master of the house, so (it is) with the totality, which lay hidden while the Father of the totality was invisible, being something which is from him, from whom every space comes forth. For this reason Jesus appeared; he put on that book; he was nailed to a tree; he published the edict of the Father on the cross. O such great teaching! He draws himself down to death though life eternal clothes him. Having stripped himself of the perishable rags, he put on imperishability, which no one can possibly take away from him. Having entered the empty spaces of terrors, he passed through those who were stripped naked by oblivion, being knowledge and perfection, proclaiming the things that are in the heart, [. . .] teach those who will receive teaching.

But those who are to receive teaching [are] the living who are inscribed in the book of the living. It is about themselves that they receive instruction, receiving it from the Father, turning again to him. Since the perfection of the totality is in the Father, it is necessary for the totality to ascend to him. Then, if one has knowledge, he receives what are his own and draws them to himself. For he who is ignorant is in need, and what he lacks is great, since he lacks that which will make him perfect. Since the perfection of the totality is in the Father and it is necessary for the totality to ascend to him and for each one to receive what are his own, he enrolled them in advance, having prepared them to give to those who came forth from him.

Those whose name he knew in advance were called at the end, so that one who has knowledge is the one whose name the Father has uttered. For he whose name has not been spoken is ignorant. Indeed, how is one to hear if his name has not been called? For he who is ignorant until the end is a creature of oblivion, and he will vanish along with it. If not, how is it that these miserable ones have no name, (how is it that) they do not have the call? Therefore, if one has knowledge, he is from above. If he is called, he hears, he answers, and he turns to him who is calling him, and ascends to him. And he knows in what manner he is called. Having knowledge, he does the will of the one who called him, he wishes to be pleasing to him, he receives rest. Each one's name comes to him. He who is to have knowledge in this manner knows where he comes from and where he is going. He knows as one who having become drunk has turned away from his drunkenness, (and) having returned to himself, has set right what are his own.

He has brought many back from error. He has gone before them to their places, from which they moved away, since it was on account of the depth that they received error, the depth of the one who encircles all spaces while there is none that encircles him. It was a great wonder that they were in the Father, not knowing him, and (that) they were able to come forth by themselves, since they were unable to comprehend or to know the one in whom they were. For if his will had not thus emerged from him—for he revealed it in view of a knowledge in which all its emanations concur.

This is the knowledge of the living book which he revealed to the aeons, at the end, as [his letters], revealing how they are not vowels nor are they consonants, so that one might read them and think of something foolish, but they are letters of the truth which they alone speak who know them. Each letter is a complete (thought) like a complete book, since they are letters written by the Unity, the Father having written them for the aeons in order that by means of his letters they should know the Father.

While his wisdom contemplates the Word, and his teaching utters it, his knowledge has revealed (it). While forebearance is a crown upon it, and his gladness is in harmony with it, his glory has exalted it, his image has revealed it, his repose has received it into itself, his love has made a body over it, his fidelity has embraced it. In this way the Word of the Father goes forth in the totality, as the fruit [of] his heart and an impression of his will. But it supports the totality; it chooses them and also receives the impression of the totality purifying them, bringing them back into the Father, into the Mother, Jesus of the infinite sweetness.

The Father reveals his bosom. Now his bosom is the Holy Spirit. He reveals what is hidden of him—what is hidden of him is his Son—so that through the mercies of the Father the aeons may know him and cease laboring in search of the Father, resting there in him, knowing that this is the rest. Having filled the deficiency, he abolished the form—the form of it is the world, that in which he served. For the place where there is envy and strife is deficient, but the place where (there is) Unity is perfect. Since the deficiency came into being because the Father was not known, therefore, when the Father is known, from that moment on the deficiency will no longer exist. As in the case of the ignorance of a person, when he comes to have knowledge, his ignorance vanishes of itself, as the darkness vanishes when light appears, so also the deficiency vanishes in the perfection. So from the moment on the form is not apparent, but it will vanish in the fusion of Unity, for now their works lie scattered. In time Unity will perfect the spaces. It is within Unity that each one will attain himself; within knowledge he will purify himself from multiplicity into Unity, consuming matter within himself like fire, and darkness by light, death by life.

If indeed these things have happened to each one of us, then we must see to it above all that the house will be holy and silent for the Unity. (It is) as in the case of some people who moved out of dwellings having jars that in spots were not good. They would break them, and the master of the house would not suffer loss. Rather (he) is glad because in place of the bad jars (there are) full ones which are made perfect. For such is the judgment which has come from above. It has passed judgment on everyone; it is a drawn sword, with two edges, cutting on either side. When the Word appeared, the one that is within the heart of those who utter it—it is not a sound alone but it became a body—a great disturbance took place among the jars because some had been emptied, others filled; that is, some had been supplied, others poured out, some had been purified, still others broken up. All the spaces were shaken and disturbed because they had no order nor stability. Error was upset, not knowing what to do; it was grieved, in mourning, afflicting itself because it knew nothing. When knowledge drew near it—this is the downfall of (error) and all its emanations—error is empty, having nothing inside.

Truth appeared; all its emanations knew it. They greeted the Father in truth with a perfect power that joins them with the Father. For, as for everyone who loves the truth—because the truth is the mouth of the Father; his tongue is the Holy Spirit—he who is joined to the truth is joined to the Father's mouth by his tongue, whenever he is to receive the Holy Spirit, since this is the manifestation of the Father and his revelation to his aeons.

He manifested what was hidden of him; he explained it. For who contains, if not the Father alone? All the spaces are his emanations. They have known that they came forth from him like children who are from a grown man. They knew that they had not yet received form nor yet received a name, each one of which the Father begets.

Then, when they receive form by his knowledge, though truly within him, they do not know him. But he Father is perfect, knowing every space within him. If he wishes, he manifests whomever he wishes by giving him form and giving him a name, and he gives a name to him and brings it about that those come into existence who, before they come into existence, are ignorant of him who fashioned them.

I do not say, then, that they are nothing (at all) who have not yet come into existence, but they are in him who will wish that they come into existence when he wishes, like the time that is to come. Before all things appear, he knows what he will produce. But the fruit which is not yet manifest does not know anything, nor does it do anything. Thus, also, every space which is itself in the Father is from the one who exists, who established it from what does not exist. For he who has no root has no fruit either, but though he thinks to himself, "I have come into being," yet he will perish by himself. For this reason, he who did not exist at all will never come into existence. What, then, did he wish him to think of himself? This: "I have come into being like the shadows and phantoms of the night." When the light shines on the terror which that person had experienced, he knows that it is nothing.

Thus they were ignorant of the Father, he being the one whom they did not see. Since it was terror and disturbance and instability and doubt and division, there were many illusions at work by means of these, and (there were) empty fictions, as if they were sunk in sleep and found themselves in disturbing dreams. Either (there is) a place to which they are fleeing, or without strength they come (from) having chased after others, or they are involved in striking blows, or they are receiving blows themselves, or they have fallen from high places, or they take off into the air though they do not even have wings. Again, sometimes (it is as) if people were murdering them, though there is no one even pursuing them, or they themselves are killing their neighbors, for they have been stained with their blood. When those who are going through all these things wake up, they see nothing, they who were in the midst of all these disturbances, for they are nothing. Such is the way of those who have cast ignorance aside from them like sleep, not esteeming it as anything, nor do they esteem its works as solid things either, but they leave them behind like a dream in the night. The knowledge of the Father they value as the dawn. This is the way each one has acted, as though asleep at the time when he was ignorant. And this is the way he has (come to knowledge), as if he had awakened. [and] Good for the man who will return and awaken. And blessed is he who has opened the eyes of the blind.

And the Spirit ran after him, hastening from waking him up. Having extended his hand to him who lay upon the ground, he set him up on his feet, for he had not yet risen. He gave them the means of knowing the knowledge of the Father and the revelation of his Son. For, when they had seen him and had heard him, he granted them to taste him and to smell him and to touch the beloved Son.

When he had appeared instructing them about the Father, the incomprehensible one, when he had breathed into them what is in the thought, doing his will, when many had received the light, they turned to him. For the material ones were strangers and did not see his likeness and had not known him. For he came by means of fleshly form, while nothing blocked his course because incorruptibility is irresistible, since he, again, spoke new things, still speaking about what is in the heart of the Father, having brought forth the flawless word.

When light had spoken through his mouth, as well as his voice which gave birth to life, he gave them thought and understanding and mercy and salvation and the powerful spirit from the infiniteness and the sweetness of the Father. Having made punishments and tortures cease—for it was they which were leading astray from his face some who were in need of mercy, in error and in bonds—he both destroyed them with power and confounded them with knowledge. He became a way for those who were gone astray and knowledge for those who were ignorant, a discovery for those who were searching, and a support for those who were wavering, immaculateness for those who were defiled.

He is the shepherd who left behind the ninety-nine sheep which were not lost. He went searching for the one which had gone astray. He rejoiced when he found it, for ninety-nine is a number that is in the left hand which holds it. But when the one is found, the entire number passes to the right (hand). As that which lacks the one—that is, the entire right (hand)—draws what was deficient and takes it from the left-hand side and brings (it) to the right, so too the number becomes one hundred. It is the sign of the one who is in their sound; it is the Father. Even on the Sabbath, he labored for the sheep which he found fallen into the pit. He gave life to the sheep, having brought it up from the pit in order that you might know interiorly—you, the sons of interior knowledge—what is the Sabbath, on which it is not fitting for salvation to be idle, in order that you may speak from the day from above, which has no night, and from the light which does not sink because it is perfect.

Say, then, from the heart that you are the perfect day and in you dwells the light that does not fail. Speak of the truth with those who search for it and (of) knowledge to those who have committed sin in their error. Make firm the foot of those who have stumbled and stretch out your hands to those who are ill. Feed those who are hungry and give repose to those who are weary, and raise up those who wish to rise, and awaken those who sleep. For you are the understanding that is drawn forth. If strength acts thus, it becomes even stronger. Be concerned with yourselves; do not be concerned with other things which you have rejected from yourselves. Do not return to what you have vomited to eat it. Do not be moths. Do not be worms, for you have already cast it off. Do not become a (dwelling) place for the devil, for you have already destroyed him. Do not strengthen (those who are) obstacles to you who are collapsing, as though (you were) a support (for them). For the lawless one is someone to treat ill rather than the just one. For the former does his work as a lawless person; the latter as a righteous person does his work among others. So you, do the will of the Father, for you are from him.

For the Father is sweet and in his will is what is good. He has taken cognizance of the things that are yours that you might find rest in them. For by the fruits does one take cognizance of the things that are yours because the children of the Father are his fragrance, for they are from the grace of his countenance. For this reason the Father loves his fragrance and manifests it in every place, and if it mixes with matter he gives his fragrance to the light and in his repose he causes it to surpass every form (and) every sound. For it is not the ears that smell the fragrance, but (it is) the breath that has the sense of smell and attracts the fragrance to itself and is submerged in the fragrance of the Father, so that he thus shelters it and takes it to the place where it came from, from the first fragrance which is grown cold. It is something in a psychic form, being like cold water which has frozen (?), which is on earth that is not solid, of which those who see it think it is earth; afterwards it dissolves again. If a breath draws it, it gets hot. The fragrances, therefore, that are cold are from the division. For this reason faith came; it dissolved the division, and it brought the warm pleroma of love in order that the cold should not come again but there should be the unity of perfect thought.

This (is) the word of the gospel of the discovery of the pleroma, for those who await the salvation which is coming from on high. While their hope, for which they are waiting, is in waiting—they whose image is light with no shadow in it—then, at that time, the pleroma is proceeding to come. The (deficiency) of matter came to be not through the limitlessness of the Father, who is coming to give time for the deficiency, although no one could say that the incorruptible one would come in this way. But the depth of the Father was multiplied and the thought of error did not exist with him. It is a thing that falls, it is a thing that easily stands upright (again) in the discovery of him who has come to him whom he shall bring back. For the bringing back is called repentance.

For this reason incorruptibility breathed forth; it pursued the one who had sinned in order that he might rest. For forgiveness is what remains for the light in the deficiency, the word of the pleroma. For the physician runs to the place where sickness is, because that is the will that is in him. He who has a deficiency, then, does not hide it, because one has what the other lacks. So the pleroma, which has no deficiency, but fills up the deficiency, is what he provided from himself for filling up what he lacks, in order that therefore he might receive the grace. For when he was deficient, he did not have the grace. That is why there was diminution existing in the place where there is no grace. When that which was diminished was received, he revealed what he lacked, being (now) a pleroma; that is the discovery of the light of truth which rose upon him because it is immutable.

That is why Christ was spoken of in their midst, so that those who were disturbed might receive a bringing back, and he might anoint them with the ointment. The ointment is the mercy of the Father who will have mercy on them. But those whom he has anointed are the ones who have become perfect. For full jars are the ones that are usually anointed. But when the anointing of one (jar) is dissolved, it is emptied, and the reason for there being a deficiency is the thing by which its ointment goes. For at that time a breath draws it, a thing in the power of that which is with it. But from him who has no deficiency, no seal is removed nor is anything emptied, but what he lacks the perfect Father fills again. He is good. He knows his plantings, because it is he who planted them in his paradise. Now his paradise is his place of rest.

This is the perfection in the thought of the Father, and these are the words of his meditation. Each one of his words is the work of his one will in the revelation of his Word. While they were still depths of his thought, the Word which was first to come forth revealed them along with a mind that speaks, the one Word in silent grace. He was called thought, since they were in it before being revealed. It came about then, that he was first to come forth at the time when the will of him who willed desired it. And the will is what the Father rests in and is pleased with. Nothing happens without him nor does anything happen without the will of the Father, but his will is unsearchable. His trace is the will and no one will know him nor is it possible for one to scrutinize him in order to grasp him. But when he wills, what he wills is this—even if the sight does not please them in any way before God—desiring the Father. For he knows the beginning of all of them and their end. For at their end he will question them directly. Now, the end is receiving knowledge about the one who is hidden, and this is the Father, from whom the beginning came forth, to whom all will return who have come forth from him. And they have appeared for the glory and the joy of his name.

Now the name of the Father is the Son. It is he who first gave a name to the one who came forth from him, who was himself, and be begot him as a son. He gave him his name which belonged to him; he is the one to whom belongs all that exists around him, the Father. His is the name; his is the Son. It is possible for him to be seen. The name, however, is invisible because it alone is the mystery of the invisible which comes to ears that are completely filled with it by him. For indeed, the Father's name is not spoken, but it is apparent through a Son.

In this way, then, the name is a great thing. Who, therefore, will be able to utter a name for him, the great name, except him alone to whom the name belongs and the sons of the name in whom rested the name of the Father, (who) in turn themselves rested in his name? Since the Father is unengendered, he alone is the one who begot him for him(self) as a name, before he brought forth the aeons, in order that the name of the Father should be over their head as lord, that is the name in truth, which is firm in his command through perfect power. For the name is not from (mere) words, nor does his name consist of appellations, but it is invisible. He gave a name to him alone, since he alone sees him, he alone having the power to give him a name. For he who does not exist has no name. For what name is given to him who does not exist? But the one who exists exists also with his name, and he alone knows it, and alone (knows how) to give him a name. It is the Father. The Son is his name. He did not, therefore, hide it in the thing, but it existed; as for the Son, he alone gave a name. The name, therefore, is that of the Father, as the name of the Father is the Son. Where indeed would compassion find a name except with the Father?

But no doubt one will say to his neighbor: "Who is it who will give a name to him who existed before himself, as if offspring did not receive a name from those who begot (them)?" First, then, it is fitting for us to reflect on this matter: What is the name? It is the name in truth; it is not therefore the name from the Father, for it is the one which is the proper name. Therefore, he did not receive the name on loan as (do) others, according to the form in which each one is to be produced. But this is the proper name. There is no one else who gave it to him. But he (is) unnameable, indescribable, until the time when he who is perfect spoke of him alone. And it is he who has the power to speak his name and to see it.

When, therefore, it pleased him that his name which is loved should be his Son, and he gave the name to him, that is, him who came forth from the depth, he spoke about his secret things, knowing that the Father is a being without evil. For that very reason he brought him forth in order to speak about the place and his resting-place from which he had come forth, and to glorify the pleroma, the greatness of his name and the sweetness of the Father. About the place each one came from he will speak, and to the region where he received his establishment he will hasten to return again and to take from that place—the place where he stood—receiving a taste from that place and receiving nourishment, receiving growth. And his own resting-place is his pleroma.

Therefore, all the emanations of the Father are pleromas, and the root of all his emanations is in the one who made them all grow up in himself. He assigned them their destinies. Each one then is manifest, in order that through their own thought (. . .). For the place to which they send their thought, that place, their root, is what takes them up in all the heights to the Father. They possess his head, which is rest for them, and they are supported, approaching him, as though to say that they have participated in his face by means of kisses. But they do not become manifest in this way, for they were not themselves exalted; (yet) neither did they lack the glory of the Father nor did they think of him as small nor that he is harsh nor that he is wrathful, but (that) he is a being without evil, imperturbable, sweet, knowing all spaces before they have come into existence, and he had no need to be instructed.

This is the manner of those who possess (something) from above of the immeasurable greatness, as they wait for the one alone and the perfect one, the one who is there for them. And they do not go down to Hades nor have they envy nor groaning nor death within them, but they rest in him who is at rest, not striving nor being twisted around the truth. But they themselves are the truth; and the Father is within them and they are in the Father, being perfect, being undivided in the truly good one, being in no way deficient in anything, but they are set at rest, refreshed in the Spirit. And they will heed their root. They will be concerned with those (things) in which he will find his root and not suffer loss to his soul. This is the place of the blessed; this is their place.

For the rest, then, may they know, in their places, that it is not fitting for me, having come to be in the resting-place, to speak of anything else. But it is in it that I shall come to be, and (it is fitting) to be concerned at all times with the Father of the all and the true brothers, those upon whom the love of the Father is poured out and in whose midst there is not lack of him. They are the ones who appear in truth, since they exist in true and eternal life and speak of the light which is perfect and filled with the seed of the Father, and which is in his heart and in the pleroma, while his Spirit rejoices in it and glorifies the one in whom it existed because he is good. And his children are perfect and worthy of his name, for he is the Father: it is children of this kind that he loves.

TEXT 19

The Gnostics: The Gospel of the Egyptians[1]

The Nag Hammadi or Coptic Gnostic Library represents a collection of "hereti cal" religious texts hidden from Church authorities in the Egyptian desert sometime in the early centuries of Christianity. Gnosticism, referred to in Greek as gnosis or knowledge was actually a theology of Egyptian mysticism that became amalgamated with certain elements of early Christianity. It emphasized "secret knowledge," that is, the gaining of insight into human behavior and the spiritual world that penetrated beneath the veneer of literal thinking. The reasons for the church's persecution of the gnostics are not surprising if one reads for example the Gnostic Apocalypse of Peter, in which Jesus Christ is quoted as saying:

> They will cleave to the name of a dead man, thinking that they will become pure. But they will become greatly defiled and they will fall into the name of error and into the hand of an evil, cunning man and a manifold dogma, and they will be ruled heretically. For some of them will blaspheme the truth and proclaim evil teaching. And there shall be others of those who are outside our number who name themselves bishop and also deacons, as if they have received their authority from God.[2]

"The Gospel of the Egyptians" represents a literary effort to set down the fundaments of Gnosticism.

---

[1] James M. Robinson (general editor), *The Nag Hammadi Library,* in English/translated and introduced by members of the Coptic Gnostic Library Project of the Institute for Antiquity and Christianity, Claremont, California, 1988, pp. 209–19.
[2] Ibid., p. 5.

THE GOSPEL OF THE EGYPTIANS

The [holy] book [of the Egyptians] about the great invisible [Spirit, the] Father whose name cannot be uttered, [he who came] forth from the heights of [the perfection, the] light of the light of the [aeons of light], the light of the [silence of the] providence <and> the Father of the silence, the [light] of the word and the truth, the light [of the incorruptions, the] infinite light, [the] radiance from the aeons of light of the unrevealable, unmarked, ageless, unproclaimable Father, the aeon of the aeons, Autogenes, self-begotten, self-producing, alien, the really true aeon.

Three powers came forth from him; they are the Father, the Mother, (and) the Son, from the living silence, what came forth from the incorruptible Father. These came [forth from] the silence of the unknown Father.

[And] from that place Domedon Doxomedon came [forth, the aeon of] the aeons and the [light of] each one of [their] powers. [And] thus the Son came [forth] fourth; the Mother [fifth; the Father] sixth. He was [. . .] but unheralded; [it is he] who is unmarked among all [the powers], the glories, and the [incorruptions].

From that place the three powers [came] forth, the three ogdoads that [the Father brings] forth, in silence with his providence, from his bosom, i.e. the Father, the Mother, (and) the Son.

The <first> ogdoad, because of which the thrice-male child came forth, which is the thought, and [the] word, and the incorruption, and the eternal [life], the will, the mind, and the foreknowledge, the androgynous Father.

The second ogdoad-power, the Mother, the virginal Barbelon epititioch [. . .] ai, memeneaimen [. . . who] presides over the heaven, karb [. . .] the uninterpretable power, the ineffable Mother. [She originated] from herself [. . .]; she came forth; [she] agreed with the Father [of the] silent [silence].

The third ogdoad-[power], the Son of the [silent silence], and the crown of the silent silence, [and] the glory of the Father, and the virtue [of the Mother. He] brings forth from the bosom the seven powers of the great light of the seven voices, and the word [is] their completion.

These are the three [powers], the three ogdoads that the Father [through] his providence brought [forth] from his bosom. He brought them [forth] at that place.

Domedon Doxomedon came forth, the aeon of the aeons, and the [throne] which is in him, and the powers [which surround] him, the glories and the [incorruptions. The] Father of the great light [who came] forth from the silence, he is [the great] Doxomedon-aeon in which [the thrice]-male child rests. And the throne of his [glory] was established [in it, this one] on which his unrevealable name [is inscribed], on the tablet [. . .] one is the word, the [Father of the light] of everything, he [who came] forth

---

Source: Pages 209–19 (4,872 words) from *The Nag Hammadi Library in English,* 3rd., completely revised ed. by James M. Robinson, general editor. Copyright © 1988 by E. J. Brill, Leiden, The Netherlands. Reprinted by permission of HarperCollins Publishers, Inc.

TEXT 19: The Gnostics: The Gospel of the Egyptians

from the silence, while he rests in the silence, he whose name [is] in an [invisible] symbol. [A] hidden, [invisible] mystery came forth iiiiiiiiiiiiiiiiiii[iii] ē[ē-ē o] ooooooooooooooooooooo uu[uuu] uuuuuuuuuuuuuuuuuuu eeee eeeeeeeeeeeeeeeee aaaaaa[aaaa] aaaaaaaaaaa ō ō ō ō ō ō ō ō o[ō ō] ō ō ō ō ō ō ō ō ō.

And [in this] way the three powers gave praise to the [great], invisible, unnameable, virginal, uncallable Spirit, and [his] male virgin. They asked [for a] power. A silence of living silence came forth, namely [glories] and incorruptions in the aeons [. . . aeons] myriads added [on . . . , the] three males, [the three] male offspring, the [male] races (IV 55, 5–7 adds: the [glories of the Father, the] glories of the great [Christ and the] male offspring, the [races]) filled the great Doxomedon-[aeon with] the power of the word of the [whole pleroma].

Then the thrice-male [child of the great] Christ whom the [great] invisible Spirit had anointed—he [whose] power [was called] Ainon—gave [praise to] the great invisible Spirit [and his] male virgin Yoel, [and] the silence of silent silence, and the [greatness] that [. . .] ineffable. [. . .] ineffable [. . .] unanswerable and uninterpretable, the first one who has [come forth], and (who is unproclaimable, [. . .] which is wonderful [. . .] ineffable [. . .], he who has all the greatnesses [of] greatness [of] the silence at that [place]. The thrice-[male child] brought praise and asked [for a power] from the [great, invisible, virginal] Spirit.

Then there appeared at [that] place [. . .] who [. . . who] sees [glories . . .] treasures in a [. . . invisible] mysteries to [. . .] of the silence [who is the male] virgin [Youel].

Then [the child of the] child Esephech [appeared].

And [thus] he was completed, namely, the [Father, the] Mother, the [Son], the [five] seals, the unconquerable power which [is] the great [Christ] of all the incorruptible ones. [. . .] holy [. . .] the end, [the] incorruptible [. . .] and [. . .], they are powers [and glories and] incorruptions [. . .] they came forth [. . .]. This one brought [praise] to the unrevealable, hidden [mystery . . . the] hidden [. . .] him in the [. . . and] the aeons [. . .] thrones, [. . .] and each one [. . .] myriads of [powers] without number surround [them, glories] and incorruptions [. . .] and they [. . . of] the Father, [and] the [Mother, and] the Son, and [the] whole [pleroma] which I [mentioned] before, [and the] five seals [and the mystery] of [mysteries]. They [appeared . . . who] presides [over . . .] and the aeons [of . . . really] truly [. . .] and the [. . .] eternal [. . .] and the [really] truly [eternal] aeons.

Then [providence came forth from silence], and the [living silence of] the Spirit, [and] the Word [of] the Father, and [a] light. [She . . . the five] seals which [the Father brought] forth from his bosom, and she passed [through] all the aeons which I mentioned before. And she established thrones of glory [and myriads] of angels [without] number [who] surrounded them, [powers and incorruptible] glories, who [sing] and give glory, all giving praise with [a single voice], with one accord, [with one] never-silent [voice . . . to] the Father, and the [Mother, and the] Son [. . . and all the] pleromas [that I] mentioned [before], who is [the great] Christ, who is from [silence, who] is the [incorruptible] child Telmael Telmachael [Eli Eli] Machar Machar [Seth, the] power which really truly lives, [and the] male [virgin] who is with [him], Youel, [and] Esephech, [the] holder of glory, the [child] of the child [and the crown of] his glory [. . .] of the five seals, [the] pleroma [that I mentioned before].

There the great self-begotten living [Word came forth, the] true [god], the unborn physis, he whose name I shall tell, saying, [. . .]aia[. . . . .]thaōthōsth[. .], who [is the] son of the [great] Christ, who is the son [of the] ineffable silence, [who] came forth from the great [invisible] and incorruptible [Spirit]. The [son] of the silence and [silence] appeared [. . . invisible . . . man and the] treasures [of] his glory. [Then] he appeared in the revealed [. . .]. And he [established] the four [aeons]. With a word [he] established them.

He brought [praise] to the great, [invisible], virginal Spirit, [the silence] of the [Father] in a silence [of the] living silence [of silence, the] place where the man rests. [. . .] through [. . .].

Then there came forth [at (or: from)] that [place] the cloud [of the] great light, the living power, the mother of the holy, incorruptible ones, the great power, the Mirothoe. And she gave birth to him whose name I name, saying, ien ien ea ea ea, three times.

For this one, [Adamas], is [a light] which radiated [from the light; he is] the eye of the [light]. For [this is] the first man, he through whom and to whom everything became, (and) without whom nothing became. The unknowable, incomprehensible Father came forth. He came down from above for the annulment of the deficiency.

Then the great Logos, the divine Autogenes, and the incorruptible man Adamas mingled with each other. A Logos of man came into being. However, the man came into being through a word.

He gave praise to the great, invisible, incomprehensible, virginal Spirit, and the male virgin, and the thrice-male child, and the male [virgin] Youel, and Esephech, the holder of glory, the child of the child and the crown of his glory, and the great Doxomedon-aeon, and the thrones which are in him, and the powers which surround him, the glories and the incorruptions, and their whole pleroma which I mentioned before, and the ethereal earth, the receiver of God, where the holy men of the great light receive shape, the men of the Father of the silent, living silence, the Father and their whole pleroma as I mentioned before.

The great Logos, the divine Autogenes, and the incorruptible man Adamas gave praise, (and) they asked for a power and eternal strength for the Autogenes for the completion of the four aeons, in order that, through them, there may appear [. . .] the glory and the power of the invisible Father of the holy men of the great light which will come to the world which is the image of the night. The incorruptible man Adamas asked for them a son out of himself, in order that he (the son) may become father of the immovable, incorruptible race, so that, through it (the race), the silence and the voice may appear, and, through it, the dead aeon may raise itself, so that it may dissolve.

And thus there came forth, from above, the power of the great light, the Manifestation. She gave birth to the four great lights: Harmozel, Oroiael, Davithe, Eleleth, and the great incorruptible Seth, the son of the incorruptible man Adamas.

And thus the perfect hebdomad which exists in hidden mysteries became complete. When she [receives] the [glory] she becomes eleven ogdoads.

And the Father nodded approval; the whole pleroma of the lights was well pleased. Their consorts came forth for the completion of the ogdoad of the divine Autogenes: the Grace of the first light Harmozel, the Perception of the second light Oroiael, the Understanding of the third light Davithe, the Prudence of the fourth light Eleleth. This is the first ogdoad of the divine Autogenes.

And the Father nodded approval; the whole pleroma of the lights was well pleased. The <ministers> came forth: the first one, the great Gamaliel (of) the first great light Harmozel, and the great Gabriel (of) the second great light Oroiael, and the great Samlo of the great light Davithe, and the great Abrasax of [the great light] Eleleth. And [the] consorts of these came forth by the will of the good pleasure of the Father: the Memory of the great one, the first, Gamaliel; the Love of the great one, the second, Gabriel; the Peace of the third one, the great Samblo; the eternal Life of the great one, the fourth, Abrasax. Thus were the five ogdoads completed, a total of forty, as an uninterpretable power.

Then the great Logos, the Autogenes, and the word of the pleroma of the four lights gave praise to the great, invisible, uncallable, virginal Spirit, and the male virgin, and the great Doxomedon-aeon, and the thrones which are in them, and the powers which surround them, glories, authorities, and the powers, <and> the thrice-male child, and the male virgin Youel, and Esephech, the holder of glory, [the child] of the child and the crown of [his] glory, the whole pleroma, and all the glories which are there, the infinite pleromas <and> the unnameable aeons, in order that they may name the Father the fourth with the incorruptible race, (and) that they may call the seed of the Father the seed of the great Seth.

Then everything shook, and trembling took hold of the incorruptible ones. Then the three male children came forth from above down into the unborn ones, and the self-begotten ones, and those who were begotten in what is begotten. The greatness came forth, the whole greatness of the great Christ. He established thrones in glory, myriads without number, in the four aeons around them, myriads without number, powers and glories and incorruptions. And they came forth in this way.

And the incorruptible, spiritual church increased in the four lights of the great, living Autogenes, the god of truth, praising, singing, (and) giving glory with one voice, with one accord, with a mouth which does not rest, to the Father, and the Mother, and the Son, and their whole pleroma, just as I mentioned <before>. The five seals which possess the myriads, and they who rule over the aeons and they who bear the glory of the leaders were given the command to reveal to those who are worthy. Amen.

Then the great Seth, the son of the incorruptible man Adamas, gave praise to the great, invisible, uncallable, unnameable, virginal Spirit, and the <male virgin, and the thrice-male child, and the male> virgin Youel, and Esephech, the holder of glory, and the crown of his glory, the child of the child, and the great Doxomedon-aeons, and the pleroma which I mentioned before; and asked for his seed.

Then there came forth from that place the great power of the great light Plesithea, the mother of the angels, the mother of the lights, the glorious mother, the virgin with the four breasts, bringing the fruit from Gomorrah as spring and Sodom, which is the fruit of the spring of Gomorrah which is in her. She came forth through the great Seth.

Then the great Seth rejoiced about the gift which was granted him by the incorruptible child. He took his seed from her with the four breasts, the virgin, and he placed it with him in the fourth aeon (or, IV 68, 3: [in] the four aeons), in the third great light Davithe.

After five thousand years the great light Eleleth spoke: "Let someone reign over the chaos and Hades." And there appeared a cloud [whose name is] hylic Sophia

[. . . . She] looked out on the parts [of the chaos], her face being like [. . . in] her form [. . .] blood. And [the great] angel Gamaliel spoke [to the great Gabriel], the minister of [the great light] Oroiael; [he said, "Let an] angel come forth [in order that he may] reign over the chaos [and Hades]." Then the cloud, being [agreeable, came forth] in the two monads, each one [of which had] light. [. . . the throne], which she had placed in the cloud [above. Then] Sakla, the great [angel, saw] the great demon [who is with him, Nebr]uel. And they became [together a] begetting spirit of the earth. [They begot] assisting angels. Sakla [said] to the great [demon Neb]ruel, "Let [the] twelve aeons come into being in [the . . .] aeon, worlds [. . . ." . . .] the great angel [Sakla] said by the will of Autogenes, "There shall [be] the [. . .] of the number of seven [. . .]." And he said to the [great angels], "Go and [let each] of you reign over his [world]." Each one [of these] twelve [angels] went [forth. The first] angel is Ath[oth. He is the one] whom [the great] generations of men call [. . . . The] second is Harmas, [who] is [the eye of the fire]. The third [is Galila. The] fourth is Yobel. [The fifth is] Adonaios, who is [called] Sabaoth. The sixth [is Cain, whom] the [great generations of] men call the sun. The [seventh is Abel]; the eighth Akiressina; the [ninth Yubel]. The tenth is Harm[upiael. The] eleventh is Arch[ir-Adonin]. The twelfth [is Belias. These are] the ones who preside over Hades [and the chaos].

And after the founding [of the world] Sakla said to his [angels], "I, I am a [jealous] god, and apart from me nothing has [come into being," since he] trusted in his nature.

Then a voice came from on high, saying, "The Man exists, and the Son of the Man." Because of the descent of the image above, which is like its voice in the height of the image which has looked out, through the looking out of the image above, the first creature was formed.

Because of this Metanoia came to be. She received her completion and her power by the will of the Father and his approval with which he approved of the great, incorruptible, immovable race of the great, mighty men of the great Seth, in order that he may sow it in the aeons which had been brought forth, so that, through her (Metanoia), the deficiency may be filled up. For she had come forth from above down to the world which is the image of the night. When she had come, she prayed for (the repentance of) both the seed of the archon of this aeon and <the> authorities who had come forth from him, that defiled (seed) of the demon-begetting god which will be destroyed, and the seed of Adam and the great Seth, which is like the sun.

Then the great angel Hormos came to prepare, through the virgins of the corrupted sowing of this aeon, in a Logos-begotten, holy vessel, through the holy Spirit, the seed of the great Seth.

Then the great Seth came and brought his seed. And it was sown in the aeons which had been brought forth, their number being the amount of Sodom. Some say that Sodom is the place of pasture of the great Seth, which is Gomorrah. But others (say) that the great Seth took his plant out of Gomorrah and planted it in the second place to which he gave the name Sodom.

This is the race which came forth through Edokla. For she gave birth through the word to Truth and Justice, the origin of the seed of the eternal life which is with those who will persevere because of the knowledge of their emanation. This is the great, incorruptible race which has come forth through three worlds to the world.

And the flood came as an example for the consummation of the aeon. But it will be sent into the world because of this race. A conflagration will come upon the earth. And grace will be with those who belong to the race through the prophets and the guardians who guard the life of the race. Because of this race famines will occur and plagues. But these things will happen because of the great, incorruptible race. Because of this race temptations will come, a falsehood of false prophets.

Then the great Seth saw the activity of the devil, and his many guises, and his schemes which will come upon his incorruptible, immovable race, and the persecutions of his powers and his angels, and their error, that they acted against themselves.

Then the great Seth gave praise to the great, uncallable, virginal Spirit, and the male virgin Barbelon, and the thrice-male child Telmael Telmael Heli Heli Machar Machar Seth, the power which really truly lives, and the male virgin Youel, and Esephech, the holder of glory, and the crown of his glory, and the great Doxomedon-aeon, and the thrones which are in him, and the powers which surround them, and the whole pleroma, as I mentioned before. And he asked for guards over his seed.

Then there came forth from the great aeons four hundred ethereal angels, accompanied by the great Aerosiel and the great Selmechel, to guard the great, incorruptible race, its fruit, and the great men of the great Seth, from the time and the moment of Truth and Justice until the consummation of the aeon and its archons, those whom the great judges have condemned to death.

Then the great Seth was sent by the four lights, by the will of the Autogenes and the whole pleroma, through <the gift> and the good pleasure of the great invisible Spirit, and the five seals, and the whole pleroma.

He passed through the three parousias which I mentioned before: the flood, and the conflagration, and the judgment of the archons and the powers and the authorities, to save her (the race) who went astray, through the reconciliation of the world, and the baptism through a Logos-begotten body which the great Seth prepared for himself, secretly through the virgin, in order that the saints may be begotten by the holy Spirit, through invisible, secret symbols, through a reconciliation of the world with the world, through the renouncing of the world and the god of the thirteen aeons, and (through) the convocations of the saints, and the ineffable ones, and the incorruptible bosom, and (through) the great light of the Father who preexisted with his Providence and established through her the holy baptism that surpasses the heaven, through the incorruptible, Logos-begotten one, even Jesus the living one, even he whom the great Seth has put on. And through him he nailed the powers of the thirteen aeons, and established those who are brought forth and taken away. He armed them with an armor of knowledge of this truth, with an unconquerable power of incorruptibility.

There appeared to them the great attendant Yesseus Mazareus Yessedekeus, the living water, and the great leaders, James the great and Theopemptos and Isaouel, and they who preside over the spring of truth, Micheus and Michar and Mnesinous, and he who presides over the baptism of the living, and the purifiers, and Sesengenpharanges, and they who preside over the gates of the waters, Micheus and Michar, and they who preside over the mountain Seldao and Elainos, and the receivers of the great race, the incorruptible, mighty men <of> the great Seth, the ministers of the four lights, the great Gamaliel, the great Gabriel, the great Samblo, and the great Abrasax, and they who preside over the sun, its rising, Olses and Hypneus and Heurumaious, and they who preside over the entrance into the rest of eternal life, the rulers Mixanther and Michanor, and they who guard the souls of the elect, Akramas and Strempsouchos, and the great power Heli Heli Machar Machar Seth, and the great invisible, uncallable, unnameable, virginal Spirit, and the silence, and the great light Harmozel, the place of the living Autogenes, the God of the truth, and <he> who is with him, the incorruptible man Adamas, the second, Oroiael, the place of the great Seth, and Jesus, who possesses the life and who came and crucified that which is in the law, the third, Davithe, the place of the sons of the great Seth, the fourth, Eleleth, the place where the souls of the sons are resting, the fifth, Yoel, who presides over the name of him to whom it will be granted to baptize with the holy baptism that surpasses the heaven, the incorruptible one.

But from now on through the incorruptible man Poimael, and they who are worthy of (the) invocation, the renunciations of the five seals in the spring-baptism, these will know their receivers as they are instructed about them, and they will know them (or: be known) by them. These will by no means taste death.

Iē ieus ēō ou ēō ōua! Really truly, O Yesseus Mazareus Yessedekeus, O living water, O child of the child, O glorious name, really truly, aiōn o ōn (or: O existing aeon), iiii ēēēē eeee oo oo uuuu ōōōō aaaa{a}, really truly, ēi aaaa ōō ōō, O existing one who sees the aeons! Really truly, aee ēēē iiii uuuuuu ōōōōōōō, who is eternally eternal, really truly, iēa aiō, in the heart, who exists, u aei eis aei, ei o ei, ei os ei (or: (Son) forever, Thou art what Thou art, Thou art who Thou art)!

This great name of thine is upon me, O self-begotten Perfect one, who art not outside me. I see thee, O thou who art visible to everyone. For who will be able to comprehend thee in another tongue? Now that I have known thee, I have mixed myself with the immutable. I have armed myself with an armor of light; I have become light. For the Mother was at that place because of the splendid beauty of grace. Therefore I have stretched out my hands while they were folded. I was shaped in the circle of the riches of the light which is in my bosom, which gives shape to the many begotten ones in the light into which no complaint reaches. I shall declare thy glory truly, for I have comprehended thee, sou iēs ide aeiō aeie ois, O aeon, aeon, O God of silence! I honor thee completely. Thou art my place of rest, O son ēs̄ ēs̄ o e, the formless one who exists in the formless ones, who exists, raising up the man in whom thou wilt purify me into thy life, according to thine imperishable name. Therefore the incense of life is in me. I mixed it with water after the model of all archons, in order that I may live with thee in the peace of the saints, thou who existeth really truly for ever.

This is the book which the great Seth wrote, and placed in high mountains on which the sun has not risen, nor is it possible. And since the days of the prophets, and the apostles, and the preachers, the name has not at all risen upon their hearts, nor is it possible. And their ear has not heard it.

The great Seth wrote this book with letters in one hundred and thirty years. He placed it in the mountain that is called Charaxio, in order that, at the end of the times and the eras, by the will of the divine Autogenes and the whole pleroma, through the gift of the untraceable, unthinkable, fatherly love, it may come forth and reveal this incorruptible, holy race of the great savior, and those who dwell with them in love, and the great, invisible, eternal Spirit, and his only begotten Son, and the eternal light, and his great, incorruptible consort, and the incorruptible Sophia, and the Barbelon, and the whole pleroma in eternity. Amen.

The Gospel of <the> Egyptians. The God-written, holy, secret book. Grace, understanding, perception, prudence (be) with him who has written it, Eugnostos the beloved in the Spirit—in the flesh my name is Gongessos—and my fellow lights in incorruptibility, Jesus Christ, Son of God, Savior, Ichthus, God-written (is) the holy book of the great, invisible Spirit. Amen.

The Holy Book of the Great
Invisible Spirit.
Amen.

TEXT 20

Hermeticists: Libellus XVI—Epistle of Asclepius to King Ammon

from The Corpus Hermeticum[1]

The Corpus Hermeticum *represents a collection of approximately 17 documents of non-Christian Gnosticism, believed to have been written by Egyptians during the early centuries* A.D. *The doctrines of the Hermetica represent the spiritual seeking of men and women who believed, like their Christian Gnostic counterparts, that personal insight brought them closer to the truth of God than the dogmas of the established religions of their day. However, it should be remembered that Christianity took several centuries to spread throughout Egypt, and during that time Christian and non-Christian theologies vied for the intellectual and spiritual attention of Egyptians. In this regard the Hermeticists melded the philosophy of Plato with Egyptian modes of thought. These writings took the form of discourses between the teacher, Hermes Trismegistus (a Greek rendering of Thoth, the Egyptian god of Wisdom) and his pupil, Tat or Asclepius or Ammon.*

It is because the Hermetica appears to have exercised such a powerful influence over Christian Gnosticism, as well as the Greek philosophy of Plato, and the Hellenized Egyptian variant called Neoplatonism, that scholarly debate continues to this day about the degree to which this Egyptian philosophy exhibited influences emanating from the Greeks, Jews, Persians, and Mesopotamians.[2] *However, as modern scholars*

---

[1]Brian P. Copenhaver, *Hermetica: The Greek Corpus Hermeticum and the Latin Asclepius in a New English Translation* (New York: Cambridge University Press, 1992).
[2]Martin Bernal, *Black Athena: The Afroasiatic Roots of Classical Civilization* (New Jersey: Rutgers University Press, 1987), p. 134.

have freed themselves from the constricting intellectual frameworks of the past, it has become apparent that all societies and religious traditions may exhibit some degree of spiritual interiority.

The Corpus Hermeticum *document titled "Libellus XVI" suggests among other things that deficiencies in the Greek language make it incapable of accurately rendering the subtleties of Egyptian philosophic religion to the reader. Walter Scott, the translator of the Hermetica from Greek, notes:*

> [The writer] must have been an Egyptian by race; and in spite of his Hellenic education, he is still strongly conscious of his Egyptian nationality. He speaks of the Greeks as foreigners, and regards them with contempt; he holds them unworthy to know the holy secrets of the true religion.[3]

Of weighty import is this discourse which I send to you, my King; it is, so to speak, a summing up of all the other discourses, and a reminder of their teaching. It is not composed in accordance with the opinion of the many; it contains much that contradicts their beliefs. . . . For my teacher Hermes often used to say in talk with me when we were alone, and sometimes when Tat was with us, that those who read my writings . . . will think them to be quite simply and clearly written, but those who hold opposite principles to start with will say that the style is obscure and conceals the meaning. And it will be thought still more obscure in time to come, when the Greeks think fit to translate these writings from our tongue into theirs. Translation will greatly distort the sense of the writings, and cause much obscurity. Expressed in our native language, the teaching conveys its meaning clearly; for the very quality of the sounds . . . , and when the Egyptian words are spoken, the force of the things signified works in them. Therefore, my King, as far as it is in your power (and you are all-powerful,) keep the teaching untranslated, in order that secrets so holy may not be revealed to Greeks, and that the Greek mode of speech, with its . . . , and feebleness, and showy tricks of style, may not reduce to impotence the impressive strength of the language, and the cogent force of the words. For the speech of the Greeks, my King, is devoid of power to convince; and the Greek philosophy is nothing but a noise of talk. But our speech is not mere talk; it is an utterance replete with workings.

I will begin by invoking God, the Master and Maker and Father and Encompasser of all, who is both One and all things; not that the One is two, but that these two are one; for the whole which is made up of all things is one. And I beg you to keep this in mind, my King, throughout your study of my teaching. For if any one attempts to separate all things from the One, taking the term "all things" to signify a mere plurality of things, and not a whole made up of things, he will sever the All from the One, and will thereby bring to naught the All; but that is impossible. It needs must be that all things are one, if they exist (and they do exist, and never cease to exist), in order that the whole which is made up of them may not be dissolved.

---

[3]Walter Scott, *Hermetica: The Ancient Greek and Latin Writings Which Contain Religious or Philosophic Teachings Ascribed to Hermes Trismegistus* (Boston: Shambahala, 1993), p. 437.
Source: Reprinted from Walter Scott, *Hermetica: The Ancient Greek and Latin Writings Which Contain Religious or Philosophic Teachings Ascribed to Hermes Trismegistus,* © 1993, Shambhala Publications, Inc.

You can see that in the earth there gush forth many springs of water and of air in its midmost parts, and that these three things, air, water, and earth, are found in the same place, being attached to one single root. Hence we believe that the earth is the storehouse of all matter; it gives forth the supply of matter, and in turn receives those things which comes from above. For in this way the Demiurgus (that is, the Sun) brings together heaven and earth, sending down true being from above, and raising up matter from below. And he . . . in connexion with himself, both drawing . . . to himself, and giving forth . . . from himself; for he lavishes light on all things without stint. For the Sun is he whose beneficent works operate not only in heaven, but also upon earth, and penetrate even to the lowest depths. The material body of the Sun is . . . ; and if there is such a thing as a substance not perceptible by sense, the light of the Sun must be receptacle of that substance. But of what that substance consists, or whence it flows in, God only knows. The Sun, being near to us in position, and like to us in nature, presents himself to our sight. God does not manifest himself to us; we cannot see him and it is only by conjecture, and with hard effort, that we can apprehend him in thought. But it is not by conjecture that we contemplate the Sun; we see him with our very eyes. He shines most brightly on all the universe, illuminating both the world above and the world below; for he is stationed in the midst, and wears the Kosmos as a wreath around him. And so he lets the Kosmos go on its course, not leaving it far separated from himself, but, to speak truly, keeping it joined to himself; for like a skilled driver, he has made fast and bound to himself the chariot of the Kosmos, lest it should rush away in disorder. And the reins are . . . .

In this wise he makes all things. He assigns to the immortals their everlasting permanence, and with that part of his light which tends upwards (that is, the light which he sends forth from that side of him which faces heaven), he maintains the immortal parts of the Kosmos; but with the light which is shed downward, and illuminates all the sphere of water, earth, and air, he puts life into the things in this region of the Kosmos, and stirs them up to birth, and by successive changes remakes the living creates and transforms them. . . . For the permanence of every kind of body is maintained by change. Immortal bodies undergo change without dissolution, but the changes of mortal bodies are accompanied by dissolution; that is the difference between immortals and mortals. And as the light of the Sun is poured forth continuously, so his production of life also is continuous and without intermission. . . .

And to the Sun is subject the troop of daemons—or rather, troops; for there are many and diverse troops of them, placed under the command of the planets, an equal number of daemons being assigned to each planet. Thus marshaled in separate corps, the daemons serve under the several planets. They are both good and bad in their natures, that is, in their workings; for the being of a daemon consists in his working. To these daemons is given dominion over all things upon earth, . . . They are also the authors of the disturbances upon earth, and work manifold trouble both for cities and nations collectively and for individual men. For they mould our souls into another shape, and pull them away to themselves, being seated in our nerves and marrow and veins and arteries, and penetrating even to our inmost organs. For at the time when each one of us is born and made alive, the daemons who are at that moment on duty as ministers of birth take charge of us,—that is, the daemons who are subject to some one planet. For the planets replace one another from moment to moment; they do not go on working without change, but succeed one another in rotation. These daemons then make their way in through the body, and enter into the two irrational parts of the soul; and each daemon perverts the soul in a different way, according to his special mode of action. But the rational part of the soul remains free from the dominion of the daemons, and fit to receive God into itself. If then the rational part of a man's soul is illumined by a ray of light from God, for that man the working of the daemons is brought to naught; for no daemon and no god has power against a single ray of the light of God. But such men are few indeed; and all others are led and driven, soul and body, by the daemons, setting their hearts and affections on the workings of the daemons. This is that love which is devoid of reason, that love which goes astray and leads men astray. The daemons then govern all our earthly life, using our bodies as their instruments; and this government Hermes called 'destiny.'

The intelligible Kosmos then is dependent on God; and the Sun receives from God, through the intelligible Kosmos, the influx of good (that is, of life-giving energy), with which he is supplied. And round about the Sun, and dependent on the Sun, are the eight spheres, namely, the sphere of the fixed stars, and the six planet-spheres, and the sphere which surrounds the earth; and the daemons are dependent on these spheres; and men are dependent on the daemons. Thus all things and all persons are dependent on God. God then is the Father of all; the Sun is the Demiurgus; and the Kosmos is the instrument by means of which the Demiurgus works. . . . He . . . governs the gods; and the daemons are subject to the gods, and govern men. Thus is marshaled the army of gods and daemons. Working through gods and daemons, God makes all things for himself; and all things are part of God. And inasmuch as all things are parts of him, God is all things. Therefore, in making all things, God makes himself. And it is impossible that he should ever cease from making; for God himself can never cease to be.

TEXT 21

Origen: A Great Theater Is Filled with Spectators

from Exhortation to Martyrdom[1]

Born into a Christian family of Alexandria, Egypt, in A.D. 185, Origen became one of the preeminent early fathers of the church. At the age of 17, he was, according to legend, spared the martyrdom suffered by his father only because his mother hid his clothes to deter him from slipping out of the house into the hands of Roman soldiers. However, a martyr's fate did eventually catch up with Origen who died in A.D. 251 of wounds suffered upon being arrested and tortured by the emperor Decius.

Throughout his life Origen was a controversial figure in the church. In persuading a wealthy Christian named Ambrose to abrogate the teaching of the prominent Gnostic theologian Valentinus, Origen obtained the man's patronage for life, enjoying new economic security. This enabled him to compose a commentary on Saint John, his interpretation of whom was aimed at refuting the teachings of Valentinus. Origen is also noted for preparing from available manuscripts in A.D. 200 the version of the Septuagint upon which our modern versions of the Bible are based.

This theologian's legacy, particularly in his definition of Christian spirituality, remains an integral part of church thought even today. He has often been called the first great scholar of the church, as well as the first great preacher and the first great devotional writer.[2]

As John Clark Smith has pointed out in The Ancient Wisdom of Origen:

> . . . he was a thinker, a man who dared to speculate, yet one greater than any Christian thinker of the ancient world because he alone first explored the territory of Scripture with great depth.[3]

---

[1] Rosan A. Greer, *Origen: An Exhortation to Martyrdom* (New York: Paulist Press, 1979), pp. 53–63.
[2] Henry Bettenson, *The Early Christian Fathers* (London: Oxford University Press, 1956), p. 27.
[3] John Clark Smith, *The Ancient Wisdom of Origen* (Lewisburg, PA: Bucknell University Press, 1992), p. 15.

Exhortation to Martyrdom became one of Origen's most renowned works. It articulated the theological principle that one means by which good triumphs over evil is in the act of giving one's life for Christ.

XVIII. A great theater is filled with spectators to watch your contests and your summons to martyrdom, just as if we were to speak of a great crowd gathered to watch the contests of athletes supposed to be champions. And no less than Paul you will say when you enter the contest, "We have become a spectacle to the world, to angels, and to men" (1 Cor. 4:9). Thus, the whole world and all the angels of the right and the left, and all men, those from God's portion (cf. Deut. 32:9; Col. 1:12) and those from the other portions, will attend to us when we contest for Christianity. Indeed, either the angels in heaven will cheer us on, and the floods will clap their hands together, and the mountains will leap for joy (Ps. 98:8), and all the trees of the field will clap their branches (Is. 55:12)—or, may it not happen, the powers from below, which rejoice in evil, will cheer. And it is in no way foolish to see by using Isaiah's words what will be said by those in hell to the ones who have been defeated and have fallen from their heavenly martyrdom. This will make us shudder all the more at the impiety of denying. For this is what I think will be said to the person who has denied, "Hell below is stirred up to meet you; all the giants who ruled the earth have been raised up for you; they raise all the kings of the nations from their thrones. They will all answer and speak to you" (Is. 14:9–10). What will the defeated powers say to those who have been defeated? And what will those taken captive by the devil say to those taken captive by denial but this, "You have been captured as we were, and you have been numbered among us"? (Is. 14:10). And if someone with a great and glorious hope in God is overcome by cowardice or by the sufferings inflicted upon him for his faith, he will hear, "Your glory has come down to hell, and your great delight. They spread decay beneath you for a bed, and the worm is your covering" (Is. 14:11). If anyone has often shone in the churches, illuminating them like the day star, with his good works shining before men (cf. Mt. 5:16), and if afterwards in the great contest he has lost the crown of such a throne, he will hear, "How have you fallen from heaven, O Day Star, who rise early in the morning? You have been trodden down to the ground!" (Is. 14:12). And this will be said to him when he has become like the devil by his denial, "He shall be thrown on the hills like a polluted corpse with many who have died pierced with swords and who come down to hell. Just as a garment stained with blood will not be clean, so neither will you be clean" (Is. 14:19–20 LXX). For how shall he be clean who is defiled with blood and slaughter, by the polluted lapse of denial, and who is stained by so great an evil?

But as it is, let us show that we have heard the saying "He who loves . . . son or daughter more than me is not worthy of me" (Mt. 10:37). Let us stand fast lest there arise in us any hesitation whether we should deny or confess, lest Elijah's word be

---

Source: Reprinted from *Origen* by Rosan A. Greer, © 1979 by The Missionary Society of St. Paul the Apostle in the States of New York. Used by permission of Paulist Press.

also said to us, "How long will you go on limping on both your thighs? If the Lord is God, follow Him" (1 Kings 18:21).

XIX. It is likely that we shall both be reproached by our neighbors and scorned by those who surround us and shake their heads at us as fools. But in these circumstances let us say to God, "You have made us a reproach of our neighbors, a scorn and a derision of those about us. You have made us a byword among the nations, a shaking of the head among the peoples. All day long my disgrace is before me, and the shame of my face has covered me, at the voice of the reproacher and reviler, at the face of the enemy and avenger" (Ps. 44:13–16). But when all this happens, it is blessed to speak to God the word uttered by the prophet in his boldness, "All this has come upon us, and we have not forgotten you, and we have not been false to your covenant, and our heart has not turned back" (Ps. 44:17–18).

XX. Let us remember that while we are in this life we should think of the paths outside life and say to God, "You have turned our steps by your path" (Ps. 43:19 LXX–44:18). Now is the time to remember that this region in which we have been humiliated is a place of distress for the soul, so that we may say in our prayers, "You have humiliated us in a place of distress, and the shadow of death has covered us" (Ps. 43:20 LXX–44:19). But taking courage let us also say, "If we had forgotten the name of our God and if we had spread forth our hands to a strange god, would not God discover this?" (Ps. 44:20–21).

XXI. Let us enter the contest to win perfectly not only outward martyrdom, but also the martyrdom that is in secret, so that we too may utter the apostolic cry "For this is our boast, the martyrdom of our conscience that we have believed in the world . . . with holiness and godly sincerity" (2 Cor. 1:12). And let us join to the apostolic cry the prophetic one, "He knows the secrets of our hearts," especially if we are led away to death. Then we shall say to God what can be said only by martyrs, "For your sake we are slain all the day long; we are accounted as sheep for the slaughter" (Ps. 44:21–22). And if fear of the judges who threaten us with death should ever try to undermine us with the mind of the flesh (cf. Rom. 8:6f.), let us then say to them the verse from Proverbs, "My son, honor the Lord, and you will prevail. Fear no one else but Him" (Prov. 7:1 LXX).

XXII. And what Solomon says in Ecclesiastes is also useful for the subject under discussion, "I praised all who have died more than the living, who are alive till now" (Eccles. 4:2). Who would so rightly be praised as the person who died of his own accord, welcoming death for his religion? This is what Eleazar was like, who welcoming death with honor rather than life with pollution went up to the rack of his own accord (2 Macc. 6:19). And this Eleazar made a high resolve worthy of his ninety years and the dignity of his old age and the grey hairs that he had reached with distinction and his excellent life even from childhood, and moreover according to the holy God-given Law. And he said, "Such pretense is not worthy of our time of life, lest many of the young should suppose that Eleazar in his ninetieth year has gone over to an alien religion, and through my pretense, for the sake of living a brief moment longer, they should be led astray because of me, while I defile and disgrace my old age. For even if for the present I should avoid the punishment of men, yet whether I live or die I shall not escape the hands of the Almighty. Therefore, by manfully giving up my life now, I will show myself worthy of my old age and leave to the young a noble example of how to die a good death willingly and nobly for the revered and holy laws" (2 Macc. 6:24–28).

I pray that when you are at the gates of death, or rather of freedom, especially if tortures are brought (for it is impossible to hope you will not suffer this from the will of the opposing powers), you will use such words as these, "It is clear to the Lord in His holy knowledge that though I might have been saved from death, I am enduring sufferings in my body, but in my soul I am glad to suffer these things because I fear Him" (2 Macc. 6:30). Such was the death of Eleazar, as it was said of him, "He left in his death an example of nobility and a memorial of courage, not only to the young but to the great body of his nation" (2 Macc. 6:31).

XXIII. As well, the seven brothers described in 2 Maccabees, whom Antiochus tortured with whips and cords when they remained steadfast in their religion, will be a powerful and noble example of robust martyrdom for everyone who considers whether he will prove to be less a man than boys who not only endured their own tortures, but also demonstrated how strong their religion was by watching their brothers' tortures. One of them became, as Scripture calls it, "spokesman" and said to the tyrant, "What do you intend to ask and learn from us? For we are ready to die rather than transgress the laws of our fathers" (2 Macc. 7:2). Why do I need to tell what pans and cauldrons, heated to torture them, they endured after each had undergone different sufferings? For the one called their spokesman first had his tongue cut out. Then he was scalped, and he bore the scalping as others bear circumcision, believing that even in this he was fulfilling the word of God's covenant. Not satisfied with this Antiochus cut off his hands and feet while the rest of the brothers and the mother looked on, thus punishing the other brothers and the mother by the sight and thinking he would shake their resolve by what he supposed fearful sights. And so, not satisfied with this Antiochus commanded that the brother, when he was utterly helpless so far as the condition of his body was concerned because of the previous tortures, should be taken still breathing to the fire in the pans and cauldrons and should be fried in a pan (2 Macc. 7:5). And when the smoke of that noblest athlete of piety's flesh, roasted by the cruelty of the tyrant, spread widely, the others encouraged one another with their mother to die nobly, consoling themselves by considering that God was watching over all these tortures. For the conviction that the eye of God is present with those who endure was enough to give them endurance. And the Judge of the athletes of piety encouraged them, being encouraged Himself and, so to speak, cheering for those who were struggling against such great sufferings. And it would be appropriate for us, as well, in such circumstances to use their words to those behaving this way and to say, "The Lord God is watching over us and in truth has compassion on us" (2 Macc. 7:6).

XXIV. When in this way the first brother had been tried as gold is tried in the furnace (cf. Wis. 3:6; Prov. 17:3), the second was brought forward for their sport. The servants of the cruel tyranny tore off the skin of his head with the hair and called on the one who had suffered to change his mind, asking him whether he would eat the idol meat rather than have his body punished limb by limb (2 Macc. 7:7). And when he refused to change his mind, he was brought forward for the next torture. He remained steadfast to the last breath, for he did not break down or yield to his sufferings. And he said to the impious tyrant, "You accursed wretch, you dismiss us from this present life, but the King of the universe will raise us up to an everlasting renewal of life, because we have died for His laws" (2 Macc. 7:8).

XXV. Then the third brother counted his offerings as nothing and trod them underfoot because of his love for God. When it was demanded, he quickly put out his tongue and courageously stretched forth his hands (2 Macc. 7:10) and said, "By leaving these behind for the laws of God, I hope to get them back from God the way He gives them to those who are athletes for His religion" (2 Macc. 7:11).

Likewise the fourth brother was tortured, bearing his torments and saying, "One cannot but choose to die at the hands of men and to cherish the hope that God gives of being raised again by Him in a resurrection that the tyrant will not have. For he will be raised not to life but to reproach and to shame" (2 Macc. 7:14).

Next the fifth brother was tortured. He looked at Antiochus and reproached him with failing to let his corruptibility cut short his arrogance, since he supposed that tyrannical authority for a few days was a great thing. And he said that even though it was so persecuted, the nation had not been forsaken by God, who would torture Antiochus and his descendants with such tortures as they had never seen (2 Macc. 7:15–17).

After him the sixth brother, when he was about to die, said, "Do not deceive yourself. Since we are paying these penalties for our sins so that we may be cleansed by our suffering, we suffer them willingly." And he said to him that he ought not to suppose he would be guiltless for trying to fight against God. For the one who fights against those who have been made divine by the Word fights against God (2 Macc. 7:18–19; cf. Acts 5:39).

XXVI. Antiochus then laid hold of the last and youngest brother; and since he was persuaded that he was a true brother of those who had counted such great sufferings as nothing and that he had the same resolve as theirs, he used other methods. Antiochus thought that he would be persuaded by appeals and by promises with oaths that he would make him rich and enviable, if he would turn away from the ways of his fathers, be enrolled among the tyrant's friends, and be entrusted with royal affairs (2 Macc. 7:24). And when he got not even the first sign of a response, since the young man paid no attention to words so foreign to what he had freely chosen for himself, Antiochus called the mother to him and urged her to advise the youth to save himself (2 Macc. 7:25). She pretended to persuade her son of what Antiochus wanted, but she mocked the tyrant and moved her son with many words about endurance. The result was that the young man did not wait for the torture to be brought, but took the initiative in summoning the officers ahead of time and said to them, "What are you waiting for, and why are you so slow? For we obey the Law given from God. It is not right to side with an ordinance contrary to the divine words." Moreover, like a king giving verdicts against those being judged by him, he pronounced judgment against the tyrant, judging him rather than being judged. And he said that since Antiochus had raised his hands against the children of heaven, he would not escape the judgment of the almighty, all-seeing God (2 Macc. 7:30–35).

XXVII. Then one could have seen the mother of such sons bearing their sufferings and deaths with good courage because of her hope in the Lord (2 Macc. 7:20). For the dews of true religion and the wind of holiness did not permit that fire of a mother's love which flames up in most women under such heavy evils to be kindled in her bowels. I think it extremely useful for what lies ahead to tell the story I have summarized from Scripture, so that we may see how much power against the harshest sufferings and the deepest tortures there is in religion and in the spell of love for God, which is immensely more powerful than any other love spell. Human weakness does not live in the same city with this spell of love for God, since it is driven abroad from the soul and has no power to act when a person can say, "The Lord is my strength and my song" (Ps. 118:14) and "I can do all things in Him who strengthens me, Christ Jesus our Lord" (Phil. 4:13; 1 Tim. 1:12).

TEXT 22

Plotinus: Are All Souls One?

from Ennead IV[1]

Modern scholars regard Plotinus (A.D. 204–270) to be the founder of Neoplatonism, the dominant non-Christian philosophical school of the ancient Mediterranean world. He was born in a town in upper Egypt named Lycopolis (modern Assyut), near the Nubian border.

At the age of 28, Plotinus began the study of philosophy in Alexandria. Upon completing his studies, a spirit of adventure led him to Persia and India, where he hoped to study Eastern thought, and then to Rome where he settled at the age of 40.

The philosophical school founded by Plotinus rejected the doctrinal complexities of Christian Gnosticism, particularly the latter's reliance on intermediaries. And yet Poltinus's own belief in the divinity within oneself would by today's philosophical reckonings be considered an integral part of Gnostic ways of thinking. This is because both philosophies contrast with the externalized God figure of mainstream Christianity in favor of a more personalized experience, that is, a more interior quest for mystical union. His disciple Porphyry relates an intriguing anecdote of Plotinus's relationship to magic:

> In fact Plotinus possessed by birth something more than is accorded to other men. An Egyptian priest, who had arrived in Rome and, through some friend, had been presented to the philosopher, became desirous of displaying his powers to him, and he offered to evoke a visible manifestation of Plotinus' presiding spirit. Plotinus readily consented and the evocation was made in the Temple of Isis, the only place, they say, which the Egyptians could find pure in Rome. At the summons a Divinity appeared, not a being of the spirit-ranks, and the Egyptian exclaimed: "You are singularly graced; the guiding-spirit within you is not of the lower degree but a god." It was not possible,

---

[1]*Plotinus: The Six Enneads,* Robert Maynard Hutchins (editor), Stephen MacKenna and B. S. Page (translators), vol. 17, pp. 205–7, 1952.

however, to interrogate or even to contemplate this God any further, for the priest's assistant, who had been holding the birds to prevent them flying away, strangled them, whether through jealousy or terror. Thus Plotinus had for indwelling spirit a Being of the more divine degree, and he kept his own divine spirit unceasingly intent upon the inner presence.[2]

The Enneads *was written in Greek and is considered to be one of the great classics of mysticism, blending the philosophies of Plato and Aristotle with ancient Egyptian philosophical religion.*

NINTH TRACTATE
Are All Souls One?

1. That the Soul of every individual is one thing we deduce from the fact that it is present entire at every point of the body—the sign of veritable unity—not some part of it here and another part there. In all sensitive beings the sensitive soul is an omnipresent unity, and so in the forms of vegetal life the vegetal soul is entire at each several point throughout the organism.

Now are we to hold similarly that your soul and mine and all are one, and that the same thing is true of the universe, the soul in all the several forms of life being one soul, not parcelled out in separate items, but an omnipresent identity?

If the soul in me is a unity, why need that in the universe be otherwise seeing that there is no longer any question of bulk or body? And if that, too, is one soul and yours, and mine, belongs to it, then yours and mine must also be one: and if, again, the soul of the universe and mine depend from one soul, once more all must be one.

What then in itself is this one soul?

First we must assure ourselves of the possibility of all souls being one as that of any given individual is.

It must, no doubt, seem strange that my soul and that of any and everybody else should be one thing only: it might mean my feelings being felt by someone else, my goodness another's too, my desire, his desire, all our experience shared with each other and with the (one-souled) universe, so that the very universe itself would feel whatever I felt.

Besides how are we to reconcile this unity with the distinction of reasoning soul and unreasoning, animal soul and vegetal?

Yet if we reject that unity, the universe itself ceases to be one thing and souls can no longer be included under any one principle.

---

[2]"Porphyry: On the Life of Plotinus and His Work" in *Plotinus: The Enneads,* translated by Stephen MacKenna (New York: Penguin Books, 1991), pp. cx–cxi.

Source: From Robert Maynard Hutchins, *Plotinus: The Six Enneads,* © 1952. Reprinted by permission of Encyclopedia Britannica, Inc.

2. Now to begin with, the unity of soul, mine and another's, is not enough to make the two totals of soul and body identical. An identical thing in different recipients will have different experiences; the identity Man, in me as I move and you at rest, moves in me and is stationary in you: there is nothing stranger, nothing impossible, in any other form of identity between you and me; nor would it entail the transference of my emotion to any outside point: when in any one body a hand is in pain, the distress is felt not in the other but in the hand as represented in the centralizing unity.

In order that my feelings should of necessity be yours, the unity would have to be corporeal: only if the two recipient bodies made one, would the souls feel as one.

We must keep in mind, moreover, that many things that happen even in one same body escape the notice of the entire being, especially when the bulk is large: thus in huge sea-beasts, it is said, the animal as a whole will be quite unaffected by some membral accident too slight to traverse the organism.

Thus unity in the subject of any experience does not imply that the resultant sensation will be necessarily felt with any force upon the entire being and at every point of it: some transmission of the experience may be expected, and is indeed undeniable, but a full impression on the sense there need not be.

That one identical soul should be virtuous in me and vicious in someone else is not strange: it is only saying that an identical thing may be active here and inactive there.

We are not asserting the unity of soul in the sense of a complete negation of multiplicity—only of the Supreme can that be affirmed—we are thinking of soul as simultaneously one and many, participant in the nature divided in body, but at the same time a unity by virtue of belonging to that Order which suffers no division.

In myself some experience occurring in a part of the body may take no effect upon the entire man but anything occurring in the higher reaches would tell upon the partial: in the same way any influx from the All upon the individual will have manifest effect since the points of sympathetic contact are numerous—but as to any operation from ourselves upon the All there can be no certainty.

3. Yet, looking at another set of facts, reflection tells us that we are in sympathetic relation to each other, suffering, overcome, at the sight of pain, naturally drawn to forming attachments; and all this can be due only to some unity among us.

Again, if spells and other forms of magic are efficient even at a distance to attract us into sympathetic relations, the agency can be no other than the one soul.

A quiet word induces changes in a remote object, and makes itself heard at vast distances—proof of the oneness of all things within the one soul.

But how reconcile this unity with the existence of a reasoning soul, an unreasoning, even a vegetal soul?

[It is a question of powers]: the indivisible phase is classed as reasoning because it is not in division among bodies, but there is the later phase, divided among bodies, but still one thing and distinct only so as to secure sense-perception throughout; this is to be classed as yet another power; and there is the forming and making phase which again is a power. But a variety of powers does not conflict with unity; seed contains many powers and yet it is one thing, and from that unity rises, again, a variety which is also a unity.

But why are not all the powers of this unity present everywhere?

The answer is that even in the case of the individual soul described, similarly, as permeating its body, sensation is not equally present in all the parts, reason does not operate at every point, the principle of growth is at work where there is no sensation—and yet all these powers join in the one soul when the body is laid aside.

The nourishing faculty as dependent from the All belongs also to the All-Soul: why then does it not come equally from ours?

Because what is nourished by the action of this power is a member of the All, which itself has sensation passively; but the perception, which is an intellectual judgement, is individual and has no need to create what already exists, though it would have done so had the power not been previously included, of necessity, in the nature of the All.

4. These reflections should show that there is nothing strange in that reduction of all souls to one. But it is still necessary to enquire into the mode and conditions of the unity.

Is it the unity of origin in a unity? And if so, is the one divided or does it remain entire and yet produce variety? And how can an essential being, while remaining its one self, bring forth others?

Invoking God to become our helper, let us assert, that the very existence of many souls makes certain that there is first one from which the many rise.

Let us suppose, even, the first soul to be corporeal.

Then [by the nature of body] the many souls could result only from the splitting up of that entity, each an entirely different substance: if this body-soul be uniform in kind, each of the resultant souls must be of the one kind; they will all carry the one Form undividedly and will differ only in their volumes. Now, if their being souls depended upon their volumes they would be distinct; but if it is ideal-form that makes them souls, then all are, in virtue of this Idea, one.

But this is simply saying that there is one identical soul dispersed among many bodies, and that, preceding this, there is yet another not thus dispersed, the source of the soul in dispersion which may be thought of as a widely repeated image of the soul in unity—much as a multitude of seals bear the impression of one ring. By that first mode the soul is a unit broken up into a variety of points: in the second mode it is incorporeal. Similarly if the soul were a condition or modification of body, we could not wonder that this quality—this one thing from one source—should be present in many objects. The same reasoning would apply if soul were an effect [or manifestation] of the Conjoint.

We, of course, hold it to be bodiless, an essential existence.

5. How then can a multitude of essential beings be really one?

Obviously either the one essence will be entire in all, or the many will rise from a one which remains unaltered and yet includes the one-many in virtue of giving itself, without self-abandonment, to its own multiplication.

It is competent thus to give and remain, because while it penetrates all things it can never itself be sundered: this is an identity in variety.

There is no reason for dismissing this explanation: we may think of a science with its constituents standing as one total, the source of all those various elements: again, there is the seed, a whole, producing those new parts in which it comes to its division;

each of the new growths is a whole while the whole remains undiminished: only the material element is under the mode of part, and all the multiplicity remains an entire identity still.

It may be objected that in the case of science the constituents are not each the whole.

But even in the science, while the constituent selected for handling to meet a particular need is present actually and takes the lead, still all the other constituents accompany it in a potential presence, so that the whole is in every part: only in this sense [of particular attention] is the whole science distinguished from the part: all, we may say, is here simultaneously effected: each part is at your disposal as you choose to take it; the part invites the immediate interest, but its value consists in its approach to the whole.

The detail cannot be considered as something separate from the entire body of speculation: so treated it would have no technical or scientific value; it would be childish divagation. The one detail, when it is a matter of science, potentially includes all. Grasping one such constituent of his science, the expert deduces the rest by force of sequence.

[As a further illustration of unity in plurality] the geometrician, in his analysis, shows that the single proposition includes all the items that go to constitute it and all the propositions which can be developed from it.

It is our feebleness that leads to doubt in these matters; the body obscures the truth, but there all stands out clear and separate.

TEXT 23

Pachomius: Instruction Concerning a Spiteful Monk[1]

*T*he establishment of monastic orders within Christianity can be traced to the work of the early Egyptian Christian Pachomius, born around A.D. 290 in upper or southern Egypt. After serving as a young man in the army of Roman Emperor Constantine, Pachomius eventually withdrew to the desert on the east bank of the Nile River where he joined a small colony of Christian hermits. Possessing a genius for administration, Pachomius was able to replace the scattered communities of hermits with smoothly functioning monastic orders of religious men and women, governed by communal rules. By the time of his death, the monasteries under his care had a membership of over 7,000.

Struggle, my beloved, for the time is near and the days have been shortened. There is no father who instructs his children, there is no child who obeys its father; good virgins are no longer; the holy fathers have died on all sides; the mothers and the widows are no longer, and we have become like orphans; the humble are crushed underfoot; and blows are showered upon the head of the poor. Therefore there is little to hold back the wrath of God from grieving us, with no one to console us. All this has befallen us because we have not practised mortification. The churches are filled with quarrellers and wrathful people; monastic communities have become ambitious; pride reigns; there is no one left who is dedicated to his neighbour; on the contrary, every man has crushed his neighbour. We are plunged into suffering. There is no prophet nor gnostic. No one wins over another, for hardness of heart abounds. Those who understand keep silence, for the times are evil. Each one is his own lord.

---

[1]Philip Rousseau, *Pachomius: The Making of a Community in Fourth-Century Egypt* (Berkeley: University of California Press, 1985), pp. 176–77.

Source: From Philip Rousseau, *Pachomius: The Making of a Community in Fourth-Century Egypt,* © 1985, The Regents of the University of California. Reprinted by permission of the University of California Press.

TEXT 24

Athanasius: Temporal Afflictions and Eternal Glory

from The Resurrection Letters[1]

While still a young Christian archdeacon of Alexandria, Athanasius gained distinction as a powerful theologian when he was called to represent the bishop of Alexandria at the Council of Nicaea in 325. It was at this synod that a creed still used by many Christian churches today was formulated. It was intended to combat Arianism, which the Roman Catholic Church had determined to be a heresy. The doctrine of Arianism defined by an elderly priest of Alexandria named Arius, represented an effort to define the Trinity through a Gnostic belief that the Father, Son, and Holy Spirit were three separate essences.

Athanasius was appointed bishop of Alexandria in A.D. 328 after the death of his predecessor. He presided over the church during particularly turbulent times for nascent Christianity. On five occasions, either because of political infighting within the church hierarchy or at the instigation of enemies in government, he was banished, first to Treves in Germany, and the second time to Rome where he pleaded his case before Pope Julius I. His third exile, where he sought refuge in the Egyptian desert among ascetics, has been viewed as the period of his greatest theological productivity, a time in which he wrote *The History of the Arian Heresy* and many letters. The importance of this time in his life may also account for the supportiveness Athanasius showed toward the Egyptian monastic movement.

The Letters of Athanasius were written between the years A.D. 329–348 on the occasion of Easter.

---

[1]Jack N. Sparks, *The Resurrection Letters of St. Athanasius*, (Nashville, TN: Thomas Nelson Publishers, 1979), pp. 48–49.
Source: From Jack N. Sparks, *The Resurrection Letters of St. Athanasius,* © 1979. Reprinted by permission of Jack N. Sparks.

CHRISTIANS TRIED FOR THEIR OWN GOOD

The other saints, having the same confidence in God, gladly accepted the same sort of testing—as Job, for example, who said, "Blessed be the name of the Lord" (Job 1:21). And the psalmist *asked* for testing: "Search me, O Lord, and try me: test my heart and my mind" (Ps. 26:2). When strength is tested and proven, even foolish people are convinced.

These saints, because they saw that the "divine fire" would cleanse them and benefit them, did not shrink back from or get discouraged by the trials they faced. Rather than being hurt by what they went through, they grew and were made better, shining like gold that has been refined in a fire (cf. Mal. 3:3; 1 Peter 1:7). As one who had gone successfully through this sort of thing said, "You have tried my heart; You have visited me at night; You have tested me and found no evil in me; I do not harm others with my mouth" (Ps. 17:3).

Rebels, on the other hand, since all they understand is eating, drinking, and dying, consider trials to be dangerous. They very quickly stumble over them, and then, having an untested and unstable faith, their evil minds run free and they fall into improper behavior (cf. Rom 1:28). Therefore St. Paul urges us to exercise our faith in the face of troubles. Having already come through them victoriously, he said, "Therefore I take pleasure in persecutions and weaknesses" (2 Cor. 12:10). In another place he said, "Exercise yourself in godliness" (1 Tim. 4:7). He knew that those who choose to live godly lives are going to be persecuted, so he wanted his disciples to be aware of the difficulties they would face. Then when the trials and afflictions did come, they would have built up enough strength to handle them easily.

You know yourself that when you've been looking forward to something, even if it's hard, you experience a secret joy when it actually comes.

MARTYRS REFINED BY THEIR SUFFERINGS

This is how the blessed martyrs were so quickly matured in Christ that they were able to keep their minds on the expected rest rather than the pain and injury their bodies would go through (cf. Col. 1:28). They had already experienced trials and troubles that had brought them a long way toward that attitude of life.

What a contrast to those people who name their estates after themselves (Ps. 49:11), and those who have their minds on hay, wood, and stubble (cf. 1 Cor. 3:12)! These people are aliens to the kingdom of heaven because they are strangers to troubles.

Oh, if they only understood that "tribulation works patience, and patience strength of character, and strong character hope, and hope does not disappoint" (Rom. 5:3–5). Then they would have exercised themselves as Paul did: "I buffet my body and keep it under subjection so that after I've preached to others, I will not be disqualified myself" (1 Cor. 9:27).

They would have gladly borne the afflictions that came along in life if they had listened to the prophetic advice: "It is good for a man to take Your yoke in his youth; let him sit alone and be silent when he has taken it up. Let him turn his cheek to the one who strikes him and accept insults. Because the Lord does not reject forever, for when He afflicts, He is gracious, according to the abundance of His tender mercies" (Lam. 3:27–32).

TEXT 25

Synesius of Cyrene (Libya): Letters to Hypatia and Euoptius[1]

One of the most remarkable female philosophers and mathematicians of all times was Hypatia of Alexandria, born around A.D. 370. The daughter of the noted mathematician and philosopher, Theon, she embraced Neoplatonism and reformed it in her own image, articulating a philosophic religion, which strove toward the attainment of liberation of the spirit through fusion with God. She was murdered by a mob of Christian zealots in 412, led by monks of the Nitrian order.

One of Hypatia's most devoted students was Synesius of Cyrene in Libya, whose life and relationships have been captured in the 156 letters of his which have survived. Because all of Hypatia's works have been lost, some of what we know of her intellectual talents is reflected in the letters Synesius wrote to her.

To the Philosopher (Hypatia)

I am in such evil fortune that I need a hydroscope. See that one is cast in brass for me and put together. The instrument in question is a cylindrical tube, which has the shape of a flute and is about the same size. It has notches in a perpendicular line, by means of which we are able to test the weight of the waters. A cone forms a lid at one of the extremities, closely fitted to the tube. The cone and the tube have one base only. This is called the baryllium. Whenever you place the tube in water, it remains erect. You can then count the notches at your ease, and in this way ascertain the weight of the water.

---

[1]Augustine Fitzgerald, *The Letters of Synesius of Cyrene* (London: Oxford University Press, 1926), numbers 15–16, 81, 124, 136.
Source: From Augustine Fitzgerald, *The Letters of Synesius of Cyrene,* © 1926. Reprinted by permission of Oxford University Press.

To the Philosopher (Hypatia)

I am dictating this letter to you from my bed, but may you receive it in good health, mother, sister, teacher, and withal benefactress, and whatsoever is honoured in name and deed. For me bodily weakness has followed in the wake of mental suffering. The remembrance of my departed children is consuming my forces, little by little. Only so long should Synesius have lived as he was still without experience of the evils of life. It is as if a torrent long pent up had burst upon me in full volume, and as if the sweetness of life had vanished. May I either cease to live, or cease to think of the tomb of my sons! But may you preserve your health and give my salutations to your happy comrades in turn, beginning with father Theotecnus and brother Athanasius, and so to all! And if any one has been added to these, so long as he is dear to you, I must owe him gratitude because he is dear to you, and to that man give my greetings as to my own dearest friend. If any of my affairs interests you, you do well, and if any of them does not so interest you, neither does it me.

To the Philosopher (Hypatia)

Even if Fortune is unable to take everything away from me, at least she wants to take away everything that she can, she who has 'bereft me of many excellent sons.' But she can never take away from me the choice of the best, and the power to come to the help of the oppressed, for never may she prevail to change my heart! I abhor iniquity: for one may, and I would fain prevent it, but this also is one of those things which were taken from me; this went even before my children.

'Aforetime the Milesians were men of might.' There was a time when I, too, was of some use to my friends. You yourself called me the providence of others. All respect which was accorded to me by the mighty of this earth I employed solely to help others. The great were merely my instruments. But now, alas, I am deserted and abandoned by all, unless *you* have some power to help. I account you as the only good thing that remains inviolate, along with virtue. You always have power, and long may you have it and make a good use of that power. I recommend to your care Nicaeus and Philolaus, two excellent young men united by the bond of relationship. In order that they may come again into possession of their own property, try to get support for them from all your friends, whether private individuals or magistrates.

To the Philosopher (Hypatia)

Even though there shall be utter forgetfulness of the dead in Hades,

'even there shall I remember thee,' my dear Hypatia. I am encompassed by the sufferings of my city, and disgusted with her, for I daily see the enemy forces, and men slaughtered like victims on an altar. I am breathing an air tainted by the decay of dead bodies. I am waiting to undergo myself the same lot that has befallen so many others, for how can one keep any hope, when the sky is obscured by the shadow of birds of prey? Yet even under these conditions I love the country. Why then do I suffer? Because I am a Libyan, because I was born here, and it is here that I see the honoured tombs of my ancestors. On your account alone I think I should be capable of overlooking my city, and changing my abode, if ever I had the chance of doing so.

To His Brother

I hope that I may profit as much as you desire from my residence at Athens. It seems to me that I have already grown more than a palm and a finger's length in wisdom, and I can give you at once a proof of the progress I have made. Well, it is from Anagyrus that I am writing to you; and I have visited Sphettus, Thria, Cephisia, and Phalerum. But may the accursed ship-captain perish who brought me here! Athens has no longer anything sublime except the country's famous names. Just as in the case of a victim burnt in the sacrificial fire, there remains nothing but the skin to help us to reconstruct a creature which was once alive—so ever since philosophy left these precincts, there is nothing for the tourist to admire except the Academy, the Lyceum, and, by Zeus, the Decorated Porch which has given its name to the philosophy of Chrysippus. This is no longer Decorated, for the proconsul has taken away the panels on which Polygnotus of Thasos had displayed his skill.

To-day Egypt has received and cherishes the fruitful wisdom of Hypatia. Athens was aforetime the dwelling-place of the wise: to-day the bee-keepers alone bring it honour. Such is the case of that pair of sophists in Plutarch who draw the young people to the lecture room—not by the fame of their eloquence, but by pots of honey from Hymettus.

TEXT 26

Paphnutius: Abba Aaron and the Miracle of the Nubian's Son

from The Coptic Histories of the Monks of Upper Egypt [1]

Because the name Paphnutius was as common to upper (southern) Egypt as Smith would be to an American, confusion sometimes arose as to which Paphnutius actually wrote *The Coptic Histories of the Monks of Upper Egypt.* Among his namesakes were a noted Coptic bishop and supporter of Athanasius, a famed Christian martyr who was killed during the persecution of Diocletian, a disciple of Macarius of Alexandria, and at least seven others known to history.[2]

The story of Abba Aaron was written in the Coptic dialect of upper Egypt and has been attributed to Paphnutius Cephalas (the Hermit), who was believed to have penned these accounts of his travels to Aswan and Philae, situated at the boundary of upper Egypt and Nubia, between A.D. 390 and 400.[3] Both cities were prominent sites from early Pharaonic times of temples and monuments to the ancient Egyptian gods. Philae was in fact often referred to as the "City of [the Egyptian goddess] Isis." It is now becoming apparent that these areas also figured more significantly than had previously been recognized in the growth of the monastic movement that spread from Egypt to Europe and the Near East.

---

[1] Tim Vivian, *Histories of the Monks of Upper Egypt and the Life of Onnophrius by Paphnutius* (Kalamazoo, MI: Cistercian Publications, 1993), pp. 120–22.
[2] Ibid., pp. 42–43.
[3] Ibid., p. 53.

98. Now it happened that on another day we were sitting with one another. A certain Nubian came out from the mountain with his son to drink water from the river. And when his young son put his hand into the river to scoop up some water to drink, a huge crocodile seized him and dragged him under and fled. Immediately his father threw himself to the ground and cried out and wept bitterly, for besides that son he had no other. Now as the man ran up the mountain crying out, he cut himself against the sharp edges of the rocks and severely injured himself. When I saw how heartbroken he was, I told my father. He got up and came to the door and gestured to the Nubian with his hand to come to him. And when he had come, Abba Aaron saw the wounds on his body, and he wiped away the blood that had run over his body and took him and brought him inside his home. He brought him in by force and made him sit down.

99. Now when he had questioned him about what had happened (he could not understand what the Nubian was saying to him), my father said to me, "Rise, see if you can find anyone on the road. Call him. Perhaps you can find someone who knows how to speak with him. When I went out I found a man from Philae who was going to Aswan riding on a donkey. I called to him and said to him, "Do you understand the language of the Nubians?" He said, "Yes." I took him to my father Abba Aaron. Now when that man saw the Nubian and the wounds all over his body, he was astonished and said to him, "How were you wounded?" and the Nubian told him what had happened. The holy man Abba Aaron took a piece of wood and gave it to him, saying, "Take it and throw it into the river where the crocodile seized your son." And he went and did as Abba Aaron had told him.

100. Now it happened that when he threw the piece of wood into the water, a huge crocodile appeared and cast the little boy up on the shore—and he had not been injured in any way! And his father took him by the hand and brought him to the holy old man Abba Aaron. And when the Nubian saw this miracle, he shouted with joy and hugged Abba Aaron and kissed him. Now the interpreter went to Philae and did not go to Aswan that day; instead, he went about proclaiming the miracle that had taken place. And when the Nubian saw the miracle that had taken place, he went home glorifying God and proclaiming what had happened. And all those who heard glorified God and the holy man Abba Aaron until this very day.

Source: From Tim Vivian, *Histories of the Monks of Upper Egypt and the Life of Onnophrius by Paphnutius,* © 1993. Reprinted by permission of Cistercian Publications.

TEXT 27

Coptic Apocrypha: The Death of Joseph

from The Coptic Apocryphal Gospels[1]

*T*he term "apocrypha" derives from a Greek infinitive meaning "to hide away." It has come to refer to biblical writings rejected by the orthodox church and thus left out of the traditional Bible. In the early centuries of Christianity, diverse sects arose, some of which were declared heretical by the established church and their writings deemed "apocryphal." An examination of these "rejected" books of the Bible offer valuable insights into the competing value systems of those times. The Coptic apocrypha were written on papyri in the dialects of upper Egypt and Nubia and reflect in some cases the influences of ancient Egyptian religion on certain elements of early Christendom. These texts are retained at the Vatican in Rome.

This is the going forth from *the* body of our father Joseph the carpenter, the father of Christ according to flesh, whose life was one hundred and eleven years. Our Saviour told the apostles his whole life on the mount of Olives, and the apostles also wrote these words, and left them in the Library at Jerusalem. And again the day on which the holy old man laid down *the* body is the twenty sixth of the month Epep; in the peace of God, Amen.

I. Now it came to pass on a day, as our good Saviour was sitting on the mount of Olives and His disciples were assembled to Him, that He spake with them, saying, O My brethren beloved and ye sons of My good Father, whom He hath chosen from among the whole world. Ye know that many times now I have told you that I must needs be crucified and taste death for the universe, and rise from the dead, and give

---

[1] J. Armitage Robinson, *Texts and Studies,* vol. IV, no. 2, *The Coptic Apocryphal Gospels* (Cambridge, England: Cambridge University Press, 1896), pp. 130–37.
Source: From J. Armitage Robinson, *Texts and Studies,* vol. IV, no. 2, *The Coptic Apocryphal Gospels,* © 1896. Reprinted by permission of Cambridge University Press.

you the preaching of the gospel, that ye may preach it in all the world, and clothe you with power from on high, and fill you with the Holy Ghost, that ye may preach to all the nations, saying to them, Repent; for it is better that a man find a cup of water in the age that is coming than all the riches of all the world. And again, Better is a single footstep in My Father's house than all the wealth of this world. And again, Better is a single hour of the righteous rejoicing than a thousand years of the sinners weeping and mourning, whose tears shall not be wiped away, neither shall they be heeded at all. Now therefore, O My glorious members, when ye go, preach to them, *saying,* A just balance and a just measure are those wherewith My Father will take account with you. And again, A single word of jest that ye shall speak shall be required of you. Even as no one can escape death, so no one can escape those things which he hath done, whether *it be* good or evil. But all these words have I told you now, *saying,* No mighty one can be saved because of his strength, neither can a man be saved because of the multitude of his wealth. Now therefore hear, and I will tell you the life of My father Joseph, the blessed old man *who was a* carpenter.

II. There was a man Joseph who was from a city *called* Bethlehem, which is the *city* of the Jews, and is the city of king David. And he learned well the wisdom and the trade of carpentry. And this man Joseph took to himself a wife according to a union of a holy marriage. And she bare him sons and daughters, four sons and two daughters; whose names are these, Judas and Josetos, James and Simon: and the names of his daughters are Lysia and Lydia. And Joseph's wife died, even as it is appointed for all men, and left James still little. And Joseph was a righteous man, glorifying God in all things. And he was without, working at the trade of carpentry, he and his two sons, living by the work of their hands, according to the law of Moses. And this righteous man, of whom I speak, this is Joseph My father according to flesh, to whom My mother Mary was betrothed for a wife.

III. And whilst My father Joseph lived as a widower, Mary also My mother, who was in every wise good and blessed, was dwelling in the temple, serving therein in purity, and she grew up until *she was* twelve years *old.* She spent three years in the house of her parents, and nine other years in the temple of the Lord. Then the priests, when they saw the Virgin living austerely and dwelling in the fear of the Lord, spake one with another, saying, Let us seek a good man and espouse her to him until the time of the marriage feast; lest by any means we let the custom of women happen to her in the temple, and we come to be under a great sin.

IV. And straightway they called the tribe of Judah, and brought out therefrom twelve peoples, according to the name of the twelve tribes of Israel. The lot fell upon the good old man Joseph, My father according to flesh. Then the priests answered and said to My blessed virgin mother, Go with Joseph, obey him, until the time comes that we make the marriage feast. My father Joseph received Mary My mother into his house. She found the little boy James in the sadness of bereavement, and was cherishing him. Therefore she was called Mary of James. Now Joseph took her into his house: and he went to the place wherein he worked in carpentry. Mary My mother spent two years in his house until the good time.

V. Now in the fourteenth year of her life I came by My own will and dwelt in her, I *who* am Jesus your life. Now when she was three months pregnant, the guileless Joseph came from the place wherein he worked in carpentry; and found My virgin mother pregnant. He was troubled and feared, and purposed to put her away privily. And from grief of heart he did not eat or drink.

VI. But in the middle of the night, behold Gabriel, the archangel of joy, came unto him in a vision, according to the command of My good Father; and said to him, Joseph, thou son of David, fear not, take Mary thy wife unto thee: for that which she will bear is of the Holy Ghost. She shall bear a Son; and thou shalt call His name Jesus; it is He that will rule all the nations with a rod of iron. And the angel departed from him. And Joseph arose from his sleep, and did as the angel of the Lord commanded him, and took Mary unto him.

VII. Now after these things there went out a decree from Augustus the king, that all the world should give in its name, each one after his city. The good old man also arose, and took Mary My virgin mother up to his city Bethlehem, for she was nigh to bear *a child*. And he wrote his name through the scribe: Joseph, the son of David, and Mary his wife and Jesus his son are of the tribe of Judah. And Mary My Mother bare Me in the way that turns to Bethlehem, by the tomb of Rachel, the wife of Jacob the patriarch, who is the mother of Joseph and Benjamin.

VIII. Satan gave counsel to Herod the great, the father of Archelaus, who beheaded John, My beloved and My kinsman. Thus he sought after Me, to slay Me, thinking that My kingdom was of this world. And Joseph was told by My Father in a vision; and he arose, and took Me and Mary My mother—I sitting on her arms and Salome following us. We went down to Egypt, and dwelt there the space of a year, until Herod's body bred worms, that he died, because of the blood of the sinless little children which he shed.

IX. Now when that lawless *man* Herod was dead, we returned to the land of Israel, and we dwelt in a city of Galilee, whose name is Nazareth. And My father Joseph, the blessed old man, was working at the trade of carpentry, whilst we lived by the work of his hands. He never ate bread for nought, doing according to the law of Moses.

X. And after this long time his body was not without power, nor were his eyes without light, nor was a single tooth in his mouth destroyed. He was not without understanding in wisdom all this time, but he was as a youth. And his life had come to one hundred and eleven years in a good old age.

XI. Now his two elder sons Josetos and Symeon took wives, and went to their house; and his two daughters also took husbands: as it is laid down for all men. But Joseph dwelt with James his youngest son. When the Virgin bare Me, I was with them in all subjection of sonship: for I did every work of mankind, sin only excepted. And I called Mary My mother, and Joseph My father; and I obeyed them in all things that they told Me. I did not answer a word unto them, but I loved them exceedingly.

XII. Now it came to pass after these things that the death of Joseph My father drew nigh, even as it is appointed for all men. When his body was sick, his angel told him, In this year shalt thou die. And when his soul was troubled, he went up to Jerusalem, and he went into the temple of the Lord, and he repented before the altar, and prayed thus, saying,

XIII. God, the Father of all mercies and the God of all flesh, the Lord of my soul and of my body and of my spirit: if the days of my life which Thou hast given me in the world, are ended; I beseech Thee, Lord God, that Thou wouldest send me Michael the archangel, to stand by me, until my wretched soul goes forth from my body without trouble and confusion. For a great fear and grief is death to all men, whether *it be* man or cattle or wild beast or creeping thing or bird: in short every creature which is under heaven, wherein is *a* soul of life, there is trouble and grief *to them,* until their soul is separated from their body. Now therefore, O my Lord, let Thine angel stand by my soul and my body, until they are separated from one another without trouble. Cause not the angel, appointed unto me from the day that Thou didst form me until now, to burn in his face with anger towards me in the path, as I come unto Thee: but let him be at peace with me. Let not those whose face is diverse trouble me in the path, as I come unto Thee. Let not those who *are* by the gates restrain my soul; neither put me to shame at Thy fearful judgment seat. Let not the waves of the river of fire be savage towards me, wherein all souls are purified, before they see the glory of Thy godhead. O God who judgest each one in truth and righteousness. Now therefore, my Lord, let Thy mercy be to me *a* consolation; for Thou art the Fountain of all good. Thine is the glory unto *the* ages of the ages. Amen.

XIV. Now it came to pass after these things, he went unto Nazareth, the city wherein he dwelt. And he lay down with the sickness wherewith he should die, even as it is appointed for all men. And his sickness was very heavy, beyond all the times that he was sick, from the day that he was born into the world. This is the manner of life of My beloved father Joseph. He was forty years *old, when* he took *a* wife, and other forty nine years living in wedlock with his wife. And she died: and he was a year alone. My mother was two other years in his house, when the priests gave her to him, when he was told by the priests, *saying,* Keep her until the time of your marriage. At the beginning of the third year, whilst she was in his house, which is the fifteenth year of her life, she bare Me on the earth in a mystery: no one knoweth it in the whole creation, save Me and My Father and the Holy Ghost, being as We are in unity.

XV. Now all the days of the life of My father Joseph, the blessed old man, are an hundred and eleven years, even as My good Father commanded. And the day wherein he went forth from *the* body, is the twenty sixth of the month Epep. And the choice gold, even the flesh of My father Joseph, began to be altered; and the silver was changed, even the mind and the wisdom. He forgot to eat and to drink: the wisdom of the craft turned into error. And it came to pass when the light arose on that day, which is the twenty sixth of the month Epep, My father Joseph was much troubled on his bed; and he uttered a great groan, and smote his hands together, and cried out in great trouble, speaking thus:

XVI. Woe to me to-day. Woe to the day that my mother brought me forth into the world. Woe to the womb wherein I received seed of life. Woe to the breasts which I sucked. Woe to the knees on which I sat. Woe to the hands which carried me, until I grew up and became sinful. Woe to my tongue and my lips, for they have been entangled often in violence and in backbiting and in false slander and in idle words of jest, full of deceit. Woe to my eyes, for they have looked upon stumbling-blocks. Woe to my ears, for they have loved to hear vain words. Woe to my hands, for they have taken things which are not theirs. Woe to my stomach and my bowels, for they have desired foods which are not theirs: and if it found anything, it would consume it more than a burning fiery furnace, and make it everywhere unprofitable. Woe to my feet, which served my body ill, taking it into no good ways. Woe to my body, for it hath made my soul waste and strange to God Who made it. What shall I do now? I am shut in on every side. Truly woe to every man who shall sin. Truly this is the great trouble, which I saw upon Jacob my father, when he came forth from *the* body: it also hath overtaken me the wretched one to-day. But Jesus, God, the mediator of my soul and of my body, doeth His will in me.

XVII. Now as My beloved father Joseph was saying these things, I arose and went in unto him as he lay down; and I found him troubled in his soul and his spirit. I said to him, Hail, My beloved father Joseph, whose old age is at once good and blessed. He answered in great fear of death, saying to Me, Hail many times, my beloved Son. Behold my soul rested within me a little, when I heard Thy voice. Jesus my Lord, Jesus my true King, Jesus my good and merciful Saviour, Jesus the Preserver, Jesus the Pilot, Jesus the Shelterer, Jesus [who holdest fast] the universe in Thy goodness, Jesus whose name is sweet in the mouth of all and very rich, Jesus the Eye that sees, the Ear that hears in truth, hear me to-day, even me Thy servant, as I beseech Thee, pouring out my tears before Thee. Thou art God in truth, Thou art the Lord in truth, even as the angel said to me many times: especially *on* the day that my heart doubted within me, because of a human thought against her, blessed *and* virgin, because she was pregnant; when I said, I will put her away privily. But as I thought on these things, the angel appeared unto me in a vision, saying unto me, Joseph, thou son of David, fear not, take Mary thy wife unto thee: for that which she will bear *is* of the Holy Ghost. Do not doubt at all concerning her pregnancy: for she will bear a Son; and thou shalt call His name Jesus. Thou art Jesus Christ, the Saviour of my soul and of my body and of my spirit.

PART FOUR

Byzantine and Romanized Carthage–Numidia

After conquering Egypt in 31 B.C., Rome continued its expeditionary sweep westwards, through the remainder of North Africa. The continent of Africa derived its name from one of these Roman colonial provinces on the Mediterranean coast. The second prominent province of Roman Africa to the west of Egypt was Numidia, which encompassed the region of present-day Tunisia and Algeria. The Numidian city of Carthage on the Tunisian coast, like Alexandria to the east, became a major center

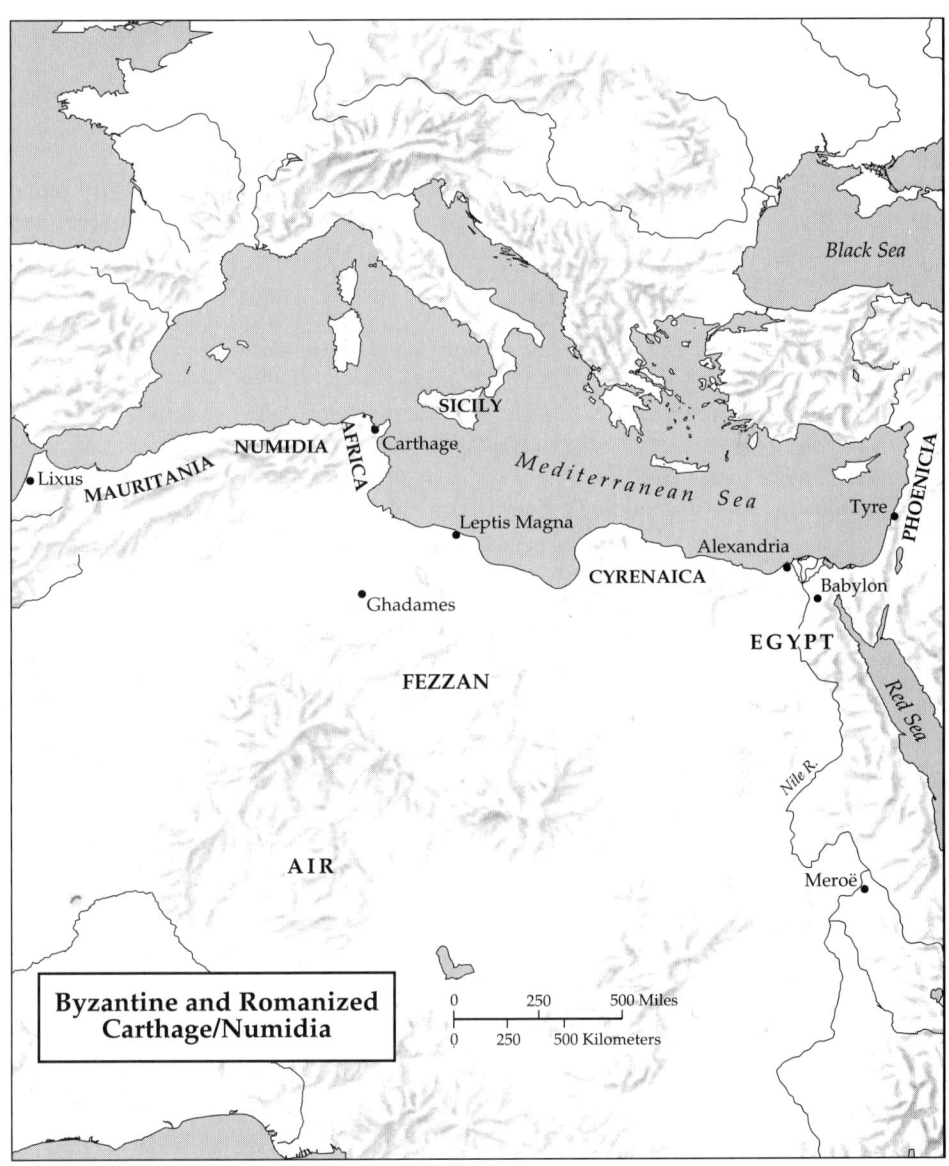

of commercial and intellectual activities. Founded by traders from Phoenicia on the coast of Lebanon in the ninth century B.C., Carthage developed into a cosmopolitan mix of Phoenicians, indigenous Berber nomadic populations, and settled farmers who had inhabited this region of Africa from earliest times. It was during the second of the Punic Wars, fought between Rome and Carthage, that the African Hannibal (247–182 B.C.) crossed the Alps with elephants and defeated the Roman army. However, in the third and final Punic War, Rome defeated the Carthaginians in 146 B.C., decimating their city in the process.

Numidian society during the subsequent period of Roman occupation exhibited two distinct classes. The ruling aristocracy of the cities exhibited strong Greek and Phoenician influences in their art and architecture, which was not the case, however, among the less acculturated lower classes of Berber farmers and nomads. As a Roman province, the coastal cities also became the residence of Roman administrators and wealthy Carthaginians who added Roman cultural elements to their already cosmopolitan lifestyle of Hellenized Phoenician–Berbers. Among this privileged class, the Latin language became the primary means of communication. However, the rural populations maintained Berber as their language and continued to regard Rome as an alien interloper in their country.

From the first century A.D., Christianity began its spread westward into this region of Africa from its Egyptian nucleus in Alexandria. And it was into this Numidian environment of brutal Roman persecution of the early Christian Church and the martyrdom of thousands that the African theologians Tertullian, Cyprian, and Augustine lived and developed theological doctrines that would define Western Christianity.

Unfortunately, far too little scholarly attention appears to have been paid to the cultural influences of Tertullian, Cyprian, and Augustine's African Berber backgrounds; and yet the North Africa in which these men who eventually achieved sainthood lived was never quite able to forget its subordinate status to Roman citizens of Italian origin because these Africans, although speaking Latin and possessors of Roman citizenship, were not viewed as equals by the indigenous citizens of Rome.

As regards Christianity of that time, J. M. Rogers asserts:

> The African Church had a special temperament of its own since the days of Tertullian, its great founding figure. Its roots did not lie in the Hellenized cities of the east, but in soil laid down by the religions of Carthage and Numidia which lingered on amid the Berber peasantry.[1]

Religious scholars consider Tertullian (A.D. 150–223/225) to have been the first and most preeminent of the early Church Fathers. A native of Carthage and a lawyer, he converted to Christianity late in life. Employing his well-honed skills as a lawyer and orator, he became one of the most noted theologians fighting the doctrinal battle against Gnosticism. To counter such teachings that, among other things, focused on Christ's divinity, Tertullian emphasized the human nature of Jesus Christ.

---

[1] J. M. Roberts, *History of the World* (New York: Oxford University Press, 1993), p. 234.

One of Tertullian's most devoted students, Cyprian (A.D. 200–258), became bishop of Carthage in A.D. 249 and was eventually martyred. Cyprian's best-known work confronted the doctrinal issue of "rebaptism," an African Christian practice that was eventually repudiated by Rome.

SAINT AUGUSTINE

While the Roman Church fought and eventually lost against Monophytism in Egypt, a new heresy erupted among the Berber Christians of Numidia; it was called Donatism. This doctrine defined a legalistic form of Christianity more akin to the Judaism found in the Torah. In the battle waged by the mainstream church against Donatism, a young African of towering intellect rose to the fore. Assuming the bishopric of Hippo (in present day Algeria), Augustine (A.D. 350–430) was not only the church's most forceful spokesman against Donatism in Africa, he became likewise the leading theologian and formulator of Roman Catholic doctrine.[2]

The degree to which Augustine's cultural marginality as an African member of the Roman Empire may have offered him new insights has yet to be explored in full. Augustine had always lived in conflicting worlds. One of them was the Christian world of his mother, Monica, a central figure in his life, whose name, however, may have derived from her own family's belief in the Berber goddess Mon.[3] Augustine had also to live in the secular world of his father Patricus, a man described as "irascible, driven," an African struggling to rise in a Roman system.[4] His family were poor members of the Latin-speaking aristocracy of naturalized Roman citizens within the larger Punic and proto-Berber speaking society of Numidia. Living all but 5 of his 76 years in Africa, he was reminded of his ethnic heritage when he finally journeyed to Rome because of his distinctively African accent.

Shortly after converting to Christianity at the age of 33, Augustine wrote *The Confessions,* a prose poem of such probing sensitivity that it has often been described as the first modern biography. In his later years, Augustine faced the doctrinal assaults of Julian, the noble-born Italian to whom Augustine was always "the African" and the battle waged against him was a "Punic War of the mind." Julian constantly reminded his followers that the African Augustine represented a contamination of the true Roman culture of the Italians and "imposed upon the Italian church a set of dogmas genuinely foreign to the spirit of the Christianity of their land."[5]

Augustine's magnum opus, *De Civitate Dei* [*The City of God*], has often been called the first true work of political science. Written after the sack of Rome by the Visigoths in A.D. 410, his work represented a powerful apologetic for Christianity, in which he defined the existence of two cities, a worldly one and a godly one. This book examined the history of the Roman Empire itself, in a way that had never before been

---

[2]Peter Brown, *Augustine of Hippo: A Biography* (Berkeley: University of California Press, 1969), p. 383.
[3]W. H. C. Frend, *The Donatist Church: A Movement of Protest in Roman North Africa* (Oxford: Clarendon Press, 1952), p. 230, and Brown, *Augustine of Hippo,* p. 32.
[4]J. J. O'Meara, *The Young Augustine* (London: Longman, 1954), p. 25, and Mallard, p. 17.
[5]Brown, *Augustine of Hippo,* p. 383.

done, in order to disprove critics who blamed the new Christian religion and the repudiation of the traditional Roman gods for the catastrophe that befell the Empire. Augustine died in A.D. 430 during the siege of Hippo by northern European Vandals who succeeded in driving the Romans from Africa. Even though the Roman Church in Africa died shortly thereafter, J. M. Roberts has nevertheless pointed out that Augustine of Hippo was able to articulate more effectively than any of his predecessors the nature of the debate that later defined the course of Church history in Europe, between predestination and free will, grace and good works.[6]

Nine years after Augustine's death, the Vandal king suffered defeat by the army of the surviving East Roman Empire called Byzantium, which was based in Constantinople. After A.D. 439 and until the Arab invasion of 705, Carthage became an Exarchate, that is, a semiautonomous province of the Byzantine Empire. Even so, the predominant population of the territory continued to be that of African Berbers.

---

[6] J. M. Roberts, *History of the World,* (New York: Oxford University Press, 1993), p. 235.

TEXT 28

Tertullian: Against the Valentinians[1]

*Q*uintus Septimus Florens Tertullianus was born into a pagan household of Latinized Berbers in Carthage around A.D. 155/160. His father may have served as a centurion in the African legion of the province encompassed by Carthage. Tertullian received his early education in Carthage and then studied in Rome to become a lawyer.

Converting to Christianity after his return to Africa six years later, the young theologian rose in the church to become one of its most influential leaders and is considered to have played a formative role in the social and theological evolution of early Christianity. He instituted, among other things, the establishment of Latin as the ecclesiastical language of the Roman Church and was especially noted for his adamant stance against the influences of Egyptian Gnosticism, whose doctrines stressed salvation through self-awareness and insight.

Tertullian's theological positions also emphasized the church's role as disciplinarian and teacher of proper moral conduct. For a brief period, around A.D. 210, he defected to Montanism. It was a sect that refused church membership to individuals not perceived to be of the highest moral stature, and also rejected the Catholic hierarchy in favor of a lay Church of the Spirit. In time Tertullian left the Montanists in order to establish a sect of his own, which lasted into the fifth century.

This theologian's most renowned writings include the many works he composed in defense of the Christian faith, including "Against Valentinus" (the Egyptian Gnostic); "Against Marcion" (an Anatolian heretic who believed that the world was created by the evil god of Judaism); and "Against Hermogenes" (a Carthaginian painter who claimed that God created the world out of preexisting matter).

---

[1] Alexander Roberts and James Donaldson (editors), *The Ante-Nicene Fathers,* vol. III, "Against the Valentinians" (Grand Rapids, MI: Wm. B. Eerdmans Publishing Co., 1951), pp. 503–20.

CHAP. I.—INTRODUCTORY. TERTULLIAN COMPARES THE HERESY TO THE OLD ELEUSINIAN MYSTERIES. BOTH SYSTEMS ALIKE IN PREFERRING CONCEALMENT OF ERROR AND SIN TO PROCLAMATION OF TRUTH AND VIRTUE.

The Valentinians, who are nÆo doubt a very large body of heretics—comprising as they do so many apostates from the truth, who have a propensity for fables, and no disciple to deter them (therefrom) care for nothing so much as to obscure what they preach, if indeed they (can be said to) preach who obscure *their doctrine.* The officiousness with which they guard their doctrine is an officiousness which betrays their guilt. Their disgrace is proclaimed in the very earnestness with which they maintain their religious system. Now, in the case of those Eleusinian mysteries, which are the very heresy of Athenian superstition, it is their secrecy that is their disgrace. Accordingly, they previously beset all access to their body with tormenting conditions; *and* they require a long initiation before they enrol (their members), even instruction during five years for their perfect disciples, in order that they may mould their opinions by this suspension of full knowledge, and apparently raise the dignity of their mysteries in proportion to the craving for them which they have previously created. Then follows the duty of silence. Carefully is that guarded, which is so long in finding. All the divinity, however, lies in their secret recesses: there are revealed *at last* all the aspirations of the fully initiated, the entire mystery of the sealed tongue, the symbol of virility. But this allegorical representation, under the pretext of nature's revered name, obscures a real sacrilege by help of an arbitrary symbol, and by *empty* images obviates the reproach of falsehood! In like manner, the heretics who are now the object of our remarks, the Valentinians, have formed Eleusinian dissipations of their own, consecrated by a profound silence, having nothing of the heavenly in them but their mystery. By the help of the sacred names and titles and arguments of true religion, they have fabricated the vainest and foulest figment for men's pliant liking, out of the affluent suggestions of Holy Scripture, since from its many springs many *errors* may well emanate. If you propose to them inquiries sincere and honest, they answer you with stern look and contracted brow, and say, "The subject is profound." If you try them with subtle questions, with the ambiguities of their double tongue, they affirm a community of faith (with yourself). If you intimate to them that you understand *their opinions,* they insist on knowing nothing themselves. If you come to a close engagement with them, they destroy your own fond hope of a victory over them by a self-immolation. Not even to their own disciples do they commit a secret before they have made sure of them. They have the knack of persuading men before instructing them; although truth persuades by teaching, but does not teach by first persuading.

CHAP. II.—THESE HERETICS BRAND THE CHRISTIANS AS SIMPLE PERSONS. THE CHARGE ACCEPTED, AND SIMPLICITY EULOGIZED OUT OF THE SCRIPTURES.

For this reason we are branded by them as simple, and as being merely so, without being wise also; as if indeed wisdom were compelled to be wanting in simplicity,

---

Source: From Alexander Roberts and James Donaldson, *The Ante-Nicene Fathers,* vol. III, © 1951 Wm. B. Eerdmans Publishing Co. Reprinted by permission of Wm B. Eerdmans Publishing Co.

whereas the Lord unites them both: "Be ye therefore wise as serpents, and simple as doves." Now if we, on our parts, be accounted foolish because we are simple, does it then follow that they are not simple because they are wise? Most perverse, however, are they who are not simple, even as they are most foolish who are not wise. And yet, (if I must choose) I should prefer taking the *latter* condition for the lesser fault; since it is perhaps better to have a wisdom which falls short in quantity, than that which is bad in quality—better to be in error than to mislead. Besides, the face of the Lord is patiently waited for by those who "seek Him in simplicity of heart," as says the very Wisdom—not of Valentinus, but—of Solomon. Then, again, infants have borne by their blood a testimony to Christ. (Would you say) that it was children who shouted "Crucify Him"? They were neither children nor infants; in other words, they were not simple. The apostle, too, bids us to "become children again" towards God, to be as children in malice" by our simplicity, yet as being also "wise in our practical faculties." At the same time, with respect to the order of development in Wisdom, I have admitted that it flows from simplicity. In brief, "the dove" has usually served to figure Christ; "the serpent," to tempt Him. The one even from the first has been the harbinger of divine peace; the other from the beginning has been the despoiler of the divine image. Accordingly, simplicity alone will be more easily able to know and to declare God, *whereas* wisdom alone will rather do Him violence, and betray Him.

CHAP. III.—THE FOLLY OF THIS HERESY. IT DISSECTS AND MUTILATES THE DEITY. CONTRASTED WITH THE SIMPLE WISDOM OF TRUE RELIGION. TO EXPOSE THE ABSURDITIES OF THE VALENTINIAN SYSTEM IS TO DESTROY IT.

Let, then, the serpent hide himself as much as he is able, and let him wrest all his wisdom in the labyrinths of his obscurities; let him dwell deep down in the ground; let him worm himself into secret holes; let him unroll his length through his sinuous joints; let him tortuously crawl, though not all at once, beast as he is that skulks the light. Of our dove, however, how simple is the very home!—always in high and open places, and facing the light! As the symbol of the Holy Spirit, it loves the (radiant) East, that figure of Christ. Nothing causes truth a blush, except only being hidden, because no man will be ashamed to give ear thereto. *No man will be ashamed* to recognize Him as God whom nature has already commended to him, whom he already perceives in all His works,—Him indeed who is simply, for this reason, imperfectly known; because man has not thought of Him as only one, because he has named Him in a plurality (of gods), and adored Him in other *forms*. Yet, to induce oneself to turn from this multitude of deities to another crowd, to remove from a familiar authority to an unknown one, to wrench oneself from what is manifest to what is hidden, is to offend faith on the very threshold. Now, even suppose that you are initiated into the entire fable, will it not occur to you that you have heard something very like it from your fond nurse when you were a baby, amongst the lullabies she sang to you about the towers of Lamia, and the horns of the sun? Let, however, any man approach the subject from a knowledge of the faith which he has otherwise learned, as soon as he finds so many names of Aeons, so many marriages, so many offsprings, so many exits, so many issues, felicities *and* infelicities of a dispersed and mutilated Deity, will that man hesitate at once to pronounce that these are "the fables and endless genealogies" which the inspired apostle by anticipation condemned, whilst these seeds of heresy were even then shooting forth? Deservedly, therefore, must they be regarded as wanting in simplicity, and as merely prudent, who produce such fables not without difficulty, and defend them only indirectly, who at the same time do not thoroughly instruct those whom they teach. This, of course, shows their astuteness, if their lessons are disgraceful; their unkindness, if they are honourable. As for us, however, who are the simple folk, we know all about it. In short, this is the very first weapon with which we are armed for our encounter; it unmasks and brings to view the whole of their depraved system. And in this we have the first augury of our victory; because even merely to point out that which is concealed with so great an outlay of artifice, is to destroy it.

Chap. IV.—The heresy traceable to Valentinus, an able but restless man. Many schismatical leaders of the school mentioned. Only one of them shows respect to the man whose name designates the entire school.

We know, I say, most fully their actual origin, and we are quite aware why we call them Valentinians, although they affect to disavow their name. They have departed, it is true, from their founder, yet is their origin by no means destroyed; and even if it chance to be changed, the very change bears testimony to the fact. Valentinus had expected to become a bishop, because he was an able man both in genius and eloquence. Being indignant, however, that another obtained the dignity by reason of a claim which confessorship had given him, he broke with the church of the true faith. Just like those (restless) spirits which, when roused by ambition, are usually inflamed with the desire of revenge, he applied himself with all his might to exterminate the truth; and finding the clue of a certain old opinion, he marked out a path for himself with the subtlety of a serpent. Ptolemaeus afterwards entered on the same path, by distinguishing the names and the numbers of the Aenons into personal substances, which, however, he kept apart from God. Valentinus had included these in the very essence of the Deity, as senses and affections of motion. Sundry bypaths were then struck off therefrom, by Heraclean and Secundus and the magician Marcus. Theotimus worked hard about "the images of the law." Valentinus, however, was as yet nowhere, and still the Valentinians derive their name from Valentinus. Axionicus at Antioch is the only man who at the present time does honour to the memory of Valentinus, by keeping his rules to the full. But this heresy is permitted to fashion itself into as many various shapes as a courtezan, who usually changes and adjusts her dress every day. And why not? When they review that spiritual seed of theirs in every man after this fashion, whenever they have hit upon any novelty, they forthwith call their presumption a revelation, their own perverse ingenuity a spiritual gift; but (they deny all) unity, *admitting only* diversity. And thus we clearly see that, setting aside their customary dissimulation, most of them are in a divided state, being ready to say (and that sincerely) of certain points of their belief, "This is not so"; and, "I take this in a different sense"; and, "I do not admit that." By this variety, indeed, innovation is stamped on the very face of their rules; besides which, it wears all the colourable features of ignorant conceits.

Chap. V.—Many eminent Christian writers have carefully and fully refuted the heresy. These the author makes his own guides.

My own path, however, lies along the original tenets of their chief teachers, not with the self-appointed leaders of their promiscuous followers. Nor shall we hear it said of us from any quarter, that we have of our own mind fashioned our own materials, since these have been already produced, both in respect of the opinions and their refutations, in carefully written volumes, by so many eminently holy and excellent men, not only those who have lived before us, but those also who were contemporary with the heresiarchs themselves: for instance Justin, philosopher and martyr; Miltiades, the sophist of the churches; Irenaeus, that very exact inquirer into all doctrines; our own Proculus, the model of chaste old age and Christian eloquence. All these it would be my desire closely to follow in every work of faith, even as in this particular one. Now if there are no heresies at all, but what those who refute them are supposed to have fabricated, then the apostle who predicted them must have been guilty of falsehood. If, however, there are heresies, they can be no other than those which are the subject of discussion. No writer can be supposed to have so much time on his hands as to fabricate materials which are already in his possession.

Chap. VI.—Although writing in Latin he proposes to retain the Greek names of the Valentinian emanations of deity. Not to discuss the heresy but only to expose it. This with the raillery which its absurdity merits.

In order then, that no one may be blinded by so many outlandish names, collected together, and adjusted at pleasure, and of doubtful import, I mean in this little work, wherein we merely undertake to propound this (heretical) mystery, to explain in what manner we are to use them. Now the rendering of some of these *names* from the Greek as to produce an equally obvious sense of the word, is by no means an easy process: in the case of some others, the genders are not suitable; while others, again, are more familiarly known in their Greek form. For the most part, therefore, we shall use the Greek names; their meanings will be seen on the margins of the pages. Nor will the Greek be unaccompanied with the Latin *equivalents;* only these will be marked in lines above, for the purpose of explaining the personal names, rendered necessary by the ambiguities of such of them as admit some different meaning. But although I must postpone all discussion, and be content at present with the mere exposition (of the heresy), still, wherever any scandalous feature shall seem to require a castigation, it must be attacked by all means, if only with a passing thrust. Let the reader regard it as the skirmish before the battle. It will be my drift to show how to wound rather than to inflict deep gashes. If in any instance mirth be excited, this will be quite as much as the subject deserves. There are many things which deserve refutation in such a way as to have no gravity expended on them. Vain and silly topics are met with especial fitness by laughter. Even the truth may indulge in ridicule, because it is jubilant; it may play with its enemies, because it is fearless. Only we must take care that its laughter be not unseemly, and so itself be laughed at; but wherever its mirth is decent, there it is a duty *to indulge it.* And so at last I enter on my task.

CHAP. VII.—THE FIRST EIGHT EMANATIONS, OR AEONS, CALLED THE OGDOAD, ARE THE FOUNTAIN OF ALL THE OTHERS. THEIR NAMES AND DESCENT RECORDED.

Beginning with Ennius, the Roman poet, he simply spoke of "the spacious saloons of heaven,"—either on account of their elevated site, or because in Homer he had read about Jupiter banqueting therein. As for *our* heretics, however, it is marvellous what storeys upon storeys and what heights upon heights, they have hung up, raised *and* spread out as a dwelling for each several god of theirs. Even our Creator has had arranged for Him the saloons of Ennius in the fashion of private rooms, with chamber piled upon chamber, and assigned to each god by just as many staircases as there were heresies. The universe, *in fact,* has been turned into "rooms to let." Such storeys of the heavens you would imagine to be detached tenements in some happy isle of the blessed, I know not where. There the god even of the Valentinians has his dwelling in the attics. They call him indeed, as to his essence, $Αἰὼν\ τέλειος$ (*Perfect Aeon*), but in respect of his personality, $Προαρχή$ (*Before the Beginning*), $Ἡ\ Ἀρχή$ (*The Beginning*), and sometimes Bythos *(Depth),* a name which is most unfit for one who dwells in the heights above! They describe him as unbegotten, immense, infinite, invisible, and eternal; as if, when they described him to be such as we know that he ought to be, they straightway prove him to be a being who may be said to have had such an existence even before all things else. I indeed insist upon it that he is such a being; and there is nothing which I detect in beings of this sort more obvious, than that they who are said to have been before all things—things, too, not their own—are found to be behind all things. Let it, however, be granted that this Bythos of theirs existed in the infinite ages of the past in the greatest and profoundest repose, in the extreme rest of a placid and, if I may use the expression, stupid divinity, such as Epicurus has enjoined upon us. And yet, although they would have him be alone, they assign to him a second person in himself and with himself, Ennoea *(Thought)*, which they also call both Charis *(Grace)* and Sige *(Silence)*. Other things, as it happened, conduced in this most agreeable repose to remind him of the need of by and by producing out of himself the beginning of all things. This he deposits in lieu of seed in the genital region, as it were, of the womb of his Sige. Instantaneous conception is the result: Sige becomes pregnant, and is delivered, of course in silence; and her offspring is Nus *(Mind),* very like his father and his equal in every respect. In short, he alone is capable of comprehending the measureless and incomprehensible greatness of his father. Accordingly he is even called the Father himself, and the Beginning of all things, and, with great propriety, Monogenes (*The Only-begotten*). And yet not with absolute propriety, since he is not born alone. For along with him a female also proceeded, whose name was Veritas (*Truth*). But how much more suitably might Monogenes be called Protogenes (*First begotten*), since he was begotten first! Thus Bythos and Sige, Nus and Veritas, are alleged to be the first fourfold team of the Valentinian set (of gods), the parent stock and origin of them all. For immediately when Nus received the function of a procreation of his own, he too produces out of himself Sermo (*the Word*) and Vita (*the Life*). If this latter existed not previously, of course she existed not in Bythos. And a pretty absurdity would it be, if *Life* existed not in God! However, this offspring also produces fruit, having for its mission the initiation of the universe and the formation of the entire Pleroma: it procreates Homo (*Man*) and Ecclesia (*the Church*). Thus you have an

Ogdoad, a double Tetra, out of the conjunctions of males and females—the cells (so to speak) of the primordial Aeons, the fraternal nuptials of the Valentinian gods, the simple originals of heretical sanctity and majesty, a rabble—shall I say of criminals or of deities?—at any rate, the fountain of all ulterior fecundity.

CHAP. VIII.—THE NAMES AND DESCENT OF OTHER AEONS; FIRST HALF A SCORE, THEN TWO MORE, AND ULTIMATELY A DOZEN BESIDES. THESE THIRTY CONSTITUTE THE PLEROMA. BUT WHY BE SO CAPRICIOUS AS TO STOP AT THIRTY?

For, behold, when the second Tetrad—Sermo and Vita, Homo and Ecclesia—had borne fruit to the Father's glory, having an intense desire of themselves to present to the Father something similar of their own, they bring other issue into being—conjugal of course, as the others were—by the union of the twofold nature. On the one hand, Sermo and Vita pour out at a birth a half-score of Aeons; on the other hand, Homo and Ecclesia produce a couple more, so furnishing an equipoise to their parents, since this pair with the other ten make up just as many as they did themselves procreate. I now give the names of the half-score whom I have mentioned: Bythios (*Profound*) and Mixis (*Mixture*), Ageratos (*Never old*) and Henosis (*Union*), Autophyes (*Essential nature*) and Hedone (*Pleasure*), Acinetos (*Immoveable*) and Syncrasis (*Commixture*), Monogenes (*Only-begotten*) and Macaria (*Happiness*). On the other hand, these will make up the number twelve (to which I have also referred): Paracletus (*Comforter*) and Pistis (*Faith*), Patricas (*Paternal*) and Elpis (*Hope*), Metricos (*Maternal*) and Agape (*Love*), Ainos (*Praise*) and Synesis (*Intelligence*), Ecclesiasticus (*Son of Ecclesia*) and Macariotes (*Blessedness*), Theletus (*Perfect*) and Sophia (*Wisdom*). I cannot help here quoting from a like example what may serve to show the import of these names. In the schools of Carthage there was once a certain Latin rhetorician, an excessively cool fellow, whose name was Phosphorus. He was personating a man of valour, and wound up with saying, "I come to you, excellent citizens, from battle, with victory for myself, with happiness for you, full of honour, covered with glory, the favourite of fortune, the greatest of men, decked with triumph." And forthwith his scholars begin to shout for the school of Phosphorus, φεῦ (*ah!*) Are you a believer in Fortunata, and Hedone, and Acinetus, and Theletus? Then shout out your φεῦ for the school of Ptolemy. This must be that mystery of the Pleroma, the fulness of the thirty-fold divinity. Let us see what special attributes belong to these numbers—four, and eight, and twelve. Meanwhile with the number thirty all fecundity ceases. The generating force and power and desire of the AEons is spent. As if there were not still left some strong rennet for curdling numbers. As if no other names were to be got out of the page's hall! For why are there not sets of fifty and of a hundred procreated? Why, too, are there no comrades and boon companions named *for them?*

CHAP. IX.—OTHER CAPRICIOUS FEATURES IN THE SYSTEM. THE AEONS UNEQUAL IN ATTRIBUTES. THE SUPERIORITY OF NUS; THE VAGARIES OF SOPHIA RESTRAINED BY HOROS. GRAND TITLES BORNE BY THIS LAST POWER.

But, further, there is an "acceptance of persons," inasmuch as Nus alone among them all enjoys the knowledge of the immeasurable Father, joyous and exulting, while they of course pine in sorrow. To be sure, Nus, so far as in him lay, both wished and tried to impart to the others also all that he had learnt about the greatness and incomprehensibility of the Father; but his mother, Sige, interposed—she who (you must know) imposes silence even on her own beloved heretics; although they affirm that this is done at the will of the Father, who will have all to be inflamed with a longing after himself. Thus, while they are tormenting themselves with these internal desires, while they are burning with the secret longing to know the Father, the crime is almost accomplished. For of the twelve Aeons which Homo and Ecclesia had produced, the youngest by birth (never mind the solecism, since Sophia *(Wisdom)* is her name), unable to restrain herself, breaks away without the society of her husband Theletus, in quest of the Father and contracts that kind of sin which had indeed arisen amongst the others who were conversant with Nus but had flowed on to this *Aeon,* that is, to Sophia; as is usual with maladies which, after arising in one part of the body, spread abroad their infection to some other limb. The fact is, under a pretence of love to the Father, she was overcome with a desire to rival Nus, who alone rejoiced in the knowledge of the Father. But when Sophia, straining after impossible aims, was disappointed of her hope, she is both overcome with difficulty, and racked with affection. *Thus* she was all but swallowed up by reason of the charm and toil (of her research), and dissolved into the remnant of *his* substance; nor would there have been any other alternative for her than perdition, if she had not by good luck fallen in with Horos *(Limit).* He too had considerable power. He is the foundation of the great universe, and externally, the guardian thereof. To him they give the additional names of Crux *(Cross),* and Lytrotes *(Redeemer,)* and Carpistes *(Emancipator).* When Sophia was thus rescued from danger, and tardily persuaded, she relinquished further research after the Father, found repose, and laid aside all her excitement, *or* Enthymesis *(Desire),* along with the passion which had come over her.

CHAP. X.—ANOTHER ACCOUNT OF THE STRANGE ABERRATIONS OF SOPHIA, AND THE RESTRAINING SERVICES OF HOROS. SOPHIA WAS NOT HERSELF, AFTER ALL, EJECTED FROM THE PLEROMA, BUT ONLY HER ENTHYMESIS.

But some dreamers have given another account of the aberration and recovery of Sophia. After her vain endeavours, and the disappointment of her hope, she was, I suppose, disfigured with paleness and emaciation, and that neglect of her beauty which was natural to one who was deploring the denial of the Father,—an affliction which was no less painful than his loss. Then, in the midst of all this sorrow, she by herself alone, without any conjugal help, conceived and bare a female offspring. Does this excite your surprise? Well, even the hen has the power of being able to bring forth by her own energy. They say, too, that among vultures there are only females, which become parents alone. At any rate, she was another without aid from a male, and she began at last to be afraid that her end was even at hand. She was all in doubt about the treatment of her case, and took pains at self-concealment. Remedies *could* nowhere *be found.* For where, then, should we have tragedies and comedies, from which to borrow the process of exposing what has been born without connubial modesty? While the thing is in this evil plight, she raises her eyes, and turns them to the Father. Having, however, striven in vain, as her strength was failing her, she falls to praying. Her entire kindred also supplicates in her behalf, and especially Nus. Why not? What was the cause of so vast an evil? Yet not a single casualty befell Sophia without its effect. All her sorrows operate. Inasmuch as all that conflict of hers contributes to the origin of Matter. *Her* ignorance, *her* fear, *her* distress, become substances. Hereupon the Father by and by, being moved, produces in his own image, with a view to these *circumstances* the Horos whom we have mentioned above; (and this he does) by means of Monogenes Nus, a male-female (Aeon), because there is this variation of statement about the Father's sex. They also go on to tell us that Horos is likewise called Metagogius, that is, "a conductor about," as well as Horothetes (*Setter of Limits*). By his assistance they declare that Sophia was checked in her illicit courses, and purified from all evils, and henceforth strengthened (in virtue), and restored to the conjugal state: (they add) that she indeed remained within the bounds of the Pleroma, but that her Enthymesis, with the accruing Passion, was banished by Horos, and crucified and cast out from the Pleroma,—even as they say, *Malum foras!* (Evil, avaunt!) Still, that was a spiritual essence, as being the natural impulse of an Aeon, although without form or shape, inasmuch as it had apprehended nothing, and therefore was pronounced to be an infirm and feminine fruit.

TEXT 29

Perpetua: The Martyrdom of Saints Perpetua and Felicitas[1]

The rich corpus of early Christian texts on martyrdom, referred to as acta martyrum, *represents a form of heroic literature, which scholars have attempted to classify according to whether the narrative represents the circumstance of actual historical personalities as opposed to fictional accounts. Herbert Musurillo has pointed out, in* The Acts of the Christian Martyrs, *that most such compositions, whether factual or fictional, follow a proscribed form:*

> In all, there is a tense dramatic movement sharpened by the brooding air of inevitability: the reader knows that there will be no quarter, no surrender. Foremost, of course, is the portrayal of the martyrs' courage in the face of the most vicious torture and humiliation, a courage shared by both sexes, by both slave and free. . . . The constant counterpoint to this theme is the often well-meant attempts of the Roman officials to weaken the martyrs' resolve, and the witty or macabre comments either of judges or of the crowd, which reflect a worldly wisdom which the Christians do not share. To these the martyrs reply with a loving charity which embraces even those who persecute them, but sometimes with a boldness which forces even the pagans to admiration.[2]

The apocalyptic account of Perpetua and Felicitas, which was written in Latin, narrates the circumstances of the trial and sufferings of two young African women who became Christian martyrs during the latter half of the second century A.D. *The 22-year-old Vibia Perpetua came from an aristocratic family residing in Thuburbo, a*

---

[1]Herbert Musurillo, *The Acts of the Christian Martyrs* (London: Oxford University Press, 1972), p. liii. This English translation derives from the Latin version of a manuscript that has also been found in Greek, C. J. M. J. van Beek, *Passi sanctarum Perpetuae et Felicitatis.*
[2]Musurillo, *The Acts of the Christian Martyrs,* pp. 182–95.

town in what is now the country of Tunisia. Felicitas was her personal slave-girl, who was pregnant at the time of their arrest.

THE MARTYRDOM OF SAINTS PERPETUA AND FELICITAS

1. The deeds recounted about the faith in ancient times were a proof of God's favour and achieved the spiritual strengthening of men as well; and they were set forth in writing precisely that honour might be rendered to God and comfort to men by the recollection of the past through the written word. Should not then more recent examples be set down that contribute equally to both ends? For indeed these too will one day become ancient and needful for the ages to come, even though in our own day they may enjoy less prestige because of the prior claim of antiquity.

Let those then who would restrict the power of the one Spirit to times and seasons look to this: the more recent events should be considered the greater, being later than those of old, and this is a consequence of the extraordinary graces promised for the last stage of time. For *in the last days, God declares, I will pour out my Spirit upon all flesh and their sons and daughters shall prophesy and on my manservants and my maidservants I will pour my Spirit, and the young men shall see visions and the old men shall dream dreams.* So too we hold in honour and acknowledge not only new prophecies but new visions as well, according to the promise. And we consider all the other functions of the Holy Spirit as intended for the good of the Church; for the same Spirit has been sent to distribute all his gifts to all, as the Lord apportions to everyone. For this reason we deem it imperative to set them forth and to make them known through the word for the glory of God. Thus no one of weak or despairing faith may think that supernatural grace was present only among men of ancient times, either in the grace of martyrdom or of visions, for God always achieves what he promises, as a witness to the non-believer and a blessing to the faithful.

And so, my brethren and little children, *that which we have heard and have touched with our hands we proclaim also to you, so that* those of *you that were witnesses may recall the glory of the Lord and those that now learn of it through hearing may have fellowship* with the holy martyrs and, through them, *with* the Lord *Christ Jesus,* to whom belong splendour and honour for all ages. Amen.

2. A number of young catechumens were arrested, Revocatus and his fellow slave Felicitas, Saturninus and Secundulus, and with them Vibia Perpetua, a newly married woman of good family and upbringing. Her mother and father were still alive and one

---

Source: From Herbert Musurillo, *The Acts of the Christian Martyrs,* © 1972. Reprinted by permission of Oxford University Press.

of her two brothers was a catechumen like herself. She was about twenty-two years old and had an infant son at the breast. (Now from this point on the entire account of her ordeal is her own, according to her own ideas and in the way that she herself wrote it down.)

3. While we were still under arrest (she said) my father out of love for me was trying to persuade me and shake my resolution. 'Father,' said I, 'do you see this vase here, for example, or waterpot or whatever?'

'Yes, I do,' said he.

And I told him: 'Could it be called by any other name than what it is?'

And he said: 'No.'

'Well, so too I cannot be called anything other than what I am, a Christian.'

At this my father was so angered by the word 'Christian' that he moved towards me as though he would pluck my eyes out. But he left it at that and departed, vanquished along with his diabolical arguments.

For a few days afterwards I gave thanks to the Lord that I was separated from my father, and I was comforted by his absence. During these few days I was baptized, and I was inspired by the Spirit not to ask for any other favour after the water but simply the perseverance of the flesh. A few days later we were lodged in the prison; and I was terrified, as I had never before been in such a dark hole. What a difficult time it was! With the crowd the heat was stifling; then there was the extortion of the soldiers; and to crown all, I was tortured with worry for my baby there.

Then Tertius and Pomponius, those blessed deacons who tried to take care of us, bribed the soldiers to allow us to go to a better part of the prison to refresh ourselves for a few hours. Everyone then left that dungeon and shifted for himself. I nursed my baby, who was faint from hunger. In my anxiety I spoke to my mother about the child, I tried to comfort my brother, and I gave the child in their charge. I was in pain because I saw them suffering out of pity for me. These were the trials I had to endure for many days. Then I got permission for my baby to stay with me in prison. At once I recovered my health, relieved as I was of my worry and anxiety over the child. My prison had suddenly become a palace, so that I wanted to be there rather than anywhere else.

4. Then my brother said to me: 'Dear sister, you are greatly privileged; surely you might ask for a vision to discover whether you are to be condemned or freed.'

Faithfully I promised that I would, for I knew that I could speak with the Lord, whose great blessings I had come to experience. And so I said: 'I shall tell you tomorrow.' Then I made my request and this was the vision I had.

I saw a ladder of tremendous height made of bronze, reaching all the way to the heavens, but it was so narrow that only one person could climb up at a time. To the sides of the ladder were attached all sorts of metal weapons: there were swords, spears, hooks, daggers, and spikes; so that if anyone tried to climb up carelessly or without paying attention, he would be mangled and his flesh would adhere to the weapons.

At the foot of the ladder lay a dragon of enormous size, and it would attack those who tried to climb up and try to terrify them from doing so. And Saturus was the first to go up, he who was later to give himself up of his own accord. He had been the builder of our strength, although he was not present when we were arrested. And he arrived at the top of the staircase and he looked back and said to me: 'Perpetua, I am waiting for you. But take care; do not let the dragon bite you.'

'He will not harm me,' I said, 'in the name of Christ Jesus.'

Slowly, as though he were afraid of me, the dragon stuck his head out from underneath the ladder. Then, using it as my first step, I trod on his head and went up.

Then I saw an immense garden, and in it a grey-haired man sat in shepherd's garb; tall he was, and milking sheep. And standing around him were many thousands of people clad in white garments. He raised his head, looked at me, and said: 'I am glad you have come, my child.'

He called me over to him and gave me, as it were, a mouthful of the milk he was drawing; and I took it into my cupped hands and consumed it. And all those who stood around said: 'Amen!' At the sound of this word I came to, with the taste of something sweet still in my mouth. I at once told this to my brother, and we realized that we would have to suffer, and that from now on we would no longer have any hope in this life.

5. A few days later there was a rumour that we were going to be given a hearing. My father also arrived from the city, worn with worry, and he came to see me with the idea of persuading me.

'Daughter,' he said, 'have pity on my grey head—have pity on me your father, if I deserve to be called your father, if I have favoured you above all your brothers, if I have raised you to reach this prime of your life. Do not abandon me to be the reproach of men. Think of your brothers, think of your mother and your aunt, think of your child, who will not be able to live once you are gone. Give up your pride! You will destroy all of us! None of us will ever be able to speak freely again if anything happens to you.'

This was the way my father spoke out of love for me, kissing my hands and throwing himself down before me. With tears in his eyes he no longer addressed me as his daughter but as a woman. I was sorry for my father's sake, because he alone of all my kin would be unhappy to see me suffer.

I tried to comfort him saying: 'It will all happen in the prisoner's dock as God wills; for you may be sure that we are not left to ourselves but are all in his power.'

And he left me in great sorrow.

6. One day while we were eating breakfast we were suddenly hurried off for a hearing. We arrived at the forum, and straight away the story went about the neighbourhood near the forum and a huge crowd gathered. We walked up to the prisoner's dock. All the others when questioned admitted their guilt. Then, when it came my turn, my father appeared with my son, dragged me from the step, and said: 'Perform the sacrifice—have pity on your baby!'

Hilarianus the governor, who had received his judicial powers as the successor of the late proconsul Minucius Timinianus, said to me: 'Have pity on your father's grey head; have pity on your infant son. Offer the sacrifice for the welfare of the emperors.'

'I will not,' I retorted.

'Are you a Christian?' said Hilarianus.

And I said: 'Yes, I am.'

When my father persisted in trying to dissuade me, Hilarianus ordered him to be thrown to the ground and beaten with a rod. I felt sorry for father, just as if I myself had been beaten. I felt sorry for his pathetic old age.

Then Hilarianus passed sentence on all of us: we were condemned to the beasts, and we returned to prison in high spirits. But my baby had got used to being nursed at the breast and to staying with me in prison. So I sent the deacon Pomponius straight away to my father to ask for the baby. But father refused to give him over. But as God willed, the baby had no further desire for the breast, nor did I suffer any inflammation; and so I was relieved of any anxiety for my child and of any discomfort in my breasts.

7. Some days later when we were all at prayer, suddenly while praying I spoke out and uttered the name Dinocrates. I was surprised; for the name had never entered my mind until that moment. And I was pained when I recalled what had happened to him. At once I realized that I was privileged to pray for him. I began to pray for him and to sigh deeply for him before the Lord. That very night I had the following vision. I saw Dinocrates coming out of a dark hole, where there were many others with him, very hot and thirsty, pale and dirty. On his face was the wound he had when he died.

Now Dinocrates had been my brother according to the flesh; but he had died horribly of cancer of the face when he was seven years old, and his death was a source of loathing to everyone. Thus it was for him that I made my prayer. There was a great abyss between us: neither could approach the other. Where Dinocrates stood there was a pool full of water; and its rim was higher than the child's height, so that Dinocrates had to stretch himself up to drink. I was sorry that, though the pool had water in it, Dinocrates could not drink because of the height of the rim. Then I woke up, realizing that my brother was suffering. But I was confident that I could help him in his trouble; and I prayed for him every day until we were transferred to the military prison. For we were supposed to fight with the beasts at the military games to be held on the occasion of the emperor Geta's birthday. And I prayed for my brother day and night with tears and sighs that this favour might be granted me.

8. On the day we were kept in chains, I had this vision shown to me. I saw the same spot that I had seen before, but there was Dinocrates all clean, well dressed, and refreshed. I saw a scar where the wound had been; and the pool that I had seen before now had its rim lowered to the level of the child's waist. And Dinocrates kept drinking water from it, and there above the rim was a golden bowl full of water. And Dinocrates drew close and began to drink from it, and yet the bowl remained full. And when he had drunk enough of the water, he began to play as children do. Then I awoke, and I realized that he had been delivered from his suffering.

9. Some days later, an adjutant named Pudens, who was in charge of the prison, began to show us great honour, realizing that we possessed some great power within us. And he began to allow many visitors to see us for our mutual comfort.

Now the day of the contest was approaching, and my father came to see me overwhelmed with sorrow. He started tearing the hairs from his beard and threw them on the ground; he then threw himself on the ground and began to curse his old age and to say such words as would move all creation. I felt sorry for his unhappy old age.

10. The day before we were to fight with the beasts I saw the following vision. Pomponius the deacon came to the prison gates and began to knock violently. I went

out and opened the gate for him. He was dressed in an unbelted white tunic, wearing elaborate sandals. And he said to me: 'Perpetua, come; we are waiting for you.'

Then he took my hand and we began to walk through rough and broken country. At last we came to the amphitheatre out of breath, and he led me into the centre of the arena.

Then he told me: 'Do not be afraid. I am here, struggling with you.' Then he left.

I looked at the enormous crowd who watched in astonishment. I was surprised that no beasts were let loose on me; for I knew that I was condemned to die by the beasts. Then out came an Egyptian against me, of vicious appearance, together with his seconds, to fight with me. There also came up to me some handsome young men to be my seconds and assistants.

My clothes were stripped off, and suddenly I was a man. My seconds began to rub me down with oil (as they are wont to do before a contest). Then I saw the Egyptian on the other side rolling in the dust. Next there came forth a man of marvellous stature, such that he rose above the top of the amphitheatre. He was clad in a beltless purple tunic with two stripes (one on either side) running down the middle of his chest. He wore sandals that were wondrously made of gold and silver, and he carried a wand like an athletic trainer and a green branch on which there were golden apples.

And he asked for silence and said: 'If this Egyptian defeats her he will slay her with the sword. But if she defeats him, she will receive this branch.' Then he withdrew.

We drew close to one another and began to let our fists fly. My opponent tried to get hold of my feet, but I kept striking him in the face with the heels of my feet. Then I was raised up into the air and I began to pummel him without as it were touching the ground. Then when I noticed there was a lull, I put my two hands together linking the fingers of one hand with those of the other and thus I got hold of his head. He fell flat on his face and I stepped on his head.

The crowd began to shout and my assistants started to sing psalms. Then I walked up to the trainer and took the branch. He kissed me and said to me: 'Peace be with you, my daughter!' I began to walk in triumph towards the Gate of Life. Then I awoke. I realized that it was not with wild animals that I would fight but with the Devil, but I knew that I would win the victory. So much for what I did up until the eve of the contest. About what happened at the contest itself, let him write of it who will.

11. But the blessed Saturus has also made known his own vision and he has written it out with his own hand. We had died, he said, and had put off the flesh, and we began to be carried towards the east by four angels who did not touch us with their hands. But we moved along not on our backs facing upwards but as though we were climbing up a gentle hill. And when we were free of the world, we first saw an intense light. And I said to Perpetua (for she was at my side): 'This is what the Lord promised us. We have received his promise.'

While we were being carried by these four angels, a great open space appeared, which seemed to be a garden, with rose bushes and all manner of flowers. The trees were as tall as cypresses, and their leaves were constantly falling. In the garden there were four other angels more splendid than the others. When they saw us they paid us homage and said to the other angels in admiration: 'Why, they are here! They are here!'

Then the four angels that were carrying us grew fearful and set us down. Then we walked across to an open area by way of a broad road, and there we met Jucundus, Saturninus, and Artaxius, who were burnt alive in the same persecution, together with Quintus who had actually died as a martyr in prison. We asked them where they had been. And the other angels said to us: 'First come and enter and greet the Lord.'

12. Then we came to a place whose walls seemed to be constructed of light. And in front of the gate stood four angels, who entered in and put on white robes. We also entered and we heard the sound of voices in unison chanting endlessly: *'Holy, holy, holy!'* In the same place we seemed to see an aged man with white hair and a youthful face, though we did not see his feet. On his right and left were four elders, and behind them stood other aged men. Surprised, we entered and stood before a throne: four angels lifted us up and we kissed the aged man and he touched our faces with his hand. And the elders said to us: 'Let us rise.' And we rose and gave the kiss of peace. Then the elders said to us: 'Go and play.'

To Perpetua I said: 'Your wish is granted.'

She said to me: 'Thanks be to God that I am happier here now than I was in the flesh.'

13. Then we went out and before the gates we saw the bishop Optatus on the right and Aspasius the presbyter and teacher on the left, each of them far apart and in sorrow. They threw themselves at our feet and said: 'Make peace between us. For you have gone away and left us thus.'

And we said to them: 'Are you not our bishop, and are you not our presbyter? How can you fall at our feet?'

We were very moved and embraced them. Perpetua then began to speak with them in Greek, and we drew them apart into the garden under a rose arbour.

While we were talking with them, the angels said to them: 'Allow them to rest. Settle whatever quarrels you have among yourselves.' And they were put to confusion.

Then they said to Optatus: 'You must scold your flock. They approach you as though they had come from the games, quarrelling about the different teams.'

And it seemed as though they wanted to close the gates. And there we began to recognise many of our brethren, martyrs among them. All of us were sustained by a most delicious odour that seemed to satisfy us. And then I woke up happy.

14. Such were the remarkable visions of these martyrs, Saturus and Perpetua, written by themselves. As for Secundulus, God called him from this world earlier than the others while he was still in prison, by a special grace that he might not have to face the animals. Yet his flesh, if not his spirit, knew the sword.

15. As for Felicitas, she too enjoyed the Lord's favour in this wise. She had been pregnant when she was arrested, and was now in her eighth month. As the day of the spectacle drew near she was very distressed that her martyrdom would be postponed because of her pregnancy; for it is against the law for women with child to be executed. Thus she might have to shed her holy, innocent blood afterwards along with others who were common criminals. Her comrades in martyrdom were also saddened; for they were afraid that they would have to leave behind so fine a companion to travel alone on the same road to hope. And so, two days before the contest, they poured forth a prayer to the Lord in one torrent of common grief. And immediately after their

prayer the birth pains came upon her. She suffered a good deal in her labour because of the natural difficulty of an eight months' delivery.

Hence one of the assistants of the prison guards said to her: 'You suffer so much now—what will you do when you are tossed to the beasts? Little did you think of them when you refused to sacrifice.'

'What I am suffering now,' she replied, 'I suffer by myself. But then another will be inside me who will suffer for me, just as I shall be suffering for him.'

And she gave birth to a girl; and one of the sisters brought her up as her own daughter.

16. Therefore, since the Holy Spirit has permitted the story of this contest to be written down and by so permitting has willed it, we shall carry out the command or, indeed, the commission of the most saintly Perpetua, however unworthy I might be to add anything to this glorious story. At the same time I shall add one example of her perseverance and nobility of soul.

The military tribune had treated them with extraordinary severity because on the information of certain very foolish people he became afraid that they would be spirited out of the prison by magical spells.

Perpetua spoke to him directly. 'Why can you not even allow us to refresh ourselves properly? For we are the most distinguished of the condemned prisoners, seeing that we belong to the emperor; we are to fight on his very birthday. Would it not be to your credit if we were brought forth on the day in a healthier condition?'

The officer became disturbed and grew red. So it was that he gave the order that they were to be more humanely treated; and he allowed her brothers and other persons to visit, so that the prisoners could dine in their company. By this time the adjutant who was head of the gaol was himself a Christian.

17. On the day before, when they had their last meal, which is called the free banquet, they celebrated not a banquet but rather a love feast. They spoke to the mob with the same steadfastness, warned them of God's judgement, stressing the joy they would have in their suffering, and ridiculing the curiosity of those that came to see them. Saturus said: 'Will not tomorrow be enough for you? Why are you so eager to see something that you dislike? Our friends today will be our enemies on the morrow. But take careful note of what we look like so that you will recognise us on the day.' Thus everyone would depart from the prison in amazement, and many of them began to believe.

18. The day of their victory dawned, and they marched from the prison to the amphitheatre joyfully as though they were going to heaven, with calm faces, trembling, if at all, with joy rather than fear. Perpetua went along with shining countenance and calm step, as the beloved of God, as a wife of Christ, putting down everyone's stare by her own intense gaze. With them also was Felicitas, glad that she had safely given birth so that now she could fight the beasts, going from one blood bath to another, from the midwife to the gladiator, ready to wash after childbirth in a second baptism.

They were then led up to the gates and the men were forced to put on the robes of priests of Saturn, the women the dress of the priestesses of Ceres. But the noble Perpetua strenuously resisted this to the end.

'We came to this of our own free will, that our freedom should not be violated. We agreed to pledge our lives provided that we would do no such thing. You agreed with us to do this.'

Even injustice recognised justice. The military tribune agreed. They were to be brought into the arena just as they were. Perpetua then began to sing a psalm: she was already treading on the head of the Egyptian. Revocatus, Saturninus, and Saturus began to warn the onlooking mob. Then when they came within sight of Hilarianus, they suggested by their motions and gestures: 'You have condemned us, but God will condemn you' was what they were saying.

At this the crowds became enraged and demanded that they be scourged before a line of gladiators. And they rejoiced at this that they had obtained a share in the Lord's sufferings.

19. But he who said, *Ask and you shall receive,* answered their prayer by giving each one the death he had asked for. For whenever they would discuss among themselves their desire for martyrdom, Saturninus indeed insisted that he wanted to be exposed to all the different beasts, that his crown might be all the more glorious. And so at the outset of the contest he and Revocatus were matched with a leopard, and then while in the stocks they were attacked by a bear. As for Saturus, he dreaded nothing more than a bear, and he counted on being killed by one bite of a leopard. Then he was matched with a wild boar; but the gladiator who had tied him to the animal was gored by the boar and died a few days after the contest, whereas Saturus was only dragged along. Then when he was bound in the stocks awaiting the bear, the animal refused to come out of the cages, so that Saturus was called back once more unhurt.

20. For the young women, however, the Devil had prepared a mad heifer. This was an unusual animal, but it was chosen that their sex might be matched with that of the beast. So they were stripped naked, placed in nets and thus brought out into the arena. Even the crowd was horrified when they saw that one was a delicate young girl and the other was a woman fresh from childbirth with the milk still dripping from her breasts. And so they were brought back again and dressed in unbelted tunics.

First the heifer tossed Perpetua and she fell on her back. Then sitting up she pulled down the tunic that was ripped along the side so that it covered her thighs, thinking more of her modesty than of her pain. Next she asked for a pin to fasten her untidy hair: for it was not right that a martyr should die with her hair in disorder, lest she might seem to be mourning in her hour of triumph.

Then she got up. And seeing that Felicitas had been crushed to the ground, she went over to her, gave her her hand, and lifted her up. Then the two stood side by side. But the cruelty of the mob was by now appeased, and so they were called back through the Gate of Life.

There Perpetua was held up by a man named Rusticus who was at the time a catechumen and kept close to her. She awoke from a kind of sleep (so absorbed had she been in ecstasy in the Spirit) and she began to look about her. Then to the amazement of all she said: 'When are we going to be thrown to that heifer or whatever it is?'

When told that this had already happened, she refused to believe it until she noticed the marks of her rough experience on her person and her dress. Then she called for her brother and spoke to him together with the catechumens and said: 'You must all *stand fast in the faith* and love one another, and do not be weakened by what we have gone through.'

21. At another gate Saturus was earnestly addressing the soldier Pudens. 'It is exactly,' he said, 'as I foretold and predicted. So far not one animal has touched me. So

now you may believe me with all your heart: I am going in there and I shall be finished off with one bite of the leopard.' And immediately as the contest was coming to a close a leopard was let loose, and after one bite Saturus was so drenched with blood that as he came away the mob roared in witness to his second baptism: 'Well washed! Well washed!' For well washed indeed was one who had been bathed in this manner.

Then he said to the soldier Pudens: 'Good-bye. Remember me, and remember the faith. These things should not disturb you but rather strengthen you.'

And with this he asked Pudens for a ring from his finger, and dipping it into his wound he gave it back to him again as a pledge and as a record of his bloodshed.

Shortly after he was thrown unconscious with the rest in the usual spot to have his throat cut. But the mob asked that their bodies be brought out into the open that their eyes might be the guilty witnesses of the sword that pierced their flesh. And so the martyrs got up and went to the spot of their own accord as the people wanted them to, and kissing one another they sealed their martyrdom with the ritual kiss of peace. The others took the sword in silence and without moving, especially Saturus, who being the first to climb the stairway was the first to die. For once again he was waiting for Perpetua. Perpetua, however, had yet to taste more pain. She screamed as she was struck on the bone; then she took the trembling hand of the young gladiator and guided it to her throat. It was as though so great a woman, feared as she was by the unclean spirit, could not be dispatched unless she herself were willing.

Ah, most valiant and blessed martyrs! Truly are you called and chosen for the glory of Christ Jesus our Lord! And any man who exalts, honours, and worships his glory should read for the consolation of the Church these new deeds of heroism which are no less significant than the tales of old. For these new manifestations of virtue will bear witness to one and the same Spirit who still operates, and to God the Father almighty, to his Son Jesus Christ our Lord, to whom is splendour and immeasurable power for all the ages. Amen.

TEXT 30

Cyprian: Heretical Baptism—The Issue between Rome and Africa[1]

Born of a wealthy pagan family, Caecilius Cyprianius (A.D. c. 200–258) had been a successful lawyer before converting to Christianity at the age of 46. Three years later so dynamic had his presence become in the church that Cyprian was appointed bishop of Carthage. He died a martyr during the Valerian persecution of A.D. 258–259 but not before exercising a profound influence on the early church.

One of the central issues of Cyprian's time and place was a controversy that erupted around the practice of rebaptism within the African church. Cahal B. Daly in his book Tertullian: The Puritan and His Influence elucidates the distinctive theological practices, which pitted African Christians against their Roman counterparts during this formative period:

> The appellation African was appropriate for a doctrine which united in its support Africans of every theological allegiance, orthodox and heterodox, Africans bitterly opposed to one another on other questions of doctrine. The Catholic bishop, Agrippinus, second occupant of the see of Carthage, the rebellious Catholic priest, Tertullian . . . the primate Cyprian, with his colleagues, pillars of orthodoxy, champions of Catholic unity, and the heretical Novatianists and Donatists, all shared the common conviction of Africa that the baptism of heretics is invalid and inefficacious and must be repeated.[2]

---

[1]Henry Bettenson, *The Early Christian Fathers: A Selection from the Writings of the Fathers from St. Clement of Rome to St. Athanasius* (New York: Oxford University Press, 1956), pp. 372–75.
[2]Cahal B. Daly, *Tertullian: The Puritan and His Influence* (Dublin: Four Courts Press, 1993), p. 41.

It was in an effort to respond to the questions surrounding African rebaptism that Cyprian wrote the treatise On the Unity of the Catholic Church *in Latin. On August 30, 257, Cyprian was summoned before the Roman proconsul in Carthage during a purge of Christians, tried, and condemned to death.*

(e) Heretical Baptism: The Issue between Rome and Africa

This decision on the baptism of those who join the Church from heresy is no new or sudden departure. A long time has passed since Agrippinus, of honoured memory, presided over a meeting of a large number of bishops, which came to this decision. From that time to this many thousands of heretics in our provinces who have been converted to the Church have not scorned or hesitated to attain the grace of the lifegiving bath and of saving baptism; rather they have embraced the opportunity rationally and gladly. . . .

(4) In a letter, of which you sent me a copy, I find it clearly stated that 'no enquiry is to be made about the minister of baptism, since the baptized may have received remission of sin in virtue of his own faith.' This is a topic which, I feel, must not be passed over: especially as in the same letter I noted a mention of Marcion, with the instruction that not even those who come into the Church from his heresy should be baptized in the name of Jesus Christ. We must therefore examine the faith of those who hold a belief outside the church, and consider whether they can obtain any grace in virtue of sharing the same faith . . .

(5) . . . The Lord instructed his disciples to baptize . . . 'In the name of the Father, and of the Son, and of the Holy Ghost . . . . Does Marcion hold this Trinity? . . . . How can one baptized among such heretics be considered as having obtained remission of sins and the grace of divine mercy through his faith, seeing that he has not the truth of the Faith itself?

I send you a copy of our brother Stephen's answer. When you read it you will be all the more cognizant of his error, for he tries to maintain the cause of heretics against Christians and the Church of God. For among arrogant claims, irrelevancies, and inconsistencies—he is an inexpert and careless writer—he goes so far as to add: 'If anyone comes to you from any heresy whatever, let there be no novel additions to the traditional procedure, namely the imposition of hands for repentance; since the heretics themselves do not baptize those who come to them from other sects, but merely admit them to communion'. . . . Thus he has judged the baptisms of all heretics to be valid and regular.

If any one objects that Novatian observes the same rule as the Catholic Church, and baptizes with the same creed as we do, acknowledges the same God the Father, the same Christ the Son, the same Holy Ghost, and therefore can lay claim to the power of baptizing, because he does not appear to differ from us in the baptismal interrogation—if anyone thinks this a valid objection, let him know in the first place that

Source: From Henry Bettenson, *The Early Christian Fathers: A Selection from the Writings of the Fathers from St. Clement of Rome to St. Athanasius,* © 1956. Reprinted by permission of Oxford University Press.

the schismatics have not one and the same rule of the creed as ours, nor the same interrogation. For when they ask, 'Dost thou believe in the remission of sins and eternal life through the holy Church?' there is a lie in their interrogation, seeing that they do not have the Church. Moreover, they admit, by their own words, that remission of sins can only be given through the holy Church; and since they do not have this they show that sins cannot be remitted among them.

(f) No Validity Outside the Church

Some of our colleagues, by a curious presumption, are led to suppose that those who have been dipped among the heretics ought not to be baptized when they join us; because, they say, there is 'one baptism.' Yes, but that one baptism is in the Catholic Church. And if there is one Church, there can be no baptism outside it. There cannot be two baptisms: if heretics really baptize, then baptism belongs to them. And anyone who on his own authority concedes them this privilege admits, by yielding their claim, that the enemy and adversary of Christ should appear to possess the power of washing, purifying, sanctifying a man. Our assertion is that those who come to us from heresy are baptized by us, not *re*-baptized. They do not receive anything there; there is nothing there for them to receive. They come to us that they may receive here, where there is all grace and truth; for grace and truth are one.

The Church is one and indivisible: therefore there cannot be a Church among the heretics. The Holy Spirit is one, and cannot dwell with those outside the community; therefore the Holy Spirit has no place among heretics.

It follows that there can be no baptism among heretics; for baptism is based on this same unity and cannot be separated either from the Church or from the Holy Spirit.

(5) . . . It is ridiculous to assert that spiritual birth—that second birth of ours in Christ through the bath of regeneration—can take place among the heretics where, it is admitted, the Spirit has no place. Water cannot of itself purify and sanctify, unless it is accompanied by the Holy Spirit.

TEXT 31

Augustine: The Miseries of the Romans in the African Wars

from The City of God[1]

Aurelius Augustinus of Hippo (A.D. 354–430), known to posterity as Saint Augustine, has often been described as one of the most influential philosophers of the Christian world. He was born into a family of Romanized Berbers who resided in a small farming community named Thagaste, in what is today Souk Ahras, Algeria. Augustine's father, Patricius, remained a pagan throughout his life. His mother, Monica, on the other hand was a devoted Christian. As a young man, Augustine found himself drawn to Manichaeism rather than Christianity. Manichaeism represented a philosophic religion of dualistic materialism that described the world in terms of good and evil as they are reflected in the battle between light and dark substances. However, he grew disillusioned with that religion as the practitioners with whom he came into contact were unable to answer questions to his satisfaction. Augustine's conversion to Christianity was depicted in his autobiographical *Confessions,* a book written with such candor and emotional insight that in many ways it prefigures the modern genre of autobiographical writing.

His thinking also appeared to have been profoundly influenced by the Alexandrian philosopher Plotinus, whose Neoplatonic mysticism articulated the principle that our innermost spirit rather than our externalities links us to the divine. In the *Confessions* Augustine explains that through a mystical experience of introspection rather than a mere process of reasoning, he found God.

---

[1]John Healey, *The City of God by Saint Augustine* (London: J. M. Dent & Sons, 1909), book III, chapters XVIII–XX, pp. 139–45.

Professor Susan Raven notes in Rome in Africa:

The young Augustine was imaginative, shrewd and ardent. He was as African as Tertullian had been—as far removed from Roman gravitas *as he was from the cosmopolitan sophistication of Constantinople. . . . He was well aware—fifteen hundred years before Freud—of the existence of the subconscious.*[2]

Knowledge to Augustine, as to the Gnostics, Hermetists, and Neoplatonists, was internal and restrictive. "Augustine argued that the ability to make true judgments never can be inserted into the mind from outside. The human teacher never can do more than help his pupil to see for himself what he already knew without being aware of it."

When Augustine became bishop of Hippo, a small city in the Roman African province of Numidia (Algeria) at the age of 37, the Christian Church faced many challenges from competing sects. The Donatists were a sect of African Christians who had rebelled against the authority of the church leadership in Rome. Augustine, on the other hand, represented those Africans who believed that the Roman Church could encompass his universalist conception of the Christian faith. In waging a relentless battle against Donatism, Augustine succeeded in restoring the authority of the Roman Church. However, he then had to face what he must surely have seen as the mirror image of the Donatists, that is, the Pelagians. This Italian-based schism insisted on purifying Christianity of what it considered to be the contamination of African doctrines. By the spring of 418, Augustine and other African bishops were able to obtain from the Emperor Honorius an edict imposing banishment on the Pelagian heretics.

During the period of this latter controversy, Augustine wrote The City of God, a book which has had a seminal impact on the later development of Christianity. Written in Latin, it offered reflections on biblical scripture, philosophy, and paganism as a means of formulating an all-embracing Christian philosophy of history. This work was also directed at critics of Christianity who insisted that human prosperity can only be maintained through devotion to the traditional Roman pantheon of gods. It likewise attempted to refute the opinion of those who blamed Christianity and the prohibition against the worship of traditional gods for the disintegration of the Roman Empire and the barbarian invasions.[3] In fact, Augustine's lifetime witnessed the final disintegration of the Roman Empire, even to the extent where the Vandal armies were besieging Hippo when he died on August 28, A.D. 430.

CHAPTER XVIII

The miseries of the Romans in the African wars, and the small stead their gods stood them therein.

But now in the wars of Africa, victory still hovering doubtfully betwixt both sides, and two mighty and powerful nations using all their might and power to reciprocal ruin,

---

[2]Susan Raven, *Rome in Africa* (New York: Longman, 1984), p. 197.
[3]Healey, *The City of God by Saint Augustine*, pp. xiv–xv.
Source: Reprinted from John Healey, *The City of God,* © 1909, J. M. Dent & Sons.

how many petty kingdoms perished herein? How many fair cities were demolished, or afflicted, or utterly lost? How far did this disastrous contention spread, to the ruin of so many realms and great estates? How often were the conquerors on either side conquered? What store of men (armed and naked) was there that perished? How many ships were sunk at sea by fight and tempest? Should we particularise, we should become a direct historiographer. Then Rome being in these deep plunges, ran headlong under those vain and ridiculous remedies: for then were the secular plays renewed by the admonition of the Sybil's books: which institution had been ordained an hundred years before, but was now worn out of all memory, in those so happy times. The high priests also renewed the sacred plays to the hell-gods which the better times had in like manner abolished before: nor was it any wonder to see them now revenged, for the hell-gods desired now to become revellers, being enriched by this continual unceasing world of men: who (like wretches) in following those bloody and unrelenting wars, did nothing but act the devil's revels, and prepare banquets for the infernal spirits. Nor was there a more laudable accident in all this whole war, than that Regulus should be taken prisoner: a worthy man, and before that mishap a scourge to the Carthaginians: who had ended the African war long before, but that he would have bound the Carthaginians to stricter conditions than they could bear. The most sudden captivity, and the most faithful oath of this man, and his most cruel death, if the gods do not blush at, surely they are brazenfaced, and have no blood in them. Nay, for all this, Rome's walls stood not safe, but tasted of some mischief, and all those within them, for the river Tiber overflowing, drowned almost all the level parts of the city: turning some places as it were into torrents, and some others into fens or lakes: this plague ushered in a worse of fire, which beginning in the market-place, burned all the higher buildings thereabouts, sparing not the harbour and temple of Vesta, where it was so duly kept in, by those not so honourable as damnable votaresses. Now it did not only continue here burning but raging: with the fury whereof the virgins being amazed, Metellus, the high priest, ran into the fire, and was half burned in fetching out of those fatal reliques which had been the ruin of three cities, where they had been resident. The fire never spared him for all he was the priest. Or else the true deity was not there, but was fled before though the fire were there still: but here you see how a mortal man could do Vesta more good than she could do him: for if these gods could not guard themselves from the fire, how could they guard their city which they were thought to guard from burnings and inundations? Truly not a whit, as the thing showed itself: herein we would not object these calamities against the Romans, if they would affirm that all these their sacred observations only aim at eternity, and not at the goods of this transitory world; and that therefore when those corporal things perished, there was yet no loss by that, unto the ends for which they were ordained, because that they might soon be made fit for the same uses again. But now such is their miserable blindness, that they think that those idols that might have perished in this fiery extremity, had power to preserve the temporal happiness of the city: but now seeing that they remained unconsumed, and yet were able to show how such ruins of their safeties and such great mischiefs has befallen the city, this makes them ashamed to change that opinion which they see they cannot possibly defend.

CHAPTER XIX

Of the sad accidents that befel in the second African war, wherein the powers on both sides were wholly consumed.

But all too tedious were it to relate the slaughters of both nations in the second African war, they had so many fights both far and near, that by their own confessions who were rather Rome's commenders than true chroniclers, the conquerors were ever more like to the conquered than otherwise. For when Hannibal arose out of Spain, and broke over the Pyrenean hills, all France, and the very Alps, gathering huge powers, and doing horrible mischiefs in all this long track, rushing like an inundation into the face of Italy, oh what bloody fields were there pitched, what battles struck! How often did the Romans abandon the field, how many cities fell to the foe, how many were taken, how many were razed? What victories did that Hannibal win, and what glories did he build himself upon the ruined Romans. In vain should I speak of Cannæ's horrible overthrow, where Hannibal's own excessive thirst of blood was so fully glutted upon his foes, that he himself bade hold: whence he sent three bushels of rings unto Carthage, to show how huge a company had fallen at that fight, that they were easier to be measured than numbered: and hence might they conjecture, what a massacre there was of the meaner sort, that had no rings to wear, and that the poorer they were, the more of them perished. Finally, such a defect of soldiers followed this overthrow, that the Romans were fain to get malefactors to go to war for quittance of their guilt; to set all their slaves free, and out of this graceless crew, not to supply their defective regiments, but even to make up a whole army. Nay, these slaves (O let us not wrong them, they are freemen now) wanted even weapons to fight for Rome withal: that they were fain to fetch them out of the temples, as if they should say to their gods, Come, pray let these weapons go, you have kept them long enough to no end: we will see whether our bond-slaves can do more good for us with them, than you gods could yet do: and then the treasury failing, the private estate of each man became public, so that each one giving what he was able, their rings, nay their very bosses (the wretched marks of their dignities) being all bestowed, the Senate themselves (much more the other companies and tribes) left not themselves any money in the world: who could have endured the rages of those men, if they had been driven to this poverty in these our times? seeing we can very hardly endure them as the world goes now, although they have store now to bestow upon stage-players, which as then, they were full fain of, for their uttermost means of safety, to spend upon the soldiers?

CHAPTER XX

Of the ruin of the Saguntines, who perished for their confederacy with Rome; the Roman gods never helping them.

But in all the disasters of the second African war, there was none more lamentable than the dissolution of the Saguntines: these inhabiting in a city in Spain being sworn friends to the Romans, were destroyed for keeping their faith to them. For Hannibal, breaking the league with Rome, gave here the first occasion of war, engirting the city of Sanguntum with a cruel and strait siege: whereof the Romans having intelligence, sent an ambassage to wish Hannibal, to raise his siege: but the Legates being despised by him, went to Carthage, whence (having done nothing) they returned without any redress for the breach of the league, and in the meantime, this city (whilom so stately) was now brought to that misery, that about eight or nine months after the beginning of the siege, the Africans took it and razed it to the very ground. To read how it perished were a horror; much more to write it: yet I will run over it briefly, seeing it is very pertinent to the argument we prosecute. First, it was eaten down with famine: for some say it was driven to feed upon the carcasses which it harboured. And then being in this labyrinth of languors, yet rather than it would take in Hannibal as a conqueror, the citizens made a huge fire in the marketplace, and therein entombed all their parents, wives, children, and friends (after they had slain them first), and lastly themselves. Here now these gluttonous, treacherous, wasteful, cozening, dancing gods should have done somewhat: here they should have done somewhat to help these distressed faithful friends of the Romans, and to save them from perishing, for their loyalty's sake. They were called as witnesses between both when the league was made between Rome and these poor men; who keeping that faith which they had willingly passed, solemnly sworn, and sacredly observed, under their protections, were besieged, afflicted, and subverted by one that had broken all faith, all religion. If the gods with thunder and lightning could frighten Hannibal from Rome's walls, and make him keep aloof from them, they should first have practised this here: for I dare aver, that with far more honesty might they have helped the Romans' friends, being in extremes, for keeping their faith to them, and having then no means nor power, than they did, and the Romans themselves, that fought for themselves, and had very good forces and purses able to repel Hannibal's powers. If they had been careful guardians of Rome's glory, they would never have left it stained with the sufferance of this sad calamity of the Saguntines. But now how sottish is their belief that think these gods kept Rome from perishing by the hand of victorious Hannibal and the Carthaginians, that could not save Saguntum from perishing for keeping her faith sworn so solemnly to the Romans? If Saguntum had been Christian and had suffered such an extremity for the Gospel (though it ought not as then to have wracked itself by fire nor sword), yet had it endured such for the Gospel, it would have borne it stoutly, by reason of that hope which it would have held in Christ to have been after all crowned by Him with an eternal guerdon. But as for these false gods, that desire to be and are worshipped only for the assurance of this transitory term of our mortality, what can their attorneys, their orators, say for them in this ruin of the Saguntines, more than they said in that of Regulus? Only he was one man, this a whole city, but perseverance in faith was cause of both calamities. For this faith would he return to his foes, and for this would not they turn to their foes. Doth loyalty then grieve the gods? Or may ungrateful cities (as well as men) be destroyed, and yet stand in their gods' liking still? Let them choose whether they like: if the gods be angry at men's keeping of their faith, let them seek faithless wretches to serve them. But if they that serve them and have their favours, be nevertheless afflicted and spoiled; then to what end are they adored? Wherefore let them hold their tongues that think they lost their city because they lost their gods: for though they had them all, they might nevertheless not only complain of misery, but feel it at full, as Regulus and the Saguntines did.

TEXT 32

Corippus: The Royal Banquet

from In Praise of Justin[1]

F*lavius Cresconius Corippus had been a sixth century* A.D. *small-town teacher in Rome's African province. However, he was catapulted to a position of fame when he first came to the attention of the Byzantine emperor after composing an epic poem in eight books called "Johannis," which detailed the African exploits of Justinian's general John Troglita. Having conquered the Vandals, the Eastern Roman or Byzantine Empire was now able to restore Africa to Roman imperial rule—Roman, but this time Eastern Roman or Byzantine, rule. Because "Johannis" remains the only surviving source of information about this period in African history, it is indeed regrettable that it has never been translated from the original Latin into English.*

In 550 Corippus, having relocated from Africa to Constantinople, composed another important historical work. This panegyric, "In Praise of Justin," eulogized Justinian I's successor, Justin II, in four books.

Meanwhile the happy emperor with his holy wife had begun to partake of the blessed joys of the imperial table, the royal banquet and the sweet gifts of Bacchus, which wild Sarepta and Gaza had created, and which lovely Ascalon had given to her happy colonists; or what ancient Tyre and fertile Africa send, and what Meroë, Memphis and bright Cyprus have: and what the ancient vines bear with their mature strength, which Ithacan Ulysses planted with his own hands, † . . . . . . † and he lived in the household of Laertes, not yet trying to avoid the dangers of the Trojan war: and the draughts that the farmer squeezed from the grapes of Methymna, fragrant, full of glassy Falernian. The ancient gifts of the Palestinian Lyaeus were mingled in,

---

[1]Averil Cameron (ed. and translator), *Flavius Cresconius Corippus, In Laudem Justini* (London: University of London, 1976), p. 104.

Source: From Averil Cameron, *Flavius Cresconius Corippus,* In Laudem Justini © 1976. Reprinted by permission of The Athlone Press.

white with the colour of snow and light with bland taste. They poured dusky chrysattic wines into the yellow metal, produced by nature without need of liquid honey, and blended in the gift of Garisaean Bacchus. Who will tell of all that the world brings forth for her rulers, all the provinces that are subject to the Roman Empire?

Though these things were there in plenty, in great luxury, only a little food was taken by his modest mouth, in his accustomed frugality, and as much drink as a sober mind will take, sober judgement keeping to the limits. The very responsibility of his rule and the clement man's own mind rightly make him partake of food only sparingly, and wisdom seeks little drink. They placed golden platters on the purple tables, made even heavier with the weight of jewels. Justinian was depicted everywhere. His picture was pleasing to the royal pair, and the happy descendants rejoiced when they saw the image of their father. You would think the holy likenesses there were real, and were standing there alive. The skill and the medium could add souls, if you, nature, did not deny the right to add life. Men's minds are allowed to live after death by their fame: their own glory keeps their name in honour.

PART FIVE

Byzantine, Coptic, and Islamic North Africa

The founding of Constantinople in A.D. 330 by the rulers of the Eastern Roman Empire, or Byzantium, transferred the locus of economic vitality eastward, undermining the central position that Alexandria had occupied for centuries. Over time a growing theological gulf echoed the economic and political divide between Egypt and the remainder of the Byzantine Empire. When in 451 the Council of Chalcedon asserted that

Christ possessed two natures, divine *and* human, the Egyptian Church rejected this doctrine and formally established its independent Coptic Orthodox Church. The latter was based on the theology of Monophysitism, which asserted a singular divine nature of Christ. After this time, Egypt saw a steady decline in the effective power and influence of its Byzantine rulers.

ISLAMIZATION

By A.D. 640 the Arab armies had conquered the area of the ancient Near East and crossed into Africa, wresting Egypt from what remained of Byzantine control. The Arabs established their new capital of Cairo near the ruins of the ancient Egyptian city of Memphis. As Arab rule consolidated its dominion over Egypt, the Arab language came to supplant the Coptic derivative of ancient Egyptian, and the Muslim religion replaced Coptic Christianity in much if not all of Egypt.

However, it was not until 690 that the Muslim army of 40,000 had built up sufficient naval strength to attack Byzantine rule in the former Roman colony of Numidia, to the west of Egypt. They overthrew the Byzantine Exarchate of Carthage in A.D. 697–698 and established dominion as well over the region that the Arabs referred to as *al-Maghrib* [the west], or Morocco. One of the most legendary figures to arise among Berber resisters to the Muslim armies was that of the Prophetess Kahina, Berber queen of the Aures mountains of eastern Algeria. She initially defeated the Muslims, but as reinforcements from Cairo continued to pour into the Berber territories, her resistance efforts eventually collapsed and she was beheaded.

The Islamization of North Africa was a slow but relentless process, spurred along by the conversion of young Berbers who joined the attractively remunerated Arab army. Also, the diffusion of the Islamic religion followed the lucrative trade routes which crisscrossed the Sahara. Not content with limiting their conquests to the African continent, the Islamic army, reenergized by a reformist movement of Moroccan Berbers called the Almoravids, began crossing over into Europe after A.D. 711 and gradually succeeded in conquering Spain. The culture of Islamic Spain in the centuries that followed became one of the most vibrant Europe had yet known.

The same religious fervor that had contributed to the establishment of Almoravid sovereignty had by the 1140s been transferred to a new group of Islamic reformers, the Almohads, led by another African Berber, Muhammad Ibn Tumart. Almohad armies wrested control from the Almoravids both in Spain and in North Africa and established their seat of control in Morocco.

EGYPT UNDER THE FATIMIDS AND MAMELUKES

From A.D. 969 to 1171 Egypt was ruled by a Shiite dynasty known as the Fatimids, replacing a dynasty established by Ibn Tulun in A.D. 868. Although of Arabized Berber origins, the founder of Fatimid rule in Egypt, Idris Ibn 'Abd Allah, claimed descent from Muhammad's son-in-law Ali and his wife Fatima. He represented a branch of the Shiite schism from orthodox Islam, which today remains prominent within Iran and parts of Iraq. In 1160 Egypt's Fatimid rulers found themselves threatened by Christian Crusaders, who had swept into North Africa and the Middle East from Europe. Saladin, the great Muslim military leader of Turkish origin, at first came to their rescue by rebuffing the Crusaders. However, he then turned around and established himself as ruler of Egypt. After his death the Turkish and Sudanese slaves whom Saladin had constituted into a military elite seized control of Egypt and established the Mameluke Dynasty, which was to reign for the 250-year period preceding the Ottoman Turkish seizure of Egypt.

COPTIC AND ISLAMIC LITERATURE

While most of Egypt converted to Islam from the eighth century onward, a vibrant community of Coptic Christians retained their mother faith. A sacred literature in the Coptic language flourished, particularly in the southern parts of Egypt. Egyptian intellectuals like Severus al-Muqaffa, who wrote *Lives of the Patriarchs* in the tenth century, played a seminal role in the writing of church biography or hagiography.

It is interesting to note that Muslim scholars were also influenced by the Coptic Christian tradition of hagiography. Egyptian Muslim scholars became renowned throughout the Islamic world for their biographical works on the life of the Prophet Muhammad and in the field of Islamic jurisprudence or *fiqh*. The Mameluke period in Egypt also witnessed the final codification of *A Thousand and One Nights,* also known as the *Arabian Nights,* which became one of the most popular foreign books to circulate in medieval Europe. Egypt also became a theological nub for Sufism, that is, Islamic Gnosticism, particularly under the leadership of Dhu al-Nun (died A.D. 860/861), a Nubian scholar believed to have been one of the early founders of Sufism.

African Muslim intellectuals of that period represented two distinct geographical foci, one centered in Egypt and the other in the Berber regions bordering and encompassing the Sahara Desert. Ibn Battuta (1304–1368/9) of Tangiers in Morocco and Ibn Khaldun (1332–1406) of Tunis constituted two of the most noted among the latter. Ibn Battuta became one of the most famous world travelers of history, recording his travels through Africa and Asia with remarkable objectivity and wit for his times. Ibn Khaldun, although he lived most of his life in Africa, had emanated from a family that had at one time been prominent Muslims in Granada, Spain. This scholar's massive work, *Al-Muqaddimah,* represents one of the most important works of political science and philosophical history ever written.

THE OTTOMAN TURKS

Egypt and North Africa fell under the dominion of the Ottoman Turkish Empire after A.D. 1517. Having conquered Constantinople in 1453, whose name they changed to Istanbul, the Ottomans had gone on to establish a vast empire encompassing eastern Europe, western Asia, and now all of the Mediterranean coast of Africa. However, Ottoman rule in Egypt deteriorated over the centuries and was unable to withstand the 1798 invasion by Napoleon Bonaparte. By allying themselves with the British, however, the Ottomans were finally able to force Napoleon's forces to leave Egyptian soil. However, this collaboration bore a heavy cost for the Ottomans. From that time Britain began to establish ever greater influence over the governance of Egypt at the expense of the titular Turkish pashas.

TEXT 33

Dhu al-Nun of Nubia: Islamic Gnosticism[1]

The Arabian armies of Muhammad swept into Egypt in A.D. 640, conquering this ancient land. Since the fifth century, Egypt and much of North Africa had labored under the dominion of the Byzantine, that is, the Eastern Roman Empire, based in Constantinople. Egyptians practiced Coptic Christianity and maintained their intellectual traditions in the Coptic language, a derivative of the last remnants of the ancient Egyptian language whose script utilized the Greek alphabet rather than hieroglyphics. Although the religion of ancient Egypt had disappeared many centuries earlier, scholars have only now begun to recognize its lingering influences on the later religious practices of the Egyptians.

From the seventh century onward, Islam began to replace Christianity in much, but not all, of Egypt. However, the orthodox Islamic faith as it spread throughout Egypt began to face a new challenge, which was represented by the powerful Gnostic tradition centered in upper Egypt and Nubia. The established Christian Church believed that it had by the fourth century stamped out Gnostic influences, which focused on the divinity within oneself rather than on external church authority. However, Gnostic impulses began to resurface within portions of newly Islamized Egypt during the tenth century, emanating, nor surprisingly, from the same desertic regions of upper Egypt and Nubia where the earliest Gnostic traditions had flourished.

Abu al-Fayd Thawban ibn Ibrahim, known as Dhu al-Nun (died A.D. 860/861), was born into this cultural environment of upper Egypt. He grew up in a Coptic or Nubian family of Ikhmin. This particular city enjoyed a long history dating back to pharaonic times in which it maintained a reputation for being an industrial center as well as a seat of learning. In Ikhmin and the surrounding areas, special devotional emphasis had from earliest times been paid to the ancient Egyptian god of wisdom and self-knowledge, Thoth. During the Greek occupation of Egypt after the fourth century B.C., Thoth became transposed into the Greek god Hermes Trismegistus,

---

[1]A. J. Arberry, *Sufism, An Account of the Mystics of Islam* (London: Routledge & Kegan Paul Publishers, 1970), pp. 53–54.

whose adherents, the Hermeticists, represented one of the earliest known practices of Gnosticism.

Islamic tradition credits Dhu al-Nun with having introduced the Gnostic spiritual path, or Sufism, into the Muslim religion, even though this religious tendency may have entered the religion from diverse sources, including Persia and Iraq as well. According to A. J. Arberry:

> Dhu al-Nun is represented in Sufi biographies as an almost legendary figure, half-mystic half-alchemist; he is said to have known the ancient Egyptian hieroglyphs and to have been familiar with the Hermetic wisdom.[2]

Guidest Thou not upon the road
The rider wearied by his load,
Delivering from the steps of death
The traveller as he wandereth?

Didst Thou not light a Beacon too
For them that found the Guidance true
But carried not within their hand
The faintest glimmer of its brand?

O then to me Thy Favour give
That, so attended, I may live,
And overwhelm with ease from Thee
The rigour of my poverty.

I die, and yet not dies in me
The ardour of my love for Thee,
Nor hath Thy Love, my only goal,
Assuaged the fever of my soul.

To Thee alone my spirit cries;
In Thee my whole ambition lies,
And still Thy Wealth is far above
The poverty of my small love.

I turn to Thee in my request,
And seek in Thee my final rest;
To Thee my loud lament is brought,
Thou dwellest in my secret thought.

However long my sickness be,
This wearisome infirmity,
Never to men will I declare
The burden Thou hast made me bear.

---

[2]Arberry, *Sufism*, p. 52.

Source: From A. J. Arberry, *Sufism: An Account of the Mystics of Islam*, © 1970. Reprinted with permission from Routledge & Kegan Publishers.

To Thee alone is manifest
The heavy labour of my breast,
Else never kin nor neighbours know
The brimming measure of my woe.

A fever burns below my heart
And ravages my every part;
It hath destroyed my strength and stay,
And smouldered all my soul away.

TEXT 34

Sawirus Ibn al-Mukaffa: The Father Gabriel

from History of the Patriarchs of the Egyptian Church[1]

By the tenth century, much of Egypt had converted from Coptic Christianity to Islam. Even so, remnants of Coptic communities remained, particularly in the southern part of the country. Their literature was almost entirely of a sacred nature, with special emphasis placed on hagiography, that is, biographies of the saints. The Coptic theologian Sawirus Ibn al-Mukaffa (A.D. 955–987) served as Bishop of al-Ushmunain, a city in southern Egypt. His History of the Patriarchs of the Egyptian Church *came to represent one of the most influential works of Coptic biography ever written.*

---

[1]Sawirus Ibn al-Mukaffa, *History of the Patriarchs of the Egyptian Church (Known as the History of the Holy Church)* (Cains, Egypt: Societé d'Archaéologie Copt, 1893), pp. 39–59.

THE FATHER GABRIEL (GHABRYÂL) IBN TURAÎK THE PATRIARCH, AND HE IS THE SEVENTIETH OF THE NUMBER OF THE FATHERS

This venerable father Gabriel (Ghabryâl) Ibn Turaîk was of the inhabitants of Cairo (Miṣr), of distinguished race, (and) from among the notables of the scribes. He sat on the patriarchal throne fourteen years and six months, and he went to his rest on the tenth of (the month of) Baramûdah (in the) year eight hundred and sixty-two of the Martyrs which corresponds to the eleventh of (the month of) Šawwâl (in the) year five hundred and thirty-nine of the Lunar (Year). His name was, while he (was) a layman, Abû'l-ᶜUlâ, a deacon in the Church of Saint Abba (Abû) Mercurius (Markûrah) at Cairo (Miṣr). He was a man of middle age, wise, good, learned, experienced, of excellent manner of life, of much alms-giving and piety, known for his love of the Prayers and the Liturgies, and for his ministration to the churches, to strangers of them. As regards Ruḍwân Ibn Walkhašî, he entered Cairo (al-Ḳâhirah) and the Calif (al-Khalîfat) invested him with the ministry (wizârat) in the year five hundred and thirty-one. And he plundered the churches of Cairo (al-Ḳâhirah) and the Khandak, and the Muslims (al-Muslimîn) burned the dwellings of the Armenians (Arman) known as Aẓ-Ẓuhrî, and they killed their patriarch and all whom they found with him of the monks in the monastery. And Ruḍwân Ibn Walkhašî (was) the first wazîr (who) ordered that the Christians (an-Naṣârâ) should not be employed in the important dîwâns nor as superintendents nor as administrators, and that they should bind their girdles about their waists, and that they should not ride on a horse. And he doubled for them and for the Jews (al-Yahûd) the capitation-tax (al-ǧizyat), and he made it of three categories, for the people who (were) rich, four dînârs and one sixth, and the people below them, two dînârs and two ḳirâṭs; and as regards the rest of their common people, one dînâr and one third and a quarter, and for him of low extraction, a dirham. And he employed in the Dîwân al-Ǧawâlî a man from the witnesses of Cairo (Miṣr), known as the Ḳâḍî al-Muhadhdhab Ibn Abî'l-Baḳâ, and the cause for this was what (had happened) through the Calif's (al-Khalîfat) employing a protégé of the califate (al-Khilâfat), the Šaikh Abû Zikrî Ibn Yaḥyâ Ibn Paul (Bûlus), the Christian (an-Naṣrânî) scribe, in the Dîwân of Investigation (at-Taḥḳîḳ). He had invested him with a coat-of-mail, and had caused him to sit within his Castle, in the Hall of the Golden Gate, in a place (which) he had set apart for him in it. And he employed with him twelve scribes from among the Christians (an-Naṣârâ), notables, in the days of the ministry (wizârat) of Bahrâm, towards the end of the year five hundred and thirty. And there was with him also two scribes from among the Muslims (al-Muslimîn), one of the two of them was known as

Source: Reprinted from Sawirus Ibn al-Mukaffa, *History of the Patriarchs of the Egyptian Church (Known as the History of the Holy Church)*, © 1893 Societé d'Archaéologie.

the Ḳâḍî al-Khaṭîr Ibn al-Bawâb, and the other, as the Ḳâḍî al-Murtaḍî Ibn atl-Tarâbulsî, both of whom Ruḍwân Ibn Walkhašî had employed in the Dîwân of the Council (al-Maǧlis) instead of him. Then he dismissed him after this, and he banished him to the region of Asyûṭ, because it was his country and the home of his ancestors; and the two mentioned scribes remained permanent, each one of them separate in his dîwân. The application of the Ġawdâlî (Tax) for the dhimah has remained until I wrote this biography. And I found in the days of the ministry (wizârat) of Ruḍwân Ibn Walkhašî (there was) a severe dearth until most of the people lacked food, and the mentioned Ruḍwân sold wheat and other things beside it in the way of red rice, black broad beans, weevilled cereals, and wheat (which) had become (rotten) from its old-ness and the length of its staying in the granaries and the depots, the silos and govern-ment stores from the days of Amîr al-Ǧuyûš for need (in times) of famine, and many things (were) at a great price, so that the Cairenes (al-Miṣriyîn) called it "historic" wheat. And the cost of bread in those days was an Egyptian (Miṣrî) raṭl for a dirham. Then God came to the aid of (His) creatures [through His mercy, and He had compas-sion on their poor, and He heard their supplication and He relieved them] and He low-ered their costs. And there happened similar to this in the year five hundred and thirty-four of the Lunar (Year). The Nile did not attain in it above fourteen cubits, and the cost (of food) became dear. When the land was dried up, the people experienced great harm by reason of the drought of the land. And Michael (Mîkhâyîl), bishop of Ṣahraǧt, undertook the renewal of the church of Minyat Ziftâ, and he consecrated it, and he cel-ebrated the Divine Liturgy in it, and he dedicated it to the name of Saint, my lord (Mârî) George (Ǧirǧis). And the Muslims (al-Muslimîn) of Minyat Ziftâ sprang upon it, and they demolished it out of their hatred for the Christians (an-Naṣârâ), and they made it a prayer-house (Masǧid). And Michael (Mîkhâyîl) the bishop stood before the wazîr Ruḍwân Ibn Walkhašî, and he cried for help from him, and he made clear to him that it was an ancient church. And he signed for him (a document) in his hand-writing to restore it and to return it to what was its former state in the way of its limits, up-wards and downwards. And he restored it and completed it, and he consecrated it, after he had endured on account of it great affliction and a great fine. And Ruḍwân contin-ued in the ministry (wizârat) until there rose up against him the soldiers and the amîrs of the State. Then he departed from the House of the Ministry (Dâr al-Wizârat) in Cairo (al-Ḳâhirah) in flight, and he did not put on his feet save one boot, and they did not give him time so that he might put on the other. And he stayed with the Dirmâwiyîn Arabs (al-ʾArab), and they took him to Syria (aš-Šam). And he stirred up a party of the Ghuzz (al-Ghuzz), and the Arabs (al-ʾArab) who had allowed him (to pass) joined themselves to him. And he came to Cairo (al-Ḳâhirah), and he halted on the top of the mountain at the place of the Observatory on the Mountain al-Mukkaṭam. And the army of the Egyptians (al-Miṣriyîn) came out against him and they fought him, and he routed them. Then they fought him in earnest, and they conquered him and defeated him. And when he saw that he was defeated, he returned to the land of Syria (aš-Šam) a second time. And the Imâm al-Ḥâfiẓ wrote to him and reassured him and appeased him, and he sent to him from among his companions one who was trust-worthy for him, and in his hand was money with which to travel, he and those with him of his companions and his followers. Then he returned accompanied by those whom he had chosen to go (with him) from among the amîrs of the State. Then the

TEXT 34: *Sawirus Ibn al-Mukaffa: The Father Gabriel*

Imâm al-Ḥâfiẓ caused him to stay with him in a Castle, and he set apart for him a great hall and its quarters and its offices, and he gathered together his sons and the sons of his sons. And he was in it honoured (and) free to do what he liked, (and) [at liberty, without fetters, and he was not under surveillance, and he was not guarded]. And as regards Bahrâm the Armenian (Arman) who was wazîr before him, when Ruḍwân caused him to come from the White Monastery, he placed him with him in his house. And when there befell Ruḍwân what occurred, our Sire al-Ḥâfiẓ transferred him to his Castle, and he besought him that he should return to his ministry (wizârat), but he did not do it and he said: "I am a monk; I am not a soldier"; and he took up his abode in the Castle being served until he died.

TEXT 35

Ahmad Ibn Yusuf al-Misri: Choicest Accounts of Ibn Tulun

The Arabization of Egypt, begun with the invasion of Muhammad's armies in A.D. 640, was complete by the tenth century. The indigenous Coptic language had been replaced in speech and writing by Arabic, except among the small community of Christians who continued to practice the Coptic Christian faith. Because the evolving literary traditions of Arabic Egypt complemented those of other Islamic areas, works from this period should not be viewed in total isolation from its larger Islamic intellectual context. At the same time, the regional flavor of Egyptian literature in Arabic offers important insights into the cultural influences of pre-Islamic Egypt as well. Just as biographies played a seminal role in the earlier Coptic literary tradition, scholars in Islamic Egypt became noted for their richly woven biographies of Muslim notables.

One of the most famed Islamic scholars of that period was Ahmad Ibn Yusuf al-Misri (d. A.D. 951). Because his mother had served as wet nurse to an Abbasid prince during a period in which his family resided in Baghdad, the son came to be known by his nickname Ibn al-Dayah ("Son of the Wet Nurse"). His most famous work was a biography of Ibn Tulun, the Turkish founder of a new dynasty in Egypt, which lasted from A.D. 868 to 905. Regarding this work of Ibn al-Dayah, Professor Ayyad notes in The Cambridge History of Arabic Literature:

> Under Ibn al-Dayah's pen, [Ibn Tulun] commands our deepest feelings of sympathy and fear. No mere extract from this unique book can do it justice, since much of the writer's art lies in the piecing together of the numerous episodes collected from eye witnesses.[1]

---

[1] S. M. Ayyad, "Regional Literature: Egypt," *The Cambridge History of Arabic Literature,* 'Abbasid Belles-Lettres,' edited by Julia Ashtiany, T. M. Johnstone, and J. D. Lathan (New York: Cambridge University Press, 1990), p. 426.

In that year he entered Tarsus with a mighty host and in great pomp . . . Abū ᵓl-ᶜAbbās al-Ṭarsūsī (who washed Ibn Ṭūlūn's body after he died), a truthful, clean-living man, said as follows: "There was in Tarsus a ragged Sufi, who had forsaken great wealth and ease to seek God, learned to weave palm-fronds from which he earned his livelihood, and campaigned year after year as a simple foot-soldier. When Ibn Ṭūlūn was in Tarsus, he used to visit him and marvel at his words. One night he said to me: 'Go before me to the house of such a one [i.e. the Sufi]; I shall follow hard on your heels. Be sure not to make him feel that deference to my rank requires his compliance, approach him humbly, but tell him how I have been longing to see him and ask him if he is willing to see me.' " Abū ᵓl-ᶜAbbās said: "I went, found him at home, and said: 'The amir Ibn Ṭūlūn sends you his greetings and says he longs to see you. He is hard on my heels.' The Sufi replied: 'I was angry with him, but your message has won me over.' I repeated Ibn Ṭūlūn's command that the message should be delivered with the utmost courtesy; the Sufi said: 'He can come when he likes.' I hurried back to Ibn Ṭūlūn and found him on his way with only a small entourage; when I told him what had passed he rejoiced and hastened to the meeting. At his approach the Sufi went up to him, saying, 'This duty we owe to our rulers,' and Ibn Ṭūlūn wept. When the two of them were alone together, the Sufi said: 'What have you got against God that you run away from him like this? You may shun him, but you cannot escape him. Spare your soul a burden which it cannot bear; do not put your trust in this world, this joyless world; remember that when you return to God, your deeds will go with you.' Ibn Ṭūlūn made no reply, but wept. 'Look,' said the Sufi, turning to me, 'He is quite racked with pain.' Then he looked up at the sky and said: 'Open his eyes; guide him; spare him Your wrath.—Go now in God's keeping, lest you infect me with the love of this world and I yield to my own judgement. God willing, I shall remember you in my prayers.' " When asked by Ibn al-Dāyah how it was that he knew what the hermit had said and could repeat it so exactly, Abū ᵓl-ᶜAbbās replied that he could not have done so, but that Ibn Ṭūlūn had a confidential secretary who wrote down everything the Sufi said so that the two of them could ponder it afterwards. He added that whenever Ibn Ṭūlūn sent an aide with a verbal message, he had the confidential secretary write it down for reference, and when the messenger came to take leave he would question him to see if he had got the message right; if he had, he was sent on his errand; if not, Ibn Ṭūlūn would throw him in jail and appoint a replacement.

Source: From Julia Ashtiany, T. M. Johnstone, and J. D. Lathan (eds.), *The Cambridge History of Arabic Literature,* © 1990. Reprinted by permission of Cambridge University Press.

TEXT 36

Ibn Tumart: The Muslim Creed[1]

From the tenth century and well into the fifteenth, large portions of Spain were ruled by two African Muslim dynasties, the Almoravids followed by the Almohades. The first represented a religio-political movement founded by Berbers of the western Sahara, who created a Muslim state extending from the borders of Senegal on the West Coast to Algeria on the Mediterranean. In the eleventh century, the Almoravids were superseded by another dynasty of Muslim Berbers, the Almohades. Their founder was Muhammad Ibn Tumart (born A.D. c. 1080), a native of the mountainous district of Sus which lies to the southwest of Morocco. A devoted and peripatetic scholar, Ibn Tumart traveled to Córdoba, Spain, in order to study the Islamic sciences and then returned to his native Africa to continue his studies in Tunisia and Egypt, and later in Iraq and Syria. In A.D. 1121 Ibn Tumart underwent a religious experience after which he proclaimed himself "the Mahdi," that is, the Savior. He began preaching a reformed version of Islamic teachings, focusing, in particular, on the Unity of God. The Almohad doctrine rejected the syncretic practices common to Berber Muslims, who tended to anthropomorphize religious imagery and proclaimed the infallibility of Ibn Tumart himself. Ibn Tumart's successor, Abu al-Muʾmin, succeeded in completing the conquest of the Almoravid territories, uniting the entire Mediterranean coast of Africa, Egypt, and Muslim Spain under the Almohad dynasty which lasted until A.D. 1269.

In the Name of Allah, the Merciful, the Compassionate

Praise be to Allah, as is due to Him, and such eulogy as He gave to Himself, and blessing from Him be upon Muḥammad and his family.

---

[1] Rachid Bourouiba, *Ibn Tumart* (Alger, Algeria: SNED, 1974).
Source: Reprinted from Rachid Bourouiba, *Ibn Tumart,* © 1974.

(1)

(On the excellence of tawḥīd, and the necessity for it, so that it is the first thing that must be acquired)

[It is related] from Ḥumrān, the client of ᶜUthmān b. ᶜAffān, from ᶜUthmān b. ᶜAffān, that the Apostle of Allah—upon whom be Allah's blessing and peace—said: "Whosoever dies in the knowledge that there is no deity save Allah will enter Paradise." Also from Ibn ᶜUmar, from the Prophet—upon whom be Allah's blessing and peace—that he said, "Islam is built upon five things, on maintaining the unity of Allah, or performing prayers, giving alms, fasting [during] Ramaḍān, and the Pilgrimage." Also from Ibn ᶜAbbās [it is related] that the Apostle of Allah—upon whom be Allah's blessing and peace—sent Muᶜādh to the Yemen saying: "You are being set over a community of the People of the Book, so let the first thing to which you summon them be to the worship of Allah. If they recognize Allah inform them that Allah has laid as incumbent duties upon them five prayers each day and night. If they conform to that inform them that Allah has laid as an incumbent duty upon them the legal alms (*zakāt*), to be taken from their property and given to their poor. If they are obedient in that let them possess in security the most precious things they possess." Another line of transmission has [instead of this last phrase, the words]: "And pay heed to the call of the oppressed, for there is no veil between it and Allah."

From this it becomes certain that worship is not genuine apart from faith and sincerity. But faith and sincerity [come not save] by knowledge, knowledge [comes not save] by seeking, seeking [comes not save] by willing, willing [comes not save] by desire and dread, desire and dread [come not save] by promise and threat, promise and threat [come not save] by the religious law, the religious law [comes not save] by trust in the Apostles, trust in the Apostles [comes not save] by the appearance of a miracle, and the appearance of a miracle [comes not save] by the permission of Allah, Most High.

(2)

It is by an intellectual necessity that one comes to know the existence of the Creator—glory be to Him. This necessary truth is something which cannot be subject to doubt and which no intelligent person can reject. This necessary truth may be said to be of three categories, (i) what needs must be; (ii) what may possibly be; (iii) what may not be. What needs must be comprises things which have to exist, e.g. a doer for a deed. What may possibly be comprises things which may or may not actually exist [at any particular moment], e.g. the coming down of rain. What may not be comprises things which cannot possibly become actual, e.g. the bringing together of opposites.

These necessary truths are all firmly established in the souls of intelligent beings. It is firmly established in their souls that a deed must have a doer, and that there can be no doubt about the existence of the doer. Of this Allah—blessed and exalted be He—has given a reminder in His Book, where He says (XIV, 10/11): "Is there doubt about Allah, Creator of the heavens and the earth?" The most High thus informs [us] that there is no doubt about the existence of the Creator of the heavens and the earth. Now that about which doubt has been removed is obviously something whose existence is known, so by this it becomes an assured thing that the Creator—glory be to Him—is known by innate knowledge (lit. by necessity of the intellect).

(3)

Also from his own creation man knows of the existence of his Creator, since he knows that he exists [now], though [there was a time when] he was not in existence. It is as the Most High has said (XIX, 9/10): "I created thee before, when thou wast not anything." He also knows that he was created "from base water," as the Most High has said (LXXXVI, 5–6): "Let man then look at that from which he was created. He was created from water that pours forth." Man also knows by innate knowledge that the water from which he was created was of single quality, undifferentiated, uncompounded, unformed, without bone or flesh, without hearing or seeing. Then all these qualities came into existence in him after that they had not been existing. So when he recognizes that they were created he also recognizes that there must have been a Creator who created them, as the Most High has said (XXIII, 12–14): "And indeed We created man of a pith of clay. Then We made him a drop in a safe receptacle. Then We created the drop into a blood-clot, created the blood-clot into a lump, created the lump into bones, and clothed the bones with flesh. Then We produced him another creature. So blessed be Allah, best of Creators."

(4)

From this one deed (viz. the creation of man) the existence of the Creator—glory be to Him—may be known, and the same would be true of a second [deed] and a third, and so on ad infinitum. From the [existence of] the heavens and the earth and all created things the existence of the Creator—glory be to Him—may be known, just as we know from the coming to be of a single movement both the fact that there must have been an agent [who caused the movement], and the impossibility of its having come to be without such an agent. Just as a single deed necessarily demands a doer, so do all deeds, and everything whose existence we know, though previously it had not existed, must be a thing produced. Thus by innate knowledge we know that night and day, men and beasts, cattle and birds, wild animals and beasts of prey, and other species of creatures are things produced, brought into existence after having been non-existent. Now if we know that one single body is a thing produced, we know that all the rest of bodies are things produced, because they are all in the same category with regard to the way in which they occupy space, suffer change, have their possibilities and peculiarities, are contingent and need an agent [who produces them]. Allah, Most High, has given a reminder in His Book that they are created, for He says (II, 164/159): "Assuredly, in the creation of the heavens and the earth, [in] the alternation of night and day, [in] the ships which run in the sea with what may be useful to people, [in] the rain which Allah sends down from the sky, whereby He quickens the earth after its deadness, and spreads abroad in it every [kind of] animal, [in] the changing about of the winds, and in the clouds set to serve between sky and earth, [in all of these] are signs for a people who have intelligence."

(5)

If it is known that they are things brought into existence after having been non-existent, it is also known that a created thing cannot possibly be a creator. Created things are of three categories, (i) rational living beings; (ii) irrational living beings; (iii) inanimate uncomprehending bodies. Now were all the individual rational beings [in the universe] to combine to restore a single finger after it had passed away they would not be able to do it. If rational beings are thus incapable how much more incapable are irrational beings, and if both rational beings and irrational beings are incapable, then inanimate bodies are still further [from being capable]. Thus it is known that Allah is the [sole] Creator of everything. It is as Allah—blessed and exalted is He—has said (XXXIX, 62/63): "Allah is the Creator of everything, and He over everything has charge."

(6)

If it is known that Allah is the Creator of everything, it is known also that He does not resemble anything, since a thing resembles only what is of its own species. The Creator—glory be to Him—cannot possibly be of the species of created things, for had He been of their species He would have been incapable with their incapacity, and had He been incapable with their incapacity it would have been impossible for Him to bring actions to pass. But we have seen that there is innate knowledge that actions do come to pass, and to deny them in spite of their existence is impossible. So hereby it is known that the Creator—glory be to Him—does not resemble that which has been created. It is as Allah—blessed and exalted is He—has said (XIV, 17): "Is then One who creates as one who does not create? Will ye not recollect?"

(7)

If it is known that any resemblance between the Creator and what has been created must be denied, it is also known that the Creator—glory be to Him—exists absolutely. Everything that has a beginning and an end, has defined limits and its proper attributes, must be something that occupies space, suffers change, has possibilities and peculiarities, is contingent and stands in need of a Creator. But the Creator—glory be to Him—has no beginning, for everything that has a beginning has a "before," and what has a "before" has an "after," and what has an "after" has a limit, and everything that has a limit is a thing produced, and everything that is produced needs a creator. The Creator, however—glory be to Him—"He is the First and the Last, the Outward and the Inward, and He knows all things" (LVII, 3). [He is] the First without any beginning, the Last without any end, the Outer without any defined limits, the Inner without any peculiar properties, existing in absoluteness without *tashbīh* and without *takyīf*. Were all intelligent creatures to combine [their intelligences] in order to ascertain how a creature sees or hears or understands they would not be able to do so, even though it is question of but a creature. If they are incapable of ascertaining how this is in the case of a creature, how much more incapable are they in the case of One Who has no resemblance to any creature and Who cannot be measured by what is intelligible? There is no similitude by which He could be measured. It is as the Most High has said (XLII, 11/9): "There is nothing at all like Him, though He is the One Who hears, the One Who sees." Imagination does not reach Him, nor does intelligence ascertain how He exists. It is as the Chosen One (i.e. Muḥammad)—upon whom be Allah's blessing and peace—said: "I do not understand how to praise Thee. Thou art as Thou hast praised Thyself," [a statement] in which he draws attention to the fact that we cannot say what He resembles or how He exists, while yet recognizing the majesty and greatness of "the Wealthy, the Praiseworthy" (XXII, 64/63). This is the extreme limit of wisdom. May Allah's peace be upon him.

(8)

Intelligence has a limit where it stops and cannot pass beyond. This limit is its incapacity to ascertain how [He exists]. It has no way of passing beyond [this incapacity] and attaining [a knowledge of how He exists], save by *tajsīm* (i.e. giving Him a body like ours and conceiving of Him anthropomorphically), or by *taʿṭīl* (i.e. depriving Him of His attributes). Those who know Him know Him by His actions, and they refuse any statements of how He, the Majestic One, comes to be, because they know what *tajsīm* and *taʿṭīl* lead to, viz. that which is impossible. Now whatever leads to the impossible is itself impossible. His deeds bear witness to His existence as Creator, unique in power, so all the ambiguous statements [of the Qurʾān] (*al-mutashābihāt*), which give rise to suggestions that He might resemble something, or that one might know how He comes to be, such as the verse about His taking His seat (VII, 54/52), and the Tradition about His coming down, and such other ambiguous statements in the Divine law, must be accepted as part of belief just as they are, but [accepted] along with denial of any *tashbīh* or *takyīf*. No one follows these ambiguous statements in the Divine law [instead of following the clear ones], save him in whose heart is deviation, as Allah, Most High, has said (III, 7/5): "Now as for those in whose hearts is deviation they follow what is ambiguous in it, seeking dissension, seeking its interpretation, whereas none knows its interpretation save Allah. Those well grounded in knowledge say: 'We believe in it [even though we do not understand it]; it is all from our Lord.' " Here the Most High informs [us] that deviators follow what therein is ambiguous, out of desire for dissension, and desire for its interpretation, and He reproves them for that. The Most High also informs [us] that those firmly grounded in knowledge say: "We believe in it; it is all from our Lord," and He praises them for that, bidding the Apostle—upon whom be Allah's blessing and peace—beware of those who follow such parts of it as are ambiguous. It is related from ʿĀʾisha—with whom may Allah be pleased—that she said: "The Apostle of Allah—upon whom be Allah's blessing and peace—was asked about this verse (III, 7/5): 'It is He Who has sent down upon thee the Book, some of whose verses are clear, which are the Mother of the Book, but others are ambiguous. Now as for those in whose hearts is deviation, etc.,' and the Apostle of Allah—upon whom be Allah's blessing and peace—said: 'When you see those who follow what therein is ambiguous, [know that] they are those whom Allah has named, and beware of them.' " No one can picture anything in his imagination save in terms of these ten limits, viz. before, after, above, below, to right, to left, in front of, behind, whole and part. But everything that is [pictured] in terms of these is accidental and demands a creator, whereas the Creator—glory be to Him—is the Wealthy, the Praiseworthy (XXII, 64/63).

(9)

If it is known that He exists absolutely, it is also known that He has not with Him any other than Himself in His kingdom, for were there with Him any other than Himself He would necessarily be bound by the limits of accidental things, since the existence of the independent other must be a thing separated out, whereas the Creator—glory be to Him—is neither joined to nor separated from. Could He be described in terms of joining and separation His existence would necessarily be something created, but the existence of the Creator as something created is impossible since it is impossible that essences be reversed. By this, it is known that He is One God, Who has no second with Him in His kingdom, as the Most High has said (XVI, 51/53): "Take not for yourselves two deities. He is only One God: Me, therefore, reverence Me."

(10)

If it is known that He is unique in His oneness, by the might and the majesty He needs must have, known also is the impossibility of anything being lacking in Him, for the Creator must needs be One who lives, One who knows, One who exercises power, One who wills, One who hears, One who sees, One who speaks, without our being able to imagine *how* this comes to be. Could He be described as being deficient in certain respects, then the bringing to pass of certain actions would be impossible for Him, for it is impossible for an ignorant person, one who is incapable, or sleeping, or dead, to be a Creator. The world as a whole bears testimony to the Wealthy, the Praiseworthy, through the fact that in it there is [evidence of] designing and forming, harmony and disharmony, that which is predetermined and that which is freely determined, that which is accurately done and that which is perfectly accomplished, [all testifying to the fact] that He—blessed and exalted is He—is "able to do whatever He wills," One Who "accomplishes that which He intends" (LXXXV, 16; XI, 107/109). He is living, self-subsistent, One whom slumber takes not nor sleep (II, 255/256). He is the One Who knows the hidden and the manifest (IX, 94/95), from Whom nothing whether on earth or in heaven is hidden (III, 5/4). He knows what is in land and sea, and not a leaf falls but He is aware of it (VI, 59). Not the weight of an atom in the heavens or in the earth escapes Him, nor what is less than that or greater (XXXIV, 3; X, 61/62). He has comprehended all things in [His] knowledge (LXV, 12), and has counted all things by number (LXXII, 28). Shall not He who did the creating know? seeing that He is the Kindly, the Well-informed (LXVII, 14).

(11)

If it is known that He necessarily exists in His eternal existence, it is also known that it is impossible that He should change from that state of might and majesty that are necessarily His, because it is impossible that real essences (*ḥaqāʾiq*) should be subject to change. Could the necessary suffer change to the possible and the possible to the impossible there would no longer be any matters certainly known. It is therefore necessarily known that He must of necessity continue existing. He has not ceased and He will not cease knowing all things that are produced as they really are in their attributes and their varied species, their times and their numbers, even before they substantially come into being. The One Who knows decreed them in His eternal existence, so they made their appearance by His wisdom, as directed by His decreeing, and they will run their course by His determining, according to a reckoning that may not be thrown into disorder and an arrangement that may not be disarranged.

(12)

Everything that He has predestined and decreed must be and cannot fail to appear. All created things are the result of His predestining and decreeing. The Creator—glory be to Him—caused them to appear just as He decreed them in His eternal existence, without anything being added or subtracted. There can be no substitution for a thing that has been decreed, nor any turning away from that which has been rendered obligatory. He brought them into existence without any intermediary and for no particular cause. He had no partner in the production of them, nor auxiliary in the task of bringing them into existence. He did not produce them from anything that was there with Him in eternity, and He set them in order without any pattern then existing that could be followed. He forged them to be an indication of what He was able to do and what He chose to do, and He set them to work as an indication of His wisdom and His economy (lit. His arranging). "He created the heavens and the earth without being worn out by creating them" (XLVI, 33/32). "His only command when He wishes any thing is to say to it: 'Be', and it is" (XXXVI, 82).

(13)

All the different varieties of creatures who have appeared as existing after they had been non-existent are in the possession of the Creator—glory be to Him. His predestining and decreeing preceded [them], measuring out their allotted portions, marking their tracks, numbering their breaths, setting limits to their terms so that nothing can lag behind its term nor get ahead of it. Nor can anyone die without having received in full his allotted portion, nor can what has been decreed for him be encroached upon. Each will enjoy the riches that have been created for him, and each may expect that which has been decreed as his. He who has been created for bliss will move smoothly into ease of life, and he who has been created for torment will move smoothly into distress. The happy man [was already] happy in his mother's womb, and the miserable man [was already] miserable in his mother's womb. All this is according to His predestining and decree. Nothing escaped His decreeing, and nothing from an atom upwards, moves in the darkness of the earth apart from His predestining and decree. "With Him everything has its measure. He is the One Who knows the hidden and the manifest, the Great, the Self exalted One" (XII, 8/9, 9/10).

(14)

The Creator—glory be to Him—is unique in equity and in welldoing. He guides and He leads astray. He exalts and He humbles. There is no ruler save Him, and no owner beside Him. Injustice and aggression are not laid to the charge of any save such as are under interdiction and judgment for having transgressed the bounds of some owner and disposed of something which they did not themselves own. Such an one is charged with injustice and aggression because there is an interdiction on him with regard to his possessions and a judgment against him for his deeds. But the Creator—glory be to Him—is under no interdiction in His control, nor is there any judgment against Him for His deeds. He is unique in [His] kingdom and oneness. [In His] sovereignty and divinity. He does in His kingdom whatever He wishes, and in His creation he passes sentence as He wills. He punishes whom He wills, and He shows mercy to whom He wills, looking for no reward and fearing no punishment. He owes nothing, and has no sentence against Him. Every act of blessing from Him is a favour, but every punishment from Him is just. "He is not to be questioned about what He does, it is they who will be questioned" (XXI, 23).

(15)

About the names of Allah, most

He has the most beautiful names (VII, 180/179). "He is the First and the Last, the Outward and the Inward, and He knows all things" (LVII, 3). "He is Allah, other than Whom there is no deity, the King, the most Holy One, the Peacemaker, the Faithful, the Guardian, the Sublime, the Mighty, the Proud" (LIX, 23). "He is the High, the Mighty" (II, 255/256), "the Great, the Self-exalted One" (XIII, 9/10), "the Wealthy, the Praise-worthy" (XXII, 64/63), "the Living, the Self-subsistent" (III, 2/1), "He who hears, He who sees" (XVII, 1), "the Knowing, the Well-informed" (LXVI, 3). "He is Allah, the Creator, the Maker, the Fashioner, His are the most beautiful names. To Him gives glory whatsoever is in the heavens and the earth, for He is the Sublime, the Wise" (LIX, 24). The names of the Creator—glory be to Him—are dependent upon His permission. He is not to be named save by the names He has given Himself in His Book, or by the tongue of His Prophet. Matters of analogy, derivation or technical usage do not come in question in regard to His names. A creature may be named "Jurist" or "liberal man" on the ground of his learning or his generosity, but there is no analogy from this to the case of the Creator—glory be to Him. A creature may be named "one who throws" or "one who kills" because of his throwing or his killing, but there is no analogy from that to the case of the Creator—glory be to Him. A creature may be called Zaid or ᶜAmr. He is born not having a name, and he adapts himself to his name, but it is not for a creature to give a decision with regard to his Creator or to name Him by a name other than such as He has given Himself in His Book. What He refrains from giving Himself in His Book he will refrain from giving Him, and what He has affirmed for Himself he will affirm for Him, without making any change or [indulging in] *tashbīh* or *takyīf*. We will name Him by His most beautiful names, and by them will we call upon Him. It is as He—blessed and exalted is He—has said (VII, 180/179): "Allah has the most beautiful names, so call upon Him by them, and leave those who deviate with regard to His names; they will be recompensed for what they have been doing."

(16)

What is said in the Divine law about the vision [of Allah] must be confidently believed in. He will be seen without there being any resemblance to creaturely things and without our knowing how. "Sight does not reach to Him" (VI, 103), in the sense that [that would involve that] He has a limit or may be encompassed or is subject to contiguousness or separation, for such categories of accidental things cannot be applied to Him. Every specialization involves some diminution or limitation involving an accidental character which must be rejected in the case of His Majesty. He—glory be to Him—is One, with none resembling Him: "He did not beget, and He was not begotten, and no one has ever been His peer" (CXII, 3/4). "Originator of the heavens and the earth, how should He have a son, seeing that He has had no female companion? He created everything, and He knows everything. That is Allah, your Lord, there is no deity save Him, Creator of everything; so worship Him, for He is in charge over everything. Sight does not reach Him, but He reaches the sight. And He is the Gentle One, the Well-informed" (VI, 101–103).

(17)

On the confirmation of a mission by miracles

By innate necessary knowledge (*ḍarūra*) is known the trustworthiness of an Apostle, through the appearance of signs such as violate the natural order of things and which accompany the proclamation of his message. The proof of this is that the one who claims to have a mission will belong to one of three classes. Either he will come with actions which are customary, such as eating, drinking, wearing clothes, and claim that they are a miracle on his part, but his claim is of no avail because they do not provide any sign of his trustworthiness. Or he will come with actions [involving some unusual skill, but one which] may be attained by [natural] ability or by instruction, such as writing, or building, or sewing, or such like acts, which he claims are a miracle on his part, but his claim is of no avail because nothing which may be attained by [natural] ability or instruction can be considered to be a genuine miracle of an Apostle. Or he may come with actions which violate the usual course of things, such as making the sea divide, or changing a rod into a serpent, or raising the dead, or splitting the moon, and claim that they are a miracle on his part. In such a case his trustworthiness is confirmed, since only the Creator—glory be to Him—could bring them about and cause them to appear as an accompaniment to the proclamation [of the Apostle's message]. The concurrence of the miracle with the proclamation is something that is perceived, and there is no way of refuting things perceived, or of making of no avail things that are [assuredly] known.

Among the miracles of [our] Prophet—upon whom be Allah's blessing and peace—is the Qurʾān. The Faithful Spirit brought it down in clear Arabic speech (XXVI, 193, 195), and Allah made it a sign of his trustworthiness. Said Allah—blessed and exalted is He—(II, 23/21): "And if ye are in doubt about what We have sent down to Our servant, then bring a Sūra like it, and summon your witnesses apart from Allah, if ye are speaking truth." So when they were unable to bring the like of what he brought his trustworthiness was known by necessary knowledge. Allah sent him to mankind as a whole, a bringer of good tidings and a warner (XXXIV, 28/27), a summoner to Allah, by His permission, and a shining lamp (XXXIII, 46/45). He sent him with compassion and mercy, specially endowed him with knowledge and dread, ennobled him with forbearance and wisdom, and guided him to the finest habits. So he delivered the message, made clear the religious law, and brought security. Then there came to him from his Lord firm conviction after religion had been perfected and [Allah's] favour completed. May Allah's blessing and peace be upon him, and on his family, on his Companions, both the Emigrants, and the Helpers, and the Followers, with all of whom may Allah's goodness be till the Day of Judgment.

And praise be to Allah, Lord of the Worlds

TEXT 37

Mamelukes of Egypt: The Young Man with the Severed Hand and the Girl

from A Thousand and One Nights[1]

A Thousand and One Nights, *also popularly referred to as* The Arabian Nights, *represents an ancient compilation of tales, reflecting diverse—Egyptian, Indian, Persian, and Baghdadian—cultural influences. An old Persian book called* Hazar Afsana (Thousand Tales) *contributes some of the stories to this rich compilation. However, it is the Cairo influence in this book which has perhaps generated the greatest degree of controversy. It has even been suggested that one of the most noted of these tales, "Aladdin and the Wonderful Lamp," might actually have been grafted onto this book in the eighteenth century.[2] In any case the primary Egyptian literary influences on this work emanated from the dynasty of the Mameluke Sultans who came to power in* A.D. *1250 and ruled until they were conquered by the Ottoman Turks in 1517. The word* mameluke *means "slave" in Arabic. The dynasty was founded by Aybak, a Turkish slave and bodyguard to the previous ruling dynasty of Egypt, the Ayyubids, founded by Saladin. The Mamelukes, like Saladin before them, became renowned for their defeat of the European Crusaders.*

The narrator of A Thousand and One Nights *is the Princess Scheherazade. She creatively commuted her sentence of death by stopping at the most suspenseful moment each evening with the promise that the story would be continued the next night.*

---

[1]Husain Haddawy, translator, *The Arabian Nights* (New York: W. W. Norton & Company, Inc., 1990), pp. 214–27.
[2]Ibid., p. xvii.

O King, I came as a stranger to your country, bringing merchandise with me, and was fated to stay here these many years. I was born a Copt, a native of Cairo. My father was a prominent broker, and when he died, I became a broker in his place and worked there for many years. One day, as I was sitting in the market of the fodder merchants in Cairo, a handsome and finely dressed young man, riding a tall ass, came up to me. He saluted me, and I rose in salute. Then he took out a handkerchief containing sesame and asked me, "How much is the measure worth?"

But morning overtook Shahrazad, and she lapsed into silence. Then Dinarzad said, "Sister, what a strange and entertaining story!" Shahrazad replied, "What is this compared with what I shall tell you tomorrow night if the king spares me and lets me live!"

The One Hundred and Tenth Night

The following night Shahrazad said:

I heard, O happy King, that the Christian broker said to the king of China:

O King of the age, I replied to the young man, "It is worth a hundred dirhams." He said, "Take a measurer and some porters and come to the al-Jawli Caravansary, by the Gate of Victory, where you will find me." I rose and went to find a buyer, making the rounds of the sesame merchants, confectioners, and fodder dealers, and got one hundred dirhams per measure. Then I took with me four teams of porters and went with them to the al-Jawli Caravansary, where I found the young man waiting for me. As soon as he saw me, he rose and led me to the storeroom, saying, "Let the measurer enter to measure, while the porters load the donkeys." The porters kept loading, one team coming and one team going, until they emptied the storeroom, carrying fifty measures in all, costing five thousand dirhams. Then the young man said to me, "Take ten dirhams per measure for your brokerage, and keep my share of four thousand and five hundred dirhams with you. When I finish selling the rest of my crop, I will come to you and take the money." I replied, "Very well," kissed his hand, and departed, surprised at his liberality.

For a month I sat waiting for him until he finally came and asked, "Where is the money?" I welcomed him and invited him to sit with me and have something to eat, but he refused and said, "Go and get the money, and in a little while I will come back to take it from you." Then he departed on assback, while I went and brought the money and sat waiting for him. But again he did not show up for a month, and I said to myself, "This is indeed a liberal young man. He has left four thousand and five hundred dirhams of his money with me, for two full months, without coming to take it." At last he came back, riding an ass, dressed in fine clothes, and looking as if he had just come from the bath.

But morning overtook Shahrazad, and she lapsed into silence. Then Dinarzad said, "What a strange and entertaining story!" Shahrazad replied, "What is this compared with what I shall tell you tomorrow night if the king spares me and lets me live!"

Source: From *The Arabian Nights: The Thousand and One Nights* by Husain Haddawy, translator. Copyright © 1990 by W. W. Norton & Company. Reprinted by permission of W. W. Norton & Company, Inc.

The One Hundred and Eleventh Night

The following night Shahrazad said:

I heard, O happy King, that the Christian broker said to the king of China:

The young man looked as if he had just come from the bath. When I saw him, I left the shop and went up to him, saying, "Sir, will you take your money back?" He replied, "What is the hurry? Wait until I sell the rest of my crop. Then I'll take it from you, next week." When he left, I said to myself, "When he comes back next time, I will invite him to eat with me."

He was absent for the rest of the year, during which I used his money, trading with it and making a great deal of profit. At the end of the year, he came back again, dressed in fine clothes. When I saw him, I went up to him and swore by the New Testament that he must eat with me as my guest. He agreed, saying, "On condition that what you spend on me will be from my own money." I replied, "Very well." Then I went in, prepared the place for him and seated him. Then I went to the market and, getting enough of beverages, stuffed chickens, and sweets, set them before him, saying, "Please help yourself." He came to the table and began to eat with his left hand. I said to myself, "Only God is perfect. Here is a young man who is handsome and respectable yet so conceited that he does not bother to use his right hand in eating with me." But I ate with him.

But morning overtook Shahrazad, and she lapsed into silence. Then Dinarzad said, "What a strange and entertaining story!" Shahrazad replied, "What is this compared with what I shall tell you tomorrow night if the king spares me and lets me live!"

The One Hundred and Twelfth Night

The following night Shahrazad said:

I heard, O happy King, that the Christian broker said to the king of China:

When we finished eating, I poured water on his hand and gave him something to wipe it with, and after I offered him some sweets, we sat to chat. I asked him, "Sir, relieve my mind by telling me why you ate with me with your left hand? Does something ail your right hand?" When the young man heard my question, he wept and recited the following verses:

> If Leyla I have for Selma exchanged,
> 'Twas not at will but by necessity.

Then he drew his right arm from his bosom and showed it to me. It was a stump, with the hand cut off at the wrist. I was astonished at this, and he said to me, "Don't wonder and say to yourself that I am conceited and have eaten with my left hand out of conceit. There is a strange story behind the cutting off of my hand." I asked, "How came it to be cut off?" Sighing and weeping, he said:

I was a native of Baghdad and the son of one of its most prominent men. When I reached manhood, I heard travelers and other people tell of the land of Egypt, and it stayed in my mind. When my father died and I inherited his business, I prepared a load of merchandise, taking with me all kinds of fabrics of Baghdad and Mosul, including a thousand silk cloaks. Then I left Baghdad and journeyed until I reached Egypt. When I entered Cairo, I unloaded at the Masrur Caravansary, where I unpacked the goods and stored them in the storerooms. Then I gave one of my servants money to prepare some food, and after I and my servants ate and I took a rest, I went out for a walk along Bain al-Qasrain Street and then came back and slept. When I arose, I opened the bales of fabric and said to myself, "I will go to some good market and find out the prices." I took samples and, giving them to one of my servants to carry, put on my finest clothes and walked out until I came to the Jerjes Market. When I entered, I was met by the brokers, who had already heard of my arrival. They took my fabrics and auctioned them, but the pieces failed to fetch even their cost. I was vexed and said to the brokers, "My pieces did not fetch even their cost." But they replied, "Sir, we can tell you how you can make a profit without risk."

But morning overtook Shahrazad, and she lapsed into silence. Then Dinarzad said, "Sister, what a strange and entertaining story!" Shahrazad replied, "What is this compared with what I shall tell you tomorrow night if the king spares me and lets me live!"

The One Hundred and Thirteenth Night

The following night Shahrazad said:

I heard, O happy King, that the Christian broker told the king of China that the young man said:

The brokers said, "We can tell you how you can make a profit without risk. You should do what the other merchants do and sell your goods on credit for a fixed period, on a contract drawn by a scribe and duly witnessed, employ a money changer, and collect your money, every Monday and Thursday. In this way you will make a profit, while you spend your own time enjoying the sights of Cairo and the Nile." I said, "This is a good idea," and took the brokers and the porters with me to the caravansary, where I took out the bales of fabric, and they carried them and went with me to the market, where I sold them on credit, on a written and duly witnessed contract, which I left with the banker. Then I left the market and returned to the caravansary.

I lived there, breakfasting every morning on a cup of wine, mutton, pigeons, and sweets, until a month went by, and the time came when my receipts began to fall due. Then I began to go to the market every Monday and Thursday and sit in the shop of one or other of the merchants, while the scribe and money changer went around to collect the money till past the afternoon prayer, when they would bring it, and I would count it and give them a receipt for it and take it and return to the caravansary.

I did this for six days, until one day, which happened to be a Monday, I went early to the bath. When I came out, I put on nice clothes and returned to my place in the caravansary, where I breakfasted on a cup of wine and then went to sleep. Then I arose, ate a boiled chicken and, perfuming myself, went to the market and sat at the shop of a merchant called Badr al-Din al-Bustani. We sat chatting for a while, when a lady, wearing a cloak and a magnificent headcloth and exhaling perfume, came up to the shop, and her beauty at once captured my heart. She saluted Badr al-Din, raising her upper veil and revealing a pair of large black eyes. He welcomed her and stood talking with her, and when I heard her speech, the love of her got hold of my heart, and I felt a sense of foreboding. Then she asked him, "Do you have a piece of silk fabric with hunting scenes?" He showed her one of the pieces he had gotten from me, and she bought it for one thousand and two hundred dirhams. Then she said to him, "With your permission, I will take it with me and send you the money next market day." He replied, "This is not possible, my lady, for this gentleman is the owner of the piece, and I have to pay him for it today." She said, "Shame on you, haven't I been buying much from you at whatever profit you wished, taking the fabric from you and sending you the money afterwards?" Badr al-Din replied, "Yes, indeed, but this time, I need the money today." She threw the piece of fabric back into the shop and said angrily, "You merchants don't respect anyone. May God blight you all." Then she turned to go.

But morning overtook Shahrazad, and she lapsed into silence. Then Dinazad said, "O sister, what a strange and entertaining story!" Shahrazad replied, "What is this compared with what I shall tell you tomorrow night if the king spares me and lets me live!"

The One Hundred and Fourteenth Night

The following night Shahrazad said:

I heard, O happy King, that the Christian broker told the king of China that the young man said:

When she threw the piece of fabric back into the shop and turned to go, I felt as if my soul was going with her and cried out to her, "For God's sake, lady, do me a favor and come back." She turned back, saying with a smile, "I am coming back for your sake," and sat in the shop facing me. I asked Badr al-Din, "Sir, what was the price we set for this piece of fabric?" He replied, "One thousand and two hundred dirhams." I said, "I will give you one hundred dirhams as a profit for it. Give me a piece of paper, and I will write you a discharge." I wrote him a discharge, took the piece of fabric, and gave it to the lady, saying to her, "Take it, my lady, and if you wish, bring me the money next market day, or better yet, accept it as a present from me to you." She replied, "May God reward you and grant you a larger share of riches and a longer life than mine." (And the gates of Heaven opened and received Cairo's prayers.) I said to her, "My lady, this piece of fabric is yours, and God willing, many like it, only let me see your face." She turned her head and lifted her veil, and when I took one look, I sighed and lost my senses. Then she let down the veil and, taking the piece of fabric, said, "I will miss you," and departed, while I remained in the shop till past the afternoon prayer, lost in another world. When I asked Badr al-Din about the girl, he said, "She is a lady of wealth, the daughter of a prince who died and left her a great fortune." Then I took my leave of him and went to the caravansary, still thinking of her, and when they set supper before me, I could not eat, and when I lay down, I could not sleep but lay awake till dawn. Then I rose, changed my clothes and, swallowing something for breakfast, hurried to Badr al-Din's shop.

But morning overtook Shahrazad, and she lapsed into silence. Then Dinarzad said, "Sister, what a strange and entertaining story!" Shahrazad replied, "What is this compared with what I shall tell you tomorrow night if the king spares me and lets me live!"

The One Hundred and Fifteenth Night

The following night Shahrazad said:

I heard, O happy King, that the Christian told the king of China that the young man said:

Hardly had I been in Badr al-Din's shop, when the lady came up, followed by a maid, and more richly dressed than before. She greeted me, instead of Badr al-Din, and said to me, "Sir, let someone receive the money." I said, "What is the hurry for the money?" She replied, "My dear, may I never lose you," and handed me the money. Then we sat talking, and I dropped some hints, by which she understood that I desired to have an affair with her. She rose hastily and went away, taking my heart with her. I left the shop and walked in the market, when suddenly a black maid came up to me and said, "My lord, my lady wishes to speak with you." I was surprised and said, "No one knows me here." She said, "My lord, how soon you seem to have forgotten her! My lady is the one who was in the merchant's shop today."

I walked with her until we came to the lane of the money-changers, and when the lady saw me, she drew me aside and said to me, "My dear, you have found a place in my heart, and from the day I first laid eyes on you, I have been unable to eat and drink." I replied, "I feel the same, and my condition speaks for my plight." She asked, "My dear, your place or mine?" I replied, "I am a stranger here and have no lodging but the caravansary."

But morning overtook Shahrazad, and she lapsed into silence. Then Dinarzad said, "Sister, what a strange and entertaining story!" Shahrazad replied, "What is this compared with what I shall tell you tomorrow night if the king spares me and lets me live!"

The One Hundred and Sixteenth Night

The following night Shahrazad said:

It is related, O happy King, that the Christian broker told the king of China that the young man said:

"I have no lodging but the caravansary. Do me a favor and let me come to your place." She replied, "Very well, my lord. Tonight is Friday night, and nothing can be done, but tomorrow, after you perform the morning prayer, ride an ass and ask for the house of the syndic Barqut abu-Shamah, in the Habbaniya quarter, and do not delay, for I will be waiting for you." I said, "Very well," and I bade her good-bye.

I waited impatiently for morning, and as soon as it was daylight, I arose, put on my clothes, and perfumed myself. Then I took fifty dinars in a handkerchief and walked from the Masrur Caravansary to the Zuwayla Gate, where I hired an ass, bidding the driver take me to the Habbaniya quarter. He set off with me and in no time brought me to a side street called al-Taqwa Lane. I bade him go in and inquire about the house of the syndic Barqut, known as abu-Shamah, and he disappeared and soon returned and said, "Very well, dismount." I dismounted and said to him, "Guide me to the house, so that you can find it when you return tomorrow to take me back to the Masrur Caravansary." He took me to the house, and I gave him a quarter-dinar and bade him go.

I knocked at the gate, and there came out two little white maids who said, "Please come in, for our mistress, being overjoyed with you, was unable to sleep last night." I walked through the hallway and came to a hall, raised seven steps above the ground and surrounded by windows, overlooking a garden that delighted the eye with running streams and all kinds of fruits and birds. In the middle of the hall there was a square fountain at whose corners stood four snakes made of red gold, spouting water, as if it were jewels and pearls.

But morning overtook Shahrazad, and she lapsed into silence. Then Dinarzad said, "What a strange and entertaining story!" Shahrazad replied, "What is this compared with what I shall tell you tomorrow night if I stay alive!"

The One Hundred and Seventeenth Night

The following night Shahrazad said:

I heard, O happy King, that the Christian broker told the king of China that the young man said:

I entered the hall, and hardly had I sat down, when the lady came up to me, bedecked in fine clothes and ornaments, with a diadem on her head. Her face was made up, and her eyes were penciled. When she saw me, she smiled at me, pressed me hard to her bosom and, setting her mouth to mine, sucked my tongue, and I did likewise. Then she said, "Can it be true, my little lord, that you have indeed come to me?" I replied, "Yes, I am with you and I am your slave." She said, "By God, since I first saw you, I have enjoyed neither food nor sleep." I said, "I have felt the same." Then we sat down to converse, while I kept my head bowed. Soon she set before me a tray with the most sumptuous dishes, such as ragout, fricassee, fritters soaked in honey, and chickens stuffed with sugar and pistachio nuts, and we ate until we were satisfied. Then the servants removed the tray, and after we washed our hands and they sprinkled them with rosewater scented with musk, we sat down again to converse, and my love for her took such hold of me that all my wealth seemed little to me in comparison with her. We passed the time in dalliance till nightfall, when the servants set before us a banquet of food and wine, and we sat drinking till midnight. Then we went to bed, and I lay with her till the morning, having never spent a better night. When it was day, I arose and, slipping under the mattress the handkerchief containing the fifty dinars, took my leave of her. She wept and asked, "My lord, when shall I see you again?" I replied, "I will be with you this evening." She saw me to the door and said, "My lord, bring our supper with you."

When I stepped out, I found the driver with whom I had ridden the previous day waiting for me, and I mounted, and he drove the ass to the caravansary. I dismounted but did not pay him, saying, "Come back for me at sunset," and he replied, "Very well," and went away. After I had a little breakfast, I went out to collect the money from the sale of my merchandise. In the meantime I ordered a roasted lamb on a bed of rice, as well as some sweets and, giving a porter directions to the lady's house, sent the food to her. Thus I occupied myself with my business till the end of the day, and when at sunset the driver came for me, I took fifty dinars in a handkerchief, adding two quarter-dinars, and rode the ass, spurring it until in no time I reached the lady's house. I dismounted and gave the driver half a dinar. Then I entered and found that the house was better prepared than ever. When she saw me, she kissed me and said, "I have missed you all day long." Then the servants set the table, and we ate until we were satisfied. Then they brought us wine, and we drank till midnight; then we went to the bedroom and lay together till daylight. When I arose, I left with her the fifty dinars in the handkerchief and went out, finding the driver waiting. I rode to the caravansary, where I slept a while. Then I went out and bought from a delicatessen a pair of home-grown geese on two platters of peppered rice. I also brought colocassia roots, fried and soaked in honey, fruits and nuts, as well as aromatic herbs and candles, and sent them all with a porter to her house. Then I waited impatiently till nightfall, when I again took fifty dinars in a handkerchief and rode with the driver to the house. Again she and I conversed, ate, and lay together, and when I arose in the morning, I again left the handkerchief with her and rode back with the driver to the Masrur Caravansary.

But morning overtook Shahrazad, and she lapsed into silence. Then Dinarzad said to her sister Shahrazad, "What a strange and entertaining story!" Shahrazad replied, "What is this compared with what I shall tell you tomorrow night, if the king spares me and lets me live!"

The One Hundred and Eighteenth Night

The following night Shahrazad said:

I heard, O happy King, that the Christian broker told the king of China that the young man said:

I continued like this, eating and drinking and giving her fifty dinars every night until one day I found myself penniless. Not knowing where to find money and saying to myself, "There is no power and no strength save in God, the Almighty, the Magnificent. This is Satan's doing," I left my lodging at the caravansary and walked along Bain al-Qasran Street until I came to the Zuwayla Gate, where it was so crowded that the gate was blocked up with people. As it had been foreordained, I found myself pressed against a soldier, so that my hand came upon his breast pocket and I felt a purse inside. I looked and, seeing a green tassel hanging from the pocket, realized that it was attached to the purse. The crush grew greater every moment, and just then, a camel, bearing a load of wood, jostled the soldier on the other side, and he turned to ward it off from him, lest it should tear his clothes. And Satan tempted me, and I pulled the tassel and drew out a little blue silk purse, with something clinking inside. Hardly had I held the purse in my hand, when the soldier felt something and, touching his pocket with his hand, found it empty. He turned to me and, raising his mace, struck me with it on the head. I fell to the ground, while the people gathered around us and, holding the soldier back, asked him, "Is it because he pushed you that you struck him with such a blow?" But he shouted at them with curses and said, "This fellow is a thief!" At that moment, I came to myself and got up, and the people looked at me and said, "This nice young man would not steal anything." Some believed him while others did not, and after much debate, some of them were about to rescue me from him, when the chief of the police and the captain and the watchmen entered through the gate and saw the crowd gathered around me and the soldier. The chief asked, "What is the matter?" and they told him what had happened [and the soldier said, "He stole from my pocket a blue silk purse containing twenty dinars."]. The chief asked him, "Was there anyone else with him?" and the soldier replied, "No." Then the chief cried out to the captain, bidding him seize me. Then he said, "Strip him naked," and when they did so and found the purse hidden in my clothes, I fell into a swoon. When the chief saw the purse . . .

But morning overtook Shahrazad, and she lapsed into silence. Then Dinarzad said, "Sister, what a strange and entertaining story!" Shahrazad replied, "What is this compared with what I shall tell you tomorrow night if the king spares me and lets me live!"

The One Hundred and Nineteenth Night

The following night Shahrazad said:

I heard, O happy King, that the Christian broker told the king of China that the young man said:

When the chief saw the purse, he seized it and took out the gold coins, and when he counted, he found twenty dinars. He was angry and, yelling at the officers to bring me before him, said to me, "Young man, there is no need to force it out of you if you tell me the truth. Did you steal this purse?" I bowed my head and said to myself, "I cannot deny it, for they found the purse in my clothes, but if I confess, I will be in trouble." At last I raised my head and said, "Yes, I took it." When the chief heard my words, he called for witnesses, and they attested my confession. (All of this took place at the Zuwayla Gate.) Then he summoned the executioner, who cut off my right hand, and he would have bidden him cut off my foot too, but as the people said to him, "This is a pitiful young man," and as I implored the soldier, who finally took pity on me and interceded for me with him, the chief left me and went away, while the people remained around me and gave me a cup of wine to drink. As for the soldier, he gave me the purse, saying, "You are a nice young man, and it does not become you to be a thief." Then he left me and went away.

I wrapped my hand in a rag, thrust it into my bosom, and walked until I reached my mistress's house and threw myself on the bed. When she saw that I was pale from the bleeding, she asked, "My darling, what ails you?" I replied, "I have a headache." Worried about me, she said, "Sit up and tell me what has happened to you today, for it is written on your face." When I wept without reply, she said, "It seems as if you are tired of me. For God's sake, tell me what is the matter with you." But even though I kept silent and did not reply, she continued to talk to me till nightfall. Then she brought me food, but I refused it, for fear that she would see me eat with my left hand, and I said to her, "I don't care to eat anything." Again she asked, "Tell me what happened to you today and what is troubling you." I said, "Must I tell you?" Then she gave me wine to drink, saying, "Drink it, for it will make you feel better and help you tell me what happened." I replied, "If I must, then give me the wine." She drank, gave me the cup, and I took it with my left hand.

But morning overtook Shahrazad, and she lapsed into silence. Then Dinarzad said, "Sister, what a strange and entertaining story!" Shahrazad replied, "What is this compared with what I shall tell you tomorrow night if the king spares me and lets me live!"

The One Hundred and Twentieth Night

The following night Shahrazad said:

I heard, O happy King, that the Christian broker told the king of China that the young man said:

When she gave me the cup, I took it with my left hand with tears in my eyes. She let out a loud cry and said, "My lord, why do you weep, and why do you hold the cup with your left hand?" I replied, "I have a boil on my right hand." She said, "Put it out, and I will lance it for you." I replied, "It is not ready yet." She kept forcing me to drink until I got drunk and fell asleep. Then she examined my right arm and found it a wrist without a hand, and when she searched me and found the purse and my severed hand wrapped in a handkerchief, she grieved for me and lamented till the morning.

When I awoke, I found that she had made me a dish of broth of five boiled chickens, and after I ate some and drank a cup of wine, I laid down the purse and was about to go out, when she said to me, "Where are you going? Sit down." Then she added, "Has your love for me been so great that you have spent all your substance on me until you finally lost even your hand? I pledge to you that I will die nowhere but at your feet, and you shall soon see the truth of my words." Then she sent for witnesses and drew up a marriage contract, saying, "Write down that everything I own belongs to this young man." After she paid the witnesses their fee, she took me by the hand and leading me to a chest, said to me, "Look at all these handkerchiefs inside; they contain all the money you brought me. Take your money back, for I can never reward you enough for your precious and dear self," repeating, "Take your money." I locked the money in the chest, forgetting my sorrow and feeling happy, and thanked her. She said to me, "By God, even if I gave my life for you, it would be less than you deserve."

We lived together, but in less than a month, she fell ill and continued to get worse because of her grief for me, and in less than fifty days, she was dead. After I buried her, I found that she had left me countless bequests, including the storeroom and the crop of sesame that you, Christian, sold for me.

But morning overtook Shahrazad, and she lapsed into silence. Then Dinarzad said, "Sister, what a strange and entertaining story!" Shahrazad replied, "What is this compared with what I shall tell you tomorrow night if the king spares me and lets me live!"

The One Hundred and Twenty-First Night

The following night Shahrazad said:

I heard, O happy King, that the Christian broker told the king of China that the young man said:

"It was because I was busy selling the rest of the goods that I did not have the time to pay attention to you and receive my money from you, but now I have at last sold everything she left me. This then is the reason why I ate with my left hand. Now, by God, Christian, you must not object to what I am about to do, for I have entered your home and eaten your food. I make you a present of all the money you are holding for me from the sale of the sesame, for it is only a portion of what the Supreme God has bestowed on me."

The young man added, "Christian, I have prepared a load of merchandise for trading; will you go abroad with me?" I replied, "Yes, indeed," and agreed to go with him at the beginning of the month. Then after I too bought merchandise, I set out with the young man until we came to your city, O King, where he bought merchandise and went back to Egypt. But it was my lot to stay here. This then is my adventure and strange story. Isn't it, O King, more amazing than the hunchback's story?

TEXT 38

Ibn Battuta: The Royal Court of the Sultan of Mali

from The Travels of Ibn Battuta[1]

*I*bn Battuta (1304–1369/9) was born in Tangiers, Morocco, into a family of Berber ethnicity. He embarked on his world travels at the age of 21 and over the course of a lifetime became one of the most reliable and expansive world travelers of medieval times. While Ibn Battuta has often been compared to the European Marco Polo (1254–1324), the former's travels covered more continents as he journeyed across North Africa to the Near East and Arabia, sub-Saharan Africa, Asia Minor, the Crimea, the Balkans, Russia, India, and then to Ceylon and China. Ibn Battuta's travelogues have become classics not merely because of the richness of his cultural experiences, but also because of the breadth of interests and insatiable curiosity he brought to observing the politics, economics, food, local mores, and women inhabiting the cultures through which he passed. In 1352 Ibn Battuta journeyed to ancient Mali. This state of sub-Saharan Africa was large and vibrant, noted for its trade in gold. It was a neighboring state to Ibn Battuta's own homeland of Morocco. Europeans of this time were largely ignorant of the states of the western Sudan. It was not, however, because these regions were completely isolated. It was rather because the Muslims controlled the lucrative gold trade across the Sahara desert with these states and kept the Europeans out.

REGARDING THE SULTAN OF MALI, MANSA MUSA

The sultan of Mali is named Mansa Sulayman. *Mansa* means "sultan" and his name is Sulayman. This man is a tight-fisted ruler, wholly lacking in generosity. On account of

---

[1]Translated by Constance Hilliard.

my illness during the time of my stay (in Mali), I was unable to hold an audience with him. He had food prepared on the occasion of the funeral for the nobleman Abu al-Hasan (may God be pleased with him), to which he invited the princes, jurisconsultants, the judge and preacher. I was also in attendance. They brought reading stools and the Qur'an was recited in its entirety. They prayed for Abu al-Hasan (may God have mercy on him) as well as for Mansa Sulayman. At the completion of the service, I came forward to greet Mansa Sulayman. The judge, the preacher and Ibn al-Faqih explained the circumstances of my health to him. He responded in their language, which was transmitted to me, thusly: "The sultan says 'Thanks be to God.'" I responded: "Praise be to God, and thanks to him in all situations."

REGARDING THE MEAGERNESS OF THEIR HOSPITALITY AND THEIR OSTENTATIOUSNESS

When I returned to my lodgings, a hospitality gift had been sent to me. Because it had been delivered to the home of the jurisconsult, he had his men bring it to the home of Ibn al-Faqih, who rushed to my house in his bare feet. Ibn al-Faqih said to me: "Stand up in order to receive the Sultan's gift." I rose, assuming that I would be presented with robes of honor and other items of value. But lo and behold, I was presented with three round loaves of bread, a piece of fried beef, and a calabash containing sour milk. I could not help but laugh and wonder at their silliness in magnifying so insignificant an offering.

REGARDING MY SUBSEQUENT TALK WITH THE SULTAN AND HIS KINDNESS

After the incident with the hospitality gift, I remained for two months without hearing anything further from the Sultan. The month of Ramadan was now upon us. In the meantime, I had developed a routine of going to the place where he held his audiences. I would greet him and sit with the jurisconsult and the preacher. I conferred with Dugha, the interpreter, who said: "If you address him, I will interpret on your behalf." It was the beginning of Ramadan and I presented myself to the Sultan, saying: I have traveled throughout the world and met the kings of foreign lands. However, I have been in your country for four months and received no hospitality whatsoever from you. How shall I describe your conduct to the other sultans whom I shall meet? He said: "Indeed, I had neither seen you nor even known about you." At that point, the jurisconsult and Ibn al-Faqih rose and addressed him saying: "He has greeted you and you have in turn sent food to him." The Sultan then commanded that a house be made ready for me and that I be given an allowance. Then, he distributed money called *zakat* to the jurisconsult, the preacher and the legists on the night of the twenty-seventh of Ramadan. He included me in this distribution, for which I received thirty-three and a

Source: Translated by Constance Hilliard

third gold pieces (*mithqals*). He was also generous to me upon my departure, giving me an additional one hundred gold pieces.

REGARDING THE SULTAN'S SITTING IN HIS THRONE ROOM

The Sultan possesses a raised throne room, which is entered from the inside of his palace. He spends much of his time in there. One side faces the audience and possesses a chamber with three wooden arches, the woodwork is covered with sheets of pounded silver. Underneath these were three more covered with pounded gold, or rather gilded silver. Woolen curtains hang from the windows. They are raised on days when the Sultan will be holding audience in the throne room. To announce his presence, a silk cord is suspended from the grill of one of the arches to which an Egyptian embroidered scarf is attached. As soon as the scarf becomes visible to the crowds, drums are beaten and horns blasted. Three hundred slaves exit the door of the palace. While some carry bows in their hands, others carry small spears and shields. The spearmen arrange themselves with some standing on each side and others seated likewise. Next, they bring two mares in saddle and bridle and two rams, which are believed to stave off the evil eye. After the Sultan has been seated, three of his slaves immediately leave to summon his deputy, Qanja Musa. The commanders arrive, included among which are the princes, the preacher, and the jurisconsults, who arrange themselves in front of and to the left and right of the armed men in the place where the audiences will be held. The interpreter Dugha stands at the door of the audience chamber adorned in magnificent robes. He wears on his head a turban with fringes, which they tie in a delightful way. He also carries a sword with a gold sheath. On his feet he wears boots and spurs. He alone is clad in boots on that day. He carries in his hands two small spears, one made of gold and the other of silver, with iron blades. The soldiers, the district governors, the pages, the Massufa clansmen, and others sit on a broad tree-lined street outside the area where the audiences will be held. Each commander maintains his followers, who are carrying spears, bows, drums, and horns of elephant tusks, in front of him. Their musical instruments are made of reeds and calabashes. They beat them with sticks, producing a melodious sound. Each commander also possesses a quiver, which he sets over his shoulder. Holding the bow in one hand, he remains mounted on a mare. Some of his men are on foot while others are mounted.

Inside the audience chamber under the arches a man will be standing. He who wishes to address the Sultan will actually speak to Dugha, who will in turn transmit the communication to the man who is standing. And he alone will speak to the Sultan.

REGARDING THE AUDIENCES THAT WERE HELD

On specified days, the Sultan sits in the palace yard, where he gives audience. A three-tiered platform has been constructed under a tree, which they refer to as *banbi*. It is covered in silk fabric and pillows. The *shatr*, an umbrella made of silk, with a gilded bird on its tip, is then raised. The Sultan makes his entrance from a gate at the side of his palace. He carries a bow in one hand, a quiver tossed over his shoulders, and a cap made of gold, with gold fringes that look like narrow-bladed knives more than a span in length. He often wears a soft, red robe made of imported Roman cloth. The praise-singers precede him, carrying gold and silver ornaments. Behind him march three hundred armed slaves. The Sultan strides at a leisurely pace, pausing often and sometimes even halting in his tracks. When he comes to the platform he stops and looks out over the crowd. Then he mounts the steps with the same dignity one might note in a preacher ascending to the pulpit. As the Sultan sits down, they beat the drums and blow the horns. Three of the slaves rush out to call the deputy and the commanders, who enter and sit down. The two mares are also brought in along with the two rams. Dugha stands at the door, while the Sultan's subjects remain in the street under the tree.

REGARDING THE MORTIFICATION OF THE BLACKS IN THE PRESENCE OF THE KING, THEIR DUSTING THEMSELVES FOR HIS BENEFIT AND OTHER SUCH ODDITIES

Blacks are the most humble of people in the presence of their king and the most excessive in the mortification they practice before royalty. They swear by his name, saying: "Mansa Sulaymanki," that is, "the law according to Mansa Sulayman." When he summons one of them during his audiences, that man undresses and dons rags, removes his turban and puts on a dirty cap and rolls his trousers and robes nearly up to his knees. He advances with the humility and demeanor of a beggar. He falls to the ground, on his elbows. He prostrates himself as he listens to what the king is saying. When one of his subjects addresses the Sultan, upon receiving the reply, the man removes the clothes from his back and throws dust on his head and over his shoulder, in the gesture of one taking a bath. I was curious as to how they escaped blinding themselves from this practice. When the Sultan addresses his council, those present remove their turbans as he talks.

From time to time, one of them might stand in his presence and recall his actions in the service of the Sultan, saying: "I did so and so on such and such a day," and "I killed so and so on such and such a day." Those who know this to be the case confirm the truth of it. They do so by drawing back the cords of their bow and releasing them, as one would when shooting. If the Sultan affirms that he has spoken the truth, the man thanks the monarch, removes his clothes, and sprinkles dust over himself. This is considered good manners among them.

Ibn Juzzayy says:

> I have been informed by a keeper of the seal, the jurisconsult, Abu al-Qasim, son of Ridwan (may God grant him strength), of the following. When al-Hajj Musa of Wangara came as ambassador from Mansa Sulayman to our lord Abu al-Hassan (may God be pleased with him), and presented himself at the Noble Assembly, one of his retainers carried with him a round basket and he dusted himself every time our lord made a complimentary remark, as would be the custom in his own country.

TEXT 39

Ibn Khaldun: "Sufism" and "Defining the Intellectual Sciences"

from The Muqaddimah[1]

*I*bn Khaldun (1332–1406) has come to be recognized as one of the most noted and insightful political philosophers of all time. He was born in Tunis, of a distinguished Arabized Berber family who also maintained roots in Moorish Spain. Much of his adult life alternated between active involvement as an administrator, teacher, and judge in the turbulent politics of North Africa and Spain. Ibn Khaldun's most noted work is the Muqaddimah, that is, the "Introduction" to his history of North Africa or Kitab alᵓIbar. While the latter work is an important source for the history of the region, it is the Muqaddimah that represents an undeniably brilliant historiography of human political and social endeavor. Ibn Khaldun's rationalist approach employed the lessons of history in an effort to grapple with the reasons for the rise and fall of human civilization. The conclusions he reached were hauntingly modern, i.e., that the answers might be found in a careful and dispassionate analysis of the economic and social structure of society. As Reynold A. Nicholson has pointed out in A Literary History of the Arabs, "[Ibn Khaldun's] intellectual descendants are the great medieval and modern historians of Europe—Machiavelli and Vico and Gibbon."[2] Ibn Khaldun also offers an important glimpse into the state of Islamic knowledge during the fourteenth century as he describes and analyzes the "intellectual sciences" as they are defined within his culture.

---

[1] Translated by Constance Hilliard.
[2] Reynold Alleyne Nicholson, *A Literary History of the Arabs* (New York: Cambridge University Press, 1962), p. 439.

SUFISM

Sufism represents one of the sciences encompassed in the religious law of Islam. It emanates from an assumption that its practices were supported by the early Muslims and Companions of the Prophet Muhammad, and their successors, as right and just. The approach of the Sufis is based on a total devotion to God, the eschewing of the material things of the world, and an abstinence from pleasures, acquisitiveness, and ambitions to which most men and women aspire. It also encourages a monastic way of life. These practices were quite common during Muhammad's generation.

However, the material ambitions of Islam's adherents increased during Islam's second century. At that time the term *sufi* was attached to those who continued to aspire to divine worship.

Over time the Sufis came to represent asceticism. They developed their own unique mode of perceiving the Divine presence through ecstatic experience. For example, humankind is distinguishable from other living creatures by its capacity to perceive. Human perceptions are of two kinds. The first is that of the sciences and material knowledge, which may be irrefutable, hypothetical, doubtful, or imaginary. In addition, humans can perceive their interior emotional states such as joy and grief, anxiety and repose, satisfaction, anger, patience, gratitude, etc. The ability to reason emanates from the perceptions and human will. It is through them that humans distinguish themselves from other animals. Knowledge emanates from factual evidence, grief and joy from the perceptions of what causes pain or pleasure, energy from repose, and sloth from exhaustion. Each of those states may represent a form of divine worship. But these states may at times represent merely a quality of the emotions such as vitality, sloth, or something else.

These states are seen in an ascending order. The Sufi initiate progresses from state to state, until he or she reaches the highest state, which is recognition of the oneness with God and *gnosis,* or self-knowledge, which leads to bliss.

In this way the Sufi initiate must progress from state to state. Fundamental to each stage is obedience and sincerity. Faith is also a necessary accompaniment of these stages that lead ever upward until one attains a recognition of oneness with God and *gnosis.* If shortcomings become apparent, then it is understood that they have been carried over from the previous stage, whether they emanate from the heart or the soul.

The Sufi initiate must as a consequence scrutinize him or herself in all actions, including their motivations which may operate below the level of their conscious awareness. The initiate becomes aware of these shortcomings through the practice of mystical experiences, and engages in self-examination in order to uncover their reasons.

Very few people share the self-scrutiny demanded of the Sufis. Negligence in this regard is virtually universal. Pious people who have not progressed to the highest stage of *gnosis* engage in acts of obedience, assisted by mystical and ecstatic experience so that they will become more aware of their human deficiencies. It should be apparent by now that the path of the Sufis is dependent on self-knowledge and upon mastery of the various types of mystical and ecstatic experiences in which their adherents engage.

Source: Translated by Constance Hilliard

In addition, the Sufis have evolved their own peculiar patterns of behavior and vocabularies, which they use for instructional purposes. Their specific terminologies apply only to commonly accepted ideas. When they wish to express ideas that may not be universally understood, they resort to a technical terminology of their own construction.

Therefore, the Sufis possess a special discipline, which is not presented in the discussions of non-Sufi religious scholars. Consequently, the science of religious law has evolved in two directions. The first is the special field of the jurisconsults, concerned with the general laws applying to acts of divine worship, customary behavior, and mutual dealings. The second is that of the Sufis. It is concerned with the exercise of piety, self-examination, the different kinds of mystical and ecstatic experience, the progression from one state to another, and the interpretation of mystical terminology.

When scholars began composing scientific texts on jurisprudence and theology, commentaries and interpretations of the Qurʾan, and other subjects, the Sufis began to develop their own body of laws governing asceticism, self-examination, proper and improper behavior in imitation of the saints.

Al-Ghazzali in his book *Kitab al-Ihya* wrote systematically about the laws governing asceticism and proper modes of behavior. He went on to describe the behavior of the Sufis and to explain their terminology.

In time, the science of Sufism became treated as a legitimate discipline within Islam. Before then mysticism had merely consisted of divine worship, and its laws had existed only within the hearts of men. In this regard, it is actually no different from the other disciplines, such as commentaries on the Qurʾan, theology, and jurisprudence.

Mystical and spiritual experience are as a rule accompanied by the transcending of the material world. The Sufi is able to perceive divine worlds which another person is incapable of perceiving. The spiritual self belongs to those worlds. It is necessary to remove the barrier to these perceptions for the following reasons. When the spirit moves from perception of the external world to that of the interior, the senses become weak but the spirit grows even stronger. The spirit continues to grow. While it was once knowledge, it has now become visual as well. The barrier of perceiving with one's senses is removed, and the soul realizes its essential nature. The spirit in this way becomes ready to receive the holy gifts, for the sciences of the divine presence and for the benefits of God. Its essential nature comes to know its own true character, drawing it ever upward into the highest sphere, which is occupied by angels. The removal of the barrier often occurs to people who engage in mystical experiences. They are then able to perceive the realities of existence in ways that others cannot.

They are also able to perceive the future. With the aid of their minds and psychic abilities they are active among the lower beings, which become obedient to their will. The great Sufis do not preoccupy themselves with the removal of these barriers, nor of involving themselves with the lower beings. They even refrain from sharing information about those things that they have not been ordered to discuss, seeing them as a discomfort to be avoided whenever possible.

In recent times, mystics have turned their attention to the removal of the barriers and to a discussion of higher stage perceptions. Their ways of attaining mystical experience may vary. They have taught diverse methods of mortifying the powers of the senses and strengthening the powers of reason with exercises, in order to nourish the soul in its growth and attainment of its essential nature. When this stage is reached, they believe that all of existence becomes a unity centered in the soul. They can then perceive the reality of their essential nature from the divine throne to a rain shower. This was the comment made by al-Ghazzali in the *Kitab al-Ihya,* after he had mentioned the various types of mystical experience.

The Sufis do not believe that removal of the barriers to *gnosis* should be undertaken unless the person so attempting is acting from forthrightness. People who fast and who retire from the world, such as sorcerers, Christians, and other ascetics, may obtain removal of the barriers without forthrightness. However, we are referring only to the removal of barriers which emanate from forthright motives. This process may be compared to that of a mirror. Whether it is convex or concave, the object perceived in the mirror is distorted. However, if the mirror is flat rather than curved, the object appears in its correct proportions. Thus, forthrightness means to the soul what flatness means to perception of an object in a mirror.

Recent Sufis who have preoccupied themselves with the removal of the barriers discuss the true nature of the higher and lower orders of being, the true nature of the divine kingdom, the spirit, the divine throne, and other such issues. Those who do not share their approach are unable to grasp the mystical and ecstatic experiences upon which they base their beliefs. The orthodox muftis disapprove of the Sufis in part but not completely. Arguments and proofs are of no use in deciding whether the Sufi approach should be rejected or accepted. This is because the practice of Sufism is based on intuitive experience.

THE VARIOUS DISCIPLINES COMPRISING THE INTELLECTUAL SCIENCES

The intellectual sciences are innate to humankind because men and women possess the gift of thought. Intellect is not restricted to any particular religion. To the contrary, the intellectual sciences are studied by all religions, whose adherents are qualified to research and master them. They have existed and been studied from the very inception of civilization, and are called the sciences of philosophy and wisdom, comprising four distinct disciplines.

1. The first of the intellectual sciences is logic. It is a science that protects our thinking from fallacies in deducing unknown facts from the basis of known information. The use of logic enables students to distinguish truth from error in his investigations. He is in this way able to deduce the truth or falsity of material objects to the degree that his own intelligence allows.
2. Through the use of logic, philosophers can examine the material world, including the minerals, plants, and animals which derive from the elements, in addition to the celestial bodies, the dynamics of motion, their origins, and the like. This discipline is referred to as "physics." It constitutes the second of the intellectual sciences.
3. Likewise, the philosophers may study metaphysical or spiritual matters. This science is called "metaphysics" and represents the third intellectual science.

4. The fourth science is the study of measurements. It is composed of four separate components, called "the mathematical sciences."

The first of the mathematical sciences is geometry. It is the study of quantification, whether of numbers or geometrical figures. These mathematical concepts may be represented in one dimension, which is the straight line, in two dimensions, which is represented with the plane, or in three dimensions, which is the study of solids. The measurements and values possessed by objects, singularly or in combination, is what is studied in geometry.

Arithmetic comprises the second mathematical science. It represents the body of knowledge reflected in the constant and variable values of numbers and quantities.

Music is the fourth mathematical science. It represents the body of knowledge relating to sounds and their modalities as well as their numerical measurement. This form of knowledge produces musical melodies.

The fourth of the mathematical sciences is astronomy. It determines the shape of the celestial spheres, determines the positions of the plants and fixed stars, and makes it possible to deduce this type of information from observation of the back and forth motions of the heavenly spheres.

The aforementioned represent the seven philosophical sciences, which should be perceived in a specified order. Logic comes first, followed by mathematics, which is composed of arithmetic, followed by geometry, astronomy, and music. Physics comes next and is followed by metaphysics. Within each of these sciences are subfields. For instance, a subfield of physics is medicine. Subfields of arithmetic are calculation, the laws of inheritance, and accounting. A subfield of astronomy encompasses the astronomical tables. They are constants used in the computation of the motions of the stars and in adjusting data in order to determine their positions when necessary. An additional subfield of astronomy is the science of astrology.

Let us then discuss each of these sciences, one at a time.

Our historical information informs us that these sciences were cultivated by the two great pre-Islamic societies, the Persians and the Romans. According to the information available to us, the sciences were greatly favored by these nations because of the sophistication of their civilizations, which directly preceded the Islamic era. In these ruling nations, the sciences flourished in their cities and throughout their regions.

The Chaldeans, and prior to them, the Syrians and their Egyptian contemporaries, were very much concerned with sorcery, astrology, and related subjects such as magic and talismans. The Persians and the Greeks learned these disciplines from the aforementioned peoples. The Egyptians, in particular, cultivated those disciplines, which enjoyed prominence among them. In time, however, subsequent religions declared these matters illegal.

TEXT 40

The Arabized Berbers: The City Girl and the Country Girl[1]

The first century A.D. Roman conquerors of North Africa employed the term Berber, or barbarians, to designate the indigenous populations of the Saharan region living outside the orbit of the Roman Empire. It was, however, the Arabized Berbers of Northwest Africa, a region also known as the Maghrib, who conquered Spain in the eighth century, bringing with them a literary form that came to be known as the "Moorish ballad." This anonymous poem of the Maghrib offers a sometimes comical reflection of the inherent tensions that exist between the urban and bedouin pastoralist cultures of the region.

---

[1] Epiphanius Wilson, *Moorish Literature* (New York: Colonial Press, 1901), pp. 207–12.

THE CITY GIRL AND THE COUNTRY GIRL

O thou who hearest me, I will recite
One of these stories I am master of—
A tale that's true. By these I move the hearts
Of lovers like to thee, and I divert
Their minds with pleasant stories. As I hear,
So I relate them, and they please my friends,
By flow of wit and eloquence of thought.
I tell of beauties' battle. And my song
Is written in perfection, straight and clear.

Thinking of naught I walked along one day
When I had gone to see some beauties fair
Whose like I ne'er have seen in city nor
In country yet. I should have said
That they were sun and moon, and that the girls
Of that time were bright stars surpassing far
The Pleiades. The stars are envious
In their far firmaments, each of
The other. That's the reason why we see
Eclipses of the sun and moon.

                              My tale
Is true. The women, like unto the stars,
Are jealous also. Two young virgins met
The day I saw them, a sad day for them,
For one was jealous of the other one.

The citizeness said to the Bedouine:
"Look at thy similars and thou shalt see
In them but rustics, true dogs of the camp.
Now what art thou beside a city girl?
Thou art a Bedouine. Dost thou not dream
Of goat-skin bottles to be filled at dawn?
And loads of wood that thou must daily cut?
And how thou'rt doomed to turn the mill all night,
Fatigued, harassed? Thy feet, unshod, are chapped
And full of cracks. Thy head can never feel
The solace of uncovering, and thou,
All broken with fatigue, must go to sleep
Upon the ground, in soot and dust to lie,
Just like a serpent coiled upon himself.
Thy covering is the tatters of old tents,
Thy pillow is the stones upon the hearth.
All clad in rags thou hast a heavy sleep
Awaking to another stupid day.
Such is the life of all you country folk.
What art thou then compared to those who live

Source: Reprinted from Epiphanius Wilson, *Moorish Literature,* © 1901, Colonial Press.

In shade of walls, who have their mosques for prayer
Where questions are discussed and deeds are drawn?"

The Arab woman to the city girl
Replied: "Get out! Thou'rt like a caverned owl.
And who art thou beside the Arab girls,
The daughters of those tribes whose standards wave
Above brave bands of horsemen as they speed?
Look at thy similars. The doctor ne'er
Can leave their side. Without an illness known
They're faded, pale, and sallow. The harsh lime
Hath filled thy blood with poison. Thou art dead,
Although thou seem'st alive. Thou ne'er hast seen
Our noble Arabs and their feats of strength,
Who to the deserts bring prosperity
By their sharp swords! If thou could'st see our tribe
When all the horsemen charge a hostile band,
Armed with bright lances and with shields to break
The enemy's strong blow! Those who are like
To them are famed afar and glorified.
They're generous hosts and men of nature free.
Within the mosques they've built and lodgings made
For *tolba* and for guests. All those who come
To visit them, bear gifts away, and give
Them praises. Why should they reside in town
Where everything's with price of silver bought?"

The city girl replied: "Oh, Bedouine,
Thou dost forget all that thou hast to do.
Thou go'st from house to house, with artichokes
And mallows, oyster-plants, and such,
Thy garments soaked all through and through with grease.
This is thy daily life. I do not speak
Of what is hid from view. Thy slanders cease!
What canst thou say of me? Better than thee
I follow all the precepts of the Sonna
And note more faithfully the sacred hours.
Hid by my veil no eye hath seen my face:
I'm not like thee, forever in the field.
I've streets to go on when I walk abroad.
What art thou, then, beside me? I heard not
The cows and follow them about all day.
Thou eatest sorrel wild and heart of dwarf
Palm-tree. Thy feet are tired with walking far,
And thy rough hands with digging in the earth."

"Now what impels you, and what leads you on,"
The country girl of city girl inquired,
"To outrage us like this and say such words
Against us, you who are the very worst
Of creatures, in whom all the vices are

Assembled? You are wicked sinners all,
And Satan would not dare to tell your deeds.
You are all witches. And you would betray
Your brother, not to speak of husbands. You
Walk all unguarded in the street alone,
Against your husband's will. And you deny
Your holy faith. The curve of heav'n will weigh
Upon you when you go to meet your God.
Not one of you is honest. O ye blind
Who do not wish to see, whence comes your blindness?
You violate the law divine, and few
Among you fear the Lord. 'Tis in the country,
Amid the fields, that women worship God.
Why say'st thou that the city women sole
Are pious? Canst thou say my prayers for me?"

"What pleasure have the country girls?" replied
The city girl. "They've no amusements there.
There's nothing to divert the eyes. Their hands
They do not stain with henna, setting off
A rounded arm. Rich costumes they wear not,
Which cost some hundred silver pieces each,
Nor numerous garments decked with precious stones.
They are not coifed with kerchiefs of foulard
With flowers brocaded. Neither have they veils
Nor handkerchiefs of silk and broidered gold.
They never have a negress nurse to bring
Their children up and run on services
Throughout the house. And yet they boast as loud
As any braggart. Why bring'st thou the charge
That I a blameful life do lead, whilst thine
Deserves reproof? Dirt in the country holds
Supreme control. The water's scarce enough
To drink, with none left for the bath. The ground
Serves you as bed, and millet is your food,
Or rotten wheat and barley."

                        Then took up
The word, and spoke the Arab woman dark:
"Who are thy ancestors? Which is thy tribe
Among all those that fill the mighty world?
You're only Beny Leqyt, and the scum
Of people of all sorts. Thou call'st thyself
A city woman. What are city men?
Thy lords don't slander folk. 'Tis only those
Who come whence no one knows who have so rude
A tongue. Thou wouldst insult me, thou, of stock
Like thine, with such a name abroad! And thou
Wouldst taunt a Qorechyte, a Hachemite
Of glorious ancestors who earned their fame.
'Tis proper for a woman born of such

A stock illustrious to vaunt herself
Upon her origin. But thou, a vile
Descendant of a conquered race!

                              "Thou call'st
Thyself a Sunnite, yet thou knowest not
The three great things their Author gave to us:
(He knows all secrets.) First is Paradise,
Then the Koran, and then our Prophet great,
Destroyer of false faiths and for all men
The interceder. Whosoe'er loves him
Doth love the Arabs, too, and cleaves to them.
And whosoe'er hates them hates, too, in truth,
The chosen one of God. Thou hatest him,
For thou revil'st my ancestors, and seek'st
To lower their rank and vilify their fame.
Think on thine evil deeds, against the day
When in thy grave thou'lt lie, and that one, too,
When thou shalt rise again, insulter of
The Arabs, king of peoples on the earth."

"The Arabs I do not at all despise,"
The city woman said, "nor yet decry
Their honor, and 'tis only on account
Of thee I spoke against them. But 'tis thou
Who hast insulted all my family, and placed
Thy race above. He who begins is e'er
At fault, and not the one who follows. Thou
The quarrel didst commence. Pray God, our Lord,
To pardon me, as I will pray him, too,
And I the Arabs will no more attack.
If they offend me I will pardon them
And like them for our holy prophet's sake.
I shall awake in Paradise some day.
From them 'tis given, far beyond all price.
Frankly, I love them more than I do love
Myself. I love them from my very heart.
He who a people loveth shall arise
With them. And here's an end to all our words
Of bickering and mutual abuse."

I told them that it was my duty plain
To reconcile them. I accorded both
Of them most pure intentions. Then I sent
Them home, and made agreeable the way.
Their cares I drove away with honeyed words.
I have composed the verses of this piece,
With sense more delicate than rare perfume
Of orange-flower or than sugar sweet,
For those kind hearts who know how to forgive.
As for the evil-minded, they should feel

The *zeqqoum*. With the flowers of rhetoric
My song is ornamented: like the breast
Of some fair virgin all bedecked with stones
Which shine like bright stars in the firmament.
Some of its words will seem severe to those
Who criticise. I culled them like unto
A nosegay in the garden of allusions.
May men of lion hearts and spirit keen—
Beloved by God and objects of his care—
Receive my salutations while they live,
My countless salutations.

       I should let
My name be known to him who's subject to
The Cherfa and obeys their mighty power.
The *mym* precedes, then comes the written *ha*.
The *mym* and *dal* complete the round and make
It comprehensible to him who reads
Mahomet. May God pardon me this work
So frivolous, and also all my faults
And errors. I place confidence in him,
Creator of all men, with pardon free
For all our sins, and in his mercy trust,
Because he giveth it to him who seeks.

The country girl and city girl appeared
Before the judge, demanding sentence just.
In fierce invectives for a while they joined,
But after all I left them reconciled.

TEXT 41

Leo Africanus: The Book Trade at Timbuctu

from A Geographical Historie of Africa[1]

Hassan bin Muhammad al-Wazzan al-Zayyati, known to history as Leo Africanus, was of Moroccan origin, born in 1493 or 1494 and educated at the city of Fez. Little is known of his early life other than that his parents had, as members of the Muslim or Moorish aristocracy, lived in Granada, Spain, when he was a young child, during the reign of the Catholic Sovereigns Ferdinand and Isabella. Captured by Christian pirates, he converted to Christianity and was thereby baptized Leo Africanus. Having traveled widely in countries that were of great interest to the Europeans but of which they knew virtually nothing, the young Moroccan was handed over to Pope Leo X. Because he spoke Spanish in addition to his native Arabic, Leo Africanus was quickly able to gain the attention of the Pope and was given his freedom. Throughout his captivity, Leo Africanus had kept the notes of his extensive travels as a young Moroccan aristocrat. E. W. Bovill writes in The Golden Trade of the Moors:

> The most important events in Leo's life in the eyes of his European contemporaries . . . were his journeys to the Western Sudan, for they enabled him to give to Europe the first detailed account of the interior of Africa, of which men's conception was so blurred that they could not distinguish fact from legend.[2]

Leo Africanus completed his book in the Italian language in 1526. It was eventually translated into English by Pory in 1600 and published as The History and Description of Africa and the Notable Things therein contained.

---

[1] Leo Africanus, *History and Description of Africa*, vol. II, translated by J. Pory, Hakluyt Society, London, 1896, pp. 824–25.
[2] E. W. Bovill, *The Golden Trade of the Moors* (New York: Oxford University Press, 1970), p. 145.

The rich king of Tombuto (as he called the governor) hath many plates and scepters of gold, some whereof weigh 1,300 poundes: and he keepes a magnificent and well furnished court. When he travelleth any whither he rideth upon a camell which is led by some of his noblemen; and so he doth likewise when hee goeth to warfar, and all his souldiers ride upon horses. Whosoever will speak unto this king must first fal down before his feete, and then taking up earth must sprinkle it upon his owne head and shoulders: which custom is ordinarily observed by them that never saluted the king before, or come as ambassadors from other princes. He hath always three thousand horsemen, and a great number of footmen that shoot poysoned arrows, attending upon him. They have often skirmishes with those that refuse to pay tribute, and so many as they take they sell unto the merchants of Tombuto. Here are verie few horses bred, and the merchants and courtiers keepe certain little nags which they use to travel upon: but their best horses are brought out of Barbarie. And the king so soone as he heareth that any merchants are come to town with horses, he commandeth a certain number to be brought before him, and chusing the best horse for himselfe he payeth a most liberal price for him.

Here [continues Leo] are great store of doctors, judges, priests, and other learned men, that are bountifully maintained at the king's cost and charges. And hither are brought divers manuscripts or written books out of Barbarie, which are sold for more money than any other merchandise. The coine of Tombuto is of gold without any stampe or superscription: but in matters of smal value they use certain shels brought hither out of the kingdome of Persia, four hundred of which shels are worth a ducate and six pieces of their gold coine with two third parts weight an ounce.

Source: From E. W. Bovill, *The Golden Trade of the Moors,* © 1970. Reprinted by permission of Oxford University Press.

TEXT 42

Ahmad al-Tijani: A Ritual Prayer[1]

Islamic revival movements aimed at revivifying the faith sprang up in the eighteenth century throughout different regions of the Islamic world. In North and Northwest Africa, a new Sufi, that is, Islamic Gnostic, movement emerged. It became known as the Tijaniyya, named after its spiritual leadership by Abu al-Abbas Ahmad Ibn Muhammad Ibn al-Mukhtar al-Tijani, who was born in 1737 in the southern region of Algeria. At this time all of North Africa labored under the suzerainty of the Ottoman Turks who had established their hegemony in Africa after first conquering Egypt in 1517.

According to Muslim historians, Ahmad al-Tijani withdrew into the desert after receiving a divine call that he should found a new movement. He eventually left his desert retreat in 1798 with a divine revelation, which he began to transmit from the city of Fez in Morocco. His rule was a strict one. "He emphasized above all the need for an intercessor between God and man, the intercessor of the age being himself and his successors."[2]

After his death the movement continued to grow and spread, especially within the Sudanic regions of Africa, south of the Sahara desert. It gained a strong following among the Fulbe or Fulani ethnicity of the western Sudan and became the rallying cry for a series of holy wars launched in the eighteenth and nineteenth centuries to purify Islam in West Africa.

O God, bless our master Muhammad, who opened what had been closed, and who is the seal of what had gone before; he who makes the Truth victorious by the Truth, the guide to Thy straight path, and bless his household as is the due of his immense position and grandeur.

---

[1]Jamil M. Abun-Nasr, *The Tijaniyya: A Sufi Order in the Modern World* (New York: Oxford University Press, 1965), p. 51.
[2]Reynold Alleyne Nicholson, *A Literary History of the Arabs,* (New York: Cambridge University Press, 1930), p. 108.
Source: From Jamil M. Abun-Nasr, *The Tijaniyya: A Sufi Order in the Modern World,* © 1965. Reprinted by permission of Oxford University Press.

TEXT 43

The Mahdi: A Proclamation[1]

*E*gypt had since 1517 been ruled by the Ottoman Turks, who had likewise established their dominion over Nubia to the south. However, by the late nineteenth century, Great Britain had stepped into the power vacuum created by the disintegrating Ottoman Empire and established its dominion over Egypt. Nubia, on the other hand, became an unexpectedly difficult challenge for the Turks to hold onto or for the British to seize. The reason lay in the emergence of a holy man of the Dongola district in Nubia who in 1881 declared himself the Mahdi, that is, the awaited savior of the Islamic faith. Muhammad Ahmad al-Mahdi belonged to a small Sufi order of Islamic Gnostics called the Sammaniyah. As "Mahdi," he promised to restore Muslim purity to the faithful of Islam. His call for a jihad prompted an enthusiastic response in the Sudan. In 1885 the Mahdi and his army seized the Sudanese capital city of Khartoum, killing the British colonial administrator Charles Gordon. Well educated in Arabic, Muhammad Ahmad al-Mahdi maintained a lively correspondence with his enemies, much of which still survives.

From Mohammed El Mahdi to All His Beloved, the Believers in God and His Book

Beloved, bear in mind that real wealth consists in obeying God, and following in the footsteps of those whom God has guided into the right path. The happy man is he who is guided by others, and the foolish man is he who follows after his own ideas. God has distinguished this holy faith by holy war. Any man who takes part in this holy war will be considered a true believer; but any man who refuses to join will be consid-

---

[1]F. R. Wingate, *Mahdism and the Egyptian Sudan* (London: Frank Cass & Co., 1968), pp. 92–93.
Source: From F. R. Wingate, *Mahdism and the Egyptian Sudan,* © 1968. Reprinted by permission of Frank Cass & Co.

ered as one of those at enmity with the Prophet. (Here follow many verses from the Kuran and Ahadith.) Why, therefore, do you disobey the Almighty God? Have you not seen how I have gained victories over the Turks and infidels, whose bodies have been burnt wherever they have been pierced with spears?

Do you seek a greater miracle than this? It is just as the miracles of the Prophet. They (the Turks) are well armed with rifles and held strong positions, but not only were they defeated, they were utterly destroyed. The cause of their destruction is, that I am a light from God, and the Prophet has confirmed me as Mahdi, and has made me sit several times on his own seat in the presence of all the khalifas and prophets, and Elias was present too with all the angels, and every believer from Adam up to the present time. In battle, the Prophet and those above mentioned are with me; he has given me the sword of victory, and has promised that not even the Thakalain (i.e. half man half jinn) can defeat me. The Prophet also informed me that God has placed a mole on my right cheek, as a mark that I am the Mahdi. He has also given me another sign, which is a banner of light carried by Izrail (the angel of death), who walks before me in time of battle. In this manner I have been enabled to capture Kordofan and all the surrounding countries, and God will also open your country for me, and by His will the whole world will submit to me, accepting me as the true Mahdi. Woe, therefore, to those who do not believe in me, for they will all be destroyed. Why did you not set forth as soon as you heard of me, in order to help in the holy war? Are you afraid of the Turks and their strength? Are you not aware that all their armies must fall into my hands? Do you not know that all the infidels will be destroyed by us? Do you not believe that I am the expected Mahdi? Do you not believe in the holy writings which speak of me? (Here follow several verses of the Kuran, etc.)

Remember that I have come by order of the Prophet. He has sent me to be your saviour, and you should therefore believe in me. The Prophet has told me that any one who disbelieves in me disbelieves in God and in His Prophet. I have quoted his own words, and he repeated them three times to me. You are aware that I am descended from the family of the Prophet. I am begotten of the forehead of his father and mother, and the father and mother of my mother are descended from the Abbassides. I am lineally descended from El Hussein (the Prophet's grandson).

I made my hejira (flight) to Masat, in the mountain of Gedir, by order of the Prophet, and by his order I came into Kordofan. From there I sent my several proclamations, and I now send this one to you. On receiving it, leave the Turks at once; do not hesitate to leave your property and children behind you; leave them, and come even to the nearest village, and fight against the Turks with all your strength. (Here follow several verses from the Kuran.)

I send you Sheikh Osman Digna, of Suakin, as your emir, in order to revive the true religion. On his arrival, join him and obey his orders, advance against the Turks, and drive them out of your country. All God's people before you have quitted their country and children, in order to conquer the land of the infidels. They did not mind death nor fatigue. The present time will now prove whether you are truly God's people. This you will be if you obey the orders of the Mahdi; but if you disobey, then you must expect nothing but the sword, and your fate will be that of all those who have disobeyed us.

PART SIX

Ethiopia and Somalia

Both Ethiopia and Somalia have escaped the invisibility suffered by so many African nations in the eyes of contemporary westerners. But these two countries have only done so as a consequence of dramatic news reportage recounting incidents of famine and civil and ethnic strife. That this northeast region of Africa spawned some of the most prolific artistic

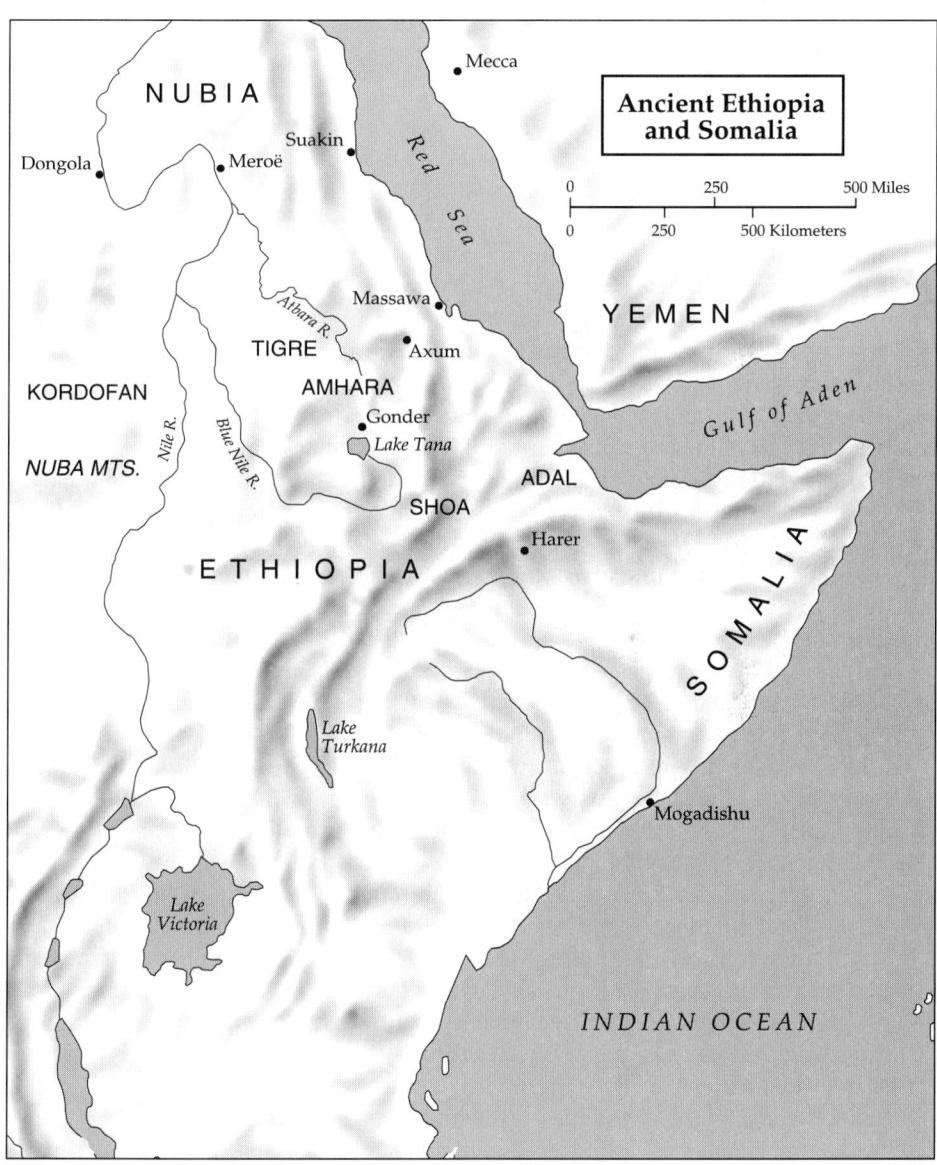

and literary cultures of the ancient world is still a little known reality, lost in today's more graphic narratives of misery and warfare.

The name *Ethiopia* derives from the Greek term for "burnt faces," and was used by Europeans in ancient times to refer to the African societies south of Egypt. What historians now know about the earliest history of the Ethiopian region is that around the sixth century B.C. Semitic-speaking hunters and traders from the Saba region of southwestern Arabia crossed the Red Sea and intermarried the Bantu-speaking populations residing in the Eritrean coastal region of Africa. Their trading settlements supplied ivory for the Persian and Indian trade.[1] The language of Ge'ez or ancient Ethiopic evolved in this region with its own alphabet derived from the Semitic script of Saba.

These early settlements over time evolved into the powerful state of Aksum, which according to the Greek shipping manual, *The Periplus of the Erythraean Sea,* conducted the most lucrative ivory trade in the entire region. At its height in the sixth century A.D., the Aksumite nobility and wealthy merchant classes built impressive temples, monuments, and tombs in stone, some of which are still standing. However, in diverting the ivory trade from the interior kingdom of Meroë, Aksum's growth almost certainly came at the expense of its Nubian neighbor on the Nile River.[2]

An Alexandrian monk named Frumentius converted the Aksumite King Ezana (A.D. 320–350) to Christianity sometime during the latter years of his reign. Influenced by the religious doctrines of the Egyptian Coptic Church, Ethiopian Christians adopted the Monophysite doctrine asserting the divinity but not the human nature of Jesus Christ.

For a period during the sixth century, Aksum had so strengthened its political base that it was able to expand across the Red Sea to encompass the Arabian region of Saba within its domain. However, it began a process of steady decline during the eighth century caused in large measure by the deterioration of an ecologically fragile agricultural environment and shifting trade patterns, which now favored the Persians and Arabs who had become unified under the Islamic banner.

Ethiopia began a long process of recovery beginning in the eleventh century. In A.D. 1150 the new Zagwe dynasty was founded by overthrowing the old Aksumite line of kings. The Zagwe rulers supported the building of monasteries and missionaries to convert ever larger elements of the Ethiopian population to Christianity. One of the most noted kings of this dynasty, Lalibela, who reigned sometime between A.D. 1200 and 1250, built monumental churches hewn out of rock that remain standing today.

Also, during this time the Ethiopian Church began to develop characteristics that stamped it as distinct from the Egyptian Coptic Church. In particular, the religious culture of Ethiopia showed itself to be more deeply influenced by elements of Judaism in beliefs and rituals, such as circumcision and dietary laws, than was the case with other Christian denominations.

In addition, Ethiopia maintained its own indigenous community of Jews numbering by the nineteenth century several hundred thousand. Even though considerable speculation had surrounded their origins, most scholars of religion now say that there

---

[1]Kevin Shillington, *History of Africa* (New York: St. Martin's Press, 1996), p. 68.
[2]Graham Connah, *African Civilization: Precolonial Cities and States in Tropical Africa.* (New York: Cambridge University Press, 1987), p. 73.

is little reason to believe that the Ethiopian Jews, referred to as *Beta Israel* or *falasha*, are anything other than one of the ancient tribes of Israel, isolated from the Jewish mainstream for more than 2,400 years. This particular community of Jews may have established communities first in Kush or Nubia and then migrated further south into Aksum during the early centuries A.D. In the Old Testament Books of Isaiah 18:7 and Zephania 3:10, reference is made to the Jewish people who reside "beyond the rivers of Abyssinia [Ethiopia]."

THE SOLOMONID DYNASTY

In the latter part of the thirteenth century, the Zagwe dynasty was overturned by a new line calling itself the Solomonid dynasty and claiming descent through the rulers of ancient Aksum to the traditional union of biblical King Solomon and the Queen of Sheba (Saba). This period ushered in what has come to be called the golden age of Ge'ez literature. Over the course of the next 250 years, literary developments paralleled the nation's political successes as it continued to maintain its defenses against its Muslim neighbors.[3]

From the beginning of its reign, the new Solomonid dynasty sought to legitimize its rule by espousing an ideology that asserted its direct descent from the union of Solomon and Sheba through the former Aksumite line of rulers. Thus, at the political behest of the Solomonid royal court sometime between A.D. 1314 and 1322, an Ethiopian monk named Isaac composed the *Kebra Nagast* (*Book of the Glory of Kings*), which remains the most venerated work of Ethiopian literature. This version of the Solomon and Sheba legend comprises in the minds of many Ethiopians the "definitive proof" that they are the descendants of the union of biblical King Solomon and the Queen of Sheba. Even though influenced by the folklore of Egypt and the Near East, this text written in Ge'ez or ancient Ethiopic was intended, without a doubt, to authenticate the rule of the new Solomonid dynasty of Ethiopia claiming purported descent from King Solomon.

Another important literary form, that of royal chronicles written by court historians, was begun during the reign of Amda Tseyon (1314–1344). Richard Pankhurst describes these narratives thus:

> [The chronicles] were in most cases produced to perpetuate and glorify the memory of the ruler for whom they were written and who probably supervised their composition from time to time. Their authors tended inevitably to present the sovereign's character and actions in the best possible light rather than to attempt any impartial assessment. There were, however, cases in which the chroniclers wrote after the death of the sovereign whose reign they described. In such cases, the authors could write with greater freedom but might seek to blacken their subject's life in order to brighten the contrast with the rulers then in power.[4]

---

[3]Albert S. Gerard, *African Language Literatures: An Introduction to the Literary History of Sub-Saharan Africa* (London: Longman, 1981), p. 8.
[4]Richard Pankhurst, *The Ethiopian Royal Chronicles* (London: Oxford University Press, 1967), pp. xii–xiii; and Gerard, *African Language Literatures*, p. 9.

At the same time, the religious needs of this ancient culture motivated the production of a prolific sacred literature. In following the 39 books of the Hebrew Bible, the 27 canonical books of the Christian New Testament, and numerous Apocryphal and Pseudepigraphic works, the Ethiopian Church created a major corpus of literature in the Ge'ez language. Among the apocalyptic books that were most popular in the Ethiopian Church was the Book of Enoch. Originally a Jewish work, this book has been preserved in toto only in the Ge'ez (ancient Ethiopic) version. Also, the Book of Kufale (Jubilees), another Jewish work of considerable importance, is preserved in complete form only in the Ge'ez version and has become of great interest to scholars.[5] Hagiographic literature on the lives of saints also held a central place in the religious traditions of Ethiopia.

Literature in Ge'ez began a steady decline during the sixteenth century, following the invasion of Ahmad al-Gran of Harar (in Somalia) who launched a successful jihad toppling Ethiopian King Lebna Dengel (1508–1540) and wrested control of the country. Al-Gran was finally overthrown and killed in 1543, and Christianity restored to Ethiopia. However, it was not before many of Ethiopia's monasteries were destroyed and their libraries burnt to the ground. The following centuries witnessed a gradual restoration of the country's Christian legacy and the emergence of the modern language of Amharic, with Ge'ez withdrawing from popular usage but remaining the language of Ethiopian Church literature.

DEFEAT OF THE ITALIANS

In the late nineteenth century, Italy became caught up in the diplomatic competition for colonial possessions, which had seized its European neighbors during that era. Between 1885 and 1886, Italy devoured the Eritrean coast on the Red Sea and established Somaliland as an Italian protectorate. Advancing into Ethiopia, the Italians met with humiliating defeat at the hands of the Emperor Menelik's army. Thus, by the early decades of the twentieth century, Ethiopia had been one of the only African nations strong enough to maintain its independence in the face of an intense scramble for Africa undertaken by the principal European powers of Britain, France, Germany, Spain, and Portugal. During World War II, however, an Italian expeditionary force of 120,000 invaded the country, sending Emperor Haile Selassie into exile in Europe. His country was liberated in 1941 by an Allied force containing thousands of troops from the British colonies of Nigeria, Ghana, and Sierra Leone.

SOMALIA

The Somali city of Harar emerged as a strong commercial center during the Middle Ages as did Mogadishu, on the Indian Ocean coast. In fact, by the fourteenth century the Mogadishu seaport had become the primary trading center for East African commerce. However, the intellectual traditions of the Somalis, perhaps given the nomadic

---

[5]Ephraim Isaac, *The Ethiopian Church* (Boston: Henry N. Sawyer Company, 1968), pp. 34–36.

nature of their populations, unlike the sedentarized, agriculturist lifestyle of their Ethiopian neighbors, tended toward the refinement of oral poetry. Little remains of early written tradition other than the chronicles of Somali conqueror Ahmad al-Gran written in Arabic by Shihab al-Din Ahmad Ibn Abd al-Qadar, and two religious books written in the local Harari language employing the Arabic script. The first of these books, called the *Book of Duties,* offers a précis of the Muslim creed. The second, *Lay of the Four Caliphs,* presents a 5,000-line poem celebrating the first four caliphs of Islam who lived during the time of Muhammad.[6]

Even so, the memories of Somali's poets have indeed been long. Poems reaching as far back as the eighteenth century are still being recited. These include the works of such bards as Raage Ugaas from the Ogaden clan who lived in the 1700s, Haaji Ali Abd al-Rahman of the Majerteyn Sultanate who also lived in the latter half of the eighteenth century, and Qamaan Bulxan of the nineteenth century.[7]

The greatest political figure of precolonial modern Somalia was Mahammed 'Abdille Hasan, born in 1864. Labeled by the British "the Mad Mullah," Mahammed 'Abdille waged a series of successful wars against the British, Italians, and the Ethiopians, all of whom sought at various times to colonize Somalia. He negotiated a temporary truce in 1905 and established a small Islamic state on the borders of Italy's newly acquired Somali colony. After Mahammed 'Abdille's death in 1920, the Italians succeeded in absorbing his state into their larger Somali colony.

---

[6]Albert S. Gerard, *African Language Literatures: An Introduction to the Literary History of Sub-Saharan African* (London: Longman, 1981), p. 13.
[7]Ibid. pp. 157–59.

TEXT 44

King Ezana: The Decline and Fall of Meroë[1]

By the fourth century A.D., the Nubian state of Meroë (located in present-day Sudan) had fallen into decline. Erosion caused by overfarming of the ecologically fragile region and the cutting down of trees to feed a massive iron smelting industry led to the exhaustion of Meroë's resource base. A once lucrative trade with Roman Egypt also had collapsed as the economic fortunes of Egypt itself declined during this period.

As the political strength of Meroë waned, a new state to the south, Aksum (later to become Ethiopia), rose to take its place. In A.D. 350 Aksumite King Ezana, also called Kasu, conquered what remained of the once great Meroë. With the original nobility of the Nubian state having fled some years before, what remained of this once great empire was now in the hands of pastoralist marauders known as the Noba, whose clans were distinguished as either "Red" or "Black."

The description of Ezana's invasion of Meroë was originally inscribed in Ge'ez or ancient Ethiopic. This early ruler of Aksum was also noted for later having converted to Christianity under the influence of a monk from Alexandria named Frumentius, and made the new faith a state religion.

---

[1] L. P. Kirwan, *Kush: Journal of the Sudan Antiquities Services,* Khartoum, vol. VIII (London: Sudan Archaeological Research Society, 1960), pp. 163–65.

TEXT 44: *King Ezana: The Decline and Fall of Meroë*

Through the might of the Lord of Heaven, (who is) victorious in Heaven and on earth over all!
ᶜĒzana, the son of (ʾElla)—ᶜAmīda, of the tribe Halēn, the King of Axum and Him(yar)
And of Raidān and of Sabaʾ and of Salḥēn and of Ṣiyāmō and of Begā and
Of Kāsū, the King of Kings, the son of (ʾElla)—ᶜAmīdā, who will not be defeated by the enemy.
Through the might of the Lord of Heaven, who has created me, of the Lord of All by whom the King is beloved,
Who will not be defeated by the enemy, no foe shall stand before me and behind me no foe shall follow!
Through the might of the Lord of All I took the field against the Nōbā, when the people of the Nōbā revolted,
When they boasted and "He will not cross over the Takkazē," said the (people of) the Nōbā,
When they did violence to the peoples Mangūrtō and Hasā and Bāryā, and the Blacks
Waged war on the Red Peoples and a second and a third time broke their oath and without
Consideration (Rücksicht) slew their neighbours and plundered our envoys and our messengers
Whom I had sent to interrogate them, robbing them of their possessions and
Seizing their lances. When I sent again and they did not hear me, and reviled me
And made off, I took the field against them. And I armed myself (?) with the power of the Lord of the Land
And fought on the Takkazē at the ford of Kemalkē. And thereupon they fled
And stood not still, and I pursued the fugitives (?) twenty-three—23—days,
Slaying (some of) them and capturing others and taking booty from them, where I came; while prisoners and
Booty were brought back by my people who marched out; while I burnt their towns,
Those of masonry and those of straw, and (my people) seized their corn and their bronze and the dried meat
And the images in their temples and destroyed the stocks of corn and cotton and (the enemy)
Plunged into the river Sēdā,—and (there were) many who perished in the water,
The number I know not—; and as their vessels foundered, a multitude of people,
Men and women, were drowned. And I took prisoner two—2—chieftains,
Who had come to spy, riding on camels,—and their names were
Yesakā,I, Būtālē,I,—also a man of noble birth ʾAngabēnāwī: and the following chieftains fell:

Source: From L. P. Kirwan, *Kush: Journal of the Sudan Antiquities Services,* © 1960 by the Sudan Archaeological Research Society. Reprinted by permission of the Sudan Archaeological Research Society.

Danōkuē,I; Dagalē,I; 'Anakuē,I; Hawārē,I; Karkarā,I; their priest,I; (the soldiers) had wounded him and taken from him a silver Crown (?) and a gold Ring(?); it was thus five chieftains who fell,
And the priest,I. And I arrived at the Kāsū, slaying (some of) them and taking (others) prisoner
At the junction of the rivers Sēdā and Takkazē. And on the day after my arrival
(I) dispatched into the field the troop Mahazā and the Harā troop and the Damaw(a) and Falh(a) and Serā'
Up the Sēdā (against) the towns of masonry and of straw; their towns
Of masonry are called 'Alwā,I, Darō,I. And they slew and took prisoners and threw (them)
Into the water, and they returned safe and sound, after they had terrified their enemies and had conquered through the power of the Lord of the Land.
And I sent the troop Halēn and the troop Lakēn(?) and
The troop Sabarāt and Falh(a) and Serā' down the Sēdā (against) the towns of straw
Of the Nōbā, 4, Neguēs,I; the towns of masonry of the Kāsū which the Nōbā had taken (were) Tabītō(?),I,
Fertōti,I; and they arrived at the territory of the Red Nōbā, and
My people returned safe and sound after they had taken (some) prisoner and slain (others) and had seized their booty through the power of the Lord of Heaven.
And I erected a throne at the junction of the rivers Sēdā and
Takkazē, opposite the town of masonry which is on this peninsula.
The Lord of Heaven has given me (as follows:) Male prisoners 214, female prisoners 415; total 629.
And men slain 602; women and children slain 156; total 700 (and) 58.
And that is, prisoners and dead (together), 1387. And booty about 10500 cattle (and) 60,
And about 51050 sheep. And I erected a throne here in Šadō.
Through the power of the Lord of Heaven who has helped me and has given me dominion.
The Lord of Heaven strengthens my dominion! And as he now has conquered my enemy, (so)
May he conquer for me, where I (but) go! As he now has given me victory and has overthrown my enemies,
(So will I rule) in right and justice, doing no wrong to the peoples. And I placed
The throne, which I have set up, and the Earth which bears it, in the protection of the Lord of Heaven who has made me King,
And if there is one who obliterates it and destroys it and tears it down,
He and his line shall be uprooted and torn (asunder); of them no trace shall remain (in the Land).
And I set up this throne through the Power of the Lord of Heaven.

TEXT 45

Isaac: Solomon and Sheba

from the Kebra Nagast[1]

*T*he thirteenth century is often called the golden age of Ge'ez or ancient Ethiopic literature. A new dynasty wrested the throne from the Aksumite rulers of Ethiopia in A.D. 1270. In order to establish their legitimacy to reign, the new rulers began calling themselves the Solomonid dynasty, claiming to be descendants of the mythical union between the Queen of Sheba and King Solomon in the Bible. It is therefore not surprising that sometime between 1314 and 1322 a member of the Ethiopian clergy named Isaac set to writing in Ge'ez an elaboration of the story of King Solomon and the Queen of Sheba. The book he wrote, the **Kebra Nagast,** legitimized the claims of the new rulers. The term **Sheba** cited in the Bible refers to the Saba region of southwestern Arabia which borders the Red Sea. However, the fact that Ethiopians have throughout their history defined this ancient queen as the mother of their nation harkens to distant recollections of that state's earliest creation when Sabaean immigrants from the Arabian peninsula intermixed with the local Africans residing in the Ethiopian region.

Often referred to as a historical romance, the **Kebra Nagast** presents the story of Makeda, the Queen of Sheba who visited King Solomon in Jerusalem attracted by tales of his great wisdom and the magnificence of his kingdom. Inspired by Solomon's wisdom and charm, she relinquished her traditional religious worship of the sun and moon and converted to worshiping the God of Israel. Solomon, captivated by her beauty and intelligence, decided to have a child with her. She returned to Ethiopia and bore Solomon a son, Menyelek.

---

[1] E. A. Wallis Budge, *The Queen of Sheba and Her Only Son Menyelek,* "The Book of the Glory of Kings" *[Kebra Nagast]* (London: Oxford University Press, 1922), pp. 17–25.

And there was a certain wise man, the leader of a merchant's caravan, whose name was TÂMRÎN, and he used to load five hundred and twenty camels, and he possessed about three and seventy ships.

Now at that time King SOLOMON wished to build the House of God, and he sent out messages among all the merchants in the east and in the west, and in the north and in the south, bidding the merchants come and take gold and silver from him, so that he might take from them whatsoever was necessary for the work. And certain men reported to him concerning this rich ETHIOPIAN merchant, and SOLOMON sent to him a message and told him to bring whatsoever he wished from the country of ARABIA, red gold, and black wood that could not be eaten by worms, and sapphires. And that merchant, whose name was TÂMRÎN, the merchant of the Queen of ETHIOPIA, went to SOLOMON the King; and SOLOMON took whatsoever he desired from him, and he gave to the merchant whatsoever he wished for in great abundance. Now that merchant was a man of great understanding, and he saw and comprehended the wisdom of SOLOMON, and he marvelled [thereat], and he watched carefully so that he might learn how the King made answer by his word, and understand his judgement, and the readiness of his mouth, and the discreetness of his speech, and the manner of his life, and his sitting down and his rising up, and his occupations, and his love, and his administration, and his table, and his law. To those to whom SOLOMON had to give orders he spake with humility and graciousness, and when they had committed a fault he admonished them [gently]. For he ordered his house in the wisdom and fear of God, and he smiled graciously on the fools and set them on the right road, and he dealt gently with the maidservants. He opened his mouth in parables, and his words were sweeter than the purest honey; his whole behaviour was admirable, and his whole aspect pleasant. For wisdom is beloved by men of understanding, and is rejected by fools.

And when that merchant had seen all these things he was astonished, and he marvelled exceedingly. For those who were wont to see SOLOMON held him in complete affection, and he [became] their teacher; and because of his wisdom and excellence those who had once come to him did not wish to leave him and go away from him. And the sweetness of his words was like water to the man who is athirst, and like bread to the hungry man, and like healing to the sick man, and like apparel to the naked man. And he was like a father to the orphans. And he judged with righteousness and accepted the person of no man (i.e., he was impartial). He had glory, and riches, which God had given unto him, in great abundance, namely, gold, and silver, and precious stones, and rich apparel, and cattle, and sheep, and goats innumerable. Now in the days of SOLOMON the King gold was as common as bronze, and silver as lead, and bronze and lead and iron were as abundant as the grass of the fields and the reeds of the desert; and cedarwood was also abundant. And God had given unto him glory, and riches, and wisdom, and grace in such abundance that there was none like unto him among his predecessors, and among those who came after him there was none like unto him.

Source: From E. A. Wallis Budge, *The Queen of Sheba and Her Only Son Menyelek,* © 1992 by the University College Oxford and Christ College Cambridge. Reprinted by permission of University College Oxford.

23. *How the Merchant returned to* ETHIOPIA

And it came to pass that the merchant TÂMRÎN wished to return to his own country, and he went to SOLOMON and bowed low before him, and embraced him, and said unto him, "Peace be to thy majesty! Send me away and let me depart to my country to my Lady, for I have tarried long in beholding thy glory, and thy wisdom, and the abundance of dainty meats wherewith thou hast regaled me. And now I would depart to my Lady. Would that I could abide with thee, even as one of the very least of thy servants, for blessed are they who hear thy voice and perform thy commands! Would that I could abide here and never leave thee! but thou must send me away to my Lady because of what hath been committed to my charge, so that I may give unto her her property. And as for myself, I am her servant." And SOLOMON went into his house and gave unto him whatever valuable thing he desired for the country of ETHIOPIA, and he sent him away in peace. And TÂMRÎN bade him farewell, and went forth, and journeyed along his road, and came to his Lady, and delivered over to her all the possessions which he had brought. And he related unto her how he had arrived in the country of JUDAH [and] JERUSALEM, and how he had gone into the presence of SOLOMON the King, and all that he had heard and seen. And he told her how SOLOMON administered just judgement, and how he spake with authority, and how he decided rightly in all the matters which he enquired into, and how he returned soft and gracious answers, and how there was nothing false about him, and how he appointed inspectors over the seven hundred woodmen who hauled the timber and the eight hundred masons who hewed the stone, and how he sought to learn from all the merchants and dealers concerning the cunning craft and the working thereof, and how he received information and imparted it two-fold, and how all his handicraft and his works were performed with wisdom.

And each morning TÂMRÎN related to the Queen [about] all the wisdom of SOLOMON, how he administered judgement and did what was just, and how he ordered his table, and how he made feasts, and how he taught wisdom, and how he directed his servants and all his affairs on a wise system, and how they went on their errands at his command, and how no man defrauded another, and how no man purloined the property of his neighbour, and how there was neither a thief nor a robber in his days. For in his wisdom he knew those who had done wrong, and he chastised them, and made them afraid, and they did not repeat their evil deeds, but they lived in a state of peace which had mingled therein the fear of the King.

All these things did TÂMRÎN relate unto the Queen, and each morning he recalled the things that he had seen with the King and described them unto her. And the Queen was struck dumb with wonder at the things that she heard from the merchant her servant, and she thought in her heart that she would go to him; and she wept by reason of the greatness of her pleasure in those things that TÂMRÎN had told her. And she was exceedingly anxious to go to him, but when she pondered upon the long journey she thought that it was too far and too difficult to undertake. And time after time she asked TÂMRÎN questions about SOLOMON, and time after time TÂMRÎN told her about him, and she became very wishful and most desirous to go that she might hear his wisdom, and see his face, and embrace him, and petition his royalty. And her heart inclined to go to him, for God had made her heart incline to go and had made her to desire it.

24. How the Queen made ready to set out on her Journey

And the Queen said unto them, "Hearken, O ye who are my people, and give ye ear to my words. For I desire wisdom and my heart seeketh to find understanding. I am smitten with the love of wisdom, and I am constrained by the cords of understanding; for wisdom is far better than treasure of gold and silver, and wisdom is the best of everything that hath been created on the earth. Now unto what under the heavens shall wisdom be compared? It is sweeter than honey, and it maketh one to rejoice more than wine, and it illumineth more than the sun, and it is to be loved more than precious stones. And it fatteneth more than oil, and it satisfieth more than dainty meats, and it giveth [a man] more renown than thousands of gold and silver. It is a source of joy for the heart, and a bright and shining light for the eyes, and a giver of speed to the feet, and a shield for the breast, and a helmet for the head, and chain-work for the neck, and a belt for the loins. It maketh the ears to hear and hearts to understand, it is a teacher of those who are learned, and it is a consoler of those who are discreet and prudent, and it giveth fame to those who seek after it. And as for a kingdom, it cannot stand without wisdom, and riches cannot be preserved without wisdom; the foot cannot keep the place wherein it hath set itself without wisdom. And without wisdom that which the tongue speaketh is not acceptable. Wisdom is the best of all treasures. He who heapeth up gold and silver doeth so to no profit without wisdom, but he who heapeth up wisdom—no man can filch it from his heart. That which fools heap up the wise consume. And because of the wickedness of those who do evil the righteous are praised; and because of the wicked acts of fools the wise are beloved. Wisdom is an exalted thing and a rich thing: I will love her like a mother, and she shall embrace me like her child. I will follow the footprints of wisdom and she shall protect me for ever; I will seek after wisdom, and she shall be with me for ever; I will follow her footprints, and she shall not cast me away; I will lean upon her, and she shall be unto me a wall of adamant; I will seek asylum with her, and she shall be unto me power and strength; I will rejoice in her, and she shall be unto me abundant grace. For it is right for us to follow the footprints of wisdom, and for the soles of our feet to stand upon the threshold of the gates of wisdom. Let us seek her, and we shall find her; let us love her, and she will not withdraw herself from us; let us pursue her, and we shall overtake her; let us ask, and we shall receive; and let us turn our hearts to her so that we may never forget her. If [we] remember her, she will have us in remembrance; and in connection with fools thou shalt not remember wisdom, for they do not hold her in honour, and she doth not love them. The honouring of wisdom is the honouring of the wise man, and the loving of wisdom is the loving of the wise man. Love the wise man and withdraw not thyself from him, and by the sight of him thou shalt become wise; hearken to the utterance of his mouth, so that thou mayest become like unto him; watch the place whereon he hath set his foot, and leave him not, so that thou mayest receive the remainder of his wisdom. And I love him merely on hearing concerning him and without seeing him, and the whole story of him that hath been told me is to me as the desire of my heart, and like water to the thirsty man."

And her nobles, and her slaves, and her handmaidens, and her counsellors answered and said unto her, "O our Lady, as for wisdom, it is not lacking in thee, and it is because of thy wisdom that thou lovest wisdom. And as for us, if thou goest we will go with thee, and if thou sittest down we will sit down with thee; our death shall be with thy death, and our life with thy life." Then the Queen made ready to set out on her journey with great pomp and majesty, and with great equipment and many preparations.

For, by the Will of God, her heart desired to go to JERUSALEM so that she might hear the wisdom of SOLOMON; for she had hearkened eagerly. So she made ready to set out. And seven hundred and ninety-seven camels were loaded, and mules and asses innumerable were loaded, and she set out on her journey and followed her road without pause, and her heart had confidence in God.

25. *How the Queen came to* SOLOMON *the King*

And she arrived in JERUSALEM, and brought to the King very many precious gifts which he desired to possess greatly. And he paid her great honour and rejoiced, and he gave her a habitation in the royal palace near him. And he sent her food both for the morning and evening meal, each time fifteen measures by the *ḳôrî* of finely ground white meal, cooked with oil and gravy and sauce in abundance, and thirty measures by the *ḳôrî* of crushed white meal wherefrom bread for three hundred and fifty people was made, with the necessary platters and trays, and ten stalled oxen, and five bulls, and fifty sheep, without (counting) the kids, and deer, and gazelles and fatted fowls, and a vessel of wine containing sixty *gerrât* measures, and thirty measures of old wine, and twenty-five singing men and twenty-five singing women, and the finest honey and rich sweets, and some of the food which he himself ate, and some of the wine whereof he drank. And every day he arrayed her in eleven garments which bewitched the eyes. And he visited her and was gratified, and she visited him and was gratified, and she saw his wisdom, and his just judgements and his splendour, and his grace, and heard the eloquence of his speech. And she marvelled in her heart, and was utterly astonished in her mind, and she recognized in her understanding, and perceived very clearly with her eyes how admirable he was; and she wondered exceedingly because of what she saw and heard with him—how perfect he was in composure, and wise in understanding, and pleasant in graciousness, and commanding in stature. And she observed the subtlety of his voice, and the discreet utterances of his lips, and that he gave his commands with dignity, and that his replies were made quietly and with the fear of God. All these things she saw, and she was astonished at the abundance of his wisdom, and there was nothing whatsoever wanting in his word and speech, but everything that he spake was perfect.

And SOLOMON was working at the building of the House of God, and he rose up and went to the right and to the left, and forward and backward. And he showed the workmen the measurement and weight and the space covered [by the materials], and he told the workers in metal how to use the hammer, and the drill, and the chisel (?), and he showed the stone-masons the angle [measure] and the circle and the surface [measure]. And everything was wrought by his order, and there was none who set himself in opposition to his word; for the light of his heart was like a lamp in the darkness, and his wisdom was as abundant as the sand. And of the speech of the beasts and the birds there was nothing hidden from him, and he forced the devils to obey him by his wisdom. And he did everything by means of the skill which God gave him when he made supplication to Him; for he did not ask for victory over his enemy, and he did not ask for riches and fame, but he asked God to give him wisdom and understanding whereby he might rule his people, and build His House, and beautify the work of God and all that He had given him [in] wisdom and understanding.

26. How the King held converse with the Queen

And the Queen MÂKĔDÂ spake unto King SOLOMON, saying, "Blessed art thou, my lord, in that such wisdom and understanding have been given unto thee. For myself I only wish that I could be as one of the least of thine handmaidens, so that I could wash thy feet, and hearken to thy wisdom, and apprehend thy understanding, and serve thy majesty, and enjoy thy wisdom. O how greatly have pleased me thy answering, and the sweetness of thy voice, and the beauty of thy going, and the graciousness of thy words, and the readiness thereof. The sweetness of thy voice maketh the heart to rejoice, and maketh the bones fat, and giveth courage to hearts, and goodwill and grace to the lips, and strength to the gait. I look upon thee and I see that thy wisdom is immeasureable and thine understanding inexhaustible, and that it is like unto a lamp in the darkness, and like unto a pomegranate in the garden, and like unto a pearl in the sea, and like unto the Morning Star among the stars, and like unto the light of the moon in the mist, and like unto a glorious dawn and sunrise in the heavens. And I give thanks unto Him that brought me hither and showed thee to me, and made me to tread upon the threshold of thy gate, and made me to hear thy voice."

And King SOLOMON answered and said unto her, "Wisdom and understanding spring from thee thyself. As for me, [I only possess them] in the measure in which the God of ISRAEL hath given [them] to me because I asked and entreated them from Him. And thou, although thou dost not know the God of ISRAEL, hast this wisdom which thou hast made to grow in thine heart, and [it hath made thee come] to see me, the vassal and slave of my God, and the building of His sanctuary which I am establishing, and wherein I serve and move round about my Lady, the Tabernacle of the Law of the God of ISRAEL, the holy and heavenly ZION. Now, I am the slave of my God, and I am not a free man; I do not serve according to my own will but according to His Will. And this speech of mine springeth not from myself, but I give utterance only to what He maketh me to utter. Whatsoever He commandeth me that I do; wheresoever He wisheth me to go thither I go; whatsoever He teacheth me that I speak; that concerning which He giveth me wisdom I understand. For from being only dust He hath made me flesh, and from being only water He hath made me a solid man, and from being only an ejected drop, which shot forth upon the ground would have dried up on the surface of the earth, He hath fashioned me in His own likeness and hath made me in His own image."

27. Concerning the Labourer

And as SOLOMON was talking in this wise with the Queen, he saw a certain labourer carrying a stone upon his head and a skin of water upon his neck and shoulders, and his food and his sandals were [tied] about his loins, and there were pieces of wood in his hands; his garments were ragged and tattered, the sweat fell in drops from his face, and water from the skin of water dripped down upon his feet. And the labourer passed before SOLOMON, and as he was going by the King said unto him, "Stand still"; and the labourer stood still. And the King turned to the Queen and said unto her, "Look at this man. Wherein am I superior to this man? And in what am I better than this man? And wherein shall I glory over this man? For I am a man and dust and ashes, who to-morrow will become worms and corruption, and yet at this moment I appear like one who will never die. Who would make any complaint against God if He were to give unto this man as He hath given to me, and if He were to make me even as this man is? Are we not both of us beings, that is to say men? As is his death, [so] is my death; and as is his life [so] is my life. Yet this man is stronger to work than I am, for God giveth power to those who are feeble just as it pleaseth Him to do so." And SOLOMON said unto the labourer, "Get thee to thy work."

And he spake further unto the Queen, saying, "What is the use of us, the children of men, if we do not exercise kindness and love upon earth? Are we not all nothingness, mere grass of the field, which withereth in its season and is burnt in the fire? On the earth we provide ourselves with dainty meats, and [we wear] costly apparel, but even whilst we are alive we are stinking corruption; we provide ourselves with sweet scents and delicate unguents, but even whilst we are alive we are dead in sin and in transgressions; being wise, we become fools through disobedience and deeds of iniquity; being held in honour, we become contemptible through magic, and sorcery, and the worship of idols. Now the man who is a being of honour, who was created in the image of God, if he doeth that which is good becometh like God; but the man who is a thing of nothingness, if he committeth sin becometh like unto the Devil—the arrogant Devil who refused to obey the command of his Creator—and all the arrogant among men walk in his way, and they shall be judged with him. And God loveth the lowly-minded, and those who practise humility walk in His way, and they shall rejoice in His kingdom. Blessed is the man who knoweth wisdom, that is to say, compassion and the fear of God."

And when the Queen heard this she said, "How thy voice doth please me! And how greatly do thy words and the utterance of thy mouth delight me! Tell me now: whom is it right for me to worship? We worship the sun according as our fathers have taught us to do, because we say that the sun is the king of the gods. And there are others among our subjects [who worship other things]; some worship stones, and some worship wood (i.e., trees), and some worship carved figures, and some worship images of gold and silver. And we worship the sun, for he cooketh our food, and moreover, he illumineth the darkness, and removeth fear; we call him 'Our King', and we call him 'Our Creator', and we worship him as our god; for no man hath told us that besides him there is another god. But we have heard that there is with you, ISRAEL, another God Whom we do not know, and men have told us that He hath sent down to you from heaven a Tabernacle and hath given unto you a Tablet of the ordering of the angels, by the hand of MOSES the Prophet. This also we have heard—that He Himself cometh down to you and talketh to you, and informeth you concerning His ordinances and commandments."

28. *How* SOLOMON *gave Commandments to the Queen*

And the King answered and said unto her, "Verily, it is right that they (i.e., men) should worship God, Who created the universe, the heavens and the earth, the sea and the dry land, the sun and the moon, the stars and the brilliant bodies of the heavens, the trees and the stones, the beasts and the feathered fowl, the wild beasts and the crocodiles, the fish and the whales, the hippopotamuses and the water lizards, the lightnings and the crashes of thunder, the clouds and the thunders, and the good and the evil. It is meet that Him alone we should worship, in fear and trembling, with joy and with gladness. For He is the Lord of the Universe, the Creator of angels and men. And it is He Who killeth and maketh to live, it is He Who inflicteth punishment and showeth compassion. Who raiseth up from the ground him that is in misery, Who exalteth the poor from the dust, Who maketh to be sorrowful and Who maketh to rejoice, Who raiseth up and Who bringeth down. No one can chide Him, for He is the Lord of the Universe, and there is no one who can say unto Him, 'What hast Thou done?' And unto Him it is meet that there should be praise and thanksgiving from angels and men. And as concerning what thou sayest, that 'He hath given unto you the Tabernacle of the Law,' verily there hath been given unto us the Tabernacle of the God of ISRAEL, which was created before all creation by His glorious counsel. And He hath made to come down to us His commandments, done into writing, so that we may know His decree and the judgement that He hath ordained in the mountain of His holiness."

And the Queen said, "From this moment I will not worship the sun, but will worship the Creator of the sun, the God of ISRAEL. And that Tabernacle of the God of ISRAEL shall be unto me my Lady, and unto my seed after me, and unto all my kingdoms that are under my dominion. And because of this I have found favour before thee, and before the God of ISRAEL my Creator, Who hath brought me unto thee, and hath made me to hear thy voice, and hath shown me thy face, and hath made me to understand thy commandment." Then she returned to [her] house.

And the Queen used to go [to SOLOMON] and return continually, and hearken unto his wisdom, and keep it in her heart. And SOLOMON used to go and visit her, and answer all the questions which she put to him, and the Queen used to visit him and ask him questions, and he informed her concerning every matter that she wished to enquire about. And after she had dwelt [there] six months the Queen wished to return to her own country, and she sent a message to SOLOMON, saying, "I desire greatly to dwell with thee, but now, for the sake of all my people, I wish to return to my own country. And as for that which I have heard, may God make it to bear fruit in my heart, and in the hearts of all those who have heard it with me. For the ear could never be filled with the hearing of thy wisdom, and the eye could never be filled with the sight of the same."

Now it was not only the Queen who came [to hear the wisdom of SOLOMON], but very many used to come from cities and countries, both from near and from far; for in those days there was no man found to be like unto him for wisdom (and it was not only human beings who came to him, but the wild animals and the birds used to come to him and hearken unto his voice, and hold converse with him), and then they returned to their own countries, and every one of them was astonished at his wisdom, and marvelled at what he had seen and heard.

And when the Queen sent her message to SOLOMON, saying that she was about to depart to her own country, he pondered in his heart and said, "A woman of such splendid beauty hath come to me from the ends of the earth! What do I know? Will God give me seed in her?" Now, as it is said in the Book of Kings, SOLOMON the King was a lover of women. And he married wives of the HEBREWS, and the EGYPTIANS, and the CANAANITES, and the EDOMITES, and the ÎYÔBÂWÎYÂN (MOABITES?), and from RÎF and KUĔRGUĔ, and DAMASCUS, and SÛREST (SYRIA), and women who were reported to be beautiful. And he had four hundred queens and six hundred concubines. Now this which he did was not for [the sake of] fornication, but as a result of the wise intent that God had given unto him, and his remembering what God had said unto ABRAHAM, "I will make thy seed like the stars of heaven for number, and like the sand of the sea." And SOLOMON said in his heart, "What do I know? Peradventure God will give me men children from each one of these women." Therefore when he did thus he acted wisely, saying, "My children shall inherit the cities of the enemy, and shall destroy those who worship idols."

Now those early peoples lived under the law of the flesh, for the grace of the Holy Spirit had not been given unto them. And to those [who lived] after CHRIST, it was given to live with one woman under the law of marriage. And the Apostles laid down for them an ordinance, saying, "All those who have received His flesh and His blood are brethren. Their mother is the Church and their father is God, and they cry out with CHRIST Whom they have received, saying, 'Our Father, Who art in heaven.' " And as concerning SOLOMON no law had been laid down for him in respect of women, and no blame can be imputed to him in respect of marrying [many] wives. But for those who believe, the law and the command have been given that they shall not marry many wives, even as PAUL saith, "Those who marry many wives seek their own punishment. He who marrieth one wife hath no sin." And the law restraineth us from the sister [-in-law], in respect of the bearing of children. The Apostles speak [concerning it] in the [Book of] Councils.

29. Concerning the Three Hundred and Eighteen [Patriarchs]

Now we ordain even as did they. We know well what the Apostles who were before us spake. We the Three Hundred and Eighteen have maintained and laid down the orthodox faith, our Lord JESUS CHRIST being with us. And He hath directed us what we should teach, and how we should fashion the faith.

And King SOLOMON sent a message unto the Queen, saying, "Now that thou hast come here why wilt thou go away without seeing the administration of the kingdom, and how the meal[s] for the chosen ones of the kingdom are eaten after the manner of the righteous, and how the people are driven away after the manner of sinners? From [the sight of] it thou wouldst acquire wisdom. Follow me now and seat thyself in my splendour in the tent, and I will complete thy instruction, and thou shalt learn the administration of my kingdom; for thou hast loved wisdom, and she shall dwell with thee until thine end and for ever." Now a prophecy maketh itself apparent in [this] speech.

And the Queen sent a second message, saying, "From being a fool, I have become wise by following thy wisdom, and from being a thing rejected by the God of ISRAEL, I have become a chosen woman because of this faith which is in my heart; and henceforth I will worship no other god except Him. And as concerning that which thou sayest, that thou wishest to increase in me wisdom and honour, I will come according to thy desire." And SOLOMON rejoiced because of this [message], and he arrayed his chosen ones [in splendid apparel], and he added a double supply to his table, and he had all the arrangements concerning the management of his house carefully ordered, and the house of King SOLOMON was made ready [for guests] daily. And he made it ready with very great pomp, in joy, and in peace, in wisdom, and in tenderness, with all humility and lowliness; and then he ordered the royal table according to the law of the kingdom.

And the Queen came and passed into a place set apart in splendour and glory, and she sat down immediately behind him where she could see and learn and know everything. And she marvelled exceedingly at what she saw, and at what she heard, and she praised the God of ISRAEL in her heart; and she was struck with wonder at the splendour of the royal palace which she saw. For she could see, though none could see her, even as SOLOMON had arranged in wisdom for her. He had beautified the place where she was seated, and had spread over it purple hangings, and laid down carpets, and decorated it with *miskât* (moschus), and marbles, and precious stones, and he burned aromatic powders, and sprinkled oil of myrrh and cassia round about, and scattered frankincense and costly incense in all directions. And when they brought her into this abode, the odour thereof was very pleasing to her, and even before she ate the dainty meats therein she was satisfied with the smell of them. And with wise intent SOLOMON sent to her meats which would make her thirsty, and drinks that were mingled with vinegar, and fish and dishes made with pepper. And this he did and he gave them to the Queen to eat. And the royal meal had come to an end three times and seven times, and the administrators, and the counsellors, and the young men and the servants had departed, and the King rose up and he went to the Queen, and he said unto her—now they were alone together—"Take thou thine ease here for love's sake until daybreak." And she said unto him, "Swear to me by thy God, the God of ISRAEL, that thou wilt not take me by force. For if I, who according to the law of men am a maiden, be seduced, I should travel on my journey [back] in sorrow, and affliction, and tribulation."

30. Concerning how King SOLOMON swore to the Queen

And SOLOMON answered and said unto her, "I swear unto thee that I will not take thee by force, but thou must swear unto me that thou wilt not take by force anything that is in my house." And the Queen laughed and said unto him, "Being a wise man why dost thou speak as a fool? Shall I steal anything, or shall I carry out of the house of the King that which the King hath not given to me? Do not imagine that I have come hither through love of riches. Moreover, my own kingdom is as wealthy as thine, and there is nothing which I wish for that I lack. Assuredly I have only come in quest of thy wisdom." And he said unto her, "If thou wouldst make me swear, swear thou to me, for a swearing is meet for both [of us], so that neither of us may be unjustly treated. And if thou wilt not make me swear I will not make thee swear." And she said unto him, "Swear to me that thou wilt not take me by force, and I on my part will swear not to take by force thy possessions"; and he swore to her and made her swear.

And the King went up on his bed on the one side [of the chamber], and the servants made ready for her a bed on the other side. And SOLOMON said unto a young manservant, "Wash out the bowl and set in it a vessel of water whilst the Queen is looking on, and shut the doors and go and sleep." And SOLOMON spake to the servant in another tongue which the Queen did not understand, and he did as the King commanded, and went and slept. And the King had not as yet fallen asleep, but he only pretended to be asleep, and he was watching the Queen intently. Now the house of SOLOMON the King was illumined as by day, for in his wisdom he had made shining pearls which were like unto the sun, and moon, and stars [and had set them] in the roof of his house.

And the Queen slept a little. And when she woke up her mouth was dry with thirst, for the food which SOLOMON had given her in his wisdom had made her thirsty, and she was very thirsty indeed, and her mouth was dry; and she moved her lips and sucked with her mouth and found no moisture. And she determined to drink the water which she had seen, and she looked at King SOLOMON and watched him carefully, and she thought that he was sleeping a sound sleep. But he was not asleep, and he was waiting until she should rise up to steal the water to [quench] her thirst. And she rose up and, making no sound with her feet, she went to the water in the bowl and lifted up the jar to drink the water. And SOLOMON seized her hand before she could drink the water, and said unto her, "Why hast thou broken the oath that thou hast sworn that thou wouldst not take by force anything that is in my house?" And she answered and said unto him in fear, "Is the oath broken by my drinking water?" And the King said unto her, "Is there anything that thou hast seen under the heavens that is better than water?" And the Queen said, "I have sinned against myself, and thou art free from [thy] oath. But let me drink water for my thirst." Then SOLOMON said unto her, "Am I perchance free from the oath which thou hast made me swear?" And the Queen said, "Be free from thy oath, only let me drink water." And he permitted her to drink water, and after she had drunk water he worked his will with her and they slept together.

And after he slept there appeared unto King SOLOMON [in a dream] a brilliant sun, and it came down from heaven and shed exceedingly great splendour over ISRAEL. And when it had tarried there for a time it suddenly withdrew itself, and it flew away to the country of ETHIOPIA, and it shone there with exceedingly great brightness for ever, for it willed to dwell there. And [the King said], "I waited [to see] if it would come back to ISRAEL, but it did not return. And again while I waited a light rose up in the heavens, and a Sun came down from them in the country of JUDAH, and it sent forth light which was very much stronger than before." And ISRAEL, because of the flame of that Sun entreated that Sun evilly and would not walk in the light thereof. And that Sun paid no heed to ISRAEL, and the ISRAELITES hated Him, and it became impossible that peace should exit between them and the Sun. And they lifted up their hands against Him with staves and knives, and they wished to extinguish that Sun. And they cast darkness upon the whole world with earthquake and thick darkness, and they imagined that that Sun would never more rise upon them. And they destroyed His light and cast themselves upon Him and they set a guard over His tomb wherein they had cast Him. And He came forth where they did not look for Him, and illumined the whole world, more especially the First Sea and the Last Sea, ETHIOPIA and RÔM. And He paid no heed whatsoever to ISRAEL, and He ascended His former throne.

And when SOLOMON the King saw this vision in his sleep, his soul became disturbed, and his understanding was snatched away as by [a flash of] lightning, and he woke up with an agitated mind. And moreover, SOLOMON marvelled concerning the Queen, for she was vigorous in strength, and beautiful of form, and she was undefiled in her virginity; and she had reigned for six years in her own country, and, notwithstanding her gracious attraction and her splendid form, had preserved her body pure. And the Queen said unto SOLOMON, "Dismiss me, and let me depart to my own country." And he went into his house and gave unto her whatsoever she wished for of splendid things and riches, and beautiful apparel which bewitched the eyes, and everything on which great store was set in the country of ETHIOPIA, and camels and wagons, six thousand in number, which were laden with beautiful things of the most desirable kind, and wagons wherein loads were carried over the desert, and a vessel wherein one could travel over the sea, and a vessel wherein one could traverse the air (or winds), which SOLOMON had made by the wisdom that God had given unto him.

TEXT 46

Shihab al-Din: The Conquest of Ethiopia

from The Ethiopian Royal Chronicles[1]

*I*n A.D. 1527 Ahmad Gran Ibn Ibrahim al-Ghazi launched a holy war against the Christian "infidels" of Ethiopia defeating the royal army of Lebna Dengel (1508–1540). As Imam of Harar in the Ogaden region of Somalia, al-Gran had overseen the growing vitality of this commercial city into which Islamic religion and culture had become deeply entrenched. After his conquest of Ethiopia, he forced the conversion of many Ethiopian Christians to Islam. Professor Donald E. Crummey describes this period thus:

> Churches were plundered, manuscripts burned, and monks and priests massacred by the thousands. Much of the cultural legacy of the country was lost . . .[2]

In the period following al-Gran's death and the expulsion of his army from Ethiopia in 1543, a revival of Ethiopian literature began. During this period many Ethiopians who had converted to Islam under pressure returned to their traditional Christian faith.[3]

The chronicle, refers to Grañ by his titles of Imam or Emir, as well as by his first name Ahmed.

Among the Somali tribes there was one called Habr Magadi from whom the Imam had claimed taxes; they had refused to pay and had cut communications and devastated the country. Ahmed advanced as far as a place called Rabud between the country

---

[1]Richard Pankhurst, *The Ethiopian Royal Chronicles* (London: Oxford University Press, 1967), pp. 149–50.
[2]Donald E. Crummey, "Church and State in Ethiopia: The Sixteenth to the Eighteenth Century," in *African Zion: The Sacred Art of Ethiopia*, edited by Roderick Grierson (New Haven, CT: Yale University Press, 1993), p. 43.
[3]Albert S. Gerard, *African Language Literatures: An Introduction to the Literary History of Sub-Saharan Africa* (London: Longman, 1981), p. 13.
Source: From Richard Pankhurst, *The Ethiopian Royal Chronicles,* © 1967. Reprinted by permission of Oxford University Press.

of the Muslims and those of the infidels (*i.e. Christians*) giving the impression that he wished to march against Abyssinia; then he suddenly turned towards the country of the Somali pillagers, who took to flight. He pursued them to a day's distance from the sea and thoroughly pillaged their country. He then returned.

The Habr Magadi, who had fled, nevertheless ravaged the country of the Girri Somalis, who were by then already in Grañ's service.

The tribe of the Girri went to plead with Ahmed, saying, "Our country has only been devastated because we have made peace with you and entered your service."

The Imam took the matter to heart; he gathered together an army and marched into the country of the Somalis until he reached the area of the Habr Magadi. . . . He defeated them, again carried off their riches, and ravaged their towns which he reduced to cinders; then he returned to his own country.

The Somalis were grieved by the pillage of their property and the ruin of their country. They went to find the Imam, having at their head Hirabu, who was followed by all the Somalis; they concluded a complete and sincere peace with Ahmed. The latter then made preparations for an expedition into Abyssinia; he gathered his troops as well as the Somalis commanded by Hirabu; they set out under his orders.

One of Grañ's early expeditions took him to Gendebelo, an important market in Ifat.

The Imam found at Gendebelo merchants who were unbelievers (*i.e. Christians*) and held goods belonging to the King of Abyssinia; the Imam killed them in the middle of the town and carried off their goods, their mules and their beasts of burden together with their packs. He stayed with his army two days at Gendebelo then he left in the afternoon to return to the country of the Muslims, taking with him the riches of the King of Abyssinia.

Trade seems to have suffered greatly at this time. The chronicler says:

The King of Abyssinia . . . had sent merchants into the country of the Muslims with gold, *wars (a yellow dye)*, ivory, musk, slaves and many other riches. The traders had sold their merchandise in the Muslim country and had crossed the sea to go to Chihr (*a market in Arabia*) and Aden, and were returning to their own land near the residence of the King. The Emir was informed. He seized their riches, which became the booty of the Muslims, and divided it among the tribes with a view to promoting the holy war. This money fortified the believers (*i.e. Muslims*) in their struggle with the unbelievers (*i.e. Christians*).

Grañ had meanwhile sent out messengers to the tribes under his control ordering them to prepare for war against the Christians. The soldiers soon answered their master's call.

The first tribe to arrive was that of the Habr Magadi . . . they showed him their arms and their equipment and gave him a display of their horse-riding; they had cavalry—what cavalry! and infantry—what infantry! Their arrival gave great joy to the Imam. . . .

As the tribesmen arrived Grañ got ready for war.

He . . . prepared to carry the holy war into Abyssinia; he equipped his troops, the soldiers and all the tribes, and to obtain arms sold the jewels of his wives and the furniture of his house without holding back anything for himself, desiring nothing but the reward promised by the very high God. . . . Then he announced his departure for Abyssinia.

Lebna Dengel was not slow to respond to the challenge. He at once rallied a very large army drawn from most of the provinces:

The King assembled his troops and reunited his army; the followers of Christianity gathered around him . . . people of Tigre, men of the Agaws, Gojam, Begemder, Angot, Qeda, Gan and the borders of the sea. All Abyssinia was in a state of alarm. The most important nobles of Tigre numbered eighty; each of them had an innumerable army under his orders. The same was the case with the people of Begemder, Angot, Qeda and Gan.

Though Grañ himself was undeterred by the size of Lebna Dengel's army most of his soldiers were terrified of it.

Many of the Muslims wanted to flee but Ahmed dissuaded them and urged them to fight; the horses were bridled for many days without either their bridles or saddles being taken off. The Imam said to those who wished to flee, "Do not run away during the night; the unbelievers will kill you when you turn your back; be patient, perhaps God will send you his help. . . ."

When the morning came almost all the troops fled; only forty cavalry and about twenty infantry remained with Ahmed; they were, however, heroes known for their bravery. The Imam and his companions pursued the fugitives and thrust them back. Then at dawn Ahmed despatched two Muslim horsemen, Ali, who was later governor of Angot, and the vizier, Nur ben Ibrahim; the Imam ordered them to make their way in front of the army and said to them, "Kill every Muslim who flees!"

The two horsemen set forth like terrible lions, crossed the river Dukham, took up a position in front of the army and thus closed its escape route. They shot four men and said, "Why do you run away?" They then swore, "By God, we will kill whosoever among you advances! Go back, stand fast, and kill the unbelievers! He among you who dies will go to paradise; he who lives will be happy."

The Muslim army, encouraged by these words, decided to fight even though it was greatly outnumbered by that of the Christians.

At the great battle of Shembera Kure, which took place in March 1529, Lebna Dengel is said to have had 16,000 cavalry and over 200,000 infantry, while Grañ had only 560 horsemen and 12,000 foot soldiers. Grañ was, however, victorious for he was very well supplied with fire-arms.

The Imam returned to his town of Harar happy, contented, triumphant and victorious.

It was not long, however, before he made a new expedition to the highlands, whereupon he announced his desire to remain there permanently as a conqueror.

The Imam had the idea of establishing himself in Abyssinia and of conquering it. He sent to the Muslim countries exhorting the people to come and join him for the holy war. But the soldiers said to him, "We will not stay in the country of the Christians; we want to go back to that of the Muslims." The Emirs said to the Imam, "Our fathers and ancestors were never accustomed to establish themselves in Abyssinia; they only made expeditions on the borders of the territories of the unbelievers, taking cattle and other things as booty before returning to the Muslim country; it is not our custom to settle in foreign lands." They obliged the Imam to give up his plan and they wanted to abandon him . . . but God prevented them. Ahmed's intimates, the Emirs and the members of his council, said to him, "The soldiers are tired; they do not want to establish themselves here; lead them back to our country and when we make another expedition, if you wish to stay, we will stay." The Imam accepted their advice. The Muslims had taken a booty such as they had never before obtained; many of the unbelievers embraced Islam and they returned with the Imam to the land of the Muslims.

Grañ, however, had by no means abandoned his ambitions. On the contrary, he was determined to establish himself permanently in the highlands. He swore that on his next expedition "he would not return from the country of the unbelievers."

When this expedition and the holy war had been decided upon he first went down to a country called Zerbah . . . then he sent to Zeila to collect arms, swords, and so forth. He ordered the purchase of cannons to make war on Abyssinia. They bought what he wanted and supplied him with seven cannons. About seventy men of Mahra (*a region in South Arabia*) also came from the coast with the intention of taking part in the holy war.

At the subsequent battle of Antakyah an olive tree standing in the centre of the Ethiopian army was cut in two by the first shot of Grañ's cannon. The chronicler claims that the Christians thereupon 'tumbled the one on the other' and were immediately defeated. The Muslim army then proceeded to ravage the country and before long had collected so much booty that "each had two hundred mules and slaves." Under these circumstances Grañ feared that his men would lose interest in the campaign and desire to return home with their booty.

The Imam gathered together all the army and said, "What are these pack animals, these mules and these slaves which you have collected? Where are you taking them?" They replied, "We are thinking of taking them to our own country; but for the time being we will take them where you wish." The Imam retorted, "Is our purpose the fighting of a holy war or the collection of pack animals, mules, baggage and slaves? If you have all these goods how can you fight against the polytheists (*i.e. Christians*)?"

"What shall we do?" they asked.

"I will tell you what to do," he replied.

Then they went out and in due course arrived at a narrow spot between the mountains. The Imam was marching at the head of the army. He stopped at a very narrow place when the soldiers came up near him. Then he said, "Throw away what you have in your hands; let no one travel with more than one mule on which he can load what the slaves carry! That is enough! I will cut off the head of anyone who disobeys me!" Then they threw away . . . everything they had with tears and cries . . . the valley and the road was full of slaves as well as the baggage which they had been carrying. . . . Then he set forth again. . . .

Looting was thereupon resumed. The army in due course arrived at a very rich church at Badeqe, a town in Shoa not far from Mount Zuquala.

Ahmed said to them, "Burn the church!" They left, arrived at Badeqe and burnt the church. They carried off the gold and pillaged and put fire to the cloth which the Christians had left in the town. . . . The Imam and his army . . . arrived at Andotnah, a town of the King. . . . There was a house there belonging to the King of Abyssinia where there were paintings: representations of lions, men and birds, painted in red, yellow, green, white and other colours. The Muslims entered this house, admired its contents and burnt it.

The army then proceeded to destroy the nearby town of Berarah before returning to their own country with the loot. Lebna Dengel, hearing this news, exclaimed:

"These Muslims have entered Berarah; they have ravaged the province; they have now returned to their own country. I will march against them, I will cross the Awash river, take up a position and fight them." Then he said to the Franks who were with him and numbered about forty, "Build me a boat like those of your country with which to cross the Awash." They built small boats.

Lebna Dengel was unsuccessful in his counter-attack and Grañ continued his offensive. The Muslim conqueror ordered the entire Christian population to accept Islam. Most of them agreed but here and there one or two persons refused. On one occasion Grañ ordered the conversion of the entire population of an area; only one man insisted on maintaining his religion. He was a nobleman called Aibes Lahati.

Ahmed invited them to embrace Islam which all of them did with the exception of this noble who said, "I will not become a Muslim; I have not come for that; I will not abandon the religion in which my fathers and grandfathers died." The Imam replied, "You are better than those who have been converted and yet you are more stubborn than they in your faith!" "As for those people," the noble answered, "they are savages; it is no dishonour for them, but if I became a Muslim I would be dishonoured in front of the King and the monks; they would say, "Aibes Lahati has embraced Islam." That would be a great shame for me; I will not abandon the religion of Mary." The Imam replied. . . . "You are a great personage among the Christians and there are family ties between us." In fact Hajirah, one of the wives of the Imam, was related to the noble, being his paternal cousin. The Imam added, "You will be of great service if you join Islam." He refused, saying, "I am your relative, I will help you, but I will remain in my religion; if you have some battle to wage against either Muslims or Christians I will fight for you." The Imam replied, "Silence! I do not want help from polytheists; you can neither help us nor harm us; surrender your horse and your arms, pay the tax and remain in your religion."

TEXT 47

Royal Chronicler: The Conquest of Ethiopia

from The Ethiopian Royal Chronicles[1]

When the Muslim conqueror, Ahmad al-Gran of Somalia, invaded Ethiopia in A.D. 1527, he deposed the Ethiopian ruler, Lebna Dengel. So devastating was this conquest for Christian Ethiopia that it is usually considered a dividing line in Ethiopian history from which that society never fully recovered. The royal chronicler of Lebna Dengel's son, Galawdewos, narrates the humiliating details of his father's defeat.

---

[1]Richard Pankhurst, *The Ethiopian Royal Chronicles* (London: Oxford University Press, 1967), pp. 50–69.

Text 47: Royal Chronicler: The Conquest of Ethiopia

Up to this time the country had neither been dismembered nor invaded by any enemy; on the contrary the Kings [of Ethiopia] had conquered many kings. Amda Tseyon defeated ten kings even before he had collected his troops. The invasion of our country by enemies began under King Lebna Dengel, the son of King Naod.

Grañ's invasion, which began in 1527, was later described in the chronicle of Lebna Dengel's son, the Emperor Galawdewos as follows:

At this period victory favoured the Muslims. . . . They dominated the church of Ethiopia. They were the victors in all fights to the east, west, north and south, and destroyed all the churches whose walls were covered with gold, silver and precious Indian stones; they put to the sword a large number of Christians and led into captivity young men and women and children of both sexes and sold them as slaves.

Many of the faithful moreover renounced the faith of the church and embraced the religion of the Muslims; it is doubtful if one in ten retained his faith.

There was . . . a great famine, the like of which had never been seen since the time of the kings of Samaria nor at the time of the destruction of the second temple.

Lebna Dengel, we are told, was unable to resist the invader.

The King was chased from his throne and wandered from desert to desert facing hunger, thirst and cold in complete destitution.

Source: From Richard Pankhurst, *The Ethiopian Royal Chronicles,* © 1967. Reprinted by permission of Oxford University Press.

TEXT 48

Royal Chronicler: The Empress Berhan Mogasa

from The Ethiopian Royal Chronicles[1]

When Iyasu II ascended the throne of Ethiopia (1730–1755), he was only a child and the actual work of government was carried out by his mother, the Empress Berhan Mogasa, popularly known as Montewab or "How beautiful she is!" The chronicler originally writing in Ge'ez describes the power of the empress, her astonishing beauty as well as the series of rebellions launched by jealous noblemen which she successfully crushed.

Iyasu II reigned for twenty-four years from 1730 to 1755. He was only a child at the time of his accession and the actual work of government was carried out by his mother, the Empress Berhan Mogasa or Walata Giyorgis, better known as Mentewab, or "How beautiful she is!" Iyasu was selected to rule by his father Bakaffa. When the latter realized that his end was near he is reported to have said:

"Make my son Iyasu reign because I have chosen him and it is he who pleases me; obey him!"

Ras Niqolawos, a relative of the Queen Mother and the principal man of state, accordingly called the nobles together.

All the dignitaries gathered together in the house of the King. . . . Ras Niqolawos placed himself in the middle of them and reported to them the order which King Bakaffa had given, namely: "Make my son Iyasu reign, place him on my throne and

---

[1] Richard Pankhurst, *The Ethiopian Royal Chronicles* (London: Oxford University Press, 1967), pp. 121–31.
Source: From Richard Pankhurst, *The Ethiopian Royal Chronicles*, © 1967. Reprinted by permission of Oxford University Press.

behave towards him as I have behaved towards you. . . !" All the dignitaries said in a single voice: "It is good! Let it thus be done! Let him reign!" There was no one who said, "Let this not be done!"

So Iyasu was placed on the throne, his mother Queen Mentewab taking her place by his side, it being understood from the outset that she would in fact be ruling the country for many years to come. Iyasu's chronicler, who recognizes Mentewab's importance in the state, devotes many lines to the beauty of this remarkable woman. Recalling the days of her late husband, the Emperor Bakaffa, he says:

When Bakaffa ascended the throne he sent wise and prudent men into all the countries to find him the most beautiful of all women. They remained many days searching for such a woman, and by the will of the Lord . . . they found a woman, among the daughters of Kings, whose eyes were as brilliant as the stars and as delightful as a grape; her face was as bright as oil; her hair was like flax, and her stature was that of a palm tree. She was called Mentewab (*"How beautiful she is!"*) and truly she was Mentewab, from whose lips there flowed milk whether she was silent or spoke, truly Mentewab whose eyes were those of the dove, truly Mentewab whose bosom was like that of bees, slim and full of sweetness, truly Mentewab obedient and wise, truly Mentewab for whom all men felt love in their hearts!

A wise and prudent man who had been one of those sent to search for this woman returned to the town (*of Gondar*) and told the King that he had found a beautiful woman. When Bakaffa learnt this he sent for Tucha Elfeyos who was Grazmatch and interrogated him about her and her family, asking: "Of what family is she?" He replied: "She is of the family of Emperor Minas, whose throne name was Admas Sagad and she is the granddaughter of Princess Yolyana." Then the King sent to Princess Yolyana a good and faithful servant of his called Issayas whom he loved more than anyone else in his service. The latter bearing the King's message said to the Princess: "Send me your daughter because I have chosen her among all women!" Princess Yolyana, hearing these words, replied: "Let the will of the Lord be done!" Then she selected clothes of silk from among her treasures and dressed her daughter with them; she anointed her with perfumes, put a ring of gold on her finger and sent her off with great pomp.

Mentewab entered into the chamber of the King, and when King of Kings Bakaffa saw her he was very happy because she was completely beautiful; he said to her: "You have no fault at all!" Then he made her sit beside him on his right hand, and had delicious foods brought and they ate and drank together. That day he knew her as Adam knew Eve . . . and she conceived that day.

Iyasu accepted the fact that his mother was the real ruler of the country.

The King of Kings Iyasu said to them: "Make my mother reign, crown her with my crown because without her my reign cannot go on!" When the dignitaries and learned men heard these words, they all rejoiced and said with a single voice: "She is worthy of it! She is worthy of it!"

TEXT 49

Bahrey: History of the Galla[1]

*A*s members of the dominant Amhara ethnic group, the Ethiopian nobility displayed an arrogant curiosity in regard to their migratory neighbors, the Oromo. Also called Galla, the Oromo ethno-linguistic group comprises more than 30 percent of the present-day population of Ethiopia. An Ethiopian court priest named Bahrey (who may actually have been of Oromo decent) composed the History of the Galla *in Ge'ez or ancient Ethiopic around 1595, during the reign of Sartsa Dengel. Bahrey served as the emperor's chaplain and may also have been the Ethiopian Church Administrator for the province of Gamo in the southwest region of the country.*

---

[1]Bahrey, *History of the Galla (Oromo) of Ethiopia; with Ethnology and History of South-West Ethiopia,* introduction by Donald N. Levine (Oakland, CA: African Sun, 1993), pp. 1–93.

History of the Galla By Bahrey

I have begun to write the history of the Galla in order to make known the number of their tribes, their readiness to kill people, and the brutality of their manners. If anyone should say of my subject, 'Why has he written a history of bad people, just as one would write a history of good people,' I would answer by saying, 'Search in the books, and you will find that the history of Mahamad and the Moslem kings has been written, and they are our enemies in religion. Likewise Giyorgis Walda Amid has written the history of the Persian kings with their childish legends, like those of Afridon and the other kings of Persia, who are now called Sofi.'

CHAPTER 1

The author of this book says: The Galla came from the west and crossed the river of their country, which is called Galanā, to the frontier of Bāli, in the time of the Haṣē Wanāg Sagad. They are two tribes called Baraytumā and Boran. Baraytumā had six children: the eldest was called Karayu, the second Marawā, the third Itu, the fourth Akaču, the fifth Warantišā, the sixth Humbanā.

The father of Boran was called Sapirā. Sapirā begot Dāča; Dāča begot Mača; Mača begot Da'alē and Jidā and these two brothers gave birth to numerous tribes. These are the sons of Da'alē: Hoko was the eldest, Čelē the second, Obo the third, and Subā was the fourth. Jidā begot Hakāko his eldest son, Gudru his second, and Liban his third.

Dāča begot the Dāč (whom he called by his own name), Kono, Bačo, and Jelē. These also gave birth to many tribes whose names are these: the children of Bačo are Uru and Ilu; the children of Dāč are Soddo, Ābo, Gāllān; the sons of Kono are Saqsaq, Liban; the sons of Jelē are Ēlā, Ābo, and Le'is; all these are called Tulamā, because they are numerous.

Originally their custom was to set out together to war; but after a long period of time they quarrelled among themselves and separated, as did Abraham and Lot, when their herds became so numerous that they said, 'Let us separate, so that thou goest to the right and I go to the left; or, I go to the right and thou to the left.'

Similarly the two tribes of Da'alē, Čelē and Hoko, and also the two tribes of Jedā (sic), Liban and Gudru, separated from their brothers and formed a confederacy, taking the name of Afrē, in the time of the *luba* which the Boran call Ambisā and the Bartumā Robālē.

Likewise, Hakāko son of Jedā (sic), and the sons of Da'alē, Ābo and Subā, made a confederacy and were called Sadača, in the time of the *luba* called Birmajē; they also gave birth to numerous tribes. These are their names: The sons of Čelē are Galām, Wabo; the sons of Hoko are Kiramo, Emuru, Jidā; the sons of Liban are Wāliso,

Source: From Bahrey, Donald N. Levine (introduction), *History of the Galla,* © 1993. Reprinted by permission of African Sun Publishing.

Kutāwē, Ameyē; the sons of Gudru are Sirbā, Malol, Čaraqā. The tribe of Hakāko is composed of Ābo, Harsu, Limu; the tribe of Subā is composed of Hagalabābo, Čurrā; the tribe of Ābo [Obo] is composed of Sayo, Abono, Tum'ē, Lēqā. All these when they are allied are called Mačā; but when they make war they call themselves Afrē and Sadačā; if they are all joined with the Tulamā they are called Sapirā.

Boran, on his side had twelve children: the eldest Dāča, the second Jelē, the third Kono, the fourth Bačo, which four are called Tulamā; the fifth was Hakāko, the sixth Obo, the seventh Subā, which three are called Sadačā; the eighth was called Čelē, the ninth Liban, the tenth Gudru, the eleventh Hoko, and these four are called Afrē.

CHAPTER 2

The Dāwē, who devastated Baṭera Amorā, belonged to the Boran; it has been said that they belong to another group, and an argument in favour of this has been seen in the fact that they have made war on the Boran. But this is a ridiculous theory and quite untrue. Those who are accurately informed declare that when the Boran quit their country, they do not all go, but those who wish to stay do so, and those who wish to leave do so; for they have no ruler who can enforce his orders, and each man does what seems best to him. Those of the Boran who stayed came out of their country by way of Kuērā; that was at the time when Fāsil attacked them and was killed by them. Then the Dāwē began to make war on the Christians, and at that time the author of this history prophesied and said, 'I fear him who killed Fāsil, for he has tasted Christian blood.' And they devastated the two districts of Batera Amorā and Waj, and it came to pass as he had foretold, for the spirit of prophecy remains with the priests. The Dāwē chased this prophet, laid waste his country, which was called Gamo, and looted all that he possessed. But let us return to the history of the Baraytumā from which we have digressed.

CHAPTER 3

Karayu [of the Baraytumā] had six children who formed many powerful tribes: the first was Liban, the second Wallo, the third Jelē, the fourth Obo, the fifth Subā, the sixth Balā. Wallo had six children: Wara, Buko, Wara Guerā', Wara Nolē'ēlu, who bear the name of Wallo; and Wara Karayu, Wara Ilu, and Wara Nolē'ali, who are known as Sadačā. Their separation dates from the time of the murder of Aboli, but they have now made peace and are leagued against us.

CHAPTER 4

Marawā Ayā begot Anā, Uru, and Abati; their children and grandchildren multiplied and formed numerous tribes. They received their name, each according to his tribe. They have neither king nor master like other peoples, but they obey the *luba* during a period of eight years; at the end of eight years another *luba* is made, and the first gives up his office. They do this at fixed times; and *luba* means 'those who are circumcised at the same time.' As to the law concerning their circumcision, it is thus: when a *luba* is formed, all the Baraytumā and the Boran give themselves a collective name, just as the king of Ethiopia's regiments call themselves by names like *Sellus haylē*, 'the Trinity is my strength,' *Badel ṣahāy*, 'the sun in victory,' or *Giyorgis haylē*, 'St. George is my strength.'

CHAPTER 5

Thus it was that he who was circumcised when the Galla began to invade the country of Bāli was called Mēlbāh; I know not the name of his father, for no man was able to tell me.

CHAPTER 6

The second *luba* was called Mudanā; his father was called Jebanā. It was he who crossed the river Wabi.

CHAPTER 7

The third *luba* was called Kilolē; he carried war towards the lowlands of Dawāro, and fought with such as the Adal Mabraq, and with the inhabitants of the region.

CHAPTER 8

The fourth *luba* was called Bifolē; it was he who devastated the whole of Dawāro and began to make war on Fatagār. He began to enslave the inhabitants, and made of them the slaves called *gabare*. Bifolē also began to drink *kosso*. The first *lubas,* which we have just mentioned, killed people—men and women, horses and mules, leaving alive only the sheep, goats, and cattle; but they had no means of killing the creature which was in their intestines, the tape-worm, which slid down their legs, as in animals.

CHAPTER 9

The fifth *luba* was called Meslē. It was he who killed the Jān Amorā corps and fought against Hamalmāl at Dago; he devastated all the towns and ruled them, remaining there with his troops, whereas previously the Galla, invading from the Wabi, had returned there at the end of each campaign. Our king Asnāf Sagad fought Meslē, starting from Āsā Zanab. And when Nur came down into his country, having done what he did, Meslē met him near Hazalo and killed a very large number of his men. Since the Galla first invaded our country there had been no such slaughter, and the troops of Nur who were killed were more in number than the troops of Awsā [Aussa] which we shall speak of in the proper place. Thus did God avenge on the Moslems the blood of his servants which they had split in Waj.

This *luba* Meslē began the custom of riding horses and mules, which the Galla had not done previously, so that he said of the *lubas* which had preceded him, 'Those who travel on two or three legs, I have made them travel on four legs.' He said, 'three legs' because they lent on their spears, as men would on their staffs when they were tired.

CHAPTER 10

These five *lubas* which we have mentioned exercised power for a period of forty years; their children were not circumcised. Those who were not circumcised abandoned their children both boys and girls, for such is their custom; but after being circumcised they reared the boys, though the girls were still abandoned for two or three years after they had been circumcised.

TEXT 50

Afawark Gabra Iyasus: Fictitious Story[1]

After the seventeenth century, literature in Ge'ez or ancient Ethiopic began to wane as did the fortunes of the Ethiopian monarchy itself. Feudal princes began vying for authority at the expense of the centralized state, precipitating a series of wars, which lasted well into the nineteenth century. By the time Ethiopia's central rulers were able to reassert their dominion, the culture of the society had evolved in dramatic ways. The ancient language of Ge'ez was no longer spoken and its writings were now confined to sacred literature. Amharic, the language of the majority Amhara ethnicity, had become the dominant language. Written in the script of ancient Ge'ez, the Amharic language spawned a new era in modern, secular literature.

Afawark Gabra Iyasus (1868–1947) became one of the most noted representatives of modern Amharic writers. He wrote Fictitious Story in 1908, a novel that combines the narrative techniques typical of oral art with the moralizing characteristics of traditional Ethiopian writing.

Wahid, Tobbya's brother, has been searching for his captured father. Wahid soon becomes the object of a long search by Tobbya and her father, who has returned in Wahid's absence.

Before sunset the songs of the birds had been a source of consolation to him, but now he was surrounded by the cries of wild beasts. He was very worried. He wanted to rest and spend the night there, but there was no shelter. If he slept where he was the wild beasts would soon devour him. Wahid was at a loss what to do. He decided to defend himself from the wild beasts rather than be eaten by them in his sleep. Furthermore he decided that he would not rest until he came to the caravan camp he had seen from afar early in the afternoon.

---

[1] An English version of Fictitious Story, entitled "Tobbya," was published by Tadesse Tamrat in Ethiopia Observer, VIII, 1964, pp. 242–67.
Source: Reprinted from Tadesse Tamrat, Ethiopia Observer, 1964.

In the meantime it was getting darker and darker. He could no longer see his way, and began to be very frightened. He thought he saw wild animals everywhere, a hyena, a leopard or a lion, laying in ambush for him! "The hyena will soon eat me up," he began to think. "The leopard will tear me to death with its cruel claws, and the lion will break my bones into pieces! Oh! Woe unto me tonight! If I escape the one I shall certainly be the prey of the other!"

What else could he do? Wahid's fear was justified. He was only a young boy. Regardless of his fears and the darkness that had engulfed him he continued his way in the direction of the camp he had seen. At one juncture of this nocturnal journey he saw what he thought was a lion. He was startled to death. His strength began to fail him. The more he looked at the terrible object the more his fears seemed to be confirmed; he thought the lion, thus created by his own fears, would suddenly jump onto him and devour him mercilessly. Wahid wanted to scare the object of his fears. He wanted to give the lion the impression that he was surrounded by many people. He then shouted with different voices to produce the effect of many persons running after it: "Courage! Courage!" he shouted. "Surround it. Don't let it go."

It was, however, simply his own imagination. There was nobody there except himself, except his own shadow which added to the darkness confused his thinking. The object that he thought a lion was simply a bush. It would not move an inch whatever his endeavours to scare it! Wahid then thought he must change his course to avoid the terrible beast. Nevertheless when he looked back in the direction of the bush he still thought that the lion was following him. Wahid gradually became almost too weak to move; his fears enormously reduced his strength. There was no shelter in which to spend the night and protect himself from wild beasts. He thought of climbing a tree and thus avoid any dangers, but by a strange coincidence there was no tree to be found there. Wahid began to worry greatly. His fears increased with every minute that elapsed. Everything around him seemed to him some wild beast ready to devour him on the spot. He changed his course every time he thought he saw a wild beast in front of him. While thus changing directions every now and then he came to a small cave which suddenly appeared on his way. He was taken aback. He was frightened to death. A cold sweat broke out over his face and body. "I just escaped one lion," he thought with complete despair, "and here I am again in front of another! I shall not be able to escape this time!" His whole body was shivering like a reed in an evening breeze. He tried to use his former stategem [sic] of scaring the object by shouting with different voices. He shouted and shouted until his throat cracked with thirst. But all was in vain. The object would not move an inch! Wahid thought he had not shouted enough and so he began to shout with more strength and intensity until he could shout no more. But all was of no effect. At last Wahid began to doubt the reality of his fears. He began to suspect that the object of his fears might just be a dark inanimate thing! He knelt down in front of the small cave and began to stare hard at it. He wanted to see if the object moved. After some minutes of close observation he thought that the object did move a little. He still stared at it, and now he thought it was even making some advance towards him! He stared so hard that his eyes were strained and filled with tears. He was, however, too frightened to make any movement himself or to clean his eyes. His tears confused his sight all the more and gave him the impression that the terrible object was heading towards him with more rapidity. Later, however, Wahid succeeded in mustering enough courage to throw some pebbles into the cave from where he was kneeling. A small bird which had been sheltering in the cave, as if by providential coincidence made a sudden noise and, slapping the leaves with its wigs [*sic*] took off and flew away in the darkness. At first this confirmed Wahid's fears. He thought that the terrible wild beast was finally about to jump on him and devour him. With this desperate idea in his head Wahid held his breath and lay flat on the ground like a dead body. He waited and waited, but nothing happened. "Am I still alive?" he asked himself. Then he began to make slight movements to see if he had been bitten by the wild beast or not. He found nothing. At first he had closed his eyes, now he reopened them with much hesitation and found out, to his surprise, that let alone a lion, not even a rabbit was in sight. He even began to breathe deeply and rose to his feet. He looked into the cave once again. It was still there. It did not move. He looked hard at it with a strange mixture of fear and wonder. "Did I not hear the terrible beast fly away, or was there no beast at all?" he thought. "I am sure I have seen it with my own eyes. Did it not bite me without my knowing?" He tried to inspect his body. There was no sign of any attack. "What could it be?" he began to ask himself. "What could it be that frightened me so much? Could it be just my own troubled imagination? Anyway it is good that nobody saw me in this frantic state! How can a man be so much deceived by his own fears?" Wahid laughed at himself and resumed his journey.

TEXT 51

Qamaan Bulxan: In Praise of a Beautiful Somali Woman[1]

*T*he nineteenth century poet Qamaan Bulxan emanated from the Ogaden clan. He was the inheritor of a long tradition of Somali adoration of poetry, a cultural trait observed by Sir Richard Burton, the British explorer who visited Somalia in 1854, who commented:

> The country teems with poets . . . the fine ear of this people causing them to take the greatest pleasure in harmonious sounds and poetical expressions, where a false quantity or a prosaic phrase excite their violent indignation.[2]

Among all the women to be seen at Qorraxey—
Those who dwell in the heart of the town
And those who dwell in the countryside around,
The splendid wives and mothers,
The no-longer wives, divorced long since,
The slips of girls with combed-up topknots,
The maidens sedate and sturdy, the strapping wenches—
Take them one and all together,
And it is Barni Sheekh who excels in beauty!

Fair of skin, her gums the colour of the deep dark sea,
She has the aspect of a crescent moon.
With her glistening curls and her date-brown hue
She is as lustrous as a pearl.

---

[1]B. W. Andrzejewski, "In Praise of Barni Sheekh," *An Anthology of Somali Poetry* (Bloomington, IN: Indiana University Press, 1993), pp. 63–64.
[2]Sir Richard Burton, *First Footsteps in East Africa,* vol. I (London: Darf Publishers, Ltd., 1894), p. 82.
Source: From B. W. Andrzejewski, "In Praise of Barni Sheekh," *An Anthology of Somali Poetry,* © 1993. Reprinted by permission of Indiana University Press.

So tall is her stature, so upright her bearing,
That you think you see a camelopard
If you glimpse her from afar.
There is strength in the build of her body
And she walks along at an easy pace,
Her left arm swinging in a graceful rhythm
That imparts beauty to her every step.

When you behold her dignified deportment,
When you feel the yearning that her character inspires
And discover the elegant beauty that God implanted in her,
Then your eyes will never cease their gazing.
The world is vast indeed
But however wide you may have roamed,

No matter what far land you may have seen,
In what country have you ever had news
Of a girl like Barni Sheekh?

TEXT 52

Mahammed ꞌAbdille Hasan: The Sayyid's Reply[1]

In the late 1800s the emperor of Ethiopia conquered the Ogaden region of Somalia, while the British annexed coastal areas of northern Somaliland and the Italians colonized the south. Mahammed ꞌAbdille Hasan (1864–1920), who later became known in the West as "the Mad Mullah," was born in the eastern part of this multifractured Somalia. In 1900 he launched a powerful jihad against the Christian infidels, both European and Ethiopian, until his movement was finally defeated. A talented poet and writer as well as militarist, Mahammed ꞌAbdille Hasan composed poetry in Somali and Arabic. B. W. Andrzejewski and I. M. Lewis in Somali Poetry *make the following observations:*

> Here, in the style of a defendant stating his case before a Somali court of arbitration, the poet neatly counters each charge made against him in a message from the British. As well as being of interest for the skill with which Sheikh Mahammed turns each charge made against him into an attack upon his accusers, the poem reveals how the nationalist leader regarded the Italian colonizers of Somalia. These, not without justice, the Sayyid sees as having been brought to his country by the British and encouraged to join the fight against him.[2]

1 Concerning your plea "Do not incite the Ogaadeen against us" I also have a complaint.
2 The people of the Ethiopian region look for nothing from you,
3 So do not press my claim against them.
4 Do not claim on my behalf the blood money which they owe me.

---

[1]B. W. Andrzejewski and I. M. Lewis, *Somali Poetry: An Introduction* (London: Oxford University Press, 1964), pp. 74–82.
[2]Ibid, p. 74.
Source: From B. W. Andrzejewski and I. M. Lewis, *Somali Poetry: An Introduction,* © 1964. Reprinted with permission of Oxford University Press.

TEXT 52: *Mahammed ʿAbdille Hasan: The Sayyid's Reply*

5   I will myself seek to recover the property and the loot which they have seized.
6   Were I to leave a single penny with them my pledge would be perverted.
7   What I claim from you is only what you yourself owe me;
8   Since you are the government the responsibility is yours,
9   Can you disclaim those whom you tricked into attacking me?
10 Do they not swim in the prosperity which they have gained from what they devoured of mine?
11 Do they not drive their livestock from the valley of ʿAado to the west?
12 What did they seek from the lands between Burao and your stations?
13 Had you a pact with them by God and by consent?
14 Or did thirst drive them mad? Fools easily lose their way.
15 And afterwards was it not into your pockets that you poured the wealth?
16 Did you not enter the amounts of the booty in your printed books and cash ledgers?
17 And have you not openly admitted this in the full light of day?
18 Are not these spoils laden upon you as upon a burden-donkey?
19 That is my statement: if you are honest with me what can you answer?
20 What profit will you gain by denial? I have clearly established my case.
21 Concerning your plea: "Do not incite the Ogaadeen against us" I also have a complaint.

*   *   *   *   *

22 As to your statement "We have not seen the sailing ship" I also have a complaint.
23 Why are you tiring yourself out, working your wiles?
24 Do you not get weary with pointless talk?
25 Who rules the sea and controls the sails and holds of ships?
26 The Italians are your followers, the foundlings whom you drive with you;
27 Had they not been led by you they would not have come to Dannood,
28 They would not have sent an expedition to Doollo and ʿIid;
29 They would not have sent their armies against me.
30 They would not have harassed me with assaults at daybreak.
31 I had no issue with the Italians until you summoned them to your aid.
32 It was you who intrigued and plotted with them;
33 It was you who said "Join us in the war against the Dervishes";
34 And they did not say "Leave us, and stop conspiring with us";
35 Did you never tire of these evil machinations?
36 Was it not through these schemes that the landings at Obbia took place?
37 Did they not greatly aid you with their arms and supplies?
38 You fools, those who attacked yesterday on your side
39 Will they not strike at me from the back if we fight tomorrow?
40 Will they be prevented from attacking me, by disclaiming their bond from you?
41 It is you who lead to pasture these weaker infidels;
42 Can I distinguish between you and your livestock?
43 As to your statement "We have not seen the sailing ship," I also have a complaint.

*   *   *   *   *

44 As to the raiders of whom you talk, I also have a complaint.
45 It is you who have oppressed them and seized their beasts,
46 It is you who took for yourselves their houses and property,
47 It is you who spoilt their settlements and defiled them with ordure,
48 It is you who reduced them to eating the tortoise and beast of prey;

49 This degradation you brought upon them.
50 If they (in turn) become beasts of prey and loot you
51 And steal small things from the clearings between your huts,
52 Then they were driven to this by hunger and famine;
53 Do not complain to me and I will not complain to you.
54 If you do not accept my statement,
55 And unless your servants confuse you with lies,
56 That I harboured them, or that I sent them against you,
57 Bring me clear evidence; otherwise it is you who are guilty of the sin.
58 As to the raiders of whom you talk, I also have a complaint.

* * * * *

59 Concerning your demand "Turn aside from the Warsangeli," I have a complaint.
60 If they prefer you, then they and I shall be at variance:
61 It is not in my nature to accept people who cringe to you.
62 But if they are Dervishes, how can I turn aside from them?
63 Do you also share their ancestry from Daarood Ismaaᶜiil?
64 Are you trying to steal towards me through my ancestor's genealogy?
65 Of late have you not turned them into gazelles, (fugitive and homeless)?
66 Have you not seen how they loathe you?
67 For have you not seized their shops and stored their goods in your houses?
68 Have you not set fire to their ships so that smoke rose from them?
69 You, with your filthy genitals, have you not hanged their men?
70 They soon found out that you would have no mercy on them.
71 You are against both worship and the Divine Law.
72 You are building a mat partition between them and the streams of Paradise and Heaven.
73 You are casting them into the raging fury and fumes of Hell.
74 Do they not see how deceitful you are?
75 Or are they well pleased with your prevarication?
76 Will they be divorced from their womenfolk and wives?

* * * * *

77 Concerning your demand "Return the camels," I have a complaint.
78 I also have suffered damage and loss;
79 You threw me on the ground and skinned my knee,
80 It was you who snatched the camels as they grazed,
81 It was you who scattered the white-turbanned army,
82 It was I who was first hammered at Gallaadi and experienced your bitterness;
83 A fool understands nothing, but the warning did not elude me.
84 The tethering rope with which you bound ᶜIise was meant for me,
85 And unless he is released at once there will be no peace in the world.
86 I uttered a cry, asserting my rights, so that I may not be wronged;
87 Do not expect generosity from me: yet shall we make a bargain?
88 And shall we agree to what is in our mutual interest?
89 Or fall upon each other? God knows who is the oppressed.
90 Oh, leave the trickery behind and decide today, now!

TEXT 53

The Ethiopian Public Health Bureau: Medical Legislation[1]

Because twentieth-century Ethiopia had escaped the fate of its colonized neighbors, it is interesting to note the free exchange of ideas and technologies which existed between Ethiopians and Europeans in the scientific and medical fields. Ethiopia possessed a long heritage of traditional medicine to which it voluntarily combined medical innovations from abroad. As early as A.D. 1521, Emperor Lebna Dengel communicated with King João III of Portugal, requesting that the European monarch dispatch to the court of the Ethiopian ruler learned physicians and surgeons.

The contemporary legislating of medical practices began in 1930. At that time the Ethiopian government established a Public Health Bureau to supervise newly legislated regulations governing the medical treatments and pharmacopoeia of modern and traditional practitioners.

1. No one could practice medicine in Ethiopia if not in possession of a diploma as a doctor of medicine issued by a recognized medical facility.

2. No one could exercise the profession of dentist without having the diploma of a medical doctor with specialisation in dentistry or a diploma or certificate of dental surgery.

3. Midwives were not allowed to deliver unless they had the relevant diploma from a foreign Government or a permit from the Ethiopian Government.

4. Midwives were forbidden to use obstetric instruments or to prescribe medicine, and, in case of difficult labour, were expected to call in a doctor of medicine.

5. No one was allowed to run a pharmacy without having a pharmacist's diploma.

---

[1]Richard Pankhurst, "The Beginnings of Modern Medicine in Ethiopia," *Ethiopia Observer* vol. IX, no. 2, 1965, pp. 114–50.
Source: Reprinted from Richard Pankhurst, *Ethiopia Observer,* 1965.

6. Medical doctors were, however, permitted to engage in pharmacy until further notice.

7. Pharmacists were not allowed to supply medical preparations or drugs without an order from a doctor of medicine, dentist or veterinary surgeon acting within their respective fields of competence.

8. Traders, grocers and other shop-keepers were forbidden from selling any medicine, simple or complex, except castor oil and sulphate of magnesium.

9. No one was permitted to exercise the veterinary art without a diploma.

10. The exercise of the profession of medicine, dentistry, pharmacy and veterinary surgery was placed under the control of the Ministry of the Interior.

11. Within three months of the promulgation of the decree all doctors, dentists, pharmacists, midwives and veterinarians had to address a request to the said Ministry for an official authorisation to exercise their profession, the request to be accompanied by evidence of their qualifications. This request in the case of Ethiopians and foreigners not registered at a consulate was to be made to the Ministry direct, and, in the case of foreigners registered at a Consulate through such a Consulate which would be responsible for authenticating the relevant diplomas.

12. A commission composed of two doctors meeting under the presidency of the Minister or the Director General of the Interior was to examine requests and diplomas and to decide whether to grant or refuse authorisations to practice.

Doctors, dentists, pharmacists, midwives and veterinarians possessing diplomas conforming with the stipulations in the above Articles: 1, 2, 3, 5 and 9 were to receive immediate authorisation to practice. Persons with diplomas inferior to those specified could, however, be allowed to continue in their profession if the commission considered their qualifications adequate.

13. As a temporary measure and as long as existing conditions warranted it the Government reserved the right to allow qualified nurses, after examination by a commission of doctors in Government employ, to treat patients in such provinces as lacked any qualified doctor.

Except in such cases no authorisation to exercise any of the professions dealt with in the decree was to be issued to anyone who did not fulfil the conditions laid down in Articles 1, 2, 3, 5 and 9.

14. The Ministry of the Interior was to keep a register of doctors, dentists, pharmacists, midwives and veterinarians authorised to practice.

15. Authorisation to exercise a medical profession could always be withdrawn from persons condemned for a crime of omission or commission.

16. Any contravention of the decree by an Ethiopian or a foreigner not registered at a Consulate was liable to a fine of from 20 to 2,000 thalers according to the gravity of the case, to be decided by the competent tribunal. Foreigners registered at a consulate were liable to the penalties applicable under their own law; where their laws did not embody analogous regulations the Ethiopian Government, acting in accord with the Consulate concerned, would take all administrative measures to assure the respect of the decree.

17. The law could be modified when the Government judged this suitable.

A law was also enacted for the strict regulation of pharmacies. Its provisions were as follows:

1. A pharmacy had to have four rooms.

2. The Ministry of the Interior had the right to prohibit the installation of a pharmacy in a building which it did not consider suitable.

3. The Ministry of the Interior reserved the right to designate to the pharmacist the town or locality in which he could establish himself. A pharmacy could not be transferred from one building, locality or town without the permission of the Ministry of the Interior.

Every pharmacy had to be supplied with all the furniture and equipment necessary for the exercise of its work.

4. Chemical products, drugs and pharmaceutical supplied were to be classified.

5. Stupefectives and poisons had to be kept in a special locked cupboard.

6. All chemical products, drugs, etc. had to be kept according to the stipulations of the pharmacopoeia.

7. Every pharmacist had to have at his disposal equipment, apparatus and a pharmacopoeia.

8. The owner of a pharmacy was obliged to declare the number and quality of his personnel which were to be registered with the Ministry of the Interior. In case of illness or other impediment the owner of a pharmacy could be represented by his assistant or by a doctor for a period of 15 days.

A pharmacist could not take an apprentice-druggist into his service without the permission of the Ministry of the Interior.

9. The owner of a pharmacy was responsible for the impeccable quality of his chemical products, drugs and pharmaceutical specialties. The name of the pharmacy and the date and price of the medicament had to be marked on prescriptions. All prescriptions had to be written in a special register together with the name of the patient, the date, the composition of the medicament and the name of the doctor. These registers had to be kept for 5 years. In cases where the doctor prescribed more than the maximum dose the pharmacist had the duty to reduce the dose unless the doctor could be consulted. If the doctor exceeded the maximum dose and confirmed this in writing the pharmacist could then execute the prescription.

The label on the medicine must bear the name of the pharmacy, the date, directions for use, and the composition of the medicament. If the medicament was prescribed for an Ethiopian the directions for use had to be written in Amharic. The label for a medicament to be applied externally had to be written on red paper. It was strictly forbidden to substitute another drug for the one prescribed without the agreement of the doctor.

10. Pharmacists were forbidden from exercising the medical art except in very urgent cases or where a doctor could not be found.

11. Pharmacists were prohibited from making an agreement with a doctor to obtain prescriptions or to dispense prescriptions written in fraudulent terms.

12. Pharmacists were obliged to be open at night and on Sundays on rota basis according to a monthly list published by the Ministry of the Interior.

13. Weights and balances, as well as measures of capacity, used in pharmacies were to be controlled once a year by the Inspector of Pharmacies.

14. The Ministry of the Interior had the right to inspect pharmacies to ensure the execution of this law, the inspection to be carried out either by the Inspector of Pharmacies or by the Public Health Commission.

15. Doctors could not open or run a pharmacy except with the permission of the Ministry of Interior. In towns where there were pharmacies doctors would not be accorded such permission.

16. Vaccines and serums whose date of efficacy had expired could not be sold. Smallpox vaccine could not be sold after 90 days of its entering the pharmacy.

17. Tincture of digitalis must be prepared by the pharmacists themselves and not be imported from abroad.

18. The regulations of the present law were applicable to hospital as to all other pharmacies.

19. Any contravention of this law was liable to a fine of from 5 to 5,000 dollars, the Ministry of the Interior reserving the right to withdraw the right to practise from any pharmacist who repeatedly broke the stipulations of the law.

Another regulation made at this time specified that druggists practicing in Ethiopia must be in possession of an assistant pharmacist's diploma or have passed a special examination given by the Ministry of the Interior after completing three years' apprenticeship in a pharmacy or drug store. Permission to practise and the sitting of the examination were both subject to a 50 dollar tax.

A comprehensive law was also issued on the possession and sale of poisonous substances; it contained the following provisions:

Law on the Possession and Sale of Poisonous Substances

1. Poisonous substances covered by the law were named in two lists, A and B, as follows:

List A

Acidum hydrocyanicum
Aconitium
Adrenalinum seu Suprareninum seu Epirenanum
Arecolinum hydrobromicum
Argentum cynanatum
Arsenum et ejus salia et preparationes
Atropinuh et ejus salia
Benzaldehydcyanhydrinum
Brucinum
Colochicinum
Coninum
Curare
Daturinum
Digitalinum, Digitoninum, Digitoxinum
Erytropheleinum
Homatropinum aceticum
  "   bijodatum
  "   bromatum

         "   cyanatum
         "   formidatum
         "   jodatum
         "   nitrocum
         "   oleinicum
         "   oxycyanatum
         "   oxydatum
         "   peptonatum
         "   praecipatatum album
         "   salicylicum
         "   tannicum
Hyoscinum (Duboisinum)
Hyoscayminum
Kalium cyanatum
Lobelinum
Natrium cyanatum
Nicotinum
Nitroglycerinum sol.
Pilocarpinum et ejus salia
Phosphorus et ejus preparationes
Physostigminum salicylicum
         "   sulfuricum
Oleum crotonis
Scopolaminum et ejus salia
Strophantium et ejus salia
Strychninum et ejus salia
Veratrinum

List B

Acidum picrinicum
Bulbus scillae
Hydrargyrum bicheoratum
         "   in pastillis

    Stupefactives were not included in either of the two lists and formed the basis of separate legislation.

    2. Doctors, dentists, pharmacists and veterinarians authorised to practise in Ethiopia were alone entitled to import, prepare, sell or otherwise dispose of, even to give away, the above poisonous substances or plants from which they could be obtained.

    3. In exceptional cases the Ministry of the Interior could authorise persons other than doctors, pharmacists, dentists or veterinarians to import, sell or utilise certain poisonous substances for industrial or agricultural use, but only under licence.

    4. It was forbidden for anyone to possess or hold poisonous substances without having proof that they were obtained by such person in conformity with the provisions of this decree.

5. It was forbidden without a licence from the Minister of the Interior, to make poisons or to cultivate plants from which they could be obtained.

6. Persons authorised to sell poisonous substances could not sell or supply commodities specified in list A except on the basis of a prescription signed by a doctor, dentist or veterinarian authorised to practise in Ethiopia or of a permit from the Ministry of the Interior.

7. The commodities on list B could only be sold or supplied by a doctor, dentist, pharmacist or veterinarian against a written receipt to persons who were proved to be trustworthy.

8. In cases where the purchaser was unable to go himself to collect the poison which he had bought it could be supplied against a receipt given by a person designated for this purpose in writing by the purchaser.

9. Sale to persons appearing to be minors was absolutely forbidden.

10. Poisonous substances had to be carefully kept in a special locked cupboard bearing the sign "POISON."

11. All poisonous substances sold had to be wrapped and bear on the packet the name of the pharmacist, the name of the poison and a label with a skull and the word "POISON".

12. Every pharmacist had to have a special balance as well as special spoons and mortars, all visibly labelled with the word "POISON." These utensils had to be kept in the cupboard reserved for the storage of poisons.

13. Any prescription given by doctors, dentists or veterinarians had to bear beside their signature their full name as well as the name and address of the person for whom it was intended. Such prescriptions had also to bear the date and the amount of the poison to be supplied.

14. Each prescription had to be noted down by the pharmacist in a special register and kept by him as a legal document.

15. It was forbidden to despense a prescription a second time without written authorisation from a doctor, dentist or veterinarian.

16. A prescription could not be given by a dentist except for dental treatment and should bear the mention "for dental treatment." Similarly a prescription could not be given by a veterinarian except for veterinary treatment and should bear the mention "for veterinarian treatment only."

17. The sale of poisonous substances was to be recorded in a special register numbered and initialed by the Ministry of the Interior. The entries had to be made at the time of the sale without leaving blank spaces or using the margins. They were to indicate the type and quantity of poisonous substances sold and the use for which they were intended, as well as the name, profession and address of the purchaser. They were to be attested to by the signature of the purchaser and by that of the person who supplied it. If the sale was made as a result of a written instruction the latter was to be kept with the register.

18. All sellers of poisonous substances had also to keep a register in which they were to inscribe in date order, without blank spaces or marginal entries, every sale of poisonous substances, wholesale or retail, which they made, with mention of the kind and quantity of poison they bought, the date of the purchase, the name, profession and address of the purchaser.

19. Pharmacists, as well as doctors, dentists and veterinarians who purchased poisonous substances from their colleagues or sold such articles to them, were obliged to keep an account of the operations in the same manner as other dealers in poisons.

20. All registers which had to be kept as a result of this decree as well as prescriptions and other documents relating to the purchase or sale of poisonous substances had to be kept for five years. They had to be available to the Ministry of the Interior.

21. To ensure the enforcement of these regulations inspectors of the Ministry of the Interior had the right at any time to inspect any premises used for the sale of poisonous substances.

22. Any infringement of the provisions of this decree was subject to a fine of from 20 to 1,000 dollars, the judge also having the right to order the confiscation of the objects concerned.

23. Anyone possessing poisonous substances without justification on the basis of this decree had to report this fact within 30 days to the Ministry of the Interior which, after examination of the case, had to decide on the method of liquidating the said poisonous substances, either by giving the owner time to sell them to persons entitled to purchase them or by purchasing them at an equitable price for the use of State hospitals.

24. After the expiry of thirty days anyone holding poisonous substances illegally would be liable to the punishments provided for in this decree.

25. The Minister of the Interior had the power to alter the list of poisonous substances mentioned in Article 1, either by addition or deletion.

Each modification of the list, should be published in the journal *Lumière et Paix* (*Light and Peace*) and be applicable after three months of such publication.

The law concerning the import and trade in stupefactives contained the following provisions.

1. The stupefactives under this law were listed as the following:

Acetylodihydrocodeinone or acetylodemethylodihydrothebaine, its salts (Acedicone), preparations and preparations of its salts.

Benzylmorphine and its salts (Peronine) and preparations.

Indian hemp, its extract, tincture, resin and preparations based on it, such as hashish, esras, shira, jamba, etc.

Cocaine, its salts, preparations and preparations of its salts.

Diacethglmorphine (Diamorphine, Heroine), its salts and preparations and preparations of its salts.

Dihydrocodeinoine, its salts (Diocodide) and preparations and preparations of its salts.

Dihydromorphine, its salts (Paramorfane) and preparations and preparations of its salts.

Dihydrooxycodeinone, its salts (Eucodoal) and preparations and preparations of its salts.

Ecgonine, its salts and preparations and preparations of its salts, esters of ecgonine and their salts and preparations.

Ethylmorphine, its salts (Dionine) and preparations and preparations of its salts.

Leaves of Coca and preparations.

Laudanone and similar preparations.

Methylmorphine (Codeine), its salts and preparations and preparations of its salts.

Morphine and its salts and preparations containing morphine and its salts, as well as preparations containing them.

Narcophine.

Noxymorphine. (Genomorphine) and its preparations.

Opium, also opium tincture, extract and other preparations.

Thebaine, its salts and preparations.

All esters of dihydrooxycodeinone, dihydrocodeinone, dihyromorphinone, acetylodihydrocodeinone or acetylomethylodihydrothebaine, dihydromorphine and their salts and preparations.

All the alkaloids of opium.

Pantopone, Opiotal and similar preparations.

All preparations produced at that time or later containing any one of the above products.

2. The import of these drugs into any part of Ethiopia was prohibited except by medical pharmacists authorised to practise.

Such persons had first to apply for a license from the Ministry of the Interior. Their request had to indicate:

1. The name and quantity of the drug which it was requested to import.
2. The name and address of the manufacturer or supplier.
3. The method of transport (e.g. post, railway, etc.) and the route of import.

Whenever the drugs concerned were not pure alkaloids but composite medicines the request had to state the percentage and nature of the alkaloids there contained.

The Ministry of the Interior had full authority to grant or refuse the request or to reduce the quantity of goods demanded. The import certificate would be subject to a dollar tax, but where the supplying country required it the Ministry of the Interior would issue free of charge a certificate attesting the legality of import of the articles concerned.

Medical pharmacists authorised to practise their profession in Ethiopia were the sole persons entitled to hold, prepare, sell or in any way supply, even free of charge, the articles specified in Article 1.

The authorised importing medical pharmacist could hold or sell these drugs at the request of a medical pharmacist authorised to practise in Ethiopia.

The method and sale of such goods was subject to the control provisions specified in Article 3 below.

The export of the products listed in Article 1 was prohibited.

4. Medical pharmacists authorised to practise had to enter details of these drugs in a special register with numbered pages: the entries, which must not be interlined, had to indicate exactly the amount of these drugs in their possession, as well as the quantities sold or used.

This information had to be presented at the end of each half year (on June 30 and December 31) to the Ministry of the Interior which had the responsibility of checking and counter-signing such information. This information had also to be presented to the said Ministry at the time of each new request to import for such drugs.

Medical pharmacists purchasing any of these drugs from their colleagues had the same responsibility as others towards the Ministry of the Interior.

Pharmacists could not sell their customers articles listed in Article 1 except against a prescription signed by a doctor authorised to practise.

The prescription had to bear not only the signature of the doctor, but also his entire name and that of the patient, both written in clearly legible characters.

Such prescriptions had to be copied into a special register kept by the pharmacist as a legal document.

It was forbidden to dispense a prescription a second time without written authorisation from a doctor.

5. In cases of emergency pharmacists could supply the following galenic preparations on their own responsibility: paregoric elixir, landanum of Sydenham and Dover powder, provided that the maximum quantity delivered did not contain more than 0.20 grammes of medicinal opium.

The pharmacist had to enter in his register the stupefactives thus supplied.

6. The Ministry of the Interior would appoint one or two doctors who would decide on all requests to import such drugs.

A special commission composed of two doctors under the presidency of the Minister of the Interior or the Director of the said Ministry would check the registers of doctors and pharmacists.

This commission was likewise charged to investigate any infringements of this law whether discovered by them themselves or brought to their attention by others. Where the person accused of breaking the law was a foreigner the commission would automatically include the consul of the country to which the foreigner belonged or by which he was represented.

7. Any illegal import, holding, sale or disposal, even free of charge, of articles listed in Article 1 by an Ethiopian subject or foreigner not registered at a consulate would be subject to a fine of from 20 to 1,000 dollars, depending on the severity of the offence.

Foreigners registered at a consulate would be liable, in case of infringement of the law, to the fines applicable in their own country or country of protection.

Any infringement of the law not published by the foreigner's own law or country of protection would render him liable to action to be taken by the Imperial Ethiopian in consultation with the consulate concerned, such action to be adopted to ensure the respect of the law.

8. Anyone possessing without a medical prescription any articles specified in Article 1 at the time of the promulgation of this law had to report the fact immediately to the Ministry of the Interior.

Medical pharmacists had the responsibility to obtain the register in which to enter the drugs covered by this law and the amount of these drugs in their possession at that time had immediately to be entered in the register.

Persons holding the specified products without authorisation had to hand them over, against receipt, to the Ministry of the Interior, if possible with the invoice of the supplier.

After examination of such products by the Government doctors the articles thus obtained would be paid for by the Ministry and put at the disposal of State hospitals.

After the coming into force of the law anyone holding articles specified in Article 1 without authorisation would be liable to the already mentioned fines.

Another law, dealing with the preparation and sale being more than 10 ccm per 100 grammes. Not more than 25 per cent. sand.

Eggs. The term "fresh eggs" could not be used for eggs more than 14 days old.

Alcohol drinks, beers, etc. Wines, liqueurs, beers and spirits were regulated by the government monopoly, the Monopole des Alcools et Spiritueax en Ethiopie.

Pastries. The materials used in the manufacture of biscuits and cakes had to conform to the regulations of this law. The use of rancid butter was forbidden.

Gelatine. If intended for human consumption had to be almost colourless, transparent and without smell or taste.

Cocoa and chocolate. The addition of sesame oil or other fatty materials to the cocoa was not allowed. Powder cocoa must not contain more than 90 per cent. water, the butter content not less than 25 per cent. There should be neither flour nor starch in the cocoa.

Chocolate must contain 33.5 to 50 per cent. of cocoa and cocoa butter and 50 per cent. to 66.6 per cent. sugar. The sale of chocolate containing more than 70 per cent. sugar was forbidden. In the case of the addition of other materials such fact had to be indicated.

6. Any violation of the articles in its law was subject to a fine of 1 to 1,000 dollars except in case of action against public health which was dealt with in Article 3.

7. The Minister of the Interior had the right to add to the regulations on quality, manufacture and composition of foodstuffs enumerated in Article 5.

PART SEVEN

West Africa

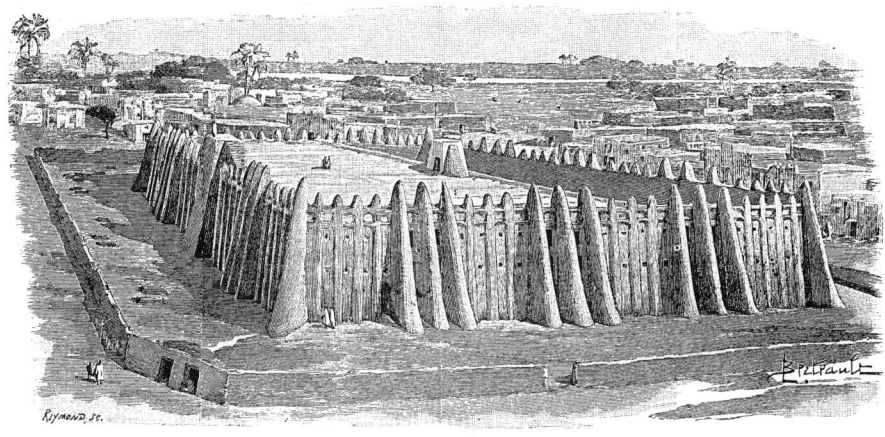

In West Africa empire-building societies, which evolved elaborate state mechanisms, labor diversification, and written traditions, coexisted alongside equally prolific but politically decentralized societies. In attempting to distinguish between the two types of polities, Western scholars had over the course of the last century propounded elaborate theories of racial classification to account for these cultural differences. The populations of the large states were often referred to as Hamitic, that is, dark-skinned Caucasoids while those of the decentralized societies as Negroid. But this classification scheme represented a false construct. While it suited the social mores of its times, it had no scientific basis since the populations of centralized states were often physiognomically indistinguishable from their decentralized neighbors.

Scholars today recognize that much of what accounts for the underlying differences between the states and their decentralized neighbors was ecological. A sizable proportion of Africa's soils are low in organic matter, erode easily, and are especially susceptible to overuse. Such factors as fertility and erosion patterns, accessibility to navigable waterways, incidence of tropical diseases, and availability of commercially desirable natural resources determined in large measure which regions would evolve the population density and economic activity needed to develop state systems rather than remain decentralized. In the absence of large scale agricultural surpluses, the presence or access to a valuable resource like gold then became the basis for empire-building.

THE WESTERN SUDAN

In the thousand years that preceded the European colonization of Africa, several powerful merchant empires evolved and eventually collapsed in the interior region of West Africa, known as the western Sudan. The wealth of these large states emanated from the long-distance trade, particularly in gold, and the states themselves served as termini of major trans-Saharan trade routes. The gold emanated, however, from the forest states to the south and its decentralized populations. These societies willingly traded gold in exchange for a commodity of even greater value in their sodium-deficient environment, i.e., salt, which was extracted from mines in the Sahara.

One of the earliest of these powerful centralized states, ancient Ghana (not to be confused with modern Ghana), was located in the region of the Niger River. It emerged sometime before the eighth century, by which time it was already known to the Moroccans as "the land of gold." Ghana was populated by the Soninke, a northern branch of the Mande-speaking peoples popularly known as Mandingoes. The economic expansion of Ghana also attested to the importance of the camel, introduced into the Sahara in the fifth century, and which served to revolutionize commerce across the desert. For the first time, the gold of sub-Saharan Africa, as well as such tropical products as ivory and exotic animal skins, became accessible to markets on the Mediterranean.

By the early thirteenth century Ghana had been superseded by Mali, situated in the plateau region between the upper reaches of the Senegal and Niger rivers. Its founder, Sundiata Keita, transformed the small, insignificant militia of Mali into a potent clan organization, using age groups as the nucleus for a vibrant, aggressive army bent on expansion. After incorporating the commercially viable areas of Ghana into Mali's expanded boundaries, Sundiata transferred the focal point of the trans-Saharan trade in gold to Mali. He likewise gained control over the crucial trade in salt, since it was this valued commodity that was traded for gold.

By the middle of the thirteenth century the kings or *mansas* of Mali dominated the entire region encompassing the bend of the Niger River to the Atlantic. Another important state of the western Sudan, Bornu, was located southwest of Lake Chad. It maintained control over the Hausa city-states of Northern Nigeria throughout much of their history. The largest and last of these great merchant empires, Songhay, maintained its capital city at Gao, situated on the banks of the Niger river. Much of what we know about the rise to power of the most renowned of the Muslim leaders of that state, the Askia Muhammad, derives from the two noted chronicles of Timbuktu, the

Tarikh al-Sudan (*History of the Land of the Blacks*) and *Tarikh al-Fattash* (*History of the Seeker After Knowledge*). However, these written sources must be juxtaposed against oral traditions, representing a dramatically different worldview, and emanating from the same time period but among the rural (rather than Islamized urban) populations. Songhay reached the apex of its power in the sixteenth century, and was finally subdued by a Moroccan invasion in 1591.

ISLAMIZATION

The diffusion of Islam into West Africa tended to follow the Saharan trade routes across the desert. The urban populations, whose economic well-being relied on the trans-Saharan trade, over time converted to Islam while much of the rural populations of these same states retained their traditional shamanistic religions and ancestral worship at least until recent times. With the Arabic language representing a *lingua franca* of this expanding Islamic world, the commercial city of Timbuktu emerged as a vital intellectual center from as early as the fourteenth century. Over time, a more fundamentalist trend emerged in West African Islam that saw the development of indigenous, non-Arabic or *ajami* literatures employing the Arabic script as well.

Beginning around the middle of the seventeenth century, the Islamized elements of the Fulani ethnicity, who inhabited regions of Senegal, Guinea, and Northern Nigeria, began waging a series of holy wars against their neighbors, which allowed them to establish theocratic states throughout large expanses of West Africa. The Fulani empire of Sokoto encompassing the Hausaland region of northern Nigeria represented the largest of the later eighteenth and nineteenth century series of states consolidated through the launching of jihad.

The intellectual output of these societies was prodigious even though much of the written literature has not survived. In many cases all that remains are references made to various lost texts by the scholars of the day. Both the use of Arabic and the utilization of the Arabic script to write indigenous languages increased literacy considerably throughout the western Sudan because of the importance the Islamic religion placed on the duty of its adherents to be able to read the Quran in the sacred Arabic language.

THE FOREST BELT

The differing ecology of the West African forest belt to the south of the savannah regions of the western Sudan created a very different economic environment from that of the western Sudan. The existence of the tsetse fly and tropical diseases made it difficult if not impossible to breed beasts of burden, whether cattle or horses. Contrary to popular belief, the immense rain forests are in fact some of the most ecologically fragile habitats in the world. This is because the dominant soils lack nitrogen, and the lush vegetation is attributable to the immense humidity and constant recycling of organic compounds before they are leached away by the abundant rains. Such factors of ecological fragility mitigate against the development of long-term surplus agriculture. Without large-scale agricultural or trade surpluses, many of the populations of the forest belt remained ethnically fragmented. The largest ethnicities in this region—the

Yoruba, Ibo, Nupe, Fon, and Asante—comprised those groups whose territories encompassed both forest and savannah and were thus able to farm more productively. Communication in the forest belt was constrained by the fact that beasts of burden could not be bred on account of the tropical disease environment. It is therefore not surprising that one of the most creative forms of expression ever devised, "drum language," evolved within this environment where communication was otherwise reduced to the speed of human movement.

The earliest known states in the region were Ife and Benin, both of which gained renown for their intricate artistic forms, particularly brass castings employing the lost wax process. The history of the Edo-speaking peoples of Benin, which came to an end in the nineteenth century after conquest by the British, began sometime in the thirteenth or fourteenth century. Enjoying an agricultural base, which employed iron age technology, Benin also participated in the long-distance trade across the Sahara through the intermediaries of Hausaland in what is today northern Nigeria. It was invaded by Britain in 1897 and subsequently collapsed.

The earliest of the Yoruba states was that of Ife, whose artists refined a West African style of bronze sculpting that has become world renowned. It was succeeded by the Oyo empire, which emerged in the seventeenth century as the dominant Yoruba state. The *alafin* or king of Oyo presided over an imperial court comprised of numerous palace and state officials, charged with maintaining an elaborate system of government administration and tax collection. Oyo began a process of steady decline during the nineteenth century and was therefore impotent in withstanding the growing British influence in the region.

An early vassal state of Benin, Dahomey broke away in order to establish its independent sovereignty in the seventeenth century. Dahomey strengthened its economic base by bartering slaves acquired in combat with European firearms. On its western borders lay the Akan states of Asante and Fante, in the coastal region that came to be known as the Gold Coast. Even as early as the fifteenth century, these peoples had traded gold with the merchant empires of the western Sudan in exchange for salt. However, as the Portuguese presence, followed by that of other Europeans, grew stronger on the coast, the Asante sought new outlets for their trade and increased their demand for European firearms. Asante grew to encompass an area of 150,000 square miles in the territory of what is today modern Ghana. Its imperial activities prompted its neighbor, Fante, to become politically centralized as a means of protecting its citizens from Asante hegemony.

EUROPEAN CONTACT AND THE TRANS-ATLANTIC SLAVE TRADE

By 1415 the Portuguese, in search of new trading networks that might bypass the Muslim monopoly on the overland trade routes, began their exploration of the west coast of Africa. The advent of the European sea-traders over time allowed the coastal kingdoms of Benin, Oyo, and Dahomey to begin trading directly with the Europeans rather than sending their gold and the trade goods through the intermediaries of the western Sudan and the trans-Saharan trade routes.

By the late seventeenth century, the commerce in slaves had eclipsed that in gold and other commodities on account of the increasing demand for cheap labor in the new American colonies. West African slaves provided a seemingly inexhaustible labor supply. In addition, they possessed some level of immunity to the tropical diseases still prevalent in the Americas, and in emanating from agricultural societies, they brought with them considerable skills in farming. So intense did slaving activities become in certain regions of West Africa that the area between the Gold Coast of modern day Ghana and the Niger Delta came to be known as "The Slave Coast."

Scholarly estimates of the numbers of Africans sold into slavery have varied from a low figure of 10 million upwards of 60 million. It is impossible to know precisely. And whatever the figure of African men and women who survived the Middle Passage across the Atlantic to arrive in the New World, an additional 20 percent died in the holds of the ships and had their bodies tossed overboard. Many times as many may also have perished on account of the incessant warfare precipitated by slaving, which brought famine and starvation to large regions of West Africa. These subsistence agricultural societies could not sustain even minimal productivity when fleeing populations were unable to sow the land. Most of the slaves were wrenched from the decentralized societies in the West African interior. Without the protections accorded by strong, state mechanisms, these became the most vulnerable populations.

Because African slave-trading societies bartered slaves for European firearms, over time it became difficult if not impossible for some of these states to remove themselves from the trade. That is, the climate of instability had become so intense that West African rulers could only protect themselves from the possibility of invasion by a neighbor hankering for captives with a large arsenal of guns, which could only be obtained if they kept a constant supply of slaves for barter.

It is also interesting to note as Roland Oliver and J. D. Fage point out, that even during those centuries, slave trading carried a stigma:

> Even though the absolute wickedness of slavery was a late discovery of the Christian conscience, the actual practice of the slave trade was so manifestly ugly, even to those who took part in it, that the prying eyes of the disinterested observer were very actively discouraged.[1]

By the 1840s the British turned to suppression of the slave trade so that European nations could establish trade in other commodities with the African continent. It was also during this period that a colony of American ex-slaves established the republic of Liberia, as a haven for freed American slaves.

European interests in African exploration after the end of the slave trade coincided with a period of fierce diplomatic competition among European states. Africa became the unfortunate canvas for their national ambitions. A few short years after the December 1884 international conference was convened in Berlin to sort out rival claims, most of the African continent had been carved up and doled out to European powers.

---

[1] Roland Oliver and J. D. Fage, *A Short History of Africa* (Penguin Books, reprinted 1978), p. 137.

TEXT 54

Ancient Mali: The Foretelling of the Great Sundiata's Birth

from The Epic of Sundiata[1]

With the decline of the ancient West African state of Ghana, a new nation arose in the Niger River valley of the thirteenth century. Its founding hero, Sundiata Keita, regaled in the oral traditions of the Mali court, represented an actual historical figure who founded the capital of his new empire at Niani, on the Niger River. Belonging to Malinke (or popularly known as Mandingo) ethnicity, he also incorporated into his new state the neighboring country of Sosso, ruled by a powerful king named Sumanguru. Like ancient Ghana and the successor state of Songhay, Mali derived much of its wealth from the trans-Saharan trade in gold. At its height Mali extended for more than 1,200 miles from the Atlantic seacoast to the borders of Hausaland in northern Nigeria.

The traditional religion of the state of Mali had originally centered around the worship of nature spirits. However, these religious practices came to be superseded in the urban portions of the empire by Islam, even though the rural sectors of the society maintained the traditional, animistic modes of worship. One can easily note in the recitation of the oral epic of Sundiata the references to Muhammad and the praises to Allah or God, even as a story of non-Islamic magical practices unfold. Such references in all probability reflect the subtle changes through which this oral tradition passed from century to century. That is, the Mande populations of Mali grew increasingly more Islamic since the time of Sundiata until the recording of this particular version of the tradition by the contemporary griot or praise singer Djeli Mamoudou Kouyate. The narrator of the epic explains his own role, thus:

> I teach kings the history of their ancestors so that the lives of the ancients might serve them as an example, for the world is old, but the future springs from the past.[2]

---

[1] D. T. Niane, *Sundiata: An Epic of Old Mali* (London: Addison Wesley Longman, Ltd., 1965), pp. 4–12.
[2] Ibid., p. 1.

TEXT 54: Ancient Mali: The Foretelling of the Great Sundiata's Birth

It was the fourteenth century ruler of Mali, however, the Mansa Musa (1312–1337), who exemplified the relentless process of Islamization in the Western Sudan. On his famed pilgrimage to Mecca in 1324–1325, he was reported to have brought with him more than 10,000 retainers and such a lavish supply of gold that it flooded the Cairo market through which the Mansa passed and depressed it for more than a decade thereafter. However, it is interesting to note that whereas the oral traditions of Mali, whose primary constituency represented the rural, farming populations of the state, give far greater weight to Sundiata than the Mansa Musa, the written traditions, representing the cultural interpretations of the urban Muslims of that country, reverse the importance of the two leaders in accordance with their historical and cultural allegiances.

Maghan Kon Fatta, the father of Sundiata, was renowned for his beauty in every land; but he was also a good king loved by all the people. In his capital of Nianiba he loved to sit often at the foot of the great silk-cotton tree which dominated his palace of Canco. Maghan Kon Fatta had been reigning a long time and his eldest son Dankaran Touman was already eight years old and often came to sit on the ox-hide beside his father.

Well now, one day when the king had taken up his usual position under the silk-cotton tree surrounded by his kinsmen he saw a man dressed like a hunter coming towards him; he wore the tight-fitting trousers of the favourites of Kondolon Ni Sané, and his blouse oversewn with cowries showed that he was a master of the hunting art. All present turned towards the unknown man whose bow, polished with frequent usage, shone in the sun. The man walked up in front of the king, whom he recognized in the midst of his courtiers. He bowed and said, "I salute you, king of Mali, greetings all you of Mali. I am a hunter chasing game and come from Sangaran; a fearless doe has guided me to the walls of Nianiba. By the grace of my master the great Simbon my arrows have hit her and now she lies not far from your walls. As is fitting, oh king, I have come to bring you your portion." He took a leg from his leather sack whereupon the king's griot, Gnankouman Doua, seized upon the leg and said, "Stranger, whoever you may be you will be the king's guest because you respect custom; come and take your place on the mat beside us. The king is pleased because he loves righteous men." The king nodded his approval and all the courtiers agreed. The griot continued in a more familiar tone, "Oh you who come from the Sangaran, land of the favourites of Kondolon Ni Sané, you who have doubtless had an expert master, will you open your pouch of knowledge for us and instruct us with your conversation, for you have no doubt visited several lands."

The king, still silent, gave a nod of approval and a courtier added, "The hunters of Sangaran are the best soothsayers; if the stranger wishes we could learn a lot from him."

The hunter came and sat down near Gnankouman Doua who vacated one end of the mat to him. Then he said, "Griot of the king, I am not one of these hunters whose tongues are more dexterous than their arms; I am no spinner of adventure yarns, nor

---

Source: From D. T. Niane, *Sundiata: An Epic of Old Mali,* © 1965. Reprinted by permission of Addison Wesley Longman, Ltd.

do I like playing upon the credulity of worthy folk; but, thanks to the lore which my master has imparted to me, I can boast of being a seer among seers."

He took out of his hunter's bag twelve cowries which he threw on the mat. The king and all his entourage now turned towards the stranger who was jumbling up the twelve shiny shells with his bare hand. Gnankouman Doua discreetly brought to the king's notice that the soothsayer was left-handed. The left hand is the hand of evil, but in the divining art it is said that left-handed people are the best. The hunter muttered some incomprehensible words in a low voice while he shuffled and jumbled the twelve cowries into different positions which he mused on at length. All of a sudden he looked up at the king and said, "Oh king, the world is full of mystery, all is hidden and we know nothing but what we can see. The silk-cotton tree springs from a tiny seed—that which defies the tempest weighs in its germ no more than a grain of rice. Kingdoms are like trees; some will be silk-cotton trees, others will remains dwarf palms and the powerful silk-cotton tree will cover them with its shade. Oh, who can recognize in the little child the great king to come? The great comes from the small; truth and falsehood have both suckled at the same breast. Nothing is certain, but, sire, I can see two strangers over there coming towards your city."

He fell silent and looked in the direction of the city gates for a short while. All present silently turned towards the gates. The soothsayer returned to his cowries. He shook them in his palm with a skilled hand and then threw them out.

"King of Mali, destiny marches with great strides, Mali is about to emerge from the night. Nianiba is lighting up, but what is this light that comes from the east?"

"Hunter," said Gnankouman Doua, "your words are obscure. Make your speech comprehensible to us, speak in the clear language of your savanna."

"I am coming to that now, griot. Listen to my message. Listen, sire. You have ruled over the kingdom which your ancestors bequeathed to you and you have no other ambition but to pass on this realm, intact if not increased, to your descendants; but, fine king, your successor is not yet born. I see two hunters coming to your city; they have come from afar and a woman accompanies them. Oh, that woman! She is ugly, she is hideous, she bears on her back a disfiguring hump. Her monstrous eyes seem to have been merely laid on her face, but, mystery of mysteries, this is the woman you must marry, sire, for she will be the mother of him who will make the name of Mali immortal for ever. The child will be the seventh star, the seventh conqueror of the earth. He will be more mighty than Alexander. But, oh king, for destiny to lead this woman to you a sacrifice is necessary; you must offer up a red bull, for the bull is powerful. When its blood soaks into the ground nothing more will hinder the arrival of your wife. There, I have said what I had to say, but everything is in the hands of the Almighty."

The hunter picked up his cowries and put them away in his bag.

"I am only passing through, king of Mali, and now I return to Sangaran. Farewell."

The hunter disappeared but neither the king, Naré Maghan, nor his griot, Gnankouman Doua, forgot his prophetic words; soothsayers see far ahead, their words are not always for the immediate present; man is in a hurry but time is tardy and everything has its season.

Now one day the king and his suite were again seated under the great silk-cotton tree of Nianiba, chatting as was their wont. Suddenly their gaze was drawn by some strangers who came into the city. The small entourage of the king watched in silent surprise.

Two young hunters, handsome and of fine carriage, were walking along preceded by a young maid. They turned towards the Court. The two men were carrying shining bows of silver on their shoulders. The one who seemed the elder of the two walked with the assurance of a master hunter. When the strangers were a few steps from the king they bowed and the elder spoke thus:

"We greet King Naré Maghan Kon Fatta and his entourage. We come from the land of Do, but my brother and I belong to Mali and we are of the tribe of Traoré. Hunting and adventure led us as far as the distant land of Do where King Mansa Gnemo Diarra reigns. I am called Oulamba and my brother Oulani. The young girl is from Do and we bring her as a present to the king, for my brother and I deemed her worthy to be a king's wife."

The king and his suite tried in vain to get a look at the young girl, for she stayed kneeling, her head lowered, and had deliberately let her kerchief hang in front of her face. If the young girl succeeded in hiding her face, she did not, however, manage to cover up the hump which deformed her shoulders and back. She was ugly in a sturdy sort of way. You could see her muscular arms, and her bulging breasts pushing stoutly against the strong pagne of cotton fabric which was knotted just under her armpit. The king considered her for a moment, then the handsome Maghan turned his head away. He stared a long time at Gnankouman Doua, then he lowered his head. The griot understood all the sovereign's embarrassment.

"You are the guests of the king; hunters, we wish you peace in Nianiba, for all the sons of Mali are but one. Come and sit down, slake your thirst and relate to the king by what adventure you left Do with this maiden."

The king nodded his approval. The two brothers looked at each other and, at a sign from the elder, the younger went up to the king and put down on the ground the calabash of cold water which a servant had brought him.

The hunter said: "After the great harvest my brother and I left our village to hunt. It was in this way that our pursuit of game led us as far as the approaches of the land of Do. We met two hunters, one of whom was wounded, and we learnt from them that an amazing buffalo was ravaging the countryside of Do. Every day it claimed some victims and nobody dared leave the village after sunset. The king, Do Mansa-Gnemo Diarra, had promised the finest rewards to the hunter who killed the buffalo. We decided to try our luck too and so we penetrated into the land of Do. We were advancing warily, our eyes well skinned, when we saw an old woman by the side of a river. She was weeping and lamenting, gnawed by hunger. Until then no passer-by had deigned to stop by her. She beseeched us, in the name of the Almighty, to give her something to eat. Touched by her tears I approached and took some pieces of dried meat from my hunter's bag. When she had eaten well she said, 'Hunter, may God requite you with the charity you have given me.' We were making ready to leave when she stopped me. 'I know,' she said, 'that you are going to try your luck against the Buffalo of Do, but you should know that many others before you have met their death through their foolhardiness, for arrows are useless against the buffalo; but, young hunter, your heart is generous and it is you who will be the buffalo's vanquisher. I am the buffalo you are looking for, and your generosity has vanquished me. I am the buffalo that ravages Do.

I have killed a hundred and seven hunters and wounded seventy-seven; every day I kill an inhabitant of Do and the king, Gnemo Diarra, is at his wit's end which jinn to sacrifice to. Here, young man, take this distaff and this egg and go to the plain of Ourantamba where I browse among the king's crops. Before using your bow you must take aim at me three times with this distaff; then draw your bow and I shall be vulnerable to your arrow. I shall fall but shall get up and pursue you into a dry plain. Then throw the egg behind you and a great mire will come into being where I shall be unable to advance and then you will kill me. As a proof of your victory you must cut off the buffalo's tail, which is of gold, and take it to the king, from whom you will exact your due reward. As for me, I have run my course and punished the king of Do, my brother, for depriving me of my part of the inheritance.' Crazy with joy, I seized the distaff and the egg, but the old woman stopped me with a gesture and said, 'There is one condition, hunter.' 'What condition?' I replied impatiently. 'The king promises the hand of the most beautiful maiden of Do to the victor. When all the people of Do are gathered and you are told to choose her whom you want as a wife you must search in the crowd and you will find a very ugly maid—uglier than you can imagine—sitting apart on an observation platform; it is her you must choose. She is called Sogolon Kedjou, or Sogolon Kondouto, because she is a hunchback. You will choose her for she is my wraith. She will be an extraordinary woman if you manage to possess her. Promise me you will choose her, hunter.' I swore to, solemnly, between the hands of the old woman, and we continued on our way. The plain of Ourantamba was half a day's journey from there. On the way we saw hunters who were fleeing and who watched us quite dumbfounded. The buffalo was at the other end of the plain but when it saw us it charged with menacing horns. I did as the old woman had told me and killed the buffalo. I cut off its tail and we went back to the town of Do as night was falling, but we did not go before the king until morning came. The king had the drums beaten and before midday all the inhabitants of the country were gathered in the main square. The mutilated carcass of the buffalo had been placed in the middle of the square and the delirious crowd abused it, while our names were sung in a thousand refrains. When the king appeared a deep silence settled on the crowd. 'I promised the hand of the most beautiful maiden in Do to the brave hunter who saved us from the scourge which overwhelmed us. The buffalo of Do is dead and here is the hunter who has killed it. I am a man of my word. Hunter, here are all the daughters of Do; take your pick.' And the crowed showed its approval by a great cheer. On that day all the daughters of Do wore their festive dress; gold shone in their hair and fragile wrists bent under the weight of heavy silver bracelets. Never did so much beauty come together in one place. Full of pride, my quiver on my back, I swaggered before the beautiful girls of Do who were smiling at me, with their teeth as white as the rice of Mali. But I remembered the words of the old woman. I went round the great circle many times until at last I saw Sogolon Kedjou sitting apart on a raised platform. I elbowed my way through the crowed, took Sogolon by the hand and drew her into the middle of the circle. Showing her to the king, I said, 'Oh King Gnemo Diarra, here is the one I have chosen from among the young maids of Do; it is her I would like for a wife.' The choice was so paradoxical that the king could not help laughing, and then general laughter broke out and the people split their sides with mirth. They took me for a fool, and I became a ludicrous hero. 'You've got to belong to the tribe of Traoré to do things like that,' said somebody in the crowd, and it was thus that my brother and I left Do the very same day pursued by the mockery of the Kondés.

The hunter ended his story and the noble king Naré Maghan determined to solemnize his marriage with all the customary formalities so that nobody could dispute the rights of the son to be born to him. The two hunters were considered as being relatives of Sogolon and it was to them that Gnankouman Doua bore the traditional cola nuts. By agreement with the hunters the marriage was fixed for the first Wednesday of the new moon. The twelve villages of old Mali and all the peoples allied to them were acquainted with this and on the appointed day delegations flocked from all sides to Nianiba, the town of Maghan Kon Fatta.

Sogolon had been lodged with an old aunt of the king's. Since her arrival in Nianiba she had never once gone out and everyone longed to see the woman for whom Naré Maghan was preparing such a magnificent wedding. It was known that she was not beautiful, but the curiosity of everyone was aroused, and already a thousand anecdotes were circulating, most of them put about by Sassouma Bérété, the king's first wife.

The royal drums of Nianiba announced the festivity at crack of dawn. The town awoke to the sound of tam-tams which answered each other from one district to another; from the midst of the crowds arose the voices of griots singing the praises of Naré Maghan.

At the home of the king's old aunt, the hairdresser of Nianiba was plaiting Sogolon Kedjou's hair. As she lay on her mat, her head resting on the hairdresser's legs, she wept softly, while the king's sisters came to chaff her, as was the custom.

"This is your last day of freedom; from now onwards you will be our woman."

"Say farewell to your youth," added another.

"You won't dance in the square any more and have yourself admired by the boys," added a third.

Sogolon never uttered a word and from time to time the old hairdresser said, "There, there, stop crying. It's a new life beginning, you know, more beautiful than you think. You will be a mother and you will know the joy of being a queen surrounded by your children. Come now, daughter, don't listen to the gibes of your sisters-in-law." In front of the house the poetesses who belonged to the king's sisters chanted the name of the young bride.

During this time the festivity was reaching its height in front of the king's enclosure. Each village was represented by a troupe of dancers and musicians; in the middle of the courtyard the elders were sacrificing oxen which servants carved up, while ungainly vultures, perched on the great silk-cotton tree, watched the hecatomb with their eyes.

Sitting in front of the palace, Naré Maghan listened to the grave music of the "bolon" in the midst of his courtiers. Doua, standing amid the eminent guests, held his great spear in his hand and sang the anthem of the Mandingo kings. Everywhere in the village people were dancing and singing and members of the royal family evinced their joy, as was fitting, by distributing grain, clothes, and even gold. Even the jealous Sassouma Bérété took part in this largesse and, among other things, bestowed fine loin-cloths on the poetesses.

But night was falling and the sun had hidden behind the mountain. It was time for the marriage procession to form up in front of the house of the king's aunt. The tam-tams had fallen silent. The old female relatives of the king had washed and perfumed Sogolon and now she was dressed completely in white with a large veil over her head.

Sogolon walked in front held by two old women. The king's relatives followed and, behind, the choir of young girls of Mali sang the bride's departure song, keeping time to the songs by clapping their hands. The villagers and guests were lined up along the stretch of ground which separated the aunt's house from the palace in order to see the procession go by. When Sogolon had reached the threshold of the king's antechamber one of his young brothers lifted her vigorously from the ground and ran off with her towards the palace while the crowd cheered.

The women danced in front of the palace of the king for a long while, then, after receiving money and presents from members of the royal family, the crowd dispersed and night darkened overhead.

"She will be an extraordinary woman if you manage to possess her." Those were the words of the old woman of Do, but the conqueror of the buffalo had not been able to conquer the young girl. It was only as an afterthought that the two hunters, Oulani and Oulamba, had the idea of giving her to the king of Mali.

That evening, the, Naré Maghan tried to perform his duty as a husband but Sogolon repulsed his advances. He persisted, but his efforts were in vain and early the next morning Doua found the king exhausted, like a man who had suffered a great defeat.

"What is the matter, my king?" asked the griot.

"I have been unable to posses her—and besides, she frightens me, this young girl. I even doubt whether she is a human being; when I drew close to her during the night her body became covered with long hairs and that scared me very much. All night long I called upon my wraith but he was unable to master Sogolon's."

All that day the king did not emerge and Doua was the only one to enter and leave the palace. All Nianiba seemed puzzled. The old women who had come early to seek the virginity pagne had been discreetly turned away. And this went on for a week.

Naré Maghan had vainly sought advice from some great sorcerers but all their tricks were powerless in overcoming the wraith of Sogolon. But one night, when everyone was asleep, Naré Maghan got up. He unhooked his hunter's bag from the wall and, sitting in the middle of the house, he spread on the ground the sand which the bag contained. The king began tracing mysterious signs in the sand; he traced, effaced and began again. Sogolon woke up. She knew that sand talks, but she was intrigued to see the king so absorbed at dead of night. Naré Maghan stopped drawing signs and with his hand under his chin he seemed to be brooding on the signs. All of a sudden he jumped up, bounded after his sword which hung above his bed, and said, "Sogolon, Sogolon, wake up. A dream has awakened me out of my sleep and the protective spirit of the Mandingo kings has appeared to me. I was mistaken in the interpretation I put upon the words of the hunter who led you to me. The jinn has revealed to me their real meaning. Sogolon, I must sacrifice you to the greatness of my house. The blood of a virgin of the tribe of Kondé must be spilt, and you are the Kondé virgin whom fate has brought under my roof. Forgive me, but I must accomplish my mission. Forgive the hand which is going to shed your blood."

"No, no—why me?—no, I don't want to die."

"It is useless," said the king. "It is not me who has decided."

He seized Sogolon by the hair with an iron grip, but so great had been her fright that she had already fainted. In this faint, she was congealed in her human body and her wraith was no longer in her, and when she woke up, she was already a wife. That very night, Sogolon conceived.

TEXT 55

Mahmud al-Kati of Songhay: The Coming to Power of the Tyrannical Sonni Ali

from the Tarikh al-Fattash[1]

The growth of the western Sudanic empire of Mali also precipitated the growing Islamization of that region of West Africa. This was particularly so in the urban areas whose economic vitality depended on the maintenance of sound commercial relations with the Muslim traders of primarily Berber ethnicity who controlled the trans-Sahran trade routes. Over time, however, Mali was eclipsed by a new state, that of Songhay, whose wealth was also based on the trade in gold across the Sahara.

Timbuktu emerged as an important center of commerce and Islamic scholarship from the twelfth century onward. During its earliest history it fell under the dominion of Mali, later the Berber Tuaregs of the Sahara, and in 1469 was incorporated into the empire of Songhay by its expansionist ruler, Sonni Ali.

The city reached its heights in the sixteenth century, during the reign of Sonni Ali's successor, the Askia Muhammad Ture. Holding the reigns of power for 35 years, he was also noted for his Muslim scholarship. Sankore was the quarter of Timbuktu where the majority of the teaching clerics lived and held their classes. Although it was not organized into a single "university," historian Robert O. Collins reminds us that the number of scholars and students there probably exceeded the number to be found in sixteenth century Oxford or Paris.[2] The fifteenth century scholar of Timbuktu, Mahmud Kati (1468–1593), belonged to a prominent Songhay family of Soninke, that is,

---

[1]Mahmud al-Kati, *Tarikh al-Fattash,* edited by O. Houdas, translated by Constance Hilliard (Paris: Ernest Leroux, 1913), pp. 43–58.
[2]Robert O. Collins, *African History* (New York: Random House, 1971), p. 10.

southern Mande, ethnicity. He became the qadi *or judge in Timbuktu and began composing his magnus opus,* Tarikh al-Fattash (History of the Seeker After Knowledge) *at the age of 50. Mahmud al-Kati became a personal friend of the most noted of the historical Muslim rulers of Songhay, that is, the Askia Muhammad Ture, and accompanied him on a famed pilgrimage to Mecca.*

The tyrannical, debauched, oppressive, and accursed Sonni or *"Chi"* Ali became the successor to Silman-Dama and the last ruler of a dynasty whose administrators also imitated this man's contemptible conduct. Always victorious, [Sonni Ali] sacked each and every country upon which he fixed his sights. Always the victor, never the vanquished, he did not spare from attack any region, city or village extending from the country of Kanta as far as Sibiridugu. He marched at the head of his cavalry, warring against the populations and ravaging their territories.

According to a text that I have perused, which was written by one of our Imams named Mahmud, the word *chi* or *koi-benendi* [in the Songhay language] means the regent of the Sultan.

The tyrant Sonni Ali exhibited such cruelty that he once shoved a child into a mortar and then forced the mother to crush him alive with a pestle. The child's flesh was then thrown to the dogs to eat.

Sonni Ali's debauchery and impiety were so outrageous that a shaykh who lived during that time in the city of Mori-Koira was asked whether this heinous prince were a Muslim or an infidel. This question arose because Sonni Ali's actions constituted those of an infidel even though he pronounced the dual profession of the Muslim faith and spoke as someone well-versed in religious matters.

Take a moment to observe from his actions, the lengths to which this man would go in impiety. He condemned learned jurisconsults to death. Oh, how many villages he destroyed, incinerating their inhabitants as well. He inflicted all manner of torture on people. Sometimes he exterminated them by fire. At other times he was known to immure human beings in a wall as a means of disposing of them. It was even said that he had opened the abdomen of a live woman so that he could rip the fetus from her body. In brief, these acts of cruelty and butchery grew so numerous that it is simply not possible to enumerate them all.

Sonni Ali was installed on the throne of Songhay in the year 69 of the ninth century of the *hegira* [September 3, 1464/August 23, 1465] and occupied power for 27 years, 4 months and 15 days, that is, until the year 897 of the *hegira* [November 4, 1491/October 22, 1492] according to what I extracted from the work entitled *Durar el-hisan fi akhbar ba'd muluk as-Sudan,* a work whose author is named Baba Guru bn al-Hajj Muhammad bn al-Hajj al-Amin Ganu.

The enemy he despised above all others were the Fulani. He could not look upon a Fulani without killing the person regardless of whether the victim was learned or ignorant, man or woman. He did not accept Fulani scholars either in his

---

Source: Translated by Constance Hilliard.

political administration or in his judiciary. He decimated the Sangare clan of the Fulani allowing only an infinitesimal fraction of them to survive, in fact a number so small that all of them could gather under the shade of a single tree.

Sonni Ali seized free Muslims, enslaved and bestowed them as gifts to other Muslims, even going so far as to pride himself for generosity in so doing.

The people of his time and the soldiers had bestowed upon him the honorific *"Dali."* Each time he interrogated anyone, that person would respond *"Dali."* One of our friends, Muhammad Wangara bn Abdallah bn Sandiuka the Fulani (May God have mercy on him) told me that he heard the jurisconsult Abu al-Abbas Sidi Ahmad Ibn Anda ag Muhammad (May God have mercy on him) claim:

> It is not lawful to give such a surname to someone because the word signifies "the most high" and should be reserved for the Almighty Lord who is God the most High. The same applies to usage of the word *"Dulinta";* those why say *"Durinta"* commit an error, because this expression signifies "slave of the Master." But, by "Master" those who utilize this expression are actually referring to the *"Chi"* [may God curse him]. As for the term *"Dali,"* it is no longer used today in addressing the ruler of Kuma or Jenne. Scrupulous people and students should pay careful attention to the preceding remark.

Sonni Ali spent his entire reign engaged in military expeditions. He maintained royal residences at Kukiya, Gao and Kabara, also known as Tila at the time. He also maintained a residence at Wara in the province of Dirma. This latter one was located in the neighborhood of the city of Ankaba, facing the city of Diendiao. However, he did not reside in any of these residences. The *Chi* who had precede him lived in Kukiya, but the *Chi* or Sonni Ali, the scoundrel, was constantly on expeditions.

At the beginning of his reign, he was headed in the direction of the city of Direi. Then, receiving intelligence as to the whereabouts of the Mossi king, Kumdao, Sonni Ali left Direi in order to engage Kumdao in battle, which he did outside the town of Kobi. The Mossi troops fell into disarray and were pursued by Sonni Ali's troops to the borders of Bambara. Komdao nonetheless was able to save his own life, return to his country, and regain his capital, which was called Arguma.

Sonni Ali then reversed his course. This time he was accompanied by the ruler of Timbuktu, Muhammad Naddai, the Askia Muhammad and his brother, the Governor Amar. The Mandinka ruler Afumba, Abubakar and the Mandinka ruler Usman also took part in this expedition.

TEXT 56

Abd al-Rahman al-Sadi of Songhay: The Destruction of Knowledge

from the Tarikh al-Sudan[1]

*A*bd al-Rahman al-Sadi (c. 1569–1655) came from a prominent Muslim family of Timbuktu in the empire of Songhay. Probably emanating from a family of Fulani ethnicity, he was named to the prestigious position of Imam at the Sankore Mosque in the city of Jenne at a young age. He later became secretary of state to the Songhay ruler. His historical work, Tarikh al-Sudan (History of the Land of the Blacks) *represents an official history of Timbuktu as well as a literary reflection of the author's own fervent nationalism. This* Tarikh *is a massive chronicle that describes, among other things, the origins of the founding Sonni dynasty of Songhay, as well as the successor Askiya dynasty. In 1590 the Sultan of Morocco, Ahmad al-Mansur, succeeded in conquering Songhay with an expeditionary force that defeated the Songhay army of Askiya Ishaq and occupied Timbuktu. The state of Songhay never fully recovered from the Moroccan invasion.*

The Tarikh al-Sudan *offers a gripping account of the decline of Songhay after the Moroccan invasion. It was this work, renowned throughout Muslim West Africa, that the European explorer Heinrich Barth rediscovered in northern Nigeria in 1853.*

---

[1]Shaykh Abd al-Rahman bn Abdullah bn al-Sadi, *Tarikh al-Sudan,* edited by O. Houdas, translated by Constance Hilliard (Paris: Adrien Masionneuve, 1964).

We know that our ancestors often entertained themselves in their council meetings with presentations of the history of the Companions of the Prophet and the Islamic Saints (may God witness their satisfaction and bestow his mercy upon them). They would also talk about the kings and princes of their country, recounting stories of the conduct of these individuals, their adventures, their prowess, expeditions and the calamities that befell them. Our ancestors enjoyed nothing so much as the retelling of these stories, which served to revitalize their spirits. They remained this way throughout their lives (may God Almighty grant them mercy).

The succeeding generation did not share the same interests. None of them sought to follow the example provided by the preceding generation. No longer could anyone be found who possessed the intellectual curiosity to study and learn about the great personalities of this world. Or, if it did happen that some might possess such an attribute, their numbers were indeed minute. From this time onwards, all that seemed to remain were those possessing spirits steeped in vulgarity, inclined towards hatred, envy, meddling, discord, gossip, backbiting, and deception—all attributes constituting the roots of the worst of the evils. (May heaven save us from a similar plague).

As a consequence, I was present at the ruin of knowledge and at its effacement. I saw it disappear along with the gold coins and small change of the realm. However, knowledge is precious in the treasures which it encases and fertile in the knowledge it bears, since it reveals insights to humankind about their homeland, their ancestors, their annals, the names and biographies of their heroes. For these reasons, I asked divine assistance and undertook to record all that I could gather on the subject of the princes of the Sudan [Land of the Blacks] and of the Songhay people. This was in order that I might recount their adventures, their history, their exploits and their battles. Having accomplished this goal, I added to this narration the history of Timbuktu, from the foundation of this city, the princes who reigned in it, the scholars and saints who inhabited it and other things as well.

Source: Translated by Constance Hilliard

TEXT 57

Hausaland: Queen Amina the Great[1]

The Hausa states of northern Nigeria emerged in the eleventh century. They were comprised of the following city-states: Kano, Gobir, Zazzau, Katsina, Rano Daura, and Garun Gabas. Early legend from the region asserts that 17 queens ruled the territory in the era before it became consolidated into the political configuration of city-states. While historians dispute the veracity of this tale as legitimate history, the existence of the later fifteenth-century female ruler of Zazzau, Queen Amina (also known as Gumsu), engenders considerably less dispute. She became renowned for her conquest of the other Hausa states. After subjecting the people of Katsina, she conquered the neighboring state of Nupe, forcing its rulers to pay tribute to her. Her reign appears to have coincided with the expansion of trade that Hausaland initiated both with the states of the western Sudan and with the gold-bearing regions of the coast.

Queen Gumsu, owner of Maradi town, never looks behind her:
Owner of the city of Yam and the land of Yemen,
And of N'gasargamu and Njimi town.
Your mortar is made of the scented Guinea-pepper wood,
You own a pestle of polished silver.
   Gumsu Amina, daughter of Talba,
A descendant of the great,
The great and the blessed,
Good morning, good morning!
You are like the moon at its full,
Like the morning star,
Precious as gold, daughter of a bush-cow, you are a bush-cow among women:
Gumsu, daughter of a lion:

---

[1]Jack Mapanje and Landeg White (editors), *Oral Poetry from Africa* (London: Longman Group, Ltd., 1983), p. 16.
Source: Reprinted from Jack Mapanje and Landeg White (eds.), *Oral Poetry from Africa,* © 1983.

She is a lion as precious as gold among all women,
Like silver, Amina, daughter of Talba:
May Allah give you the long life of a frog
And the dignity of an eagle.

TEXT 58

Hausaland: Matters of State

from The Kano Chronicle[1]

*T**he Hausa ethnicity inhabiting northern Nigeria and its surrounding regions represents one of the largest linguistic groups on the African continent. Its present-day population numbers over 10 million. Throughout much of its history, the seven city-states of Hausaland—Daura, Kano, Rano, Katsina, Zazzau, Gobir, and Garun Gabas or Biram—were ruled independently. Each of them evolved from walled towns that were able gradually to gain control over the surrounding villages and incorporate these populations into the growing city-states. This political configuration continued until Hausaland came under the ethnic domination of the Fulani who established the nineteen-century Sokoto Caliphate.*

The Kano Chronicle represents one of the most significant written documents of early Hausaland history. It was written in Arabic at an uncertain point in the past and maintained by the Islamic scholars of Kano, the most important of the former Hausa city-states of Northern Nigeria. The Chronicle offers a detailed dynastic history of the Kano city-state and also provides considerable detail about the reign of each of this important city-state's rulers.

In the name of God, the merciful, the compassionate. May God bless the noble Prophet.

This is the history of the lords of this country called Kano. Barbushe, once its chief, was of the stock of Dâla, a black man of great stature and might, a hunter, who slew elephants with his stick and carried them on his head about nine miles. Dâla was of unknown race, but came to this land, and built a house on Dâla hill. There he

---

[1]H. R. Palmer, *Sudanese Memoirs,* vol. I (Portland, OR: International Specialized Book Service, 1967), pp. 97–99.
Source: From H. R. Palmer, *Sudanese Memoirs,* vol I., © 1967. Reprinted by permission of International Specialized Book Service.

lived—he and his wives. He had seven children—four boys and three girls—of whom the eldest was Garagéje. This Garagéje was the grandfather of Buzame, who was the father of Barbushe. Barbushe succeeded his forefathers in the knowledge of the lore of Dâla, for he was skilled in the various pagan rites. By his wonders and sorceries and the power he gained over his brethren he became chief and lord over them. Among the lesser chiefs with him were Gunzago, whose house was at the foot of Gorondutse to the east. After him came Gagiwa, father of Rubu, who was so strong that he caught elephants with rope. There were also Gubanasu, Ibrahim, Bardóje, Nisau, Kanfatau, Doje, Janbére, Kamakúra, Sáfataro, Hangógo, and Gartsangi. These were next to Barbushe in rank. Tsanburo lived at Jigiria, and Jandámisa at Magum. The last named was the progenitor of the Rumáwa. From Gogau to Salamta the people traced their descent from Rumá, and were called Rumáwa because they became a great people. Hambaro's house was at Tanagar. Gambarjado, who lived at Fanisau, was the son of Nisau. All these and many more there were—pagans. From Toda to Dan Bakóshi and from Doji to Dankwoi all the people flocked to Barbushe on the two nights of Id—for he was all-powerful at the sacrifical rites.

Now the name of the place sacred to their god was Kakua. The god's name was Tchunburburai. It was a tree called Shamuz. The man who remained near this tree day and night was called Mai-Tchunburburai. The tree was surrounded by a wall, and no man could come within it save Barbushe. Whoever else entered, he entered but to die. Barbushe never descended from Dâla except on the two days of Id. When the days drew near, the people came in from east and west and south and north, men and women alike. Some brought a black dog, some a black fowl, others a black he-goat when they met together on the day of Jajibere at the foot of Dalla hill at eve. When darkness came, Barbushe went forth from his house with his drummers. He cried aloud and said: "Great Father of us all, we have come nigh to thy dwelling in supplication, Tchunburburai," and the people said: "Look on Tchunburburai, ye men of Kano. Look toward Dâla." Then Barbushe descended, and the people went with him to the god. And when they drew near, they sacrificed that which they had brought with them. Barbushe entered the sacred place—he alone—and said "I am the heir of Dâla, like it or no, follow me ye must, perforce." And all the people said: "Dweller on the rock, our lord Amane, we follow thee perforce." Thus they spoke and marched round the sacred place till the dawn, when they arose, naked as they were, and ate. Then would Barbushe come forth and tell them of all that would befall through the coming year, even concerning the stranger who should come to this land, whether good or ill. And he foretold how their dominion should be wrested from them, and their tree be cast down and burnt, and how this mosque should be built. "A man shall come," said he, "to this land with an army, and gain the mastery over us." They answered, "Why do you say this? It is an evil saying." Barbushe held his peace. "In sooth," said he, "you will see him in the sacred place of Tchunburburai; if he comes not in your time, assuredly he will come in the time of your children, and will conquer all in this country, and forget you and yours and exalt himself and his people for years to come." Then were they exceeding cast down. They knew well that he did not lie. So they believed him and said: "What can we do to avert this great calamity?" He replied, "There is no cure but resignation." They resigned themselves. But the people were still grieving over this loss of dominion at some distant time, when Bagoda, a generation later, came with his host to Kano. There is a dispute, however. Some deny this, and say that it was Bagoda's grandson who first reached Kano, and that he and his son died at Sheme. He, at all events, entered Kano territory first. When he came, he found none of Barbushe's men, save Jambere, Hambarau, Gertsangi, Jandamissa, and Kanfatau. These said, "Is this man he of whom Barbushe told us?" Jambere said, "I swear by Tchunburburai if you allow this people within our land, verily they will rule you, till you are of no account." The people refused to hearken to the words of Jambere, and allowed the strangers to enter the country, saying: "Where will Bagoda find strength to conquer us?"

So Bagoda and his host settled in Garazawa and built houses there. After seven months, they moved to Sheme. The district from Jakara to Damargu was called Garazawa; from Jakara to Santolo was called Zadawa; from Santolo to Burku was called Fongui; from Banfai to Wasai was called Zaura. From Wateri to the rock of Karia was called Dundunzura; from Santolo to Shike, Shiriya; from Damargu to Kazaure, Sheme; from Burku to Kara, Gaude; from Kara to Amnagu, Gija; from Karmashe to Ringim, Tokawa. Now the chiefs whom Bagoda found holding sway over this land acknowledged no supreme lord save Tchunburburai and the grove of Jakara. Jakara was called "Kurmin Bakkin Rua," because its water was black, and it was surrounded by the grove.

The pagans stood in awe of the terrors of their god and this grove, which stretched from Gorondumasa to Dausara. The branches and limbs of its trees were still—save, if trouble were coming on this land, it would shriek thrice, and smoke would issue forth in Tchunburburai, which was in the midst of the water. Then they would bring a black dog and sacrifice it at the foot of Tchunburburai. They sacrificed a black he-goat in the grove. If the shrieks and smoke continued, the trouble would indeed reach them, but if they ceased, then the trouble was stayed. The name of the grove was Matsama and the name of Tchunburburai was Randaya.

The greatest of the chiefs of the country was Mazauda, the grandfather of Sarkin Makafi. Gijigiji was the blacksmith: Bugazau was the brewer: Hanburki doctored every sickness: Danbuntunia, the watchman of the town at night, was the progenitor of the Kurmawa. Tsoron Maje was "Sarkin Samri," and Jandodo was "Sarkin Makada Gundua da Kuru." Beside these there was Maguji, who begot the Maguzawa, and was the miner and smelter among them. Again there was Asanni the forefather of minstrels and chief of the dancers. Bakonyaki was the archer. Awar, grandfather of the Awrawa, worked salt of Awar. He was Sarkin Rua of this whole country. In all there were eleven of these pagan chiefs, and each was head of a large clan. They were the original stock of Kano.

TEXT 59

Uthman dan Fodio: The Proper Treatment of Women

from Nur al-Albab[1]

The Fulani of West Africa constitute one of the most misinterpreted groups in African history. Because of their early focus on Islamic learning, nineteenth-century scholars insisted on defining them as "Hamitic," that is, a subgroup of the Caucasoid race. While the nonliterate pastoral Fulani tended to share more physical characteristics with the lighter-skinned Berbers of the Saharan Desert, scholars of those times merely overlooked the fact that the learned, urbanized Fulani were physically indistinguishable from their black neighbors.

In 1804 a learned cleric of Fulani ethnicity, Uthman dan Fodio (1754–1817), launched a jihad, against the Hausa rulers of what is today northern Nigeria. Even though Hausaland had since the fourteenth century been nominally Islamic, dan Fodio preached against the syncretic practices emanating from their animist past, which had crept into the practice of the Islamic faith. Conquering the principal Hausa cities of Kano, Katsina, and Zaria, he had by 1810 consolidated his rule over a new Islamic Caliphate of Sokoto encompassing all of northern Nigeria and the surrounding regions. While a skillful military leader, dan Fodio was primarily a scholar and theologian. Nur al-Albab (The Light of Consciousness) *like his other works written in Arabic emphasize the goal of purifying West African Islam from syncretic practices.*

---

[1]Thomas Hodgkin, *Nigerian Perspectives: An Historical Anthology* (New York: Oxford University Press, 1975), pp. 254–55.

Most of our educated men leave their wives, their daughters, and their captives morally abandoned, like beasts, without teaching them what God prescribes should be taught them, and without instructing them in the articles of the Law which concern them. Thus, they leave them ignorant of the rules regarding ablutions, prayer, fasting, business dealings, and other duties which they have to fulfil, and which God commands that they should be taught.

Men treat these beings like household implements which become broken after long use and which are then thrown out on the dung-heap. This is an abominable crime! Alas! How can they thus shut up their wives, their daughters, and their captives, in the darkness of ignorance, while daily they impart knowledge to their students? In truth, they act out of egoism, and if they devote themselves to their pupils, that is nothing but hypocrisy and vain ostentation on their part.

Their conduct is blameworthy, for to instruct one's wives, daughters, and captives is a positive duty, while to impart knowledge to students is only a work of supererogation, and there is no doubt but that the one takes precedence over the other.

A man of learning is not strictly obliged to instruct pupils unless he is the only person in the country competent to fulfil this office; in any case he owes in the first place his care to the members of his family, because they have priority over everyone else.

Muslim women—Do not listen to the speech of those who are misguided and who sow the seed of error in the heart of another; they deceive you when they stress obedience to your husbands without telling you of obedience to God and to his Messenger (May God show his bounty and grant him salvation), and when they say that the woman finds her happiness in obedience to her husband.

They seek only their own satisfaction, and that is why they impose upon you tasks which the Law of God and that of his Prophet have never especially assigned to you. Such are—the preparation of foodstuffs, the washing of clothes, and other duties which they like to impose upon you, while they neglect to teach you what God and the Prophet have prescribed for you.

Yes, the woman owes submission to her husband, publicly as well as in intimacy, even if he is one of the humble people of the world, and to disobey him is a crime, at least so long as he does not command what God condemns; in that case she must refuse, since it is wrong for a human creature to disobey the Creator. The recompense for a woman who submits to her husband will be double, but only if she has first obeyed God and the Prophet. . . .

Source: From Thomas Hodgkin, *Nigerian Perspectives: An Historical Anthology,* © 1975. Reprinted by permission of Oxford University Press.

TEXT 60

Abdullah dan Fodio: The Intellectual Background of the Jihad[1]

Like his older brother, the nineteenth-century jihad leader Uthman dan Fodio, Abdullah was also a learned Islamic scholar. He composed several works in Arabic detailing his religious and political beliefs. The text from which this selection is drawn, The Repository of Texts—Those of the Shaykhs from Whom I Gained Knowledge, *was written in 1812 for the benefit of Fatima, the daughter of his nephew, Muhammad Bello.*

Now the needy of God, ʿAbdullāh Ibn Muḥammad says: It occurred to my heart that I should record in writing the shaikhs from whom I acquired knowledge and by whom I profited, in order to make them known. . . .

And the first of them was my father from whom I learnt the Qur'ān. He was Muḥammad, and his nickname was Fūdī. . . . Its meaning in our language is 'one learned in the law'. . . .

. . . Musa [Jukullu, my father's ancestor] . . . came with our tribe from the country of the west, which is Futa Tura, according to what we have heard, and he was one of their chief men until he came with them to the country of Kunni, and they were the first who lived in it before the Hausas and the Tuareg, until subsequently they spread through the country of the Hausas. They were the origin of the tribe of the Fulani, and their language was the language of the Fulani, . . . and their origin, according to

---

[1] Thomas Hodgkin, *Nigerian Perspectives: An Historical Anthology* (New York: Oxford University Press, 1975), pp. 240–43.
Source: From Thomas Hodgkin, *Nigerian Perspectives: An Historical Anthology,* © 1975. Reprinted by permission of Oxford University Press.

what we have heard, is from the Christians of Rūm, to whom came the armies of the Ṣaḥāba. . . .

Now among the shaikhs from whom I acquired knowledge was the Commander of the Believers, my uterine brother, ʿUthmān ibn Muḥammad. . . . Now the virtues of this Commander of the Believers are well known, horsemen having brought them from the east and west, and we will not cause tedium by mentioning them. My father left me in his hands after the reading of the Qurʾān, and I was at that time thirteen years of age. I read with him *al-Ishrīnīyāt, al-Witrīyāt,* and the Six Poets, and I learned from him the science of the Unity from the Sanūsī books and their commentaries, and from other works. It was rarely that a book on the science of the Unity reached our country, and I knew of it, and did not copy it down from him. I learnt from him syntax. . . . I learnt from him also the knowledge of mysticism which belongs to the forming of good character in oneself and that which belongs to perfecting oneself in science, such as made me independent, if God wills, of other than him. I received from him certain books on law, from which were to be learnt what is obligatory on the individual. . . . I learnt from him Qurʾanic exegesis from the beginning of *al-Fātiḥa* to the end of the Qurʾān, more times than I can tell. I learnt from him the science of tradition which comes by knowledge, such as al-ʾIrāqi, and that which comes by oral tradition, such as al-Bukhārī which trained me for [the study of] other works. I learnt from him also the science of arithmetic, the elementary [part] of it, the easy [part], and by the praise of God I came to reflect on religion through the abundance of his light, and through his informative writings, both in Arabic and in languages other than Arabic. He never composed a book from his first work until the present time, except I was, for the most part, the first to copy it down from him. I accompanied him at home and abroad. I did not leave him from the time that I was a youth, until my present age of almost fifty years. Praise be to God for that! . . .

. . . I cannot now number all the shaikhs from whom I acquired knowledge. . . . Many a scholar and many a seeker after knowledge came to us from the East from whom I profited, so many that I cannot count them. Many a scholar and many a seeker after knowledge came to us from the West, so many that I cannot count them. May God reward them all with his approval. . . . Here I collect them for you in verse in order to make the memorizing of them easy. . . .

> My shaikhs in the science of grammar and accidence
> Were our maternal uncle, namely ʿAbdullāh. . . .
> And Mujji, Ibrāhīm Barnūwa and Mandara. . . .
> And from ʿAbd al-Raḥmān, son of Muḥammad,
> Problems in grammar; he gave me permission to pass on what I wished.
> And our companion al-Firabrī, a reference for logic,
> He is high above every star! . . .
> The shaikh of our shaikhs, and our pattern Jibrīl
> Was my cloud letting down rain in that he gave us
> Licence to pass on what he had related on the authority of his shaikhs,
> And taught us the science of The Unity, the greatest favour done to me. . . .
> From al-Ḥājj Muḥammad my paternal uncle, the son of Rāj,
> I listened to the *Ṣaḥīḥ* of al-Bukhārī the perfumed. . . .
> For the two sciences of prosody and rhyme with the Rāmiza
> And [the science of] the numerical values of the Qurʾān

Ibrāhīm Mandara was my drinking place.
And many a scholar or student other than these
Have profited me with sciences, from the East and the West.
May God give all of them, and the one who loves them
To drink of the showers of abundant flowing rain of approval. . . .

TEXT 61

Al-Kanemi/Bello: The Case For and Against Holy War

from Infaq al-Maysur[1]

Muhammad Bello was the son of the nineteenth-century Fulani founder of the Sokoto Empire in northern Nigeria, Uthman don Fodio. An astute political leader and prolific scholar in his own right, Muhammad Bello was especially preoccupied in his writings with theories of Islamic government and politics. Infaq al-Maysur (Expenditure on What Is Available) *represented his most significant work. This treatise contains an especially elucidating correspondence that was exchanged between Bello and the ruler of the rival state of Bornu, Muhammad al-Amin ibn Muhammad al-Kanemi (d.1837).*

(i) al-Kanemi. The Case against the Jihād

Praise be to God, Opener of the doors of guidance, Giver of the means of happiness. Prayer and peace be on him who was sent with the liberal religion, and on his people who prepared the way for the observance of His law, and interpreted it.

From him who is filthy with the dust of sin, wrapped in the cloak of shame, base and contemptible, Muḥammad al-Amīn Ibn Muḥammad al-Kanemi to the Fulani '*ulamā*' and of their chiefs. Peace be on him who follows His guidance.

---

[1]Thomas Hodgkin, *Nigerian Perspectives: An Historical Anthology* (New York: Oxford University Press, 1975), pp. 261–67.
Source: From Thomas Hodgkin, *Nigerian Perspectives: An Historical Anthology,* © 1975. Reprinted by permission of Oxford University Press.

The reason for writing this letter is that when fate brought me to this country, I found the fire which was blazing between you and the people of the land. I asked the reason, and it was given as injustice by some and as religion by others. We were perplexed, so I wrote to those of your brothers who live near to us asking them the reason and instigation of their transgression, and they returned me a weak answer, not such as comes from an intelligent man, much less from a learned person, let alone a reformer. They listed the names of books, and we examined some of them, but we do not understand from them the things which they apparently understood. Then, while we were still perplexed, some of them attacked our capital, and the neighbouring Fulani came and camped near us. So we wrote to them a second time beseeching them in the name of God and Islam to desist from their evil doing. But they refused and attacked us. So, when our land was thus confined and we found no place even to dwell in, we rose in defence of ourselves, praying God to deliver us from the evil of their deeds; and we did what we did. Then when we found some respite at the present time—the future is in the hands of God—we decided to write to you, because we believe that writing is better than silence, even if it makes no impression on you. Know that if an intelligent man accepts some question in order to understand it, he will give a straightforward answer to it.

Tell us therefore why you are fighting us and enslaving our free people. If you say that you have done this to us because of our paganism, then I say that we are innocent of paganism, and it is far from our compound. If praying and the giving of alms, knowledge of God, fasting in Ramaḍān and the building of mosques is paganism, what is Islam? These building in which you have performed the Friday prayer, are they churches or synagogues or fire temples? If they were other than Muslim places of worship, then why did you pray in them when you captured them? Is this not a contradiction?

Among the biggest of your arguments for the paganism of the believers generally is the practice of the amirs of riding to certain places for the purpose of making almsgiving sacrifices there; the uncovering of the heads of free women; the taking of bribes; embezzlement of the property of orphans; injustice in the courts. But these five charges do not require you to do the things you are doing. As for this practice of the amirs, it is a disgraceful heresy and certainly blameworthy. It must be forbidden and disapproval of its perpetrators must be shown. But those who are guilty of it do not thereby become pagans; since not one of them claims that it is particularly efficacious, or intends by it to associate anything with God. On the contrary, the extent of their pretence is their ignorant idea that alms given in this way are better than otherwise. He who is versed in the books of *fiqh,* and has paid attention to the talk of the imams in their disputation—in connection with the prohibition of offering alms and sacrifice to tombs—will know the test of what we have said. Consider Damietta, a great Islamic city between Egypt and Syria, a place of learning and Islam: in it there is a tree, and the common people do to this tree as did the non-Arabs. But not one of the '*ulamā*' rises to fight them or has spoken of their paganism.

As for uncovering the head in free women, this is also *ḥarām,* and the Qur'ān has prohibited it. But she who does it does not thereby become a pagan. It is denial which leads to paganism. Failing to do something while believing in it is rather to be described as disobedience requiring immediate repentance. If a free woman has prayed with the head uncovered, and the time passes, but she does not repeat the prayer in accordance with what we know they say in the books of *fiqh,* surely you do not believe that her prayer is not proper because she has thereby become a pagan?

The taking of bribes, embezzlement of the property of orphans and injustice in the courts are all major sins which God has forbidden. But sin does not make anyone a pagan when he has confessed his faith. And if you had ordered the right and forbidden the wrong, and retired when the people did not desist, it would have been better than these present doings. If ordering and forbidding are confined within their proper limits, they do not lead to anything more serious. But your forbidding has involved you in sin, and brought evil on you and the Muslims in this world and the next. . . .

Acts of immorality and disobedience without number have long been committed in all countries. Egypt is like Bornu, or even worse. So also is Syria and all the cities of Islam. There has been corruption, embezzlement of the property of orphans, oppression and heresy in these places from the time of the Bani Umayya [the Umayyad dynasty] right down to our own day. No age and no country is free from its share of heresy and sin. If, thereby, they all become pagan, then surely their books are useless. So how can you construct arguments based on what they say who are infidel according to you? We take refuge with God from confusion in religion and following erroneous opinion. . . .

We have indeed heard of things in the character of the Shaikh ᶜUthmān ibn Fūdī, and seen things in his writings, which are contrary to what you have done. If this business does originate from him, then I say that there is no power nor might save through God, the most high, the most glorious. Indeed we thought well of him. But now, as the saying is, we love the Shaikh and the truth when they agree. But if they disagree it is the truth which comes first. We pray God to preserve us from being those of whom He said:

> "Say: 'Shall we tell you who will be
> the greatest losers in their works?
> Those whose striving goes astray
> in the present life, while they think
> that they are working good deeds.' "

And from being those of whom he also said:

> "But they split in their affair between them
> into sects, each party rejoicing in
> what is with them."

Peace.

(ii) Bello. The Case against Bornu

In the name of God, the compassionate, the merciful. Prayer of God be on him after whom there is no prophet. Praise be to God who has preserved the religion of Islam by the laws in his Qur'ān for the believers who seek guidance; who has wiped out that which Satan has put in the hearts of those who rule them oppressively, and in whose hearts there is sickness, the hard-heartedness of the idolators; who has preserved the laws in the Qur'ān by his saying:

> 'It is We who have sent down the Remembrance
> and We watch over it.'

Prayer and peace on our lord Muḥammad, lord of the prophets, the sayer who keeps the true knowledge from the false sayings of all its enemies, who preserves it from the alterations of the interpolators, the boastings of the triflers and the comments of ignorant people. Prayer and peace also on all his people and companions and on those who follow them in the better way until the day of judgement.

From Muḥammad Bello ibn Amīr al-Mu'minīn ᶜUthmān ibn Fūdī to al-Ḥājj al-Amīn ibn Muḥammad al-Kanemī, peace and sincere greeting.

We have occupied ourselves with the letter which you wrote to those of our people who are your neighbours asking for an explanation of the true state of affairs. We have given it full consideration, and have understood from it what our intellect could perceive. Briefly, we have understood from it that you desire us to follow the word of God, may He be exalted, when He says:

> 'If two parties of the believers fight
> put things right between them.'

Secondly you have put forward certain arguments. . . . But, by God, I tell you, my brother, that, if the Lord is kind to you, and you look on us with the eye of justice, it will be seemly for you to find that these are false arguments and mischief-making words, refutable contentions for the most part and worthless propositions. It is indeed seemly for me not to reply, but I am constrained to do so through solicitude for the ignorance of the *talaba,* so that they may not follow you because of your great conceit and mischief-making, and think that you are right in this way of acting. My intention is neither disputation nor quarrelling.

This is so that you will learn in the first place that what made it proper for us to permit our people neighbouring on you to fight Bornu was the continual receipt of news (of which we mastered the contents) from those who mixed with the people of Bornu and knew their condition, to the following effect. It was that they make sacrifices to rocks and trees, and regard the river as the Copts did the Nile in the days of the Jāhilīya. It was also that they have shrines with their idols in them and with priests. We have seen the proof of this in your first letter where you say: 'Among the biggest of your arguments for the paganism of the believers generally is the practice of the amirs of riding to certain places for the purpose of making alms-giving sacrifices there.' Then you explained that they do not wish by this to associate anything with God; nor do they believe that it has influence on events, the extent of their claim being that alms given in this way are better than otherwise. But it is not hidden from the meanest intelligence that this claim warrants no consideration. The verdict depends on what is seen. And God controls what is secret. Him whom we have seen sacrificing to rocks and trees we have charged with paganism. These matters are among those for which we have charged Bornu with paganism.

For what caused the Amir of Bornu (according to what has reached us) to inflict harm on the believers among the Shaikh's people near to you until they were obliged to flee? What caused him to begin to fight them, unless we were in alliance with the Hausa kings to assist them? It is manifest that he would not have risen to assist the Hausa kings had he not approved of their religion. And certainly the approval of paganism is itself paganism. To fight them is permitted, since the *jihād* against paganism is incumbent on all who are able.

It must be clear to you that what we have said is evidence of the paganism of the Amir of Bornu. You also must know that legal judgement about a country is determined by the religion of its sultan. If he is a Muslim, then the country is *dār al-Islām;* if he is a pagan, then the country is *dār kufr*. Only those ignorant of the words of the *'ulamā'* will deny this. . . .

If you had confined yourself to saying that the Bornuans had repented and desisted from what they were at, it would have been better than all this talk and clamour. For the latter is a weak argument for preventing the fighting to anyone who acknowledges the truth. But we did not know previously, and nothing reached us at all to show, that they had repented. However in the autumn of this year we received messages concerning you which indicated this. We have therefore sent our messenger to you in order that we may confirm this information, and so that he may bring back an account of the true state of affairs. If the matter is as we hear, then we shall despatch our messenger, Gidado Lima, to assemble our chiefs of the east. You will send those whom you please to conduct your affairs and whom you trust behind your back; and a meeting will take place in Siko. And those assembled will make a treaty according to such bonds and convenants as they find mutually acceptable, and fighting will stop. Let peace be established. In this connection we have delayed raiding Bornu this year, though we intended to. If the matter is as I have said, namely that they have repented and desisted, then let the fighting stop, for it is repugnant to our relationship, and peace is necessary between us. . . .

You say that generations of *'ulamā'* and reformers from among the imams have passed, and they have not used such arguments as these, nor charged the generality of believers with paganism, nor drawn the sword of oppression in this way, even though this heresy and immorality have been present in all countries in all ages. You say that the verses of the Qur'ān which we cite, indicating what are crimes in the sight of God, are not hidden from old women and children, let alone learned *'ulamā'*. You mention that we can do what the ancients did, though they were princes in God's name, but that more is not possible, since this generation is not created to be more virtuous or stronger or more learned than the first Muslims. The answer to this is that we have made war on Bornu only because of what I have already mentioned. There is nothing more; though it is permitted to struggle against even less than that, as will appear. The statements in your premises and the contentions you have used to elucidate them amount only to refutable arguments. How can it be said that it is not legal, for him who is able, to reform immortality or put an end to corruption? It is not right for an able man to point to learned men who in the past have not bothered to change it or speak of it. By my faith, that is of no avail. . . .

We have indeed attempted many times to initiate with you the peace which you ask for, and we have not ceased to write to you concerning it every year. But we think that probably our messages do not reach you, And that you do not receive intelligence of them. Please God there may be a suitable reconciliation. May God direct us and you to the good. . . .

TEXT 62

Samuel Anla Ogun Johnson: Yoruba System of Numbers[1]

Tradiational mathematics among the Yoruba peoples of Nigeria was based on a vigesimal system of numeration. That is, the base of computation was the number 20, unlike the decimal system of 10 which has evolved in the west. This Yoruba system relied heavily on subtraction functions, such as expressing the number 95 as 20 × 5 minus 5.

---

[1] Reverend Samuel Johnson, *The History of the Yorubas: From the Earliest Times to the Beginning of the British Protectorate* (London: Routledge & Kegan Paul Ltd., 1921), pp. 1–1v.

1. Simple Enumeration

1	Eni	50	Àdọta
2	Èji	55	Arundilọgota
3	Èta	60	Ọgota
4	Erin	65	Àrundiladọrin
5	Àrun	70	Àdọrin
6	Efa	75	Àrundilọgorin
7	Eje	80	Ọgorin
8	Ẹjọ	85	Àrundiladọrun
9	Esan	90	Àdọrun
10	Èwa	95	Àrundilọgorun
11	Òkanla	100	Ọgorun
12	Èjila	200	Igba
13	Ètala	300	Ọdunrun
14	Erinla	400	Irinwo
15	Èdogun	500	Edegbẹta
16	Èrindilogun	600	Egbẹta
17	Ètadilogun	700	Edegbẹrin
18	Éjidilogun	800	Egbẹrin
19	Òkandilogun	900	Edegbẹrun
20	Ogun	1,000	Egbẹrun
21	Òkanlelogun	2,000	Egbàwá
22	Èjilelogun	3,000	Egbẹdogun
23	Ètalelogun	4,000	Egbaji
24	Èrinlelogun	5,000	Edegbata
25	Edọgbọn	6,000	Egbata
26	Érindilọgbọn	7,000	Edegbarin
27	Étadilọgbọn	8,000	Egbarin
28	Ejidilọgbọn	9,000	Edegbarun
29	Òkandilọgbọn	10,000	Egbarun
30	Ọgbọn	20,000	Egbawa or
35	Arundilogoji		Okẹ kan, *i.e.*, one bag (of cowries).
40	Òjì		Higher numbers as 40,000, 60,000, etc.
45	Arundiladọta		being so many bags.

2. Quantitative or Numeral Adjectives

One	Ọkan	Thirteen	Mẹtala
Two	Méji	Fourteen	Merinla
Three	Méta	Fifteen	Medogun
Four	Mérin	Sixteen	Merindilogun
Five	Márun	Seventeen	Metadilogun
Six	Méfa	Eighteen	Mejidilogun
Seven	Méje	Nineteen	Mọkandilogun
Eight	Méjọ	Twenty	Ogun
Nine	Mésan	Twenty-one	Mekanlelogun
Ten	Méwa	Twenty-two	Mejilelogun
Eleven	Mókanla	Twenty-three	Metalelogun
Twelve	Méjila	Twenty-four	Metrinlelogun

continued

Source: Reprinted from Reverend Samuel Johnson, *The History of the Yorubas*, © 1921, Routledge & Kegan Paul, Ltd.

TEXT 62: Samuel Anla Ogun Johnson: Yoruba System of Numbers

Twenty-five	Medogbon	Eighty	Ogorin
Twenty-six	Merindilogbon	Eighty-five	Marundiladorun
Twenty-seven	Metadilogbon	Ninety	Adorun
Twenty-eight	Mejidilogbon	Ninety-five	Marundilogorun
Twenty-nine	Mokandilogbon	One hundred	Orún
Thirty	Ogbon	One hundred and ten	Adofà
Thirty-five	Marundilogoji	" " " twenty	Ogofa
Forty	Oji	" " " thirty	Adoje
Forty-five	Marundiladota	" " " forty	Ogoje
Fifty	Adota	" " " fifty	Adojo
Fifty-five	Marundilogota	" " " sixty	Ogojo
Sixty	Ota	" " " seventy	Adosan
Sixty-five	Marundiladori	" " " eighty	Ogosan
Seventy	Adorin	" " " ninety	Mewadinigba
Seventy-five	Marundilogorin	Two hundred etc., etc.	Igba

3. Numismatics

One cowry	O ókan	140 "	Ogoje	
Two cowries	E éji	150 "	À-adojo	
Three cowries	E éta	160 "	Ogójo	
Four "	E érin	170 "	À-adosan	
Five "	A árun	180 "	Ogosan	
Six "	E éfà	190 "	Ewadinigba	
Seven "	E éje	200 "	Igbiwo	
Eight "	E ejo	210 "	Ewalerugba	
Nine "	E ésan	220 "	Ogunlugba	
Ten "	E éwa	230 "	Ogbonwolerubga	
Eleven "	O-ókanla	240 "	Ojulugba	
Twelve "	E-éjila	250 "	A-adotalerugba	
Thirteen "	Eetala	260 "	Otàlugba	
Fourteen "	Eerinla	270 "	A-adorinlerugba	
Fifteen "	Eedogun	280 "	Orinlugba	
Sixteen "	Eerindilogun	290 "	A-adorunlerugba	
Seventeen cowries	Eétadilogun	300 "	Odunrun	
Eighteen "	Eejidilogun	400 "	Irinwo	
Nineteen "	Oókandilogun	500 cowries	E-edegbèta	
Twenty "	Okòwo	600 "	Egbèta	
Twenty-five "	E edogbon	700 "	E-edegberin	
Thirty "	Ogbonwo	800 "	Egbèrin	
Forty "	Ogoji	900 "	E-edegberun	
Fifty "	À-adota	1,000 "	Egbèrun	
Sixty "	Ogota	1,200 "	Egbèfa	
Seventy "	À-adorin	1,300 "	E-edegbèke	
Eighty "	Ogorin	1,400 "	Egbèje	
Ninety "	À-adorun	1,500 "	E-edegbèjo	
One hundred "	Ogorun	1,600 "	Egbèjo	
110 cowries	À-adofa	1,700 "	E-edegbèsan	
120 "	Ogofa	1,800 "	Egbesan	
130 "	À-adoje	1,900 "	Egbadin-ogorun	

continued

2,000 "	Egbàwá	7,000 "	Edegbarin
2,200 "	Egbokanla	8,000 "	Egbarin
2,400 "	Egbèjila	9,000 "	Edegbarun
2,500 "	Egbètaladin-ogorun	10,000 "	Egbarun
2,600 "	Egbetala	15,000 "	Edegbajo
2,800 "	Egbèrinla	16,000 "	Egbajo
3,000 "	Egbèédogun	18,000 "	Egbasan
3,500 "	Egbejidilogundin-ogorun	20,000 "	Egbawa (Oke kan)
3,600 "	Egbejidinlogun	30,000 "	E-edogun
4,000 "	Egbaji	32,000 "	Erindilogun
4,500 "	Egbetalelogundin-ogorun	34,000 "	Etàdilogun
5,000 "	Egbedogbon	36,000 "	Ejì-dilogun
5,500 "	Egbetalelogbondin-ogorun	38,000 "	Òkàndilogun
6,000 "	Egbata	40,000 "	Egbagun (Oke meji)

The Ordinal

The first	Ekini	The twenty-fifth	Ikedogbon
" second	Ekeji	" thirtieth	Ogbon
" third	Eketa	" thirty-fifth	Ikarundilogoji
" forth	Ekerin	" fortieth	Oji
" fifth	Ekarun	" forty-fifth	Ikarundiladota
" sixth	Ekefa	" fiftieth	Adota
" seventh	Ekeje	" fifty-fifth	Ikarundilogota
" eighth	Ekejo	" sixtieth	Ogota
" ninth	Ekesan	" sixty-fifth	Ikarundiladorin
" tenth	Ekewa	" seventieth	Adorin
" eleventh	Ikokanla	" seventy-fifth	Ikarundilogorin
" twelfth	Ikejila	" eightieth	Ogorin
" thirteenth	Iketala	" eighty-fifth	Ikarundilogorun
" fourteenth	Ikerinla	" ninetieth	Adorun
" fifteenth	Ikedogun	" ninety-fifth	Ikarundilogorun
" sixteenth	Ikerindilogun	" hundredth	Ogorun
" seventeenth	Iketadilogun	" hundred and first	Ikokanlelogorun
" eighteenth	Ikejidilogun	From the first to the ninth—Ikokanle to	
" nineteenth	Ikokandilogun	Ikokandin—the tenths merge into those of	
" twentieth	Ogun	simple enumeration.	
" twenty-first	Ikokanlelogun		

Adverbs of Number

One by one	Okankan	Ten by ten	Mewa-mewa
Two by two	Meji-meji	Continue to reduplicate the numerals up to	
Three by three	Meta-meta	nineteen by nineteen then—	
Four by four	Merin-merin	Twenty by twenty	Ogo-gun
Five by five	Marun-marun	Thirty by thirty	Ogbogbon
Six by six	Mefa-mefa	Forty by forty	Ogogoji
Seven by seven	Meje-meje	Fifty by fifty	Aradota
Eight by eight	Mejo-mejo	Sixty by sixty	Ogogota
Nine by nine	Mesan-mesan	Seventy by seventy	Aradorin

continued

Eighty by eighty	Ogogorin		
Ninety by ninety	Aradorun		
Hundred by Hundred	Ogogorun		

Thus from one to nineteen the numbers are reduplicated, also from 21–29; 31–39; 41–49; and so on, but for 20, 30, 40, 60, 80, 100 only the reduplication of the first two letters takes place, *e.g.,* Ogogun, Ogbogbon; for 50, 70, 90, the same occurs only the euponic "r" takes the place of "d" *e.g.,* Aradota for Adodota; Aradorun for Adodorun.

Adverbs of Time

Once	Erinkan	Forty times	Igba-ogoji
Twice	Erin-meji	Fifty "	Igba-adota
Thrice	Erin-meta	Sixty "	Igba-ogota
Four times	Erin-merin	Seventy "	Igba-adōrin
Five "	Erin-marun	Eighty "	Igba-ogorin
Six "	Erin-mefa	Ninety "	Igba-adorun
Seven "	Erin-meje	Hundred "	Igba-ogorun
Eight "	Erin-mejo		
Nine "	Erin-mesan		
Ten "	Erin-mewa		

The same to nineteen times.

Twenty times	Igba-ogun
Thirty "	Igba-ogbon

Thus "Erin" is prefixed to all the numerals, but the multiples of ten take "Igba" before them.

Note.— "Erin" is usually softened to ee, *e.g.,* èèkan, eèmeji, and so forth.

ANALYSIS OF THE NUMERALS

From one to ten, different terms are used, then for 20, 30, 200 and 400; the rest are multiples and compounds. Thus 11, 12, 13 and 14 are reckoned as ten plus one, plus two, plus three and plus four; 15 to 20 are reckoned as 20 less five, less four, less three, less two, less one, and then 20.

In the same way we continue 20 and one, to 20 and four, and then 30 less five (25) less four, and so on to 30, and so for all figures reckoned by tens.

There is no doubt that the digits form the basis of enumeration to a large extent, if not entirely so. Five, ten, twenty, *i.e.,* the digits of one hand, of two, and the toes included, and their multiples form the different stages of enumeration.

Beginning from the first multiple of 20 we have ogoji, a contraction of ogun meji, *i.e.,* two twenties (40), Ogota, three twenties (60), Ogorin, four twenties (80), Ogorun, five twenties (100), and so on to ten twenties (200), when the new word *Igba* is used.

The intermediate numbers (30 having a distinct terminology), 50, 70, 90, 110, 130 to 190 are reckoned as: 60 less ten (50), 80 less ten (70), a hundred less ten (90), and so on to 200.

The figures from 200 to 2,000 are reckoned as multiples of 200 (400, however, which is 20 × 20, the square of all the digits, has a distinct terminology, Irinwo or Erinwo, *i.e.,* the elephant of figures—meaning the highest coined word in calculation, the rest being multiples).

Thus we have Egbeta, a contraction of Igba-meta, *i.e.,* three two-hundreds (600), Egberin, from Igba-merin, four two-hundreds (800), Egberin, five two-hundreds (1,000), and so on to Egbàwá, ten two-hundreds (2,000), which in its turn forms the basis of still higher calculations.

The intermediate figures of 300, 500, 700, 900, 1,100 to 1,900 are reckoned as 100 less the multiple above them, *viz.*, Odunrun, contracted from Orún-din-ni-irinwo, *i.e.*, 100 less than 400 (300), Orún-din-ni-egbeta, 100 less than 600 (500), Orún-din-ni-egberin, 100 less than 800 (700); and so on to 2,000.

By a system of contraction, elision, and euphenic assimilation, for which the Yoruba language is characteristic, the long term Orún-din-ni (Egbeta or Egberin and so on) is contracted to Edé or Odé, *e.g.*, Edegbeta (500), Edegberin (700), Edegberun (900) and so on.

But the multiples of 200 do not end with ten times, although that figure is the basis of the higher calculations, it goes on to the perfection (or multiple) of the digits, *viz.*: twenty times (two hundred); thus we have Egbokànla, that is, Igba mokànla, 11 two-hundreds (2,200); Egbejila, twelve two-hundreds (2,400); and so on to twenty two-hundreds or Egbaji, that is, twice two thousand (4,000).

With this ends the multiples of 200. The intermediate figures of 2,300, 2,500, 2,700, 2,900 are reckoned the same way as before, *viz.*: 100 less than the next higher multiple.

As already mentioned, Egbàwá (or Egba), 2,000, forms the basis of still higher calculations; the multiples of Egba are Egbaji, two two-thousands (4,000); Egbata, three two-thousands (6,000); Egbarin, four two-thousands (8,000) on to Egbawa, ten two-thousands (20,000), which in its turn forms the basis of the highest calculations.

The intermediate figures of 3,000, 5,000, 7,000, 9,000, 11,000 onwards are reckoned as 1,000 less than the multiple above them. The more familiar terms for 3,000 and 5,000, however, are Egbe dogun, or fifteen two-hundreds, and Egbedogbon, 25 two-hundreds.

For those figures beyond 20,000 the contracted forms which are generally used are: Òkànla (for Egbamokanla) 11 two-thousands; Èjila, Età la on to Egbagun, *i.e.*, 20 two-thousands, *i.e.*, forty thousand.

Summary.—Thus we see that with numbers that go by tens five is used as the intermediate figure—five less than the next higher stage. In those by 20, ten is used as the intermediate. In those by 200, 100 is used, and in those of 2,000, 1,000 is used.

The figure that is made use of for calculating indefinite numbers is 20,000 Egbawa, and in money calculation especially it is termed Oke kan, *i.e.*, one bag (of cowries). Large numbers to an indefinite amount are so many " bags" or rather "bags" in so many places.

TEXT 63

The Yoruba of Nigeria: Hymns to the God Shango[1]

The population of the former Ife and Oyo empires of Nigeria are referred to as the Yoruba, one of the largest linguistic groups in Nigeria. These farming peoples began forming centralized states as early as the eleventh century. Their artists became especially well known for the realistic depictions of human figures made of bronze castings and terracottas.

It was on account of the transatlantic slave trade that certain elements of the religious traditions of the Yoruba people became transmitted to the western hemisphere. Their theology encompassed an ancestor cult as well as a pantheon of deities. The god of the sky, Olorum, created the Yoruba's founding ancestor, Oduduwa, who begat the political and divine institutions of the state. Shango represented the powerful and feared god of thunder. The Yoruba kings reigned with the aid of a military establishment called the Ogboni society and with the societal respect bestowed by the institution of divine kingship.

SHANGO I

Shango is the death who kills money with a big stick
The man who lies will die in his home
Shango strikes the one who is stupid
He wrinkles his nose and the liar runs off
Even when he does not fight, we fear him
But when war shines in his eye
His enemies and worshippers run all the same

---

[1] Alan Lomax and Raoul Abdul (editors), *Three Thousand Years of Black Poetry: An Anthology* (Dodd, Mead and Company, 1984), p. 12.
Source: Reprinted from Alan Lomax and Raoul Abdul, *Three Thousand Years of Black Poetry: An Anthology,* © 1984.

Fire in the eye, fire in the mouth, fire on the roof
The leopard who killed the sheep and bathed in its blood
The man who died in the market and woke up in the house

SHANGO II

Shango is an animal like the gorilla
A rare animal in the forest
As rare as the monkey who is a medicine man
Shango, do not give me a little of your medicine
Give me all! So that I can spread it over my face & mouth
Anybody who waits for the elephant, waits for death
Anybody who waits for the buffalo, waits for death
Anybody who waits for the railway, waits for trouble
He says we must avoid the thing that will kill us
He says we must avoid trouble
He is the one who waited for the things we are running away from

TEXT 64

The Ibo of Southeastern Nigeria: Night One

from The Ozidi Saga[1]

The Ibo (Igbo) inhabit southeastern Nigeria and currently number more than 16 million. Traditionally engaged in subsistence farming, the Ibo have throughout much of their history maintained decentralized political structures of autonomous village groups ruled by a council of elders. These communities were held together by common religious and ethical beliefs, age groupings and such institutions as title and secret societies. The traditional religion of the Ibo centers around devotion to ancestral spirits and nature. Oracles maintain a potent and highly respected role in these beliefs.

The Ozidi Saga has come to be an important epic recited among the populations of Iboland, even though its genesis may have been that of neighboring Benin. An oral epic, Isidore Okpewho observes:

> is fundamentally a tale about the fantastic deeds of a man or men endowed with something more than human might and operating in something larger than the normal human context and it is of significance in portraying some stage of the cultural or political development of a people.[2]

However, this particular version was recorded by Clark-Beklederemo among the Ijo of the Niger Delta in 1963.

> Traditionally, The Ozidi Saga takes seven days to perform. . . . The story of Ozidi opens with the ancient city-state of Orua casting about for a candidate to fill its fatal vacant throne. It is the turn of the seventh and last quarter to present the candidate. In the council hall there is open disagreement between two brothers qualified for elec-

---

[1] J. P. Clark-Beklederemo, *The Ozidi Saga* (Washington, D.C.: Howard University Press, 1991), pp. 1–25.
[2] Isidore Okpewho, *The Epic in Africa: Towards a Poetics of the Oral Performance* (New York: Columbia University Press, 1979), p. 34.

tion. Ozidi, the younger and the hero, would rather his family waived their turn; but his idiot elder, Temugedege, rages for his right, and promptly is granted ascension by the Olotu set, the city lords, all of them no lovers of Ozidi.[3]

NIGHT ONE

Caller: O STORY!
Group: YES!
So it happened. There lay the forest of Orua, the forest of Tarakiri. Long ago in this forest of Tarakiri, there was indeed a great city, deep there in the forest of Orua.
An enormous city it was.
Seven districts there were to it.
In this city of seven wards, there were more than enough warlords, but the man called Ozidi was the hero of all the town.
Behind him were lieutenants.
Although he had deputies, Ozidi being the foremost champion in town was the most alert of men.
As the city flourished, its citizens enthroned one king after another.
From each ward, a king.
Now each time they installed a king in a ward, it was always Ozidi holding the front of the fight until a man was captured and brought back for the magnification of their king.
After taking a man to glorify the king, came the showering of money over him, then they would cook and offer him a variety of dishes. That was how they fared.
But while they feasted like that, the kings did not live and reign long.
Some of the kings died in the first month.
Others died in two months.
And so in this state they installed king after king, until having crowned all their seven kings, only Ozidi's district was left.
Now in Ozidi's district there were no people.
All the people there were dead.
He and his brother alone were left.

With them like that, the townspeople after looking steadily at this matter, spoke out:
"Yes, with the matter as it is, if we do not go to install a king in that district, we would have insulted them.
Therefore, let us go there, and install in Ozidi's district a king."
Now the brother of Ozidi, Temugedege was his name.
He was the elder of the two.
Arriving there, [they called out]:
"Oh, Ozidi!"
"Yes, what is it?"

---

[3]*The Ozidi Saga*, p. xli.

Source: From J. P. Clark-Beklederemo, *The Ozidi Saga*, © 1991. Reprinted by permission of Howard University Press.

TEXT 64: *The Ibo of Southeastern Nigeria: Night One*

"Well, in your district the position is now like this; the crown is yours now to wear, others have all been through it; and they all are dead.
Since it's now your turn at the throne, will you please tell your brother so that we can crown him king?"
As they finished, Ozidi replied:
"Yes, greetings to you all.
Citizens, you have done very well. This crown does not fit us of this district.

I and Temugedege, that is all the district.

If there is any other person around, that person cannot be found.
So take the crown and place it on whoever you please."
"Well, this is not proper!" the people were saying when Temugedege himself rose there in rage.
How he fumed!
"You Ozidi, your silly-evil head—so it is the food I eat that now hurts your eyes?
So the meal I eat hurts your eyes so much that you have come out to say you disapprove of the office I should fill? I certainly shall sit on the throne."
After Temugedege has spoken in this tone, Ozidi said he well understood: "Go and sit on your throne."
Thus the city took the crown and placed it on Temugedege.
Next all rose as a body.
On rising like that, as soon as day broke, how Temugedege watched out for royal tributes, with a chewing-stick this long, far out it stretched, and loud, loud, and loud he chopped away at it, and every now and again he would peer this way, crane his neck that way, then peer back again.
Ozidi's bowel became bile.

Believe me, he paced past the man, stared at him, and pacing past him again, took another look at the man.

"Oh, Temugedege, what folly!

Day has grown this big, right now it is ten o'clock, and is it not time the people of this town came and greeted us?

Is it not time they brought drinks for us to take?

Now you're chewing your big stick, if you chew away long enough you will soon tire."
The other paid no heed. So it went on until such a time, it came to eleven o'clock.

"No, I'm tired of this!"
Next he jumped into his house, and brought out a bottle of gin.
"Temugedege, take! Take this and rinse your mouth of chewing-stick.
If it is state ones you are expecting, you will wait for so long, you may as well be dead."
Temugedege now laughed:
"Hi hi, hi, hi, oh, Ozidi, thanks!

You too have done well."
"Is that so? Is it now I have done well?"
"Oh, yes!"
So with the gin he rinsed his mouth of chewing-stick.
When day broke a second time, waiting again was time wasted.
Anther day, and waiting was time again ill-spent.
So it went on for seven days. When it came to the seventh day, yes, by my word, Ozidi's bowels turned bad.
Said Ozidi:
"Oh, was this what you people agreed on? Now I've heard."
Even as he spoke, Ozidi's rage mounted against the city, and he cut the town down with abuse:
"Look, this state or Orua, this territory of Tarakiri, so you have made a slave of me; I who have gone and killed men for you to grace your kings; so you, now that my brother is king, I being the man of the small ward, have indeed refused to come by my house up till this day, may your heads all be laid down and chopped up piecemeal.

May you perish to a man.

Let not one of you be left standing.

Indeed are you men?"

He abused them to that end, he abused them to this end.

Then he retired to his compound.
Once he entered his house, the townspeople met in council:
"Is it this fellow without family has cut up the town from one end to the other; is it because he is the strong man? The way he has cut the state to shreds, let's go and show him something.

Tomorrow we shall go to war; when we have told him that, let's all take cudgels and only cudgels; let none take a sword.

Ozidi, if cut with a matchet is not dented; if shot with a gun suffers no bullet-hole; if struck with a spear cannot be pierced: that's the kind of man he is.

You all know him well.

Therefore, when everybody has taken stick and only stick, let us lay an ambush in the forest and when he comes let us hit at him all together, and since he has no magic charm against cudgels, we shall fell him down. Once he falls down, we'll decapitate him, and carry off his head to Temugedege for him to be king!"

Hear hear! it's agreed!"
So they held consultations through the night, then at dawn, they all entered the forest, took to the road.

They took up positions all round the route.

They prepared for the fight, and not being goats, they kept to the front.

In no time, the rest of the raiders, all of them leading warriors, filled the front.

Then they sent a messenger:
"Go and tell Ozidi, tell Ozidi to hurry up, tell Ozidi to come here at once."
As soon as this was said, a man ran to summon Ozidi:

"Oh, Ozidi, right now Agbogidi and his group, Ogueren and his gang, Ofe and his followers, Azezabife and his fighters, indeed everybody has moved in.

Therefore you are to come at once and join them—so they said."

At this, leaping at a bound and rearing on the floor of his house, he asked:

"Is it the true Ijo thing?"
"Oh yes."

"Why didn't they as much as say so?

Say I've heard and will come."

Having said so, he rushed into his shrine.

As he came out, a male lizard ran towards his head—with short hurried steps, it leapt out and fell on his path. His wife now clung to him. Orea, she who was called so, now clung to him:

"Ah, my husband, don't go!"

Caller: O STORY!
Group: YES!

"My husband, you must not go.
Don't go to them.
Stay, it's right even if they go alone to bring your brother honour.

You yourself must not go."
Then he asked, whether it was he the hero of all the state that should not go?
Of course he had to go.
His wife pleaded:
"Do not go!"
But although she implored, he did not agree.
There, straight he stood, and once he leapt out, and snatched his sword, he raced out.
The woman raised a lament:

> Oh Ozidi my man, my man, my man, my man!
> Oh leader of the vanguard, my man, my man, my man, my man!
>
> Oh my leader of men, my man, my man, my man, my man, my man!
> Oh Ozidi my man, my man, my man, my man, my man!

By now, he could not tell whether anyone was wailing or not.
Heedless he rushed in.

As he charged on like that, the moment he burst upon the forward troops, everybody there fell down rolling, one over the other they rolled.
They fell rolling, trampling down all the grass blades.
He halted.
"What, by what thing are you scared of me?
Look, don't be afraid of me.
I am Ozidi—or aren't I?
How! Will you not stay with me, are you so scared of me you flee?"

Caller: O STORY!
Group: YES!

As he spoke, he stood like this looking at them, and since they merely stared at him, he plunged onwards.
So he sped onward, and as he came upon the group of commanders, each of them had a cudgel; and sweeping in like that, many at the mere sight of him, on seeing his eyes and body alone, fell down milling on the ground.
Next, almost at once, they fell upon him from behind, blow after blow.
When he raised his sword like this, the ground became one rolling mass.
Yes, soon, they hit him again blow upon blow.
He tried to lift his hand but cramp seized it.
So it went on, because these were his own people, because he had no thought of killing them, he let his sword drop, and his hand went limp.
And so they pummelled him, pummelled him until he tumbled down.
When they had struck him down, they hacked at his head but could not cut through.
Though they sawed at it with matchet till they wearied, it was all drudgery.
They tried it this way but the same strain.
Thoroughly tired out, they sent a man in a hurry with this message to Ozidi's wife:
"Right now your husband has slain a great warrior, but to cut his neck has been impossible.
Therefore be swift and send at once that secret for cutting up captive heads."
So briefed, the man ran off to tell Orea.

The moment he delivered his message to Orea, she said:
"Yes, I know.
My husband it is they have murdered. Look, go and carve him up, and bring to me his head.
When you have gone and plucked leaves of the coco-yam and covered up his face, cut him up, and only then can you cut through."
As she spoke, the messenger sped off. The messenger on that take-off ran without stop, and upon meeting them [burst out]:
"Here, here, it's coco-yam leaves!
Gather in coco-yam leaves.
Fetch them here to cover up his head, then cut away and you can cut through."
And truly, when they cut down coco-yam leaves and covered up his face, and cut again, like fish, they cut with ease and it took.
Having cut him up to carry, Azeza said:

TEXT 64: *The Ibo of Southeastern Nigeria: Night One*

"Bring it here, let me carry it.
I'm Az<u>e</u>za.
It was I with my staff hit the man first."

And so once they left it to Az<u>e</u>za, and Az<u>e</u>za snatched up the head to place it on his own head, the moment he placed it there, he could not move.
He walked up this way, there was no way; he walked up this way, there was no way; he walked up this way, there was no way; there was no longer road anywhere.

Caller: O STORY!
Group: YES!

Now, as soon as Az<u>e</u>za turned full on the road, to press on was impossible.

Now he took up song:

> SONG

Solo: Look, I am Az<u>e</u>zabife
Chorus: Az<u>e</u>za Az<u>e</u>zabife!

(*Repeated seven times*)

Upon my word, Az<u>e</u>za did not know again where to go.

He went this way, there was no road; he went this way, there was no road.

Said <u>O</u>fe:
"Halt! halt!

Now, bring it round to me."

And so as he pulled to a stop, <u>O</u>fe stepped straight into the place.
The man called <u>O</u>fe stood no higher than this, a downright dwarf was he, an out and out midget of a man.

As he snatched up Ozidi's head to place on his own head, the man's wife, Ozidi's wife, <u>O</u>rea, this woman at home, now spoke:

"If that road stays blocked like that, I shall not see my husband's head to weep over.

Oh, my husband, please open up the way for them so that they can bring your head to me."

She offered in this way sacrifice at home.

As she worshipped at the shrine, <u>O</u>fe lifted the head swiftly to his shoulder, but to go forward, to move on, came a blackout, so that moving this way, all was dark.

> SONG

Solo: <u>O</u>fe m<u>e</u> gbudumano
Chorus: Kpainzama, kpainzazama e Kpainzama, kpainzama e

(*Repeated four times*)

Caller: O STORY!
Group: YES!

Now when Ofe rushed in with the head, the road opened out—into one straight stretch of land.
As Ofe marched off with the head, the rest milled behind him.
Song rose aloud, it rose aloud, went on and on, until they emerged from the forest of Orua into town.
Emerging, they made straight for the house of Temugedege.
On to Temugedege's place they marched, and arriving there, upon my word, straightaway, they hurled the head down on the grounds of Temugedege.
Having dumped it, [they said]:
"Temugedege, here is for your coronation.
Take it as your royal skull.
That's it, take it!"
When Temugedege looked closely at the head, it was his brother's face.
"Oh, Ozidi, my brother, my brother, my brother, my brother, brother!
Ah, what is this, people of Ado have done hard by me, my brother, oh my brother, brother!
Men of Orua, you have done me a terrible thing. Oh my brother, oh my brother, my brother!
Ah, Ozidi, oh my brother, my brother.
My own general, my brother, oh my brother, my brother!"
While he wailed, Orea, the wife, came out; quickly, she carried off the head. As she did so, all fled out of sight.

Each fled straight for home.
And so she carried off the head, and setting it upon her lap, broke down weeping:
"Ah, Ozidi, my man, my man!
The man who was warned but would not listen, my man, oh my man!
He who held the front and rear of all fights, my man, oh my man!
The general is gone, oh my husband, my husband!
Oh Oreame, come over and see, my man, my man, oh my man.
Oh, Ozidi, my man, oh my man, my man!"

TEXT 65

The Ashanti of Ghana: A Drum Prayer[1]

The drum literature of West and central Africa represents one of the most intriguing literary forms known to human culture. As Ruth Finnegan explains: "That this is indeed a form of literature rather than music is clear when the principles of drum language are understood."[2] It is, in fact, the tonal quality of certain African languages that enables percussive instruments to convey meanings in poetic form. The rhythmic patterns of the drums enhance the intelligibility of the message.

The Ashanti ethnic group of the West African coastal state today known as Ghana represents one of the most noted cultures in the region to have perfected drum literature. The political organization of the Ashanti was until modern times decentralized, although the paramount ruler, or Asantehene, presided over a confederation of provincial leaders. The power of the Asantehene, represented by the "golden stool," was held in check by a council comprised of the queen mother and provincial leaders. Ashanti theology acknowledges a belief in an Earth Spirit, a Supreme God in heaven, and the spirits of the ancestors.

> (Spirit of) Earth, sorrow is yours,
> (Spirit of) Earth, woe is yours,
> Earth with its dust,
> (Spirit of) the Sky,
> Who stretches to Kwawu,
> Earth, if I am about to die,
> It is upon you that I depend.
> Earth, while I am yet alive,
> It is upon you that I put my trust.

---

[1] Ruth Finnegan, *Oral Literature in Africa* (London: Oxford University Press, 1970), pp. 481–82.
[2] Ibid., pp. 481–82.
Source: From Ruth Finnegan, *Oral Literature in Africa,* © 1970. Reprinted by permission of Oxford University Press.

Earth who received my body,
The divine drummer announces that,
Had he gone elsewhere (in sleep),
He has made himself to arise.
(As) the fowl crowed in the early dawn,
(As) the fowl uprose and crowed,
Very early, very early, very early.
We are addressing you,
And you will understand.
We are addressing you,
And you will understand . . .

(Spirit of) the fibre, Ampasakyi,
Where art thou?
The divine drummer announces that,
Had he gone elsewhere (in sleep),
He has made himself to arise,
He has made himself to arise;
(As) the fowl crowed in the early dawn,
(As) the fowl uprose, and crowed,
Very early, very early, very early.
We are addressing you,
And you will understand;
We are addressing you,
And you will understand.

Oh Pegs, (made from) the stump of the Ofema tree,
(Whose title is) Gyaanadu Asare,
Where is it that you are?
The divine drummer announces that,
Had he gone elsewhere (in sleep),
He has made himself to arise,
He has made himself to arise.
(As) the fowl crowed in the early dawn,
(As) the fowl uprose and crowed,
Very early, very early, very early.
We are addressing you,
And you will understand;
We are addressing you,
And you will understand . . .

(Spirit of) Asiama Toku Asare
Opontenten Asi Akatabaa,
Asiama (who came from) the God of the Sky,
Asiama of the Supreme Being,
The divine drummer declares that,
Had he gone elsewhere (in sleep),
He has made himself to arise,
He has made himself to arise.
(As) the fowl crowed in the early dawn,

(As) the fowl uprose and crowed,
Very early,
Very early,
Very early,
We are addressing you,
And you will understand.

[Oh] Boafo Anwoma Kwakyie,
Kwakyi, the tall one,
Kwakyi Adu Asare,
Whence camest thou?
Thou camest from Mampon-Kontonkyi, the place where the rock wears down the axe.
Mampon Kontonkyi Aniampam Boafo Anwoma Kwakyi,
Kon!
Who destroys towns, Firampon,
Alas!
Alas!
Alas! . . .

[Oh] Adu Boahen,
Boahen Kojo,
Whence was it that thou camest?
Thou camest from Mampon Akurofonso,
The place where the Creator made things.
Adu Gyamfi with an eye like flint, (whose title is) Ampafrako.

The Shadows were falling cool,
They fell cool for me at Sekyire
The day dawned,
It dawned for me at Sekyire,
Who is Chief of Sekyire?
The Chief of Sekyire is Kwaitu,
Kwaaye knows Afrane Atwa,
Boatimpon Akuamoa,
Akuamoa, whom we even grow weary of thanking, for his gifts,
Akuamoa, you were of the royal blood since long, long ago.
Thou camest from Mampon Kontonkyi, where the rock wears away the axe.
Kon!
Akuamoa Firampon,
Alas!
Alas!

TEXT 66

James C. Minor of Liberia: Letters[1]

The nation of Liberia was founded in 1822 by a group of African-American freed slaves. The territory upon which it was established was inhabited by several West African ethnic groups, including the Kru, Kpelle and the Vai. However, the twentieth-century history has been a difficult one, as the rule by Americo-Liberians has been challenged by the country's indigenous ethnicities. Although English was the official language throughout Liberia's history, and Christianity the religion of its American founders, the cultural and linguistic influences on the country have been diverse. The Vai, for instance, influenced by Islamic culture, invented their own unique script, which is still used by some of the elderly in that society.

In 1826, James Cephas Minor was emancipated from slavery in Virginia and established a new life for himself in Liberia. His correspondence to John Minor, the son of his former master, and to Ralph R. Gurley, an officer in the American Colonization Society, which established Liberia, offers fascinating insights into the circumstances of the times.

1 / JAMES C. MINOR TO JOHN MINOR

Monrovia, Liberia, Feb. 11, 1833

Dear Sir: I received your letter of the 20 inst. by the arrival of the ship Lafayette, with an hundred and fifth-four emigrants. Among the emigrants was Mr. [Burwell Minor] in whose care came your letter and an arithmetic called Colburn's Sequel, a book that

---

[1] Bell I. Wiley (editor), *Slaves No More: Letters from Liberia 1833–1869* (Lexington, KY: The University Press of Kentucky, 1980), pp. 15–21.
Source: Copyright © 1980, from *Slaves No More,* by Bell I. Wiley. Reprinted with permission of The University of Kentucky.

is of great service to me, and I am very much obliged to you for it. You also recommend to my care Mr. [Burwell Minor], a young man sent out by your Mother. He is now comfortably situated at Caldwell, one of our Middle Settlements. He is working for 75 cents a day. He was down here on yesterday. He intends working by the day until he can purchase some farmer's tools to commence farming for himself.

We express great joy and thankfulness to your Mother and her offspring for permitting of his liberation and greater thanks to that God who overrules the heavens and the earth and holds in his hand the hearts of the sons and daughters of man and directs their course whithersoever he pleases, even in bringing them across the waters of the great deep. Truely his mind is in obsure darkness, but he seems to see the light of prospect from afar and is cheered.

Affairs of the colony appear quite smooth at present. The war horn is not heard here. The Natives are more friendly with us. Our recaptured Africans seem somewhat persumptuous at times. I thank you for the papers and the book which my worthy friend, Mrs. [Minor] sent me, called the Pilgrim's Progress. All these were received and are much valued by me. I hope many months will not elapse before I shall receive more presents of the same kind from you all. Though I have nothing to send you in return but good will, and that I am trying to live a Christian's life in this dark and benighted land.

On the 16th of January the bark Hercules arrived in our port with an hundred and seventy emigrants from Charleston, South Carolina. They are pretty well. And on the 20th the ship Lafayette arrived with an hundred and fifty-four emigrants from Baltimore, Maryland, all I believe in good health. We have been favoured with the above mentioned numbers to come over on this side the great waters to join this federal head so to speak. We are looking every hour for the arrival of the ship Jupiter. We hope many months will not pass away before we shall see our harbour glittering with ropes [barques] that have been the bearers of the people destined to return to the land of their forefathers.

Let me say something of the above named [Burwell] whom your Mother sent over. When he first approached my presence I had no knowledge of him; but the name he bore, after a little discourse, caused me to recognize him. He is now comfortably situated at Caldwell, the middle settlement, where he can make a crop. When he first arrived, he acted like a young horse just out of the stable—he tested [his] freedom. I gave him the best instruction I could.

There is, as you will see, inserted in the 10th No. of the Liberia Herald, three extensive buildings lately erected solely for the accommodation of new comers. Ho! all ye that are by the pale faces' laws oppressed, come over to the above mentioned destiny. The Charleston people (the most of them) are very intelligent. The major part of them are living in Monrovia, keeping shops.

You are desirous to know the exact number of the Colonists. I will give it as near as I can (counting the two last arrivals), 2829 in all. Good news from Canada.

While I was penning the foregoing lines, my ears were assailed with shouts of praise and hallelujahs to God and the Lamb forever; it is about ten o'clock in the night. They proceeded from a young man who has been for some time under conviction of sin. He lives near us. Suddenly he experienced the love of Almighty God shed abroad in his heart. The same miraculous scene took place in my own heart on the Sabbath day, 29 of January, 1831; Oh, the wonders of redeeming grace! On this subject I could pen nothing but what you are acquainted with.

Remember, I beseech thee, that I wish to become one of the blowers of the Gospel trumpet. That I cannot be without such books as are adapted to prepare me.

Since my exit from death unto life there has been a new church erected, called the Second Baptist Church of Monrovia, the paster of which is the Rev. Colin Teage. Our new church moves slowly, for want of funds to defray the expense. I trust we will not always be in this barren state. I would offer a petition but am doubtful whether or not it would be received or noticed. Nothing do I hear of the coloured inhabitants of the town of Fredericksburg migrating to Liberia. The laws of Virginia surely must be more favourable to the man of color than the laws of South Carolina. Surely they do not shrink back for the fabrications of its enemies. Will they still lay down in Turkish apathy? Africa is a land of freedom. Where else can the man of color enjoy temporal freedom but in Africa? They may flee to Hayti or to Canada, but it will not do. They must fulfil the saying of Thomas Jefferson: "Let an ocean divide the white man from the man of color." Seeking refuge in other parts of the world has been tried; it is useless. We own that this is the land of our forefathers, destined to be the home of their descendants.

You are not aware perhaps that there has recently been a new settlement established at Grand Bassa, under the superintendance of Mr. Wm. Weaver. It is a place that many will resort to. The settlement at Grand Bassa is located in a very good place, and the inhabitants comfortably situated. Our infant commerce is stretching out her hands and inviting the weary wanderers of the Ocean to call. If your readers will peruse the Liberia Herald they will see for themselves the number of vessels that arrive and depart in the course of a month.

I have given you my brightest ideas on things at present that I am capable of doing. Pardon my errors and overlook my inferior discoveries. Remember my best respects to the family and particularly my friend, Mrs. [Minor]. I remain your friend, JCM

2 / JAMES C. MINOR TO RALPH R. GURLEY

Monrovia, Liberia, Ocb. 12, 1833[?]

De[ar] Rev. Sir: In behalf of the Colonial printing office of Liberia I embrace this opportunity of addressing the Board of Managers of the American Colonization Society to inform them that we are yet in want of some Buckskin or Ball [?] Stocks for the use of the Col[onial] Print Office and if we cannot get them in short we cannot do anything without them. Yours humble servant,   James C. Minor, Col. Printer

3 / JAMES C. MINOR TO RALPH R. GURLEY

Monrovia, Liberia, April 6th, [18]34

Rev. and Dear Sir: I embrace this opportunity of informing the Board of Managers of the American Colonization Society through you that I have been for the last four years in the government employ, and found that it is a mere living from hand to mouth, and have come fully to the determination to desist from the office as Colonial Printer on or before the first of June next [18]34, unless my present salary is raised from $25.00 per month, or

$300.00 per annum. It does not give bread to eat Scarcely, much less any thing else, and the manner in which I received my payment is so irregular that I cannot pay my debts.

Perhaps I may stop the Press on the close of the fourth vol. of the Herald. With much Respect Yours,

James C. Minor, C[olonial] P[rinter]

4 / JAMES C. MINOR TO SAMUEL WILKESON

To Honorable S. Wilkeson,   Monrovia, April 10th, 1841
Gen. Agt. of the Am. Col. Socty

Sir, you may be somewhat astonished at receiving a communication from the undersigned, having never previously written to you, but it may not be less my duty than that of any other of the citizens of this commonwealth to write on a subject so important and so interesting to us all as the one on which I say a few words in support of the gentlemanly conduct of our present Governor, and in contradiction of some of the most flagrant charges set up against him; which seem to have had their origin in the hot bed of the recent excitement in our heretofore peaceful community. These charges have been trumpeted to the world as worthy of everlasting remembrances and to be handed down to posterity. They have been listed high by the towering code of confusion.

Whereas, there has been a multiform catalogue of misrepresentation (and false ones too) alledged by sundry persons residing in these colonies against Thomas Buchanan, Esq., Governor of this commonwealth, and among which misrepresentations he is accused of habitual intoxication, nocturnal reveling, a common stroller in the street, ludeness and in fact of every thing that characterizes the immoral man, and to these is added the accusation of his drawing his sword from his cane in the court house while presiding as Chief Judge, and threaten the jury with the arm of his power, if they did not bring in a verdict to suit his own notions and interpretation of the law, contrary to their own judgment.

To the foregoing misrepresentations and accusations as set forth by some [and] entertained and cherished by others, I pronounce that I am an entire stranger and have no personal knowledge of such a course of conduct pursued by His Excellency Governor Buchanan. But to the contrary, so far as my knowledge goes, both his private and public deportment has been pursued with even tenor; he has acted the perfect gentleman. He has received from [some] of our citizens, in our public meetings (the occasion is well known to you) the unkooth and vulgor terms, "it is an untruth," "it is a falsehood," but he did not return them.

He has been vigilant in having the laws of the Colony passed by the Colonial legislature and given to him regularly enforced (though, by me, some of them were thought severe). He has been faithful in making known at each annual session of the Council the proceedings of his official acts during the year. He has manifested his friendship for us, and deep interest he has in our welfare, by his vigilence, and active zeal in defending our rights, and in addition to that, offered, as it were, in Ga-toomba's woods, his life in the defence of our colony. He has affected amicable treaties with the ruthless and turbulent tribes around us. He has been the means of spreading the fame of the Colony far and wide and won [on] her behalf the affections of many who heretofore stood aloof, but are made nigh by the influence of a man of standing among his own nation.

I have been a resident here for more than 12 years and have witnessed the conduct of every Governor that has governed since my arrival here, and previous to his arrival as governor of this commonwealth, and can say of a truth, and that too with the full assurance of the sanction of this community, none has ever pursued a more even tenor of their way or governed with more wisdom or promptness than our present governor; he has done honor to himself, and to Colony; he has been seen in the battle field, on the parade ground, in the house of worship, at the table of the Lord's Supper, in his private as well as public capacity, and he has always been the gentleman, and have now or in no other instance descended below that Standard.

In addition to his other usefulness, some have learned the correctness of speech and measurably the bounds of etiquette; otherwise they would have been reduced to the necessity of going to some famous house of learning. Now may it please your honor not to publish my letter. I am willing that you should make any remarks that you may think proper but not to publish this letter unless you publish it without my name, or with the letter M—but not my name more than M.

Having thus given you the history and conduct of our worth[y] Governor, as far as I am competent to do [and] hoping you pardon all errors and redundancies. I have the honor to be yours, With Much Respect, James C. Minor

5 / JAMES C. MINOR TO RALPH R. GURLEY

To Rev. R. R. Gurley, *Monrovia, January 27, 1844*
General Agent of the American
Colonization Society

Sir, you may be somewhat astonished at seeing my name at the bottom of a communication addressed to you, though doubtless you may have seen it in the Herald of Liberia; but from the nature of some existing circumstances I am induced to address you with a few lines making certain inquiries, setting forth and shewing my reasons for thus writing.

I herewith transmit to you a copy of the Special Ordinances of the Board of Managers of the American Colonization Society, respecting real estate in Liberia passed February 27th 1832. Now these ordinances have been regarded and observed by all of the Executive Officers that have ever governed here from the time it arrived here until the present administrator, Governor Roberts, who favors the opinion that the Board has virtually repealed these ordinances by granting the Maryland Code as the legal principals in the Colony, when in every deed they have said nothing about the repealing of these ordinances in no way whatever; but in their adaptation of the Code, they have only submitted it for such parts of it to be taken out and annexed to the colonial laws as did not conflict with any of their existing laws of the Colony; and not that the Board intended that any of their special ordinances or acts should be annulled by the authority of this commonwealth, which is minor to that of the Board.

Was not these ordinances intended to secure to all who were then citizens and all who should hereafter become so, the right of maintaining a spot of ground to rest the sole of their feet upon? Is it not plainly said to all in these Ordinances that after a certain day, namely, the first of January 1833, that you shall not sell the land or real property of persons for debts incurred after that time? Unless these Ordinances be revived, if ever they have been annulled, the people here will soon, many of them I mean, have no house or home. Now in the general rage of affairs and by the interpretation of the Laws by the Governor, the Sheriffs are making havoc among the people by selling of land. In short there will be orphans pilled [piled] upon orphans entirely destitute of house, home, friends or the wherewithal to be maintained when the very courts that ought to be their father and friend takes away from the orphans the last remains of their support, notwithstanding the Ordinances referred to guarantee the possessor of real property the entire right of willing his property to whom he will. Governor Buchannan, though he had the Maryland Code as sanctioned by the Board, gave Credit to and sealed these ordinances and regarded them as being too far above his control for him to annul, and how can his successor do otherwise is a mystery. In the case of David White's two orphans is a fair specimen of approaching destruction of which circumstances you will doubtless be informed by the Executor of that estate. The Governor has refused to give me any farm land. Am I entitled to any or not? I came to this country in the ship Harriet, 1829, while under age and now I think I ought to have my farm land. Please inform me. Excuse my bad writing.

Yours truly, James C. Minor

PART EIGHT

Central Africa

Equatorial Africa represents the second largest forest in the world, the Amazon being first. The rain forest of the Zaire (or Congo) River Basin, i.e., "the jungle," constitutes the single most prevalent perception of Africa held in the popular imagination. The extraordinarily fragile ecology of this vast region, which straddles the equator, has often been misunderstood, and so, as a consequence, have the cultural environments of

East and Central Africa in the Nineteenth Century

its peoples. Because that riverine area also encompasses savannah clearings in addition to the lush rain forests, the economic livelihoods of its inhabitants have varied. The densest areas of the rain forest were traditionally inhabited by pygmy hunters, while the populations of the savannas and forest clearings developed several strong state systems based on agriculture and trade.

THE CENTRALIZED STATES

The kingdom of Kongo represented one of the earliest and most significant of the state systems which evolved in this region. It emerged at the mouth of the Zaire or Congo River sometime in the fourteenth century. By the 1480s when the Portuguese began arriving off the coast of west-central Africa, this kingdom of Bakongo ethnicity was already thriving. As a consequence of Portuguese ambitions for trading in the region, they initiated diplomatic relations with Kongo. Taking sides in a Kongo dynastic dispute, the Europeans in 1506 assisted a Christian convert in seizing the throne. He took the title Afonso I and ruled until 1543.

To the south of the Kongo kingdom emerged an important rival state, that is, the Mbundu-speaking kingdom of Ndongo. The king's title, *ngola,* later came to represent the country itself. As the demand for African slaves in the New World grew relentlessly, the Angolan rulers during the sixteenth century expanded their dominion over the surrounding region, taking captives to be sold into slavery. Angola evolved during this period into the principal supply center for the Brazilian slave trade. However, Angola, like the Kongo, became torn apart by the constant intrusions of the Portuguese into their political disputes. The efforts of the latter, in addition to the Dutch and French whose primary interest was the perpetuation of slaving activities, eventually led to the depopulating of vast regions within central Africa.

In the southern region of the Congo and the coast of Angola, the Luba kingdom evolved during the fifteenth century, and its Lunda neighbor a century later. These kingdoms became so powerful in the region that they were able during the eighteenth century to extend their commercial networks, in slaves and ivory, across the expanse of central Africa, from the Angolan coast to the Indian Ocean. Slave-trading activities were so vigorously engaged in by the Portuguese, Dutch, and French that large regions of equatorial Africa were depopulated.

The eventual nineteenth century suppression of the slave trade allowed farming to reemerge as the economic basis of these societies. Cultivation expanded from millet to include corn, cassava, and palm oil.

THE PYGMIES AND OTHER DECENTRALIZED SOCIETIES

The central African region is often the most overlooked when attention is paid to the history and cultures of the African continent. This is because the ecologies of the region dictated that fewer centralized states could be sustained by the environment. Thus, the most densely forested areas of the equatorial area also tended to sustain small, decentralized political communities engaged primarily in hunting and fishing.

Certainly, the most universally recognized of these groups are those popularly placed under the heading of "pygmies." Fascination with the small-statured peoples can be observed as early as Egypt's sixth or fourth dynasty in the third millennium B.C. A tomb inscription of Pharaoh Pepi II makes reference to an expedition he sent to discover the source of the Nile. Various clans and lineages exist, with one of the largest being the Mbuti pygmies of the Ituri Forest of the Kongo or Congo. However, the pygmies, as with all hunter-gatherer populations, over the centuries have had to adjust to the encroachment of African agriculturalists, with whom symbiotic ties of barter and cultural amalgamation have been made.

TEXT 67

Afonso of Kongo: The Evils of the Slave Trade[1]

The kingdom of the Congo or Kongo arose in the early centuries A.D., in the west-central region of Africa traversed by the Zaire River. A farming people, the Congolese were also skilled in metal-working, pottery, and weaving. In 1506 a contender for the throne, Nzinga Mbemba, seized control of the country through a dynastic dispute. He was aided by the Portuguese who had by this time established a presence on the West African coast. After his conversion to Christianity, Mbemba came to be known as King Afonso I. In maintaining diplomatic ties with the Portuguese, he was thus able to communicate his wishes and displeasures both to the Portuguese king as well as to the pope in Rome.

During his reign, Afonso exchanged letters with the king of Portugal as well as with the pope in Rome. As a Christian convert, King Afonso I also made political use of that religion as a royal cult, which served to undermine the tradition-based authority of his political competitors. Employing guns purchased from the Portuguese, Afonso embarked on a path of conquest that significantly enlarged the political domain of the Kongo.

As the transatlantic slave trade began to expand in the sixteenth century, Afonso embarked on a series of military campaigns with neighboring states, thus increasing the number of captives who could be sold on the coast as slaves. However, Afonso I also used his political influence with the Portuguese to protect his own subjects from enslavement. Nevertheless, in time the ruler of the Kongo became disenchanted with the Portuguese, fearing that their slaving activities were undermining his royal authority. The Kongolese king issued an edict curtailing Portuguese activities to the area around the capital city of Mbanza Kongo, also called San Salvador.

---

[1]Basil Davidson, *The African Past: Chronicles from Antiquity to Modern Times* (New York: Curtis Brown, Ltd., 1964), pp. 191–94.

[1526] Sir, Your Highness [of Portugal] should know how our Kingdom is being lost in so many ways that it is convenient to provide for the necessary remedy, since this is caused by the excessive freedom given by your factors and officials to the men and merchants who are allowed to come to this Kingdom to set up shops with goods and many things which have been prohibited by us, and which they spread throughout our Kingdoms and Domains in such an abundance that many of our vassals, whom we had in obedience, do not comply because they have the things in greater abundance than we ourselves; and it was with these things that we had them content and subjected under our vassalage and jurisdiction, so it is doing a great harm not only to the service of God, but the security and peace of our Kingdoms and State as well.

And we cannot reckon how great the damage is, since the mentioned merchants are taking every day our natives, sons of the land and the sons of our noblemen and vassals and our relatives, because the thieves and men of bad conscience grab them wishing to have the things and wares of this Kingdom which they are ambitious of; they grab them and get them to be sold; and so great, Sir, is the corruption and licentiousness that our country is being completely depopulated, and Your Highness should not agree with this nor accept it as in your service. And to avoid it we need from those [your] Kingdoms no more than some priests and a few people to teach in schools, and no other goods except wine and flour for the holy sacrament. That is why we beg of Your Highness to help and assist us in this matter, commanding your factors that they should not send here either merchants or wares, because it is *our will that in these Kingdoms there should not be any trade of slaves nor outlet for them.* Concerning what is referred above, again we beg of Your Highness to agree with it, since otherwise we cannot remedy such an obvious damage. Pray Our Lord in His mercy to have Your Highness under His guard and let you do for ever the things of His service. I kiss your hand many times.

At our town of Congo, written on the sixth day of July.

João Teixeira did it in 1526.

The King, Dom Afonso.

[On the back of this letter the following can be read:

To the most powerful and excellent prince Dom João, King our Brother.]

The Origins of Slaving

[1526] Moreover, Sir, in our Kingdoms there is another great inconvenience which is of little service to God, and this is that many of our people [*naturaes*], keenly desirous as they are of the water and things of your Kingdoms, which are brought here by your people, and in order to satisfy their voracious appetite, seize many of our people, freed and exempt men; and very often it happens that they kidnap even noblemen and the sons of noblemen, and our relatives, and take them to be sold to the white men who are in our Kingdoms; and for this purpose they have concealed them, and others are brought during the night so that they might not be recognized.

Source: From Basil Davidson, *The African Past,* Copyright © 1964 by Basil Davidson. Reprinted by permission of Curtis Brown, Ltd.

And as soon as they are taken by the white men they are immediately ironed and branded with fire, and when they are carried to be embarked, if they are caught by our guards' men the whites allege that they have bought them but they cannot say from whom so that it is our duty to do justice and to restore to the freemen their freedom, but it cannot be done if your subjects feel offended, as they claim to be.

And to avoid such a great evil we passed a law so that any white man living in our Kingdoms and wanting to purchase goods in any way should first inform three of our noblemen and officials of our court whom we rely upon in this matter, and these are Dom Pedro Manipanza and Dom Manuel Manissaba, our chief usher, and Gonçalo Pires our chief freighter, who should investigate if the mentioned goods are captives or free men, and if cleared by them there will be no further doubt nor embargo for them to be taken and embarked. But if the white men do not comply with it they will lose the aforementioned goods. And if we do them this favor and concession it is for the part Your Highness has in it, since we know that it is in your service too that these goods are taken from our Kingdom, otherwise we should not consent to this . . . .

A Call for Aid

[1526] Sir, Your Highness has been kind enough to write to us saying that we should ask in our letters for anything we need, and that we shall be provided with everything, and as the peace and the health of our Kingdom depend on us, and as there are among us old folks and people who have lived for many days, it happens that we have continuously many and different diseases which put us very often in such a weakness that we reach almost the last extreme; and the same happens to our children, relatives and natives owing to the lack in this country of physicians and surgeons who might know how to cure properly such diseases. And as we have got neither dispensaries nor drugs which might help us in this forlornness, many of those who had been already confirmed and instructed in the holy faith of Our Lord Jesus Christ perish and die; and the rest of the people in their majority cure themselves with herbs and breads and other ancient methods, so that they put all their faith in the mentioned herbs and ceremonies if they live, and believe that they are saved if they die; and this is not much in the service of God.

And to avoid such a great error and inconvenience, since it is from God in the first place and then from your Kingdoms and from Your Highness that all the good and drugs and medicines have come to save us, we beg of you to be agreeable and kind enough to send us two physicians and two apothecaries and one surgeon, so that they may come with their drug-stores and all the necessary things to stay in our kingdoms, because we are in extreme need of them all and each of them. We shall do them all good and shall benefit them by all means, since they are sent by Your Highness, whom we thank for your work in their coming. We beg of Your Highness as a great favor to do this for us, because besides being good in itself it is in the service of God as we have said above.

[Extracts from letter of King Afonso to King of Portugal dated Oct. 18, 1526. By hand of Dom João Teixeira.]

TEXT 68

The Ovimbundu of Angola: Katiukaila and His Wife Ngeve[1]

*I*n the sixteenth century a new state arose among the Ndongo subgroup of the Mbundu peoples, who inhabited the territory on the southern border of Kongo. The title of its ruler, that is, ngola, came to signify the name of the country, Angola. One of the most famous leaders of this state was Anna Nzinga, who came to the throne in 1623. The Portuguese, having reached Angola in 1483, became engaged in a series of conflicts with the rulers of Angola, because of the unwillingness of the Angolan rulers to support Portuguese slaving activities. However, even without the support of the interior states, the Portuguese were able to transform the coast of Angola into one of the primary entrepots for the slave trade.

Among the Mbundu descendants of the Ndongo state are the two principal subgroups. The Kimbundu occupy the coastal regions of Angola and the Ovimbundu inhabit the interior and south of the country. The oral literature of both groups is characterized by a rhythm created through verbal repetition and by the use of common themes such as the dilemmas created by regional differences in marital customs and by complicated in-laws.

Once there was a country in which it was law that a man must promise, when he married, to be buried with the corpse of his mother-in-law, whenever she should die.

In that country was a girl named Ngeve, who was desired by a young man named Katiukaila. When he came to discuss engagement with her parents, they explained to him the ancient custom of their country that every man marrying a girl from this country must first promise that he will consent to be buried along with the girl's mother, even if he is not yet senile when his mother-in-law dies. After the young man had

---

[1]Merlin Ennis, *Umbundu: Folktales from Angola* (Boston: Beacon Press, 1962), pp. 174–77.
Source: From *Umbundu: Folktales from Angola* by Merlin Ennis, © 1962 by Merlin Ennis. Used by permission of Beacon Press, Boston.

heard of this custom, he replied, "I love this girl Ngeve very much, so I will consent to make the promise you demand if you will consent to our engagement." The terms were agreed upon, he courted Ngeve, they became engaged, and finally they married.

After they were married, everything went along well. But after about six months, the mother-in-law became sick and died. Messengers came and informed the daughter and son-in-law of her death. Realizing that her husband would be buried along with her mother, the wife killed a fowl and cooked mush and fowl for him. Katiukaila took only small portions of the mush and fowl from the dish, saying to his wife, "My name is Katiukaila." Then he put on his best clothes and shoes, which came from Mbaka, for at that time his people had already begun trading at Mbaka.

He accompanied his wife to the village of her people, where he would be buried, and she would weep the death of her mother and the burial of her husband. When they came to the village, they found some people were hewing boards for the coffin, while others were digging the grave. He presented eight yards of cloth, the amount needed to cover the coffin of his mother-in-law.

When the men of the village had finished hewing boards and nailing them together for the coffin, they went to find if the grave had been dug. The grave had been dug, and so they took the corpse of the mother-in-law, and took the son-in-law to the grave.

When they arrived at the grave, it appeared that it was not deep enough, for the son-in-law had brought with him twelve boxes of possessions and a bed to lie upon. Katiukaila told them that the grave was not deep enough. The grave diggers dug and dug until the grave was very deep. Then they put in the coffin with the dead woman in it, and put in the twelve boxes and the bed belonging to the man.

The man went into the grave and reclined on his bed, which was on top of his twelve boxes of possessions. It appeared that the grave was still not deep enough, for the man reclining on his bed and boxes could not be covered up. He came out and they took out his boxes and bed so that they could dig still deeper.

At this point, Katiukaila posed a question to those gathered by the grave: "All you people gathered here know my name. Who am I?"

They said, "You are Katiukaila, meaning 'you do not return.' "

Then he said to them, "That is right. You have put me into the grave, and you have taken me out again. I cannot return into the grave now, for you have already said, 'You do not return.'"

Then Katiukaila had men carry away his boxes and his bed to his village. He went there with his wife, who was much pleased. They left behind her people, filling the grave and burying the corpse.

TEXT 69

The Luba of Zaire: Nkongolo's Origins

from The Luba Genesis Myth[1]

The Luba are an agricultural people, inhabiting the savannah south of the rain forests of Zaire. Their lands include the Shaba region, known since ancient times for the mining of copper. This Bantu-speaking population was thus able to develop a class of artisans who displayed remarkable artistic skill in metalworking, particularly of copper and iron.

The first Luba empire emerged sometime in the late fourteenth or early fifteenth century. The oral historians who resided at the Luba royal court were known as the "men of memory." Thomas Q. Reefe explains in The Rainbow and the Kings that "the Luba genesis myth is not transmitted as a fixed text from one generation to the next. Rather, it is recited in free form as a set of unlabeled episodes strung together on a central story line."[2]

The oral traditions speak of a founding ancestor, Nkongolo, who consolidated the small, weaker kingdoms of the region into a powerful, centralized state, which was bound by common religious practices. He was followed by a heroic hunter named Ilunga Kalala who expanded the boundaries of the state and initiated the ruling lineage of the Luba. Proclaiming themselves nature spirits, the Luba kings were able to draw from the common traditions of ancestor worship in order to establish the respect of their subjects for their divine right to rule. In examining the oral traditions of the Luba and other populations, historians like Philip Curtin note that the following myths should not always be taken literally. He observes:

> Nkongolo may represent one man, but he may equally represent a whole dynasty of Songye rulers that was replaced by a new dynasty founded by Ilunga Kalala; or Nkongolo may represent a world-view rather than a genuine historical person or dynasty.[3]

---

[1] Thomas Q. Reefe, *The Rainbow and the Kings: A History of the Luba Empire to 1891* (Berkeley: University of California Press, 1981).
[2] Ibid., p. 23.
[3] Philip Curtin, et al. *African History*, (Boston: Little Brown, 1978), p. 254.

1. Nkongolo's Origins Before the lands of the Luba were inhabited, a man named Kyubaka Ubaka ("Maker of Huts") and a woman named Kibumba Bumba ("Pottery Maker") dwelt east of the upper Zaire River. They lived apart from one another and were unaware of each other until one day Kyubaka Ubaka discovered Kibumba Bumba cutting wood. By watching two hyenas coupling, they learned how a man and woman have sexual relations. Kibumba Bumba gave birth to twins: a boy named Kyungu and a girl named Kabange. There followed several generations of twins with these same names. They killed fish by poisoning the water, and they captured game in pit traps. People moved a bit further west each generation until the upper Zaire River had been crossed and the lands of the Luba were inhabited. One of the offspring of the line of Kyubaka Ubaka and Kibumba Bumba was named Mwamba.

2. Nkongolo's Qualities: Redness and Cruelty Mwamba's mother was named Seya, and he took the name of Nkongolo ("The Rainbow"). Nkongolo was red, and wherever he travelled the land turned red. Nkongolo was noted for his cruelty, for when he stood up he leaned on spears which pierced people lying at his feet. With the curved *nkololo* knife used to scrape out the insides of mortars, he would cut off the noses, ears, arms, or hands of people who displeased him. This is why he is remembered as *Nkongolo Mwamba mujya na nkololo* ("Nkongolo Mwamba who dances with the *nkololo* knife").

3. Nkongolo and the Ants and Termites (This episode is interchangeable with episode 15 below.) When Nkongolo was a boy he saw a group of black driver-ants destroy the much more numerous termites, and this inspired him to be a leader. Nkongolo came to rule many people and he was known as a *mukalanga* (a conqueror, i.e., a self-made ruler, as opposed to a *mulopwe,* a sacral king). Nkongolo's court was at the village of Mwibele on the shores of Lake Boya ("Mushroom Lake").

4. Mbidi Kiluwe and Mwanana's Dog One day Mbidi Kiluwe ("Mbidi the Hunter") came from the east accompanied by his hunting dogs and his companions. Mwanana, his sister, had a famous hunting dog named Lion who had disappeared, and she blamed Mbidi Kiluwe, so Mbidi Kiluwe came in search of the animal.

5. Mbidi Kiluwe's Wanderings Mbidi Kiluwe was carried over the upper Zaire River from the east at the Kiluba river crossing. He went over the Lomami River, and his followers continued west and founded the kingdoms of Lukungu and Mutombo Mukulu. Mbidi Kiluwe went further west to the Lunda. There he slept with Luija Konda and made her pregnant, and then he came back. She gave birth to a son named Mwata Yamvo. Mbidi Kiluwe's royal praise-phrase commemorating his return from the regions west of the Lomami was *Ukata ku nsulo kwa Lomami kinemo kyashibikilako kya makasu ku mutwe* ("He searched for the source of the Lomami, his bowstring was cut, and he returned with his hands on his head"). That is, Mbidi Kiluwe went west of the Lomami River and shot all his arrows—sent followers westward to settle new areas. He is said to have been particularly fond of his bow, and when it broke he returned weeping as women do, with hands on head.

6. Mbidi Kiluwe at the Pool Mbidi Kiluwe arrived, accompanied by a servant, at a pool near the village of Mwibele. The servant hid himself, and Mbidi Kiluwe

---

Source: From Thomas Q. Reefe, *The Rainbow and the Kings: A History of the Luba Empire to 1891,* © 1981 by Thomas Q. Reefe. Reprinted with permission from the University of California Press.

climbed into a tree beside the pool. Two sisters of Nkongolo came to the pool to draw water. They saw the reflection of a man's face in the pool, and they looked up and saw Mbidi Kiluwe in the tree. He jumped down, and they were struck by his very black skin and his handsome features. He told them to go to their brother and announce his arrival. They returned to the village, and one sister told Nkongolo the news, but Nkongolo did not believe her and named her Mabela ("Liar"). The other sister confirmed the news with a sad and wondering gaze in her eyes, and Nkongolo named her Bulanda ("Sadness"). Nkongolo then believed them, and he had Mbidi Kiluwe brought to his village.

7. Mbidi Kiluwe's Royal Behavior Nkongolo ate and drank in full view of his people. He offered Mbidi Kiluwe food and drink, but Mbidi Kiluwe refused the offer. His servant said that Mbidi Kiluwe ate and drank in private, hidden from the gaze of all people. The servant explained how a special two-door kitchen hut had to be made in which Mbidi Kiluwe's sacred cooking fire was guarded and in which he could eat. When Mbidi Kiluwe drank, he was hidden by a screen held by two wives kneeling with their backs to him. When he was done he snapped his fingers as a signal for the screen to be lowered. Nkongolo then learned many other things about truly royal behavior from Mbidi Kiluwe.

8. Mbidi Kiluwe's Filed Teeth Later on, Nkongolo asked his sisters if they had ever seen Mbidi Kiluwe laugh, and they said no. Nkongolo decided that he wanted to see Mbidi Kiluwe laugh. The next time he saw Mbidi Kiluwe, Nkongolo told him a dirty joke and Mbidi Kiluwe laughed. Nkongolo saw that Mbidi Kiluwe's two front teeth had been filed and immediately commented on this unusual features. Mbidi Kiluwe took this comment as an insult and decided to return to his homeland in the east.

9. Mbidi Kiluwe Commissions Mijibu Kalenga Nkongolo had given his two sisters to Mbidi Kiluwe as wives and both were pregnant. Before leaving, Mbidi Kiluwe summoned his wives and the god Mijibu Kalenga to a meeting. He told them if the children born were black-skinned like himself, then they were his children, but if they were born red-skinned, then they were Nkongolo's offspring. Mbidi Kiluwe commissioned Mijibu Kalenga to look after his children, and he gave the god a basket containing a magic iron ball, a magic rubber ball, and specially shaped arrows. Mbidi Kiluwe told Mijibu Kalenga that if his children followed him to his homeland, they should carry with them one of the special arrows so that he could recognize them.

10. Mbidi Kiluwe at Kiluba River Crossing Mbidi Kiluwe then returned to the east. He arrived at Kiluba on the upper Zaire River, and Mbidi Kiluwe told the ferryman that if he saw a red man, he should not let that man cross. If, however, the person was truly black-skinned, he should be ferried across. Mbidi Kiluwe was then carried over the river and returned to his home in the east.

11. Unusual Birth of Kalala Ilunga Bulanda gave birth to a black-skinned son named Kalala Ilunga ("Ilunga the Warrior"). The child was precocious, for he was born uttering his own royal praise-phrases: *Kantangala Mwadi Kalonzo, kana kawa butwidile ku nyansha bekadilanga mukunda* ("Kantangala Mwadi Kalonzo, the child who was born in the morning, he cries out"); *Eami monji wa mutandabela ulupuka dito utwela dito* ("I am the long [umbilical] cord which stretches from one forest to another forest"). Mabela gave birth to a boy named Kisula. Kalala Ilunga grew up in the village of his maternal uncle Nkongolo and quickly became famous as an athlete and hunter.

12. The Masoko *Game* When Kalala Ilunga was an adult, Nkongolo challenged him to the *masoko* game (the Luba version of marbles, played with the nuts of the *musoko* vine). Before the game, Kalala Ilunga went to Mijibu Kalenga and told him of Nkongolo's challenge. Mijibu gave him the magic iron ball that Mbidi Kiluwe had left for him. Kalala Ilunga used his iron ball, which was more powerful than the ones used by Nkongolo, and won the game. Kalala Ilunga then proclaimed himself *Dikoko dya mabalajya, kele bukidi, ulengela bamashinda kulowa* ("The wild *dikoko* fruit, though it has blotches [signs of coming ripeness] it does not ripen quickly; people wear a path in going to look for its fall"). Thus, he stated that he was invincible and that people would have to wait a long time before he died.

13. The Bulundu *Game* Nkongolo then challenged Kalala Ilunga to a game of *bulundu* (a kick game played with a ball made from latex). Once again, Kalala Ilunga went to Mijibu Kalenga, who gave him the magic rubber ball left by his father. When Nkongolo and Kalala Ilunga played the game and Kalala Ilunga kicked his rubber ball, it rolled into Nkongolo's cooking hut and bounced around destroying all the utensils.

14. Nkongolo's Mother's Laugh Nkongolo's mother witnessed these defeats, and she laughed at him. This enraged Nkongolo and he had his mother buried alive. That is why when someone laughs out of turn or in a boorish fashion he is warned with the proverb *Kisadi malwa kyasepele ina Nkongolo* ("It was a dreadful laugh that Nkongolo's mother laughed").

15. Kalala Ilunga and the Ants and Termites (This episode is interchangeable with episode 3 above.) Kalala Ilunga noticed large black ants carrying off termites, which he took as a sign that he should make war. He then attacked Nkongolo's people and killed some of them.

16. The Pit Trap The loss of the games and the loss of his men infuriated Nkongolo. He decided to kill Kalala Ilunga, who was sent away to collect tribute and conquer people while secret preparations were made for his return. A pit trap was dug. Spears were placed in the bottom, and mats were placed over the hole to hide it. Upon his return, Kalala Ilunga was summoned by Nkongolo to dance in front of him. The god Mijibu Kalenga was forewarned of the pit trap, and he told Kalala Ilunga to listen to the message the drummer would send during the dance. Kalala Ilunga began to dance, but every time he approached the pit trap, Mungedi, the drummer, beat on his signal drum a warning message: *Utomboka, ushinshila! Utomboka, ushinshila! Munshi mudi bwine nkala! Munshi mudi bwine nkala!* ("As you dance, spring back! As you dance, spring back! There is death below! There is death below!"). Kalala Ilunga became suspicious and threw his spear into the mats, revealing the trap. Kalala Ilunga vaulted over the heads of the crowd assembled to watch him dance. He ran to Mijibu Kalenga, who gave him one of the special arrows of recognition left by his father. Kalala Ilunga then fled east and was carried across the upper Zaire River by the Kiluba ferryman.

17. Mijibu Kalenga and Mungedi in the Tree Nkongolo had Mijibu Kalenga and Mungedi climb up into a large *muvula* tree on a ladder made from vines. The vines were cut away and Mijibu Kalenga and Mungedi were told to call back Kalala Ilunga, since they had helped him escape. Mungedi beat out the recall on his signal drum, and Mijibu Kalenga did the same on the royal double bells: *Kalala Ilunga impungwe manyema, nafu, namone malwa, namone kintu kyokimonanga amo enka nyaa! Kalala*

Ilunga pinga bukidi, nafu, namone malwa, namone kintu kyokimonanga! ("Kalala Ilunga, come back, I am dying, I see evil, I see a thing I have never seen before! Kalala Ilunga, return quickly, I am dying, I see evil, I see a thing I have never seen before!"). Kalala Ilunga did not come back, and Mijibu Kalenga and Mungedi remained trapped in the tree. Mijibu Kalenga told Mungedi to grab onto his belt and they would fly away, but Mungedi was afraid and refused. So Mijibu Kalenga flew away and escaped, while Mungedi died in the tree.

18. *Nkongolo at Kiluba River Crossing*   Nkongolo and his forces pursued Kalala Ilunga to Kiluba, but the ferryman hid the canoes from this red-skinned man. Nkongolo then had his people construct rafts from the papyrus reeds growing along the shore, but the rafts sank and the people drowned. Nkongolo's people next built a bridge, but it broke and many people perished. Nkongolo then returned to Mwibele.

19. *Return of Kalala Ilunga*   Kalala Ilunga assembled an army from among the people of his father's realm, and he crossed the upper Zaire River to conquer Nkongolo.

20. *Nkongolo and the Island*   Nkongolo heard of Kalala Ilunga's coming. He fled Mwibele village with his followers and went downstream on the Luguvu River to its junction with the Lomami River. There, near the village of Mwadi Katoloka, he set people to diverting part of the Lomami around a piece of land in order to make a fortified island. However, before the work was completed Kalala Ilunga's army appeared, and Nkongolo had to flee westward across the Lomami River.

21. *The Caverns of Kai*   Nkongolo fled to the caverns of Kai on the Luembe River. Kalala Ilunga and his followers approached Kai and searched for Nkongolo, but they could not find him. One day, the wife of a titleholder stumbled upon Nkongolo's hiding place while she was looking for firewood. She told Kalala Ilunga and led him and his warriors to the caverns during the night. The next morning Kalala Ilunga and his men captured Nkongolo as he came out of a cave to sun himself.

22. *The Miraculous Anthill*   Nkongolo was executed, and his head and genitals were severed from his body and placed in a sacred basket. Kalala Ilunga and his followers brought the basket to Nkongolo's former realm. One day they arrived at the village of Kimona. The sacred basket was placed on the ground overnight, and, when everyone awoke the next morning they found that an anthill had risen in its place. This was taken as a sign that the spirit of Nkongolo wished to remain at Kimona village, and that is why the place phrase of the village is *Kimona kyamwene Nkongolo* ("The place that Nkongolo saw [chose]"). Kimona then became the first sacred village (*kitenta*) of the Luba.

23. *Kalala Ilunga Becomes Mwine Munza*   Kalala Ilunga and his followers moved on and established a court on Mwilunde wa Nkonda hill near the village of Makwidi in the region called Munza. He then took the title *Mwine Munza* ("lord of Munza"), and all the country brought him tribute. He remained at Munza, and no region remained outside his control. Many of his praise phrases reflect this: *Ami ne dibwe dya kyalantanda; kekudipo ntanda ya shile* ("I am the great rock that spreads all over the lands; there is no land that it does not reach"); *Ami nkidopo mukalo na muntu* ("I have no boundaries with any man").

24. *The Lost Heir*   Mwine Munza had most of his children killed, lest too many offspring become rivals to succeed him. Only two children survived. One was a normal son named Kazadi Milele. The other was an abnormal son covered with animal

hair, named Ilunga Mwila and known by several descriptive phrases: *Ilunga Mwevu/Ilunga wa Lwevu* ("Ilunga the bearded one"); *Ilunga kya Moya* ("Ilunga with hair on his body"); and *Ilunga kya Maimbi* ("Ilunga with pubic hair"). Mwine Munza was furious that Ilunga Mwila resembled an animal and told his titleholders *mwelwa* and *kitapa* (the royal executioner) to kill his son. Instead, they consulted with the titleholder called *twite,* who advised them to hide the child in case he was needed in the future. *Twite* took Ilunga Mwila to be raised at Bisonge, the region to the north that is the southern border for the Songye people, where Ilunga Mwila's maternal kin lived. As proof that his animal-like son had been killed, Mwine Munza was shown a spear covered with the blood of an animal.

Kazadi Milele died while away from the court on a mission for his father. Kazadi Milele's head was placed in a sacred basket which was deposited at Shinta village, just west of the Lomami River, which became the sacred village dedicated to his worship. Mwine Munza was distraught at the news of Kazadi Milele's death, for he feared there would be no male heir to transmit the qualities of sacral kingship to later generations.

Twite then asked Mwine Munza in an oblique way whether he would accept that which he had previously refused, for wise titleholders never ask their king a direct question. Mwine Munza was puzzled by the question but responded affirmatively. *Twite* then went to Bisonge and brought Ilunga Mwila back. Mwine Munza was so overjoyed that the sacral kingship was saved that he made *twite* his chief counselor and designated him "father to the king." Ilunga Mwila then called out his praise phrase, *Ilunga Kibipile, kyakanengele, kyakanengelelanga mu lubelo* ("Ilunga the Ugly One, I was not wanted for I had no beauty, but now I am accepted [glorious] in the concourse of my people"). Ilunga Mwila succeeded to the kingship upon Mwine Munza's death, but he only ruled for a short time. When Ilunga Mwila died his sacred village was established at Kalongo.

25. *The Adulterous Son* Kasongo *Mwine Kibanza* ("Kasongo lord of Kibanza") succeeded Ilunga Mwila. He established his court at Myumbu village near the Luguvu River in the region of Kibanza. Kasongo Mwine Kibanza had four children who were physically abnormal. They were ineligible to rule, because deformed or blemished royal males threatened the health of the people and the well-being of the realm. Later, he had physically normal children. The first of these was Ilunga Mpunji; others included Manyono, Ngoye Mufungwa, Kabamba, Kapole, Disolwa Mutole, and Ndibu Yakubwanga. Ilunga Mpunji was caught in adultery and his father's senior wife, and Kasongo Mwine Kibanza had them drowned in the Luguvu River. Manyono then drowned himself at the same spot in the river in grief over his brother's death. The spirits of Ilunga Mpunji, Manyono, and the senior wife came back to the area of Kasongo Mwine Kibanza's court as a leopard, a lion, and an elephant, and they killed people. Kasongo Mwine Kibanza consulted the diviner of the spirit Nkulu, who told him to put cooked food and beer at a crossroads. This was done, and when the three animals came to eat and drink, they were killed.

TEXT 70

The Yaka of Southwest Zaire: Treatment for Female Infertility[1]

The historical culture of the former Luba empire of Zaire is closely tied to that of its southern neighbor, Lunda. In an expansionist impulse of the seventeenth century, Lunda extended its dominion over the Yaka people, an ethnic group inhabiting the southwest region of Zaire on the border with Angola. Until that time the Yaka had maintained an autochthonous or decentralized social structure organized matrilineally and engaged primarily in subsistence agriculture supplemented by hunting and fishing on the Kwango River. The material culture of the Yaka evolved high levels of artisanal skill in basket weaving, metalworking, and herbal-based therapies.

My grandfather Waana gathered together the matrimonial goods necessary for marrying a woman of the Mbela Khuumba lineage into his homestead.
Upon it, my in-laws, Mbela Khuumba, have set a rule [thus indicating the prohibitions for the descendants issuing from this marriage]: "Now that you take the bride, I, Mbela Khuumba declare: in this clan no member will throw either earth or charcoal on another, no one shall be bitten, and the knife of the night [of sorcery] will not be exhibited."
I speak with authority owing to my ancestor N-ziinga [to whom these prohibitions were given].
[A question from someone present:] These young women [Madila and Leewo], to whom have they been given? [What rights does Waana have over them?]
[Waana's answer:] A portion of the matrimonial goods given for marrying the mother [Khuumba] of these young women has been returned to me.
Subsequently, all the avuncular rights and duties have been handed to me.

---

[1]Rene Devisch, *Weaving the Threads of Life: The Khita Gyn-Eco-Logical Healing Cult Among the Yaka* (Chicago: The University of Chicago Press, 1993), pp. 289–92.
Source: From Rene Devisch, *Weaving the Threads of Life,* © 1993. Reprinted by permission of The University of Chicago Press.

Suunga has hunted a buffalo. It is with this kill that the case began. The buffalo has been eaten and the man has been killed. [Waana nearly lost his avuncular rights when he was accused of conspiring against Suunga, who was fatally ensorcelled on his return from a buffalo hunt.]

The divining oracle revealed that the sorcerous death of Suunga had been caused by the patriarch of the Mangaya clan and by the victim's uncles Moombo and Waana.

My ancestor fell ill and said: "What shall I do?" Moombo replied: "Let's go pay the cadaver. The one who is responsible for men is the one intended by the oracle." [In order to receive the ritual tonics from their uncle, Waana and Moombo paid their share to Mbela Khuumba of the mortuary goods for Suunga. They hereby recovered some innocence.]

"Here are ten thousand cowries [as compensation offered to Mbela Khuumba for Suunga's death]; there is no fabric." They returned; they had paid and settled the question [and recovered their avuncular rights].

My ancestor died and grandfather Luvwela succeeded him [in the exercise of the avuncular responsibilities in the Waana matriline]. At this time Luvwela invited me to attend in the initiation of Maa Khuumba, the mother of Madila and Leewo; Maa Khuumba suffered from a *maawa* possession. We then invited the therapist Kha N-dima, to organize the initiation.

When we went there [to the home of Kha N-dima] we were told that Maa Khuumba could not be properly initiated in the *maawa* cult because *maawa* spirits had been abusively fostered to kill uterine kin, and such possession would therefore have brought about Khuumba's death. "Treat her without her having to enter into trance."

They treated Khuumba to make her to come out of the influence of *maawa*.

Moombo, who was an accomplice in Suunga's death, said: "Why does Waana give tonics to Madila and Leewo?" [Moombo had killed Khuumba's brother, Suunga.]

Waana [represented by Luvwela], who held the avuncular rights, said: "If it were true that I do not have the right to exercise the avuncular duties, let these tonics be of harm" [though they proved to be beneficial].

This young man Kasela went to Waana who knows Mbela Khuumba [Waana and Mbela Khuumba share the avuncular rights].

But this young man Kasela went to Waana to get the dog: that is what caused his death. He was given the dog but no one followed him [to collect the payment for the dog, or to offer tonics to his mother or sisters Leewo and Madila].

I don't know if it was the patrikin Mbaya who first wished that he die.

When this young man Kasela died his eldest sister Madila [unjustly] accused me, saying, "You, great-granduncle Waana, are a sorcerer; you and our patriarch Mbaya have eaten him [Kasela]."

"Woman, I have eaten no one." This is what I told her.

Since then these young women have suffered greatly. When consulted, the oracle declared: "Waana is a sorcerer [in thwarting the fertility]; let him give up his avuncular rights."

[Granduncle Moombo then took up his responsibilities for Madila and Leewo:] "I Moombo am here." The oracle accused Waana of sorcery, namely of having taken the lives of uterine descendants [like Kasela] to avenge for Mangaya who did not share the income from his avuncular duties.

When my ancestor Waana was still alive [and exercised his avuncular duties], did some die [because of him]? We were not the ones who intervened; it was they who acted as uncles. [Moombo had exercised the avuncular duties without either have the right or being delegated to do so by Waana.]

But today problems have appeared in the matriline [with the illness of Madila and Leewo, as witness to a lack of proper reciprocity between the different generations of uncles].

Waana has given up [his avuncular rights]: "Listen, ancestor N-ziinga, grandfather Luvwefwa." They are lying. I am a direct descendant of ancestor N-ziinga.

I have taken one full basket, a hen, and five cloths from what Moombo paid in order to recover his avuncular rights [as authorized by Waana].

When Moombo came to discuss the affair [with Waana of avuncular rights] I was in the village and said nothing. When they consulted the diviner, the oracle asked: "Who chased Waana away [took from him his avuncular rights]? [Waana did not prevent Moombo from his avuncular duties yet the oracle had asked why Waana had stopped patronizing Moombo.]

Waana's oath attesting his legitimacy of avuncular rights is cited.

If it is not true that I today demanded that I be given goats [to compensate for Moombo's abuse of the avuncular rights under my guardianship], that the young women came to me [to solicit my care] and that I belong to the Waana clan, that the members of this lineage [these young women] are afflicted. If it is not true that I have been given the matrimonial goods for their mother Khuumba, and if it is not I myself who have given her in marriage to Mbaya, then may you yourselves be afflicted.

If it is not true that Waana gave his daughters [and uterine descendants] in marriage and that the divinatory oracle has never accused him of ensorcellment in relation to a death among you.

If I have remained to watch over the place that you, Khuumba, have left, if I know two or three things [if Waana has ensorcelled these women], as did their mother Khuumba, may the members of this lineage suffer. I have not been involved in any case of ensorcellment, I, Yikafiinga, whom Waana has engendered. It is Waana who has gathered the matrimonial goods in order that I be born [the speaker really belongs to the lineage of Waana, his classificatory father who has died].

Even if their father Mbaya has something against them, I have nothing to do with the affair; I have not attended the meetings of the sorcerers organized by Mbaya.

May the health of these young women be renewed; I myself am the uncle responsible for them and I have received the prohibitions concerning them from Mbela Khuumba himself so that the uterine life flow may be transmitted and be fertile.

These young women belong to me.

Mbela Khuumba is also responsible for the *khita* and *mbwoolu* cults; I myself am responsible for the *yihoonda khita* cult.

These young women are my uterine descendants; may their health be renewed. I and Mbela Khuumba, these young women are ours.

Waana ends his oration by handing over a hen to the young women and anointing them with kaolin clay.

Mbela Khuumba then offers the following speech, declaring that he is the great-great-granduncle of the young women and the owner of the *khita* cult. He further acknowledges that the young women have come under the *khita* spell that he is able to lift.

When I was still young someone else acted as their uncle. Since then I have grown up, my eyes have been opened and I, Mbela Khuumba, have become their uncle.

Each one exercises his avuncular responsibilities in his own way. But today the quarrels have become too numerous. [Those in exercise of avuncular duties have abused of their rights.]

According to the oracle, the *khita* cult operative in the Mbela Khuumba matriline has caused the women's affliction.

Today I have been given these children. I speak the truth; you, the many ancestral shades, listen to my appeal. These children have fallen under the power of the *khita* affliction. [Mbela Khuumba testifies before his ancestors that he is the great-great-granduncle responsible for the ailment pertaining to the *khita* cult.]

I myself am the root of the tree of uterine descent which has branched out into the family of Waana. Today, may the health of these young women be renewed if I am rightly in charge of the *khita* and *mbwoolu* cults.

TEXT 71

The Nyanga and the Pygmies of Gabon: The New Laws

from The Mwindo Epic[1]

*T*he Nyanga represents an ethnicity inhabiting Gabon and the region of Zaire west of Lake Kivu. They are believed to have migrated in ancient times from Rwanda and the Ugandan states of Bunyoro and Toro. In penetrating the rain forests of Zaire and Gabon, the Nyanga came into contact with several pygmy or Twa groups. As a consequence, the influences of pygmy culture on the Nyanga have been great. Certain ritual offices held only by pygmies became attached to the Nyanga sacred chiefs. Daniel Biebuyck and Kahombo Mateene describe that relationship in the following terms:

> [The pygmies] are chief's hunters, they hold various ritual offices connected with the chief's enthronement, they provide the chief with one of his ritual wives, and they are traditionally the chief's bards, experts in narrating and singing the longer epic tales.[2]
>
> The Mwindo Epic *recited by pygmy bards details the exploits of its hero of the same name, which presumably occurred sometime in the remote past. Several versions of this epic exist throughout the region inhabited by the Nyanga. Although the content is parallel, different adventures detail greater or fewer feats of Mwindo.*

After Mwindo had taken rest, he assembled all his people. They arrived. He told them: "I, Mwindo, the Little-one-just-born-he-walked, performer of many wonderful things, I tell you the news from the place from where I have come in the sky. When

---

[1]Daniel Biebuyck and Kahombo C. Mateene (editors and translators), *The Mwindo Epic: From the Banyanga (Zaire)* (Berkeley: University of California Press, 1971), pp. 143–45.
[2]Ibid., p. 2.
Source: From Daniel Biebuyck, Kahombo C. Mateene, *Mwindo Epic: From The Banyanga (Zaire)*. Copyright © 1971 The Regents of the University of California. Reprinted with permission of University of California Press.

I arrived in the sky, I met with Rain and Moon and Sun and Kubikubi-Star and Lightning. These five personages forbade me to kill the animals of the forest and of the village, and all the little animals of the forest, of the rivers, and of the village, saying that the day I would dare to touch a thing in order to kill it, that day (the fire) would be extinguished; then Nkuba would come to take me without my saying farewell to my people, that then the return was lost forever." He also told them: "I have seen in the sky things unseen of which I could not divulge." When they had finished listening to Mwindo's words, those who were there dispersed. Shemwindo's and Nyamwindo's many hairs went say "high as that" as the long hairs of an *mpaca*-ghost; and in Tubondo the drums had not sounded anymore; the rooster had not crowed any more. On the day that Mwindo appeared there, his father's and his mother's long hairs were shaved, and the roosters crowed, and that day (all) the drums were being beaten all around.

When Mwindo was in his village, his fame grew and stretched widely. He passed laws to all his people, saying:

> May you grow many foods and many crops.
> May you live in good houses; may you moreover live in a beautiful village.
> Don't quarrel with one another.
> Don't pursue another's spouse.
> Don't mock the invalid passing in the village.
> And he who seduces another's wife will be killed!
> Accept the chief; fear him; may he also fear you.
> May you agree with one another, all together; no enmity in the land nor too much hate.
> May you bring forth tall and short children; in so doing you will bring them forth for the chief.

After Mwindo has spoken like that, he went from then on to remain always in his village. He had much fame, and his father and his mother, and his wives and his people! His great fame went through his country; it spread into other countries, and other people from other countries came to pay allegiance to him.

> Among children there are none bad; whether he be disabled, or whether he not be disabled, he must not be rejected. So then there is nothing bad in what God has given to man.
>
> Heroism be hailed! But excessive callousness either pushes a man into a great crime or brings him a great one, which (normally) he would not have experienced. So, whosoever in a country is not advised will one day carry excrements—and to experience that is terrible.
>
> Mutual agreement brings about kinship solidarity; the one who will save his companion is unknown; it is like the chief and his subordinates. So, the world is but made of mutual aid. So, then, may the chief safeguard (his) subordinates and the subordinates safeguard the chief. Kingship is the stamping (of feet); it is the tremor of people.
>
> Even if a man becomes a hero (so as) to surpass the others, he will not fail one day to encounter someone else who could crush him, who could turn against him what he was looking for.

TEXT 72

The Fang of Gabon and Cameroon: Hymn to the Sun[1]

The Fang peoples, today numbering approximately 300,000, live within the West African rain-forest belt region encompassed by the modern nations of Gabon and Cameroon. In the middle of the eighteenth century, the Fang began migrating from the southern parts of Cameroon into the rain forests of Gabon. They may have been propelled to flee their homeland because of incessant slaving activities in the region. Philip Curtin and others explain that by 1800

> they had become forest dwellers, having adapted very quickly to the new environment. Fang traditions tell symbolically of a compact with the Pygmies who taught them to survive and thrive by hunting, and elephant hunting became a staple of the export trade.[2]

The Fang also brought with them to their new forest settlements their former livelihood as subsistence farmers. They were thus able to continue cultivation of traditionally grown root crops and bananas, and supplemented their diets with hunting and fishing. The Fang secret societies play a significant role in the practice of their nature religion.

---

[1] Ulli Beier (editor), *African Poetry: An Anthology of Traditional African Poems* (New York: Cambridge University Press, 1960), p. 22.
[2] Philip Curtin, et al., *African History* (Boston: Little, Brown, 1978), p. 423.

HYMN TO THE SUN

The fearful night sinks
trembling into the depth
before your lightning eye
and the rapid arrows
from your fiery quiver.
With sparking blows of light
you tear her cloak
the black cloak lined with fire
and studded with gleaming stars—
with sparking blows of light
you tear the black cloak.

Source: From Ulli Beier, *African Poetry: An Anthology of Traditional African Poems,* © 1960. Reprinted with permission from Cambridge University Press.

PART NINE

East Africa

Most scholars of human origins concur that the eastern region of the African continent probably served as the cradle of humankind. Discoveries pioneered by Dr. Louis Leakey in the Olduvai Gorge of northern Tanzania, the Lake Turkana area of Kenya, and the Omo river valley in Ethiopia suggest the existence of tool-making hominid populations

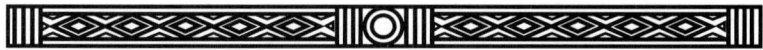

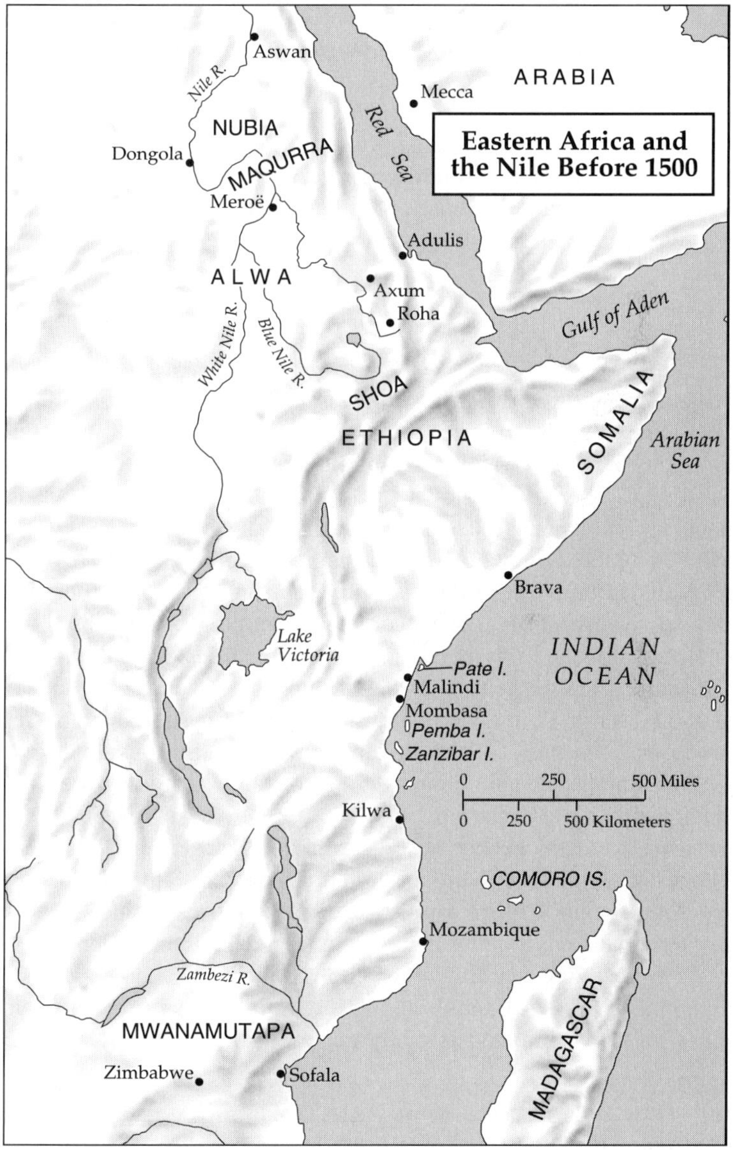
Eastern Africa and the Nile Before 1500
Aswan
Nile R.
ARABIA
Mecca
Red Sea
NUBIA
Dongola
MAQURRA
Meroë
Adulis
ALWA
Axum
Roha
White Nile R.
Blue Nile R.
Gulf of Aden
SHOA
ETHIOPIA
SOMALIA
Arabian Sea
Brava
Lake Victoria
INDIAN OCEAN
Pate I.
Malindi
Mombasa
Pemba I.
Zanzibar I.
0 250 500 Miles
0 250 500 Kilometers
Kilwa
COMORO IS.
Mozambique
Zambezi R.
MADAGASCAR
MWANAMUTAPA
Zimbabwe
Sofala

inhabiting these areas as much as one and a half to two million years ago. The earliest homo sapiens began to appear sometime between 100,000 and 400,000 years ago and are believed to have begun migrations that created the demographic characteristics of the globe as we today know it.

As for those populations who remained, Iron-Age farming populations, speaking languages classified within the Bantu linguistic family, began to absorb in some cases, displace in others, the Khoisan-speaking aboriginal populations as early as the first millennium B.C. Archaeological evidence suggests iron-working populations inhabiting regions of Rwanda, Burundi, and Tanzania from the seventh century B.C., who may have migrated from the Congo River Basin area. By the early centuries A.D., iron-working agriculturalists cultivating sorghum, millet, and melon spread throughout much of the eastern, central, and southeastern part of the African continent. The breeding of livestock occurred among those groups inhabiting those regions devoid of tsetse fly carriers of "African sleeping sickness."

THE SWAHILI COAST

The Swahili culture of the East African coast evolved over the course of the last 2,000 years, as the Bantu-speaking peoples of the area intermarried with Arabs who had settled along the East African coast for trading purposes. The resulting composite of cultures that emerged came to be known as Swahili, derived from the Arabic word for coast, i.e., *sahel*. The language itself is primarily Bantu in morphology, to which has been contributed a large number of Arabic loan words.

The rise of Islam after the seventh century contributed an even more powerful and stable trading environment for African commerce with both the Arabs and Persians, as ever larger markets opened for such lucrative commodities as gold, ivory, and slaves. The East African coastal ports of Kilwa and Zanzibar in Tanzania, Mogadishu in Somalia, and Mombasa in Kenya vied with one another for supremacy in regard to the lucrative trade with the African interior for such commodities as gold, ivory, and exotic skins. Over time the Swahili language developed its own literature as well, particularly through the medium of narrative poetry.

By the early sixteenth century, however, the Portuguese were finally able to establish a presence on the East African coast where they came into competition with the Swahili and Arab traders for control of the lucrative African trade. These Portuguese settlements were made possible by innovations in navigation, implemented during the latter part of the preceding century, which allowed them to become the first Europeans ever to circumnavigate Africa, thus entering the Indian Ocean from the south. The rise of Portuguese influence initiated a steady decline in the commercial societies of the East African coast.

THE SOCIETIES OF THE INTERIOR

Commercial activity was not, however, restricted to the East African coast. The gold-trading inland state of Great Zimbabwe rose to its greatest heights between the thirteenth and fifteenth centuries. So perplexed were later European travelers at the sophistication of Zimbabwe's stone ruins that they often concocted elaborate if somewhat preposterous theories of medieval European penetration of these regions. They did so in order to explain archaeological structures that Europeans of the time considered the indigenous Africans to be incapable of having constructed.

Nor were the intellectual traditions of East Africa limited to the coastal and trading societies. It is merely that the existence of written traditions in Swahili and Arabic among these populations have made their cultures more readily accessible to outsiders over the course of the past several centuries. Nonetheless, pastoralist societies as well as iron age cultures of agriculturalists were known to have been present in large parts of the interior of East Africa, including what is today Uganda, Tanzania, Kenya, Rwanda and Burundi, Malawi, and Zambia, as early as the second or third centuries B.C. While farming played a major role in maintaining the economic viability of these societies, cattle raising became a vital source of wealth and status in many of these societies as well. Not surprisingly, the oral traditions of these interior societies often reflected their societies' valuation of cattle in addition to the warrior traditions of cattle raiding.

In the regions of modern-day Uganda, farming populations and pastoralists began establishing first small chiefdoms and then larger centralized states from about A.D. 1000 onward. In the southwest region of Uganda, a cattle-grazing clan, the Chwezi, belonging to the Tutsi and Hima ethnicities, consolidated a number of these chiefdoms into a state called Kitara around A.D. 1450. The dynasty of the Chwezi was absorbed into the newly emerging kingdom of Bunyoro, founded by Luo-speaking peoples. A second state organized by the populations of the same ethnicity became Buganda, which began to rival Bunyoro from the seventeenth century onward.

To the south the Tutsi clans, during the eighteenth century, evolved two large kingdoms, Rwanda and Burundi. Within these aristocratic kingdoms the Tutsi developed elaborate rituals and myths of ancient origin in order to legitimize their elite position among the Hutu farming populations.

Centralized states in East Africa co-existed alongside smaller, decentralized societies such as the Kikuyu of Kenya. This Bantu-speaking population established agricultural communities throughout Kenya, unified by lineage, cultural, and age groups rather than political centralization.

THE COMING OF THE EUROPEANS

Searching for a sea route that would allow them to circumvent Muslim control of the lucrative overland trade with the Orient, the Portuguese had advanced sufficiently in maritime technology to allow Vasco da Gama in 1498 to circumnavigate Africa. Setting up small settlements on the coast of East Africa shortly thereafter, Portugal hoped to wrest control of the East African trade in gold, ivory, and tropical skins from the Swahili and Arab traders.

After the fifteenth century, the Portuguese succeeded in diverting the gold trade from the Swahili commercial networks. Thus, the coastal city-states of Kilwa, Lamu, Pate, and Zanzibar went into a steady and inexorable decline.

The Portuguese presence on the East Coast of Africa was followed by that of the British in the early 1800s, who established a military presence under the guise of suppressing the East African slave trade. The European partitioning of Africa at the end of the nineteenth century left Britain in control of much of the East African coast.

TEXT 73

The Dinka of Southern Sudan: Divorce—A Woman's Song[1]

One of the principal ethnicities occupying the southern region of the present-day country of Sudan is the Dinka. This pastoralist population inhabits the basin of the White Nile and speaks a language belonging to the Nilo-Saharan language family. Throughout its history the Dinka has maintained a fierce resistance against the spread of Islam, which began absorbing their northern neighbors from the seventh century onward. As a consequence, a sharp line of demarcation and occasional bouts of open warfare continue to separate the southern, predominantly Dinka portions of the modern nation of the Sudan from the northern, Arabic-speaking portion of that country. Religious practices among the patrilineal Dinka range from various Christian denominations to animism.

Within the traditional religious belief system articulated by the Dinka priest-chiefs, we find the concept of immortality deeply imbedded. For this reason a common practice dictates that the widow should continue to bear children in her deceased husband's name with the participation of his surviving kinsmen. Farming and cattle herding represent the economic mainstays of the region.

Agorot de Biong of Pajok lineage was divorced for dubious reasons by Micar of Col's lineage of clan Padeek. It was alleged that she had caused the death of her child by concealing some wrong. She herself felt that she was divorced because of her fading hearing ability. The situation was altogether uncertain. This song was composed to state her case, but the marriage was dissolved.

> We are agitated, the man of the house Shining Dark-Light and I,
> We are a sparrow and a hawk in chase at home

---

[1] Francis Mading Deng, *The Dinka and Their Songs* (London: Oxford University Press Inc., 1973), pp. 219–23.

Neglected girl, remain in peace
O abandoned girl left all alone
Unheeded girl, remain in peace
O girl neglected.
It is rumoured that the son of Jok has left his wife.
"No, we have no conflict with Nyantiwit," [he said]
"We have no conflict with the daughter of Biong."
Do not deny it
Micar, I will leave to the astonishment of our people.
"Thank God" were the words he sent to the sky
Grass of the Pelican has gone to the river, the river of spirits
He has gone to wash away the evil spell;
Have you now spoken with the spirits?
Mijak, have you and the spirits untied the calves?
It is a thing that did not occur
In the family of Col, only old age kills men.
Stand bewildered, daughter of the son of the White One.
People say a big thing has befallen us
The son of the clan Padeek and me;
What the left handed of Jok Anguek has done is bewildering to people
Even to the brown Arabs;
We met on the way, Deng Thokloi and I
Deng de Rahma of Dhakam tribe;
The Arab said to me, "Why have you left your home?
What have you done wrong at home when you have given birth?"
The case of the daughter of the left-handed is painful
Even to the Arab friends of the clan of Arob de Biong
Deng de Rahma paces back and forth
The Arab paces up and down,
"Alas, there is nothing good that does not spoil."
O Deng Thokloi, there is nothing good that does not spoil.
Word is spreading over the land: the daughter of Biong is divorced.
"Which one of the girls?"
"Is it not the girl for whom sons of noble men unpegged their herds to cover the plains?"
Leave the wife of "the Meek" to walk in peace
The wife of the man with no words
She will find her home.
He is a gentleman who never feared his tongue
Nothing will cross his path,
Even if he travels to reach the land of the Arabs
He will remain the husband of the Noisy One
Even if he travels to reach the land of Agar
May the husband of the Noisy One go in peace.
The gentleman has divorced the daughter of a chief:
I will explain to the people of our country

Source: From *The Dinka and Their Songs* by Francis Mading Deng. Copyright © 1973 by Francis Mading Deng. Used by permission of Oxford University Press, Inc.

I am divorced because of "Yes"
"Yes" has severed us, my husband and me
The marriage is spoiled for an empty cause
The marriage is spoiled for nothing
It is finished, it is over
All is ended between us, the bull of Ajak and me.
I never quarrelled with the people of the house
I was a girl attacked holding my peace.
I did not quarrel with the praised man of the house
I was a girl attacked holding my peace.
People ask me, "Daughter of Biong
What have you done wrong in your house?"
Theft, there is none in me
The daughter of Biong is self-composed
O our people, nor have I been seduced
To have a case taken into the court-byre or under the tree
A woman dismissed from the house with no fault
I walked away like a hyena surprised by dawn.
It is said that I am carrying a disease
I am carrying the medicine of the Falata,
The evil pushed away by the tip of a shaft
Like the black viper.
Cobra-spotted of Kwol, the Honoured Pied One
Do not believe what people say,
Do not believe that word of the Pattern of Saddle-bill
The word of the father of Arek,
A healthy person is not beaten into sickness.
And what now that I have left him to his home until the star goes to Alei?
Daughter of the camp of Milang, leave the house
The marriage has refused itself.
Col said, "Are you leaving before I go to court?"
O Cobra-Spotted of Ajak, I am leaving;
What a thing we have started with the son of my father
Dancing Head, Lueth, the Shade of the Crested Crane
O Marial of Clan Padeek, do not preach to me
I am as though I were burnt by fire
The words of the land are burning me,
O Pattern of the Saddle-bill, I am trapped with a trap
Flames have burned my face;
O brother, I do not hate you.
A woman begins her quarrel with a child but will reach the man.
Because of my quarrel with Lueth
I cannot leave with no one at the cooking hearth
Awien, daughter of Rial, please kindle the fire
Daughter of the clan of Agueng de Kwol
We are the blood of Monydhaang de Kwol of Jok's clan
We are not orphaning ourselves daughter of Biong d'Acuol.
It is ended between us, the bull of Ajak and me.
He charged at me, the man behaved like a rhino
We divorced in the moonless part of the bad month of August

What will he eat?
He will live on Yom, the Cow of Dau Dancing Leopard
Akol, cow of my sister Abul.
Abyei, Crossing Wild Dogs, fetch the cow from Maker, the camp of Abyor
The Great Camp of Dent, Reverberating Drums,
Fetch the cow Yom, from the son of the girl of our clan Pajok,
Tell the son of Makuany de Deng d'Ayuel
To give me the cow, Yom,
Our relationship is spoiled with the family of Baar Shining-Dark Shade
In the clan of Col, the Hairy, brave men do not die
I have brought death to the family of Baar;
But I do not know the wrong I have done
O mother, daughter of Ajing, the Spotted Leopard,
O Arob de Monytooc!
Our great clan of Biong d'Allor has always perished
We are the ancient victims of death;
Our clan of Allor de Monydhang has always been mortal
We are the ancient victims of death.

TEXT 74

John Nyakatura: The Attack on Rwanda

from The History of Bunyoro-Kitara[1]

Around the end of the fifteenth century or the beginning of the sixteenth, a Luo-speaking people gained suzerainty over the rules of the state of Kitara, located in the area of Uganda between lakes Victoria and Albert. The ruling Chwezi clan, which were of combined Hima and Tutsi ethnicity, succumbed to these new political leaders, who consolidated the kingdom of Bunyoro.

John Nyakatura, a Ugandan born in 1895, witnessed the decline of traditional Bunyoro society resulting from the British consolidation of colonial rule. He wrote Abakama, *that is,* The History of Bunyoro-Kitara *in the Runyoro language of Uganda*, which was later translated to English. Mr. Nyakatura describes the early influences in his life that provided the motivation for him to undertake this historical work completed in 1938:

> I sustained serious injuries on my leg as a result of the punishment "my Father" inflected on me for defying his orders to attend to the goats and for having chosen to listen to his stories instead. I still bear a big scar on this leg—a lasting testimonial to my profound interest in history. Fortunately, whatever I heard from him became deeply rooted in my head as traditional tales.[2]

The Attack on Rwanda and Other Countries

After three years in Nkore, Chwa was persuaded by the people of the Bachwezi clan—the Abafumura—to invade Rwanda, where many cattle also existed. Thereupon

---

[1] J. W. Nyakatura, *Anatomy of an African Kingdom: A History of Bunyoro-Kitara*, translated by Teopista Muganwa (New York: NOK Publishers, Ltd., 1973), pp. 73–74.

[2] Ibid., p. xix.

Source: Reprinted from J. W. Nyakatura, *Anatomy of an African Kingdom: A History of Bunyoro-Kitara*, © 1973.

he mobilized his men and moved against Rwanda. But, suspecting during the march that some of his men had deserted and had bolted back to Kitara, he decided to estimate their number by ordering everyone to be in possession of a stone. This incident took place at Birenga hill. When they arrived at a sandy river in Nyaruyanja village he ordered them to throw down their stones. The stones thus thrown down formed three big heaps and two small ones. He ordered this exercise to be repeated in order to make sure that he had sufficient men for the invasion.

At dawn he encountered King Kahindira of Rwanda [Ruanda] and a battle was fought. Kahindira was beaten and his cattle captured, many of which Chwa I sent to Kitara. Chwa himself settled in Rwanda for four years and Rwanda thus became the main center for his raiding expeditions. He attacked many countries to the west of the lacustrine region and even went beyond Lake Kivu. He died in Rwanda. (Usually when an Omukama died, his officials tried to hide the fact. From this developed the custom of saying that the king has been lost or has been swallowed up.)

During the four years he ruled Rwanda, Chwa I gave that country a taste of good administration. He reorganized it after the pattern he was used to in Kitara. In the Chronicles of Rwanda, the Kitara occupation of that country is said to have been of great importance because Chwa I left a legacy of good administration.

After the death of Chwa, his men decided to return to Kitara. [This would seem to suggest that their hold over that country was very precarious. It would even suggest that they might have been driven out of the country.] During their return journey they passed through Nkore, where they were challenged by Omugabe Ntare. Apparently Ntare had learnt of the death of Chwa and the decision of his followers to return to Kitara. So he ambushed them and killed some of them, thus avenging his earlier defeat. The defeat of the Bakitara was primarily due to the lack of a leader in the absence of Chwa, to give them inspiration. It is not surprising therefore that many of them fled in the heat of the encounter and many of those who stood their ground were cut to pieces. Ntare captured Chwa's palace, including his household.

In Bunyoro-Kitara Chwa did not leave any heir. And because of his prolonged absence, a lady called Mashamba was put on the throne as regent. Mashamba was a *Mubiitokati* [princess] as well as the *Batebe* [the official sister of the king]. The kingmakers were not disposed to offer the throne to a prince of a distant relation to the ruling line [lest he might make his position permanent]. The elevation of Mashamba was therefore a temporary measure [necessary to avoid a breakdown in administration]. Meanwhile concerted attempts were made to find an acceptable successor to the throne.

The search soon switched to the captured ladies in Chwa I's household who had become his queens [*abago*]. It happened that there was one called Ihembe, who belonged to the Babiito clan. Ihembe had been at the last stages of pregnancy when she disappeared. Thereupon the kingmakers secretly sent out people to look for her and the child.

Omukama Chwa I was not buried in Kitara, but in Rwanda. His mother was the lady Runego of the Bagweri clan. Her other son was called Nyarwa, as we saw. For the weeping of lady Runego after the disaster at Karokarungi, that kingdom's name became known as Nkore and Kitara became known as Kyaka.

TEXT 75

The Buganda of Uganda: Daoura[1]

The Luo-speaking peoples, who had founded the early sixteenth century kingdom of Bunyoro in the Great Lakes region of what is modern-day Uganda, also established several tributary states around its perimeter. Buganda emerged as the most significant of these satellite kingdoms, eclipsing Bunyoro from the eighteenth century onward. The cultivation of bananas became the economic basis of this centralized state, occupying a region of abundant rainfall whose soil was noted for its fertility.

Although located within the East African interior, Buganda was not isolated from the powerful cultural influences and challenges presented both by Islam and Christianity. The Kabakas sought to exploit the networks offered by both during the precolonial period without succumbing to either. Making use of extensive trade relations in both orbits and importing weapons from the coast, the nineteenth century **Kabakas, or rulers, of Buganda had expanded into much of the territory of a declining Bunyoro. The last and one of the most noted Kabakas of Old Buganda was Mutesa I (1856–1884),** who was especially noted for accelerating this process of imperial expansion at Bunyoro's expense.

Daoura had children; when he was old and advanced in years he said to them: "I am old; I can no longer govern Buganda, take possession of it; become the masters of your realm."

They answered him:

"Father, we are young, how can we take possession of Buganda when you are not dead? How can we succeed you while you are still alive?"

They refused.

---

[1]Blaise Cendrars, *The African Saga* (Westport, CT: Greenwood Publishing Group Inc., 1927), pp. 201–203.
Source: From Blaise Cendrars, *The African Saga,* © 1927. Reprinted with permission of Greenwood Publishing Group, Inc.

"If you will not take the kingdom," said Daoura, "leave it to me."

He called Seroganga the moukopi and said to him: "Come, I will tell you something." Seroganga came, and Daoura said to him: "Will you take me to your home and hide me?"

"Lord, I will hide you."

"Good," said the king. "Return; when it is dark, come; we will go away and you shall hide me. I am tired of the kingdom; I don't want it any more."

He said to one of his slaves and to three of his wives: "Come, we are going to hide ourselves."

He rose, set out, and went to the moukopi's home. Seroganga led him into the forest, built a house there and closed it.

"My friend," said the king, "never tell anyone that I am in the forest."

"My lord, I will not betray you."

Daoura stayed in the forest. His mother asked the notables: "Where has the king gone?"

They replied: "He has disappeared."

"Go and consult a witch-doctor" said the queen-mother.

They went to a witch-doctor. He said: "Come early tomorrow, all the people of Buganda. The best-dressed one is the one who has the king. When you see one better dressed than all the rest, seize him; he will tell you where the king is."

Seroganga said to Daoura: "My lord, I am going to a feast."

"Do not betray me."

"No, lord."

He went to Rousaka. The queen-mother called him.

Seroganga swore, saying: "I saw Daoura last night."

Namasou said to him: "Seroganga!"

He swore again. "I saw Daoura last night."

"How finely you are dressed."

Seroganga said again: "I saw Daoura last night."

"Daoura disappeared a long time ago, yet you saw him last night."

"Lord," said Seroganga, "I did not see him, I only swore."

The queen-mother said to the notables: "Seize him and kill him!"

They took hold of him. Then Seroganga said:

"Do not kill me, lords; let me go, and I will take you into the forest, to Hanyanya, where the king is."

"Let Seroganga go," said the queen-mother, "and he will take you into the forest to the king."

He walked in front of all the notables and chiefs and led them along the road; they came to the forest.

When they saw the king they went down on their knees. Daoura said to Seroganga:

"I told you not to betray me to the people. You have not done so. Who brought them here?"

"Lord," replied Seroganga, "they were about to kill me."

"Since you have betrayed me, let them do so!"

Daoura killed him. Then he left the forest, came back to Buganda, resumed his royal state and was saluted by all the notables.

TEXT 76

The Bahima of Ankole (Uganda): I Who Encircle the Foe[1]

The region of Ankole lies south of Lake Victoria and to the west of the Buganda inhabited regions, in the territory of present-day Uganda. The Bahima who occupy the Ankole region of western Uganda have throughout their history engaged in a cattle-raising economy. Not surprisingly, cattle raids as a means of conveying the heroic exploits of Bahima warriors became a standard part of the literary culture of that society. The praise poems of the Bahima were characteristically delivered in a style whereby the reciter would snap his finger and thumb at the close of each stanza and the chorus would offer the refrain, "Eeeeee."

As part of the initiation process of Bahima boys, they would be anointed with praise names based on qualities unique to each of them. Over the course of a man's career, his virtues would be appended to the original praise poem as honorific titles, which were deeply respected by that society.

1. I Who Am Praised thus held out in battle among foreigners along with The Overthrower;
2. I Who Ravish Spear In Each Hand stood out resplendent in my cotton cloth;
3. I Who Am Quick was drawn from afar by lust for the fight and with me was The Repulser of Warriors;
4. I Who Encircle The Foe, with Bitembe, brought back to the beasts from Bihanga;
5. With Bwakwakwa, I fought at Kaanyabareega,
6. Where Bantura started a song that we might overcome them.
7. Thus with my spear, I and Rwamujonjo conquered Oruhinda;
8. The Banyoro were afraid on the battlefield of Kahenda;
9. The cocks of Karembe had already crowed;

---

[1]H. F. Morris, *The Heroic Recitations of the Bahima of Ankole* (London: Oxford University Press, 1964), pp. 42–48.
Source: From H. F. Morris, *The Heroic Recitations of the Bahima of Ankole*, © 1964. Reprinted by permission of Oxford University Press.

10. I Who Am Nimble with The One Whom None Can Dislodge felled them at Nyamizi.
11. At Nkanga, I seized my spear by its shaft-end;
12. At Kanyegyero, I The Binder Of Enemies took them by surprise;
13. Thereafter was I never excluded from the counsels of princes, nor was Rwangomani;
14. I Who Rescue With The Spear had seized him so that we might fight together.

* *

1. I Who Take No Rest went for the cattle!

2. With Rwakakuuto, I went for them as they stood without the kraal;
3. Hearing the cries of their master they scattered.

4. I Who Take Myself Over Mountains made for the hills of Butumbi along with Iremezo;
5. I Who Stand Staunch saved the beasts which were weary.

6. He Who Protects His Companions pressed on at noon towards Kyamakanda;
7. He Who Never Surrenders His Chief was with The Provoker Of Vengeance;
8. He Who Is Of Value to Friends slew at Ruyanja.

9. At Kajwamushana, they captured the foe whilst the frogs were croaking;
10. They fought on without ceasing until they had vanquished them.

11. He Who Is Truculent fulfilled his word and The Slayer of The Enemy was with him;
12. He Who Grasps His Weapons Firmly slew the foe.

13. At Ruti-rw'amabaare, he supported Bashenya as he used his spear;
14. He heard the praise song of The One Who Belabours The Foe as they triumphed.

15. I Who Do Not Wait For The Dawn To Break Over Kamburara;
16. The night at Migina seemed like four to them.

17. At Kikonkoma, I joined a group of the Abariita;
18. At Rwabuhura, he had already gone with them.

19. He Who Moves Quickly vowed to fight at Nyiigongo;
20. I Who Overcome The Enemy, they did not leave me behind but they chose me.

21. Rugorami fought at Buhingo;
22. The brown cattle were followed by warriors.

23. He Who Opposes The Foe advanced upon them;
24. He Who For The Foe Brings Disaster caused much blood to flow.

25. For a great distance, I put them to flight at Nyarwanya;
26. He Who Is Direct In Attack drove before him those who were fleeing.

27. He Who Does Not Fear Black Steel and He Who Scatters The Foe
28. Rescued The Trouble Bringer and brought him home.

TEXT 77

Chronicler: The Arrival of Vasco da Gama

from The Kilwa Chronicle[1]

Swahili is an Arabic-derived term meaning "coastal people." The language Kiswahili represents a centuries-old amalgam of African Bantu and Arabic, which evolved among the trading populations of that region sometime before the ninth century A.D.

The city of Kilwa developed from the eleventh century onward and rose to become the most prominent of the East African trading city-states. It represented a melding of cultures, languages, and economic interests on the part of the African rulers and Arab traders of Oman and the Persian Gulf who developed an especially lucrative trade in African gold. The Kilwa Chronicle is a historical text of unknown East African origins that was written in Arabic and detailed the political developments of this important city-state.

In the late fifteenth century, the Portuguese navigator Vasco da Gama was commissioned by the crown to lead an expedition opening the sea route to India by circumnavigating the African continent. Da Gama's ships rounded the Cape of Good Hope on November 22, 1497, and made their way up the East African coast, stopping in the important port cities of Mombasa and Malinda. These developments were duly noted by the writer of The Kilwa Chronicle during that time.

---

[1]G. S. P. Freeman-Grenville, *The East African Coast* (London: Oxford University Press, 1962), pp. 47–48.

During al-Fudail's reign there came news from the land of Mozambique that men had come from the lands of the Franks. They had three ships, and the name of their captain was al-Mirate [Admiral Vasco da Gama]. After a few days there came word that the ships had passed Kilwa and had gone on to Mafia [an adjoining island to the northward]. The lord of Mafia rejoiced, for they thought they [the Franks] were good and honest men. But those who knew the truth confirmed that they were corrupt and dishonest persons who had only come to spy out the land in order to seize it. And they determined to cut the anchors of their ships so that they should drift ashore and be wrecked by the Muslims. The Franks learnt of this and went on to Malindi [a trading city on the Kenya coast]. When the people of Malindi saw them, they knew they were bringers of war and corruption, and were troubled with very great fear. They gave them [the Franks] all they asked, water, food, firewood, and everything else. And the Franks asked for a pilot to guide them to India, and after that back to their own land—God curse it!

Source: From G. S. P. Freeman-Grenville, *The East African Coast,* © 1960 by G. S. P. Freeman-Grenville. Reprinted with permission of G. S. P. Freeman-Grenville.

TEXT 78

Chronicler: Intrigues

from The Pate Chronicle[1]

The Pate Chronicle *represents a court history that details the political evolution of the East African coastal city-state of Pate. It is written in Swahili (employing Arabic characters) and begins around A.D. 1204. Pate was in fact an island that benefited from the lucrative trade in gold organized between Arab merchants and the Bantu-speaking African rulers of East Africa. For a brief period during the fourteenth century, Pate was able to extend its control over the other city-states of the coast. Even though the original version was believed to have been destroyed in the bombardment of Witu in 1890, several versions have remained.*

In the year 1177 [of the Hegira] Sultan Ahmad died, and a Queen Mwana Khadija, sister of Bwana Tamu the Younger, reigned. She reigned seven years, and after that the Mazaru'i intrigued with the Pate people and they put Sultan Omari on the throne.

Then there were two rulers in one country and they fought together for five years inside the city. Afterwards Sultan Omari was defeated and he fled to the Bajuns at Faza.

Mwana Khadija sent her soldiers and ameers to fight him at Faza and he fled again and took a *dhow* and made for Barawa.

He fled secretly, but the soldiers of the Mwana Khadija followed him and came up with him in the way in their *dhows*.

When he saw that he would be seized he wrote on a piece of paper and threw it into the water, and at that place there sprang up behind his *dhow* a shoal of sand.

---

[1]G. S. P. Freeman-Grenville, *The East African Coast* (London: Oxford University Press, 1962), pp. 265–69.
Source: From G. S. P. Freeman-Grenville, *The East African Coast,* © 1960 by G. S. P. Freeman-Grenville. Reprinted with permission of G. S. P. Freeman-Grenville.

Even today it is there, and the Bajuns call it Sultan Omar's shoal.

The reason was that he was a great medicine man, but magic does not stay the decree of Allah and his luck was small. So he went to Barawa and stayed there one year till he gained strength to return to Pate of one accord with the people of Pate and the Mazaru'i.

He entered Pate and seized his house, called Diwani, and half the town. Then war returned to Pate, and after one year they broke into his house at Diwani and he was killed.

His brother's son, called Fumoluti, took his place and fought with Mwana Khadija.

In the year 1187 Mwana Khadija died.

So Sultan Fumoluti reigned, for the people of Pate saw that it was better to leave off strife because of the trials they had endured for many days. So he reigned over the whole town and all were of one accord, the people of Pate, the Mazarui, the people of Amu and Siu, and even the Bajuns.

The people of Pate said, "It were better that we leave off fighting and that he reign over the whole country, for our town has been laid waste."

For in the time of Sultan Omari and Mwana Khadija everybody cut down the cocoa-nut palms and fruit trees, everybody destroyed the property of his neighbour. For five years they were not able to cultivate or to trade or to do any work whatsoever. So a great famine raged till people ate oats and the skin seats of chairs. For this reason they were pleased that peace should reign and that their country might rest.

So they remained two and a half years, and after that time the great men who were of Mwana Khadija's faction made intrigues. These people said, "What sort of a Sultan is this? We do not want him, for he is of lowly origin."

For the mother of Sultan Fumoluti bin Sheikh was of humble birth, and her father's profession was that of a fisherman.

This fisherman had three daughters, one of whom was called Mwana Sukari binti Kae.

One night during Ramadhan her father was lying in his plantation and his daughter was fanning him, when the star of destiny passed over them.

Her father pointed it out to his daughter and said to her, "My child, Allah will bless you so that you give birth to Sultans."

On the next evening the father of this Sultan Fumoluti passed the house of the fisherman and saw his daughter and loved her very much. He demanded her of her father and married her and took her to his home. She gave birth to this Sultan Fumoluti and one girl, who became Bwana Fumomadi's mother, and another boy, so she had three children.

Now from that time no other has reigned at Pate save descendants of that woman whose father prayed to Allah on her behalf.

So now by reason of the humble origin of his mother the Pate people refused to be governed by this Sultan Fumoluti, and the great men of Pate took counsel and made plans to destroy him.

Now the Sultan was a man of great strength and a brave warrior, so they said, "Who will confront him and smite him?"

They were in the midst of saying these words when a man called Fundi Suleimani, a craftsman, came forth. He drew near to the counsel of the free born.

They said to him, "What do you want here? You have no manners to disturb our privacy." He replied, "The secret thing you desire I will do it for you." They said to him, "You are a lowly person, you will not dare do the thing we wish to do." He replied, "I will do what you want and more."

Now the reason was this: the artisan Suleimani had had a very beautiful wife. Long ago, Sultan Fumoluti when a youth had taken her from him. Now that he had obtained the status of a free man he said to himself, "Now I will take my revenge that I may cure the old sore that is in my heart."

When the elders heard this, they knew that he would do truly as he had said. So they said to him, "If Allah will we will attend the levée and you must come and stand behind the Sultan. When the Mazaru'i governor enters the levée the Sultan will stand up for him, then strike him and we will be ready to seize his house."

Next day they went to the levée according to their agreement. When the Mazaru'i governor entered the Sultan rose, placing his hand on his sword. Suleimani struck him a sword cut, and the blow severed five fingers, and striking the regal chair cut off its arm.

Sultan Fumoluti's sword fell on the ground and he stooped and picked it up with his left hand. Now Suleimani's sword was broken with the blow, and there remained only the stump, with which he struck the Sultan on the right arm.

When Fumoluti had seized his sword in his left hand he struck Suleimani, who ran away and fell, outside, split in two halves.

Then the Pate people attacked Sultan Fumoluti, and he drew nigh to them and smote them with his left hand and killed twenty-five men. So they fled away, and two of their number hid themselves under a cow. Everybody fled, and his brother was killed there. When they had fled he went to the door and fastened it, and his own people and Bwana Sheikh, his son, were not present.

When they received tidings they came running and passed in by the back way, and Bwana Sheikh entered and found his father exhausted from loss of blood.

He said to his son, "Listen, my son, I give you my dying exhortation that you may act on it. I am finished and after me they will kill you."

"Now if you want my counsel go and take Bwana Fumomadi and put him here in my place. It is he who is able to avenge me, for the soldiers here belong to his father and his aunt. When these soldiers see him as ruler of the town they will come to their master. If you refuse to follow my advice you will die before me, for they will come again at once and come up into this house."

As they were in the midst of saying these words Bwana Fumomadi and his friends arrived. For when he had received the news he was not able to wait patiently because Fumoluti was his younger maternal uncle.

When Sultan Fumoluti and his son saw Bwana Fumomadi they said, "This is indeed Sultan Bwana Kombo."

So Fumoluti spake and said to Bwana Kombo, "I gave this your brother just now my dying exhortation to obey you. Now I give you my dying request. Do not follow the counsels of the Pate people. Stand by yourself and avenge me, and Allah will give you a great kingdom, and you will defeat your enemies."

"Also follow the counsel of this your brother, Bwana Sheikh, for he is wise, moreover he is a valiant man and will be of service to you against your enemies. So you must love him and help him to a high place in your kingdom, and I will then be pleased with you, for he has nothing now."

When the Nabahans and the Pate people knew that Bwana Kombo had been given the kingdom by his uncle, and that the uncle was still alive, they made an attack on the house.

So Bwana Sheikh and Bwana Kombo and their soldiers and relations fought well and resisted them.

Then the Pate people took Bwana Fumomadi's brother and made him Sultan in their quarter in place of Mwana Khadija his aunt.

They fought three days till on the fourth day, at night, Sultan Fumoluti died.

Some people said that he put his arms into burning oil, and others that he said, "There cannot be a Sultan with a stump for a right arm for how can his hand be kissed? Moreover, I will not live to be called Sultan 'stump-arm,' " and so he died.

So in the year 1190 Sultan Bwana Fumomadi reigned.

When Fumoluti was dead Sultan Bwana Fumomadi told a crier to beat the horn in the town the same night and proclaim that the Sultan was dead, and that he had taken his place, and that this was the Sultan's dying bequest. Moreover, that he who wanted war must make war with the new Sultan, and he who wanted peace must come early in the morning to the burial.

So when the morning had dawned Bwana Fumomadi and his clan buried his uncle.

Those people of the other quarter did not come, so Bwana Fumomadi knew that they were still wanting to make war.

Now of those in that quarter there were two of Bwana Fumomadi's brothers; one was he whom they had set up as Sultan, and the other followed his brother.

Now this faction was the strongest, but half of the people and soldiers, when they saw how Bwana Fumomadi reigned, came over to him because they loved him most, and they were in the beginning soldiers of his father.

So Bwana Fumomadi, when he had gained strength, fought the other faction and took their town, leaving only forty houses in the whole town. After that he seized all these houses till there was left only forty people in one house, and these were very great men.

Then he wrote a letter and sent it to his two brothers who were there, saying, "I have pardoned you, come out from there and leave me to fight it out with the remainder. You will order this kingdom equally with me, but to me will be left the name of Sultan only." They answered him, "If you want us to come out you must make peace with us together with these forty people of ours. We cannot leave them."

When their letters came, Bwana Fumomadi consulted with his cousin Bwana Sheikh, and the latter said, "If you leave these people they will make trouble again directly they have gained strength. It will not do to leave them."

"Now if your brothers have refused to come out it is best that you treat all these alike and eradicate this evil that our country may be saved, for it has suffered troubles for many days."

So he asked his brothers again to come out and they refused.

So Bwana Fumomadi did not hesitate, he sent soldiers to assault the house from back and front, and they killed everybody. Then he took either by stratagem or force every man who had been a ringleader amongst the rebel soldiers of Pate, Amu, Siu or Ozi, and killed him.

For this reason he obtained a great kingdom and sat on the throne for thirty-three years without there being trouble anywhere in his kingdom.

The whole outlook became clear, so that even now women say when the sun comes out and there are no clouds, "Today the heavens are refulgent like the sovereignty of Bwana Fumomadi."

So the country of Pate flourished, and he turned out the Mazaru'i and they had no concern with it any more. Since they had come to Pate no one had been able to govern any more without their aid, but Sultan Fumomadi put an end to this state of affairs.

Now he was the last of the great Sultans of the Nabahans; after him there came not anyone who obtained a kingdom like his, for he restored the grandeur of the ancient kingdom with his own hands.

He loved his subjects and his soldiers and he spent much money. He was a clever man, powerful and brave, and he did not consent to have his subjects oppressed.

TEXT 79

Abdallah Ibn Nasir: Lament for Greatness

from the Utendi wa Inkishafi[1]

A written literature in the Swahili (Kiswahili) language of East Africa, employing the Arabic alphabet, emerged sometime before the seventh century. It represented the intellectual output of a centuries old cultural amalgam of the Bantu and Arabic populations who engaged in trading activities along the coast. One of the most popular forms of poetic expression to evolve among the Swahili was the narrative poem referred to as the utendi.

Saiyid Abdallah ibn Nasir (c. 1720–c. 1820) is often considered the most gifted Swahili writer of the late eighteenth century. In "Lament for Greatness" he wrote about the decay of the once opulent and elegant city-states of Pate and Lamu, using their disintegration as a metaphor to convey the impermanence of earthly wealth and power. Utendi wa Inkishafi had been rendered in English either as The Soul's Awakening or Introspection.

I put first 'In the Name of God'   as I compose this poem   and I write 'The Merciful One'   and after that 'The Benign One'.
I want to put praise first   lest the curious ask   saying, Have you deprived us of the praising   and so spread a wrong that has no like?
Praise having been offered   illuminating us like a lamp   prayers and peace follow on   let us pray for the Prophet Muhammad.
And for his kinsfolk of the clan Qinan   and for his four named Companions   let us pray for them all together   may prayer and compassion leave their mark on them.

---

[1] Lyndon Harries, *Swahili Poetry* (London: Oxford University Press, 1962), pp. 91–103.
Source: From Lyndon Harries, *Swahili Poetry,* © 1962. Reprinted by permission of Oxford University Press.

TEXT 79: Abdallah Ibn Nasir: Lament for Greatness

O my Lord Allah, Granter of requests   let us pray for the Prophet who came
      and who of Thy One-ness, O Lord of slaves   taught us the meaning.

When the full measure is complete   of setting in order prayer and praise   let me
      make clear my treatise   which I purpose in my heart.

My inner intention   is to make a necklace, entwining it   shining with large
      pearls   and to put little pearls at the end.

I will make a clasp by correcting it   arranging the pearls on every side   and let
      me call its name *Inkishafi*   so that the darkness of sins be withdrawn from me.

May the darkness of ignorance be effaced   and light and radiance give forth
      brightness   and whosoever reflects (on what I write)   let it be pardon to
      him who repents.

My preface is now ended   I wish to give counsel to my heart   which is
      overcome by the lusts of the world   with the wiles of Satan which deceive.

O my heart, why dost thou not awake?   but what is it that deceives thee?
      Thou dost not explain to me for me to discern it   if it have a countenance may
      I not reject it?

O my heart, why dost thou not explain it?   Let us say thou art clever to
      discriminate   but knowest thou not that the world is vanity?   Why dost
      thou follow its turmoiled paths?

This world is a raging sea   it has coral reefs and much insubordination
      who rides it knows it is a tyrant   responsible for every loss.

It is like a well without a bottom   a place where the tossing bull
      who approaches it breaks his horns   without succeeding at all in drinking its
      water.

Or look at the dust in a ray of light   when the sun rises   if one gets near to
      grasp it   he sees nothing he can hold on to.

Or look at the mirage when it glistens   when the sun is at the meridian
      the thirsty one says, There is water   and runs to take of it.

When he goes he finds only the sun's fire   (not) the water he wants, so he rends
      himself   gaining nothing but trouble   and so it is unceasing remorse for
      him.

All vices and hardships   the difficulties and troubles which you have had
      (they come from) this world which you love   with its very base condition and
      its troubles.

The world is corrupt, cleave not unto it   it loves not man but only the infidel
      How does it come about that you, so able to comprehend   should fight with
      dogs and be (thus) profaned?

For me it possesses only what is evil   it abounds in much cunning   it is very
      fierce at striking a glancing blow   dealing men a coup de grâce over and over
      again.

How many who have passed through this world   enjoying life after their fashion
      and (the world) upset their apple-cart (lit. their deliberations)   and they fell
      only to gnaw the finger of repentance?

The noose of death met up with them   and they gnawed their fingers in remorse
      and their world obliterated them   saying, Depart, keep away from me.

(The world) says, Get going, this is it   this is the end of further tarrying
      The merchandise of pride and arrogance   you have dealt in it, I can witness.

The arrow of death pierces them   (death) enters deep into their mortal flesh
    Don't let the wide-mouthed be so aghast   saying, Who is it? what has happened?
Rendering up their lives   the depriver of pleasure (death) walks with them
    without (so much as) a cougher who coughs   nor one who from the Journey can refrain.
How many alarums were alerted   You were warned (but) you were not ready
    When will you stop this presumption?   Tell me the end of it and listen.
By this my beard, O heart   thou art not converted by my counsel   thou dost barter thy future life to the world   by too much deception and you have chosen it.
Listen well to what I tell you   O soul, behold, a lantern in the wind   nothing can prevent its being put out   at once you see it has been extinguished.
Or look at the roaring fire   in the forest-glade in the thickets   a cloud comes down in the hot season   and (the fire) is put right out and you cannot revive it.
O heart, kneel prostrate before Him   Come then, please take heed   lest the accursed Satan laugh at you   and tomorrow see you even as he is himself.
This world that thou desirest   what is its good that you so love   it has no eternal quality, it does not last   If thou hadst dominion (over it) what wouldst thou do with it?
Was not the prophet Solomon   ruler of men and of jinns   yet did not (earth) banish him and cheat him?   If it were another, what then would (earth) do to him?
How many children (of earth) have you seen   and been certain of their subsequent happiness   but now the houses of the earth (i.e. graves) enfold them in the sepulchre which enshrouds them?
How many rich men have you seen   who shone like the sun   who had control of the weapons of war   and stored up silver and gold?
All the world paid them homage   and their world was straight ahead for them   they walked with heads held disdainfully   and eyes closed in scorn.
Swinging their arms and arching their necks   while behind and in front crowds accompanied them   everywhere they live there are seats of honour and troops of soldiers attend them.
Their lighted houses were aglow   with lamps of crystal and brass   the nights were as the day   beauty and honour surrounded them.
They decorated (their houses) with choice porcelain   and every goblet was engraved   and in the midst they put crystal pitchers   amongst the decorations that glittered.
The rails for the decorations to please the eye   I swear by God the All-Wealthy were of teak and of ebony   placed rank upon rank in order to look fine.
The men's halls hummed with chatter   and the harem chambers rang out with laughter   with noise of talk from slaves and servants   merriment and shouts of joy waxed loud.
And while they lay down for rest   they had masseurs and fanners   and gay-robed women, the minstrels   singing melodies ceaselessly.

TEXT 79: Abdallah Ibn Nasir: Lament for Greatness

On lovely couches well-chosen   upon beds of padded cushions   with pillows of green at head and foot   worked with braided skein.

Folded fabrics they arranged   above the divans to cover them   they were sprinkled with rose-water   attar and sandal-wood they anointed themselves with these.

Yet even though wealth has its boasting   they were taken on the great Journey   and descended to the mansions of the grave   where the crumbling earth demolished them.

Now they lie in a town of finger's span   with no fine curtains nor cushions   and their bodies are destroyed   for the constraint of the grave has come upon them.

Their perspiration is at an end   the pus and the blood oozes out of them   maggots pass down through noses and mouths   the beauty and the countenances are transformed.

They have all become food for insects   who eat their bodies   the termites and the ants lay them waste   and the snake and the scorpion have them encoiled.

Their radiant faces are become dark-hued   the likeness of a bear or of a baboon   their skins are lacerated   their bones and flesh are shrivelled.

Their lighted mansions are uninhabited   the young of bats cling up above   you hear no whisperings nor shoutings   spiders crawl over the beds.

The wall-niches for porcelain in the houses   are now the resting-place for nestlings   owls hoot within the house   mannikin birds and ducks dwell within.

Young vultures perch on the rails   and young doves arch their necks   and flap their wings in lazy fashion   wild pigeons and swallows have built there.

In the houses the cockroach rustles   the cricket calls in the mens' halls   stilled is the hum in the ante-rooms   for silence and darkness encloses all.

The courtyards are overgrown with bush   with lots of weeds and liana   people fear the outside doors   for silence and darkness cover them.

If you do not believe and say it is a lie   go to their houses and turn your neck   if you call you get no reply but an echo   the voice of men has come to an end.

O heart, you have not yet understood   when alarums come, are you not perturbed?   yet you have ears to hear   I consider, for these matters which follow.

So now, my heart, for your part I will ask you also   explain to me entirely so that I can understand   Where are the parents who bore you?   tell me where they are, that I may greet them.

Where now is Ali b. Nasir   and his brother-in-law Abu Bakr   and Sharifs Aidarus and Muhadhar?   where did they go yonder?   show me the way they went.

I tell you so listen to me   they have been made mock of in the darkest of mansions   where there is no light nor brightness   these are the resting-places to which they have descended.

Where is Kiungu and those who filled the halls?   and the good Shaikhs of Sarambi?   they sleep in the mansions of the dust   the grave-boards strain hard upon them.

Where are the brave men of Pate sultanate   men of noble and shining mien?
> they have been forced into the mansions of the eternal sands   sovereignty and might have been removed from them.

There were lords and viziers   who went with troops of soldiery   wide-yawning
> graves opened up for them   the fetters of death enshackled them.

There were judges, dispensers of justice   students of books who proved things
> leaders of people in the right paths   yet they were called and all have answered.

Ah me, where are the dove-like women   balm for the eyes, soothers of passion?
> they are all gone and departed   now they have gone and faded right away.

TEXT 80

Mwana Kupona: A Dying Woman's Advice to Her Daughter

from the Utenda wa Mwana Kupona[1]

Utendi *or its feminine form* utenda *represents the traditional Swahili narrative poem. One of the most popular to come down through history is the* Utenda wa Mwana Kupona. *A wealthy widow, Mwana Kupona binti Msham (c. 1810–1860) came from Pate. She wrote this poem in 1836 as an instruction for her seventeen-year-old daughter. It has been noted by scholars like Alice Werner that young girls from Pate and Lamu from privileged families were often highly educated and adept at composing Swahili poetry.*

At one time Western scholars assumed that the essence of the verses contained in Utenda wa Mwana Kupona *offered a direct ethical lesson in female obedience to her husband. However, Ann Biersteker in "Language, Poetry, and Power" has reflected on the powerful but subtle role of irony in this poem. Ms. Biersteker notes:*

> [It] mocks rather than flatters "husbands," whether those "husbands" are literal spouses or political rulers who are intellectually limited . . . [and] through skilled use of language those who are otherwise powerless can manipulate those who are powerful. [It thus becomes] a poem composed to "beguile" the unwary, be they young daughters, naive husbands, scholars, or other outsiders anticipating straightforward cultural messages in Swahili poetry.[2]

---

[1] Lyndon Harries, *Swahili Poetry* (London: Oxford University Press, 1962), pp. 73–87.
[2] Ann Biersteker, "Language, Poetry, and Power: A Reconsideration of 'Utendi wa Mwana Kupona' " in Kenneth W. Harrow, *Faces of Islam in African Literature* (Portsmouth, NH: Heinemann Educational Books, Ltd., 1991), p. 59.

Attend to me my daughter   unworthy as I am of God's award   Heed my last
    instructions   for it may be that you   will apply yourself to them.
Sickness has seized upon me   and has now lasted a whole year   I have not had
    a chance to utter   a word of good advice to you.
Come forward and seat yourself   with ink and paper   I have matters at heart
    that I have longed to tell you.   Now that you are near   Write, In the Name
    of God   name Him and the Beloved   together with his Companions.
When you have thus acknowledged   the Name of God the Mighty   then let us
    pray for His bounty   as God shall deem fit for us.
A son of Adam is nought   and the world is not ours   nor is there any man
    who shall endure for ever.
My child, accept my advice   together with my blessing   God will protect you
    that He may avert you from evil.
Take this amulet that I give you   fasten it carefully upon a cord   regard it as a
    precious thing   that you may cherish it with care.
Let me string for you a necklace   of pearls and red coral   let me adorn you as a
    beautiful woman   when it shines upon your neck.
For love let me give you a clasp   a beautiful one without flaw   wear it upon
    your neck   and you shall perceive benefits.
While you shall hold to my counsel   my child, you shall escape trouble
    you shall pass through this world   and cross over to the next.

In the first place, hold fast to the Faith   do not neglect to fulfil the *faradh*
    and the *sunnah* when they are possible   and the *wajibu,* to perform them.
Secondly, be of good behaviour   with a discrete tongue   that you be as one
    beloved   wherever you shall enter.
Thirdly, be truthful   what you undertake take pains to do   a person who holds
    not to justice   do not follow in his path.
Further, my child, learn how to behave   before people of rank   when you see
    them at any place   hasten to pay them respect.
When they enter do you rise up   and let your heart rejoice   afterwards conduct
    them forth   when they wish to go their way.
Make yourself entertaining   by words without guile   but do not make
    impertinent jokes   which people dislike.
Talk with them cheerfully   of things which give them pleasure   but when
    words might give offence   it is better to hold oneself silent.
Neither maintain opinions   on matters you have not perceived   as for gossiping
    and whispering   be on your guard, I tell you.
Do not associate with slaves   except during household affairs   they will draw
    you into disgrace   as perhaps I have told you.
Go not about with foolish people   who know not how to control themselves
    as to persons who are immodest   avoid any contact with them.
Little mother, listen to this counsel   for a woman there are five blessings
    whereby she may get peace   in the next world and this.
They are of God and His Prophet   her father and mother, she must know them
    the fifth is her husband   much has this been affirmed.
Let your husband be content with you   all the days that you dwell together
    on the day on which ye are chosen   may he be happy and attribute it to you.

Source: From Lyndon Harries, *Swahili Poetry,* © 1962. Reprinted by permission of Oxford University Press.

And should you die before him   do you seek his blessing   that you may go forth exalted   thus shall you find the right road.
And on the Day of Resurrection   the award is with your husband   he will be asked what he shall wish   and as he wishes it will be done.
If he wish that you go to Paradise   you will forthwith be brought there   if he says that you go to the fire   without escape you will be put there.
Live with him befittingly   do not provoke him to anger   if he rebukes you, do not answer back   try to control your tongue.
Keep faith with him   what he desires do not withhold   you and he dispute not together   a quarreller is always hurt.
When he goes out take leave of him   and when he returns pleasantly greet him   then set ready for him   a place of ease-taking.
When he rests do not betake yourself off   draw near to him, caress him   and for cooling air let him not lack   someone to fan him.
When he sleeps do not arouse him   and don't speak with a loud voice   stay there, rise not from your place   so that if he wakes he has to search for you.
When he awakes delay not   prepare a meal for him   and take care of his body perfuming him and bathing him.
Shave him that his skin be smooth   and let his beard be trimmed   let him enjoy ablution and incense   morning and evening.
Look after him like a child   who knows not how to speak   One thing you must look well to   the household expenses and income.
Be gay with him that he be amused   do not oppose his authority   If he brings you ill   God will defend you.

My child, be not a sloven   do as you see done   to sweep and washout the bathroom   do not scorn to do it at once.
As to bathing and perfuming yourself   and plaiting your hair   and stringing jessamine blossoms   and strewing them upon the coverlet.
Do you adorn yourself with finery   that you remain like a bride   put anklets upon your ankles   and bracelets upon your arms.
And necklace and clasp   remove them not from your neck   your body deny not the fragrance   of rosewater and dalia powder.
Remove not the rings from your fingers   nor lack henna on your fingernails   cease not to put wanda below your eyes   and upon your eyebrows.
Let your house be well kept   so that you honour your husband   when people foregather there   then will they bring you praise.
That which he desires in his heart   do you also follow that   as for a matter offensive to him   do not be the one to indulge in it.
Whenever you need to go out   be sure to ask leave   when you see that he is vexed   return and sit yourself at home.
Wait upon his permission   that he may be truly content   do not loiter by the way   when the fourth hour has passed.
And do not gossip by the way   nor uncover from within the *shiraa*   let your eyes be downcast   and your countenance modest.
Return quickly to your home   that you may sit with your lord   make ready cushions and rugs, so that you may take your ease together.
And exalt your husband   spread his praises abroad   but do not make obligations for him   which he cannot fulfil.
That which gives you, accept from him   with a heart that rejoices   what he does not (ask) of his own accord   you have no need to tell him.

When you look upon his face   reveal your teeth in a smile   that which he tells you hold to it   except to rebel against the Highest.
My child, be not sharp-tongued   be like me, your mother   I was married ten years   yet we did not quarrel one single day.
I was wed by your father   with happiness and laughter   we did not abase our mutual respect   all the days that we lived together.
Not one day did we quarrel   he met with no ill from me   and from him none did I encounter   until the time when he was chosen.
And when death came   he repeatedly told me his content   and resigned himself in peace to God   while my heart was filled with grief.
From that time unto this day   I yet cease not from lamentation   when I remember the ease   and plenty of our accustomed life.
If people heed one another   for ever they share fond memories   but those who strive against each other   regret it for eternity.
The instructions of your husband   with faithful care discharge them   and your kindred and relations   love them, I adjure you.
Whenever you see friends   who are your equals by birth   if they bid you welcome   hasten to visit them.
And if they lay out a meal   and you are asked, eat it then   but do not leave a long delay   before returning to your home.
And do not be discourteous   eat until you are satisfied   if not yet content, do not confess it   when told that the dish be removed.
All people who are safe to trust   at your home, then let them be friends   do not be fond of quarrelsome people   overcome them by avoiding them.
Do not love those who affect elegance   with the arrogance of wealth   while it despises the poor   and disparages to them their lot.
She who loves you, love her   she who dislikes you, go to her   by kindness disperse her ill-feeling   mayhap she will be appeased.
And when there comes one in need   my child, to you, do not embarrass her   with what skill you are able   hasten to assist her.
My child, hearken to these words   I pray you do not ignore me   you will behold the advantage of them   for the life to come and this.
This is the end of my words   directing you, my daughter   now I will entreat God   that He receive of me a prayer.
For all that we have said   a child of Adam is but empty folly   the Lord, He it is who is Powerful   to destroy and to preserve.
I pray to Thee, O Beneficent One   grant to me aid   for the words that are upon my tongue   and for all that are in my heart.
All things of which I have spoken   O Lord, receive in trust for me   and as to those which remain unsaid   I pray thee, grant me favour.
Take for me into Thy care my children   and my kinsman, a young brother   that their names may endure   and spread abroad in all lands.
O Lord, preserve Thou my kindred   and their children and mine   may they increase in this world   with help and prosperity.
And the company of Islam   O my Lord of mercy   may their needs be fulfilled   that their hearts may rejoice.
O Lord God, my children   I have given to Thee in trust   protect them, O Lord and Master   cease not to look after them.
I have given them to Thee in this world   That Thou protect and cherish them   grant them to me hereafter in Heaven   in the presence of the holy Prophet.

Look upon them with compassion   guide them in the right path   remove them from the troubles   of the next life and of this.
To Thee I cease not to pray   nor do I still my tongue   O Comforter and Protector   bring me to the end of my sufferings.
As I stand a suppliant   yield to me readily, force not upon me   a death without blessings   of pardon and salvation.
Remove from me the evil malady   which has forcibly seized upon me   my sins and ill-doings   O Lord, forgive to me.
Although things be hard for us to bear   yet to Thee they are but small matters   take from me the fever of sickness   mayest Thou relieve me speedily.
I pray to Thee, the All-Benevolent   ward off from me fears   by reason of the Day of Arafat   and the Festival of the Sacrifice.
By these glorious days   of the Pilgrimage and the Kaaba   save me, O Lord, save me   send down to me deliverance.
O God O God   O Lord O Lord   O Fulfilment of all desire   answer me as I call upon Thee.
I call upon Thee, O Lord God   by Thy beautiful Names   nine and ninety   one hundred less one.
So let me hearken to the learned   as they tell me, Know thou   this prayer of the Faith   if one prays, ever it is granted.
And I, who am Thy poor handmaiden   one burdened with many troubles
I pray Thee, lighten them   O Lord, do thou unburden me.
    I pray to Thee in haste   as to matters of which I cannot judge   do Thou bring to me every happiness   mayest Thou deliver me from evil.
O Lord, fulfil for me matters   which I cannot accomplish   nor can I think of even one of them   that they shall come to pass.
Lord, do thou cause me to rejoice   bring the good near to me   remove the evil from me   so that I do not meet with it.
Keep me safe in this world   among the number of the Faithful   that when I die I may go to Paradise   the abiding-place of the Saved.
I have composed this poem   amid trouble and grief   by Thy dispensation, O Judge   and by Thy decrees, All High.
    I have composed it in sickness   my heart is without understanding   read it, O true believers   that you may follow the true path.
And the reason for composing   is not poesy nor minstrelsy   I have a young innocent child   and I wish to instruct her.
And I desire to warn her   that mayhap she shall realize   and follow the Lord God   together with her man.

Read, all you women   so that you may understand   that you may bear no blame in the presence of God the Highest.
    Read, you who are sprouts of wheat   obey your menfolk   so that you may not be touched by the sorrows   of the after-life and of this.
She who obeys her husband   hers are honour and charm   wherever she shall go her fame is published abroad.
She who composed this poem   is one lonely and sorrowful   and the greater of her sins   Lord, Thou wilt her forgive.
O heart, these things of men I state   the Pen of God has written their fate (lit. got them)   and you, for certain, will be even as they   unless you have your own (belief, Islam) to which you hold fast.

O heart, beware, be not a firebrand   abandon false pride, hold to the right   your friends are saved, so be thou saved also   lest the fire of Hell take you.
Know that earth's day shall be changed   and the seven heavens will be moved from their place   the moon will be stilled and the sun   but fire and heat will not cease from us.
The day of the burning spleens inwardly   and people's roofs being torn off, where will you flee for succour?   show me a refuge that I can depend on it as well.
Consider the day when the multitudes shall stand   for every deed to be revealed   the time when the oppressed shall bend the knee   saying, O Lord, judge between him and me.
Judge me, for this man has oppressed me   by your judgement which is strict   and God the All-Powerful will judge   As he did him ill, so shall he pay.
The recompense for them who are oppressed   is not the nugget-gold nor washed gold   they take no money though they be given it   in nought but virtue is their payment.
And he who has neither merit nor reward   is fastened by the jaw like unto a horse   and is made to carry the sins of the oppressed   and is told, Come on, carry them for him.
O heart, take thought of Jahannam   with its chains and ropings   when the Judge doth proclaim to it   it says, I am here, let me give forth answering cry.
Cometh the trumpet's fearsome blast   sounding like the voice of an ass   the sinner cringes, with the face of an ape   the fire and the flames engulf him.
Then there is Hawiya, listen hard   it is a fierce fire, it has no repose   when the rebel enters it he tastes conflict   he finds his breath fail him.
The fire of Sairi, understand it well   it is a fierce fire in flames   there is much smoke and bubbling   serpents and pythons dwell there.
And the fire of Ladha, also, listen   if cast in that fire at once you burn   you find that lumps of flesh come off   you see your joints split apart.
Know again about this same Hutama   its glowing fire with its roaring   it breaks the bones, it rives the flesh   the brains and pus gush out.
Now I will end, now I put the ending   he who follows and attends these words shall gain at length a good end   O Lord, we pray Thee, grant us this.
O Lord, bless him who is the composer (of this poem)   and he who has finished (these verses is) a humble bard   Prayer and peace be their safeguards (who read them)   O Lord, let thy favour come down to them.

TEXT 81

The Masai of Kenya: Proverbs[1]

The Masai, noted within the Western imagination as tall, lanky warriors, represent a pastoralist people who inhabit the Great Rift valley of Kenya. Throughout their history cattle has constituted the basis of family wealth to the point where they evolved cultural mores, according to Professor Robert July, that "forbade the taking of things from the earth."[2] As a nomadic population, the Masai live in roving bands and subsist on the meat and milk of their herds.

The language of the Masai belongs to the Nilotic linguistic family, which places them in a closer cultural proximity to the Luo of Kenya and Uganda, and the Nuer of southern Sudan than the Bantu-speaking Kikuyu, their immediate Kenyan neighbors. But not surprisingly, the Masai and the Kikuyu have through geographic proximity and occasional intermarriage come to share a number of common customs. As is customary in a number of African societies, age grades play a role in social stratification. Additionally, a man is allowed to marry once he has ascended from boy to warrior caste. As is common with pastoralist societies, the Masai are patrilineal.

The myths, legends, and proverbs of the East African Masai, as in most oral societies, convey the ethical values and religious beliefs which define their culture.

---

[1]Naomi Kipury, *Oral Literature of the Masai* (London: Heinemann Educational Books, Ltd, 1983), pp. 173–77.
[2]Robert W. July, *A History of the African People* (New York: Charles Scribner's Sons, 1980), p. 139.

PROVERBS ON WISDOM AND FOOLISHNESS

One head does not consume all knowledge
(There are limits to one person's knowledge.)

Foolishness kills (attacks) he who owns it.
A foolish person gets himself into trouble through his own foolishness.
(We begin by being foolish, but we later become knowledgeable.)

There is no one who is clever when he is cheated.
(A man may think he is clever, but someone else could be a better trickster.)

It is the eye which has travelled that is clever.
(People are known to gain experience and knowledge when they travel outside their own home areas.)

Even the circumciser is directed.
(Even a specialist, like the circumciser, could go wrong and needs to be directed.)

Wisdom does not have a white head (grey hair).
(This proverb has two meanings:
(i) Wisdom does not age;
(ii) Wisdom is not restricted to the aged.)

The ones who are seated are clever and so are the ones arriving.
(Same as the proverb above.)

An adviser does not advise himself.
(Even a clever person may require assistance from others.)

PROVERBS ON PATIENCE, IMPATIENCE, AND PERSEVERANCE

The stomach does not wait for a pot that is cooking.
(Some issues need urgent attention.)

Do not pick the stomach before it is ready.
(When it is still cooking.)

Do not be impatient, but wait until an issue has taken place.
(Often said when a person acts or speaks on an issue before it is even mentioned.)

Undergoing treatment hurts, but it also helps.
(You have to go through difficulty in order to achieve the positive things in life.)

It is not the rushing that matters, it is doing it properly.
(Slow but sure; or in Swahili: *Haraka haraka haina baraka.*)

Water cannot be drunk while it is flowing.
(You have to wait until you have seen the direction matters are taking before you react.)

Source: From Naomi Kipury, *Oral Literature of the Masai,* © 1983. Reprinted by permission of Heinemann Educational Books (E.A.) Ltd.

PROVERBS ON FAIRNESS

Kill me but bring my intestines back home.
(If you must perform a good or bad deed, remember to observe the proper rites and behaviour; do not over-react in the heat of the moment.)

Do not smear me with the dirt from the honey that I did not eat.
(Do not draw in innocent people, if you get into trouble.)

Poison does not write on the thigh.

PROVERBS OF PUNCTUALITY AND SEQUENCE

It cannot be treated when the bones are still there.

You cannot pull out the meat from the inside when the outside one is still there.

A new idea (custom) follows an old one.
(If an idea is good it is copied and followed.)

The hare has gone before the club.
(In other words, you acted later than you should have, therefore, you had better time your actions properly if you wish to attain a certain goal.)

The day (sun) does not eat news.
(You can't turn back the clock while you are doing something, for the day (time) passes. Said when one is slow or slack or when he has many other things to do in the day.)

One who has left (on a journey) does not make concrete plans.
(Because he may never know what may happen.)

TEXT 82

The Kikuyu of Kenya: The Lost Sister— Two Versions

The Kikuyu represent the largest ethnicity in Kenya. This Bantu-speaking people occupy the highland area of south-central Kenya, and are believed to have migrated to this region from Somalia in the thirteenth century. As iron age farmers since early times, they have traditionally cultivated millet, sorghum, and yams. Political organization was decentralized, where even village life was rejected in favor of individual homesteads. However, the culture and religious practices, rather than political structures among the Kikuyu, created a unified sense of nation.

It was the Kikuyu farmers who during the colonial period organized themselves into various groups, including the Mau Maus in the 1950s to resist European expropriation of their fertile farmlands. Institution of the age grade which furnished the capstone to national solidarity—a system which the Kikuyu shared with their Masai neighbors with whom they warred, traded, and occasionally intermarried.

THE VERSION BY NJARGE

A long time ago, a young warrior and his sister lived together in a house. They lived alone, because their parents had died when they were children. The house stood by itself; there were no other homesteads nearby. The name of the young man was Wagacharaibu, and the girl was called Mweru. Wagacharaibu had beautiful hair that reached to his waist, and all the young women admired him greatly, so that he often went away from home a long distance to see his friends, and Mweru was left by herself.

Source: From W. Scoresby and Katherine Routledge, *With A Prehistoric People: The Akikuyu of British East Africa,* © 1910, Edward Arnold Publisher, London.

One day, when Wagacharaibu came back after he had been away, Mweru said to him, "Three men came here last night when I was all alone. Each had a club, and each had a spear. If you go away and leave me alone, I know that they will come back and carry me off."

But Wagacharaibu only said, "You talk nonsense," and he went away again as before.

The three men with the three clubs and the three spears came back, as Mweru had said they would, and they seized the girl by the neck and the legs, and they lifted her up and carried her away.

When Wagacharaibu came home again, he went to the house and found it empty. As he went to the house, he heard a girl's voice crying on the opposite hillside.

The voice was that of his sister, and it said, "Wagacharaibu, men have come and carried me away. Go into the house, you will find the gruel on the stool."

Wagacharaibu cried aloud, and said, "Who will shave the front of my head now that you are gone? We have no neighbors!"

He plunged into the grass after Mweru. The farther he went, the farther she was carried away from him. He heard her voice, and she heard his voice, but they could not see one another. He followed for a month, and he became very hungry. He wore a hat such as men used to wear in the old days: it was a piece of goatskin, and it had two holes cut in it and strings to tie under the chin, and the skin stood out over the forehead so that rain could not touch the face. One may see such hats even now in the mountains where there are many trees and much rain, and also among the Masai. Because he was very hungry, Wagacharaibu cut a piece of the leather from his hat and ate it, and he felt strong again.

He went on for a second month, and again a third month, until the hat was all finished. Then he took his garment of skin and ate that, and so he went on a fourth month, and a fifth month, until he had travelled a year and four months, and his cape was finished.

He was again hungry. When he came to a big homestead, he went inside, and he saw a woman cooking food. He begged for some food, and she gave him some. She did not hand him the food in a nice vessel, but in a broken piece of an old pot. That night, he slept there, and the next morning he went out with the little son of the woman to frighten the birds from the crops, because the grain was nearly ripe. He took stones and threw them at the birds. As he threw a stone, he would say,

"Fly away, fly away, little bird,
As Mweru has flown away,
Never to be seen again."

The little boy listened. He went home and, when Wagacharaibu was not near, he told his mother the words the stranger had said, but she paid no attention to the tale of her son and did not listen to it.

The next day, the same thing happened, and the third day the woman herself went to the fields, and she heard the words of Wagacharaibu:

"Fly away, fly away, little bird,
As Mweru has flown away,
Never to be seen again."

The woman's name was Mweru, and she said, "Why do you say those words to the birds?"

He said, "I once had a sister named Mweru. She was lost, and I have followed her many months and years, but I have not seen her again."

The woman put her hand over her eyes and wept, for she was his sister.

She said, "Are you truly my brother?" for she did not recognize him, so changed was he by his long travels. She said, "Your hair is unkempt, and your clothes are not as they were. I did not know you. But you shall be once more dressed as in time past, and I shall see if you are really my brother, Wagacharaibu."

She went to her husband, who had carried her away in the old days, and she got four sheep and three goats. The four sheep were killed, and Wagacharaibu ate of the flesh and became big and strong once more. His sister took some of the fat and dressed his hair, and put fat on his shoulders. Of the three goats, two of which were black and one white, she made a cape. Then she took a spear and gave it to him. It was the spear her husband had carried when he came to the little house when she was alone, she gave that spear to her brother. She put on his arms brass and iron armlets, and ornaments on his legs and around his neck.

Then she said, "Now I see that you are indeed my brother, Wagacharaibu."

The husband of Mweru loved Wagacharaibu, and he gave him twenty goats and three oxen, which was much more than the dowry of his sister, but he gave it because of the affection he bore him. He built him a house in the homestead, and gave him thirty goats as dowry for a wife.

Wagacharaibu brought a young woman to the house, and his goats increased and multiplied. He took ten of the goats and his sister's husband gave him twenty in addition, and he had the dowry for a second wife.

Wagacharaibu did not go back to his old life, but lived with the sister he had lost and with her husband.

THE VERSION BY NAGATUU

Once there were a brother and sister who lived together. Their mother died, leaving many goats, and the brother looked after the goats in the daytime. But in the evening, he went away from home, because he was very handsome and had many friends. The name of the girl was Wachera; the name of the brother was Wamwea.

One day, when her brother returned, Wachera said to him, "Two men were here yesterday. If you go away and leave me, they will carry me away."

But he said, "You talk nonsense."

She said, "I am speaking the truth. When they take me, I shall take with me a gourd full of sap that is like fat, and I shall let it drop along the path, so that you can follow my trail."

That night, when Wamwea brought the goats home, Wachera made a great feast and gruel, but he went away again.

When Wamwea came back the next morning, he found the homestead empty, for his sister had been carried away as she had said. But he saw the track where, drop by drop, she had let fall the sap that is like fat. Wamwea followed over hill and dale, and ever and again he heard her voice crying from the opposite side of the hill.

"Follow after where you see the trail."

The following day, the sap began to take root and to spring up into little plants, but he did not see his sister.

At last, he returned to his home to herd the livestock. He took the oxen and goats out to feed, but he had no one to prepare food for him when he returned at night, and if he himself prepared the food there was no one to care for the stock. So he killed a goat and ate it, and when it was finished he killed another, and so on until all the goats were finished. Then he killed and ate the oxen one by one; they lasted him months and years, for the herd was large. But at last they were all gone, and then he thought of his sister.

The plants that had sprung up were by this time grown to trees. They marked the way she had gone, so he journeyed for one and a half months. At the end of that time, he came to a stream. By the stream were two children getting water, and he said to the younger, "Give me some water in your gourd."

But the child refused.

The elder child spoke to the younger, and said, "Give the stranger water to drink, because our mother said, 'If you ever see a stranger coming by way of the trees he is my brother.'"

So Wamwea and the children went up to the homestead, and he waited outside. Wachera came out, and he knew her at once. But she did not know him, for he was not dressed as before, with ochre and fat. He came into her house, and she gave him food, not in a good vessel but in a potsherd. He slept in the house, but on the floor, not on the bed.

Next day, he went out with the children to drive the birds from the crops. As he threw a stone, he would say,

> "Fly away, little bird,
> As Wachera flew away
> And never returned."

Another bird would come, and he would throw another stone and say the same words again. This happened the next day, and the next, for a whole month. The children heard him and so did others.

They said, "Why does he say the name 'Wachera'?"

They went and told their mother.

At last, she came and waited in the grass. She listened to his words, and said, "Surely this is my brother, Wamwea."

She went back to the house and sent for a young man. She told him to go and tell Wamwea to come to her, for, she said, 'He is my brother."

The young man went and told Wamwea what his sister had said, but he refused to come.

He said, "I have dwelt in the home of my sister, and she has given me no cup for my food but a potsherd," and he would not go back.

The young man returned to Wachera, and told her what her brother had said.

She said, "Take ten goats, and go again and tell him to come to me."

The young man took the ten goats, and said, "Your sister has sent these ten goats."
But Wamwea refused, and the young man returned.
Wachera said, "Take ten oxen, and give them to my brother."
But Wamwea would not return.
Wachera sent him ten cows, and ten more cows, and still Wamwea refused to come in.
Wachera told her husband how she had found her brother, and how he would not be reconciled to her.
Her husband said, "Send him even more beasts."
So Wachera sent ten more cows, then ten more, until Wamwea had received forty cows, in addition to the goats and the oxen that Wachera had sent earlier.
The heart of Wamwea relented then, and he went into the house of his sister.
She killed a goat, and took the fat and dressed his hair and his shoulders, for, she said, "I did not know you, you were not adorned as before."
After Wamwea had been reconciled to his sister, he decided that he should have eight wives, so Wachera's husband sent to all his relatives in the area, and they brought in goats for the dowry. Wamwea provided a dowry for eight young women; some dowries were thirty goats, others forty. Other relatives came; they built for the wives eight houses near the dwelling of Wamwea.
So Wamwea and his wives lived near the homestead of his sister.

TEXT 83

King Macemba of the Yao (Tanzania): Facing Invasion[1]

The Bantu-speaking Yao people who inhabit southern Tanzania had over the centuries transformed their primary economic livelihood from ivory-hunting to that of long distance traders, whose commercial relations tied the interior to the coastal city-state of Kilwa.

However, in the late nineteenth century, Germany's empire-building impulses in East Africa brought it into direct conflict with the Yao. Macemba or Machemba, the Yao ruler, writing in Swahili, composed a stern letter to Hermann von Wissmann, commander of the German forces.

I have listened to your words but can find no reason why I should obey you—I would rather die first. I have no relations with you and cannot bring it to my mind that you have given me so much as a *pesa* [fraction of a rupee] or the quarter of a *pesa* or a needle or a thread. I look for some reason why I should obey you and find not the smallest. If it should be friendship that you desire, then I am ready for it, today and always; but to be your subject, that I cannot be . . . If it should be war you desire, then I am ready, but never to be your subject . . . I do not fall at your feet, for you are God's creature just as I am . . . I am sultan here in my land. You are sultan there in yours. Yet listen, I do not say to you that you should obey me; for I know that you are a free man . . . As for me, I will not come to you, and if you are strong enough, then come and fetch me . . .

---

[1]Basil Davidson, *The African Past* (New York: Curtis Brown, Ltd., 1964), p. 358.
Source: From Basil Davidson, *The African Past,* Copyright © 1964 by Basil Davidson. Reprinted by permission of Curtis Brown, Inc.

TEXT 84

The Shambaa of Tanzania: The Kilindi Are Born Liars

from The Mbegha Myth[1]

The Shambaa of northeastern Tanzania and southern Kenya are today a relatively small (numbering 272,000) Bantu-speaking population of agriculturalists. Their principal crops include maize, cassava, pigeon peas, and beans. Sometime around the eighteenth century certain clans within the Shambaa ethnic group consolidated the diverse village communities of their region into a centralized state. Regional commerce in salt and iron enriched the coffers of this primarily agricultural state.

Steven Feierman in his work *The Shambaa Kingdom* outlines the founding myth of that society, recited in the Shambaa language:

> Mbegha was a hunter who used dogs to hunt wild pigs in the land of Ngulu, south of Shambaai. He was denied his rightful share of an inheritance by his lineage mates who said that he was a kigego, that is, a mystically dangerous being. Because as an infant he had cut his upper teeth first, his presence was causing his kinsmen to die. Mbegha fled at night and sought refuge soon after at a place called Kilindi, where he made blood partnership with a son of the chief.[2]

Thus begins the saga of Mbegha, whose heroic and adventurous exploits eventually led the Shambaa to crown him their king.

---

[1]Steven Feierman, *The Shambaa Kingdom: A History* (Madison: University of Wisconsin Press, 1974), p. 162.
[2]Ibid., pp. 43–44.

"The Kilindi are born liars. Do not rely on the word of any of them, it will not be true. A Kilindi will take two stones and hit you with one, and if you ask him why he hit you with a stone, he will show you the other and say, with what did I hit you? A stone? but here is my stone. That is the way they act. Now we agree to do as [Chanyeghea] asks; but when he is in power and has the dominion he will turn on us and say Pay me your dead. You have killed my uncles, you have taken their property, you have sold my brothers, you have given my uncles' wives in marriage, now hand over the adulterers. . . . Now we have driven out the Kilindi, we have taken their property and given their wives to others. We have become their enemies and even if we accept this matter we will never make with them any agreement whatever. That is our decision."

Source: Reprinted from Steven Feierman, *The Shambaa Kingdom,* © 1974, University of Wisconsin Press.

TEXT 85

The Kamba of Kenya and Tanzania: Medical Treatments[1]

The Kamba who inhabit the region to the east of present-day Nairobi represent the fourth largest ethnic group in Kenya, after the Kikuyu, Luhya, and Luo. Their traditional medical practitioners are noted throughout the region. The medical treatments presented in the following selection reflect the accumulated knowledge of traditional healers passed down intergenerationally from earliest times. Even so, the form in which they are here offered represent the field work of Professor Charles M. Good in the Kilungu Hills east of Nairobi between June 1977 and July 1978.

ILLNESSES AND REMEDIES RECOMMENDED BY TWO KILUNGU HERBALISTS

The following lists contain information on the uses of specific plant medicines (*miti shamba*) prescribed by Nzeki and Kutenga. The latter are the fictive names of two persons who were among the most professionally active herbalists (*akima wa miti*) practicing in Kilungu Hills in 1978. These lists represent a portion of the material acquired through several hours and multiple sessions of systematic questioning and discussion with each practitioner. Both men were generous with their time and patient in accommodating us with thoughtful answers to the numerous questions put to them. The lists contain only a portion of the illnesses that TMPs [traditional medical practitioners] in Kilungu collectively treat. However, they are fairly representative and include most of

---

[1]Charles M. Good, *Ethnomedical Systems in Africa: Patterns of Traditional Medicine in Rural and Urban Kenya* (New York: The Guilford Press, 1987), Appendix.
Source: From Charles M. Good, *Ethnomedical Systems in Africa,* © 1987. Reprinted by permission of The Guilford Press.

the commonest conditions presented to local herbalists. In Kutenga's case a few therapeutic tools and first aid procedures are also included.

Extensive, additional research is necessary to determine the degree to which these combinations of drug plants are typical among Kilungu TMPs or unique to specific individuals. The value of these lists is that they provide scholars, and those who make decisions about national and local health programs, with otherwise scarce empirical information about diseases, illness syndromes, and therapeutics at the community level.

Kutenga's Remedies

1. Headache (*kwalwa ni mutwe*).
2. "Peptic ulcer" (*kavoo/kavaso*).
3. Fever (*ndetema*).
4. "Pneumonia" (*kyambo*).
5. Edema (*mwimbo*).
6. "Syphilis" (*teko*).
7. Gonorrhea (*kisonono*).
8. Continuous menstruation (*kuua nthakame kuma ukani*). Juices in the stem of *mwany'a nthenge,* a climbing plant, are squeezed into patient's mouth. Patient also chews bark of *muthika* (*Warburgia ugandensis?*) and swallows the juices.
9. Infertility (*ngungu*). Juices of *mwany'a nthenge* plant are swallowed. Barks of *mwaitha* (*Dalbergia lactea?* or *Entada leptostachya?*) and *mukolekya* are crushed and soaked in water, which is thereafter drunk.
10. Epilepsy (*mung'athuko*). Leaves of *musanduku* (*Eucalyptus sp.*) are used.
11. Stomach ache (*kwalwa ni ivu*). Leaves of *muteta* (*Strychnos henningsii?*), *mukenia* (*Polygala sphenoptera?*), *mutula* (*Ximenia caffra?*), and *muthaa* are squeezed and the juices swallowed.
12. Chest pain (*kwalwa ni kithui*). Root of *mwany'a nthenge* plant are dried and crushed and mixed with water.
13. Infant gastroenteritis (*nyunyi*). Barks of *mukenea* (*Fagara chalybea?*) and *mukolekya* are crushed and mixed with water. *Mathimoti* (oil-like medicine available in shops) is applied on depressed fontanelle and chest.
14. Swelling in abdomen associated with a nonspecific disease of the pancreas (*ndumo*). Root of *mwany'a nthenge* is dried, crushed, and added to water. Patient drinks this.
15. Pain in joints (*mutambuko*). Root of *mulingula* is dried, crushed, and added to water. Patient drinks this.
16. Diarrhea (*kwituua*). Root of *mulingula* is dried, crushed, and added to water. Juices squeezed from roots of *kyuvi* and *mutula* are swallowed.
17. Whooping cough (*mutitino*). Barks of *mukoleyka* and *muthika* (*Warburgia ugandensis?*) are crushed and added to soup or water.
18. Excessive bleeding. Juice of sugar cane is squeezed on the wound to stop bleeding.

19. Eliminate numbness. Stem of *mukungula,* a climbing plant, is dried and crushed to a powder, mixed with milk and drunk. "It helps the blood to circulate and removes numbness from a part of the body."
20. Local anesthesia. Leaves and stems of *isongosya* and *isoambumbu* tree are warmed near a fire; white latexlike substance is then squeezed out and eventually applied to affected area for about 5 min. Numbness lasts up to 1 hr.
21. Repair of wound—for example, in case of cut on lower leg. Roots of *mukulila* are dried and crushed into powder form, which is applied to wound and covered with gauze. If this does not work well, add stems of *mukoiwa.*
22. Snake bite (*kuumwa ni nzoka*). First spits on wound. A powder made from crushed and dried stem of *ndonga* tree is then rubbed into wound. If fang marks are not large, small cuts are made at the site and the powder is rubbed into them.

Kutenga mentions 28 different plants and one shop preparation (*mathimoti*) in the list above. Only seven of these plants are used for more than one illness or treatment. They are *mwany'a nthenge* (six illnesses or treatments), *mukolekya* (four), *mulingula* (three), *mukenia* (two), *muthika* (two), *mwaitha* (two), and *mikoi wa ulenge.*

Nzeki's Remedies

1. Headache (*kwalwa ni mutwe*).
2. "Peptic ulcer" (*kavoo/kavaso*).
3. Fever (*ndetema*).
4. "Pneumonia" (*kyambo*).
5. Edema (*mwimbo*).
6. "Syphilis" (*teko*).
7. Gonorrhea (*kisonono*).
8. Worms (*nzoka sya nda*). For adults, roots of *mukolekya* and *muuka (Microglossa densiflora?*) and stems of *musoka* are boiled. Patient drinks the decoction. For children, leaves and bark of *muteta (Strychnos henningsii?*) and stems of *muuku* are boiled and patient drinks decoction.
9. Pancreatic (nonspecific) disease (*wasyungu*). First, the herbalist lifts up the sternum bone (*kavoo*). A powdered medicine prepared from the crushed and burnt root of *mulingula* is then added to water, tea, or porridge and given to patient.
10. Eye disease/conjunctivitis (*uwau wa metho*). Leaves of *mukengeka (Cassia singueana?*) are squeezed and juice is dropped into patient's eyes. Juice of *muti (Aspilia pluriseta* or *A. mossambiensis*) is commonly used in treating children.
11. Teething problems (*uwau wa ini*). Applies soda ash (*iati*) on child's gums.
12. Stiff neck/transient deviation of neck (*mukiki*). Applies saliva on patient's neck and massages the area.
13. Upper abdominal-rib cage swelling (*iwethyu*). Associated with *kavoo/kavaso.* Patient is given a mixture of *mulingula, mutheketha, kauthilu,* and *kiema uvunyie.*

14. Kidney disease (nonspecific) (*mbio*). Herbalist (1) applies oil on his hands and lifts up small ribs which are pushing into the flesh covering the kidneys; or (2) puts a stone in cold water and then places it on the affected region. It then heals.
15. Liver disease (nonspecific) (*itema*). Leaves of *muthiati* are boiled and patient drinks the decoction.

PART TEN

Southern Africa

Archaeological evidence suggests that a population of hunter-gatherers and pastoralists known as the San peoples, of which the !Kung formed a subgroup, were the earliest settlers of southern Africa. Their languages constituted the Khoisan linguistic group, identified by the unique consolidated "click" sounds that eventually found their way into some of the Bantu languages as well. The Khoisan hunter-gatherers and pastoralists sometimes traded with the Bantu-speaking farming populations

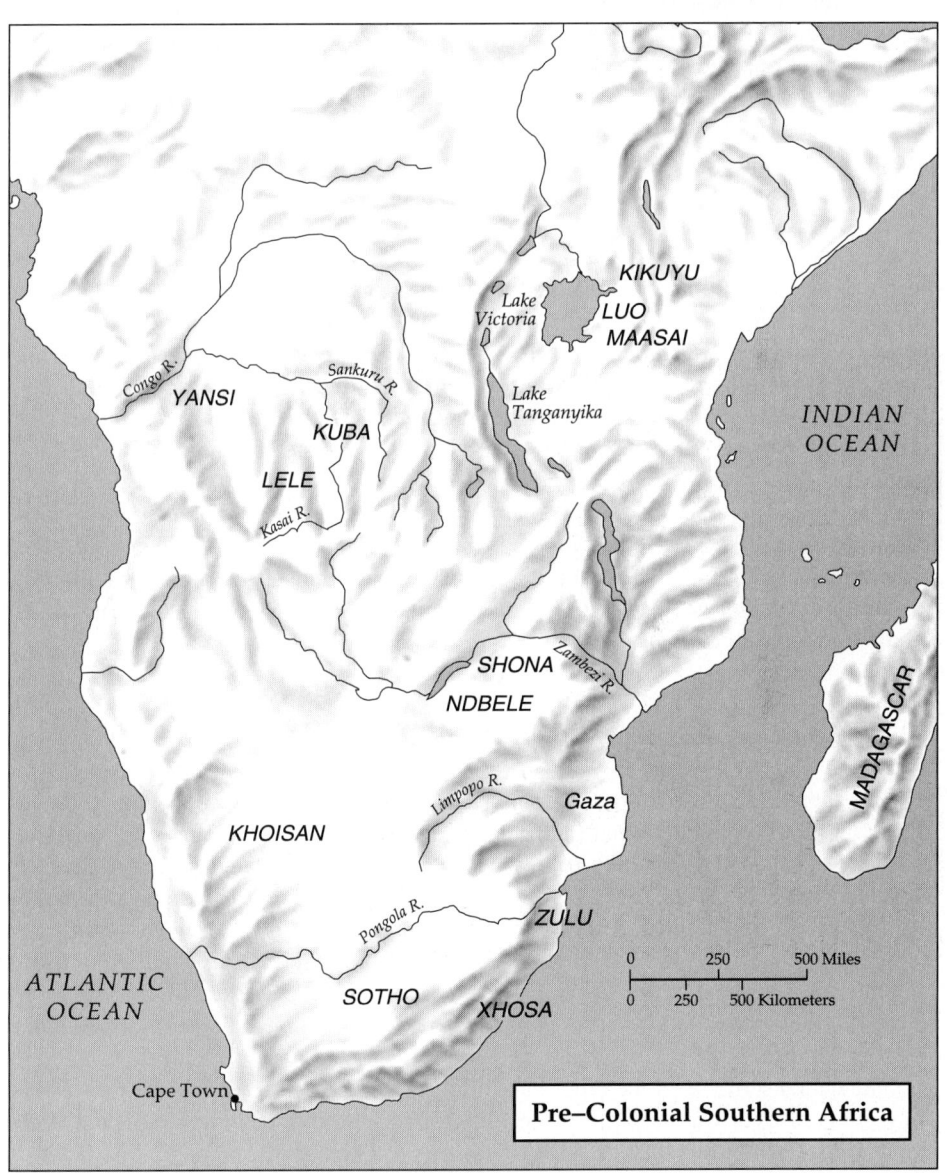

who had perhaps as early as the first centuries of the Christian era begun migrating from East Africa into this southern region.

The Bantu-speaking populations of farmers were composed of two primary linguistic branches. The first were the Sotho–Tswana peoples of Lesotho, Botswana, and South Africa. The second group encompassed the Nguni-speaking peoples, that is, the Zulu and Xhosa of South Africa and Ndebele of Zimbabwe. In the territory of present-day South Africa, the Sotho–Tswana traditionally inhabited the plateau region, known as the high veld to the west of the Drakensburg mountain range, while their Nguni-speaking neighbors occupied the eastern side, known as Natal. These peoples spoke "click" languages that suggest a close tie and history of intermarriage with the Khoisan populations from which these unique linguistic styles apparently emanated.

Among the Sotho–Tswana-speaking peoples, a cosmogony revolved around the existence of a single supreme being, *Modimo*. He controlled the weather, particularly the rain, and was ultimately responsible for good harvests or famine. But he could only be contacted through the medium of the spirits of the ancestors and the intermediary intervention of the chief, as spiritual leader of his people. Initiation ceremonies were central in defining the tradition from childhood into full adult life and marriageability. Every few years initiates of about the same age were drawn from families right across the chiefdom. After the ceremonies, the newly initiated adults were formed into age-classes.

The Nguni populations shared many of the same cultural characteristics as the Sotho–Tswana. Like the Sotho–Tswana, the religious beliefs of the Nguni centered around the worship of a supreme God and contact with the spiritual world through the medium of one's ancestors. The social division into age-classes was also a critical feature of Nguni social structure.

THE EUROPEAN PENETRATION OF SOUTH AFRICA

In 1652 the Dutch East India Company under the leadership of Jan van Riebeeck founded a refreshment station at the Cape of Good Hope on the southern tip of Africa in order to provision its seamen following maritime routes around Africa to Asia. In the century that succeeded this Dutch settlement, the Khoisan populations suffered the greatest tragedy of their history. A series of wars launched by the Dutch against this indigenous people, aided by a smallpox epidemic brought by European ships to the settlement, led to the extermination of large portions of the Khoisan. Many of the survivors were enslaved, and others were forced to migrate into the desolate Kalahari desert of Namibia.

The Dutch settlers, on the other hand, flourished in these fertile agricultural lands. They evolved over time a cultural and linguistic identity separate from that of the motherland. Calling themselves Afrikaners, they spoke a new language, "Afrikaans," derived from its Dutch linguistic roots. The growth of Afrikaner agricultural settlements soon brought these Europeans into conflict with the Bantu-speaking African farmers, namely the Zulu and Xhosa. As both Africans and Europeans vied for farmland, a series of wars erupted beginning in 1779. While the Africans were able to hold the Europeans at bay initially, the tide eventually turned because of the superior European military technology.

The British, however, succeeded in seizing control of the Cape Colony from the Dutch-Afrikaners in 1795, creating a second European wave of settlers to the southern African region. By the early nineteenth century, the British also launched a series of wars against the Nguni-speaking Xhosa in order to dislodge the Africans from fertile farmlands coveted by the Europeans. Because the Afrikaners, also known as Boers, were also anxious to escape British domination, they launched a large-scale migration into the interior which brought them into direct military confrontation first with the Xhosa and then with the more northern-based Zulu.

These Afrikaner migrations, which came to be known as the Boer Trek, established permanent European colonies in the interior. In response to the resultant land pressures, the Zulu nation emerged in the Natal region between the Drakensburg Mountains and the coast, under the leadership of Shaka, who was born around 1787, son of Zulu chief Senzangakhona and his wife, Nandi. A military genius, Shaka reorganized the social institutions of the Zulu in order to reconstitute his society into a military machine operating under a concept of total warfare. The age groupings within traditional Nguni society were transformed into permanent age regiments. Shaka also instituted the military tactic of stabbing enemy soldiers rather than merely throwing spears from a safe distance. The expansion of the Zulu kingdom came at the expense of its African neighbors, precipitating the *mfecane,* that is "the crushing." It constituted a series of wars fought between 1816 and 1840 by Shaka against the neighboring populations, including the Xhosa, who were the southernmost of the Nguni peoples.

Tensions between African and Europeans escalated once again in the late nineteenth century on account of the discovery of diamonds and gold in a region of South Africa inhabited by Nguni-speaking populations. By the 1870s the British had succeeded in subduing African resistance in South Africa. The British industrialist, Cecil Rhodes, organized the De Beers company to exploit the diamond mines in those territories in which the Afrikaners had expropriated land from the Nguni-speaking Africans. The British then initiated a new conflict, the Boer War (1899–1902), in which they succeeded in gaining dominion over the Afrikaner inhabitants of the mineral-rich provinces of the Transvaal and the Orange Free State.

The English-speaking South Africans of British descent maintained political control until 1949 when the Afrikaners regained the reins of government and attempted to subdue permanently the African political threat through the creation of a rigid system of segregation called *apartheid.* However, in one of the most remarkable twists of history this century has seen, the African resistance to European control finally prevailed when the leader of the African National Congress who had been jailed for 27 years, Nelson Mandela, won a democratic election in South Africa, thus becoming the first African president of the country in 1990.

GREAT ZIMBABWE AND MONOMATAPA

North of South Africa, in the former British colony of Rhodesia (and modern day Zimbabwe), lay the stone-walled ruins of Great Zimbabwe, a prosperous state dating from the ninth century. Its vibrant economy was based on the trade in gold, which was extracted from its mines and transported to the Swahili traders on the East African coast. It was finally abandoned around A.D. 1450 possibly because of the exhaustion of its timber, gold, and salt resources. J. D. Fage explains in *A History of Africa* that

> The most splendid achievements at Great Zimbabwe can be dated to the fourteenth and fifteenth centuries, and are associated with growing prosperity, indicated by the presence for the first time in any large quantity of imported porcelains and beads.[1]

Because it was difficult for European colonizers of the last century to imagine that the Shona ethnicity inhabiting the region could have created these structures in ancient times, colonial historians posited a wild array of theories to explain these sophisticated ruins. The suppositions ranged from beliefs that the populations of Great Zimbabwe were a lost tribe of Israel, to a wandering band of Portuguese settlers, to, according to one "authoritative" report, a landing site for extraterrestrials. Contemporary scholars, however, agree that the iron-using populations of Great Zimbabwe represent the ancestors of today's Shona-speaking peoples who inhabit the region. While the intellectual traditions of that era are lost, the cultural activity of the Shona-speaking populations of Zimbabwe from pottery design to gold ornamentation and folk narrative remain a vibrant legacy of their flourishing past.

Monomatapa, a state consolidated by King Matope before his death in A.D. 1480, arose about 300 miles to the north of Great Zimbabwe. As was the case with many other societies, the inhabitants of Monomatapa practiced divine kingship whereby

> The king was revered as a god and lived on a most lavish scale with his court of wives, concubines, and officials. His audiences were held in public but he himself remained behind a screen which concealed him from suppliants who came creeping and clapping their hands to show proper homage.[2]

The Portuguese, who had arrived on the East African coast in the early 1500s, launched an invasion force against Monomatapa, hoping to seize control of the gold mines. However, their expeditionary force fell to disease and local African resistance, leaving the state of Monomatapa beyond European control during that period. The regions encompassed by ancient Zimbabwe and Monomatapa became the British colonial possession of Rhodesia after the suppression of Shona and Ndebele resistance in the late 1890s.

---

[1] J. D. Fage, *A History of Africa,* 2nd ed. (London: Unwin Hyman, 1988), p. 131.
[2] Robert W. July, *A History of the African People* (New York: Scribner, 1970).

TEXT 86

The Shona of Zimbabwe: The Clan Praises of the Daughters of the Moyo Wakapiwa Clan[1]

The Bantu-speaking Shona peoples represent the primary ethnic group inhabiting the southeast African nation of Zimbabwe. They are noted for their cultivation of millet, sorghum, corn, peanuts, and potatoes. Cattle are kept for purposes of calculating a family's wealth and paying the bride-price rather than strictly for economic breeding purposes.

The early history of the Shona centers around the state of Great Zimbabwe, named for the stone enclosures whose hauntingly impressive ruins survive to this day. That kingdom emerged sometime before the fourteenth century. It strengthened its local economy of agriculture and cattle breeding by trading gold mined in its territories and transported to the Swahili city-state of Kilwa on the East African coast. The site of Great Zimbabwe was abandoned around A.D. 1450 due to the depletion of its gold and salt resources.

Shortly thereafter, a Shona-populated successor state emerged to the north of Great Zimbabwe, which came to be known as Monomatapa. It too grew prosperous from the gold trade and waged several successful wars against the Portuguese who had established a trading presence on the East African coast in the late sixteenth century.

---

[1]A. C. Hodza, *Shona Praise Poetry* (London: Oxford University Press, 1979), pp. 246–48.

However, by the seventeenth century that African state had sunk into permanent decline, its civil authority undermined by dynastic disputes, internal strife, and continuing Portuguese intrusions.

The Clan Praises of the Daughters of the Moyo Wakapiwa Clan

Thank you, Lady Moyo,
    Whose breast hangs down
    Like a fruit of the sausage tree;
    Grasping it, it is just like someone climbing a tree;
    Suckling a child, you have to keep holding it;
    If you let it fall, it presses upon the child and it dies.
You have done a kindness, Lady Moyo loved by everyone,
    Whose breast covers your husband,
    So that he forgets his home;
    Lady Moyo,
    Those who speak about you say,
    "The beauty of the Lady Moyo
    is in her breast.
    But to feel her leg
    Gives pleasure that lasts a mile."
    Lady Moyo Mukonde,
    Whose teeth are like milk,
    And whose face is black and glossy as a starling;
    Lady Moyo,
    Whenever you are sad, the sky seems overcast too.
You have done a service, Daughter of Zirowosehwa;
    My dear one, close as a bead-belt to me.
It is your kindness, Lady Moyo;
    You sprinkled the ant-heap with your spittle,
    and it was soaked through and through.
    It was hoed to plant food,
    and the people ate and were filled;
    Lady Moyo;
    You never go to bed hungry.
You have done a kindness, One on whom everyone relies;
    Wherever you go there is acclamation.
A service has been rendered, Lady Moyo;
    Soothing shade to the weanling;
    Where you are the girls gather to play;
    Lady Moyo,
    Whose neck is so long, a louse must rest upon its climb.
We thank you, Lady Mwenda
    and the Lady Munombirei,

Source: From A. C. Hodza, *Shona Praise Poetry,* © 1979. Reprinted by permission of Oxford University Press.

Who walk with dignity as elephants do,
And whose lips are firm as gristle on the bone.
There, Do not call it abuse,
    it is your totem.
You have done a service, Those who lie at Daranjiva,
    where the father of Dimwa is and Chimunda.
Thank you, Those who lie at Matsvitsi and Chikura.
Thank you, Those of Dikitira.
Thank you, Those who lie at the Mucheranegombe.
Thank you, Those at Wona.
Indeed, a service has been rendered
It is clear to all, Child of Zirewosehwa.

TEXT 87

The Zulu of South Africa: Shaka and the Princess Mkhabayi

from The Zulu Epic of Shaka the Great[1]

The most noted military leader of Zulu history, Shaka (1787–1828), was born the son of a minor Zulu king. As a child he accompanied his mother into exile, forced to flee their homeland for political reasons, and seek refuge at the court of the Zulu leader Dingiswayo. As a young man, Shaka first became military commander to Dingiswayo and then assumed the throne after the king's assassination by members of a rival clan.

Shaka built the weak Zulu clan into a powerful, militaristic empire. He reorganized the army into regiments arranged by age classes, and instituted new fighting techniques such as the use of the assegai, *a long blade spear that allowed his soldiers to fight at close quarters, instilling ever greater terror in an enemy more accustomed to the largely ineffectual throwing of spears at a distance. By incorporating defeated people into the Zulu nation, he continued to expand both the political and military base of his power. Hemmed in by the expanding presence of Afrikaners (of Dutch origin) and British settlers in the region of the Cape Coast, he launched a brutal series of wars against the kingdoms to his north, which came to be known as the* mfecane *or crushing.*

Shaka the Great revealed himself to be both a brilliant military strategist as well as tactician. Through a series of skillful maneuvers, he rose to the pinnacle of power among the Nguni-speaking peoples, even though he also had to confront political intrigues instigated by his ambitious half-brothers and mediated by his aunt, the Princess Mkhabayi.

---

[1]Mazisi Kunene, *Emperor Shaka the Great: A Zulu Epic* (London: Heinemann Educational Books, 1979).

Such was the growing power of the Zulus:
Eastwards it expanded, following the sun's directions.
At the vast village-city of Princess Mkhabayi
The sun opened its inner womb of forgetfulness.
Her mind was said to equal ten men of the Assembly.
Many sought to hear her great and fearless thoughts;
Large possessions travelled to her royal city of Nquthu.
The great princess often narrated ancient stories of the Zulus.
In mid-thought, she would stare as if she had seen a spirit;
Her ideas flashed like lightning.
She was black like the deep shadows of the forest,
Like the eternal powers that hang over the earth.
When she walked her footfalls echoed into water,
Proud and confident like one who fears neither life nor death.
It was because of this people cast down their eyes,
Breaking twigs like children before her.
In her presence people waited their turn.
When she spoke only her voice, round and beautiful, was heard:
"Zulu and Qwabe were children of Malandela.
Qwabe, like elder brothers, lacked the zealousness of his brother.
He was slow to think and slow to act.
He prided himself only in the glories of his father, King Malandela,
Not like Zulu who was always thinking of new things.
Even at the Assembly he was never silent.
His sharp mind grasped the thoughts of others like a scorpion's clasp.
For this he was popular at the Assembly;
Often his absence stirred a protest: 'Where is the prince?'
Because of this Qwabe resented his brother,
But still there was nothing he could do,
For, indeed, the heir must please;
He must derive his power from the importance of his position.
Not so the unhappy lot of others
Who must strive and survive through intrigue and sharp intellect.
Zulu, by his alertness, did not enhance his brother's name,
Nor did his followers bow down to their future king.
He was as hard and unbending as a winter cane.
These quarrels threatened to break the bonds of kinship.
The wise King Malandela decided: to preserve peace
He must allot Zulu his own special place,
Removing him from the ancient lands and graves of his Forefathers.
He said: 'My son, take this portion of your father's wealth
And never let it graze in your brother's fields.'
He gave him his choicest breed of white cattle,
Implanting among them a giant black bull.
Prince Zulu moved with all his wealth to his own region.
He vowed: 'By my prosperity these lands would be the envy of all.'
Indeed his prophecy came true.

Source: From Mazisi Kunene, *Emperor Shaka the Great: A Zulu Epic,* © 1979. Reprinted by permission of Heinemann Publishers Oxford.

He nurtured a special stock, which he fed with the softest grass.
As it grazed passers-by stood and watched in awe.
He put his cattle in separate corrals and grazing lands
According to their variety of colours.
His royal village became the attraction of many peoples—
Indeed, it was the envy of many princes.
From the collection of followers and admirers
He formed the first home of the Zulu people:
To this day we speak as descendants of this wise prince.
So long as there are people on earth, so long shall our nation be."
As she finished talking it was clear to everyone
Shaka was to her mind the reincarnation of this prince.
He fulfiled the promise made to them by the Ancestors.
The wily Princess knew no great history is without heroes:
Great countries are those that boast a great Ancestry.
Indeed, artists embellish their past to inspire their children.
For this she sang the song of Zulu and broke into tears:
"Those who worship foreign gods are swallowed by them.
The greatness of our land lies in the glory of our children.
As we fight our battles, we create their tales."
Like the poet who moulded the sacred staff,
Carving it from the ebony plant of the ancient forest,
Thus, too, did the princess tell the tales of the Forefathers.
In honour of her the poet said: "Father of the wily ones,
Crafty daughter of the River Snake.
As you tell a tale you lead a man to his doom!
You overcame the wizards;
You destroyed Mkhongoyiyana near the Mngadi villages;
You demolished Bheje amongst the diviners.
Thou vast quagmire of Menzi,
That trapped people and was nourished by them.
This is true of Nohela of Mlilo.
Great fire that burns amongst all the mountains,
It seized Nohela and swallowed him.
The cow that bellowed from the hill of Sangoyana,
Its voice boomed and exploded into heaven.
The distant villages of Gwabalanga heard its moaning.
(He was the son, Mndaba of the Khumalo clan).
After reaching puberty the young woman spoke no more.
Some began to gossip about her, commenting on her turbulent mind.
She caused the hunters to capture the birds without effort.
As they seized them she stared at them in the eye.
She opened all the gates for people to enter
But members of her family had to enter through the small gates.
She, the devourer of the magic herbs who surrounded the enemies,
The Mhlathuzi river is going to overflow at broad daylight!
She, the fieldmouse that opened the paths to the land of Malandela,
And said: 'Only those of Malandela
Shall travel along these sacred routes.
She said, only they shall take the direction they choose.' "

As kingdoms grow they breed their own internal enemies,
Spawning those who desire to eat the fruit of power
And extinguish the rays of the sun.
Such was the fate of Shaka's rule.
While acts of heroes blazed with grandeur at the memorial cairn
There were those who ached with festering grudges,
Who, like Prince Dingane, often generated hatreds against Shaka.
Prince Dingane often swore aloud by his father's sovereignty.
He and Prince Mhlangane never fully acclaimed their brother's rule:
They planted seeds of doubt about his war tactics and reign.
Shaka heard these rumours.
Loyal followers urged him to eliminate these troublesome voices
But Shaka only said: "These are my brothers.
How can I kill those who are the children of my father?
Besides, who would rule the country should I die in battle?"
Indeed Shaka himself never filled the royal grounds with royal issue.
His children were secretly given to relatives or removed.
Fearing his displeasure, old women became adept at keeping secrets.
Even the King's favourite woman of the Cele clan
Never boasted his child, despite her endless pleas;
Nor did the King soften to the tears of Nandi.
Encouraged by the absence of an heir
The princes frantically plotted against their brother.
They spoke to Princess Mkhabayi, hoping to win her sympathy,
But she never swerved: she spoke profusely in praise of Shaka.
She proclaimed publicly:
"Shaka is the only ruler who shall make our nation great.
He does not hoard the loot of wars like others
Or breed large numbers of princes and princesses,
Who by their conceit often squander what is rightly of the nation."
Kingdoms and states and empires are kept intact by their poets—
It is they who embellish their tales, making the future desirable.
Thus, too, did Princess Mkhabayi inspire loyalty to Shaka's rule.
Of the people of Zululand it was said:
They walk high with crowns of red feathers on their heads.
They stare into the dome of the sky, unafraid.
From the south, from the north, and from the sun's nocturnal home,
People sing the great anthems of the Zulu nation.

Day after day the regiments built up their anger against Zwide,
Pointing their spears to his region and composing fierce anthems;
Mgobhozi often provoked him with tales of Zwide's rule and cruelty.
More ardent than others was the uFasimba regiment;
They requested to be the first in battle against Zwide.
It was not long before the sparks of war exploded in Nguniland.
Zwide, unable to restrain his anger,
Shouted to the mountains the slogans of war:
"Young boy of Senzangakhona,
You swore at me in the hearing of nations.
I, son of Langa, King of Kings, I heard your blasphemy

When you called me an old, dried-up cow-hide;
Yet I was senior to you and as old as your father.
I shall yet tear up the sinews of your youth!'
Though not yet fully prepared for this war,
Shaka set out, vowing: "I shall cut the tongue of this he-goat."
Shaka said to Mgobhozi: "Anger is not enough in this war.
I have sent a message to my relatives of the Qwabe clan,
Asking them to give me support against this fierce Zwide.
It is hard for us to tackle this challenge alone—
Our army still suffers the wounds of the Qokli battle.
The assault of Zwide would be too heavy on our troops.
Besides, in the south we need an opening for retreat."
While Mgobhozi agreed with these words
He was not convinced of Shaka's judgement.
He said: "My lord, I doubt if the Qwabes shall join us.
Would they not rather wait the outcome of war?
Remember, my lord, there are ancient grudges in your families."
While Mgobhozi was talking and arguing against these high expectations
A messenger was heard, announcing to the king:
"I did go, my lord, to Phakathwayo of the House of Malandela,
Telling him: 'My lord of the House of Zulu borrows some shields.
The wild man Zwide is out on a rampage again.'
King Phalathwayo just laughed, making fun of my words.
He said: 'Go back to him and say I ask him this question:
Does he not know the custom of Nguniland,
Not to swear at those senior and older than him?
Those who breach the laws should suffer the consequence.
They should be punished even if they be of our house and family.
Tell him these words come from Phakathwayo, the son of Khondlo.
Tell him I have, indeed, observed for some time his conceit.
He has scattered and terrorized even those under my protection!' "

It was as though Shaka had been hit on his chest:
He was spitting and swearing inaudible words of anger.
He said: "I shall teach him. I am the grandson of Jama!
Go back to him, then. Tell him to get ready for battle.
I shall not delay, I, Nodumehlezi, the son of Menzi."
He summoned his army from all the hills and valleys;
Phakathwayo's ears were deafened by the sound of war songs.
Yet it was no war to tell one's grandchildren about.
Soon the Qwabe army was thrown into disarray.
Indeed, many had denounced this war,
Saying it would open the door to enemies.
The Zulus returned, still itching for fiercer battles,
Eager to settle their scores against their true enemy, Zwide.
When he heard of the swift defeat of Phakathwayo
He said to his supreme commander General Soshangane:
"Do you see how skillfully the boy of Senzangakhona fights?
Had he desired it he would have destroyed the Qwabe nation,
But he only gave a warning blow,

Fighting as though preparing for some ultimate battle;
For now many are full of praise,
Lauding his generous gesture of preserving his relatives.
I want you to destroy this growing monster:
I want you to return with his head.
If you fail it is your head I shall demand."
The Ndwandwes prepared for war like numerous teams of locusts.
Even the young sharpened their light spears.
Everyone talked once again of this war as a war to end all wars,
Certain it would determine the supreme master of the earth.
Many swore no war would ever be so fearful.
It was said from the battlefields only messengers should survive.
From the poet, generations thereafter shall ask:
"What great issues could provoke so fearful a war?"
Of the War-of-the-Hurricanes he shall only shed tears:
Old age and time shall seal his mouth.

The Zulu regiments swarmed like flying ants after rains,
Eager to challenge and defeat Zwide's army.
Shaka now launched his army in all directions;
He sent a command to the regions of the battlefield,
Ordering the season's harvest to be reaped at once.
Every grain and food-store was to be razed to the ground and burnt.
Nothing was to remain in all the summer fields.
Shaka knew as he planned these stratagems
Zwide's army carried no supplies
But relied on the loot extorted from the conquered peoples.
Shaka's army carried its own provisions through the young carrier boys.
No sooner had the two armies come close to each other
Than Shaka shouted a battle command to all Zulu generals,
Ordering them to disengage with speed and to retreat.
The Ndwande army followed, bewildered by this action,
Thinking perchance the large Zwide army
Had intimidated the unprepared Zulu army.
Up and down the smaller and larger hills they chased after them,
At intervals accelerating their speed but beaten down by the sun,
Their sandalled feet blistered from the hot earth.
The fingers of hunger restrained their zeal.
Everywhere they found only burnt harvests.
They charged into every grain pit
Like dogs famished for a full five-day cycle.
They were like hens digging frantically after rains.
Trapped, they still followed the Zulu army.
Across a winding stream they halted.
There they conferred on the ways to overtake the Zulu army,
But the Zulus launched endless forays and attacks.
General Soshangane spoke his concern to General Zwangendaba:
"I think I can see what snares they are laying for us—
As our army is drained by exhaustion they shall attack full-scale.
Go to all regiments and announce to them:

'The Zulus fight to protect large stores of grain and meat.'
Then each man shall fight, hoping to gain by his effort.'
General Zwangendaba conveyed this message
Though he knew it was only to keep up their spirits.
The Zulus spread their lines around them, singing their battle songs.
The Ndwande army milled together in confusion.
Without warning they suddenly scattered in all directions,
Disrupting the commander's schemes and stratagems.
Shaka let loose on them his troops,
Causing further panic among the tired Ndwande troops.
In disorder they attempted to throw their missiles
But the Zulus crept closer, forcing them onto an incline.
Like winter leaves they fell on the broken ground.
Humiliated and defeated, the Ndwandwes began to retrace their steps.
The ancient poet enshrined this occasion in the great epic:
"The chaser of men who chases without stopping—
How I loved him as he pursued Zwide, the son of Langa,
Following him from the regions of the rising sun
And making him seek sanctuary in the land of the setting sun.
Zwide was the man whose little shoulders he broke in two,
Like an old man surprised by a youth!
Fierce one, whom they announce in terror
As they flee from their homes.'
The poet tells us how General Soshangane
Sent word to Zwide, saying:
"Your army has been lost to Shaka of Senzangakhona."
Soshangane himself broke off from Zwide,
Inviting all forces hostile to him to desert the ageing monarch.
He crossed the plains to the north,
Where he set up the great Gasa kingdom.
But the grudges of battle die hard:
There the Zulu army pursued him many years after.
It was as though Soshangane had blasphemed the king's name,
So great was the eagerness to bring him to justice.
Only Zwangendaba returned with the depleted army.
Ahead of him Shaka sent a section of his own army
Who, by singing Zwide's victory songs, lured them to their defeat.
The Mbonambi and Siphezi regiments set Zwide's capital in flames,
Sending the troublesome ruler to flee for his life.
Thus was avenged the many peoples and rulers
Whom Ntombazi had kept for ridicule in her house.
It was this macabre house that was kept intact;
Here the Zulus ceremonially buried all Zwide's victims,
Performing all rites appropriate to them.
From every direction anthems of victory were sung.
The regiments shouted their battle call: "Zulu power is eternal."
From the lands of the setting sun
The voice of triumph travelled to the regions of the rising sun.
King Macingwane of the Chunus shook on his throne.

Listen to the heroes as they narrate their tales of battle.
Zulu, the son of Nogandaya of the Zungu clan said to Mgobhozi:
"We attacked them at night when they hoped to sleep,
Believing we, too, should rest like all armies of Nguniland
Who never attack in darkness.
Confused and blinded by night, each man stabbed the one next to him.
Only with the star of dawn did we return to our camp.
Vakaza, the son Heshane, Msinga, the son of Noti,
Vumazwe, the brave son of the Zondi family,
Moyeni who was loved by women: all died there.
Mgobhozi of-the-Mountain could see clearly the truth of this episode.
He said: "We have succeeded in digging out the root of an evil tree—
What remains are only little plants.
Their stems shall be cut by the little boys."
He referred to the little kingdoms that bordered the south.

No celebration in the whole history of the Zululand
Shall exceed in glory the one held on this occasion.
Even old ladies constantly spoke of it in awe.
Festival songs were no longer sung with the voices of children
But combined those of the Ndwandwe and the Mthethwa nations.
Through these the Zulu nation swelled in numbers;
Even their dances affected a multitude of styles.
Thus many stared in wonderment as the dancer of the Jali clan
Moved slowly, thrusting his foot forward,
While tall young men circled him in snake movements.
At intervals they touched the ground with their toes.
Finally ten thousand troops entered the arena!
Even the Ancestors heard their dancing,
For the Forefathers always rejoice in our joys.
They stand at the passes of their divine mountains, watching us,
Happy to see the huge rounds of our feasts.
Was it not known to everyone
That Dingiswayo's spirit was there,
Celebrating with his children the downfall of his enemy?
Was it not acknowledged by Jama's children
That his spirit saw with pride the fulfilment of his dream?
Shaka caused many eyes to stare as he emerged,
Adorned for the festival in colours of triumph.
On his shoulders were epaulettes of the soft otter skin
And on his head was the long feather of the loury bird.
He carried a large white shield centred with a deep black spot.
The poet, inspired by this spectacle, declaimed:
"The glorious feather that bends over beyond the Nkandla forest,
Arching to devour the crowds of men!"
The majesty that was Shaka was embellished with white tails;
His arms were covered with ivory amulets.
As he stood facing the noonday sun his body glistened,
Radiating the secrets of mind and contentment.
All around him sat the royal women:
Next to Shaka sat Nandi, the Queen Mother.

Her body was covered in a long robe of leopard skin;
Her arms were round, full and gentle.
On them were ornaments bequeathed by queens and kings of many lands
Who sought favours and protection from her son.
Princess Mkhabayi sat near her own regiments
Who were famed everywhere for their fierceness.
The great ministers of the land sat in a circle around the king,
Their headrings glistening from the sun's fire.
The poets of the land sang their new songs,
Each declaiming the great episodes of battles.
They commented in turn on the epic-histories of the Zulu nation;
They sang of the great heroes of ancient times;
They sang the old poems of Jubinqwanga;
Yet none could surpass in skill Magolwane,
Who was the beautiful voice of the Ancestral Spirit.
He scattered words like sparks of fire.
He beat the ground with his ceremonial stick.
His voice trembled and boomed to the cliffs.
He sang the great epics:
"The black thunderhead of Mageba
That roared over the mountains of Nomangci—
It exploded behind the village of Kuqhobekeni
And the bellies of men were chilled.
It seized the shields of the Maphela and the Mankayiya regiments.
The little melons were left half eaten by iziMpaka regiment.
He seized Nomahlanjana, the son of Zwide, of the Mapheleni regiment;
He swallowed up Nobengula, the son of Zwide, of the Mapheleni regiment;
He killed Mpepha, the son of Zwide, of the Mapheleni regiment;
He killed Dayingubo, the son of Zwide, of the Mapheleni regiment;
He seized Sonsukwana, the son of Zwide, of the Mapheleni regiment;
He eliminated Zwide's wife of Lubongo clan;
He destroyed Mtimona, the son of Gaga, of the Mapheleni regiment;
He killed Mhondo-phumela-kwezinde of the Mapheleni regiment;
He killed Ndengezi-mashumi of the Mapheleni regiment;
He destroyed Sihlamthini among those of Zwide;
He killed Nqwangube, the son of Lundiyane.
He was our hero, as he turned his shield in all directions.
Come back, Great Destroyer, it is enough!"
As Magolwane declaimed his epic
Great crowds acclaimed and cheered his words.
Their voices resounded from a distance like a waterfall:
They were like a million singers heard all at once.
The evening, with its many vessels, brings together the singing voices.
The teller of tales sits on the mountainside,
Listening and humming his song in homage;
From many hills, the poems of excellence are sung.
The night feeds the dream and those of future times.
From the upper regions the teller of tales speaks:
"We sing a new great song:
From the power of life, each generation gives birth
Until by the thickness of their numbers their dust darkens the sun.

TEXT 87: *The Zulu of South Africa: Shaka and the Princess Mkhabayi*

Someone is pregnant.
The child shall rejoice in what is to come
A son of our nation follows the dark path to the forest.
He shall open the way for the children;
Because of him the sun shall wait,
Lingering in the east until he has arrived.
To accompany him it opens its giant centre,
Exposing the path into the end of the earth.
Our nation shall live and multiply forever.
We are the Children of the Palm Race."
Such were the songs of the oracle
But no one was listening,
Except one young boy whose body he entered,
Generating in it a great power,
Binding his lips until the Forefathers had spoken.

In the remote regions people celebrated.
They sang of Mbonambi, of Ntenjana, of Siphezi,
Of uFasimba, of Jubinqwanga, of amaWombe, of uDlambedlu regiments.
They composed songs and poems about their heroes.
General Mdlaka was the theme of many songs and legends;
For his skill in battle he was nicknamed "Shaka's spirit."
It was said he laughed loud as he fought in battle.
Of all commanders none inspired to greater acts of courage than he.
Boy detachments swore by his name:
They vowed to equal and surpass their seniors in all things.

Women regiments danced to their own battle songs.
Young men and women sang from distant hills:
"Our land shall stretch beyond the horizon.
Of what use is fear?
Great is the feast in Zululand—let all people come.
Listen to the women singing across the river.
They are the women of Baqulusi regions.
They sing of the festival.
They give warning to Macingwane of Luboko.
They threaten Mvelase of the Thembus."
Such were the songs that cemented the bonds of clans and nations.
Those who narrate tales of ancient times tell us
Despite all this Nandi still yearned for her own grandchild.
When she heard how Mbuzikazi of the Cele clan
Might yet bear the king a child
She made elaborate plans to save it.
She said: "I shall steal this child and make it my own.
I shall bring it up secretly under my care,
Nourishing it as I did my own children."
Nandi sent a message to the king:
"I suffer constantly from ill health.
Of all the royal women
I trust the gentle and kindly daughter of the Cele clan;

I ask that in this condition she alone attends me."
By such a ruse she hoped to hide this pregnancy.
Months passed; people began whispering;
Words of gossip spread like a new season's crop.
It was Mbopha's wife who exposed the secrets.
She said to her husband, the chief of the royal household:
"It seems many surprises shall come from Nandi's household.
I am a woman. I know the craftiness of other women.
I know a woman when her body has become beautiful.
Such is the state of the favourite woman of the king.
The king himself seems ignorant of this truth.
He does not know his household grows in secret."
She planted these words in the sharp ears of Mbopha,
Knowing he craved to be the king's most favoured councillor.
He was weak and flatterable.
No sooner had this been whispered to his ear
Than he hurried to report to the king:
"My lord, I bring news that is disturbing to me.
To speak of it I must expose the secrets of your right hand,
But I speak only to fulfil the duties of my office.
I love my king sincerely:
I know our whole future depends on him.
It is our task to do as ordered.
By your laws many nations have been brought together—
To follow them is to fulfil the vision of our greatness;
To overlook them is to destroy our very nation.
For this reason I am bound to tell all secrets
Though our Forefathers have said:
'Affairs of families hurt only the outsider.' "
Thus did Mbopha throw words to soften the king.
Shaka's eyes moved, keen to know Mbopha's story
Even before Mbopha could tell it.
For rulers often prefer to be ahead of their underlings.
Through their eyes they learn the secrets of their subjects.
Shaka spoke slowly and carefully:
"Mbopha, son of Sithayi, I have put you above everyone,
Trusting you and believing in you.
I did not ask you to distinguish for me what deserves my judgement.
These rumours have already reached my ears
But I waited for you to tell me the whole truth.
Thus, I order you no longer to swallow words;
Indeed, much more important affairs demand my attention."
Mbopha was restless; he still spoke in fragmented thoughts:
"My lord, I am frightened to tell the truth,
Yet I have the command of my king.
By your command I speak of the Female Elephant, Mother Nandi.
She and the beloved daughter of the Cele clan
Hide from you a secret child born to your house."
It was as if something had stabbed the king.
He stood up suddenly and said:
"Mbopha, son of Sithayi, do you know what you are saying?

TEXT 87: *The Zulu of South Africa: Shaka and the Princess Mkhabayi*

Have you got the full truth of this tale?"
Mbopha shivered, alarmed at this reaction.
He was like someone who had uttered words of war.
Mbopha's sweat ran over his face;
He moved his cold buttocks from side to side.
The great son of Senzangakhona filled the house with anger.
He spoke to Mbopha solemnly and said:
"Son of Sithayi, I want you to leave me alone.
I want to put into place my thoughts.
Such news is too heavy for my shoulders.
Go, before my anger overwhelms me,
Choosing you to thrust its whirlwind blade,
Thus making me a target of blame among the Zulu people."
As he spoke, his mind seethed like a volcano.
He groaned like a young tiger at its first kill.
He sat alone on one side of the house, brooding,
His thoughts racing like a pain.
For the first time in the whole span of his life
His desires had been flagrantly violated by his parent.
His house seemed enveloped in darkness.
He laughed at the many thoughts that came to his mind.
All day long Shaka kept alone.
Even Mgobhozi never got near to assuage his mind.
It was as thought he was dressing for some festival.
As he stepped on to the open ground,
"Go to my mother. Tell her before the sun sets tomorrow
I shall have arrived at the grounds of her royal residence."

No sooner had the early morning spread its seeds of light
Than Shaka began bedecking his elaborate adornments.
It was as though he was dressing for some festival.
As he stepped on to the open ground,
His very footfalls seemed to echo his inner thoughts.
He was slow of movement and slow of speech.
With a small army of bodyguards he travelled through mountains and valleys.
In the whole journey he seldom spoke.
At Nandi's royal city he rested, eager to put together his words.
After his respite he headed for Nandi's special residence.
There she waited for him;
She sat leisurely on a multi-coloured mat.
With a stammer he began to speak to her,
His anger choking him:
"Mother, many times I have endured great pains
But never have I ever faced so great a challenge.
The one closest to me has betrayed me!
Mbopha tells me you harbour what shall be the death of our house.
A child, supposedly mine, has been kept away from me;
Yet I am still convinced never could my parent act against me.
What example would I be setting for the army?
What wise general would ask of his men what he himself would not do?
Yet something deeper eats into my mind:

Of all living beings you are the only one I truly trust,
Nor have I criticized or condemned your own deeds
But of late you have opened the doors to my enemies.
Perhaps in my deeds I was blinded by my heart
When I vowed never to allow enemies to cross our path.
I ask you to give me some richer explanation!
How have I erred? How have I wronged you?"
The old, experienced Nandi calmly answered:
"Shaka, my son, no one is gifted in all things.
You have many types of knowledge and experiences
But one aspect still remains obscure to you:
The heart that yearns to fulfil its dreams and fantasies.
It is not out of evil that people act against others,
But love sometimes obscures itself in acts of cruelty.
The older I get the greater are my concerns.
Thus by my own love I am weakened.
I had hoped when these two voices sing to each other
The dynasty of your house shall nourish forever our land.
I live alone, despite all the abundance;
I have never had peace since I first spoke to you.
But all that I utter now is not enough.
Only one thing troubles me above all else:
I fear Mbopha; I fear him as I fear a snake.
Often I feel he shall bring great tears to our house.
Even now our talks no longer have meaning
Since, by his orders, he has killed the very child I loved.
Such a man is dangerous!
He kills today; he shall always thirst for more blood."
Shaka was quiet, his mind deeply absorbed in thought.
He was uncertain whether to condemn Mbopha utterly
Or to uphold his act as one of devotion to his master.
Besides, by this deed he had weakened his own case;
Yet a dutiful councillor must elevate the nation's laws.
Having sorted out his thoughts he said:
"I understand the deep truths in your words.
I endorse them, too, in accordance with your thinking.
But there are still other demands of power
Whose laws and rules remain obscure to you.
The command of our Ancestors demands acts greater than ourselves.
I am a king, who must rule over many nations of Zululand.
It is by these laws I myself must abide.
They must extend beyond the circumstance of self.
I have ordered the army not to marry except by special command.
I, too, must follow these laws, whatever the consequences.
I must elevate the glory that attends to our nation and army.
If I fail to choose only what satisfies my own appetite,
Then there shall be greater disasters than ever before.
It would be better if the nation of Zululand
Had not been roused in its nest of peace.
People follow the example of their heroes;

They imitate the image that best fulfils their fantasies.
Should I fail, the nation itself shall disintegrate.
I explain all this only because it is you.
To follow the heart is noble,
Yet it does not rule the thoughts and minds of men.
Often it doubts, it hesitates and abounds in self-recrimination.
Yet a leader must act decisively where others flee in terror.
He must walk unafraid and unintimidated by all shadows.
These things must inspire others to greater triumphs.
Our spirits no longer follow the same path.
Yours suffers the emptiness of plenty
But mine is the spirit of a restless traveller.
It must forever be thrilled by the strangeness of things.
Your own visions bear their own truth—
Perhaps this way they nourish their own worlds.
It is possible that your fears about Mbopha are true,
But I have no way to remove him as the nation's honoured councillor.
His task is to see what I cannot see,
To be the nation's agent and to protect its king.
What would the nation say
If, because of my own whim, I removed him from power?
Will people not complain: 'This is no ruler of people.
He succumbs to his parent and follows personal fears."
I cannot follow the heat of my anger
And say, because of his deed Mbopha must die.
Besides, whoever shall assume his power
Shall abide by the same rules and the same authority.
It is wiser, then, to retain the man whose mind I know
Than to seek those whose hearts take time to fathom.
I ask you, then, to see things with my eyes
In the same way I have always championed your truth,
Even though at times it cut against my plans and feelings."
As he spoke Nandi stared at him kindly and said:
"Mlilwana, you shall escape any trap laid for you.
For in truth you sense the desires and needs of people.
You sift and weigh all acts of men.
I love you, my son, despite all the pains I suffer for it.
But know I have the heart of a woman.
All this enthusiasm about wars does not excite me.
Even though I listen and praise these battles and heroes
It is only to fulfil what is highest in your mind.
I thank you for your insight into my desire for a child.
This understanding alone nourishes me with deep fulfilment.
It is this I treasure above all else;
It shall yet console me in my loneliest moments."
Shaka hugged his parent to remove the sadness in her eyes.
Even Nandi wept tears of joy.
While Shaka displayed all this affection
His mind had not forgotten Mbopha's unsolicited act.
He remembered now many strange incidents:

How Mbopha would be heard laughing at Dingane's residence,
Then next he would be heard at the home of Prince Mhlangana.
Many reported their suspicions to the king
But Shaka knew: men in positions of authority
Often attract to them many secret enemies
Through their arrogance they became detestable to all.
Such had become of Mbopha, the son of Sithayi.
He swelled with conceit, avoiding those whom he once honoured.
He opened and closed the royal gates at will,
Deciding who should see the king and when.
Abusing his power, he spread the hostile words of the princes,
Creating a spate of poisonous talk.
Shaka, learning of these stories, approached Mkhabayi.
Speaking solemnly he said:
"Great and wise one, you were here before us.
I ask you to share with me your great wisdom.
My brothers are always criticizing my actions
Despite all I have done for them.
As the head of our house I have given them all they need.
Their complaints are never spoken directly to me
But are secretly conveyed to those who are not members of our family;
Yet I have vowed to them our family together must rule,
Giving to each other the harshest and the best advice.
Even now I hesitate to rush into things,
Yet all their violent words begin to challenge my authority
And make us appear a family in dissension."
The wily daughter of Jama, assuming her composure, said:
"Shaka, my son, listen to me.
There is no ruler in this world without fault.
Your brothers criticize only out of love,
Proud of the family you share together.
In truth, this is how they elicit the truth from your enemies.
Above all, they never can be wiser than you.
Even as they criticize your actions
They know it is only to enhance their own reputations.
You should only laugh at whatever talk is reported to you.
Words often assume a fierceness when reported by others."
Through such words did Mkhabayi restore the peace in the family.
She was not like Nandi of the Mhlongos.
She took pleasure in accompanying her regiments with a song;
She declaimed the great epics of her Forefathers and heroes.
Her warm and friendly words consoled Shaka's heart.
He said to Mgobhozi: "It is true, in all large families
The young frequently challenge their elders,
Yet the strong bonds of family survive."
As he spoke many pleasant thoughts passed through his mind.

TEXT 88

The Xhosa of South Africa: Custom Requires the Traditional Response[1]

As with the Bantu-speaking Zulu of southern Africa, the Xhosa people, who currently number approximately 4 million, represent a subgroup of the Nguni ethnicity. This farming population, organized into a central state under the leadership of powerful kings, had been living in the Transkei region of South Africa several centuries before the arrival of European settlers. The nineteenth-century migration of the Afrikaners (of Dutch origin) into Xhosa territories precipitated a number of bloody wars, which resulted in the displacement of the Africans from their farmlands. In modern times the Xhosa have represented a dominant group within the ruling African National Congress of South Africa.

This is how the traditions in the land of the Xhosa came into existence, the way they were in the beginning.

As time passed, men wondered, "How are we going to go about doing things, since all activities require a leader?"

When this issue was raised, someone said that they ought to go to the homestead of the royal residence—that is, the royal residence for us Xhosa of Gcalekaland.

Someone responded, "Two young men should be sent. Let them go to the royal residence and ask, 'What shall we do about this?'"

---

[1]Nongenile Masithathu Zenani, *The World and the Word: Tales and Observations from the Xhosa Oral Tradition* (Madison: University of Wisconsin, 1992), pp. 117–22.
Source: From Nongenile Masithathu Zenani. Edited with an Introduction by Harold Scheub. *The World and the Word: Tales and Observations from the Xhosa Oral Tradition,* © 1992, University of Wisconsin Press. Reprinted by permission of University of Wisconsin Press.

A school was about to be established; this was the beginning of education. The thing called a "school" was to be established for the first time. The Xhosa had not known what a school was to this time.

Later, the men assembled here, and the young men were asked, "Did you go to the royal residence?"

The two young men who had been sent there said, "We did go to the royal residence."

"And whom did you find there?"

"We arrived at the royal residence, and the king was there."

"Who was the king at that time?"

"It was Sarhili."

It happened that the name of the king at that time was Sarhili, a prince of a man.

These men had now returned, and they were being asked, "What does the king say?"

The young men said, "Well, the king says that he does not know what a 'school' is, he does not know what 'education' is. Nor does he know what 'to study' means."

The young men finished speaking, and a councillor of the royal residence, a councillor who was loyal to that king, stood up.

He said, "Well, your report sounds right. King, don't allow your blood to boil. Here in the land of the Xhosa, there has never been this 'studying.' There's never been a 'school.' We aren't accustomed to that. It's not in the nature of things to have a 'school,' as far as we Xhosa are concerned. Now then, King, you must look at this matter with care, what a 'school' and 'studying' will mean in the land of the Gcaleka, of the Xhosa. Through the years, we have felt that our traditions are strong. We never thought that we required schools. Anyone who insists that we do need schools is implying that our traditions are not sufficiently strong. What do you say to that, King?"

It was quiet, then, it was quiet. After a long time, the king hesitantly stood and said, "Our land is not now what it used to be. We don't know the 'school.' And 'studying,' too—we don't know it. Now some say that we must have this 'studying.' The question is, will our traditions, will the things that we do, harmonize with that 'education'?"

From among that mass of people assembled in the royal residence, another man got up. He said, "Well, King, we understand what you're saying. But time edges forward. And it's not enough just to hear one's name. One must also be able to identify it on paper. A person should know his name not just when he hears it, but also when he sees it written. I'm a member of the Qwathi clan, and I've had occasion to go to Johannesburg. Now when I got to Johannesburg, I had to identify myself by my 'surname.' The concept of a 'surname' was foreign to me. I didn't know it. This is what they mean by 'surname': they want to know your grandmother who bore your father. I wanted to get confirmation of this, so I hesitated, I was confused. Finally, I asked some others, 'Who was my father's father?' A young man of the Mvulane clan told me that my father was borne by a daughter of the Qocwa clan. Now all this happened when I was trying to understand what they meant in Johannesburg by 'surname,' something that is not familiar to us. I pretended that I was skilled in the use of 'surnames'; I gave the appearance of being spontaneous about this. So I told them my 'surname.' I explained that 'surname' idea at my home when I returned from Johannesburg, when my contract of nine months had expired—that's the length of time we had contracted for in Johannesburg. I worked at Mqandatye's. I told my father about this.

"I said to him, 'Father, how can something like the matter of "surname" be taken by me to the royal residence? I don't know Xhosa tradition. I may have tampered with the traditions of the Xhosa by my actions in Johannesburg. I am a child; you are experienced. Over there at the royal residence, I'll be asked about Xhosa traditional things. Really, Father, it's more fitting that I go with you when I go to the royal residence.'

"Then my father told my mother, 'Nosenti, do you hear what this young man has been saying?'

"And she said, 'What does he say?' Then Nosenti said to her husband, 'What he is saying is this: he cannot go to the royal residence alone because they'll want to know the origin of ancient Xhosa traditions.'

" 'But this young man says that he should go with me, Nosenti. He says that he should go to the royal residence to tell about his experiences in Johannesburg when he worked at Mqandatye's.'

"Nosenti said, 'No, really, this is what the young man said. This is how it is, Sozekelwa, this is what happens when our children go to find employment with he white men. Our children board the trains and go off to the white man. Then they return with things that puzzle us. Now he says that he wants you to go with him to the royal residence, so that he can explain this matter of "surnames." We don't know "surnames." You must go with him, then, and explain what this child is saying. You can fill in the gaps in the statements that he makes. And there is also the matter of the school. Here, they say that a school is necessary so that a person may know his name, so that a person may know what is being said. We do not know these things because we have never gone to any school. We talk about things in our own customary way here, and we are comfortable with the things that we speak. But if something new comes up, you should not just oppose it because you do not know how it will turn out when you have opposed it.' "

The fellow agreed with his wife, and he took the journey with his son. He agreed with what his wife, Nosenti, said in support of her son's statement.

So it was that they discussed the matter of the possibility of having a school, something that had never before been present among the Xhosa—a school, education, the idea that the people should be "taught."

When he arrived at the royal residence, he said, "Well, here we are. We're busy, we've got journeys of our own to take. We don't know why we've been called here."

"We want to know if the establishment of a school among us will prove to be dangerous to us."

A man, who was believed to be an expert on the matter because he knew what a "school" was, stood up and said, "No, the school is not dangerous."

The fellow who had come with his son and wife said, "Speak up!"

He raised his voice and said, "Well, it's only a school, where people study. That's all there is to it. There's no danger."

The other man got up and said, "Who says so? Who says that studying should take place? And what is it that should be studied?"

The expert, getting up again, repeated his statement: "No, the government says that studying should take place."

This one said, "What is the government? What is this thing called 'government'? Where is this government? Who is it, really? Where does it live?"

The other said, "No, no, the government is another great one, a great one, like you notables. The government is like you, except that he is a white person. And he does not live with you. But he does look after your welfare."

The other one said, "How does he look after our welfare? Where is he now? Because in the past, we did not have to dip our cattle. We did not have to pay taxes."

It was said, "There you are, sitting at home. And this thing comes along to the effect that you must bring your tax. Now if the government was actually there, then why didn't he help us? We're suffering. Where was that government when we needed it?"

The expert said, "No, you should know that, at the time you were suffering, the government had no knowledge that you were being harmed because you were far from him. You've never even talked with him."

This one said, "Well then, the government had no knowledge that we were suffering because we didn't speak with him because he is so far away from us. But what pains did he take to come and find out from those of us who were in the bad situation of which he knew nothing?"

That one said, "No, consider all facets of it. You ought to study in this 'school.' When you have studied in the school, you'll know how to speak with the government. You'll be able to inform him of your serious sufferings, so that he'll realize that you've been harmed. We must move quickly. Forget the irrelevant things. There's just one point at issue here. Let's not get involved in peripheral matters that will only keep us here. The question is, Should there be a school, so that a person may know his name? We'll learn soon enough what one gets out of this 'education.' "

The other said, "No, he'll *get* nothing from 'education'! But he'll be *given* enlightenment. He'll know where to go to get help, how to write, and he'll know a lot of other things. He'll be able to say what a thing is!"

Another said, "All right then, if that's the way it is. How many schools are there to be in a village?"

The councillor at the royal residence got up and said, "Well, we'll only waste time if we go on in this way. When the schools begin, there won't be nine or ten of them. One school will be established, and if that is seen to be a good thing, then another will be set up."

The other fellow got up again, and said, "My ancestral name is Mdladla. I don't want to hear something discussed in isolation, unrelated to anything else, so that we don't have a clear direction in our argument. Will someone tell me what we've come here for? People are talking, but others say that nothing has been said yet. What have we been talking about all this time? The things that are being mentioned are the precise things that should be mentioned. Now, if you don't understand what is being said, then ask your neighbor about it, someone from your own village. Ask him to listen for you. The rest of us understand that what is being said is that there should be schools. All of us, as we sit here, understand that it is being recommended that something called a 'school' should be established here. And it is said that, because of this 'school,' a person will know his name and be able to write it. It is said that he shall recognize his name when it is written. It is therefore concluded that a 'school' will help us. Some of us want others to understand how it is that we have suffered. Now, this is supposed to be a time of enlightenment. Do you refuse to be persuaded? Do you insist that you won't have anything to do with this school business? What is your position?" So he said, and then he sat down.

This fellow got up then, and said, "Well, I understand the argument, but I'm quite old already, and I've never heard of this school nonsense before! At home, milk used to be poured out into a spoon, then we'd drink it. At home, all that we talked about was in regard to what ought to be done concerning our home. If there were a misunderstanding between my aunt and my father, the people were called together and the case was judged in court. Nothing was written down. Now I wonder. You want things for writing. Is it because things will work out better then? Perhaps, without knowing it, you are misleading yourselves with all this writing business because this is how we live, according to the laws of the Xhosa and of nature and tradition.

"But I'll accept whatever you decide because it is obvious that I am alone in the matter of which I speak. But keep in mind that Xhosa custom is traditional. It is of ancient tradition, and it requires traditional responses. No young upstart dares issue a command related to the school concerning traditional Xhosa custom, and then expects that this is healthy for the society. My younger sister is a doctor. And she never came close to a school! Even though she has never been to a school, she has told us significant things in that home of ours. What did she do over there in our home? Well, this is one thing that she did. When there was a falling out between our father and my uncle, she told them, 'Uncle, would you take the time to come and visit me, so that you'll have a better understanding of why you're really quarreling with your elder brother? You see, Uncle, there's this one fault in you: you do not realize that this elder brother of yours knows the customs of your home better than you do. On the day when the "sickness" took over me, you were not present—when I was in this sick state, being initiated into the profession of medicine, being developed into a fully qualified doctor. But this is how we do it in this homestead. A plant must be picked in the fields, then applied to the person. Then a white goat must be slaughtered. Now then, Uncle, you're not very close to my father, and that puzzles me. After all, I'm your daughter too. You should help to put me together. You should speak the healing word to me. But you didn't speak the healing word to me because you don't get along, you don't know how it ought to be done.'

"Then that woman's father did indeed get together with his younger brother and said, 'This woman is posing a problem for us. Clearly, she's more important than we are because she knows the traditional Xhosa mind, the origins from deep down, from long ago. Now then, how shall we approach this problem? The young woman should be summoned; the people should also be called. And this young woman should speak of this matter while the people are present, so that they may or may not concur. We don't know whether they'll agree with what she says or if they'll side with us in our disagreement with what she says.' "

Things went on, and the assembly was still discussing the matter the following week.

TEXT 89

William W. Gqoba: The Cause of the Cattle-Killing at the Nongqawuse Period[1]

The year 1856 was a time of great social stress for the Xhosa people who had suffered a series of defeats and dislocations by their Zulu neighbors as well as the European colonialists. In this environment of anxiety for the future, a young Xhosa girl named Nongqawuse rose to prominence claiming to be a youthful soothsayer bearing a message from the ancestral spirits—that the people should kill their livestock and destroy their foodstores. William W. Gqoba, a Xhosa historian and poet, was 17 years old when this event occurred and recorded its details in the following account.

It so happened that in the Thenjini region of Gcalekaland, in the ward of headman Mnzabele, in the year 1856, two girls went out to the lands to keep the birds away from the corn. One was named Nongqawuse, daughter of Mhlakaza, and the other the daughter of a sister of Mhlakaza's. Near a river known as the Kamanga two men approached them and said, "Convey our greetings to your people, and tell them we are So-and-So and So-and-So" (giving their names). And the names by which they called themselves turned out to be the names of people who were known to have died long ago. They went on to say: "You are to tell the people that the whole community is about to rise again from the dead. Then go on to say to them all the cattle living now

---

[1] A. C. Jordan, *Towards an African Literature:* (Berkeley, CA: University of California Press, 1973), pp. 70–75.
Source: From A. C. Jordan, *Towards an African Literature.* © 1973. Reprinted by permission of the University of California Press.

must be slaughtered, for they are reared with defiled hands, as the people handle witchcraft. Say to them there must be no ploughing of lands, rather must the people dig deep pits (granaries), erect new huts, set up wide, strongly built cattlefolds, make milksacks, and weave doors from buka roots. The people must give up witchcraft on their own, not waiting until they are exposed by the witchdoctors. You are to tell them that these are the words of their chiefs,—the words of Napakade (Forever), the son of Sifubasibanzi (the Broad-chested).

On reaching home the girls reported this, but no one would listen to them. Everybody ridiculed them instead. On the following day, they went again to keep the birds away from the corn, and after some time, these men appeared again and asked if the girls had told the people at home, and what the people had said in reply. The girls reported that their message had simply been a thing of laughter, no one believing them. "The people simply said we were telling stories." This happened in Gcalekaland near the mouth of the Gxara.

The men then said: "Say to the elders that they are to call all the chiefs together from Gcaleka's, Tato's, Ngqika's and from the Gqunukhwebe, and they must tell the news to them."

On the following morning, Mhlakaza and some other men went to the lands, but these strangers did not reveal themselves. They were heard without being seen. It was only Nongqawuse and the other girl who heard them, and it was Nongqawuse who interpreted what was being said by the spirits. They said: "Tell those men to go and call the chiefs and bring them here. Only then shall we reveal ourselves."

Some men then went to Rili's royal place at Hohita, and there the strange news was related by Mhlakaza's daughter. Then Rili sent out Botomani, a minor chief, to go and verify this thing. Botomani went, but the strangers did not reveal themselves. Then Rili sent messengers to tell the chiefs that there were people who had been heard by Mhlakaza's daughter to say all the chiefs must be called together to meet the chief Napakade, son of Sifubasibanzi, near the mouth of the Gxara.

From Tato's came Maramnco, son of Fadana, accompanied by Shele, son of Zizi. From the Ndungwane came Dulaze, son of Qwesha, related to Ndarala. From the Tshatshus came Mpeke, son of Mfeneni. From the Ngqika came Namba, great son of Maqoma. From the Gcaleka section came Rili and Lindinxiwa, sons of Hintsa, together with Ngubo, son of Mlashe, and Nxiti, son of Lutshaba. From the Ndlambes came Nowawe, son of Ndlambe. From the Gqunukwebe came Dilima, son of Pato. All these men made their way to the home of Mhlakaza near the Gxara.

On arriving there, they were told that Nongqawuse desired that the numbers to go to the Gxara be reduced, and that those who were to go must be mostly chiefs. This in truth was done.

As the people were rather fearful, it happened that as they drew near the River Kamango, their throats went dry, and they felt thirsty. Meanwhile Nongqawuse, beautifully painted with red ochre, led the way. Then those who were thirsty were heard to say: "Is one who is thirsty allowed to drink?"

Nongqawuse replied, "He who does not practice witchcraft may drink without fear."

Thereupon Dilima, hero son of Pato, removed his kaross and stooped to drink. Then one by one the other men of Nomagwayi wase Mbo followed suit.

The Vision

Just at this time, there was a tremendous crash of big boulders breaking loose from the cliffs overlooking the headwaters of the River Kamanga, whereupon, the men gazed at one another wondering, for they were seized with fear. It seemed that some unknown thing on the cliffs was going to burst into flames.

While they stood wondering, the girl was heard saying, "Just cast your eyes in the direction of the sea."

And when they looked intently at the waters of the sea, it seemed as if there were people there in truth, and there were sounds of bulls bellowing, and oxen too. There was a huge formless black object that came and went, came and went and finally vanished over the crests of the waves of the sea.

Then it was that all the people began to believe.

The army in the sea never came out to meet the chiefs, and even what they said was not heard by any besides Nongqawuse. After it had vanished, she said: "The Chiefs yonder say you are to return to your homes and slaughter all your cattle and, in order that the resurrection may hasten, you are not to rear any cattle. You are not to plough the fields, but make big new pits (granaries), and these you will suddenly find full of corn. Erect new huts and make many doors. Shut yourselves in your huts, because on the eighth day, when the community returns in the company of Napakade, son of Sifubasibanzi, all the beasts on the land and in the rivers, and all the snakes will be roaming the land. You are also to take out all the old corn in the pits and throw it away. In order to survive, you are to use many doors to close each hut, fasten every door tightly, and abstain from witchcraft."

She went on to say that there was another chief, mounted on a grey horse. His name was Grey, eitherwise known as Satan. All those who did not slaughter their cattle would become the subjects of the chief named Satan, and such people would not see the glory of our own chief, Napakade, son of Sifubasibanzi.

That then was the cause of the cattle-killing of 1856 to 1857.

In the midst of this there appeared another young girl from the house of Nkwitshi of the Kwemta clan, in the Ndlambe section near the Mpongo. Her name was Nonkosi. The message of this girl was one with Nongqawuse's. She used to lead the people to a pond there at the Mpongo, and there used to see abakweta dancing on the surface of the water, and they thought that they heard the thudding of the oxhide, accompanied by a song, to which the abakweta danced. Truly, the people were so deluded that they went so far as to claim that they had seen the horns of cattle, heard the lowing of milk-cows, the barking of dogs, and the songs of milkmen at milking time.

The Orders of the Chiefs

On reaching their homes, the chiefs assembled their subjects and made known the news of the ancestors who were expected to return to life, fresh and strong, of the promised coming-to-life again of the cattle they were about to slaughter and of those that they had slaughtered long ago.

Nongqawuse had said that anyone who, on slaughtering his ox, decided to dispose of its carcass by barter, should nevertheless engage its soul, in order that on its coming back to life it should be his property. And she had said that all those who did not slaughter their cattle would be carried by a fierce hurricane and thrown into the sea to drown and die.

The community was split in two. One section believed that the resurrection of the people would come some day, but not that of the cattle. Thereupon, father fell out with son, brother with brother, chief with subjects, relative with relative. Two names emerged to distinguish the two groups. One group was named amaTamba (the Submissive), that is, Nongqawuse's converts. The other was called amaGogotya (the Unyielding), that is, those who were stubborn and would not kill their cattle. So some slaughtered their cattle, and others did not.

The Eighth Day

As the killing of the cattle went on, those who had slaughtered hurriedly for fear of being smelt out began to starve and had to live by stealing the livestock of others. Then everybody looked forward to the eighth day. It was the day on which the sun was expected to rise red, and to set again in the sky. Then there would follow great darkness, during which the people would shut themselves in their huts. Then the dead would rise and return to their homes, and then the light of day would come again.

On that day the sun rose as usual. Some people washed their eyes with sea-water at the mouth of the Buffalo. Some peered outside through little apertures in their huts, while those who had never believed went about their daily outdoor tasks. Nothing happened. The sun did not set, no dead person came back to life, and not one of the things that had been predicted came to pass.

Such then was the Nongqawuse catastrophe. The people died of hunger and disease in large numbers. Thus it was that whenever thereafter a person said an unbelievable thing, those who heard him, said: "You are telling a Nongqawuse tale."

TEXT 90

Lesotho: Moshoeshoe I[1]

The Bantu-speaking Sotho of southern Africa today number more than 4 million people and encompass under their linguistic rubric the Tswana and Pedi ethnicities as well. The powerful, centralized nation of Basotho developed into what is today the independent nation of Lesotho, which is surrounded on all sides by South Africa.

Moshoeshoe (born c. 1786) emerged the leader of the Mokoteli clan of the Sotho, who had been displaced by the mfecane, *that is, a series of wars launched by Shaka Zulu in the 1820s. In the new territory in which he settled his peoples, Moshoeshoe built a powerful confederation of chiefdoms, all of whom opposed the Zulu. The new Sotho kingdom built by Moshoeshoe evolved into the independent state of Lesotho, which was able to maintain its sovereignty within the physical boundaries of the South African state.*

    You who are fond of praising the ancestors,
Your praises are poor when you leave out the warrior,
When you leave out Thesele, the son of Mokhachane;
For it is he who is the warrior of the wars:
Thesele is brave and strong,
That is Moshoeshoe-Moshaila.
    When Moshoeshoe started to govern the Sotho,
He started at Botha-Bothe:
Thesele, the cloud, departed from the east,
It left a trail and alighted in the west
At Thaba Bosiu, at the hut that is a court.

---

[1]Jack Mapanje and Landeg White (editors), *Oral Poetry from Africa* (London: Longman Group, Ltd., 1983), pp. 11–12.
Source: Reprinted from Jack Mapanje and Landeg White, *Oral Poetry from Africa,* © 1983.

Every nation heard,
And the Pedi heard him too.
Moshoeshoe, clear the road of rubbish
That the Maaooa may travel with pleasure,
And travel with ease.
The Ndebele from Zulu's heard too.

Lay down the stick, son of Mokhachane,
Sit down:
The village of the stick is not built,
"What can you do to me?" does not build a village:
The village that is built is the suppliant's, Thesele,
Great ancestor, child of Napo Motlomelo,
Protective charm of the Beoana's land.

The cave of the poor and of the chiefs,
Peete's descendant, the brave warrior,
He is loved when the shields have been grasped,
When the young men's sticks have been grasped.

TEXT 91

Botswana: Medicinal Plants[1]

The southern African nation of Botswana is populated by the western division of the Sotho peoples, who speak the Tswana language. As early as the thirteenth century, Tswana kingdoms were known to have existed in the region of the western Transvaal. By the twentieth century this population had come to number approximately 4 million people. Remaining a British protectorate until 1960, Botswana was thereby able to retain indigenous sovereignty and escape the oppression of South Africa and its apartheid system.

As is customary in other parts of the African continent, traditional healers in Botswana have over the centuries developed a vast reservoir of natural and herbal substances used to treat a range of human maladies.

Mpitipiti *Abrus precatorius L. ssp. africanus Verdc.*

(BMP 679) (*LEGUMINOSAE*)

Habitat
Planted in herbalist's garden. Grows normally only in shaded, well watered areas.

Plants identified in immediate environment:

Medicinal uses:
Red painful eyes.

---

[1] Inga Hedberg and Frants Staugard, *Traditional Medicinal Plants: Traditional Medicine in Botswana* (Gabosone, Botswana: Ipeleng Publishers, 1989), Appendix.
Source: Reprinted from Inga Hedberg and Frants Staugard, *Traditional Medicinal Plants: Traditional Medicine in Botswana,* © 1989, Ipeleng Publishers.

Dose and regimen:
Thorn is stuck into aril. Seed is covered with vaseline. Burn seed with matches (while on thorn). Smoke eyes with the burning seed. Then grind seed between fingers and put powder into eyes. Use at night only.

Ethnomedical information:
Other common names available: 78.
86 pieces of information available.

Biological information on extracts:
157 pieces of information available.

Compounds present:
152 pieces of information available.

Literature references:
112 literature references available.

Motsididi   *Abutilon austro-africanum Hochr.*

(BMP 252)   (*MALVACEAE*)

Habitat:
Flat area in closed shrub/tree savanna. Compact grey loam.

Plants identified in immediate environment:
Combretum apiculatum.

Medicinal uses:
Stomach pain.

Dose and regimen:
One cup of powdered roots mixed with cold water is taken two to four times per day.

Mogoloreomoswu   *Abutilon fruticosum Guill. & Perr..*
(BMP 691)   (*MALVACEAE*)

Habitat:
Dense shrub savanna with small trees. Coarse, pale orange sand.

Plants identified in immediate environment:
Dichrostachys cinerea/Acacia karoo/Peltophorum africanum.

Medicinal uses:
All sicknesses.

Dose and regimen:
Roots are folded and boiled with water. One half cup of the fluid is taken twice a day until recovery.

This medicine must be drunk immediately after preparation or else it is spoiled.

Motsididi *Abutilon sp.*
(BMP 266) *(MALVACEAE)*

Habitat:

Plants identified in immediate environment:

Medicinal uses:
Stomach pain in pregnant women.

Dose and regimen:
One cup of water boiled with fresh roots is taken once a day.

Mogokatau (BMP 480) *Acacia arenaria Schinz*
Mosokelateng (BMP 499) *(LEGUMINOSAE)*

Habitat:
Shrub/low tree savanna close to road verge. Pale grey, fine loose sand (BMP 480). Woodland with small amount of herbaceous ground cover, almost no grass. Slightly compacted, pale grey sand (BMP 499).

Plants identified in immediate environment:
Acacia tortilis/Grewia spp. (BMP 480).
Colophospermum mopane (BMP 499).

Medicinal uses:
1. A cough remedy (BMP 480).
2. Tuberculosis (BMP 480).
3. Dry cough and chest pain (BMP 499).

Dose and regimen:
Ad 1, 2. One teaspoon of water boiled with roots is taken three times a day (BMP 480).
Ad 3. One half cup of water boiled with roots is taken twice a day (BMP 499).

Mogotho *Acacia erioloba E. Mey.*
(BMP 191) *(LEGUMINOSAE)*

Habitat:
Open shrub/tree community on small plateau between rocky outcrops. Compacted grey/brown loam.

Plants identified in immediate environment:

Medicinal uses:
Nose bleeding.

TEXT 92

The !Kung of Namibia: Tactics in Springbok Hunting[1]

The !Kung of the Kalahari Desert in Namibia (formerly Southwest Africa) also occupy parts of the neighboring country of Botswana. They represent a subgroup of the San traditional hunter-gatherer peoples. Facing extermination by European settlers, from the seventeenth century onward, this population found itself continually displaced from the fertile and temperate savannah regions of the Cape of Good Hope. The !Kung were eventually forced into the desert regions of southern Africa. The present-day population of the San peoples numbers little more than 50,000.

The languages of these populations are especially noted for a fascinating clicklike consonantal sound employed by Khoisan speakers. This sound is designated with the symbol "!" in writing.

TACTICS IN SPRINGBOK HUNTING

This man [who stands at 5], he has ostrich feathers upon sticks. Therefore, he sticks (into the little bushes) a large stick with ostrich feathers (upon it) here [at 6], because he wants it to look like a man who ( ) stands, so that the springbok may see it, when they go towards the (lesser) feather brushes. For, the springbok would (otherwise), turning back, pass behind him, when he was driving the springbok for the other people, the springbok would, turning back, pass behind him, at the place where ( ) he had stood, calling them. He runs forward from it. Therefore, he sticks in a feather brush at it [at 6]. He goes, also to stick in a little feather brush, which is short [at 7]; while he

---

[1]W. H. I. Bleek and L. C. Lloyd, *Specimens of Bushmen Folklore* (London: G. Allen & Company, Ltd., 1911).
Source: Reprinted from W. H. I. Bleek and L. C. Lloyd, *Specimens of Bushmen Folklore*, © 1911, G. Allen & Company, Ltd.

intends, with the little feather brush which is very small ( ) to drive the springbok, as he wishes that the foremost one may run, passing through, may run passing by the man who lies between [at 9]; he is the one to whom he (the man who drives the springbok) intends the foremost to run. Therefore, the springbok do thus, when ( ) this man shoots the springbok which follows the leading one, they divide nicely; because, the springbok which was following the other turns aside, it darts aside, while the springbok which had been following it ( ) turns aside [in an opposite direction], while they, springing aside, divide at the noise of the arrow on the other one's skin, that and (the noise of) the feathers, which went so quickly.

Credits

Photos
Part I: Queen Nefertiti; Art Resource, NY, © Erich Blessing
Part II: Granite Sphinx; © British Museum
Part III: Greek cross and ankhs; Art Resource, NY, Borromeo
Part IV: Votive head of bull; Museé du Louvre, M. et P. Chuzeville, photographs
Part V: Egyptian calligraphy; By permission of the British Library, 1405 ff370v 371r
Part VI: King Solomon & Queen Sheba; Art Resource, NY, Giraudon
Part VII: African mosque; Stock Montage, Inc.
Part VIII: Congo ruler with ambassadors; Stock Montage, Inc.
Part IX: Ruins of the Great Mosque of Kilwa; Art Resource, NY, © Werner Forman
Part X: Zimbabwe Temple; © Harold N. Howard

Maps
Maps courtesy of Mapping Specialists, Ltd., Madison, WI